GUNS

ILLUSTRATED®
2006 38th Annual Edition

Edited by
Ken Ramage

© 2005
by Gun Digest Books

Published by

Our toll-free number to place an order or obtain
a free catalog is (800) 258-0929.

Manuscripts, contributions and inquiries, including first class return postage, should be sent to the
GUNS ILLUSTRATED Editorial Offices, KP Books, 700 E. State Street, Iola, WI 54990-0001. All materials
recieved will receive reasonable care, but we will not be responsible for their safe return. Material
accepted is subject to our requirements for editing and revisions. Author payment covers all rights and
title to the accepted material, including photos, drawings and other illustrations. Payment is at our
current rates.

CAUTION: Technical data presented here, particularly technical data on handloading and on firearms
adjustment and alteration, inevitably reflects individual experience with particular equipment and
components under specific circumstances the reader cannot duplicate exactly. Such data presentations
therefore should be used for guidance only and with caution. KP Books accepts no responsibility for
results obtained using these data.

Library of Congress Catalog Number: 0072-9043

ISBN: 0-87341-664-3

Designed by Patsy Howell & Tom Nelsen

Edited by Ken Ramage

Printed in the United States of America

GUNS ILLUSTRATED Staff

EDITOR
Ken Ramage

CONTRIBUTING EDITORS

Holt Bodinson – Ammunition, Ballistics & Components
J. W. "Doc" Carlson – Blackpowder Review
John Haviland – Shotgun Review

John Malloy – Handguns Today: Autoloaders
Layne Simpson – Rifle Review
John Taffin – Handguns Today: Six-guns & Others

ABOUT THE COVERS

Revolvers and autoloaders from Gary Reeder Custom Guns in Flagstaff, Arizona appear on both the front and back covers of this 38th edition of GUNS ILLUSTRATED®. Today's custom gun business evolved from the Pistol Parlor gun shop founded some 25 years ago – and still operated by Reeder's wife, Colleen.

Initially, Reeder customized only single-shot pistols–– the T/C Contender and Remington XP-100––then expanded into an ever-increasing offering of custom revolvers based predominantly on Ruger single-action and double-action revolver models, plus one from Freedom Arms.

Today Reeder offers custom autoloading pistols (*via Kase Reeder Custom Guns*), and numerous custom revolvers–– including the hunting revolvers and autoloading pistols on our covers––plus custom single-shot pistols based on the Thompson/Center Contender and Encore, custom hunting rifles, one-of-a-kind firearms and restoration services.

THE FRONT COVER:

Two handguns from Reeder's extensive line include (*top to bottom*) the Ultimate 10, and the 510 Hunter. Kase Reeder produced the Ultimate 10, a full custom 10mm built on a stainless steel Rekon frame, with a six-inch slide, adjustable rear sight with a tritium front sight, and other custom features.

The 510 Hunter is built upon either the Ruger Blackhawk or Super Blackhawk and is chambered for a new cartridge, the 510 GNR, which reportedly delivers terminal ballistics comparable to the 500 Linebaugh, but with considerably less recoil. Standard features on this revolver include a six-inch octagon barrel, and the new Gunfighter Grip made of red laminated cherry wood.

THE BACK COVER:

Two more guns from Reeder's custom line include (*top to bottom*) the Rekon Kommander and the BMF (*Best Made Firearms*). From Kase Reeder comes the Rekon Kommander, his latest full-custom 1911-style autopistol in 45 ACP. The pistol has just about every custom feature there is, including a tactical accessory rail on the custom frame.

The BMF single-action is chambered for the 500 Maximum and is designed to be the ultimate backup gun. Reeder advises this revolver is not for the average handgunner. Numerous options are available.

NOT SHOWN:

The Vampyre Slayer is a special limited-edition 1911-style 10mm autopistol built by Kase Reeder to the customer's specifications. Comes in a coffin case, with three extra magazines.

For more information on these, and other Reeder guns and services (*including Kase Reeder guns*), contact Gary Reeder Custom Guns at 2601 7th Avenue East, Flagstaff, Arizona 86004/928-526-3313; Website: **www.reedercustomguns.com**

CONTENTS

PAGE 41

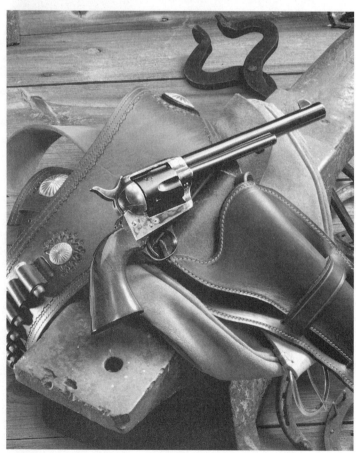

CATALOG OF ARMS AND ACCESSORIES

PAGE 22

PAGE 66

PAGE 58

PAGE 50

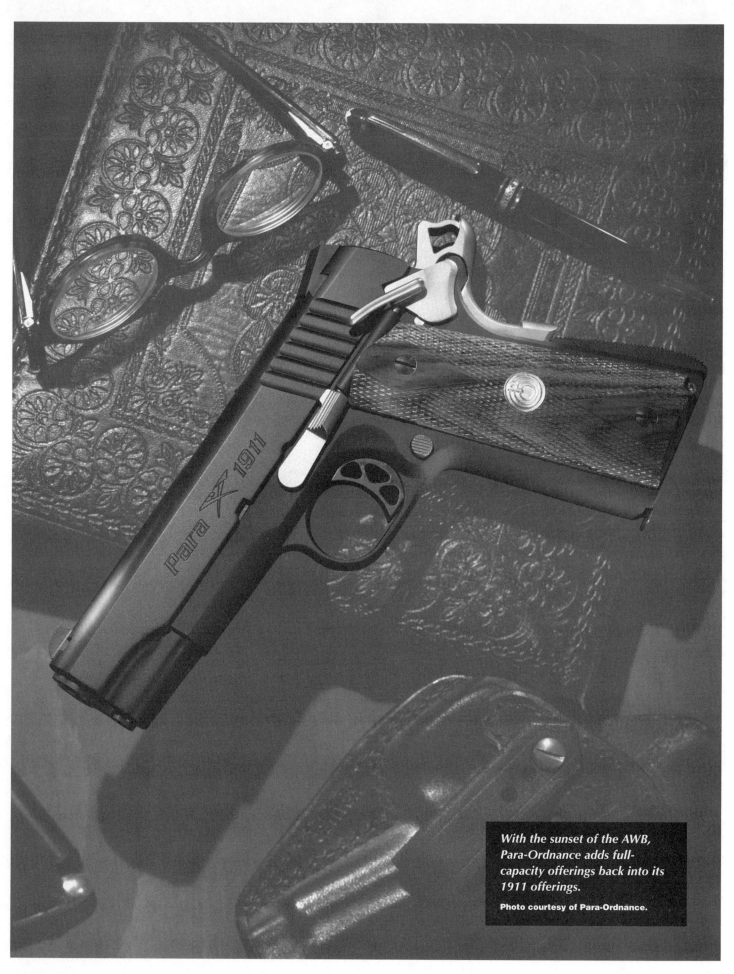

With the sunset of the AWB, Para-Ordnance adds full-capacity offerings back into its 1911 offerings.

Photo courtesy of Para-Ordnance.

AUTOLOADING PISTOLS

by John Malloy

The biggest recent news concerning the autoloading handgun scene was probably not mechanical, but political. As those with an interest in firearms know now, the so-called "Assault Weapons Ban" (AWB) was allowed to sunset at its appointed time on September 13, 2004. Then, George W. Bush was reelected President of the United States on November 4, 2004.

This report is not really a place for political commentary. However, some aspects of the political situation affect autoloading handguns directly, so it is perhaps appropriate to discuss them briefly here. The now-defunct AWB was thought by many to deal only with "assault" rifles. However, perhaps most of the effect was actually felt in relation to semiautomatic handguns.

The AWB banned the manufacture of 19 specific firearms, most of them rifles, guns that were deemed to be "assault weapons." Also, "copycat" models were banned if they had any two cosmetic features considered offensive, such as a flash suppressor or a bayonet mount. The false picture presented to the public by the major media was that the rifles that had been banned, such as the semiautomatic AR-15 and AK-47 clones, were really machineguns.

However, semiautomatic handguns, hardly mentioned by the major media, were addressed in greater detail in the law. Only two specific handgun models, the TEC-9 and the SWD M-10 (the "MAC-10") were specifically banned.

However, manufacturers were prohibited from making any autoloading pistol that used a detachable magazine and had two or more arbitrary features. Such features included a magazine outside the pistol grip, a threaded muzzle that could accept various accessories, a shroud around the barrel, a weight of 50 ounces or more, or just being a semiautomatic version of a full-automatic firearm.

A major provision of the "Assault Weapon Ban" was the prohibition on the manufacture of "ammunition feeding devices" that held more than 10 rounds. This restriction most affected manufacturers of autoloading handguns. With most rifles that are designed to use extended magazines, the magazine protrudes below the lower line of the rifle. Thus, rifles designed for greater capacity magazines could just substitute a shorter 10-round magazine.

The overwhelming majority of automatic pistols, however, have the magazine contained within the pistol's grip frame. The frame is of a size and shape to accommodate a magazine of a certain size and shape. Thus, decreased-capacity pistol magazines had to be redesigned—not only to hold just 10 rounds and fit the pistol and work properly—but to prevent any efforts to later increase the capacity. The innovations in plugged and distorted magazines that resulted might make an interesting

historical collection—one that should remind us never to let such legislation become the law of the land again.

It is good that this bad law, which was based largely on emotion, and without any support of facts or logic, has been allowed to sunset. However, the effect of the AWB is not completely gone. A number of laws in different areas essentially duplicated the federal law, and they are still in effect. Since the sunset, anti-gun organizations have made an effort to

AMT is back, and the DAO Back Up pistols, in 380 and 45 ACP, are once again in production. The larger 45-size frame will also be offered in other calibers.

introduce bills in state legislatures that would, in effect, reestablish the AWB in the affected states.

So, the issue has not gone away. Unfortunately, neither has the federal "Assault Weapons Ban." It was not deleted from federal law; it just remains on the books, dormant, because the sunset clause has removed from it the force of law. We can bet that the antis will continue their efforts to either strike out the sunset language or to write an even more restrictive bill. However, for the present, pistol shooters can legally acquire new magazines that were actually designed for their handguns, and can enjoy "politically-incorrect" features on new guns.

The failure of the anti-gun forces to prevent sunset of the AWB was a prelude to the elections of November 4, 2004. The gun rights issue had been a strong factor in the 2000 elections, and the Democrats' 2004 presidential candidate, John Kerry, made an effort to disguise his two-decade anti-gun voting record. He appeared in TV ads as a hunter and shooter. The facts of his record, coupled with his incredibly bizarre descriptions of his hunting experiences, worked against him. George W. Bush was reelected for a second term as president, and the number of reportedly pro-gun legislators in both the House and Senate increased.

The Bush administration is not perfect, but is basically in accord with firearms rights. The Bush Justice Department released an exhaustively-researched report concluding that the Second Amendment "secures an individual right to keep and bear arms." So, drastic federal anti-gun legislation seems unlikely within the next few years. However, efforts to continue and expand bans of certain firearms and "high-capacity" magazines can be expected to continue at state and local levels. Autoloading pistols always seem to be the objects of such proposed legislation.

Perhaps we should make an effort to dispense with the terminology that the anti-gun forces use. They use the term "high-capacity" as something sinister and evil. A 13-round magazine for a Browning Hi-Power is not really a "high-capacity" magazine—it is the magazine for which the pistol was designed. Thus, it is a "normal-capacity"

or "full-capacity" magazine. The 10-round magazines we were forced to use for a decade were "reduced-capacity" or "restricted-capacity" magazines.

Now, then, as far as the guns themselves are concerned: the fighting in Iraq, the threat of terrorism and the continuing need for personal protection have kept interest in autoloading handguns high. Most autoloaders introduced recently are suitable for personal protection, or for police or military use. The 45 ACP cartridge seems still to be king of the hill as far as new introductions are concerned. Several companies have introduced new 45s for the first time.

The tried-and-true Colt/Browning 1911 still reigns as the most-used design. For each of the past few years, a company that had never before made a 1911 brought out its version of the classic design. This year we add another two companies, Taurus and United States Fire Arms.

Old names are returning, and it is good to see them back. To the Detonics and Whitney pistols reintroduced last year, we can now add AMT and AutoMag offerings. The Iver Johnson name is also back, offering, among other things, another new 1911 line!

State and local restrictions, no matter how illogical, have to be considered by the manufacturers. In order to sell their products in all states, some handgun makers have had to add internal locking devices, magazine disconnectors and other mechanical devices, and have to be able to supply restricted-capacity 10-round magazines for those who live in areas where magazine freedom has not reached.

Frame rails have become more popular. More organizations and more shooters seem to like the option of hanging various things from their pistols. With polymer-frame pistols, similar frames may be moulded with or without a rail, and some manufacturers offer both varieties.

Laser sighting devices have also become more popular. If a shooter does not want to attach a laser device to his pistol, he can opt for laser grips. Such grips have the batteries, switches and beam generators contained entirely within the grips. At least one American manufacturer, Smith & Wesson, now offers some handguns that are

factory-equipped with laser grips.

As a reason to buy a new pistol, why not a commemorative model to celebrate an anniversary? A number of anniversary models—including anniversaries for pistols and companies and organizations—are offered this year.

Interest in pistol-caliber carbines continues to grow, and the option of larger magazine capacity has perhaps given that category of firearms special favor this year. The pistol-caliber carbines are generally not covered along with traditional hunting and target rifles, so we'll give them at least a little attention here.

Please keep all this in mind, and let's take a look at what the companies are doing:

ADCO

The 45 ACP ADCO TT45 was introduced last year, and it has now been joined by versions in 9mm and 40 S&W. The new pistols were introduced, logically so, as the Models TT9 and TT40. These polymer-frame pistols, made in the Czech Republic and based on the CZ 75 mechanism, weigh 26 ounces. With the federal magazine capacity restrictions lifted, the 9mm has 15+1 capacity, and the 40 holds 12+1. For those in states that still restrict magazine capacity, reduced-capacity 10-round magazines are available.

American Derringer

Almost unnoticed among the variety of derringers and other non-autoloading handguns made by this Texas company, a stainless-steel 25 auto has been in the line for some time. With the increased interest in 25-sized 32 autos, the company investigated revising the pistol into a 32. The prototype apparently worked well, but production of the 32 would have required extensive redesign of the pistol and tooling. A decision was made to drop the work on the 32. The 25, a stainless-steel pistol with wood grips, remains in the line.

AMT/Automag

To the disappointment of many shooters, AMT ceased production of its line of innovative stainless-steel pistols in late 2001. However, in 2004, the Crusader Group acquired the assets, and selected AMT pistols are once more being offered. By early 2005, the double-action-only (DAO) BackUp pistols had been returned to production. They are available in 380 and 45 ACP calibers. The original larger BackUp was also made in five other calibers (40 S&W, 9mm, 38 Super, 357 SIG, and 400 Cor-Bon), and smaller numbers of these additional chamberings are now in the works.

The AutoMag II, the first-ever production autoloading pistol for the 22 Winchester Magnum Rimfire (22 WMR), is now back in production, in three barrel lengths. Lengths offered are the original 6-inch, 4 1/2-inch and 3 3/8-inch variants. A new version in 17 Hornady Magnum Rimfire (17 HMR) was scheduled for late 2005. The AutoMag III, in 30 Carbine, is also being returned to production.

Parts and magazines for AMT and AutoMag pistols will be available, and will work with previously-made guns. Magazines will be available for all models and all calibers. (see also CRUSADER)

Armscor

Armscor offers a line of 45-caliber Philippine-made 1911 pistols, and has recently introduced some changes. All 1911 pistols made under the Armscor name now have external extractors and fully-supported barrels. Guns made under the Rock Island name have the original 1911 features.

Still considered prototypes *(although they made it into the 2005 catalog)* are two new 9mm pistols. Of CZ 75 style, one has a steel frame, and the other has a polymer frame.

Beretta

A number of companies have taken an established pistol design and used it as the basis for a pistol-caliber carbine. Beretta, on the other hand, has taken its successful Storm Cx4 carbine and, with that as a concept, has developed a companion Storm pistol. The new Px4 Storm pistol was shown for the first time at the January 2005 SHOT Show. The new Beretta pistol is a polymer-frame pistol that

The AutoMag brand has returned, and the AutoMag II in 22 Winchester Magnum Rimfire, is back in production.

uses the same magazines as the Storm carbine. It is designed around what Beretta calls a "modular concept."

The emphasis toward potential law-enforcement acceptance is obvious. The Storm pistol can meet just about any specifications a department might have. To fit different hand sizes, the pistol has three interchangeable grip backstraps. Reversible magazine-release buttons—of different sizes—are included to further customize the gun to the shooter. The safety lever also comes in two different interchangeable sizes. Available at first as a conventional double-action (DA), Beretta's vision is that the trigger mechanism can be customized to include the options of conventional DA with or without a manual safety, and two types of double-action-only (DAO) mechanisms.

The locking system is a new rotary barrel arrangement, and the recoil spring is held captive. Takedown is simple, and the pistol frame has a Picatinny accessory rail moulded in. The new Storm pistol is available now in 9mm and 40 S&W, has a barrel length of 4 inches and an overall length of 7-1/2 inches. The 9 weighs 27-1/2 ounces and has 17+1 capacity. The 40 weighs 29 ounces, with 14+1 capacity. Rumors are that a 45-caliber version will also be introduced, and this seems logical, but there was no official confirmation.

Bersa

Bersa Thunder 9 and Thunder 40 double-action pistols were designed for larger-capacity magazines, but had to be sold with 10-round magazines. As of January 2005, the

The new Beretta Storm Px4 pistol has interchangeable grip backstraps and controls of different sizes to customize a pistol to the shooter's hand.

The action of Browning's Buck Mark rifles is essentially the same as that of the Buck Mark pistols.

The Browning Buck Mark target rifle has a heavy bull barrel and can use a variety of optical or electronic sights.

Browning's Buck Mark Sporter is an open-sight carbine based on the Buck Mark pistols.

The Browning Buck Mark Field Target Rifle has a heavy barrel and laminated stock.

The lightest carbine in Browning's Buck Mark rifle line is the Field Carbon rifle with a carbon composite barrel. Weight is about 3-1/2 pounds.

Bersa 9mms will be shipped with 17-round, and 40s with 13-round magazines. Extra full-capacity magazines will be available as separate items. Bersa pistols are imported by Eagle Imports.

Browning

Browning has introduced a number of new variants of its popular 22-caliber Buck Mark pistol.

One version is called the Buck Mark Hunter. It features a round, heavy 7 1/4-inch barrel with an integral scope mount base. The pistol has a Pro-Target adjustable rear sight, and a fiber-optic Truglow front sight from Marble. Cocobolo target-type grips are furnished.

The Buck Mark Camper Stainless is a stainless-steel version of the existing Camper pistol, and has a 5 1/2-inch tapered bull barrel.

Two stainless-steel versions of the Buck Mark Standard pistol are now available, one with a flat-sided 5 1/2-inch barrel, and the other as a 4-inch-barrel "Micro" version.

The Buck Mark 5.5 Field pistol has a 5 1/2-inch bull barrel that sports target sights and a full-length mounting rail for optical or electronic sights. The 5.5 Target pistol is similar, and also has the front and rear sights hooded—a potential help when shooting in bright sunlight.

The 22-caliber carbines based on the Buck Mark pistol mechanism *(called "Buck Mark rifles" by Browning)* have proven popular. Several different variants are now available. There is a Sporter with open sights, and also Target and Field Target heavy-barrel variants. A lightweight rifle with a carbon composite barrel weighs only about 3-1/2 pounds. All Buck Mark rifles have 18-inch barrels.

Bushmaster

With the sunset of the "Assault Weapons Ban," Bushmaster is again able to offer models and features not available for a decade. Of interest to us here are the 223-caliber Carbon 15 pistols that Bushmaster offered for the first time last year, which are now freed from weight restrictions.

Recall that Bushmaster acquired Professional Ordnance last year, and thus became a pistol—as well as a rifle—company. Their Carbon 15 pistols feature the same controls as the Bushmaster AR 15-type rifles, but the upper and lower receivers are of Carbon 15 material, bringing the weight down substantially.

The Type 21 pistol, which has a 7 1/4-inch barrel, is now joined by the Type 21S. The new 21S has added a forend/handguard surrounding the barrel, and a full-length optics rail.

The Type 97, with a 7 1/4-inch fluted stainless-steel barrel, is now also offered as the 97S. This new version has a handguard, a full-length upper optics rail, and a lower accessory rail.

A conversion kit to upgrade Type 21 and Type 97 pistols to Type 21S configuration is also available.

Century

Century International Arms carries a line of new Bulgarian Arcus pistols *(based on the Browning "Hi-Power")* in 9mm chambering, and the Bulgarian Makarov pistols in 9x18mm. Century also carries the innovative line of Korean Daewoo "tri-fire" pistols, in 9mm and 40 S&W.

In addition to their newly-manufactured pistols, Century is handling surplus CZ 52 pistols, and has a limited stock of surplus German Lugers and P-38s.

The company recently dropped its line of Philippine-made 45-caliber 1911-type pistols.

Charles Daly

The ZDA pistol, announced by Charles Daly last year, is now a new catalog item. The Zastava-made conventional double-action pistols are available in 9mm or 40 S&W calibers.

The Ultra-X pistol, a very compact double-column polymer-frame 45 of 1911 style, was not approved for importation last year. Charles Daly hoped to have everything worked out so the Ultra-X would be available here by late 2005.

Ciener

Jonathan Arthur Ciener now has in production 22 Long Rifle (22 LR) conversion kits for the Browning Hi-Power pistol and its clones.

Interest in 22 LR conversions for centerfire pistols dates back to the Colt Ace units of the pre-WWII days. In the last fifteen years, Ciener has become a dominant force in such conversions, previously offering kits for 1911, Glock, Beretta and Taurus pistols, as well as for a number of long guns.

22 LR conversion kits obviously let a shooter shoot more for less money. The kits are not firearms, and can generally be purchased without restrictions and shipped directly to a buyer. Use of a conversion kit can extend the usefulness of a pistol in a location that may restrict the number of firearms a person may possess.

Ciener's new Browning kits are offered in two styles, Standard and Hi-Power Plus. The standard unit has fixed sights, while the Plus unit has adjustable sights. Finishes are matte black, gloss black and silver. The units work on both 9mm and 40-caliber Hi-Power pistols.

Cobra

Cobra Enterprises has made a subtle name change, and is now Cobra Enterprises of Utah, Inc. The company still offers pistols similar to those formerly marketed under the Davis, Lorcin, Republic and Talon names. New items now offered are holsters and rebuild kits for older pistols.

Colt

The original Colt 1911, made to World War I specifications, became a catalog item last year, and is now in full production.

The Series 70 pistol is now made in a lightweight Officer's version. The new variant has a 4 1/4-inch barrel, a short "officer's" grip and Novak sights.

A new heavy-barrel 38 Super is being offered. The barrel of the new 38 Super is the same diameter as that of the 45, and fits the 45's barrel bushing.

Crusader

The formation of this new group was announced in September 2004, and although the name may be new to some, to others, the name "Crusader" may evoke memories of the limited-production High Standard Crusader revolver of the late '70s and early '80s. Yes, High Standard is indeed part of the new Crusader Group, which also includes the resurrected AMT and AutoMag lines. Other companies included are Firearms International, Inc., and Arsenal Line Products. (see also AMT / AUTOMAG, and HIGH STANDARD)

CZ

2005 was the 30th anniversary of the CZ 75 pistol, which was introduced in 1975, when Czechoslovakia was still hidden behind the Iron Curtain. Reports of the new pistol at that time were vague, but some thought it to be the best new pistol design introduced. It does seem to have stood the test of time. To commemorate this 30-year milestone, CZ-USA offered a limited run of a special 30th anniversary edition.

The 30th Anniversary pistols will have special serial numbers from 1 to 1000. The pistols are special CZ 75B pistols, chambered for the 9mm cartridge, and featuring high-polish blue, special engraving, inlays, plated controls and blond-finish birch grips. A 15-round magazine comes with each gun.

It is nice to again have design-capacity magazine options, and CZ will now ship full-capacity magazines with the appropriate models.

CZ also introduced a new 40 S&W version of its CZ 75 Compact. The steel frame has an accessory rail, and the pistol has an ambidextrous manual safety. Magazine capacity is 10 rounds. The barrel on the new compact is 3.87 inches, and the gun weighs about 38 ounces.

DETONICS

Detonics USA reintroduced the Detonics pistol last year, and the 45-caliber compact version, the CombatMaster, is now in production and has been shipping since February 2005. Detonics president Jerry Ahern says that a very few CombatMaster pistols will also be made in 357 SIG, 40 S&W, 38 Super and 9mm.

Eventually the "commander-size" ServiceMaster and then later, the full-size target-ready ScoreMaster will be added to the line.

Before then, though, Detonics had planned a surprise. The new Detonics StreetMaster was scheduled to debut during early 2005. Ahern, a leading authority on concealed carry, felt there was a niche that had not been addressed in the world of concealed carry and personal protection. The new StreetMaster has the same abbreviated frame as the compact CombatMaster, but has a 5-inch barrel and a full-length slide to match. In a number of situations, such a pistol would be

Top: 2005 was the 30th anniversary of the CZ 75 pistol, and the Czech company has brought out a special commemorative version with engraving, gold-plated parts and special grips.
Bottom: The CZ 75 Compact pistol is now available in a new 40 S&W version.

easier to carry and conceal than many conventional pistols, while offering the advantages of the longer barrel. With spacers, full-length magazines can be used to offer a full-size grip. The new StreetMaster has been given the trademarked model number 9-11-01.

FNH USA

FNH expanded their FNP line of polymer-frame pistols with two new models in production. The FHP 40 is a 40-caliber pistol with a 4-inch barrel. It is available with 16-round or 10-round magazines, depending on the location of the sale. Interchangeable mainspring housings allow the gun to be fit to the shooter's hand. A rail is made as part of the frame, for attaching lights, lasers or other accessories. Action and controls are the same as the previously-introduced FNP 9.

There is also a new FNP 9. It is a compact version with a 3.8-inch barrel, and an overall length of 7 inches. Weight is about 25 ounces. As with the new 40-caliber pistol, 16- or 10-round magazines are available. The new polymer pistol line now has a magazine disconnector.

The interesting Five-seveN pistol is now available in a new model, the USG. The new refined version of this lightweight polymer pistol has a more traditionally-shaped trigger guard, reversible magazine release, and a textured grip. The pistol's 5.7x28 cartridge, originally designed for FN's P90 machinegun, had previously been available only to law enforcement. Now, a new sporting round, designated SS196, is available. Because of the small diameter of the cartridge, the magazine capacity is 20 rounds. A 10-round magazine is also available. It will be interesting to follow future sporting interest in this combination.

Glock

The 45 Glock Automatic Pistol (45 G.A.P.) cartridge was introduced two years ago and the Model 37 pistol in that new caliber went into production last year. It was seemingly just a matter of time before compact and subcompact 45 G.A.P. versions were introduced. That time

came at the January 2005 SHOT Show, when the new Models 38 and 39 were announced. The compact Model 38 has 8+1 capacity, while the Model 39 subcompact holds 6+1.

Heckler & Koch

2005 was the 25th anniversary of HK's interesting squeeze-cocking P7 pistol. To celebrate, the company brought out a limited commemorative edition of the P7M8, with special engraving and checkered walnut grips. The guns are packaged in wood presentation cases, each with a special commemorative coin. Only 500 of the commemorative P7s will be made.

For 2005, the company offered some of the most popular HK pistols with tan, green or grey frames. These will be offered on a limited basis for five models—the USP 40, the USP 40 Compact, the USP 45, the USP 45 Tactical and the Mark 23.

High Standard

In September 2004, High Standard Manufacturing Company became part of the Crusader Group. Recall that the Crusader revolver was one of the last new products of the old High Standard company before its demise in 1984. Rejuvenated in 1993, High Standard continued its line of 22-caliber target pistols, and added 45-caliber pistols based on the 1911 design.

For 2005, the company has added several new 45s, and two now carry the Crusader name. The Crusader Model 1911 and Crusader Combat pistols are embellished 1911 pistols with 5-inch and 4 1/4-inch barrels, respectively. A shorter version, with a 3 7/8-inch barrel, will also be available. There is also a new military-specification Parkerized 45, the Model of 1911 USA.

One question is sure to be asked, so here is the answer: There is no official word as to whether or not the Crusader revolver will ever be put back into production. All we know is that it was not a possibility before, and there is at least some possibility now.

High Standard will incorporate the services of a company historian, and will offer factory letters for Hi-Standard pistols. (see also CRUSADER)

The new Glock Model 38 is a new compact pistol chambered for the 45 G.A.P. cartridge. An accessory rail is molded into the polymer frame.

A new Glock subcompact pistol is chambered for the 45 G.A.P. cartridge. The small Model 39 does not have a rail incorporated into the frame.

Hi-Point

Hi-Point Firearms offers a line of affordable pistols in 380, 9mm, 40 S&W and 45 ACP. The company also produces what is perhaps the most popular line of pistol-caliber carbines in America. Available in 9mm and 40, the carbines have been limited to 10-shot magazines. Now, with the AWB's magazine ban no longer in effect, Hi-Point plans to offer magazines of larger capacity, but none were yet available for inspection at the January 2005 SHOT Show.

Hornady

What is Hornady, a company involved with ammunition and components, doing in this report? Ah, it is here because Hornady has taken an interest in keeping surplus firearms shooting, and has offered a new line of rifle and handgun cartridges and components. The first autoloading pistol cartridge, just made available, is the 9mm Steyr. A lot of nice shootable old 1911/1912 Steyr pistols sit unused now, and fresh new ammunition can get them out and shooting. The new Hornady ammo is distributed by Graf & Sons.

Iver Johnson

The Iver Johnson name has returned, and the new company offers some interesting autoloading pistols. With the name dating back well over a century, Iver Johnson has been located in New England, in Arkansas, and now in Rockledge, Florida. The present company is connected with Essex Arms of Vermont, which acquired the tooling for the Arkansas-made Iver Johnson 30-caliber carbines. Because Essex already made 1911 slides and frames, it seemed a logical move to add complete 1911 pistols to the new Iver Johnson line of M1 carbines and other guns.

The Iver Johnson 1911s are offered in 45 ACP chambering, and also as 22-caliber pistols. 45-caliber guns are made with steel frames and slides, while the 22s have aluminum frames and slides. A pretty extensive line of pistols is offered, with adjustable- and fixed-sight variants, in 5-inch or 4 1/4-inch barrel lengths. Blue or stainless finishes are available, along with two-tone options. The guns are made in Vermont and shipped to Florida for distribution.

In addition, the nice little Iver Johnson X300 "Pony" 380 ACP pistol will be offered once again. Initial production was planned for late 2005. This 6+1 capacity 380 pistol goes back a long way, and it will be good to have it available again.

Kahr

Kahr has expanded its lightweight polymer-frame DAO line. Expanded it up to 45-caliber! Kahr's first 45 ACP pistol to actually bear the Kahr name *(we won't count the Auto-Ordnance/Thompson 1911 45s that Kahr also makes)* weighs only a bit over 20 ounces, with magazine. It features a textured black polymer frame with a stainless-steel slide. The barrel is 3-1/2 inches long, and is polygonally rifled. The pistol feels good in the hand, and has a 7 1/2-pound trigger. Capacity is 6+1, and each P45 comes with two magazines.

Kahr also introduced a value-priced pistol to appeal to the concealed-carry market. The CW9 is a 9mm with a 3 1/2-inch barrel and has 7+1 capacity.

In the Thompson 1911 line, Kahr has introduced two new Custom models, one with a stainless-steel frame, and

The new Thompson Custom pistol from Kahr has a beavertail tang, extended safety and other custom features.

one with an aluminum frame. Both versions have stainless slides, adjustable triggers, beavertail tangs, extended manual safety levers and other features.

Kel-Tec

Kel-Tec continues its line of lightweight polymer-frame personal-protection pistols in 9mm, 380 and 32 ACP.

The company has a knack for coming up with interesting model designations for its firearms. Recall that their 380 ACP pistol is the Model P-3AT. I get a kick out of saying that aloud. Their 223 carbine is the SU-16, in which the SU represents a "Sport Utility" rifle.

The company's pistol-caliber carbine, the SUB 2000, has a number of interesting features. For one, it folds in half, with a folded overall length of 16 inches, which is also the barrel length. It is offered in 9mm and 40 S&W calibers. The carbine can be ordered with a number of different frames, to fit standard pistol magazines used in Smith & Wesson, Glock, Beretta, SIG, or Kel-Tec pistols. Thus, a shooter with a favorite 9mm or 40-caliber pistol of one of these types can have a Kel-Tec SUB-2000 carbine that uses the same ammunition—and the same magazines—as his pistol.

Kimber

Interest in 1911 pistols is strong, and Kimber addressed that situation with

Pistol-caliber carbines are popular now, and Malloy tries out what is perhaps the most popular of all, the Hi-Point 9mm carbine. Magazines with capacity of more than 10 rounds are now legal for such carbines.

The pistol-caliber Kel-Tec SUB 2000 carbine can be folded to an overall length of only 16 inches.

the introduction of a number of new 1911 variants. Here are some of them.

The 45-caliber LAPD "SWAT" pistol is now available in a stainless-steel version, as the Stainless TLE/RL.

The Stainless Target II is the same as the existing full-size stainless 45 ACP target pistol, but is available in 9mm and 10mm chamberings.

The Pro TLE/RL II in 45 ACP is a blued version with a 4-inch barrel. This shorter variant uses a bushingless barrel-to-slide arrangement. The frame is standard size and includes an accessory rail.

The Stainless Pro TLE/RL is a stainless-steel version of the above pistol.

The Tactical Pro II 9mm, except for caliber, is the same as the 45 ACP version, including lightweight aluminum alloy frame, checkered front strap, and laminated grips.

Two 38 Super pistols have joined the Kimber line. The Stainless II 38 Super is a full-size pistol with polished flats and fixed sights. The Stainless Target II 38 Super is the same basic pistol with adjustable sights.

Kimber claims to be the largest maker of 1911-style pistols. Their goal seems to be to make a variant that will appeal to every individual 1911 shooter, no matter what his preferences.

La Prade

Full-capacity magazines are finally again permissible for ordinary citizens to have, and a number of sources can provide them. Some, like La Prade, can also supply extended magazines. With the growing popularity of pistol-caliber carbines, these can be used

to good effect with such carbines, as well as with pistols. The extended magazines can be useful for plinking, law enforcement, for some forms of competition, and for personal protection. La Prade offers Glock magazines in capacities of 33 rounds (9mm), 29 rounds (40 S&W, 357 SIG), 29 rounds (10mm) and 25 rounds (45 ACP). An extended magazine in a Mech-Tech, Kel-Tec or Olympic carbine designed to accept Glock magazines would make an impressive piece of equipment. They will work in the appropriate Glock pistols too, of course.

For those who need one, La Prade also has the last remaining supply of original Bren Ten magazines.

Les Baer

Les Baer Custom has been in business 25 years, and it seemed the appropriate time for a 25th Anniversary Model 1911. The guns will be engraved, and will feature real (legal) ivory grips. White gold inlays of the legend "25th Anniversary" and Baer's signature are on the slide. Only 25 pistols will be made.

A new addition to the Baer line is the "Recon" pistol. A 5-inch 1911 custom pistol, the frame is machined with a Picatinny rail. A SureFire X-200 light comes standard with the pistol.

Llama

The latest Llama catalog does not list any large-capacity pistols, but the Spanish gunmaker has supplied them in the past, and the importer has announced that they will again be available. In addition, normal-capacity

magazines will be available for those large-capacity pistols previously sold with 10-rounders. The Llama Max-II pistols will be available with 13-round magazines for the 45-caliber Llama Max-II, and 17-rounders for the 9mm version. Import Sports, of New Jersey, imports Llama pistols.

Olympic

The Whitney Wolverine 22-caliber pistol, featured last year as a pre-production item, has advanced to the production stage. By February 2005, the first production run of 5000 pistols was well under way. Seven hundred Whitney pistols had been completed, but the supply of magazines had not kept up with pistol production. By the time you read this, the Wolverine may be on dealers' shelves.

The OA-93, Olympic's big 223-caliber pistol based on the AR-15 design, had been outlawed by the 1994 AWB because of its weight. In response, Olympic had brought out the OA-98, a pistol of similar design, but drastically lightened to get the weight under 50 ounces. The lightening included putting holes in every component possible, giving the big pistol an interesting ventilated appearance. Now, the original OA-93

La Prade offers new extended Glock magazines that will hold 33 rounds (9mm), 29 rounds (40 or 357 SIG), 29 rounds (10mm) and 25 rounds (45 ACP).

and the light OA-98 will both be part of Olympic's product line. Barrel length for both pistols is 6-1/2 inches.

The company also makes a variety of pistol-caliber carbines in 9mm, 40, 10mm and 45 ACP. These guns are all based on the AR-15 design.

Para-Ordnance

Recall that Para-Ordnance was the leader in increased-capacity frames for 1911-type pistols. With the sunset of the AWB, Para adds full-capacity offerings back into its 1911 line.

The company can hardly be said to be lacking for new 1911 offerings. Para has introduced six new models of its PXT (Power Extractor) line. Variants are available with double-action (DA) or single-action (SA) triggers, and with high-capacity or single-column magazines. A Para-Ordnance communication states that the question now is not, "Do I want single-action or double-action, and do I want High Capacity or Single Stack?" but "Which Para do I want?" The company certainly does offer a variety. All the new pistols are in 45 ACP.

The OPS is a single-action, single-column compact pistol. Its 3 1/2-inch barrel gives it an overall length of 7 inches. In stainless steel, it has "Griptor" grasping grooves, other niceties, and Cocobolo stocks.

The stainless-steel Lt. Colonel (LTC) is a single-action, single-column pistol with a 4 1/4-inch barrel and length of 7-3/4 inches. Capacity is 7+1, and the weight is 35 ounces.

The "Hi-Cap LTC" is a similar pistol with a wider frame and 14+1 capacity.

Top: Para's new LTC pistol is a stain-less-steel single-column pistol with a 4 1/4-inch barrel.
- *Middle: The Colonel is Para's 14+1 steel pistol with a 4 1/4-inch barrel and Para's LDA trigger.*
Bottom: The 10+1 Para Nite Hawg is a compact 24-ounce pistol.

The last of the single-action versions added is the S12.45 Limited. This pistol features a 3 1/2-inch barrel and what Para calls "Sterling" finish—all stainless steel with a black slide that has polished sides. Capacity is 12+1.

Two LDA (Light Double Action) pistols have been introduced. The Stealth Carry is a compact 30-ounce single-column pistol with a 3-inch barrel and a capacity of 6+1.

The Colonel is a high-capacity LDA pistol with a 4 1/4-inch barrel and a weight of 37 ounces. A full 14 + 1 capacity and lots of other niceties.

Para seems to have gone hog-wild with some of its nomenclature. Recall that the "Warthog," a small 10+1 45-caliber pistol with a 3-inch barrel, was introduced last year. This year, the "Nite Hawg" has been added, essentially a Warthog in covert black finish. The "Hawg 9" is a similar pistol in 9mm. The "Slim Hawg" is a new 3-inch 45 with a single-column magazine that gives 6+1 capacity.

Rohrbaugh

The little Rohrbaugh 9mm pistol has been standardized with a revised frame. Pistols with the new frames have fired 5000 rounds without a problem. Serial numbers for the revised-frame pistols now have an "R" prefix. The all-metal pistol weighs 12.8 ounces, and measures 5.2 x 3.7 inches. Carbon-fiber grips are now standard. Still, two models are offered, the Model R9 (without sights) and the Model R9S (with sights). With a capacity of 6+1, the Rohrbaugh is the smallest, lightest, flattest 9mm pistol made. Reportedly, it has received attention from troops going to Iraq—it can be carried inconspicuously and uses the military 9mm ammunition.

Ruger

Sturm, Ruger & Company slipped a mid-year model, the P345, in on us since the last edition. In 45 ACP, this new polymer-frame pistol is available in a blued-slide or stainless-slide manual-safety version, and a stainless-steel "decocker-only" version. The new Ruger 45s are slimmer than the company's previous offerings, and seem to feel good in most hands. With

*Above: **Ruger's new Mark III Hunter is in stainless steel, and has a long 6 7/8-inch fluted barrel.***
*Below: **The new Ruger P345 is available in a blued version with a manual safety.***
*Bottom: **A Ruger P345 with a stainless slide and a decocker is available.***

barrel lengths of 4.2 inches, the pistols are 7-1/2 inches in length. Weight for either variant is 29 ounces. Each pistol comes with two 8-round magazines.

The Mark III semiauto, in 22 Long Rifle, is the latest incarnation of the original Ruger Standard pistol of 1949. The magazine release has been moved from the butt to the left side of the frame, and a loaded chamber indicator is on the left side of the receiver. The Mark III series pistols come with Weaver-type scope adapters, as well as new internal locking devices and magazine safeties. A 17 Mach 2 version is now also available. The Mark III 22/45 variant has the controls in the same positions as the 1911-style pistols.

For 2005, the Mark III series offered a special version, the Mark III Hunter. It is of stainless steel, with a 6 7/8-inch barrel, and the barrel is fluted. It features adjustable sights that are a departure from the traditional square-notch type. The rear sight has a V-notch, and the front sight is a round "HiViz" light-gathering sight. Don't like the front-sight color? No problem. Six interchangeable "LitePipes" are included. A scope-mounting base is also included, for which the receiver is already drilled and tapped.

Ruger has made a number of subtle changes on a number of models. Internal locks, magazine disconnectors and other mechanical devices have been added to appropriate

models. Such guns now meet the mishmash of state laws, and can now be sold in every state.

Ruger is proud that the company was able to fill a rush order from the U. S. Army for 9mm pistols. The pistols were needed in a hurry, and Ruger was able to deliver an order for 5000 9mm P95 pistols within 30 days.

Ruger 9mm pistols are now supplied with the 15-round magazines for which they were designed. Except, of course, where state or local regulations still limit magazine capacity. There, reduced-capacity magazines can be supplied.

Ruger's pistol-caliber carbines logically use Ruger pistol magazines. The 40-caliber version still comes with a 10-round magazine, but the 9mm variant now comes with a 15-round magazine.

Sigarms

Sigarms introduced a number of new pistols this year. One of the most noteworthy is the X-Five. Although SIG has an actual real 1911 in their line now, the X-Five is a stainless-steel P226 pistol modified for single-action firing, and with a 5-inch barrel and with 1911-style controls. The new pistol offers shooters the choice of 9mm or 40

S&W. Magazine capacities are 19 for the 9mm and 14 for the 40. The pistols have fired groups of under 2 inches in factory testing, and the pistol is suited for the Limited category of IPSC (International Practical Shooting Confederation) shooting.

The polymer-frame SP2022 is available in 9mm, 40 and 357 SIG. With slightly modified controls and a standard accessory rail, the pistol was accepted by a U. S. Army unit, which ordered 5000 of the new guns in 9mm chambering. Mechanism is conventional double action, and the standard magazine holds 12 rounds.

The new 22 LR Mosquito pistol was introduced at the January 2005 SHOT Show. With a polymer frame and standard rail, adjustable sights and new locking devices, the 22-caliber Mosquito is about 90 percent the size of the P226. Trigger mechanism is conventional double action. The new blowback 22 has several safety and lock features, and a 10-shot magazine is standard.

The P229 and P226 DAK pistols are double-action-only guns with a new trigger system. Pull is 6-1/2 pounds, and the mechanism allows second-strike capability in case of a misfire. These pistols were available to law enforcement last year, and are now available for commercial sales.

SIG 1911 "commander-size" and "officers-size" pistols will become available in the near future. To be called the GSC (Granite Series Compact) models, the new smaller guns will be made without the accessory rail of the full-size pistol.

Sigarms puts out a number of limited-edition arms each year. It certainly would seem to be a way to keep collectors happy, as they could get at least one new SIG every year. This year, a number of limited editions were offered. Perhaps the most eye-catching were the P239 and P232 pistols with multicolored "rainbow" titanium slides.

Smith & Wesson

All right, S&W brought out another big new headline-stealing revolver, the 460 S&W Magnum, but there were plenty of new items introduced in the autoloading pistol lines.

Three existing pistols are now offered with fitted Crimson Trace Lasergrips. The variants available

Top: *The right side view of the Smith & Wesson 410 S.*
Bottom: *A new stainless-steel SW 1911 factory-equipped with Crimson Trace olive-drab Lasergrips.*

Top: *1911 with olive-drab Lasergrips, right view.*
Bottom: *The 40-caliber S&W 410 S comes from the factory with Crimson Trace Lasergrips.*

Top: *The Lasergrip-equipped carbon-steel SW 1911 PD, right view.*
Bottom: *A carbon-steel SW 1911 PD, with a 4 1/4-inch barrel, is fitted with tan Lasergrips.*

with these laser grips are the 1911PD 45 ACP with 4 1/4-inch barrel, the standard SW1911 stainless-steel full-size pistol, and the 410S, a double-action, double-column-magazine gun in 40 S&W caliber.

Smith & Wesson, once it decided to make 1911-style pistols, went into it in a big way. Six new 1911 models have now been added to the line. The 1911 scandium-frame full-size pistol with a 5-inch barrel is now available, a larger variant of the original scandium compact pistol that had been recently introduced. A new full-size pistol is now in the line, with frame and slide made of carbon steel, instead of stainless steel.

A special Doug Koenig variant has a blued carbon-steel slide on a stainless frame. Lots of the niceties that many shooters prefer are standard on this model.

A Doug Koenig variant in 38 Super is also available from the S&W Performance Center. This hand-built pistol may perhaps be the company's first handgun in the 38 Super chambering since its experimental big-frame revolver in that caliber back around 1929.

Two additional five-inch-barrel 1911 models are now available. They are similar to the Performance Center models introduced last year, but made of stainless steel. One has a satin finish over its entire surface. The other has the flats polished.

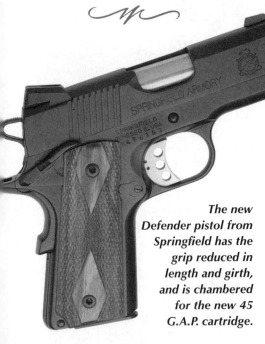

The new Defender pistol from Springfield has the grip reduced in length and girth, and is chambered for the new 45 G.A.P. cartridge.

In the 22-caliber line, S&W had added a new Model 22A pistol, this variant with polished sides on the barrel and slide, and a "Hi-Viz" front sight.

Because the Walther PPK does not meet the arbitrary BATF standards for importation, Smith & Wesson, under license from Walther, is now making the PPK here, in 380 ACP. The new gun is smaller and about 3 ounces lighter than the PPK/S that previously replaced the PPK.

Springfield

Springfield's Parkerized military-style 45-caliber 1911-A1 pistols were well-received last year. Now, with the sunset of the AWB, the company has introduced a Parkerized GI-type full-size pistol with a "Hi-Cap" magazine. Specifications are essentially the same as the other military-style pistols, but the frame is wider to house a 13-shot magazine. Other high-capacity competition pistols have also been added to Springfield's line.

In addition, some additional models have been added to the company's line of single-column 45-caliber 1911-style pistols. Most, but not all, are competition variants.

With the acceptance of the 45 G.A.P. cartridge, Springfield last year chambered its XD polymer-frame pistol in that caliber. For 2005, the company thought that those with smaller hands might favor a 1911 with the grip scaled down for that shorter cartridge. The result was the new lightweight 1911 Defender pistol in 45 G.A.P. The new little pistol weighs only 23 ounces, with a grip 1/8-inch shorter front-to-back and 1/4-inch less in circumference.

Steyr

The striking-looking polymer-frame Steyr Model M pistol came on the scene several years ago, then disappeared. For some time, we were unable to learn whether it was even being made any more. This question has now been answered. At the January 2005 SHOT Show, the somewhat redesigned Steyr M-A1 pistol was displayed. The new pistol is available

A Smith & Wesson 38 Super, the Doug Koenig Professional Series, is now available.

S&W's new Model 22A pistol has a HI-VIZ front sight and polished sides on the barrel and slide.

in 9mm and 40S&W *(and 357 SIG on request)*, with a 15-round magazine for the 9 and a 12-rounder for the 40 and 357. The new Steyr pistols still feature the interesting triangular sight system. Literature accompanying the new pistols listed only an Austrian address, so importation arrangements were still uncertain.

STI

2006 is the 30th anniversary of the International Practical Shooting Confederation (IPSC), and STI International is building special commemorative pistols to celebrate that occasion. Work on the pistols began in 2005 and was scheduled to continue into 2006. The pistols are made in 9mm, 40 S&W and 45 ACP. With 5-inch barrels, the two-tone guns

Left: Springfield has introduced a new full-size high-capacity competition pistol, the Loaded Leatham Trophy Match, in 40 S&W. A similar pistol is available in 45 ACP.
Middle: Springfield has added a Hi-Cap pistol to its line of Parkerized GI-style 45-caliber 1911s.
Right: Some new Springfield models are essentially cosmetic changes to the company's 1911 45-caliber line, such as this striking-looking black stainless-steel combat version.

One of Taurus' new 1911 pistols is a blue version with a beavertail tang, ventilated hammer and trigger and other features.

will have "saber tooth" serrations on the slide, and special slide engraving for the IPSC 30th anniversary.

Taurus

The DAO Taurus Model 24/7 was introduced in 9mm and 40 S&W calibers. Now, it has been offered in 45 ACP. The new polymer-frame 45 pistol is available with either a stainless or blued slide. The grip has ergonomic finger-indexing "Memory Pads" that aid in providing a consistent grip. Contrary to competition practice, the magazine release is recessed. The frame extends into an accessory rail that allows attachment of a light or laser. A manual safety lever (not common on a DAO pistol), a firing pin block, and the key-operated Taurus Security System are incorporated in the design. The 45-caliber 24/7 has a 12+1 round capacity. The earlier 9mm and 40 S&W pistols now are available in their full design capacity—17+1

for the 9 and 15+1 for the 40.

Taurus' new PT745 is a new lightweight 45 that comes in under 21 ounces. A polymer-frame pistol, it has a 3 1/4-inch barrel and the single-column magazine holds seven rounds. Similar to the company's Millennium Pro pistol, the PT745 is available with either a blued or stainless slide.

Another new 1911! Taurus displayed two variants of its brand-new PT 1911 at the January 2005 SHOT Show. At that time, the pistols were so new that the two displayed were the only two specimens in the United States. Taurus' new 1911 has the basic Colt/Browning mechanism, and includes other features. Both the blued steel and the stainless versions of the pistol exhibited similar features. Many of the niceties that seem to appeal to modern shooters, such as beavertail tang, ambidextrous safety, Heinie sights and lowered ejection port, are on the Taurus 1911 pistols. The exhibited pistols seemed to have trigger guards that

were somewhat thicker than usual, and had rather shallow grasping grooves on both the front and rear of the slide.

The Taurus PT 922, which went through several incarnations and was finally standardized last year, is gone. The 22-caliber autoloader has been dropped from the line and is no longer being produced.

United States Fire Arms

United States Fire Arms Manufacturing Company has made a name for itself by recreating early Colt revolvers. With the continuing current interest in the 1911 semiauto pistol, would it not be logical for the company to pay some attention to the early Colt autoloading pistols? By early 2005, they had done just that.

Two new 45 automatics were introduced by the firm. Mechanically, they are 1911s, but they have a "retro" appearance that makes them look even earlier, and that ties in with the company's other products.

The first one was named the "Model of 1910 Commercial." It has the burr hammer of the older Colt Model 1905 pistol, and also has that earlier pistol's wide, flat walnut grips with small-head grip screws. It has a long trigger, the 1905–type tiny sights, and a commercial-grade high-polish finish. The markings are taken from the 1905, and the caliber is marked, "Calibre 45 Rimless Smokeless."

The "later" version was called the "Model 1911 Military," and has a number of features of the original Model 1911. The gun has a wide hammer spur and a short tang, as did the early 1911s. However, it also sported the 1905 walnut grips and the small grip screws. Each of these 1911 guns will come with a reprint of the 1917 manual, "Description of the Automatic Pistol, Caliber .45 Model of 1911."

The U. S. Fire Arms automatics do not really replicate any particular historical firearm. However, they capture the flavor of the old Colts made in the early days of the automatic pistol in our country.

Walther

The Walther PPK is back. The original PPK fell afoul of the arbitrary BATF point system, and could not be imported. It was replaced by the PPK/S. In early 2005, Walther and Smith & Wesson announced that the little gun would be manufactured by S&W under license in the United States.

Also new in Walther's lineup is the Model P99QA with its polymer frame finished in desert sand color. Recall that QA stands for "Quick Action" and indicates the striker is partially pre-cocked by the movement of the slide, allowing a short 8-pound pull. The war in Iraq has created some interest in sand-colored pistols, and the new

Walther addresses this interest. Strangely, it is available only in 40 S&W chambering. One might have expected it to also be in the NATO-standard 9mm, as are the other series P99QA pistols.

Wildey

The JAWS Viper pistol, a joint venture between Wildey and the country of Jordan, has finalized its design. Parts are now in production, and the initial production run has been sold, even before final production.

Several interesting things were on display by Wildey at the January 2005 SHOT Show. One was the actual pistol used in the "Death Wish 3" motion picture, which starred Charles Bronson.

A Wildey Colt was also displayed. About 5 years or so ago, a small number of Wildey pistols were made by the company for Colt and were so marked. These interesting pistols were reportedly made with three barrels each, for 45 Winchester Magnum, 45 Wildey Magnum and 475 Wildey Magnum. About seven pistols were left undelivered when the arrangement ended. These are interesting collectible items.

Selected Wildey arms, including the Wildey carbine, are now available with a muzzle brake. The 18-inch-barrel Wildey carbine is perhaps taking the concept of the pistol-caliber carbine to its logical extreme. Chambered for 44 AutoMag, 45 Winchester Magnum, 45 Wildey Magnum and 475 Wildey Magnum, it can certainly be considered suitable for a range of game hunting beyond the capability of most traditional pistol cartridges. ✺

Top: A stainless-steel variant of Taurus' new 1911 pistol also has a beavertail tang and other special features, such as an extended manual safety.
Middle: The Walther PPK in 380 ACP is back, made under license in the United States by Smith & Wesson.
Bottom: The JAWS Viper is in final form, and parts are being produced for the first production run.

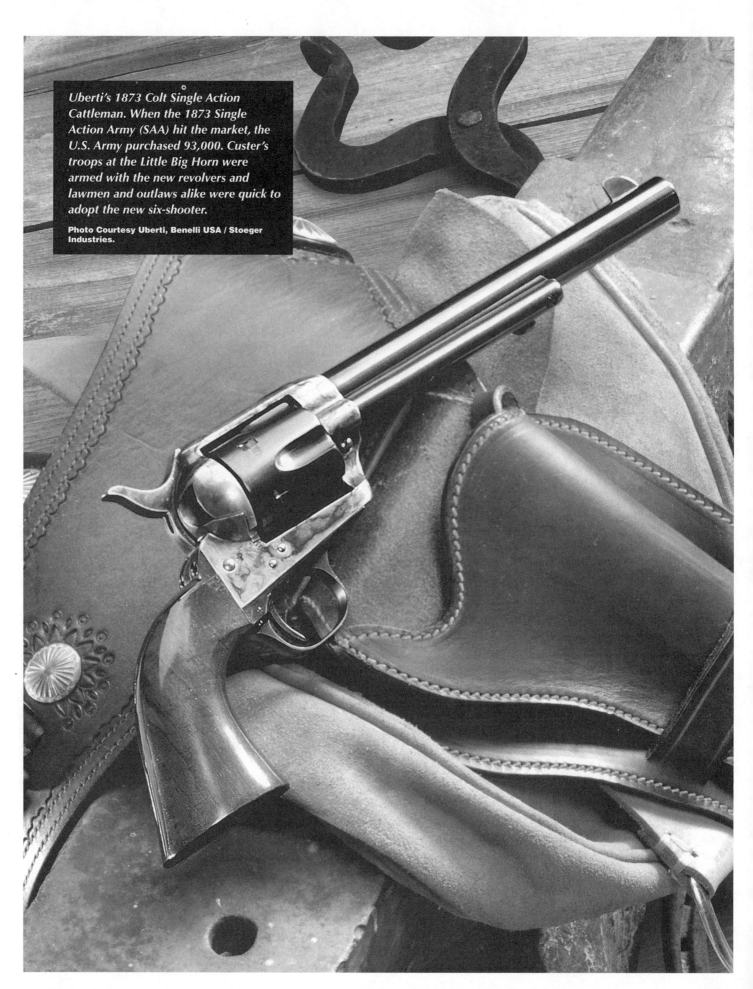

Uberti's 1873 Colt Single Action Cattleman. When the 1873 Single Action Army (SAA) hit the market, the U.S. Army purchased 93,000. Custer's troops at the Little Big Horn were armed with the new revolvers and lawmen and outlaws alike were quick to adopt the new six-shooter.

Photo Courtesy Uberti, Benelli USA / Stoeger Industries.

REVOLVERS, SINGLE-SHOTS & OTHERS

by John Taffin

Life used to be so simple! When McDonald's first opened up they had a walk-up window offering two choices: a hamburger or cheeseburger. The choice of the latter was usually predicated on whether one had the extra four cents or not. Today, one has to choose between the drive-through or walk-in, and then be faced with a menu board larger than the square footage in the floor plan of most houses. The same situation now applies to the firearms industry. In 1955, if one wanted a Ruger 357 Blackhawk, the situation was almighty simple; there was only one: blued, with a 4 5/8-inch barrel. One year later, shooters could have any 44 Magnum Blackhawk desired as long as it was a 6 1/2-inch version, also blued. The Super Blackhawk arrived in 1959 and, until well into the 1980s, it was only offered in a blued 7 1/2-inch model.

Over the years, most gun manufacturers have followed McDonald's lead. Ruger alone offers a total of 40 new choices this year, handguns and long guns combined. If we factor in all models from the rest of the major manufacturers I guess there are at least 100 new choices.

It's time to take our annual look at the state of handguns: single-action and double-action six-guns, as well as single-shot pistols.

Ruger

There is good news and bad news from Ruger this year. The bad news: After a dozen years of production and nearly three-quarters of a million units manufactured, the Vaquero has been removed from production. However, the greater good news is that the Vaquero is being replaced by an even better single-action six-gun: the New Vaquero. The original Vaquero was a virtually indestructible single-action six-gun built on the same frame size as the 44 Magnum Super Blackhawk. If there was any complaint about the Vaquero, it was its size and bulkiness. The New Vaquero addresses this "problem."

Several years ago Ruger's Bill Ruger, Jr., Steve Sanetti and Bob Stutler sat down for a brainstorming session and one of the results we are now seeing is the New Vaquero, a much improved, downsized version. The original Vaquero was larger than the traditional Single Action Army; the New Vaquero is basically the same size as the Colt Model P and its replicas. In addition to its smaller, easier-to-carry size, several other improvements have been made to the New Vaquero. The

Production Manager Bob Stutler, with Ruger's latest single action, the New Vaquero.

Above: Two great choices for the handgun hunter are Ruger's Bisley and Super Blackhawk 44 Magnum models.

ejector rod head is now larger, allowing more comfort and positive action when ejecting spent shells, and the cylinder now lines up correctly with the ejector rod. In the old Vaquero, the audible *click* as the cylinder was rotated told us we had gone too far and the cylinder had to be backed up slightly for the ejector rod to enter the chamber mouth; with the New Vaquero the *click* says we are there, and the cylinder is lined up correctly with the ejector rod.

When the first Ruger six-gun, the Single-Six 22, appeared in 1953 the grip frame was virtually identical in size and shape to the 1st Generation Single Action Army. This XR3 frame was carried over to the 357 Blackhawk of 1955 and the 44 Magnum version one year later.

In 1963 the grip frame was changed to XR3-RED, allowing more room between the back of the trigger guard and the front of the grip strap. It has taken more than four decades to go back to the original; however, the New Vaquero has the 1950s XR3 size and shape. The New Vaquero grip frame is also slightly narrower than the old and, combined with the checkered rubber grips, which are also slimmer than the original Vaquero's wooden grips, makes it feel awfully good in my hand. In fact, these are the best-feeling Ruger single-action factory stocks I've ever experienced and I've been shooting Ruger single-action six-guns exactly a half-century this year. Instead of the medallion found in all Ruger stocks since 1953, these new checkered rubber grips have the Ruger Eagle molded into the grip itself.

The New Vaquero will be initially offered in 357 Magnum and 45 Colt, in both blue/case-colored and stainless steel versions in barrel lengths of 4-5/8 and 5-1/2 inches, with the 45 Colt also offered in the longer 7 1/2-inch barrel length. They should be very popular not only with cowboy action shooters but with all six-gunners appreciating traditionally-sized and styled single actions. I certainly hope Ruger will eventually offer it in 44 Special. WARNING: These New Vaqueros are for standard 45 Colt loads only, not the "Heavy Ruger Loads" listed in many loading manuals and articles.

Ruger's other single-action offering, which will probably be sold out by the time you read this, is their 50th Anniversary Model of the 357 Blackhawk. Although it is built on the New Model action instead of the three-screw action of the original, this Anniversary version has the 4 5/8-inch barrel, Micro-style rear sight, and checkered hard rubber grips with a black eagle medallion as did the

Ruger's New Vaquero is available in both blued and stainless steel versions, chambered in 357 Magnum or 45 Colt.

original Blackhawk in 1955, and it is also the same size as the New Vaquero, having the same old-style XR3 grip frame, and the capability of taking a lot of six-gunners back to their roots. This special Ruger is only to be offered for one year; however, in talking with Ruger President Steve Sanetti I was given hope this basic model could stay in the catalog and also be offered in other chamberings *(hint: 44 Special)* and barrel lengths. If you feel the same as I do, a short letter to Ruger would help to influence the decision.

One of the best bargains out there for the handgun hunter has been Ruger's Hunter Model. First introduced in 1992 in 44 Magnum with a 7 1/2-inch solid ribbed heavy barrel cut for Ruger's scope rings, this is a stainless steel six-gun made for heavy-duty outdoor use. Two years ago the Bisley Model version arrived with the Ruger Bisley Model grip frame, hammer, and trigger, and this was then followed one year later by a 22 Single-Six version with an extra cylinder chamber in 22 Magnum. Now for this year Ruger has added the fourth 7 1/2-inch stainless steel, scope-ready Hunter Model to the catalog chambered in 17HMR with an extra cylinder for the 17 Mach 2. With these four Hunter Models, Ruger has covered all the bases when it comes to hunting big game, small game, or varmints.

At the other end of the six-gun spectrum, Ruger is offering something special for those who like truly big-bore packin' pistols. Ruger's Super Redhawk, probably the most durable and strongest double-action revolver ever offered, is now cataloged in a much more convenient carrying version. Until this year the Super Redhawk, whether chambered in 44 Magnum, 480 Ruger or 454 Casull, was offered only in 7 1/2- and 9 1/2-inch barrel lengths, and scope-ready for the handgun hunter. This year Ruger has gone really radical by cutting the barrel even with the extended frame, for a barrel length of only 2-1/2 inches. Known as the Alaskan, this new Super Redhawk will have a rounded trigger guard and trigger, rubber Hogue Monogrip, no cuts in the frame for scope rings, and will be chambered in 480 Ruger and 454 Casull. I expect it to be very popular with those spending

Top: The 22 LR/22 Magnum and bottom: the 17HMR/17 Mach 2 models have now joined the ranks of handgun hunting choices for hunters.

a lot of time outdoors and needing a very powerful but portable six-gun.

Smith & Wesson

Two years ago Smith & Wesson introduced the new "world's most powerful revolver" with the X-frame Model 500 chambered in 500 S&W Magnum. Now from S&W comes the second chambering in the X-frame: the 460XVR, or X-treme Velocity Revolver. While the 500 in its most powerful loading uses a 440-grain bullet at 1650 fps, the 460 becomes the factory-chambered big-bore revolver velocity king with a 200-grain 45-caliber bullet at 2300 fps.

Smith & Wesson notes this is the most powerful 45-caliber production revolver in the world, with over 2400

ft/lbs of muzzle energy (fpe) and "incredibly low perceived recoil." Several factors come together to help tame the 460: namely, a weight of 73 ounces, a compensated 8 3/8-inch barrel and special recoil-reducing grips made of a rubber-like substance called Sorbothane. One can well imagine what the recoil would feel like in a traditional-sized revolver of 48 ounces. In addition to the 200-grain load, Cor-Bon also offers a 250-grain bulleted load at "only" 1900 fps. The 460 will also accept 454 and 45 Colt loads.

The Model 460XVR comes drilled and tapped for a scope mount base, has a fully adjustable rear sight mated with a black blade front sight with a gold bead, and an interchangeable HI-VIZ green dot front sight is also included. Something new for Smith & Wesson

Smith & Wesson's extremely popular X-frame Model 500 is now available with a Hi-Viz front sight.

Now anyone can shoot as fast as Jerry Miculek, or at least dream about it, with S&W's Jerry Miculek Model 625 chambered in 45 ACP and wearing stocks designed by Jerry.

Smith & Wesson is now offering this Airweight with Crimson Trace Laser Grips

in this revolver is gain-twist rifling, which means the twist becomes faster towards the muzzle. This is not a new idea by any means as it has even been used in muzzle-loading rifles and cap 'n ball revolvers. Like the Model 500, the 460XVR is a double-action six-gun crafted of stainless steel with a satin finish and five-shot cylinder.

Another great old standby revolver, the Model 66, has been dropped from production. However, it has been replaced by the slightly larger L-frame Model 620. It is still stainless steel, with a Model 66-style barrel without the heavy underlug, and has a seven-shot cylinder. The Model 65 has also been upgraded to a fixed sight, seven-shot L-frame 357 Magnum, the Model 619, with a standard barrel without an enclosed ejector rod housing. Smith & Wesson's first stainless steel revolver, the Model 60, is available in a new version having a five-inch barrel with an enclosed ejector rod and adjustable sights. This 357 Magnum five-shooter should be a very popular, relatively lightweight trail gun.

Jerry Miculek, the "World's Fastest Revolver Shooter," a title he holds for such remarkable feats as 12 shots from one six-shot revolver in less than three seconds, now has his name on a standard production gun from Smith & Wesson, the Model 625 Jerry Miculek Professional Series. This is a stainless steel double-action revolver with a 4-inch heavy underlug barrel, adjustable rear sight paired with a gold bead/black post front sight, and chambered in 45 ACP (full-moon clips recommended). Also included are Jerry's specially designed wooden stocks and a wide Miculek Speed trigger.

The 44 Special is also back at Smith & Wesson with the Model 21-4 Thunder Ranch Special. This is the first fixed-sight, 4-inch, blued, six-shot 44 Special since the original Model 21 was dropped 40 years ago. Thanks to Clint Smith's collaboration with Smith & Wesson, we have a real no-nonsense, big-bore fighting six-gun in the Model 21-4. The original run of these "Special" 44 Specials have the Thunder Ranch gold logo on the right side; however, expect later production models to be blued without the logo and chambered in 44 Special, 45 ACP, and 45 Colt. Thank you, Clint Smith and Smith & Wesson.

There was a time I would not even consider laser grips; however, my experience with Crimson Trace Laser Grips has changed my mind and I now find them exceptionally useful. These ingenious grips take the place of regular grips and, when a small button in the front strap of the grip is depressed as one takes a normal shooting grip, a small red beam appears on the target.

Now Smith & Wesson is offering two J-frame six-guns already equipped with Crimson Trace Laser Grips. The 15-ounce 38 Special stainless steel 2-inch Model 637 and the 13.5-ounce 32 Magnum black matte 2-inch Model 432PD both come with Crimson Trace Laser Grips already installed. For those having concealed weapon permits, especially women who do not shoot a lot, either one of these could be very useful.

Taurus

As usual, Taurus has a full line of new six-guns for this year. The single-action Gaucho was prematurely announced last year; however, by now it should be readily available in blue, blue/case-colored, and stainless steel versions. The Gaucho is offered in both 45 Colt and 357 Magnum and barrel lengths of 5-1/2 and 7-1/2 inches, all with fixed sights, black rubber grips, four-click action, half-cock loading notch, and a transfer bar safety. Those I have handled seemed exceptionally smooth.

The Taurus Raging Bull, chambered in 44 Magnum, 454 Casull, and 480 Ruger, has been popular with handgun hunters and big-bore revolver shooters for several years. Joining the lineup is the newest Bull, the 500 Magnum. This 10-inch version features a

ported heavy-underlug barrel, adjustable rear sight mated with a black post front, smooth trigger and black rubber finger groove grips with the trademark recoil-reducing red cushion insert along the back strap. Capacity is five shots; weight 4 1/2 pounds.

Taurus also offers an easy-packing big-bore six-gun—the Model 444 Ultralite, a 4-inch Raging Bull-sized, six-shot double-action 44 Magnum with a titanium cylinder. Designed for

The new high-velocity revolver champion, with a 200-grain bullet at 2300 fps, is Smith & Wesson's 460XVR chambered in 460 S&W Magnum.

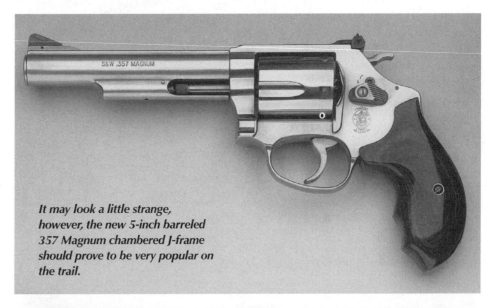

It may look a little strange, however, the new 5-inch barreled 357 Magnum chambered J-frame should prove to be very popular on the trail.

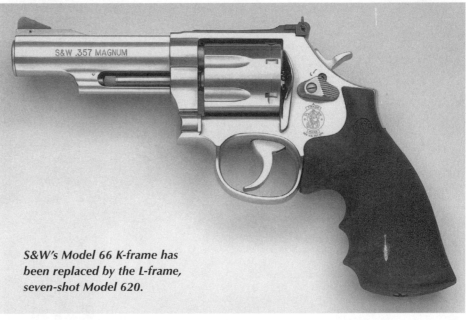

S&W's Model 66 K-frame has been replaced by the L-frame, seven-shot Model 620.

The Taurus Gaucho single action (above) is now here in stainless steel or (below) blued steel in 357 Magnum and 45 Colt.

Taurus is now offering the 500 S&W Magnum chambered in the very popular Raging Bull.

Another Raging Bull offering from Taurus is the long-cylinder .410/44-40 revolver.

portability, the 444 Ultralite weighs 28 ounces, and is equipped with fiber-optic sights, smooth trigger and Raging Bull cushioned-insert rubber grips. A second 44 Magnum offered by Taurus is the slightly smaller five-shot Tracker with a 4-inch barrel, Ribber grips, and ported heavy-underlug barrel. Of all steel construction, the Tracker 44 weighs 34 ounces. Both models are offered in either blue or stainless steel.

The last two new big-bore revolvers from Taurus are the Model 44-Ten Tracker and 44-Ten Bull, featuring elongated cylinders to handle the .410 shotgun shell or 44-40 revolver round. Both are available in blue or stainless steel, with a fiber-optic front sight and cushioned insert grips. The Raging Bull version features a ventilated, ribbed barrel. Weights are 32 ounces for the Tracker version and 39 ounces for the Bull model.

Taurus also has several interesting little guns. The very popular 38 Special five-shot Model 85 is now available with Ribber grips, while the IB (Instant Backup) double actions are offered in both blue and stainless versions in either a five-shot 9mm or eight- shot 17 HMR. The Triad Model 85 takes 38 Specials, or 357s plus 9mms with a provided clip. There is also a larger Tracker Triad with a seven-shot cylinder.

All Ruger, Smith & Wesson and Taurus handguns either now have—or soon will have—internal locking devices, which are now required by many cities and states. This is a fact of life in today's society, and whether we like it or not, they are not going to go away.

Colt

What does the Colt Python have in common with the New Service, Official Police, Officers Model Match, Detective Special, King Cobra, and Anaconda? All are great six-guns and all, including the Python, are now gone. The Python arrived in 1955 and was soon regarded as the Cadillac of double-action revolvers. Now it is gone.

The only revolver left in the Colt catalog is the Single Action Army. It is now offered in barrel lengths of 4-3/4, 5-1/2 and 7-1/2 inches, blue/case hardened or nickel plating and in six chamberings:

Left: This eye-catching six-gun, the 444 Ultralite, is Taurus' entry into the lightweight 44 Magnum arena. The red cushion insert along the back strap really helps reduce felt recoil.

Middle: The Taurus IB (Instant Backup) is available in both 17 HMR and 9mm.

Right: The Taurus Tracker Triad, with felt recoil-reducing Ribber grips, handles 38 Specials, 357 Magnums, and 9mms—all from the same cylinder.

32-20, 38 Special, 357 Magnum, 38-40, 44-40 and 45 Colt. The major question is whether or not Colt can continue to compete in the civilian handgun market, offering only the Single Action Army and the 1911 Government Model. They have a very small share of the latter market and must compete with imported replica single actions, as well as American-made single-action six-guns from United States Firearms and Ruger. Most six-gunners would truly be saddened to see Colt disappear from the civilian firearms scene; however, it seems pretty obvious Colt must do more to survive.

Freedom Arms

The single-action six-guns from Freedom Arms, whether a full-sized Model 83 or the mid-frame Model 97, are expensive—there is no doubt about that. However, I have yet to hear of any owner of a Freedom Arms revolver saying they are not worth the money.

All of Freedom Arms' six-guns are crafted of stainless steel, and the full-sized Model 83 is offered in both a bright, brushed Premier Grade or less expensive matte finished Field Grade. Whichever finish is chosen, both are built with the same materials

and attention to detail and tight tolerances. Premier Grade Model 83s are offered in 475 Linebaugh, 454 Casull and 357, 41 and 44 Magnums, while the Field Grade comes in the same chamberings, plus the 22 Long Rifle. Both models feature adjustable sights with standard barrel lengths of 4-3/4, 6, 7-1/2 and 10 inches; other lengths and octagon barrels are offered on a custom basis. Currently the only fixed-sight Model 83 offered is the Premier Grade chambered in 454.

The Model 97 is available only in the Premier Grade with adjustable-sighted models chambered in 45 Colt, 44 Special, 41 Magnum—all with five-shot cylinders—while the 357 Magnum, 32 H&R Magnum, 22 Long Rifle and 17HMR all have six-shot cylinders. All versions are available with a 4 1/4-, 5 1/2-, or 7 1/2-inch barrel, with 10-inch barrels available on the latter three chamberings. Fixed-sight models are also available in 45 Colt, 357 Magnum, and 32 H&R Magnum.

With these Freedom Arms Model 83s the handgun hunter can tackle anything, any-where. Top guns are chambered in 454 Casull, while the bottom six-guns are both 475 Linebaughs.

Freedom Arms also offers auxiliary cylinders in 45 Colt, 45 ACP and 45 Winchester Magnum for the Model 83 in 454 Casull; in 480 Ruger to fit the 475 Linebaugh, and 22 Magnum for the 22 Long Rifle Model 83. Optional cylinders for the Model 97 include 45ACP, 38 Special, 32-20, 22 Match, 22 Magnum and 17 Mach 2. All Freedom Arms' cylinders have been unfluted; however, they may now be ordered with flutes, and both the Model 83 and Model 97 are now offered with a rounded butt.

Magnum Research

This is the home of the 50 AE Desert Eagle semi-automatic pistol, however Magnum Research also offers the BFR *(Biggest, Finest Revolver)*, a stainless steel single-action six-gun offered in a variety of frame sizes and calibers. With standard "Short Cylinder" and frame, the BFR is found in 454 Casull, 475 Linebaugh/480 Ruger, 50 AE and 22 Hornet, while the Long version is chambered in 45-70, 444 Marlin, 410/45 Colt, 450 Marlin, 30-30, and even in the relatively new 500 S&W.

All BFRs are totally American-made featuring all stainless steel construction, cut-rifle barrels, free-wheeling 5-shot cylinders, adjustable

▼ *The Magnum Research BFR is offered in a standard model with a "short" cylinder.*

▼ *A long cylinder version for such cartridges as the 45-70 or 500 S&W Magnum.*

sights, hand-filling grips—and the retail price has just been reduced to $899, making it the least expensive way to get into a really big-bore six-gun. Magnum Research also offers scope mount bases and rings, as well as both leather and Cordura holsters. I have fired BFRs chambered in 475, 500, and 45-70, finding them all to be superbly accurate and smooth-operating.

United States Firearms

USFA is putting out beautiful traditionally styled single-action six-guns! The main frame and the hammer

are case-colored in what is described as Armory Bone Case, the balance of the six-gun is finished in a deep, dark Dome Blue color, and the standard grips are checkered hard rubber with a "US" molded into the top part of the grip. On all the USFA single actions I have examined, these stocks are perfectly fitted to the frame and feel exceptionally good in my hand.

One of the things I always look for in the fitting and finishing of single action six-guns is the radiusing of the lower part of the back of the hammer and the two "ears" formed by the backstrap where it screws into the mainframe on both sides of the hammer. A well-made single action will exhibit a smooth mating of the contours of all three. USFA six-guns are very nearly perfect in this area, and the same careful fitting can also be found where the top of the face of the hammer meets the top strap. The fit of the trigger guard to the bottom of the mainframe is so perfectly done one can run a finger over the area and not feel where one part begins and the other ends. The same is true where the backstrap meets the mainframe.

The front of the ejector rod housing as well as the cylinder are both beveled which not only looks good and feels good, it also provides for easier holstering. Markings on these six-guns include the

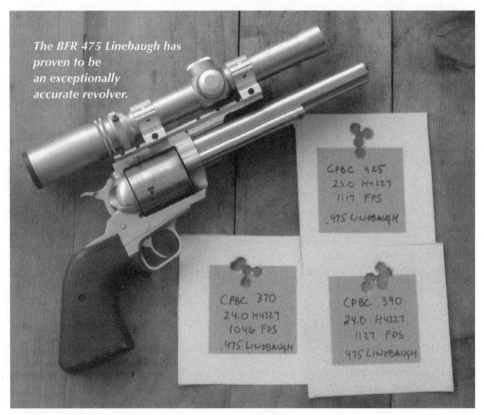

The BFR 475 Linebaugh has proven to be an exceptionally accurate revolver.

serial number in three places: the butt, in front of the trigger guard and on the mainframe in front of the trigger guard screw. This is exactly as the original 19th-century single action armies were marked. Trigger pulls are set at three pounds. Cylinders lock up tight both in the hammer down or cocked position.

All USFA six-guns are totally American-made and available with a V-notch or square-notch rear sight perfectly filled in by a front sight that also has a square profile, rather than tapering to the top. Shooters also have a choice of a cross pin or screw-in "black powder" cylinder pin latch. Chamberings for USFA single actions include the 45 Colt, of course; however, other choices include 32 WCF (32-20), 41 Long Colt, 38 Special, 38 WCF (38-40), 44 WCF (44-40), 45 ACP, 44 Russian and 44 Special. The latter can be marked, and properly chambered as "RUSSIAN AND S&W SPECIAL 44" as early Colt single actions were marked, while 38 Specials can also be marked on the left side of the barrel with "COLT AND S&W SPECIAL 38" just as were early 20th-century revolvers.

The less expensive Rodeo is the same basic six-gun as the Single Action Army except it comes with a matte blue finish instead of the beautiful finish of the standard revolver. The Rodeo has proven so popular it is now offered in several chamberings and all three standard barrel lengths. In addition to the Single Action Army that is also offered in an ejectorless Sheriff's Model, USFA offers a Flat-Top Target version patterned after the target models of the 1890s. The Omni-Potent is a special USFA single action with a grip frame reminiscent of the 1878 Colt Double Action. It is available in all calibers and barrel lengths as well as a target version, all with checkered wood grips and a lanyard ring, and what may be the ultimate belly gun—The Snubnose, with a 2-inch barrel *sans* ejector rod housing.

Hartford Armory

Hartford Armory began manufacturing their version of the Remington Models 1875 and 1890, chambered in 45 Colt and capable of handling +P+ loads, last year. As with any new endeavor it is always a slow process getting everything

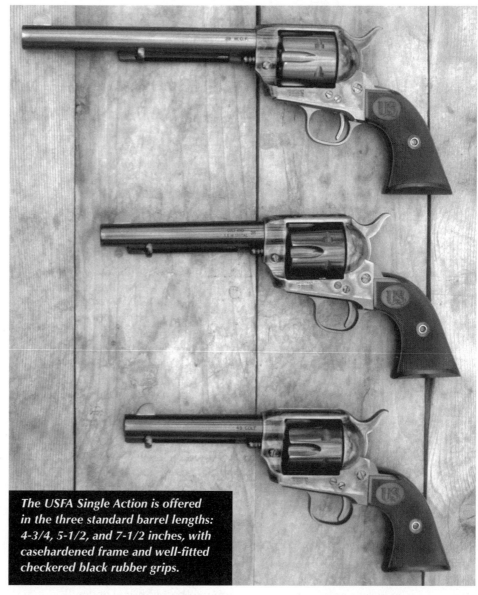

The USFA Single Action is offered in the three standard barrel lengths: 4-3/4, 5-1/2, and 7-1/2 inches, with casehardened frame and well-fitted checkered black rubber grips.

up and running smoothly, however the kinks have been smoothed out and Remingtons are now coming through regularly. These high-quality Remingtons are being produced on thoroughly modern, totally up-to-date machinery using the finest American-made

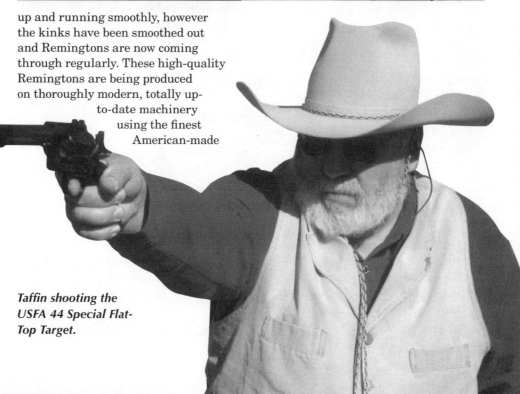

Taffin shooting the USFA 44 Special Flat-Top Target.

4130 and 4140 steels with forged mainframes, not cast. Hartford Armory has deviated from the original design in only one way: making the cylinder approximately 1/8-inch longer to allow use of today's 45 Colt ammunition. The original Remington cylinders were even shorter than those in the Colt Single Action Army, and many of the modern rounds offered in 45 Colt are deliberately made long enough to preclude their being used in Colt Single Actions or replica Remingtons as they are simply are not strong enough to handle +P or Heavy Duty 45 Colt hunting loads. However, Hartford Armory's Remingtons are strong enough to handle any factory 45 Colt ammunition currently offered; even strong enough to be chambered in 44 Magnum.

The grip frame of the Remington raises the comfort level considerably when using heavy loads since the backstrap is slightly straighter and also comes up higher, much like the design found on the original Colt Bisley Model and the current Freedom Arms and Ruger Bisley model. Both the 1875 and 1890 Hartford Armory Remingtons come from the factory with smooth actions, easy-to-operate hammers and the trigger pull set at around three pounds. Both models feature a beautifully polished blue finish, with a case-hardened hammer and loading gate, as on the originals. Cylinder lockup is tight with no movement side-to-side or front-to-back. The barrel/cylinder gap will not accept the smallest feeler gauge I have, which is 0.002-inch. Hartford

Armory Remingtons are available only through Taylor's & Co. They are available in blue or stainless steel, with 5 1/2- or 7 1/2-inch barrels and chambered in 45 Colt, 44 Magnum, 44-40 and 357 Magnum.

Gary Reeder

In the 1920s Elmer Keith set about to build the perfect six-gun, the result being his #5SAA, a 5 1/2-inch 44 Special. Gary Reeder is now offering six-guns, built on his frames, of the #5 Improved that is based on Elmer's #5 as it appeared in the 1929 *American Rifleman*. Reeder has made a few changes: better sights, a standard cross-pin cylinder pin latch and a transfer bar safety conversion combined with a standard single-action style action. For loading and unloading, the loading gate is opened and the hammer put on half-cock, even though it has a transfer bar safety.

Reeder's Deluxe Grade all-steel #5 in 44 Special is of polished stainless steel, fully engraved, with an octagonal barrel. Sights are fully adjustable with an interchangeable front sight feature, stocks are elephant ivory, and the grip frame is like no other. Keith had very small hands, which is evident in the design of his #5 grip frame. Reeder has maintained the same basic grip frame while making it more useable by adding 3/8-inch to the length.

The #5 Improved was designed around the 44 Special and will also be available in 45 Colt. The standard Field Grade #5 with walnut stocks has a base price of $1295,

with full engraving, octagon barrel and custom stocks available.

As a companion piece to the #5 Improved, Reeder offers the Improved #6, which is nothing more than a slightly larger #5 Improved that can handle the 44 Magnum, as well as the 41 Magnum and a five-shot version in 454. The Deluxe Grade Improved #6 has a 5 1/2-inch octagon barrel, is also fully engraved, and is fitted with Mongolian stag stocks.

Thompson/Center

For nearly four decades the T/C Contender has been the single-shot pistol by which all other single shots are measured. It was definitely the leading force in long-range silhouetting and remains one of the best choices for the handgun hunter. A few years back, a second version was added to the Thompson/Center lineup: the Encore. The Contender, now in its second stage as the easier-opening G2, handles most revolver and rifle cartridges up to 30-30 pressures, while the Encore is reserved for high-pressure cartridges such as the 454 Casull and the 308 Winchester.

Since the mid-1960s, the Contender has been offered in a long list of chamberings—including just about every six-gun, semi-automatic pistol, and levergun cartridge. It has been especially favored by handgun hunters in 30-30 and 44 Magnum. Current offerings include 22 Match, 22 Hornet, 357 and 44 Magnum, and 45 Colt/.410-bore with 12-inch barrels, while the selection with the Super 14 barrel includes 17HMR, 204 Ruger, 22 Match, 22 Hornet, 223 Remington, 7-30 Waters, 30-30, 375 JDJ, 44 Magnum, 45-70, and 45 Colt/410. When I was participating in long-range silhouetting my favorite chamberings were the 357 and 30-30.

Encores are catalogued with 12-inch barrels in 223, 44 Magnum, 454 Casull, and 45 Colt/410. The longer barrel Encore has a near-rifle length of 15 inches and is offered in a range of rifle cartridges including 204 Ruger, 22 Hornet, 223 Remington, 22-250, 243, 25-06, 270 Winchester, 7mm-08, 308, 30-06, 375 JDJ, 45-70, 45 Colt/.410. Both the Contender and Encore are offered with blued barrels and frames with walnut stocks and forearms, while a few models are offered in stainless

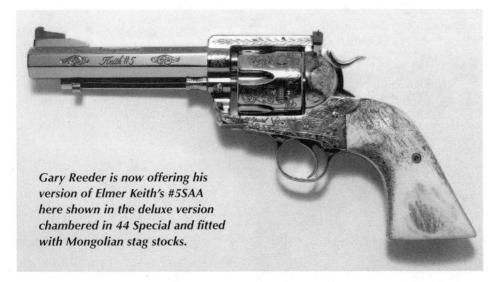

Gary Reeder is now offering his version of Elmer Keith's #5SAA here shown in the deluxe version chambered in 44 Special and fitted with Mongolian stag stocks.

steel. The T/C rubber grip is a desirable addition for the harder-kicking Encores.

Thompson/Center has a new owner. Greg Ritz, who has been with T/C for quite a while and may be seen regularly hunting on television, is a true shooter and should prove a very valuable asset not only to Thompson/Center but all shooters.

SSK Industries

It is virtually impossible to mention Thompson/Center single-shot pistols without thinking of SSK Industries and the genius of J.D. Jones. J.D. is one of the world's top handgun hunters using custom SSK T/Cs to take virtually everything. I started handgun hunting with one of SSK's early efforts, the 430 JDJ, nearly 30 years ago; moved up to the 45-70, and then settled on the 375 JDJ for large game and the superb 6.5 JDJ for deer-size game. The latter is based on the 225 Winchester case expanded and blown out to 6.5mm. It kills all out of proportion to its paper ballistics, especially when loaded with the 120-grain Speer SP at 2400 fps.

With the coming of the Encore, SSK moved up a notch and offers custom barrels in any safe chamberings, including several wildcats such as the 6.5 Dreadnought based on the 30-06 case. Two of the most recent chamberings are the 500 S&W and 460 XVR. In addition to standard Encores chambered in 22-250, 308, and 7mm-08, I also use J.D.'s barrels chambered in the aforementioned Dreadnought and 500 S&W. If it can be done safely, SSK can provide a custom Encore barrel in virtually any rifle chambering. SSK also offers the ONLY scope mounting system for really hard-kicking handguns, the T'SOB. It works and is the only one I recommend for the heavy-hitters.

Mag-Na-Port

Even before J.D. Jones started SSK Industries, his good friend and hunting buddy, Larry Kelly, started helping shooters reduce recoil by the EDM process known as Mag-na-port. The little trapezoidal-shaped ports were cleanly cut into barrels electronically and reduced muzzle flip. Kelly soon began offering not only the Mag-na-port feature but also custom handguns design for the handgun

Top: T/C's G2 Contender is a very popular hunting handgun, especially in the 14-inch version.
Bottom: For high-pressure cartridges such as the 454 Casull, 308, and 30-06, T/C offers the Encore, here in stainless steel.

hunter. The Stalker conversions were, and are, accomplished on big bore Ruger, Smith & Wesson, and Freedom Arm six-guns, with specially tuned actions, Mag-na-porting, sling swivels, and scopes mounted using SSK's T-SOB system.

Now Larry Kelly is retired and Mag-na-port is headed up by son Ken who offers several new packages for the new generation of six-guns.

Smith & Wesson's new line of revolvers are traveling in two directions: The 500 and 460 Magnums are two extremely powerful cartridges in very large and heavy revolvers; on the other hand S&W offers the 357 and 44 Magnum in very lightweight revolvers made of scandium and titanium. The answer to help tame recoil, especially on the very lightweight guns, is Mag-na-porting.

European American Armory

EAA has entered the single-shot market. Thor is the latest single-shot pistol from Tanfoglio, via EAA. Chambered in 45-70, the grip frame is 1911-shaped and Hogue's checkered rubber grips with finger grooves provide a very secure hold.

Thor is built heavy-duty with a 1/2-inch block of steel containing the firing pin. To open the action, the hammer is placed on half-cock, the 1911-style "magazine" release button is pushed in and the other hand pushes down on the top of the barrel. A cartridge is inserted, the receiver is pushed down into place and the action locks. To fire, the hammer is fully cocked. There is a thumb safety and grip safety; again, just as on a 1911.

Barrel length, including the entire cartridge, is 14 inches and the top of the massive receiver has a scope mount integrally machined. Thor is finished in matte black, appropriate for a gun with this name, and comes with a matching matte black Leupold M8-4x scope mounted in quick-release rings. Thor is also available in 444 Marlin and 308 Winchester.

Replica Single Actions

I've been hoping and watching for it since Navy Arms first introduced the Schofield Model in the early 1990s. I knew it had to be close when Navy followed with the Model #3 Russian. Now it is here. *Beretta/Uberti* has announced the New Model #3—patterned after the original Smith & Wesson New Model #3 of the

Top: The Ruger Super Redhawk becomes a much easier to pack six-gun with the Mag-Na-Port 480 Advantage conversion. Bottom: Some of the nastiest recoil imaginable is found in the 12-ounce S&W 360Sc 357 Magnum. Mag-na-porting helps tame the muzzle flip.

1880s. The original was chambered in 44 Russian, a few in 44-40. For some reason, Beretta/Uberti chose to go with the 45 Colt. The prototype at the SHOT Show was a Target Model hurriedly finished in matte black; production models will be polished blue. It felt very good, with a smooth action, and I hope they chamber it for one of the original cartridges. Beretta/Uberti also displayed nickel-plated Bisley models looking very close to the originals of the 1890s.

By the time you read this, **Cimarron Firearms** hopes to have the cartridge conversion Model 1858 Remington complete with ejector rod housing. They continue to offer the Colt-style cartridge conversions with both the 1851 Navy and 1860 Army grip frame, as well as the 1871-72 Open-Top. The Model P is offered in blue/case-colored, nickel-plated and in a variety of calibers—as well as stainless steel—in all three standard barrel lengths, chambered in both 357 Magnum and 45 Colt. Their Evil Roy Model P—designed by Gene "Evil Roy" Pearcy with checkered wood stocks, tuned action, and easy-to-see square sights—is proving to be very popular with western action shooters.

EMF continues to offer the Great Western II in blue and nickel finishes and has now added stainless steel models. They also offer a full line of traditionally styled 1873 Colt-style Hartford Models as well as the Pinkerton, Buntline, and Bisley Models—plus the replica Remington Model 1875. EMF's Great Western II is produced by Pietta, which also manufactures the Heritage Single Action. The latter, with a 4 3/4-inch barrel, nickel plating, and well-fitted and shaped American walnut stocks, will retail for only $329.

Navy Arms, as mentioned was the first to offer an S&W single action: the Schofield, followed by the Model #3 Russian. The Schofield, in 45 Colt or 38 Special, is offered in the 7-inch Cavalry, 5-inch Wells Fargo, and 3 1/2-inch Hideout Models, while the Model #3 Russian is offered only in the traditional 6 1/2-inch, and chambered in 44 Russian. In addition to the standard 1873 Single Action, Navy also has The Gunfighter, specially tuned with checkered rubber grips, silver-plated backstrap and trigger guard, all three traditional barrel lengths and chambering choices of 45 Colt, 44-40, and 357 Magnum.

In addition to being the exclusive distributor of the American-made Hartford Armory Remingtons, **Taylor's & Co.** has a full line of traditional-styled 1873 single actions as well as the Bisley Model, round-butted Birdshead, stainless steel Outfitter, and the compact Stallion. New this year is the "TR Presidential" with enhanced photo engraving. Taylor's is the first to offer a specially tuned Ruger New Vaquero as the HandleBar Doc Signature Series. Taylor's also offers a full line of R&D drop-in cylinders to convert cap and ball revolvers to cartridge firing. These include 45 Colt to fit Uberti, Pietta, and ASM Remingtons and Ruger Old Armies as well as 38 Special cylinders for steel frame Pietta or Uberti 36-caliber Remingtons.

Kenny Howell of **R&D** is also doing conversions and offering conversion kits on 1851/1861 and 1860 cap and ball six-guns. These conversions consist of a cartridge cylinder complete with loading gate and a lined barrel to 38LC/38 Special on all models or 44 Colt on the 1860. He is also offering a five-shot 45 Colt cylinder kit, which matches up with the existing barrel on the 1860. These are quality conversions all the way.

Custom Six-Guns On Old Model Ruger Blackhawks

Skeeter started it *(Skeeter Skelton, that is)* with an article in the April 1972 issue of *Shooting Times* about converting old model Rugers and

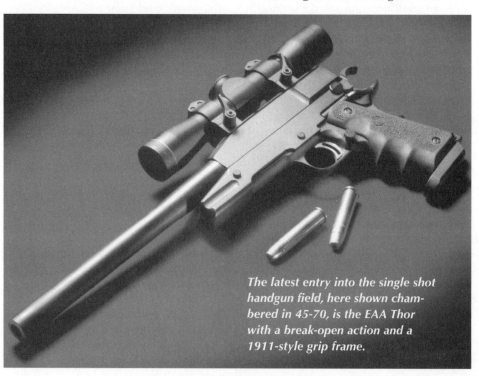

The latest entry into the single shot handgun field, here shown chambered in 45-70, is the EAA Thor with a break-open action and a 1911-style grip frame.

the S&W Highway Patrolman to 44 Special. Skeeter went Home in 1988 and I have been doing my best to continue to spread the word about the wonders of the 44 Special in general—especially when chambered in a three-screw Ruger, whether it started life as Flat-Top or Old Model 357 Magnum. Unlike the New Model Ruger Blackhawk, which is built on the larger 44 Blackhawk frame, the three-screws manufactured from 1955-1972 all have Colt single action-sized frames. Bill Ruger expected to chamber his original Flat-Top Blackhawk in 44 Special; however, the arrival of the 44 Magnum changed all that and he instead brought out a larger-framed 44 Flat-Top in 1956.

Whether starting with a Highway Patrolman or three-screw Ruger for the conversion, it is necessary to re-chamber the cylinder and either re-bore the barrel or use an available 44 Special barrel. This was not a problem with the Smith & Wesson conversion thirty years ago when original 44 Special Model 24 barrels were still available. Today, they are nearly impossible to find. The Ruger conversion is much easier to accomplish since a Ruger 44 Magnum

barrel can be used, or one may start with 44 barrel stock, which is much easier to fit to a single action than a double-action revolver requiring a cut out and lock up for the ejector rod.

Here then are ten 44 Special conversions on three-screw Rugers by five different gunsmiths, another custom 44 by a very special friend, and if you look closely you may even catch a glimpse of that other Special, the 41. Feel free to use any of these ideas, or better yet contact one of the four remaining six-gunsmiths, as Bill Grover has been called Home.

HAMILTON BOWEN: Pictured are four 44 Special Blackhawk conversions and one 41 Special Blackhawk with case-colored frame and hammer—all by Hamilton Bowen. Three of the 44s are on Flat-Tops, one on an Old Model, and the 41 on a Flat-Top frame. The latter has to be one of the most beautiful single-action six-guns in existence. Two of the 357 Flat-Tops are now a matched pair of 4 5/8-inch bright blue 44 Specials with stag grips. The third one had been ridden hard and put up wet and although it was mechanically fine, the finish was pitted in places. This has been made

▲ *Mike Harvey of Cimarron Firearms shows an engraved and nickel-plated 1871-72 Open-Top.*
▼ *Some replica single actions available today are,* clockwise from top right, *EMF's Model 1875 Remington, Navy Arms Model #3 Russian, and two from Cimarron—an Original Finish Model P and an 1871-72 Open-Top*

into a real workin' 44 Special six-gun with a bead blasted finish. The final 44 Special conversion by Bowen on an Old Model frame is fitted with a 7 1/2-inch barrel, polished grip frame, and black micarta grips by Charles Able.

DAVID CLEMENTS: David Clements is another custom six-gunsmith building many big-bore New Model conversions, however, he also turns out some fine three-screw 44 Special six-guns.

BEN FORKIN: Ben Forkin of Montana began his gunsmithing career the right way, working under Hamilton Bowen. All of the custom three-screw Blackhawks mentioned thus far have 4 5/8- or 7 1/2-inch barrels. Using a recently purchased like-new 6 1/2-inch 44 Magnum Flat-Top barrel, we decided to do a 5 1/2-inch 44 Special complete with case hardened mainframe and hammer. Ben performed his usual action work: smoothing, tuning, and tightening; re-chambered the cylinder to 44 Special cutting it to use .430-inch Keith bullets; cut the 44 Magnum barrel to the proper length and fitted it with a post front sight mated with a Bowen adjustable rear sight. He finished off the package with one of Belt Mountain's #5 base pins.

BILL GROVER: In the late 1980s I saw a very special 44 Special on a Ruger Old Model. The barrel was 4-5/8 inches long, the grip frame was polished bright, and the grips were made from the horns of a bighorn sheep. This special six-gun was shown to me by Bart Skelton as it had belonged to his dad Skeeter before he died and then belonged to gunwriter John Wootters. Two three-screw 357 Blackhawks went off to Bill Grover of Texas Longhorn Arms.

Grover and I put our heads together on this one so a double influence can be seen. The cylinder has been re-chambered to 44 Special tightly to allow the use of .429-inch diameter bullets but kept to minimum dimensions for long case life. Barrel/cylinder gap was set at 0.0025-inch. The Ruger XR3 grip frame and steel ejector housing were not discarded,

The Cimarron "Evil Roy" is especially designed for cowboy action shooters with square sights, tuned action, and checkered wooden stocks.

Middle Left: **Taylor's & Co. now offers the R&D drop-in cylinder, chambered in 45 Colt, for the Ruger Old Army.**
Bottom Left: **Not a New Frontier but rather a Ruger OM converted to 44 Special, with an auxiliary cylinder in 44-40 and a New Frontier barrel fitted by David Clements. Custom stocks are by Larry Caudill.**

Two easy-packing 44 Specials: the blued version by Andy Horvath and the nickel-plated "Baby" by R.G. Baer.

but put back for use on the other 44 Special Grover was building. In their place Grover fitted steel Colt parts, a Colt backstrap and trigger guard, which now wears one-piece ivories, and a Colt ejector housing along with a bullseye-head ejector rod.

The second 44 Special six-gun from Grover was built with a 7 1/2-inch barrel using a 10 1/2-inch Ruger Super Blackhawk barrel. The XR3 grip frame of #SS4 now resides on this six-gun along with rosewood stocks. This long-range six-gun made to complement the #SS4 packin' pistol also wears a Number Five front sight and a Number Five base pin.

R.G. BAER: Bob Baer is not a working gunsmith but simply a special friend who likes to customize his own six-guns. An Old Model three-screw 357 Ruger Blackhawk was turned over to him with instructions to simply build me a special gun, his choice of style and caliber. Having seen, handled, and shot many of Baer's creations from short barrels

to long barrels, from round butts to lanyard rings, from 22s to 357s to 44s, with all kinds of artistic touches, I knew I would not be disappointed.

Since Baer had a pretty good idea where my heart lies, the conversion is a 44 Special. The front and rear edge of the grip frame are tapered for greater comfort, with no sharp edges to emphasize recoil, and the fancy walnut grips have been expertly fitted to the bright polished aluminum grip frame. The aluminum ejector rod housing is also polished bright while the rest of Baby, as Baer dubbed it, is finished in satin hard nickel plating. To aid in the project, gunsmith Keith DeHart expertly re-chambered the cylinder and furnished the 3 1/4-inch barrel. The total package is a very easy to pack 30 ounces.

ANDY HORVATH: About 20 years ago Horvath was asked if he could do a round-butted, 4-inch barrel 44 built on a Ruger 357 three-screw Blackhawk, a real 44 Special packin' pistol. The answer came back

affirmative and off went a 6 1/2-inch 357 three-screw Blackhawk, a 7 1/2-inch Super Blackhawk barrel, and some special items I had been saving for just such a project.

Recently I have had the pleasure of working with one of Horvath's latest 44 Specials. Starting with a Flat-Top 357 Blackhawk, Andy re-chambered it to 44 Special, fitted it with a full-ribbed heavy barrel from a S&W 44 Magnum with an undercut post front sight, re-contoured the front edge of the top strap to blend in perfectly with the ribbed barrel, then fitted it with an abbreviated style #5 base pin. The finish is a deep, high polished blue set off perfectly by a case hardened frame and hammer. It was very difficult to even consider returning this test gun—so I bought it.

Yes, things were much simpler in the old days when so few choices were available. Today's handgunner can sincerely say that sometimes progress can be wonderful. Have a great six-gunnin' year!

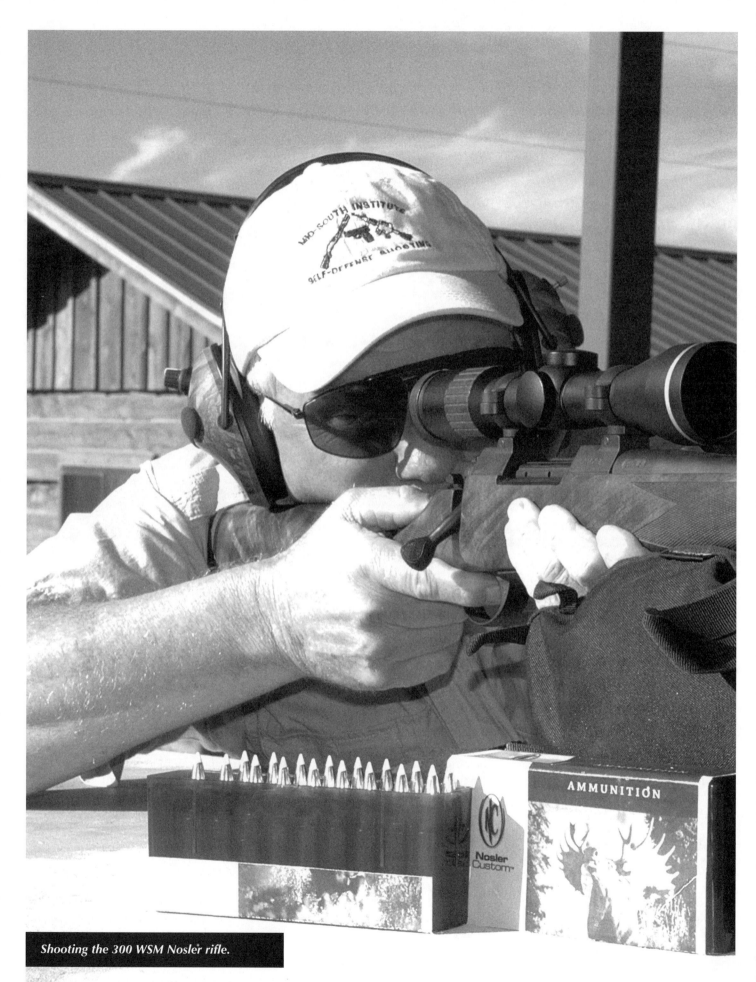

Shooting the 300 WSM Nosler rifle.

RIFLES TODAY:

RIFLE REVIEW

by Layne Simpson

T he Barrett M468 is an AR-15-style autoloader in 6.8mm Remington SPC. To mention but a few of its features: dual spring extractor system, folding front sight, heavy-duty gas block and two-stage trigger. Overall length, with 16-inch barrel, is 35-1/2 inches and it weighs 7-1/4 pounds.

Benelli

The R-1 rifle I used on a hunt for whitetail deer in 2004 was exactly like the one I carried a few years back while hunting driven boar and stag in the Transylvania Mountains of Romania. At that time its only chambering options were 308 Winchester, 30-06 and 300 Winchester Magnum, but you can now buy one in 270 WSM or 300 WSM as well. It doesn't take a lot to kill a Texas deer, so I stuck with the 308 Winchester and used Fusion ammunition from Federal. I could not have asked for better performance from a bonded-core bullet. Here is the really interesting part: The new line of ammunition will cost the same as Federal Power-Shok ammo, which is a bargain considering it is loaded with bullets of bonded-core design. We hunted until dark each day and the 3-10x Burris Euro Diamond scope worn by the rifle I hunted with proved to be incredibly bright.

On that same hunt I took a rather large boar with a Benelli turkey gun loaded with Federal's new TruBall

You can also buy the Benelli R1 in 30-06, 300 Winchester Magnum, 270 WSM and 300 WSM, but since Texas whitetails don't take a lot of killing, I chose one in 308 Winchester to take this buck back in November of 2004. I also used Federal ammo loaded with the new Fusion, bonded-core bullet and it worked great.

version of the 12-gauge rifled slug load. The range was just under 70 yards. The Foster-style slug is the same one Federal has been offering for many years, but a plastic ball and special wad are loaded in the shell behind it to improve accuracy. During the hunt, I did not have an opportunity to seriously check out the accuracy of the new load in the Benelli, but after arriving back home I tried it in two other guns, a Thompson/Center TCR

83 rifle wearing a slug barrel and a Winchester Model 1300 pump gun. Both had smoothbore barrels and both wore scopes. The TCR barrel has a bore diameter of 0.729-inch with no choke constriction, while the bore of the Model 1300 measures 0.733-inch, with 0.003-inch of constriction (Light Skeet). In the Model 1300, the TruBall load averaged 3.31 inches for five, five-shot groups at 50 yards compared to 4.28 inches for the load it has replaced

in the Federal ammunition lineup. In the TCR, it was 2.73 inches for the new and 4.66 inches for the old.

The lineup of Uberti rifles imported by Benelli continues to grow, with a copy of the Colt Lightning being the latest addition. It will be offered in 357 Magnum and 45 Colt.

Browning

Since Browning and U.S. Repeating Arms, maker of Winchester rifles, are both owned by the same parent company, and since both have a close working relationship with the other Winchester that makes ammunition, it comes as no surprise to see those two companies first in line to offer rifles with "325 WSM" stamped on their barrels. Simply the 300 WSM case necked up for an 8mm bullet, the new cartridge is slated to become available in a number of Browning rifles in plenty of time for the 2005 hunting seasons. A-Bolt variants chambered for it will include both right- and left-hand versions of the Hunter, Micro Hunter and Medallion, as well as the Stainless Stalker and Composite Stalker. The year 2005 will also see more A-Bolt variants available in 25 WSSM, a super-short cartridge that duplicates the performance of the 25-06 Remington.

Latest edition of the BLR is the short-action Lightweight with pistol grip stock and 20- or 22-inch barrel in various chamberings ranging in power from the 22-250 to 325 WSM. It weighs 6-1/2 pounds in standard chamberings and a quarter-pound more in the magnums. Moving from big-game rifles to rifles better suited for plinking and small-game hunting, we can now buy the BL-22 in *(surprise!)* 17 HM2. Except in this case it is called the BL-17 and offered in several styles, one with an octagonal barrel and two others with satin-nickeled receivers.

Charles Daly

A real sleeper among small-game rifles, the new Superior II bolt gun has a 22-inch barrel and a walnut stock of classical style with oil finish and cut checkering. The receivers of rifles in 22 LR and 17 HM2 are grooved for scope mounting while those in 22 WMR and 17 HMR are drilled and tapped. The detachable magazine holds five rounds and it weighs six pounds.

Cimarron

Reproductions of several Sharps single-shot rifles are now available from Cimarron. The Texas Ranger Carbine has a 22-inch barrel in 45-70 or 50-70, and is a copy of the 1859 percussion military carbine converted to centerfire. Then we have the Cimarron Big Fifty with a 34-inch barrel in 50-90 or 50-100, either of which Billy Dixon would have been proud to own. Two other Sharps replicas are the Professional Hunter and Pride of Plains, both in 45-70. Also available is a copy of the Winchester Low Wall single shot in 22 LR, 22 Hornet, 30-30, 32-20, 38-40, 357 Magnum, 44-40 and 44 Magnum.

Cooper Arms

Only a very few companies build rifles as accurate as those built by Cooper Arms, and even fewer companies build rifles as handsome. I know of no other company building rifles that are both custom rifle handsome and target rifle accurate. I will go even further by saying that if I had to pick five companies that build the most handsome rifles in America, one of them would have to be Cooper Arms. And since Dan Cooper guarantees his centerfire rifles to shoot three bullets inside half an inch at 100 yards, the beauty of his rifles is more than skin deep. His guarantee for rimfire rifles in 17 HM2,

17 HMR, 22 Long Rifle and 22 WMR is 1/4-inch for five shots at 50 yards.

Three model variations are available in centerfire varmint rifles, Varminter, Montana Varminter and Varminter Extreme. Most of the popular chamberings are available with some of the more interesting being 17 Ackley Hornet, 17 Mach IV, 19 Calhoun, 218 Mashburn Bee, 22 PPC and 220 Weatherby Rocket. I have owned a Varminter Extreme in 17 Remington for several years and it refuses to shoot groups bigger than half an inch at 100 yards with the Berger 25- and 30-grain bullets, and the Hornady 20-grain V-Max. Big-game rifles include the Classic, Custom Classic and Western Classic, the latter with an octagonal barrel and case-colored receiver. Actions range from short enough to be just right for the new 6.8mm Remington SPC to long enough to handle the old 25-06 and Ackley's improved version of same. In addition to the standard chamberings, there are other options such as the 6x45mm, 243 Winchester Improved, 6mm-284, 25x45mm and 257 Roberts Improved. As I write this, all Cooper rifles are single shots––but my crystal ball says I will be writing about the new repeaters next year.

During the 2004 season I took a very nice pronghorn buck while hunting with Mike Ballew of the Whittington Center near Raton, New Mexico and the rifle I used was a Cooper Model 22 Custom Classic in 6.5-284 Norma. Believe me when I say photos do not do its English walnut stock justice. All Cooper rifles come with a test target fired at the Montana factory and, while the one in the box with my rifle was fired at 50 yards, it was still quite impressive since it measured a mere 0.008-inch. That, my friends, is the thickness of two pages in the fine publication you are now holding in your hands. The load used to fire that group consisted of the Federal 210M primer, Hornady case, and 47.0 grains of Reloder 22 behind the 140-grain Sierra MatchKing. Using the same load, I was not able to duplicate the accuracy of the factory group but I figure the 0.37-inch average I did manage to squeeze off at 100 yards was good enough. In fact, of the dozen handloads I tried in the rifle, only one

The latest version of the short-action, lightweight Browning BLR has a curved grip and is chambered for various cartridges from the old 22-250 to the new 325 WSM.

averaged greater than minute-of-angle, and it came close at 1.08 inches. Five of the loads averaged less than half an inch. One of my three most accurate recipes was recommended by the folks at Sierra—46.7 grains of IMR-4831 and the 140-grain MatchKing for an average of 0.29-inch. The other two loads were 47.0 grains of VihtaVuori N165 and the Hornady 140-grain A-Max (0.34-inch) and 46.7 grains of IMR-4831 behind the Sierra 142-grain MatchKing for an average of 0.38-inch. The Cooper rifle was also quite accurate with custom ammo loaded by Nosler; the 120-grain Ballistic Tip load I used on the antelope hunt averaged 0.33-inch at 100 yards. Average muzzle velocity of that load was 3025 fps.

CZ-USA

By the time you read this, the CZ 527 should be available in 6.8mm Remington SPC. Over in the rimfire department there is the 542 in 17 HM2 with a 22 1/2-inch barrel and walnut stock. The varmint version has a heavier 21-inch barrel. Both have five-round detachable magazines.

Ed Brown Products

The EBP family of rifles continues to grow. In addition to rifles with serious names like Tactical, Light Tactical and Marine, there is a nine-pound varmint rifle and big-game rifles called Damara (6-1/4 pounds), Denali (seven pounds), Savannah (7-1/2 pounds) and Bushveld at 8-1/2 pounds. All EBP rifles wear McMillan synthetic stocks; a camo finish on the Marine and black on all the rest. Most of the popular chamberings, from 204 Ruger to 458 Lott, are available.

During the 2004 season I took a very nice elk in Utah with a Denali chambered for a cartridge that some say is not big enough to kill an elk, the 270 Winchester. The rifle wore a Zeiss 3-9x scope. The ammo I used was Hornady Light Magnum loaded with the 130-grain InterBond bullet and it averaged about 1-1/2 inches for three shots at 100 yards. I found it interesting that the Hornady loading of the ancient old 270 Winchester is actually faster than Winchester's loadings of the 270 WSM with the

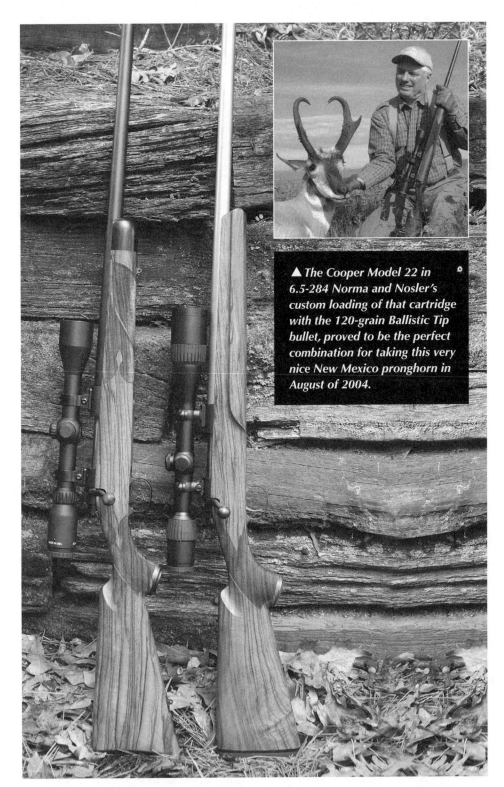

▲ The Cooper Model 22 in 6.5-284 Norma and Nosler's custom loading of that cartridge with the 120-grain Ballistic Tip bullet, proved to be the perfect combination for taking this very nice New Mexico pronghorn in August of 2004.

At left is my new Cooper Model 22 in 6.5-284 Norma and at right is my old Cooper Model 21 in 17 Remington. Both will consistently shoot five bullets inside half an inch at 100 yards.

same bullet weight. And this is in barrels of the same length. I recently completed a thorough comparison of those two cartridges in a couple of Weatherby Vanguard rifles, both with 24-inch barrels. The Hornady 130-grain Light Magnum load averaged 3218 fps versus 3152 fps for the fastest Winchester load (130-grain Ballistic Silvertip). The pessimist would say the new cartridge is 66 fps slower than the old cartridge. The

The new Ultra Varmint version of the Handi-Rifle has a stock of radical styling (for H&R) and is available in 204 Ruger, 223 Remington and 22-250.

A reproduction of the Winchester Model 92, the Puma from Legacy is available in a number of interesting chamberings, including 454 Casull and 480 Ruger.

optimist would say the new cartridge comes within 66 fps of duplicating the performance of one of the finest big-game cartridges ever developed.

Empire Rifles

All rifles from Empire are built around newly-manufactured Mauser 1898 actions in the square bridge style, and they ooze quality from every pore. Stocks are available in synthetic or high-grade walnut. You can get a light rifle in calibers ranging from 257 Roberts to 338 Winchester Magnum, or a heavy rifle in really serious chamberings ranging from 375 H&H Magnum to 505 Gibbs. Five grades are available: Field, Guide, Professional, Express and Empire. The fancier the name the more you pay and you will pay a lot for the Empire with its custom stock and hand engraving. These are very nice rifles and the list of options goes on and on.

Harrington & Richardson

Latest chambering available in the H&R Handi-Rifle is the 500 S&W, a pistol cartridge that behaves like a rifle cartridge when fired in a long barrel. Also new is the Ultra Varmint with a stock of radical styling *(for H&R)* in 204 Ruger, 223 Remington and 22-250.

Kimber

Everybody who is anybody is offering a rifle in 17 Hornady Mach 2,

and Kimber is no exception. Called the Kimber 17, several variations are being built. The Classic Varmint has a walnut stock and 20-inch stainless steel barrel with lightening flutes; the Pro Varmint is the same except for its gray laminated wood stock. Weights are six pounds, nine ounces for the former and two ounces more for the latter. Also wearing a walnut stock, another variation called the Hunter has a 22-inch barrel of lighter contour and this lowers its weight to 6-1/2 pounds. The SVT with its high-comb laminated stock and beavertail forearm has an 18 1/2-inch barrel and weighs seven pounds, nine ounces. Like all Kimbers, these have a three-position safety, free-floating barrel and receiver drilled and tapped for scope mounting. As centerfire rifles go, new chamberings are 204 Ruger, 223 Remington and 22-250 in the Model 84M, and the 325 WSM in the Model 8400.

Legacy Sports International

The New Howa Model 1500 Lightning weighs about 7-1/2 pounds and is available in 14 chamberings ranging from 223 Remington to 338 Winchester Magnum. Blued steel and stainless steel barreled actions are available with black and camo synthetic stock options. And now you too can own a lever-action rifle with an oversized finger lever like Chuck Connors once carried on TV. A member of the Puma family of Winchester Model 92 knockoffs, it is called Large Loop Lever and is

available in 45 Colt and 357 Magnum. Other Puma variants are available in other interesting chamberings as well, including 480 Ruger and 454 Casull.

Marlin

The most handsome rifle I have seen lately, and perhaps the most handsome Marlin ever, is the four-millionth Model 336. Marlin built the rifle and then commissioned the craftsmen at Doug Turnbull Restorations to transform it into a one-of-a-kind, heirloom-quality work of art with styling that takes us back to the turn of the 20th century. It is chambered to 38-55 Winchester. Marlin donated the rifle for auction at the 2005 SHOT Show with the proceeds going to the Hunting & Shooting Sports Heritage Fund and its efforts to protect and enhance America's hunting traditions and firearm freedoms.

Moving on to handsome big-game rifles you and I can afford, Marlin now offers the ever-popular Model 336 in nine different variations, all with cut-checkered wood stocks. Chamberings are 30-30, 35 Remington, 444 Marlin, 45-70 and 450 Marlin and 410 smoothbore. Marlin never describes its Model 336 as the most accurate lever-action rifle available but during the past few years I have shot several in all calibers except 35 Remington, and each one averaged less than two inches at 100 yards for five-shot groups. Some bolt-action rifles are not as accurate.

The Model 1894 family of rifles and carbines also continues to grow and the 32-20 chambering is back in the lineup for 2005. Called the Model 1894CL, its half-length magazine holds six rounds, and its 22-inch barrel has a rifling twist rate of 1:20 inches. Overall length is 39-1/2 inches and it weighs six pounds. Can the 218 Bee and 25-20 be far behind? Other variations include the Model 1894 (blued steel) and Model 1894SS (stainless) in 44 Magnum, Model 1894FG in 41 Magnum and Model 1894C in 357 Magnum. The "cowboy" versions, with their octagonal barrels in various calibers including 32 H&R Magnum, are quite nice, too.

If your guess is the new Model 717M2 autoloader is chambered for the 17 Mach 2 you are correct. Its detachable magazine holds seven rounds, it has an 18-inch barrel with a 1:9 inch rifling twist rate and it weighs five pounds. Overall length is 37 inches. The Monte Carlo-style stock is described by Marlin as walnut-finished laminated hardwood. This neat little small-game rifle has a last-shot bolt hold-open feature and its receiver is grooved for scope mounting. Also new is the Model 917VSF in the same caliber, a bolt gun with stainless steel-barreled action, laminated wood stock and detachable magazine. It is basically last year's Model 917VS with a fluted barrel.

The new Model 717M2 autoloader from Marlin is chambered for the 17 Hornady Mach 2.

The Marlin 1894 is now available in 32-20 Winchester, and a very nice little outfit it is.

Nosler

So what is the name Nosler doing in a report on rifles? The rifle I shot had something more than its name in common with Nosler bullets—it was incredibly accurate. To see what such a rifle looks like, you have only to turn to my Testfire report elsewhere in this edition.

Remington

The 6.8mm Special Purpose Cartridge (SPC) was developed as a military cartridge for the AR-16/M-16 rifle and its mission is to deliver quicker stops on bad guys than the 5.6x45mm *(or 223 Remington to us civilians)* is capable of. It is now being promoted by Remington as a low-recoil deer cartridge with the ability to deliver a 115-grain, 270-caliber bullet at about the same level of energy at 200 yards as the 30-30 Winchester does at 100. Of course, this is comparing the performance of a pointed bullet in the 6.8mm to a bluntnose bullet in the 30-30. When loaded to maximum velocity with a 150-grain spitzer and fired in my T/C G2 Contender rifle, the 30-30 equals the 6.8mm in power at all ranges. But that's beside the point to those who do not handload.

The Model Seven AWR now being offered in 6.8mm SPC by Remington was still a long way off back in early September of 2004 when I headed to the far north for caribou so I had to make-do with a short-action Model 700 from Remington's custom shop. I tried all four factory loads in that rifle and the 115-grain Core-Lokt Ultra whipped 'em all in accuracy, including the load with Sierra's MatchKing

bullet of the same weight. The CL-U load also accounted for a nice caribou bull. My most accurate handloads consisted of Benchmark powder and two bullets; Hornady's 130-grain SST and Sierra's 135-grain MatchKing. Velocity was around 2400 fps.

Those of us who have had a few custom rifles built through the years have long known that the extremely rigid Remington XP-100 single-shot action is one of the best available to wrap a varmint rifle around. On top of that, there was a time when the one in 221 Fire Ball was cheap enough to buy and throw away everything except the action. Remington has now made such a rifle available to the shooting

masses by introducing its Model XR-100 Rangemaster in 204 Ruger, 223 Remington and 22-250. It is a mixture of XP-100 single-shot action, Model 700 bolt handle and 40-XB trigger, all nestled in gray laminated wood with thumbhole-style buttstock, and beavertail forearm replete with 1955 Buick-style cooling vents. The trigger is adjustable down to about 24 ounces and the medium-heavy barrel is 26 inches long. This one gets my vote as the long-range varmint rifle to be seen in the field with during the next decade or so. I only wish it was available in 220 Swift as well.

I now have two favorite Model 700 variations. When I am in the mood

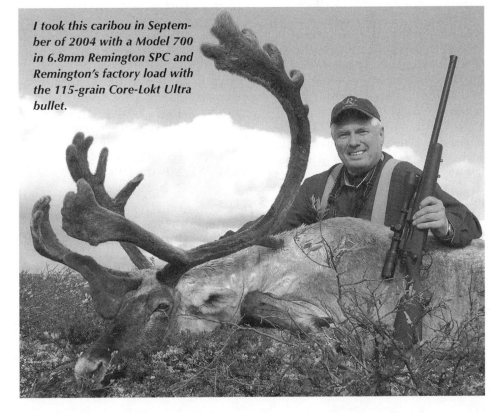

I took this caribou in September of 2004 with a Model 700 in 6.8mm Remington SPC and Remington's factory load with the 115-grain Core-Lokt Ultra bullet.

for checkered walnut and blued steel, the Model 700 CDL is the rifle you are likely to see me toting over hill and dale. It reminds me a lot of the old Model 700 Mountain Rifle, but it has a 26-inch barrel for squeezing maximum speed from the magnum cartridges for which it is chambered. I had two bulls on my caribou license so after bumping off one with the 6.8mm SPC, I took the other a few days later with a Model 700 CDL in 7mm Remington Magnum. Back home, it consistently shot inside an inch at 100 yards with Remington's 140- and 160-grain Core-Lokt Ultra factory loads with a number of groups measuring close to half an inch. Its other chamberings are 243 Winchester, 270 Winchester, 7mm-08, 7mm Ultra Mag, 30-06, 300 Winchester Magnum and 300 Ultra Mag. Darned nice rifle, and one of the more handsome ever built by Remington. It and the Model 700 in 6.8mm SPC I used on the caribou hunt wore 2.5-10x Bushnell Elite 4200 scopes with the RainGuard lens coating, and they earned their keep in all that rain. My favorite Model 700 for rough weather hunting, by the way, is the XCR which is short for Xtreme Conditions Rifle.

Last in line and price but certainly not last in value are break-action, single-shot, over-under and side-by-side rifles at unbelievably low prices. All are members of Remington's new Spartan Gunworks line of firearms. The SPR18 single-shot is available in 223 Remington, 243 Winchester, 270 Winchester and 30-06. The SPR94 over-under combination gun is available in 22 LR, 17 HMR and 22 WMR over a 410-bore shotgun barrel or 12-gauge over 223, 308 and 30-06. The SPR22 is a side-by-side double in 30-06 or 45-70. Standard features include chrome-lined, hammer-forged barrels, all-steel receivers, fully adjustable open sights, scope mounting rail atop the receiver, walnut stock and forearm and one-inch carrying sling swivels. Made in Russia, "they strong like bear".

Rogue River Rifle Co.

The Chipmunk is every kid's idea of the perfect rifle and it is now available in 17 HM2 and 22 LR and in a left-hand version as well. TruGlo sights are now standard on all models, and the new stainless steel rifles won't rust as quickly when handled by sticky little hands. The latest variant is called the Barracuda and its stock is unlike anything you have ever seen worn by a Chipmunk.

Rossi

When it comes to break-action, single-shot firearms, nobody offers more choices than Rossi. Inline muzzleloaders, smoothbore shotguns, slug guns with rifled barrels, centerfires, rimfires, you name it and they probably have it. A number of two-barrel sets are available too, with 22-250 and 20-gauge one of the latest additions. The Muzzleloader Plus One pairs offer several combinations, such as a 50-caliber inline barrel matched up with a barrel in 12-gauge or 243 Winchester. The options are so great in number they fill up the latest Rossi catalog.

Ruger

The curved steel buttplate on the stock of the Mini-14 Ranch Rifle has been replaced with a black rubber pad. Also new to this little rifle is a matte finish on the stainless steel and a military-style front sight blade with protective ears. The Mark II Frontier version of the Model 77 rifle is rated at only six pounds. That, along with a barrel length of 16 inches and a stock length-of-pull of only 12-5/8 inches, makes it a compact and lightweight package. Using Ruger rings, you can attach a regular scope to the receiver or, if you are so inclined, you can attach a long-eye relief scope to a quarter-rib out on the barrel. The rib appears to have been robbed from Ruger's No. 1 single-shot rifle. The stock is laminated wood and, like Henry Ford might have said had he built rifles rather than automobiles, you can have any chambering you want so long as the chambering you want is 243 Winchester, 308 Winchester, 300 WSM or 7mm-08. Other news from Prescott includes the 17 HM2 in the Model 77/17, and the 204 Ruger in the No. 1A Light Sporter and Mark II Target Rifle.

Sako

Biggest news from Finland is the Sako Quad, a handsome little bolt-action rifle with 22-inch interchangeable barrels and magazines in 17 HM2, 22 Long Rifle, 17 HMR and 22 WMR. The rifle can be purchased with one barrel or in a combo package with all four barrels. Switching barrels takes mere seconds. The Quad weighs 5-3/4 pounds, has a black synthetic stock and pull weight of its single-stage trigger is adjustable from two to four pounds. I have one of these on the way and will let you know how well it works next year.

Moving on to centerfire rifles, we have a new variation of the Model 75 called Grey Wolf. Its barreled action is stainless steel and as its name might imply, its laminated wood stock is gray in color. Barrel lengths are 22-1/2 inches for standard cartridges ranging from 223 Remington to 30-06, and 24-1/2 inches for Winchester's short magnums in 270, 7mm and 300

Ruger's Ranch Rifle has undergone a number of upgrades, including a rubber butt pad and a military-style front sight with protective ears.

As its name implies, the Sako Model 75 Gray Wolf has a gray laminated wood stock. It is available in a variety of chamberings from 223 Remington to 300 WSM.

I like switch-barrel rifles and am looking forward to working with the new bolt-action Quad from Sako. It can be bought with one barrel or with four interchangeable barrels and magazines in 17 HM2, 22 LR, 17 HMR and 22 WMR. What fun!

calibers. A similar rifle called the Custom Single Shot is offered in 308 Winchester only and one wonders why it is not also available in various 22-caliber varmint chamberings––and perhaps even 243 Winchester.

Savage

Savage recently brought back the Stevens name with the introduction of an economy-grade knockabout shotgun in side-by-side style and the new Model 200 centerfire rifle is a continuation of that resurrection. Basically a no-frills version of the Savage 110, it is available with both long and short actions in a variety of calibers. The action is pillar-bedded into a synthetic stock.

Shilen, Inc.

Shilen does not build rifles but the company does make some of the world's most accurate barrels. Something

some folks don't realize is the guys at Shilen will rebarrel rifles. I recently had them install a 26-inch benchrest-grade barrel in 257 Weatherby Magnum on a highly tuned Remington Model 700 action. It consistently averages half an inch for three shots at 100 yards with Weatherby factory ammo loaded with the Nosler 115-grain Ballistic Tip. Shilen offers two types of 257 Weatherby Magnum chambers. One duplicates the freebore of Weatherby factory rifles in that caliber. Another cuts a shorter chamber throat, but factory ammo can still be fired in it. Shilen also offers excellent match-grade triggers for the Model 700. One is for big-game rifles and the other with its two-ounce weight of pull is for use on a target rifle.

Springfield, Inc.

About a week before writing this I watched GUN DIGEST editor Ken

Ramage shoot the new Socom II rifle from Springfield and he kept asking for more ammo. The latest variation of the ever-popular M1A1, its 16-1/4 inch barrel is in 7.62mm NATO *(or 308 Winchester to we civilians)* and it comes with a 10-round magazine *(20-rounders are also available)*. It has a black synthetic stock *(what else?)* and an extremely loud muzzle brake. Iron sights consist of the standard adjustable aperture at the rear and a tritium-imbedded post with protective ears up front. Four Picatinny rails on the top, bottom and sides of its ventilated forearm *(called Cluster Rail System by Springfield)* have more than enough room for scopes, red dot sights, lasers, flashlights and other gadgets and gizmos that make a gun like this fun to shoot. Overall length is a compact 37 inches, which is why its manufacturer bills the Socom II as just the ticket for close-quarters work.

Due to its interchangeable barrels in various calibers, the Thompson/Center G2 rifle can be many different things to many different hunters and in my case, the 30-30 barrel and a handload with the Hornady 150-grain SST bullet was what I needed to harvest this whitetail on a December 2004 hunt in Kansas.

Taylor's & Company

This company offers a reproduction of the Winchester Model 92 in three versions, standard, saddle ring carbine and takedown, the latter available with 20- or 24-inch octagon barrel. Chambering options are 32-20, 32 H&R Magnum, 38 Special, 357 Magnum, 38-40, 44-40 and 45 Colt. Stock and forearm are American walnut with an oil finish.

Thompson/Center

The trim little G2 Contender rifle has three new barrel options for 2004. All are 23 inches long. The one in 6.8mm Remington SPC is an excellent choice for a youngster's first centerfire, or for anyone who is looking for a low-recoil rifle capable of taking deer out to 250 yards or so. I have not fired the T/C barrel in this caliber, but the one built by SSK Industries for my G2 Contender rifle will consistently shoot the Hornady 130-grain SST and Sierra 135-grain MatchKing bullets inside three inches at 300 yards. And it is just as accurate with Remington ammo loaded with the 115-grain Core-Lokt Ultra bullet.

Due to its interchangeable barrel design, the G2 Contender has the capability of being many things to many different hunters and when wearing a 45-caliber barrel it is one of my favorite inline muzzleloaders. We all assumed that barrels above 45 caliber are too large in diameter to squeeze into the small G2 receiver but those clever engineers at T/C have now proven us wrong by introducing a 50-caliber barrel for it. They accomplished this by reducing the diameter of the breech of the barrel enough to fit inside the receiver but leaving the rest of the barrel full diameter to keep recoil at a manageable level. The receiver of the prototype I shot a few groups with had a case-colored finish from the T/C custom shop and that along with its excellent accuracy made me want to take it home. The third new barrel is a smoothbore chambered for the 28-gauge shell which is okay by me since I use the 28 for more of my upland hunting than anything else with the possible exception of the .410. It will come with interchangeable chokes in Improved Cylinder, Modifed and Full.

The G2 Contender rifle barrel, by the way, is not the same as the old Contender carbine barrel. It measures 23 inches long and 0.800-inch at the muzzle, compared to 21 inches long and 0.610-inch at the muzzle for the carbine barrel. It will work on both the old and

new Contender receivers, but its larger diameter does require the use of a different forearm. On average, I find the heavier barrel to be more accurate and yet, at a weight of about seven pounds, the G2 rifle is plenty light for long-distance walking. I know this to be true because I used one back in December while hunting deer in Kansas. Many years ago I shot metallic silhouette with a T/C Contender pistol in 30-30 Winchester, but I had never worked with a Contender rifle in that chambering until the Kansas hunt. Unlike rifles with tubular magazines, a single shot is safe to use with pointed bullets so the handload I settled on consisted of the Federal 210M primer, Winchester case and 34.0 grains of H4895 behind the Hornady 150-grain SST. Muzzle velocity averaged close to 2400 fps. Prior to the hunt I shot the G2 rather extensively and it would consistently keep five bullets inside four inches at 300 yards with that load, and it would do the same with the Hornady 150-grain InterBond pushed along by the same powder charge. It shot flat enough too; when zeroed three inches high at 100 yards, either bullet landed just about dead-on my point of aim at 200 yards and halfway between the first and second tick marks of the Ballistic Plex reticle of the Burris 3-10x Euro Diamond scope worn by the rifle. I was prepared to shoot that far but did not have to. With no more than 15 minutes of shooting light left in the day, the buck stepped out of the woods at about 200 yards for his last meal of green winter wheat.

While in Kansas I also had a ball hunting fox squirrels with a prototype of T/C's Classic autoloader in 17 Hornady Mach 2. This particular version is called Model R55 due to design changes necessitated by cycle timing difference of the 17 HM2 cartridge. A floating balance weight riding beneath the barrel is designed to be adjusted at the factory for the 17 HM2 or 22 Long Rifle cartridge. Another new addition is a trapdoor compartment in the buttstock for stowage of an extra magazine, or a small candy bar should you be so inclined. The handsome little rifle I shot functioned perfectly. I did not have the opportunity to ventilate enough paper targets with it to be more specific about its accuracy but I got the impression that you will not believe your eyes when you shoot your first groups with one. The trajectory of the 17 HM2 is quite flat. With the rifle zeroed dead-on at 50 yards, it was only about an inch low at 100 yards. Inside 40 yards, the Hornady ammo I was shooting seemed to be more effective on body shots to bushytails than 22 Long Rifle hollowpoints, but once it reaches 60 yards or so that tiny 17-grain bullet really begins to run out of steam fast. From that point on you'd best hold those crosshairs on the head.

Tikka

I never cease to be amazed at how much accuracy is available for so few dollars in Tikka rifles. A T3 Lite in 270 Winchester I have been working with will keep a number of factory loads and handloads inside an inch at 100 yards. Some of the groups I fired with the T3 Tactical in 223 Remington measured less than half an inch. For many years I have been telling various firearms manufacturers that a serious varmint rifle needs a stock with a height-adjustable comb due to the great variations in mounting heights among varmint scopes with their various objective diameters. Its adjustable stock is one of the primary reasons I chose the T3 Tactical for most of my varmint shooting during 2004. I am happy to say that the comb of the fiberglass-reinforced polymer stock of the new-for-2005 Super Varmint is also adjustable for height. The new rifle also inherited the five-round magazine of the Tactical as well as a Picatinny rail atop the receiver that will allow any scope to be positioned to suit the individual shooter. The trigger is easily adjustable in the two to four pounds range, and it can be done without removing the stock. It has a heavy 23 1/2-inch barrel in 223 Remington, 22-250 or 308 Winchester. They claim the Super Varmint is capable of half-inch groups at 100 yards and, since it is basically a civilianized version of the Tactical, I'd say that's probably no brag.

Also new for 2005 is the T3 Big Boar. Its 19-inch barrel is available in 308, 30-06 and 300 WSM; it weighs 6-1/2 pounds.

Ultra Light Arms (New)

Melvin Forbes who, many years ago, raised the performance bar for

This year's Tikka T3 Super Varmint has a lot in common with last year's T3 Tactical which I am shooting here, including a height-adjustable comb and Picatinny rail atop its receiver.

extremely light big-game rifles, has added the various WSSM chamberings to his already lengthy list of options for the original Model 20 rifle. In case you have not noticed this little company that could, four other centerfire actions are also available: Model 24 in standard cartridges ranging from 25-06 to 338-06, Model 28 in mid-length magnums from 264 Winchester to 358 Norma; Model 32 in full-length magnums from 7mm STW to 358 STA, and Model 40 in serious stuff such as 416 Rigby and 458 Lott. And as might be expected, the Model 20RF is now available in 17 HM2.

USRAC

If you have been putting off the purchase of a Winchester Model 9422 for the past 33 years you had best not procrastinate any longer because U.S. Repeating Arms is dropping the sweet little rifle from production. That leaves the Marlin 39A as the only high-quality lever-action 22 rimfire being produced in America. USRAC is saying farewell to the 9422 by producing a run of limited-production rifles called the Tribute series. A total of 9,422 will be built and when those along with the 222 Custom Tribute rifles are gone, there will be no more. Rifles in 22 Long Rifle and 22 WMR will be built, some with a 20 1/2-inch barrel and straight-grip stock, others with a 22 1/2-inch barrel and a curved grip. All will have upgraded walnut stocks and special engraving on their receivers.

Moving from bad news to plinkers and small-game hunters to good news for varmint shooters and big-game hunters, there are now even more Model 70 options available. They include the Super Grade III with its handsome walnut stock in both standard and limited-edition Rocky Mountain Elk Foundation versions. The RMEF rifle is available in 300 WSM and 325 WSM, while the other one is offered in those two—plus seven other chamberings ranging from 25-06 to 338 Winchester Magnum. Then we have the Model 70 Ultimate Shadow Blued which is, with one exception, exactly like the Camo Ultimate Shadow Stainless we already had. All seven stubby and super-stubby chamberings from 223 WSSM to 325 WSM are available. Also available in those same calibers is a blued steel version of the old Model 70 Coyote Stainless and the Coyote Lite in both blued and stainless. The latter two have synthetic stocks replete with aluminum bedding block and ventilation slots. And in case you have not noticed, the Model 70 Featherweight and Sporter II are available with left-hand actions. Moving on to rifles that shoot only one time between loadings, the Model 1885 Low Wall is now available in 17 HM2, and you can buy its High Wall mate in three WSM chamberings: 270, 7mm and 300.

Unlike the rimfire version of the Model 94, the centerfire version is still alive and well and available in more

The new Vanguard Compact from Weatherby comes with two stocks, one short enough for a youngster, the other long enough to be used once he or she grows up. The price is no higher than "youth" rifles sold by other companies with one stock.

After the Tribute version is gone, there will be no more Winchester Model 9422 rifles.

than a dozen configurations. Many years ago, the only way to mount a scope on a 94 was over on the left-hand side of its receiver, or out on the barrel. Its top-ejection of spent cases ruled out mounting a scope atop the receiver. Then came 94s with the Angle-Eject feature and suddenly Marlin was not the only company making a lever action rifle with a tubular magazine that ejected cases eastward when you were shooting north. USRAC is now offering a Model 94 designed to be used with a forward-mounted scope which brings everything back full circle. Called the Timber Scout, it has a Weaver-style scope mounting base attached out on its 18-inch barrel and it is available in 30-30 and 44 Magnum. Those who are so inclined have the option of removing the base from the barrel and mounting a scope back on the receiver where it is supposed to go, or you can forego glass sights entirely and use the rifle with its open sights as John Browning meant for it to be used. As Model 94s of current production go, my favorite is the Trails End Hunter Octagon. It has a 20-inch barrel and it is available in 25-35, 30-30 and 38-55. I'd probably buy one in 25-35 if it wore a Marble's tang sight like the one worn by the Legacy series of rifles.

Volquartsen Custom

Tom Volquartsen's goal in designing his new Evolution rifle was to come up with an autoloader in 223 Remington with the accuracy of a match-grade AR15, but one that looks more like a sporting rifle than a battle rifle. He has done just that. The gas-operated Evolution uses AR-15 magazines and is available in 223 Remington and 204 Ruger.

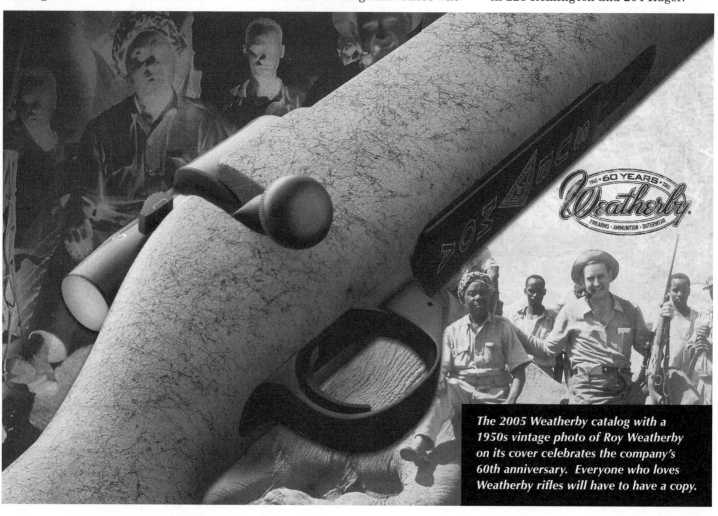

The 2005 Weatherby catalog with a 1950s vintage photo of Roy Weatherby on its cover celebrates the company's 60th anniversary. Everyone who loves Weatherby rifles will have to have a copy.

Its barrel, and the receiver with its integrally-machined Picatinny scope mounting rail, are stainless steel, and both are made by Volquartsen. Same goes for all other component parts. The rifle is made for varmint-shooting so it is no lightweight at 10 pounds. The relatively heavy barrel is 20 inches long. I will not be surprised to see the Evolution shoot five bullets inside half an inch at 100 yards on a regular basis. Equally interesting is Volquartsen's Fusion takedown rifle in four rimfire calibers. You can learn more about it in my "Testfire" report elsewhere.

Weatherby

Roy Weatherby founded his company in 1945, which makes it 60 years old in 2005. The special catalog the company is printing to celebrate those six decades of fame and success is a must-have item for Weatherby rifle fans. And for those of us who are especially addicted, there are commemorative baseball caps, coffee mugs, t-shirts and embossed tin signs. Mention of the name Weatherby has always brought to mind rifles that are strong, accurate, handsome and chambered for super-quick cartridges but the company has become just as widely known for its shotguns in autoloading, over-under and side-by-side persuasion. And we must not overlook the fact that as hunting clothing goes, Weatherby wool is *"weally"* wonderful. I know this to be true because it has kept my young and tender body warm in terribly cold places ranging from a deer stand on the plains of Iowa in December to the Transylvania mountains of Romania.

The Vanguard family of Weatherby rifles continues to grow in both model variations and chambering options. Whereas the standard Vanguard is guaranteed to keep three bullets inside 1-1/2 inches at 100 yards, the new SUB-MOA version is guaranteed to put three inside minute-of-angle when fed Weatherby factory ammunition or specified premium-grade ammo from Remington, Federal and Winchester. Blued and stainless steel versions are available, both with pillar-bedded, fiberglass/carbon fiber stocks available in six different color patterns. Both rifles have 24-inch barrels in 223

The Weatherby Vanguard is now available in about any chambering your heart might desire, and the one in 270 WSM I used to take this mule deer is new for 2005.

Remington, 22-250, 243 Winchester, 270 Winchester, 308 Winchester or 30-06––or you can choose among seven magnums: the 257 Weatherby, 270 WSM, 7mm Remington, 300 Winchester, 300 WSM, 300 Weatherby or 338 Winchester. As might be expected, the 270 WSM and 300 WSM are on the same short Vanguard action as the 223 Remington and other short cartridges. The trigger is adjustable for weight of pull and sear engagement. I used one in 270 WSM on a mule deer hunt in Wyoming during the 2004 season and it worked quite nicely.

Weatherby has taken the new Compact version of its Vanguard rifle a step beyond what we have seen from other rifle companies. Youngsters have a tendency to eventually outgrow the extremely short length of pull of the stocks of other so-called "youth" rifles so the better idea from Weatherby comes with two stocks. That way, your son or daughter can start out with the hardwood stock and its 12 1/2-inch pull and then, a few years later, switch to the synthetic stock with its standard 13 1/2-inch pull. The concept also allows Dad to sneak off and hunt with the rifle while junior is in school. Even more good news is the fact that suggested price of the complete package is less than some of the other short-pull rifles that come with only one

stock. Its trigger is fully adjustable too. The Vanguard Compact weighs 6-3/4 pounds and has a 20-inch barrel in 22-250, 243 Winchester or 308 Winchester. It is the kind of rifle any kid would absolutely love to grow up with.

So far, Weatherby's best-selling Vanguard has been the Synthetic Package. It comes with a factory-mounted and bore-sighted 3-9x Bushnell banner scope and an Uncle Mike's nylon carrying sling with quick-detach swivels, all in a hard plastic carrying case. Barrel length is 24 inches with the following standard chambering options: 223 Remington, 22-250, 243 Winchester, 270 Winchester, 308 Winchester and 30-06. Magnum chamberings include 257 Weatherby, 270 WSM, 7mm Remington, 300 Weatherby, 300 Winchester, 300 WSM and 338 Winchester. During the 2004 season I took a nice pronghorn buck in Wyoming with the Synthetic Package in 257 Weatherby Magnum and Weatherby factory ammo loaded with the 115-grain Nosler Ballistic Tip bullet. Accuracy averaged 1-1/4 inches at 100 yards.

NOTE: Autographed copies of Layne's full-color, hardback books *Shotguns and Shotgunning, and Rifles,* and *Cartridges For Large Game* are available for $39.95 plus $6 for shipping and handling from High Country Press, 306 Holly Park Lane, Simpsonville, SC 29681. Also available are softcover editions of his *The Custom Model 1911 Pistol and Shooter's Handbook,* either priced at $30.95 plus $4 s&h.

The Charles Daley
Country Squire

SHOTGUNS TODAY:

SHOTGUN REVIEW

by John Haviland

Shotguns have always been imported into America. This year, though, the number of guns arriving on America's shores have increased substantially, with established American companies putting their names on foreign shotguns. Whether this is a good trend remains to be seen. Certainly these imported guns are taking sales away from American-made shotguns.

Beretta

The Beretta UGB25 Xcel is an inertia-operated autoloading trap gun that breaks open like a hinge action. A Beretta spokesman said the main reason for the break-open feature is to show others the gun is unloaded. A large lever on the left side of the receiver tilts the barrel breech up so the chamber can be loaded. A carrier on the right side of the receiver holds a second shell for shooting doubles. Fired cases eject out the bottom of the gun.

The UGB25 Xcel softens recoil with a stock-mounted spring reducer, GelTek pad and an over-bored barrel with a lengthened forcing cone. The butt pad and comb are adjustable for a custom fit and to move shot pattern impact. The gun weighs eight to nine pounds, depending on barrel length and configuration.

The Xtrema autoloader has added some features and is now called the Xtrema2. The Kick-off recoil reduction system somewhat tames the kick of 3 1/2-inch 12-gauge shells with two hydraulic dampeners incorporated into the recoil pad. The Kick-off system can also adjust length of pull. A new trigger group also provides a shorter trigger travel, crisp pull and quick reset. The gun's forearm is more slender with flutes for the fingertips to grip and rubber inserts to help absorb recoil. All metal of the Xtrema2 is coated to resist corrosion.

Beretta has restyled four of its shotgun models as the King Ranch Shotguns. The Silver Pigeon, EELL Diamond Pigeon and Silver Pigeon IV over/unders and AL391 Teknys autoloaders feature receivers engraved with scenes of the Texas King Ranch, and their checkering incorporates the King Ranch's running W brand.

Bill Hanus Bird Guns

The BSA Royal 20-gauge side-by-side is made in Spain and is available with 26- or 28-inch barrels. The barrels have 3-inch chambers and chrome-lined bores. Three screw-in choke tubes are included. A single selective trigger and automatic ejectors eliminate the motions of picking a trigger to select a barrel to shoot and pulling fired shells out of the chambers. Wood is Turkish walnut with laser-cut checkering. The sideplates are case-colored and engraved.

Mr. Hanus also sells the Briley Diffusion spreader choke tube for the Royal. Rifling is cut into this skeet tube which imparts a spin to the shot as it leaves the muzzle and results in a wide pattern for jungle shots on quail in the mesquite or ruffed grouse in the alders.

Browning

Browning has further refined its Citori 12- and 20-gauge line with three new models of these over/unders, and

The EELL Diamond Pigeon over/under features a receiver engraved with scenes of the Texas King Ranch and its checkering incorporates the King Ranch's running W brand.

The AL391 Teknys autoloader features a receiver engraved with scenes of the Texas King Ranch and its checkering incorporates the King Ranch's running W brand.

The Kick-off recoil reduction system at least somewhat tames the kick of 3 1/2-inch 12-gauge shells with two hydraulic dampeners incorporated into the recoil pad.

*The Beretta **UGB25 Xcel** is an inertia-operated autoloading trap gun that breaks open like a hinge action.*

The Xtrema autoloader has added some features and is now called the Xtrema2.

two new grades of Lightnings. The Citori Super Lightning combines the styling and weight of the Lightning and Super Light, and wears a blued receiver with gold borders with 26- or 28-inch barrels. The Classic Lightning Feather is pretty much the same style, but with an aluminum receiver that

reduces gun weight by about one pound. The Classic Lightning features a silver nitrate receiver and an oil-finished walnut stock with a muted glow. The Grade IV Lightning features a grayed receiver with engraving of various sporting scenes. For example, the 12-gauge model illustrates pheasants on the left side and mallards on the right. The Grade VII features 24-karat gold inlays of pointers and mallards. Both grades are available in .410-bore and 28, 20 and 12 gauges.

The Citori XT Trap has been spiffed up with features like Golden Clays engraving, high-grade wood and Midas Grade choke tubes. It also features the Gracoil recoil reduction system and an adjustable comb.

Browning has expanded its line of Gold autoloaders. The Gold Fusion High Grade features a high-grade Turkish walnut stock and forearm and a silver nitride receiver engraved with mallards and a Labrador

Above: Browning Cynergy 20-gauge with a Texas bobwhite quail.
Inset: Shooting the Browning Cynergy 20-gauge over/under with the blue sky of Texas in the background.

The Charles Daly autoloader is now available in a left hand Field Hunter model.

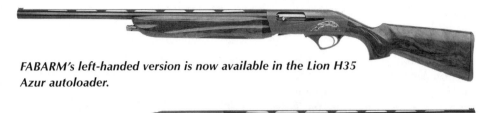

FABARM's left-handed version is now available in the Lion H35 Azur autoloader.

Cosmetic changes made to the Lion H35 Azur autoloader, include a couple of ceramic inlays on the receiver flats and laser-cut checkering patterns that flow along the forearm and through the grip.

The Beta Grade IV is an upgrade of FABARM's side-by-side. The Grade IV includes a wood butt plate, Arabesques and animal motifs on the side plates and titanium coating on the forearm bracket.

retriever on the 12-gauge model. The 20-gauge engraving features quail and a pointer. The stock is adjustable with shims that move comb height 1/8 of an inch up and down. A HiViz TriComp sight system keeps the barrel in your peripheral vision.

A Golden Clays version of the Sporting Clays and Ladies Sporting Clays has added. Both guns wear a motif featuring gold enhancements of a pheasant transforming into a clay bird on the right side and a quail changing into a clay bird on the left side. The ladies version wears a stock with slightly smaller dimensions to fit smaller shooters and a somewhat thicker stock to help absorb recoil.

The Cynergy over/under was introduced last year in 12 gauge and is joined this year by 20 and 28 gauges. The Cynergy shotguns feature a trigger system that uses an actuator to reverse the direction of the impact force from the pin to the striker. Browning states this results in a crisper and lighter trigger pull with a greatly reduced lock time and overtravel. The 20- and 28-gauge Cynergy guns each weigh about 6-1/2 pounds.

The new 20-gauge and 28-gauge Cynergys also feature the Browning Inflex Recoil Pad that Browning claims reduces recoil by 25 percent. If you can get past its less than attractive looks, the recoil pad works well. A couple of friends and I shot the 20- and 28-gauge guns at Texas bobwhite quail last winter. Even shooting Winchester Super-X 1 ounce loads in both gauges, the guns recoiled so little I rarely lost the sight picture. That allowed taking a quick second shot. The guns are available in Field and Sporting versions.

Charles Daly

The Charles Daly autoloader is now available in a left-hand model. The Field Grade 12-gauge wears either a black synthetic stock to match its receiver and barrel, or full camouflage. Barrel lengths are 24, 26, or 28 inches with 3 screw-in choke tubes. The barrel bore is also chrome-lined.

FABARM

The Beta Grade IV is an upgrade of FABARM's side-by-side. The Grade IV includes a wood buttplate, Arabesques and animal motifs on the side plates and titanium coating on the forend bracket.

The Specialists over/under has had a coat of MAX 4 Camouflage added.

Cosmetic changes have been made to the Lion H35 Azur autoloader, including ceramic inlays on the receiver flats and laser-cut checkering patterns that flow along the forearm and through the grip. A green fiber optic insert has been added to the rear top of the receiver to remind shooters to keep their cheek planted firmly on the comb. A rubber and wood butt pad are included. A left-hand version is also available.

Ithaca

The Turkey Slayer Guide Gun wears the new Accu-Grip pistol grip stock that helps absorb some of the recoil from turkey loads and helps hold the gun still for a long period. A Tasco 30mm Red Dot Sight comes mounted and bore-sighted to help place the tight shot pattern on target when fired through the Triple X Ithaca Turkey choke. A Quake Industries sling and Doskocil hard-side case accompany each gun.

The Home State Shotgun is a limited edition Model 37 Featherlight pump 12-gauge that features the map of an individual state, its banner, name, motto and year of statehood. A stock inlay depicts the official seal of the state. The right side of the receiver carries a flowing banner etched with the edition limit.

The Collector Edition I "One of 100" is limited to 100 guns per state. Grade I will be limited to 100 guns and Grade II to 10 guns. The etchings on both sides of the gun's receiver are plated 24-karat gold. The trigger, safety and magazine cap are also plated with gold.

The Edition II Museum Edition is limited to 10 guns per state. Each of these guns begins as an Edition I gun and from there is hand-engraved over most of the metal, even the muzzle.

The Guide Series Slug gun features a blued finish with a rifled 12- or 20-gauge 20- or 24-inch barrel and Monte Carlo black laminate stock with a ring-tailed forearm. The receiver is drilled and tapped for a scope.

Harrington & Richardson

H&R has started importing a line of autoloading and over/under shotguns.

The Excell Auto 5 autoloading 12-gauge has a 3-inch magnum chamber, 5-shot magazine, magazine cut-off, ventilated recoil pads and ventilated rib barrels. Excell models include the Synthetic, Walnut, Waterfowl with 28-inch ventilated rib barrels, Turkey with a 22-inch barrel and fiber optic sights and Combo with a 28-inch ventilated rib barrel and 24-inch rifled barrel. All come with four screw-in chokes and weigh 7 pounds.

The Pinnacle over/under 12- and 20-gauge models have single selective triggers and selective automatic ejectors. They also feature vent rib barrels and three choke tubes. The stocks are walnut-stained with checkering, curved grips and recoil pads. The 12-gauge gun weighs 6-3/4 pounds and the 20-gauge 6-1/2 pounds.

Kimber

Kimber named its over/under shotgun Augusta after a small town along Montana's Eastern Front of the Rocky Mountains. It is thus only fitting that Kimber's new side-by-side 20-gauge is named after Valier, a town a short distance to the north.

The Valier is a sidelock made in Turkey with 26- or 28-inch barrels and double triggers. A lever on the left plate can be turned out for access to the sideplates. The gun weighs 5 pounds, 14 ounces. The Grade I has no ejectors and wears somewhat plainer Turkish walnut. It retails for $4422. The Grade II has selective automatic ejectors and wears much fancier wood. It costs five grand.

Krieghoff

The K-80 Trap Special Combo has a fully adjustable rib on both its over/under barrels and an "unsingle" barrel for point-of-impact adjustments. Built around the K-80 receiver, the Trap Special comes with 32-inch over/under barrels and 34-inch "unsingle" barrel. A Monte Carlo trap stock with adjustable comb designed for the high-post rib is standard. The rib can be adjusted so the gun shoots from fairly flat (60 percent/40 percent), to a full pattern high (100 percent). The point-of-impact of the over/under barrels can be individually adjusted to different points of impact by changing the front hanger.

Legacy Sports

Legacy's new line of imported Khan shotguns include seven over/unders. The guns include Field models with extractors on the 28-inch barrel of the 12-gauge, and the 26-inch barrel of the 20- and 28-gauge, and .410 bore. Weights run from 5.7 pounds for the

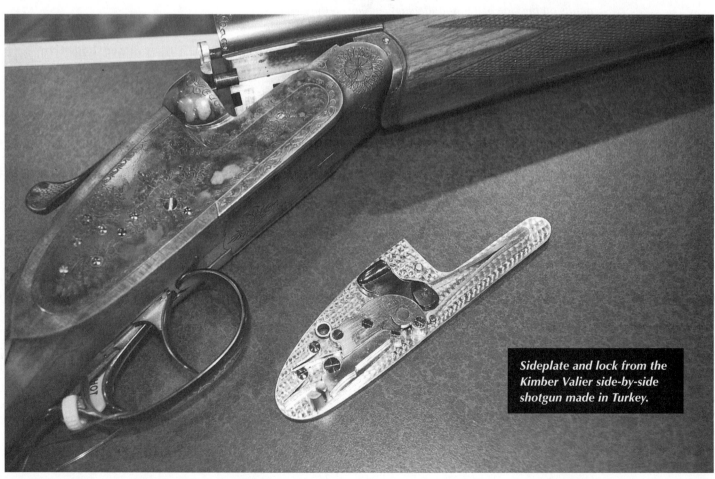

Sideplate and lock from the Kimber Valier side-by-side shotgun made in Turkey.

.410 to 7.7 pounds for the 12-gauge. The Deluxe and Clays models in 12 and 20 include more brightly finished metal and wood, and ejectors. The .410 wears fixed chokes, while the other gauges come with five screw-in chokes.

The Escort shotguns have several additions. The Escort semi-auto Youth wears a 22-inch barrel and shorter length of pull. Several models have had bores plated with chrome, with outsides coated with black chrome. A 12-gauge 3 1/2-inch magnum is also available. Cantilever scope mounts have also been added to the Slug models.

The Escort pump line has expanded to include a 12-gauge MarineGuard with a nickel-plated 18-inch barrel, and Field Hunter models with multi-chokes in 26-inch barrels. New camo patterns have also been added to several models, as well as HiViz fiber optic front sights.

Marlin

Marlin has owned the famous name of L.C. Smith since 1971 and is now putting the name on over/under and side-by-side guns made by Fausti Stefano of Italy.

The LC12-OU 12-gauge features a 3-inch chamber in 28-inch ventilated rib barrels with three screw-in choke tubes, single selective trigger, and selective automatic ejectors. It wears a checkered walnut stock with a fluted comb and recoil pad. The gun weighs 7-1/4 pounds.

The LC12-DB 12-gauge double barrel features a 3-inch chamber, a single trigger, selective automatic ejectors, three choke tubes (IC, M, F), 28-inch barrels with a solid rib and a bead front sight. Its walnut stock is checkered, and has a fluted comb, a beavertail forearm and a recoil pad.

The LC20-DB is pretty much the same gun, but in 20-gauge with 26-inch barrels and a weight of 6 pounds.

Mossberg

Mossberg calls its 935 Magnum the most reliable value-priced 12-gauge 3 1/2-inch autoloader ever made. The gun features an over-bored barrel and a self-regulating gas system to take the sting out of recoil. The gun weighs 7-3/4 pounds and includes 22-, 24-, 26- or 28-inch barrels with a front fiber optic

Legacy's Escort shotgun is now available in 12-gauge 3 1/2-inch Magnum.

The Escort semi-auto Youth wears a 22-inch barrel and shorter length of pull.

The Escort pump line has expanded to include a 12-gauge MarineGuard with a nickel-plated 18-inch barrel.

Legacy's new line of imported Khan shotguns include seven over/unders. The guns include Field models with extractors on the 28-inch barrel of the 12-gauge and 26-inch barrel of the 20- and 28-gauge and .410-bore.

bead and three screw-in choke tubes. Five camo patterns are available.

The 930 autoloader is a 12-gauge 3-inch version of the 935. The 930 weighs 7-1/2 pounds and wears a ported barrel, three choke tubes, receiver drilled and tapped for scope mounts and a cocking indicator.

The 535 All-Terrain Shotgun (ATS) is another inexpensive 3 1/2-inch 12 gauge. The pump shotgun is similar to the established Mossberg 500. With a simple barrel change a hunter can outfit the 535 to hunt upland birds, waterfowl, turkey and deer.

The 500 Bantam pump 20 gauge features a 12-inch length of pull. It also comes with stock spacers and an extra recoil pad that lengthens its synthetic stock to 13 inches. When a young shooter has outgrown that stock, a certificate with the gun is worth 50 percent off the price of a full-size stock. The gun comes in Turkey, Field, Slug and Field/Deer Combo models.

Remington

Remington has added features and improvements to several of its guns and is importing a line of budget-priced guns made in Russia.

Let's start with the big guns for big birds. The Model SP-10 Magnum is now covered with Mossy Oak Obsession camouflage. The Model 870 Special Purpose Turkey Super Magnum Thumbhole is covered with the same camo. The thumbhole stock makes holding the gun in alignment easier for a longer time when a gobbler is strutting just out of range. The thumbhole stock and R3 recoil pad also take up a lot of the kick from magnum turkey loads. The Model 870 Express Super magnum is now available with a 28-inch barrel and a coat of Fall Flight camo.

The Model 11-87 Sportsman is Remington's most dependable autoloader in a plain wrapper that is easy on the checkbook. The 11-87 Sportsman comes in 12- and 20-gauge versions with 26- or 28-inch barrels with ventilated ribs and a screw in Modified choke tube. The slug hunting model has a fully rifled 21-inch barrel and cantilever scope base. Its comb is raised to position the eye behind a scope.

The youth model 20-gauge wears a 21-inch barrel and 13-inch length of pull. All models include a matte-black metal finish, black synthetic stock and forearm with swivel studs. The youth Model 870 Express Jr. NWTF Jakes gun is a lightweight 20-gauge pump featuring an 18 1/2-inch ventilated rib barrel and a synthetic stock with 12-inch length of pull. The stock and forearm are camouflaged in Skyline Excel camo with a "Team NWTF" medallion embedded into the stock. The receiver and barrel have a black matte finish. A portion of the proceeds from every "Team NWTF" gun will be donated to

Remington's youth Model 870 Express Jr. NWTF Jakes gun is a lightweight 20-gauge pump featuring an 18 3/4-inch ventilated rib barrel, and a synthetic stock with 12-inch length of pull. The stock and forearm are camouflaged in Skyline Excel camo with a "Team NWTF" medallion embedded into the stock.

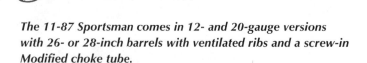

Remington's Model 11-87 Sportsman slug hunting model has a fully rifled 21-inch barrel and cantilever scope base. Its comb is raised to position the eye behind a scope.

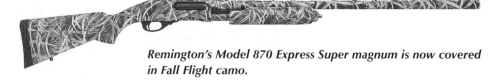

The 11-87 Sportsman comes in 12- and 20-gauge versions with 26- or 28-inch barrels with ventilated ribs and a screw-in Modified choke tube.

Remington's Model 870 Express Super magnum is now covered in Fall Flight camo.

The Model 870 Express Super Magnum Synthetic shoots all lengths of 12-gauge shell. The gun is available with a 26- or 28-inch vent rib barrel with a Modified screw-in choke, matte finish and a black synthetic stock.

The Model 870 Special Purpose Turkey Super Magnum Thumbhole is covered with the same camo. The thumbhole stock makes holding the gun in alignment easier for a longer time when a gobbler is strutting just out of range.

the National Wild Turkey Federation.

The Model 870 Express Slug Gun wears a fully rifled, heavy contour barrel in either 12 or 20 gauge. The cantilever scope mount base is attached to the barrel and extends back over the receiver. Mounting the scope on the barrel, instead of the receiver, makes for more accurate shooting because the play between the barrel and receiver are removed. These pump shotguns feature a non-glare matte finish on all exterior metalwork and all-weather black synthetic stocks and fore-ends.

The Model 870 Wingmaster Dale Earnhardt Tribute is the third shotgun in a four-year limited edition series. Earnhardt's love of the shooting sports and his achievements in the world of NASCAR racing are captured in this special edition Model 870 Wingmaster. Remington will donate a portion of the money from each shotgun sold to the Dale Earnhardt Foundation, which supports wildlife initiatives and children's educational programs.

This 12-gauge pump wears a 28-inch light-contour ventilated rib barrel and American walnut stock and forearm with a high gloss finish and cut checkering. Engraved on the polished blued receiver is Earnhardt's likeness, his signature and scrollwork on the left side. On the right side of the frame is engraved "7 Time Winston Cup Champion" banner. The signature and banner are inlayed in 24 karat gold.

The 870 Wingmaster Jr. is a shotgun for young shooters just starting out. The lightweight 20-gauge wears an 18 3/4-inch ventilated rib barrel and an American walnut stock with 12-inch length of pull, cut checkering and high-gloss finish. The barrel features an ivory front sight and steel middle bead, along with Rem Choke tubes for Improved Cylinder, Modified and Full chokes.

The Model 870 Express Super Magnum Synthetic shoots all lengths of 12-gauge shell. The gun is available with a 26- or 28-inch vent rib barrel with a Modified screw-in choke, matte finish and a black synthetic stock. The Model 870 Express Youth Synthetic Combo covers birds and big game. A 20-inch fully rifled barrel with sights is just right for deer, while a 21-inch ventilated rib barrel with a screw-in Modified choke tube and bead sight covers birds and clay targets.

Remington's Model 870 Wingmaster Dale Earnhardt Tribute is the third shotgun in a four-year limited edition series. Earnhardt's love of the shooting sports and his achievements in the world of NASCAR racing are captured in this special edition Model 870 Wingmaster.

The 870 Wingmaster Jr. is a shotgun for young shooters just starting out. The lightweight 20-gauge wears an 18 3/4-inch ventilated rib barrel and an American walnut stock with 12-inch length of pull, cut checkering and high-gloss finish.

The Athena D'Italia is Weatherby's newest entry into the box lock side-by-side market. The gun is chambered in 12-, 20- and 28-gauge and weighs 6-3/4 to 7-1/4 pounds.

Remington has started importing a variety of break-action guns made in Russia under the Spartan Gunworks name. They include single-shot shotguns that sell for $89 at the local Wal Mart. The Spartan name also includes single-shot rifles, side-by-side and over/under shotguns, rifle/shotgun combinations and side-by-side rifles.

Rossi

The Rossi fully rifled slug gun is ported at the muzzle to help control the punishing recoil of slug rounds. The barrel is equipped with fiber optic sights. The 12- and 20-gauge single shots are drilled and tapped for the installation of an included scope mount base.

Weatherby

The Athena D'Italia is Weatherby's newest entry into the boxlock side-by-side market. The gun is chambered in 12-, 20- and 28-gauge and weighs 6-3/4 to 7-1/4 pounds. The 12- and 20-gauge have a screw-in improved cylinder, modified and full chokes, while the 28 gauge wears fixed Improved Cylinder and Modified chokes. The chrome-lined barrels are back-bored and have extractors and automatic ejectors. The trigger guard has a rolled edge to eliminate cutting the finger when reaching for the double triggers. The stock has a straight grip and laser-cut checkering of diamond-shaped webs Weatherby calls "New Scottish." Full engraving is included on the false sideplates. The gun stores in a foam-lined hardcase.

Winchester

New to the Super X2 line is the Super X2 Light Field Model 12-gauge which weighs about 6-1/2 pounds with a 26- or 28-inch barrel.

The new 1300 Practical Defender will rid the garden of carrot-robbing rabbits, and protect against strange things that go bump in the night. The Defender features a composite stock, 22-inch barrel with screw-in chokes, adjustable open sights and an 8-round magazine.

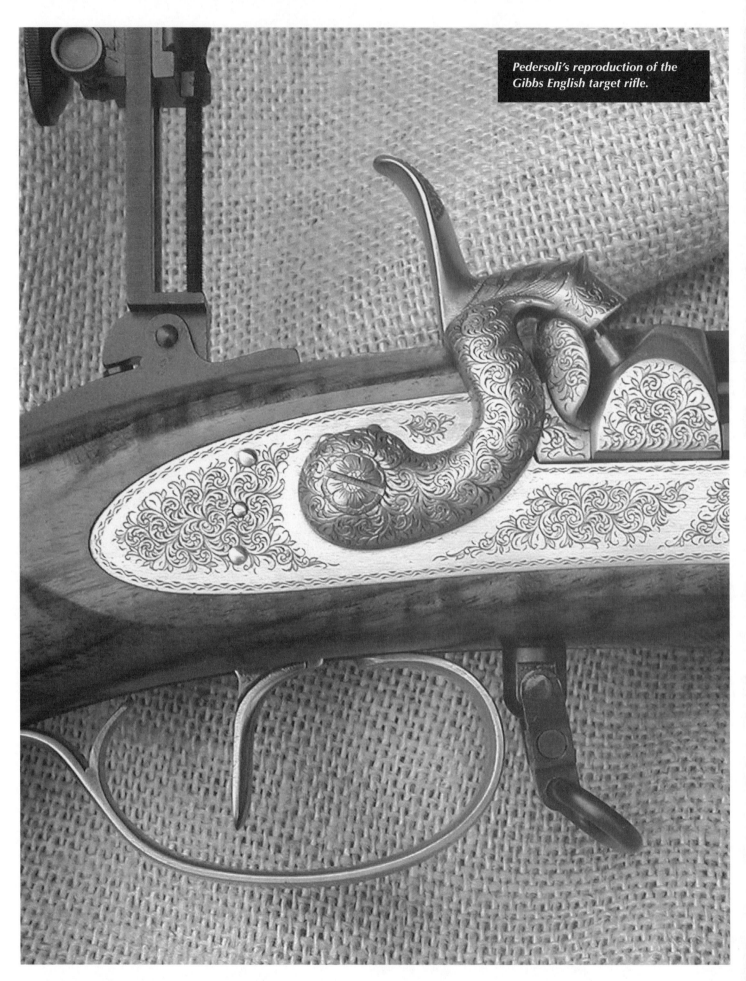

Pedersoli's reproduction of the Gibbs English target rifle.

TODAY'S MUZZLELOADING:

BLACKPOWDER REVIEW

by Doc Carlson

Whether one is interested in hunting, target shooting, re-enacting or just plinking, the available selection of blackpowder firearms is such that if an interesting gun can't be found, the person isn't trying very hard. There is bound to be a blackpowder-eating firearm out there to appeal to everyone, regardless of his (or her) area of interest in the sport. There are more types of muzzleloaders available today than a couple of hundred years ago. Now, let's take a quick look at some of the guns and accessories offered in today's marketplace.

One of the myths that has grown up around the muzzleloading firearms of yesterday is the statement that the early Kentucky rifles were of a "small caliber" and that they were the first rifled firearms made. Actually, most of the early long rifles were between 50- and 60-caliber. European rifles were made with rifled barrels well before the Kentucky rifle came on the scene. Why did the "smaller caliber" myth come about? It's probably a matter of semantics. European rifles—English and German primarily—of the time were of rather large caliber, often running well over 60-caliber. So, compared to them, the Kentucky rifle of 55-caliber was smaller. The really small calibers: 36, 40, etc., were made much later, after the golden age of the Kentucky long rifle. They arrived after most of the large game of the East—

forest buffalo, bear and such—was gone. After that, most hunting was for small game and the Eastern deer.

The large-caliber English rifles and German Jaegers were fine hunting guns. The stock design handled recoil very well and the large-caliber round ball was a consistent killer. I'm happy to say there is a rekindling of interest in these big-bore guns of yesteryear. If you like to hunt with traditional guns, using patched round ball, bigger is definitely better. Large round balls land with authority—the Brits and Germans knew what they were doing.

James A. Gefroh

James A. Gefroh, a Colorado gunsmith, is one of the custom gunmakers who is keeping the large-caliber English and German rifles alive. He builds jaeger- and English-pattern rifles in calibers ranging from 62 (20-bore) through 69 (14-bore), 72 (12-bore), 775 (10-bore)—all the way up to the very impressive 83 (8-bore) for game animals that tend to bite back. The same style can be had in a smoothbore fowler for bird hunting, if the customer desires.

His basic rifle is made with a figured black walnut stock, hooked breech, and tapered barrel utilizing Forsythe-type rifling specifically designed for shooting large round balls. Included are double-set triggers, fixed open sights, ebony nose cap, browned furniture, either flint or percussion ignition in

right- or left-hand configurations. No carving or stock embellishments are included in the basic rifle. It is a true working rifle of the period.

However, if one is interested in adding some fancy upgrades, several options are available. These include more highly figured wood, either American black or English walnut, original-style relief carving, silver wire inlay, or a relief sterling silver animal head set in ivory and surrounded by silver wire inlay. The prices for these upgrades are very reasonable, considering the amount of labor involved. I would certainly add all the upgrades that I could afford; after all, we look at our firearms more than we actually shoot them. It might as well be pretty, as well as useful. The rifles that Gefroh builds are truly works of art that will become family heirlooms.

Both styles of rifles, English and German, have a stock design that handles the recoil of the large calibers very well. As the rifles are made on a special order basis, stock dimensions are made to fit the owner/shooter. They point like a well-fitted shotgun, allowing fast target acquisition, something very important in the hunting field.

Gefroh's rifles have taken large game animals in both Africa and North America. His rifles have been used by very satisfied owners to take the Big Five in Africa. Gefroh, himself, has taken elephant, rhino, Cape buffalo and leopard in Africa, as well as most

▲ *English half-stock sporting rifle by James Gefroh.*
▶ *Fine-figured black walnut and clean checkering, as well as crisp lines and tight inletting, are typical of Gefroh rifles.*

of the plains game of that country.

Any hunter that enjoys traditional muzzleloading rifles and fowlers for his hunting activities should take a long look at the firearms of James Gefroh.

Pedersoli

The Italian manufacturer, Pedersoli, is one of the top names in the manufacture of traditional-type blackpowder firearms. Their catalog contains an amazing selection of reproduction firearms of the blackpowder era. All periods and countries are represented in a wide range of styles and ignition systems. Civilian and military arms are included.

One of the newest additions to the line of traditional rifles is the Gibbs Target Rifle. This faithful copy of a target rifle made in 1865 by the well-known English gunsmith, George Gibbs, reproduces the peak of the development of the muzzleloading

target rifle. The original rifles won many medals and trophies in shooting matches of the time and the Pedersoli reproduction is also winning in competitions around the world.

The rifle is available in 45-caliber utilizing a six land-and-groove barrel with a 1:18 inch twist. It is intended for use with a .451-inch elongated bullet, similar to what one sees being used in the 45/70 cartridge. This highly accurate rifle features an oil-finished walnut pistol grip

half-stock with an ebony grip cap and forend tip. There is no provision for a ramrod, typical of target rifles of the period. The blued 35 1/4-inch barrel is round, tapered slightly, with an octagon breech area. The percussion bar-type lock shows a pleasing color case-hardened finish. The steel buttplate and trigger guard are blued. Sights are a windage-adjustable front with 15 inserts and spirit level, and a tang-type rear sight, adjustable for elevation.

This outstanding reproduction target rifle has shown very good accuracy at long-range shooting from 100 to 600, 800–or even

Pedersoli's well-made reproduction Gibbs English target rifle—a real match-winner.

1000 yards. The good-looking English style rifle would be a nice addition to any gun cabinet.

Dixie Gun Works

In 1855 Colt Manufacturing brought out their Colt-Root revolving rifle, an attempt to come up with a repeating rifle for both the military and civilian market. They were made in various models and barrel lengths in calibers from 36 through 64, as well as a shotgun version in 10- and 12-gauge. Less than 20,000 were made. Of those, less than 10,000 were the Military Rifle model.

Dixie Gun Works is now marketing a copy of the Colt/Root full stocked military rifle M1855. This six-shot revolving cylinder rifle is 44-caliber, utilizing a .454-inch ball. The blued barrel is 31-1/2 inches long, rifled 1:38 inches and is slightly tapered. The birch military configuration full stock is oil-finished and the furniture is blued steel. The cylinder is full fluted, as were the originals, and the big side-hammer is color case-hardened. Sights are a one-piece blued blade front coupled with a rear sight having two flip-up blades; again, as original. The full-length forearm is

held by two blued steel barrel bands. A steel ramrod is installed under the forearm, and there is a ramrod extension hidden under the middle butt plate screw to extend the ramrod for cleaning. Sling swivels complete the picture of this Civil War military rifle.

The 1855 Colt/Root was issued to Union forces during the War of Northern Aggression, as some call it. It was issued to Berdan's Sharpshooters, the 9th Illinois Volunteer Cavalry, the 21st Ohio Volunteer Infantry and some Wisconsin regiments. This well-made and nicely finished new offering from Dixie will undoubtedly find a home among Civil War re-enactor groups.

Traditions

There are some states that require flintlock ignition for their muzzle-loading hunting seasons and there

The new Root revolving rifle from Dixie Gun Works.

are folks out there that merely like to hunt with the more primitive ignition system. Up to now, blackpowder was the only useable propellant for these guns since the use of replica blackpowder, such as Pyrodex, was not practical. Traditions Performance Firearms now claims to have an answer. According to Traditions, their PA Pellet Flintlock will fire reliably with Pyrodex—either loose powder or pellets.

The lock, called a "Super Flintlock" by Traditions, has an improved frizzen and a deepened pan. The specially-hardened frizzen throws a massive shower of hot sparks and the deepened pan holds more priming powder for flawless ignition, according to the manufacturer. The specially-designed breech plug directs the fire from the pan through the touchhole and funnels it forward to the base of the Pyrodex pellets for fast, sure ignition. The 26-inch 50-caliber octagonal barrel is rifled with a 1:48 twist to handle patched round ball, sabotted bullets or bore-size slugs. The barrel is easily removable from its hooked breech. The breech plug can be screwed out and the barrel cleaned from the breech, as if it was an inline gun. Sights are the easily seen Tru-Glo fiber optic front and

rear. The ramrod is solid aluminum for durability since a broken ramrod in the hunting woods is a real disaster. The rifle is recommended for up to 150-grain loads of Pyrodex or blackpowder.

The rifle is made with a blued finish and hardwood stock in both right- and left-hand models. It is also available with a black synthetic stock and either a nickel or blue barrel. If camo is your interest, the gun is offered with a nickel barrel and Mossy Oak stock or, new this year, an all-camo version with both stock and barrel covered with Hardwoods HD finish.

The focusing of modern technology on the venerable muzzleloader is producing some surprising results. Improvements in powders, primers and bullets, coupled with modern design features of the guns themselves, are rapidly putting the muzzleloader on an equal footing with the modern cartridge rifle-carrying hunter.

Ultimate Firearms

Ultimate Firearms is putting just such a gun on the market. Called the Ultimate Muzzleloader, this bolt-action modern-looking rifle has some serious innovations. The rifle

uses a 45 Magnum brass case to carry a Magnum Rifle primer. The case slips over an enlarged nipple in the breech of the rifle and effectively seals against blowback gasses during the firing sequence. The flash of the primer is directed through the nipple to the main charge (*recommended as four 50-grain pellets of Pyrodex or Triple 7*). The unique nipple-breech system causes a "controlled burn" (called a controlled detonation by the company) that allows 200 grains of Pyrodex or Triple 7 to be consumed in the 50-caliber barrel, resulting in unheard-of velocities and flat trajectories for a muzzle-loading arm. The priming system produces a flame temperature many times hotter than the standard #209 primer.

The gun shoots pretty flat out to 200 yards, with 100-yard and 200-yard groups nearly on top of each other. Accuracy is very good. Groups measuring 1/2-inch at 100 yards and 3-3/4 inches at 500 yards have been shot with sabotted bullets and 200-grain charges, according to the manufacturer. The gun cleans easily. There is no blowback of powder gasses into the action thanks to the sealing characteristics

Ultimate Firearms' new ultra-modern hunting rifle—200-grain loads recommended!

Traditions Pyrodex pellet–firing flint-lock rifle.

of the primer/nipple system.

The rifle uses a Howa action with a stainless steel barrel and custom trigger system. They are available in three models. The BP Xpress Hunter features a thumbhole stock of laminated wood in one of four colors: Autumn Dawn, Nutmeg, Pepper and a multicolored "Ghost." The BP Xpress Infinity adds an aluminum bedding system with a free-floating barrel and a limb-saver recoil pad. The top-of-the-line BP Xpress Remington 40X Ultra uses the aluminum bedding system in a figured walnut Monte Carlo stock with laser-carved grip and forearm panels, ebony forend tip and the owner's initials carved into the stock.

This new rifle appears to be opening a new era in muzzleloading. The long-range trajectory and accuracy claimed for this rifle is truly eye-opening for this old patched round-ball shooter. We'll be watching this one with interest.

Austin & Halleck

Austin & Halleck, maker of some very nice muzzleloading rifles, both inline and traditional types, is developing a new in-line rifle that is certainly different from the ordinary. Some years ago, Thompson/Center had a rifle they called the Scout Rifle. The little slab-sided rifle had a center-hung hammer and was made with either a 21- or 24-inch round 50-caliber barrel, as I remember. The look and feel of the rifle reminded one of the venerable Model '94 Winchester. It had the same quick handling qualities that have made the Model '94 one of the most popular and recognizable guns in history. Alas, the tooling for the little rifle was lost in a fire at the T/C plant, so the little gun is gone.

Austin & Halleck has gone one better. Their new rifle looks like a Model '94 with a ramrod. The 50-caliber barrel is loaded from the muzzle, the same as any muzzleloader. The lever is cycled to open the bolt, similar to the '94, and a #209 primer is inserted into a cut in the face of the bolt. The bolt is levered closed and firing is accomplished as the center-hung hammer is tripped by pulling the trigger. The result is a front-loading rifle with all the handling

LaserLyte laser bore-sighter makes a difficult job easy.

characteristics of the Model '94. The fit, finish and quality of this handy rifle are what we have come to expect from the Austin & Halleck folks. Time will tell how this new and very different muzzleloader will be accepted by hunters and shooters—it's certain to attract attention in hunting camp.

Bore-sighting a muzzleloader presents something of a problem because it is difficult to peer through the bore at a distant object, or collimator screen, since we don't have easy access to the rear end of the bore. Even the in-lines require breech plug removal, to be able to look through the barrel. Further, most of the boresights on the market don't seem to lend

Austin & Halleck 420 LR Monte Carlo in-line rifle.

Austin & Halleck 320 LR Camo in-line rifle in Realtree-Hardwoods pattern.

Austin & Halleck Flintlock Mountain Rifle.

themselves to muzzleloaders, due to the higher trajectories of the breed.

A company called **LaserLyte** has a laser boresight that does work very well for the front-loader guns. The laser is projected by a small unit that plugs into the end of the barrel, and is aligned with the bore by expandable plugs. The laser is bright enough to be easily seen at 25 and 50 yards, even on rather bright days. It is even useable at 100 yards when the laser is pointed at a reflective target (*included in the kit*). The kits are available with expandable stubs that handle up to 50-caliber, and 20- and 12-gauge stubs are available also. Kits come with either one laser projector for single-barrel guns, or with two to regulate double-barrel rifles and shotguns. I've been using one of these kits in my own shop and find it very accurate. I've used the collimator-type boresight—they work fine, but the laser dot gives a more accurate picture of where the bore is pointing, and makes sight settings easier, in my view. This is a great tool to have—whether you are building guns, installing sights, or just want to check your favorite firearm before going hunting.

Cash Manufacturing

Cash Manufacturing has been making accessories for the muzzleloading crowd since the '60s. He has always catered to the traditional shooter, making reproductions of accessories that were used in the heyday of the muzzleloader. He recently stepped into the modern world of the inline with two very nice cappers.

The first of these is a straight-line capper for either the four- or six-wing musket caps. It holds 12 caps and has a convenient side-loading slot with a tension spring release. The second is a straight-line capper designed to hold 12 #209 primers. Both these are aimed at the in-line rifles that use either musket caps or the #209 shotgun primer. The straight-line design makes getting the cap or primer into the tight recesses of the inline a much easier job. Both cappers are finely crafted of brass and will probably outlast your rifle.

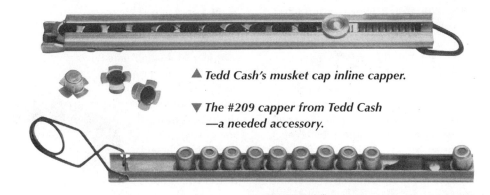

▲ *Tedd Cash's musket cap inline capper.*

▼ *The #209 capper from Tedd Cash —a needed accessory.*

▶ *Cartridge grade (right) is intended for the large-bore cartridges used in the black-powder cartridge silhouette competition.*

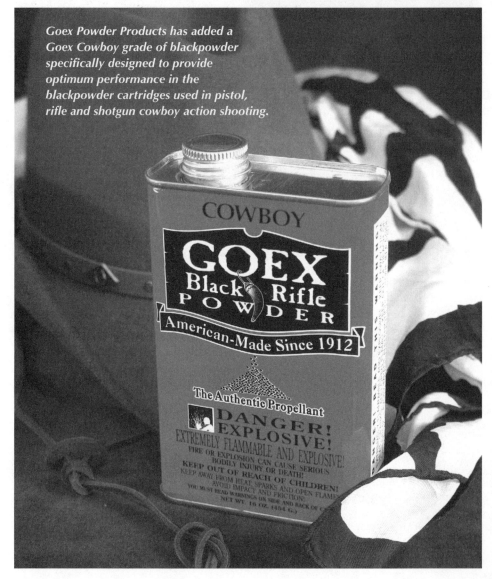

Goex Powder Products has added a Goex Cowboy grade of blackpowder specifically designed to provide optimum performance in the blackpowder cartridges used in pistol, rifle and shotgun cowboy action shooting.

These new ideas from Tedd Cash make handling the inline just a bit easier and certainly makes carrying the caps and primers very handy.

Hoppe's

Hoppe's, a name that almost every shooter is familiar with, has added to their line a new blackpowder cleaner and solvent. This soap-based solvent is equally effective in removing the residue of blackpowder, Pyrodex, Triple 7—or any of the other replica blackpowders. It also cuts lead and plastic fouling. As it dries, it leaves a microscopic layer of rust inhibitor and dry lube that penetrates into the pores of the steel, protecting the bore and making repeat cleanings easier. It effectively replaces the barrel seasoning and break-in process, according to the Hoppe's folks.

Hoppe's Number 9 solvent was the number one powder fouling cleaner for many, many years. The distinctive, instantly identifiable smell was always associated with fine firearms. I'm told that women who wished to meet hunters and/or gun enthusiasts would put a drop of Hoppe's Number 9 behind their ear instead of perfume. It would draw them like bees to honey.

Goex Powder Products

Goex Powder Products, the continuation of the old DuPont powder company, has some new additions to their product line. They have added a Goex Cowboy grade of black powder specifically designed to provide optimum performance in the blackpowder cartridges used in pistol, rifle and shotgun cowboy action shooting. This is in addition to their regular granulations of 1Fg, 2Fg, 3Fg, 4Fg and Cannon grade—plus Cartridge grade, intended for the large-bore cartridges used in the blackpowder cartridge silhouette competition.

They have a new replica blackpowder also, called Pinnacle. This low-pressure powder is available in 2Fg and 3Fg grades and produces the same velocities and accuracy as

blackpowder without the smoke and smell, while producing less fouling than conventional blackpowder.

Goex also now has a line of blackpowder-loaded cartridges called Black Dawg Cartridges. They are available in a wide range of chamberings for rifle, pistol and shotgun. Long-range cartridges such as 45/70, 45/90, 45/120 and others are loaded for use in the big single-shot rifles. Bullets are cast of a soft alloy, lubed with SPG lube and the cartridges are loaded, of course, with blackpowder. These should find a ready market among cowboy action shooters, and others who like to shoot the old blackpowder loads and don't want to reload.

Hodgdon Powder Company

Triple 7, the very low residue replica blackpowder from the Hodgdon Powder Company, is now available in new packaging that is more convenience to blackpowder hunters. The new 50-grain, 50-caliber pellets come in a pack containing four tubes, each containing six of the pellets. This will

Hodgdon's new packaging for their Triple 7 pellets will be handy for hunters.

allow the hunter to slip one or two of the tubes in his pocket–or possibles bag–and have enough reloads for the average hunt. The tubes protect the pellets from damage until needed and are a handy reloading accessory.

Remington

One of the problems with #209 primers in muzzleloading guns has been the formation of a ring of fouling just above the breech plug where the projectile rests in the loaded barrel. This ring of hard fouling seems to be due to the hot #209 primer. Now Remington is making a #209 primer designed specifically for muzzleloader shooting. Remington promises the new primer will dramatically reduce fouling and make reloading easy, while maintaining velocity and accuracy between shots without swabbing. Remington claims 15 to 20 times less fouling than with the standard #209 primer. Difficulty in reloading for a second shot, without swabbing with a damp patch, has been a problem with the in-lines for some time. It is especially troublesome when using sabbotted bullets. Hopefully, this new Remington Kleenbore primer will reduce this problem.

Modern technology continues to improve the blackpowder field. The lot of the blackpowder shooter and hunter has never been easier. Just when you think nothing can be improved, American ingenuity steps forward. Old Jim Bridger and Daniel Boone would be amazed.

AMMUNITION, BALLISTICS & COMPONENTS

by Holt Bodinson

I t's been an active year for acquisitions and consolidations. Western Powder buys Accurate Arms. American Ammunition acquires Triton, and Powerbelt purchases West Coast Bullets.

We needed some new cartridges and we got them. Winchester fielded its "stomper," the 325 WSM while S&W teamed up with Cor-Bon to roll out its "stomper," the 460 S&W. For shooters who don't quite need a "stomper," Remington civilized the mild-mannered 6.8mm Remington.

Speaking about new cartridges, keep an eye on NATEC's polymer-cased 223 and 308 ammunition. There may be a manufacturing revolution in the making.

Green is in. Lead-free bullets and primers continue to make inroads in every major line. Among the more interesting developments was Bismuth's introduction of Bismuth-core 55-grain/223 bullets.

Heavier-than-lead, non-toxic shot is hot. Federal introduced "Heavyshot" while Winchester fielded "Xtended Range High Density" shot. Meanwhile Hevi-Shot introduced "Hevi-Steel" as a lower cost alternative to its original product.

Graf & Sons, teamed with Hornady, is giving the old warhorses a new lease on life with fresh components and loaded ammunition for the 6.5 Carcano, 6.5 Jap, 7.5 Swiss, 7.65 Argentine, 7.7 Jap, 8x56 Hungarian, 9mm Steyr and 455 Webley. For those who own those great old quality Model 99 Savages in 303 Savage, Huntington has arranged with Norma to make a special run of the brass.

Finally, Federal has been tinkering with the internals of shotshells and has commercialized some great design breakthroughs with their new "Flight control" wad and "TruBall" smoothbore slug.

It's been an innovative year indeed in the ammunition, ballistics and components business.

Accurate Arms Company

New owner. Western Powders Company, the largest master distributor of reloading powders in North America and originator of the Ramshot powders, has purchased Accurate Arms and moved it to its home base, Miles City, Montana. Western says the existing line of Accurate Arms powders will be maintained with no disruption of service or availability. www.accuratepowder.com

Aguila

No new products but a great new color catalog this year that is full of photographs and ballistic data. Aguila's 22 rimfire line continues to be outstanding with both the heaviest loading (60 grains) and the highest velocity (1700 fps) loading. www.aguilaammo.com

Alliant

With ten shotgun powders, three pistol powders and six rifle powders in the line, look for a new target shotshell powder from Alliant around mid-year. Until then, it's a corporate secret! www.alliantpowder.com

Ballistic Products

When it comes to shotshell reloading components, Ballistic Products is the place to shop. In stock at all times are all the well-known brands of commercial components, plus Ballistic Products' own designs and the best of the European component lines. To simplify the reloading process, they are even pre-packaging components with instructions for assembling "Master" steel duck/goose, pheasant, sporting clays, and 20-gauge field

Barnes is applying its Triple-Shock technology to a line of big-bore solids carrying the name "Barnes Banded Solids."

loads. You just have to add the shot and powder. There's a new slug for rifled bores load this year. The name is LBC BluForce and it's a sabot/slug system that features their hardened 0.650-inch diameter Dangerous Game slug mated with a ribbed, breakaway sabot designed for barrels with a 0.750-inch land diameter. By all means, send for their fascinating catalog. www.ballisticproducts.com

Barnes

Building on the phenomenal success they have had with the performance, accuracy and shooter acceptance of the "Triple-Shock" X-bullet, Barnes is adding fourteen new bullets to the line: a 53-grain 224; 120-grain 6.5mm; 110-grain 6.8mm; 150-grain 270; 120-grain 7mm; 130-grain 308; 180-grain 8mm (325 WSM); 210-grain 338; 225-grain 358; 270-grain 375; 350 and 400-grain 416; and 450- and 500-grain 458. Under the banner of "Barnes Banded Solids," the folks from Utah have carried their grooves over to their dangerous game

bullet line with the introduction a 270- and 300-grain 375; 350 and 400-grain 416; and 450- and 500-grain 458. And if that looks like big medicine, there's a new 750-grain 577 Nitro pill in the Coated X-Bullet (XLC) series. Anticipating the unveiling of the 460 S&W, Barnes is producing a new 200-grain 460 (*actually 0.451"*) spitzer boattail bullet in the XPB line. What's interesting is the adoption of the Barnes line by many of the major ammunition makes such as Federal, Cor-Bon, Black Hills, Sako and Sellier & Bellot. "Unleaded" may be the future! www.barnesbullets.com

Berger Bullets

It's catch-up time this year with the focus being the production of Berger's five new 20-caliber pills weighing from 30 to 50 grains. www.bergerbullets.com

Bismuth Cartridge Co.

Bismuth-core 223-caliber varmint bullets? They're here. Bismuth is entering the jacketed rifle bullet

world with a 55-grain hollowpoint. Because of their length-to-weight ratio, the new Bismuth bullets require a minimum twist of 1:10. The NATO 1:7 twist is even better. Along the same environmentally friendly lines is a new series of 21-gram 12-, 20-, and 28-gauge shells featuring Eley's "Kleena-Wad" and #8 shot. The Kleena-Wad is made from natural fibers, keeps the barrel virtually residue free, and can be shot in environmentally sensitive areas because it rapidly decomposes. A side benefit of the Bismuth 21-gram load is that it contains the same pellet count as a lead 24-gram loading. Velocity of the 12-gauge, 21-gram load is 1450 fps. www.bismuth-notox.com

Black Hills Ammunition

The Black Hills are famous for gold, and the Black Hills Gold line is famous for being one of the greatest premium hunting ammunition lines ever assembled. Its even better this year with the addition of Nosler AccuBond bullets in the 308, 30-'06, 270 WSM, 300 WSM, 300 WM and 7mm Remington Magnum. Famous for their match-grade ammunition, Black Hills has matched the 175-grain Sierra MatchKing to the 300 WSM at 2950 fps which should keep the paper punchers and tactical snipers in clover. And speaking of match ammunition, Black Hills has just been awarded the U.S. Army contract for 9mm, 45 ACP and 223 match ammo and continues to furnish the USMC Rifle Team with 77-grain molycoated MatchKing loads. You can buy the exact match load from Black Hills, so be sure to see their complete catalog at www.black-hills.com

Calhoon

While James Calhoon makes his proprietary double hollowpoint, "Slick Silver" varmint bullets in 20- and 22-caliber, his first love remains the 19-caliber. Now there are three Calhoon

Bismuth wins the "environmentally friendly" award by utilizing natural fiber shotgun wads and adding Bismuth cores to their 223-caliber varmint bullets.

Black Hills Ammunition upgrades its premium "Gold" line even further with the addition of AccuBond bullets.

19-caliber cartridges: the 19 Calhoon (Hornet) at 3600 fps; the 19-223 at 4000 + fps, and the brand new 19 Badger at 3750 fps. Calhoon can provide complete custom conversions based on the CZ rifle models or re-barrel kits for your own gun. www.jamescalhoon.com

CCI

You've heard of slam-fires occurring in semi-automatic military-style rifles when using ammunition primed with a rather sensitive primer. Or even look at the tiny firing pin sign on chambered, but not fired, rounds from firearms like the AR15, AK, and SKS. CCI has a solution—military spec primers that combine a tougher primer cup with a magnum primer charge for military ball powders. Called CCI "Arsenal" primers, the Small and Large Rifle primers use the same reloading data as CCI's 250 and 450 primers and should be on your dealer's shelves as you read this. CCI just improved the 17 HMR with a new 20-grain "GamePoint" bullet that mushrooms just like a big game bullet. The idea is to save game meat and predator hides. The muzzle velocity of the new load is 2375 fps, and it is said to deliver sub-MOA levels of accuracy. www.cci-ammunition.com

Cor-Bon

The Cor-Bon/Smith & Wesson team has done it again. Last year it was the development of the 500 S&W Magnum. This year it's the 460 S&W Magnum with a 200-grain bullet at 2300 fps. If the full-powered 500 S&W is a bit much, Cor-Bon has developed a light target load featuring a 350-grain FMJ at 1,200 fps. Child's play! Expanding their DPX (Deep Penetrating X) line utilizing proprietary Barnes X and Triple Shock bullets, Cor-Bon has added a new "Hunter" line that includes a variety of handgun and rifle calibers. The light-kicking "Pow'Rball" line offered under the Glaser label has been enhanced with a 165-grain bullet at 1075 fps for the increasingly popular 45 GAP, and oh, yes, the 45 GAP gets a 145-grain Glaser Safety Slug at 1325 fps, too. www.corbon.com

Dakota Arms

Dakota Arms has teamed up with Todd Kindler, founding editor of the *Small Caliber News*, to chamber Kindler's wildcats, the Tac 20, 17 Tactical, 17 VarTag, 20 VarTag, and 22 VarTag. Kindler's 17 and 20 Classics have been renamed the 17 and 20 Dakotas. www.dakotaarms.com

Federal

This is the year for Fusion bullets, super-dense shot, a new concentrator wad, a smoothbore slug that shoots like a sabot round, and some speedy upland loads. Federal's new Fusion rifle bullet is a boattail bonded-core design in which the jacket is plated to the core—plus it's priced at the level of conventional jacketed bullets. Watch for a variety of grain weights in all the popular calibers from 243 Winchester to 300 WSM.

"Heavyshot" is Federal's response to the success of Hevi-Shot. Heavyshot is remarkable stuff. It is 25 percent more dense than Hevi-Shot, 37 percent more dense than lead, and the pellets of this soft tungsten-iron shot are completely round, uniform and consistently sized. It will first appear in Federal's 12-gauge MagnumShok turkey loads featuring a new "Flightcontrol" wad that stays with the shot column longer, separates from it more smoothly, and consequently delivers more highly concentrated patterns. Watch for the Flightcontrol wad in waterfowl loads this year.

Recent slug designs have been focused on sabots and rifled shotgun bores leaving the old smoothbore slug gun to whither on the vine. No longer! Federal has come up with a conventional Foster-type slug that is mated to its driving wad by a plastic ball. Called TruBall, the slug riding on a ball is centered in the wad and the bore. Shooting an open-sighted 18-inch smoothbore slug barrel in a Remington 870, I have achieved 3 1/4 - 3 3/4-inch three-shot groups at 100 yards with the new TruBall ammunition. That's sensational!

Finally, Federal is introducing this year a number of faster upland game loads (1350-1500 fps) for those of us who are a bit slow in getting off a shot at a cackling rooster or a blur of a grouse. www.federalcartridge.com

Fiocchi

"Super Crusher" is a great name for Fiocchi's latest 12-gauge target load consisting of 1 ounce of hi-antimony lead #7.5 and 8 shot at 1400 fps. And then there's the "Paper Crusher"—a paper-hulled version of the same load but a hundred feet slower at 1300 fps.

Fiocchi's 40 S&W offerings have been updated with a 165-grain JHP at 1100 fps and a 165-grain truncated cone encapsulated base projectile at 1140 fps. www.fiocchiusa.com

Garrett Cartridges

If you're pursuing big or dangerous game with a 45-70, you can't do any better than using one of Randy Garrett's superior loads. Two, new + P loadings for modern 45-70 rifles

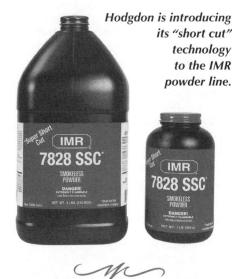

Hodgdon is introducing its "short cut" technology to the IMR powder line.

are a 500-grain Speer AGS tungsten core solid at 1,530 fps and a 500-grain Woodleigh Weld-Core at 1600. Either one is capable of penetrating a Cape buffalo from stem-to-stern. www.garrettcartridges.com

Goex

Goex is back in the non-corrosive, replica blackpowder business with the introduction of "Pinnacle Black Powder" in FFG and FFFG. We've missed the old Clear Shot brand. Pinnacle looks like blackpowder, shoots consistently with little fouling build-up and offers an indefinite shelf life. A new granulation called "Cowboy Action Cartridges" in Goex's standard blackpowder line is designed specifically for 40-grain loads or less. Speaking about cowboy cartridges,

GOEX is now marketing a complete line of blackpowder-loaded, SPG lubed, Black Dawge cartridges for rifle, pistol and scatterguns. Let the boom begin. www.goexpowder.com

Graf & Sons

There's no excuse for not shooting those old surplus rifles of any nationality. Loaded for them by Hornady, Graf now offers 6.5 Jap, 6.5 Carcano, 7.5 Swiss, 7.65 Argentine, 7.7 Jap, 8x56 Hungarian, 9mm Steyr and 455 Webley ammunition at attractive prices, plus special Hornady runs of the component bullets to reload those calibers. Based on my testing, this is premium quality ammunition. Graf is also importing the Privi Partizan brand of ammo in 6.5 Carcano, 7.5 French, 7.5 Swiss and 7.65 Argentine at sensational prices. Stock up while you can. www.grafs.com

Hevi-Shot

Hevi-Shot introduces Hevi-Steel that is 16-20 percent heavier than premium steel shot. Take a 3-inch 12-gauge hull, fill it with 1-1/8 oz. of Hevi-Steel, send it off at 1550 fps and you have Hevi-Steel, aka "Our Fast Little Brother." Two other innovations this year are Hevi-Shot 13, the heaviest shot made to date, and standard 12g/cc Hevi-Shot in the form of T-sized shot for a line of 12-gauge predator shells, named appropriately, "Dead Coyote." www.hevishot.com

Hevi-Shot's new predator loading for the 12-gauge features T shot.

Hodgdon Powder

After acquiring the IMR Powder Company last year, Hodgdon is refining the IMR line. The first improvement, which will prove to be a boon for handloaders, is a "super short-cut" version of IMR7828. Grains of the new IMR7828SSC are 35 percent shorter than the older cut length, yield the same burn rate, and run through a powder measure as slick as ball powder. With the reduced size of the grains, IMR7828SSC also yields 4 percent more case capacity, which can be an asset when compressed charges are called for. Great new packaging for Triple Seven 50-caliber/50-grain pellets. They're now offered in a blister pack that contains four clear plastic tubes with six pellets in each tube. Perfect for the hunt. Look for a new complimentary "IMR Smokeless Powder Guide" with updated data for the most recent cartridge introductions like the 204 Ruger and 25 WSSM. www.hodgdon.com

Hornady

Smith & Wesson's new 460 Magnum is getting a special 200-grain SST loading from Hornady. The polymer-tipped spitzer SST bullet is loaded to a velocity of 2250 fps, and when sighted-in 3 inches high at 100 yards, drops only 3.8 inches at 200 yards. Flat indeed! The SST bullet design is being carried over to Hornady's shotgun slug line as well with an initial 12-gauge offering with a muzzle velocity of 2050 fps. Look for lots of new Hornady component brass in all of the popular rifle and handgun calibers, plus hard-to-find numbers like 6.5-284, 376 Steyr, 405 Winchester, 458 Lott, and 475 Linebaugh. If you pursue big game, there are three new InterBond (bonded softpoint) bullets being offered this year: 375-caliber/ 300-grain; 416-caliber/400-grain; and a 45-caliber/500-grain. Lots of new rifle, pistol and shotgun additions to Hornady's "TAP" personal defense ammunition line. See them at www.hornady.com.

Huntington

Need some 303 Savage cases? Huntington just had Norma make a run. Here's the one-stop source for common and oddball components for any

Hornady's new 300-grain SST bullet churns up 2,050 fps in the 2 3/4"/12-gauge.

cartridge you can imagine reloading plus all the RCBS products and parts. Where can you find a complete inventory of Hornebar, Hirtenberger, Norma, Sako, RWS, Walter Gehmann and Dakota cases? Huntington's, of course, and the same can be said for bullets. Don't miss their extensive reference catalog at www.huntington.com

Lapua

Just when you think the 22 Long Rifle can't be improved, it is. Lapua has developed a special 22 Long Rifle bullet design that offers many of the qualities of their coated centerfire bullet line. Named "Signum," the form of the projectile and its lubrication provide decreased bore friction and bullet form integrity. See it at www.lapua.com

Liberty Shooting Supplies

Earlier this year, I was looking for an unplated lead bullet for the 8mm Nambu. Remembering that Liberty Shooting Supplies casts the most extensive array of bullet designs I know of, I went searching there and found exactly what I was looking for. If you enjoy shooting quality cast bullets, sized and lubricated to your specifications, take a look at their catalog. Liberty will also cast from your moulds. www.libertyshootingsupplies.com

Magtech

Magtech's "First Defense" line of 100-percent copper hollowpoint ammunition for law enforcement and personal defense is now available in 38 Special, 357 Magnum and 380 Auto—plus the same bullet technology has

been carried over to a new "Hunting" line featuring the larger handgun calibers. For the cost-conscious plinkers, Magtech is offering its most popular handgun calibers in 250-round boxes. www.magtechammunition.com

Meister Bullets

This well-known brand of hard cast bullets is expanding this year to include a 167-grain 30-30 Winchester; 170-grain 32-40 Winchester and 330-grain 500 S&W bullets. www.meisterbullets.com

NATEC

Building on their success with 223 polymer-cased ammunition, NATEC is bringing the technology to bear on the 308 Winchester which will be loaded with a 144-grain tracer, 150-grain FMJBT and Sierra GameKing, and a 168-grain Sierra MatchKing. The claimed benefits for the polymer-cased ammo are reduced weight (*35 percent in the case of the 308 Winchester*) and, because of its insulating qualities, improved propellant combustion and reduced heat transference to the firearm. www.natec-us.com

Norma

If we gave awards for the most beautiful and pro-hunting catalog

in the industry, Norma would be this year's winner hands down. Get it. It's a collector's item. Three new cartridges have been added to the line this year: 270 WSM, 7mm-08 Remington and the 470 Nitro Express. Norma's bonded-core Oryx bullet is now being loaded in an expanded list of big-game calibers. Here's something unique, a ballistics software program that can be accessed through the Norma website at www.norma.cc.

Northern Precision

I suspect those long, northern winters in upstate New York give Northern Precision the time to invent the most interesting array of 358, 416-, 429-, 452, and 458-caliber bullets in the industry. Just consider a 200-grain varmint bullet for the 416 Remington for a moment. Northern makes it. This year it's bonded-core spitzers for the 454 Casull and 250-grain bonded-core flat-points for the 356 Winchester. Call for their catalog at (315) 493-1711.

Nosler

This past hunting season, my wife and I shot Nosler AccuBonds exclusively in her 308 Winchester and my 300 WSM. The accuracy and performance of this bonded-core bullet has to be experienced to be appreciated. New in the AccuBond line this year are a 110-

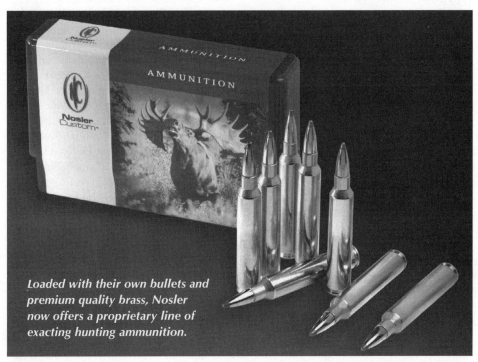

Loaded with their own bullets and premium quality brass, Nosler now offers a proprietary line of exacting hunting ammunition.

grain/257-caliber; 150-grain/30-caliber; 200-grain/8mm (loaded in the 325 WSM) and 180-grain/338-caliber. Nosler is also getting into the brass and ammunition businesses. Nosler brass, which is weight-sorted to one-half a grain, deburred and chamfered, is now available for the 223 Remington, 22-250 Remington, 243 Winchester, 270 Winchester, 7mm Remington Magnum, 308 Winchester, 30-'06 and 300 Winchester Magnum. The biggest news is that Nosler is offering its own line of precision ammunition direct to the consumer using a variety of components for decimal and metric calibers ranging from 218 Bee to 416 Rigby. www.nosler.com

Old Western Scrounger

When Dangerous Dave states that "we carry the largest and finest inventory of obsolete ammunition, bar-none," you had better believe it. Do you need 20mm Vulcan brass and a press big enough to load it? Or 11mm Mannlicher clips? How about 577 Snyder, 22 Remington Jet, 32 Winchester Self-Loader, 33 Winchester, 9x56 Mannlicher/Schoenauer, 43 Mauser, or 50-140 Sharps ammunition supplied in the most picturesque boxes ever created? The Old Western Scrounger is the place to go. www.ows-ammunition.com

PMC

A big push is on at PMC to bring new calibers into its environmentally friendly PMC Green line featuring frangible copper-polymer bullets and primers made without any heavy metal compounds. Added this year are a 100-grain loading for the 30-'06 and a 77-grain loading for the 380 Auto. The bullets are so frangible they disintegrate harmlessly when fired into steel plate only 3 inches from the muzzle. Over in the rimfire line are an ultra-quiet 22 Super Subsonic featuring a 20-grain bullet at 500 fps, a high-speed 22 Short, and the 17PMC outfitted with a 20-grain bullet at 1800 fps. www.pmcammo.com

Powerbelt

Big news! Powerbelt buys West Coast Bullets and will continue and expand the extensive West Coast cast line under

the named "Accura." A few of the new introductions will be hollowpoints and new coatings on top of the standard copper-clad coating. The newer coatings, called "Black Pearl" and "Sterling," permit the use of the cast bullets in Glocks, yielding higher velocities, lower pressures and better accuracy. Also being introduced is a new 40- and 45-caliber frangible line featuring sintered, copper-plated bullets. Powerbelt is expanding its highly popular copper-clad muzzleloading bullet line, that features an attached plastic gas seal, with the introduction of a 45-caliber 175-grain and a 50-caliber 223-grain. Both bullets feature a poly tip named the "Aerotip." www.powerbeltbullets.com

Remington

Tactical goes practical with the rollout of the 6.8mm Remington (Special Purpose Cartridge) and a Model 7 to shoot it in. If it's as successful as Remington's domestication of the 5.56mm in the guise of the 223 Remington, it will be successful indeed. The sporting load consists of a 115-grain PSP Core-Lokt Ultra Bonded bullet at 2775 fps, just right for lightweight rifles and recoil-sensitive shooters. The successful Managed-Recoil line has been extended with a 125-grain PSP Core-Lokt at 2660 fps in the 308 Winchester and a 150-grain loading at 2650 in the 300 Winchester Magnum. There's even a new Premier STS Low-Recoil 12-gauge loading of 1-1/8 oz. of #9s for those extended shoot-offs at Skeet.

A revolutionary new muzzleloading battery-cup primer for in-line and break-action rifles is making its debut. Remington has designed a unique nickel-plated Kleanbore primer that dramatically reduces chamber fouling, permitting more shots to be fired before the need to clean the old smokepole.

The super accurate, green-tipped Premier AccuTip bullet lines keep growing with the introduction of 32- and 40-grain bullets for the 204 Ruger; a 140-grain in the 280 Remington; a 35-grain pill for the 22 Hornet; and a 17-grain green tip for the wee 17 MACH2.

Keeping shooting affordable, Big Green is expanding its UMC lines with a 50-grain JHPs at 3410 fps in the 223 Remington and 3800 fps in the 22-250 Remington, as well as a 230-

grain JHP and FMJ at 835 fps in the new 45 GAP. Responding to slug gun hunters who favor a nice light rifled 20-gauge gun, Remington is introducing a 1 oz. Buckhammer slug at 1550 fps.

In shotshells, the old "Heavy Game" load label for shotshells has been replaced by "Pheasant Loads," and at the top of the list is the Nitro Pheasant line featuring copper-plated, 4-percent antimony shot in loads like 1-3/8 oz. of #4, 5, 6 at 1300 fps in the 2 3/4-inch 12 gauge and 1-1/4 oz. of #5, 6 in the 3-inch 20 gauge. To compete with the imports, a new Gun Club line of 12- and 20-gauge shells in #7-1/2, 8, 9 has been created.

Big Green is pushing its reloading components line. Watch for some snappy-looking plastic bags of Remington brass and bullets on your dealer's shelves.

Sierra Bullets

The bulletsmiths are right on top of the latest component market with the addition of 32- and 39-grain BlitzKings for the hot new 20-caliber cartridges—plus there's a super sleek 175-grain 7mm MatchKing that is making its appearance this year. That reminds me, if you haven't tried the 175-grain 308 MatchKing with a BC higher than that of the traditional 180-grain MatchKing, you've been missing out on one of the finest 30-caliber match bullets ever fielded. www.sierrabullets.com

Speer

Building on their successful introduction last year of a 38 Special Gold Dot HP loading for snubbies, Speer has expanded this much-needed concept with loads designed specifically for the short-barreled 9mm, 357 Magnum, 40 S&W, 44 Remington Magnum and 45 Auto. Guess what the line is called? "Short Barrel," of course! www.speer-bullets.com

SSK

JD Jones has finally outdone himself with the 620 JDJ. The new round for the T/C Encore is based on a shortened and fire-formed 577 Nitro case expanded to take a 600 Nitro bullet. JD is getting 1000 fps with a 1000-grain bullet from an Encore with a 12-inch barrel. T-Rex-grade ammunition! www.sskindustries.com

Triton

Whatever happened to Triton? It has been revived by American Ammunition, which recently acquired Triton's assets. Quik-Shok 9mm, 40 S&W and 45 ACP ammunition is once again available featuring the pre-stressed Quik-Shok core bullet that splits into three pieces upon impact. Triton Hi-Vel ammunition may be reintroduced by year's end. www.a-merc.com

Ultramax

Producing quality reloaded ammunition at great savings to the consumer, Ultramax has added three new loadings for the 500 S&W this year. The Ultramax line now includes rifle, pistol and cowboy loadings. www.ultramaxammunition.com

Vihtavuori and Lapua

Vihtavuori and Lapua have expanded their website this year. See their products at www. vihtavuori-lapua.com.

Western Powders

Western Powders buys Accurate Arms! See the comments under Accurate Arms. www.westernpowders.com

Winchester Ammunition

Winchester needed a "thumper" in their short magnum line for game like elk, moose and bear. This year they have it, the 325 WSM. A 325? Actually, it's an 8mm or 323 that combines the velocity of the 300 WSM with the punch of the 338 Winchester Magnum. Two new bullets have been designed for the 325 WSM—a 200-grain AccuBond CT loaded to 2950 fps in the Supreme line and a 220-grain Power-Point at 2840 fps that's been added to the Super-X line. A sleek 180-grain Ballistic Silvertip at 3060 fps fills out the Supreme series for lighter big game. Teamed with super-short-action Winchester Model 70s and Browning A-Bolts, the

Winchester continues to upgrade its 500 S&W offerings this year with a Platinum Tip.

325 WSSM is sure to generate a lot of excitement in the big-game hunting field. I've used it on Texas Nilgai, and it's not unusual to break both shoulders of the big bulls with the 200-grain AccuBond. That's performance! Nosler's AccuBond bullet is one of the most consistently accurate bullets ever made.

Given a Lubalox coating by Winchester, it is called an AccuBond CT and this year Winchester is adding a 110-grain loading to the 25-06 and 25 WSSM; and a 140-grain loading to the 7 WSM and 7mm Remington Magnum.

The ever popular 300 WSM is getting some added versatility as well with two new loadings: a 165-grain Fail Safe at 3125 fps and a 150-grain Power-Point at 3250 fps. For the varmint hunting clan, Big Red is adding the 17 HMR and the 204 Ruger to its cartridge offerings while elevating the 22-250 to light big status with the addition of a 64-grain Power-Point loading at 3500 fps.

The powerful 500 S&W is getting quite a play this year, so Winchester will be offering a 400-grain Platinum Tip HP at 1800 fps to the Supreme line for bone-crunching effectiveness.

Speaking about bone crunching, Winchester's 1 oz. Foster-type 12-gauge Power-Point rifled slug has been redesigned for improved accuracy and given a velocity of 1700 fps. Turkey hunters will be happy with the

introduction of Xtended Range High Density shot. That's perfectly round shot that's 10 percent heavier than lead producing denser patterns and higher pellet energy and penetration. The new shot in sizes #5 and #6 will be loaded in the 3 1/2-, 3- and 2 3/4-inch 12-gauge cases. A new 3-inch 20-gauge turkey load consisting of 1-5/16 oz. of #4, #5, #6 lead shot at 1200 fps joins the Supreme High Velocity Turkey line, and it should be a dilly. For those tough old fall roosters, Winchester is pumping up the 3-inch 20 gauge with 1-1/4 oz. of copper-plated #4, #5 and #6 at a sizzling 1250 fps in its Super Pheasant line.

The little .410 is receiving some welcome attention this year with a Super Sport AA sporting clays load consisting of 1/2 oz. of #7-1/2 at 1300 fps; a 3/4 oz. Super-X loading of #4, #6 and #7-1/2 at 1100 fps in the 3-inch case; and a full 1/4 oz. Super-X rifled slug for the 3-inch hull at a sizzling 1800 fps.

Speaking about "sizzling," the full 12-gauge Supreme High-Velocity Buckshot line will be receiving hard copper-plated OO buck roaring out at 1450 fps this year. Keeping the cost of steel shot shells in line, Winchester is introducing a 7/8 oz. loading of #2 and #4 at 1500 fps for the 3-inch 20 gauge in its economical Xpert Steel lineup. It's been a busy year at Winchester Ammunition! www.winchester.com

SHOOTER'S MARKETPLACE
PRODUCT NEWS FOR THE ACTIVE SHOOTING SPORTSMAN

The companies represented on the following pages will be happy to provide additional information – feel free to contact them.

Doug Turnbull Restoration
Big Bore Classics

Turnbull Restoration Big Bore Classics Rifles are constructed using original and new manufactured Model 1886 Winchester & Browning Rifles. Available in calibers: 45-70, 45-90 & 50-110 (50 Express). For more information contact us at:

6680 Route 5 & 20, P.O. Box 471 Bloomfield, NY 14469
Phone: 585-657-6338 Email: turnbullrest@mindspring.com Website: www.turnbullrestoration.com

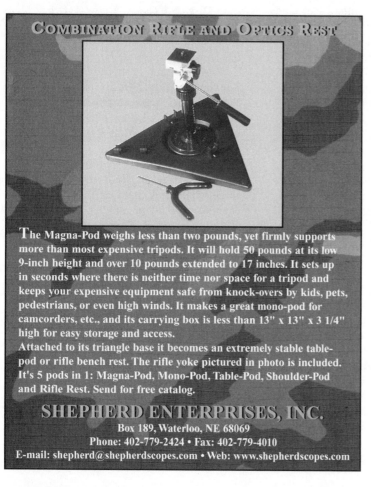

COMBINATION RIFLE AND OPTICS REST

The Magna-Pod weighs less than two pounds, yet firmly supports more than most expensive tripods. It will hold 50 pounds at its low 9-inch height and over 10 pounds extended to 17 inches. It sets up in seconds where there is neither time nor space for a tripod and keeps your expensive equipment safe from knock-overs by kids, pets, pedestrians, or even high winds. It makes a great mono-pod for camcorders, etc., and its carrying box is less than 13" x 13" x 3 1/4" high for easy storage and access.

Attached to its triangle base it becomes an extremely stable table-pod or rifle bench rest. The rifle yoke pictured in photo is included. It's 5 pods in 1: Magna-Pod, Mono-Pod, Table-Pod, Shoulder-Pod and Rifle Rest. Send for free catalog.

SHEPHERD ENTERPRISES, INC.
Box 189, Waterloo, NE 68069
Phone: 402-779-2424 • Fax: 402-779-4010
E-mail: shepherd@shepherdscopes.com • Web: www.shepherdscopes.com

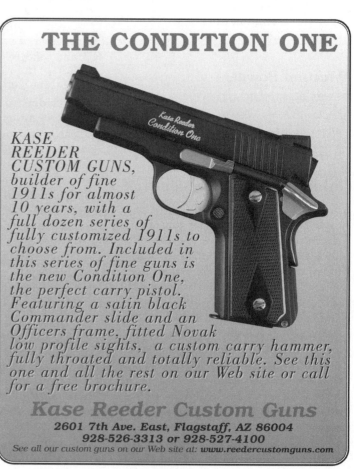

THE CONDITION ONE

KASE REEDER CUSTOM GUNS, builder of fine 1911s for almost 10 years, with a full dozen series of fully customized 1911s to choose from. Included in this series of fine guns is the new Condition One, the perfect carry pistol. Featuring a satin black Commander slide and an Officers frame, fitted Novak low profile sights, a custom carry hammer, fully throated and totally reliable. See this one and all the rest on our Web site or call for a free brochure.

Kase Reeder Custom Guns
2601 7th Ave. East, Flagstaff, AZ 86004
928-526-3313 or 928-527-4100
See all our custom guns on our Web site at: www.reedercustomguns.com

2006 GUNS ILLUSTRATED Complete Compact CATALOG

GUNDEX

GUNDEX

GUNDEX

SEMI-CUSTOM

HANDGUNS

RIFLES

SHOTGUNS

BLACKPOWDER

AIRGUNS

COMPENDIUM

MANUFACTURER'S
DIRECTORY

GUNDEX

GUNDEX

GUNDEX

GUNDEX

GUNDEX

Browning Luxus Grade B2

Browning Luxus Renaissance Argent

Browning Luxus Renaissance OR

Ed Brown Classic Class A

Ed Brown Kobra Carry

Kimber Ultra CDP

Kimber Custom Target II

BRILEY 1911-STYLE AUTO PISTOLS

Caliber: 9mm Para., 38 Super, 40 S&W, 10-shot magazine; 45 ACP, 8-shot magazine. **Barrel:** 3.6" or 5". **Weight:** NA. **Length:** NA. **Grips:** Rosewood or rubber. **Sights:** Bo-Mar adjustable rear, Briley dovetail blade front. **Features:** Modular or Caspian alloy, carbon steel or stainless steel frame; match barrel and trigger group; lowered and flared ejection port; front and rear serrations on slide; beavertail grip safety; hot blue, hard chrome or stainless steel finish. Introduced 2000. Made in U.S. From Briley Manufacturing Inc.

Price: Fantom (3.6" bbl., fixed low-mount rear sight, armor coated lower receiver), from **$1,900.00**
Price: Fantom with two-port compensator, from **$2,245.00**
Price: Advantage (5" bbl., adj. low-mount rear sight, checkered mainspring housing), from **$1,650.00**
Price: Versatility Plus (5" bbl., adj. low-mount rear sight, modular or Caspian frame), from **$1,850.00**
Price: Signature Series (5" bbl., adj. low-mount rear sight, 40 S&W only), from **$2,250.00**
Price: Plate Master (5" bbl. with compensator, lightened slide, Briley scope mount), from **$1,895.00**
Price: El Presidente (5" bbl. with Briley quad compensator, Briley scope mount), from **$2,550.00**

BROWNING HI-POWER LUXUS

The legendary Browning Hi-Power pistol still produced in Belgium is available in four grades in the Luxus series: Grade II, Renaissance Argent, Grade B2 and the gold-finished Renaissance OR. Other specifications NA.
Price: From **$4,391.00**

ED BROWN CLASSIC CUSTOM AND CLASS A LIMITED 1911-STYLE AUTO PISTOLS

Caliber: 45 ACP; 7-shot magazine; 40 S&W, 400 Cor-Bon, 38 Super, 9x23, 9mm Para. **Barrel:** 4.25", 5", 6". **Weight:** NA. **Length:** NA. **Grips:** Hogue exotic checkered wood. **Sights:** Bo-Mar or Novak rear, blade front. **Features:** Blued or stainless steel frame; ambidextrous safety; beavertail grip safety; checkered forestrap and mainspring housing; match-grade barrel; slotted hammer; long lightweight or Videki short steel trigger. Many options offered. Made in U.S. by Ed Brown Products, Inc.

Price: Classic Custom (45 ACP, 5" barrel), from **$2,895.00**
Price: Executive Elite (45 ACP, 5" barrel), from **$2,195.00**
Price: Executive Carry (4.25" bbl., has "bobtail™" modification to reduce overall length), from **$2,295.00**
Price: Kobra (45 ACP only, 5" bbl., completely hand-fitted with heavy dehorning), from **$1,995.00**

Price: Kobra Carry (45 ACP only, 4.25" bbl., has exclusive snakeskin pattern on frame, top portion of mainspring housing and slide), from **$2,195.00**
NEW! Price: Executive Target, (45 ACP, 5" government model, features exclusive 25 lpi checkering and Bo-Mar adjustable sights), from **$2,370.00**

KIMBER CUSTOM II 1911-STYLE AUTO PISTOLS

Caliber: 9mm Para., 38 Super, 9-shot magazines; 40 S&W, 8-shot magazine; 45 ACP, 7-shot magazine. **Barrel:** 5". **Weight:** 38 oz. **Length:** 8.7" overall. **Grips:** Black synthetic, smooth or double-diamond checkered rosewood, or double-diamond checkered walnut. **Sights:** McCormick low profile or Kimber adjustable rear, blade front. **Features:** Machined steel slide, frame and barrel; front and rear beveled slide serrations; cut and button-rifled, match-grade barrel; adjustable aluminum trigger; full-length guide rod; Commander-style hammer; high-ride beavertail safety; beveled magazine well. Other models available. Made in U.S. by Kimber Mfg. Inc.

Price: Custom II (black matte finish) **$730.00**
Price: Custom Royal II (polished blue finish, checkered rosewood grips) **$886.00**
Price: Custom Stainless II (satin-finished stainless steel frame and slide) **$832.00**
Price: Custom Target II (matte black or stainless finish, Kimber adj. sight) **$945.00**
Price: Custom Compact CDP II (4" bbl., alum. frame, tritium three-dot sights, 28 oz.) **$1,141.00**
Price: Custom Pro CDP II (4" bbl., alum. frame, tritium sights, full-length grip, 28 oz.) **$1,141.00**
Price: Ultra CDP II (3" bbl., aluminum frame, tritium sights, 25 oz.) **$1,141.00**
Price: Gold Match II (polished blue finish, hand-fitted barrel, ambid. safety), from **$1,168.00**
Price: Stainless Gold Match II (stainless steel frame and slide, hand-fitted bbl., amb. safety) .... **$1,315.00 to $1,345.00**

Les Baer Thunder Ranch Special

Volquartsen Stingray

Rock River Arms Limited Match

LES BAER CUSTOM 1911-STYLE AUTO PISTOLS
Caliber: 9mm Para., 38 Super, 40 S&W, 45 ACP, 400 Cor-Bon; 7- or 8-shot magazine. **Barrel:** 4-1/4", 5", 6". **Weight:** 28 to 40 oz. **Length:** NA. **Grips:** Checkered cocobolo. **Sights:** Low-mount combat fixed, combat fixed with tritium inserts or low-mount adjustable rear, dovetail front. **Features:** Forged steel or aluminum frame; slide serrated front and rear; lowered and flared ejection port; beveled magazine well; speed trigger with 4-pound pull; beavertail grip safety; ambidextrous safety. Other models available. Made in U.S. by Les Baer Custom.

Price: Baer 1911 Premier II 5" Model (5" bbl., optional stainless steel frame and slide), from **$1,498.00**
Price: Premier II 6" Model (6" barrel), from **$1,675.00**
Price: Premier II LW1 (forged aluminum frame, steel slide and barrel), from **$1,835.00**
Price: Custom Carry (4" or 5" barrel, steel frame), from **$1,728.00**
Price: Custom Carry (4" barrel, aluminum frame), from **$2,039.00**
Price: Swift Response Pistol (fixed tritium sights, Bear Coat finish), from **$2,339.00**
Price: Monolith (5" barrel and slide with extra-long dust cover), from **$1,660.00**
Price: Stinger (4-1/4" barrel, steel or aluminum frame), from ... **$1,552.00**
Price: Thunder Ranch Special (tritium fixed combat sight, Thunder Ranch logo), from **$1,685.00**
Price: National Match Hardball (low-mount adj. sight; meets DCM rules), from **$1,425.00**
Price: Bullseye Wadcutter Pistol (Bo-Mar rib w/ adj. sight, guar. 2-1/2" groups), from **$1,560.00**
Price: Ultimate Master Combat (5" or 6" bbl., adj. sights, checkered front strap), from **$2,530.00**
Price: Ultimate Master Combat Compensated (four-port compensator, adj. sights), from **$2,558.00**

ROCK RIVER ARMS 1911-STYLE AUTO PISTOLS
Caliber: 9mm Para., 38 Super, 40 S&W, 45 ACP. **Barrel:** 4" or 5". **Weight:** NA. **Length:** NA. **Grips:** Double-diamond, checkered cocobolo or black synthetic. **Sights:** Bo-Mar low-mount adjustable, Novak fixed with tritium inserts, Heine fixed or Rock River scope mount; dovetail front blade. **Features:** Chrome-moly, machined steel frame and slide; slide serrated front and rear; aluminum speed trigger with 3.5-4 lb. pull; national match KART barrel; lowered and flared ejection port; tuned and polished extractor; beavertail grip safety; beveled mag. well. Other frames offered. Made in U.S. by Rock River Arms Inc.

Price: Elite Commando (4" barrel, Novak tritium sights) **$1,395.00**
Price: Standard Match (5" barrel, Heine fixed sights) **$1,150.00**
Price: National Match Hardball (5" barrel, Bo-Mar adj. sights), from **$1,275.00**
Price: Bullseye Wadcutter (5" barrel, Rock River slide scope mount), from **$1,380.00**
Price: Basic Limited Match (5" barrel, Bo-Mar adj. sights), from . **$1,395.00**
Price: Limited Match (5" barrel, guaranteed 1-1/2" groups at 50 yards), from **$1,795.00**
Price: Hi-Cap Basic Limited (5" barrel, four frame choices), from **$1,895.00**
Price: Ultimate Match Achiever (5" bbl. with compensator, mount and Aimpoint), from **$2,255.00**
Price: Match Master Steel (5" bbl. with compensator, mount and Aimpoint) **$5,000.00**

STI COMPACT AUTO PISTOLS
Caliber: 9mm, 40 S&W. **Barrel:** 3.4". **Weight:** 28 oz. **Length:** 7" overall. **Grips:** Checkered double-diamond rosewood. **Sights:** Heine Low Mount fixed rear, slide integral front. **Features:** Similar to STI 2011 models except has compact frame, 7-shot magazine in 9mm (6-shot in 40 cal.), single-sided thumb safety, linkless barrel lockup system, matte blue finish. From STI International.

Price: (9mm or 40 S&W), from **$746.50**

VOLQUARTSEN CUSTOM 22 CALIBER AUTO PISTOLS
Caliber: 22 LR; 10-shot magazine. **Barrel:** 3.5" to 10"; stainless steel air gauge. **Weight:** 2-1/2 to 3 lbs. 10 oz. **Length:** NA. **Grips:** Finger-grooved plastic or walnut. **Sights:** Adjustable rear and blade front or Weaver-style scope mount. **Features:** Conversions of Ruger Mk. II Auto pistol. Variety of configurations featuring compensators, underlug barrels, etc. Stainless steel finish; black Teflon finish available for additional $85; target hammer, trigger. Made in U.S. by Volquartsen Custom.

Price: 3.5 Compact (3.5" barrel, T/L adjustable rear sight, scope base optional) **$640.00**
Price: Deluxe (barrel to 10", T/L adjustable rear sight) **$675.00**
Price: Deluxe with compensator **$745.00**
Price: Masters (6.5" barrel, finned underlug, T/L adjustable rear sight, compensator) **$950.00**
Price: Olympic (7" barrel, recoil-reducing gas chamber, T/L adjustable rear sight) **$870.00**
Price: Stingray (7.5" ribbed, ported barrel; red-dot sight) **$995.00**
Price: Terminator (7.5" ported barrel, grooved receiver, scope rings) **$730.00**
Price: Ultra-Light Match (6" tensioned barrel, Weaver mount, weighs 2-1/2 lbs.) **$885.00**
Price: V-6 (6", triangular, ventilated barrel with underlug, T/L adj. sight) **$1,030.00**
Price: V-2000 (6" barrel with finned underlug, T/L adj. sight) **$1,095.00**
Price: V-Magic II (7.5" barrel, red-dot sight) **$1,055.00**

**Gary Reeder
1 Asterisk**

**Gary Reeder
Bandit**

**Gary Reeder
Belle Star**

**Gary Reeder
Black Widow**

**Gary Reeder
Coyote Classic**

**Gary Reeder
Classic Hunter**

**Gary Reeder
Doc Holiday Classic**

GARY REEDER CUSTOM GUNS REVOLVERS

Caliber: 22 WMR, 22 Hornet, 218 Bee, 356 GMR, 41 GNR, 410 GNR, 510 GNR, 357 Magnum, 45 Colt, 44-40, 41 Magnum, 44 Magnum, 454 Casull, 475 Linebaugh, 500 Linebaugh. **Barrel:** 2-1/2" to 12". **Weight:** Varies by model. **Length:** Varies by model. **Grips:** Black Cape buffalo horn, laminated walnut, simulated pearl, black and ivory micarta, others. **Sights:** Notch fixed or adjustable rear, blade or ramp front. **Features:** Custom conversions of Ruger Vaquero, Blackhawk Bisley and Super Blackhawk frames. Jeweled hammer and trigger, tuned action, model name engraved on barrel, additional engraving on frame and cylinder, integral muzzle brake, finish available in high-polish or satin stainless steel or black Chromex finish. Also available on customer's gun at reduced cost. Other models available. Made in U.S. by Gary Reeder Custom Guns.

Price: 1 Asterisk (Full custom M1911. Stainless or blued finish. Full combat features including see-thru Lexan grip panel, from **$995.00**

Price: 45 Backpacker (weighs 28 oz., comes in 45 Long Colt, all stainless except for lightweight aircraft aluminum gripframe, black Micarta grips, not recommended for Plus P ammo), from **$995.00**

Price: 510 Hunter (octagonal bbl., set back trigger, adjustable sights, 510 GNR 5-shot, built on customer furnished Ruger frame), from **$1,295.00**

Price: African Hunter (6" bbl., with or without muzzle brake, 475 or 500 Linebaugh. Built on customer's gun), from **$1,295.00**

Price: Alaskan Hunter (4-1/2" bbl., 5-shot unfluted freewheeling cylinder, black Micarta grips, soft satin vapor honed finish), from **$1,295.00**

Price: Alaskan Survivalist (3" bbl., Redhawk frame, engraved bear, 45 Colt or 44 Magnum), from **$995.00**

Price: American Hunter (475 Linebaugh or 500 Linebaugh, built to customers specs on furnished Ruger frame), from **$1,395.00**

Price: Arizona Ranger (choice of calibers and barrel lengths, stainless or Black Chromex finish, engraved with original Arizona Ranger badge), from **$850.00**

Price: Badlands Classic (all stainless, 4-1/2" bbl., high polished, fully engraved, Gunfighter grip and cowboy pearl grips), from **$850.00**

Price: Bandit (3-1/2" bbl., special Lightning style grip frame built on a Ruger Vaquero frame, engraved, set back trigger, Colt-style hammer), from **$1,095.00**

Price: Belle Starr Classic (engraved with gunfighter grip, 32 H&R), from **$850.00**

Price: Black Widow (4-5/8" bbl., black Chromex finish, black widow spider engraving), from **$850.00**

Price: BMF (500 Maximum or 500 Linebaugh, 4" barrel, round butt), from **$2,395.00**

Price: Border Classic (Built on customer furnished Schofield; 3" bbl., full scroll engraving, solid silver Mexican coin front sight, custom grips), from **$1,095.00**

Price: Classic 45 (shoots 45 Colt, 45 ACP or 45 Schofield without moon clips, built to customer specs on customer furnished Ruger frame), from **$1,295.00**

Price: Classic 475 (Built on customer furnished base gun. 475 Linebaugh, 5 shot; satin black finish, gunfighter grip, set-back trigger, from **$1,295.00**

Price: Cowtown Classic (stainless finish, engraved with imaged symbolizing the old west, from **$850.00**

Price: Coyote Classic (chambered in 22 Hornet, 22 K-Hornet, 218 Bee, 218 Mashburn Bee, 17 Ackley Bee, 17 Ackley Hornet, 256 Winchester, 25-20, 6-shot unfluted cylinder, heavy 8" barrel, Super Blackhawk gripframe, finish of satin stainless, satin Black Chromex or high polished, comes with laminated cherry grips and Gunfighter grip), from **$1,295.00**

Price: Doc Holliday Classic (3-1/2" bbl., engraved cards and dice, white pearl grips), from **$850.00**

Price: Double Deuce (8" heavy bbl., adjustable sights, laminated grips, 22 WMR 8-shot), from **$995.00**

Price: Gamblers Classic (2-1/2" bbl., engraved cards and dice, no ejector rod housing), from **$850.00**

Price: Improved #5 (field grade or deluxe grade, many options to choose from **$1,2950.00**

Gary Reeder
Rio Grande

Gary Reeder
Southern Comfort

Gary Reeder
Ultimate Black Widow

500 Linebaugh Long

500 Linebaugh

Price: Kodiak Magnum (heavy 8-1/2" bbl. with deep crown and tight
barrel/cylinder gap, satin vapor honed finish), from $850.00
Price: Lawman Classic (Full custom Vaquero, two-tone finish,
Lawman-style engraving, special Lawman gripframe with
lanyard ring), from $950.00
Price: Lonestar Classic (7-1/2" bbl., highly polished, to a mirror finish,
engraved with items relevant to the state of Texas), from $850.00
Price: Long Rider Classic (45 long Colt, choice of barrel lengths,
midnight black trigger and hammer, gold rings), from $950.00
Price: Montana Hunter Series (45 long Colt, 4-5/8" bbl., all stainless
steel, 5-shot, soft satin finish, walnut grips), from $1,295.00
NEW! Price: Night Hawk (4" bbl., dual purpose as conceal carry
or hunting revolver), from $1,095.00
Price: Night Rider (7-1/2" bbl., fully engraved with contrasting
light colored stag grips), from $850.00
Price: O.K. Corral Classic (12-1/2" bbl., engraved with western
trappings, Black Chromex finish), from $950.00
Price: Professional Hunter (stretch frame stainless 5-shot available in
calibers including 475 Maximum and 500 Maximum), from $2,395.00
Price: Rio Grande Classic (built on any caliber Vaquero in barrel
length of choice, Gunfighter grip, engraving is old southwest type
with a few western features, specially designed base pin,
long tapered hammer, from $1,095.00
NEW! Price: Sidewinder (3-1/2" bbl., snake scales over entire
frame and barrel, black micarta grips), from $950.00
Price: Southern Comfort (5-shot cylinder, heavy duty base pin,
tear drop hammer, special set back trigger, interchangeable
blade system, special gripframe, satin Vapor Honed finish),
from $1,295.00
Price: Texas Ranger Classic (45 long Colt, 5-1/2" bbl. with other
calibers and barrel lengths available, engraved with Texas
Ranger badge, gunfighter grip, simulated pearl handles,
Black Chromex finish), from $950.00
Price: Tombstone Classic (3-1/2" bbl. with gold bands, notch sight,
birdshead grips), from $850.00
Price: Trail Rider Classic (7-1/2" bbl., more lengths available,
fully engraved with western trappings, pearl grips), from $950.00
Price: Ultimate 41 (410 GNR 5-shot, built on customer
furnished Ruger frame), from $1,195.00
Price: Ultimate 44 (ported, special recoil-taming grip frame,
sling swivels, 44 Mag. 5-shot, built on customer furnished
Ruger Hunter), from $1,395.00

Price: Ultimate 50 (choice of barrel lengths in any centerfire
caliber, 5-shot stainless steel 50 Action Express,
freewheeling cylinder), from $1,295.00
Price: Ultimate 410 GNR (5-shot 410 GNR freewheeling cylinder),
from $1,295.00
Price: Ultimate 480 (choice of barrel lengths in any caliber,
full vapor honed stainless steel, satin finish Black Chromex
or two-toned finish, 5-shot cylinder, heavy barrel, Gunfighter grip,
full action job, custom laminated grips, freewheeling cylinder,
Belt Mountain base pin), from $1,195.00
Price: Ultimate 500 (built on stretch frame in 500 S&W, 5-shot.
Choice of bbl. lengths, gunfigher grip, set-back trigger, from $2,495.00
Price: Ultimate Back Up (3-1/2" bbl., fixed sights, choice of
animal engraving, 475 Linebaugh, 500 Linebaugh built on
customer's gun.), from $1,395.00
Price: Ultimate Black Widow (475 Linebaugh or 500 Linebaugh,
heavy duty 5 shot cylinder, heavy high grade barrel, Gunfighter
Grip with black Micarta grips, Belt Mountain base pin), from . . $1,395.00
Price: Ultimate Vaquero (engraved barrel, frame and cylinder, made to
customer specs), from $950.00
Price: Western Classic (standard fieid grade and deluxe grade, many
options to choose from) $1,295.00
Price: Wichita Classic (41 Special, stainless steel pins
and screws) $1,095.00

LINEBAUGH CUSTOM SIXGUNS REVOLVERS
Caliber: 45 Colt, 44 Linebaugh Long, 458 Linebaugh, 475 Linebaugh, 500
Linebaugh, 500 Linebaugh Long, 445 Super Mag. **Barrel:** 4-3/4", 5-1/2",
6", 7- 1/2"; other lengths available. **Weight:** NA. **Length:** NA. **Grips:**
Dustin Linebaugh Custom made to customer's specs. **Sights:** Bowen
steel rear or factory Ruger; blade front. **Features:** Conversions using
customer's Ruger Blackhawk Bisley and Vaquero Bisley frames. Made in
U.S. by Linebaugh Custom Sixguns.
Price: Small 45 Colt conversion (rechambered cyl., new barrel),
from $1,200.00
Price: Large 45 Colt conversion (oversized cyl., new barrel,
5- or 6-shot), from $1,800.00
Price: 475 Linebaugh, 500 Linebaugh conversions, from $1,800.00
Price: Linebaugh and 445 Super Mag calibers on 357 Maximum
frame, from $3,000.00

Gary Reeder Ultimate Encore

Gary Reeder Kodiak Hunter Dall Sheep

SSK Industries Contender

GARY REEDER CUSTOM GUNS CONTENDER AND ENCORE PISTOLS
Caliber: 22 Cheetah, 218 Bee, 22 K-Hornet, 22 Hornet, 218 Mashburn Bee, 22-250 Improved, 6mm/284, 7mm STW, 7mm GNR, 30 GNR, 338 GNR, 300 Win. Magnum, 338 Win. Magnum, 350 Rem. Magnum, 358 STA, 375 H&H, 378 GNR, 416 Remington, 416 GNR, 450 GNR, 475 Linebaugh, 500 Linebaugh, 50 Alaskan, 50 AE, 454 Casull; others available. **Barrel:** 8" to 15" (others available). **Weight:** NA. **Length:** Varies with barrel length. **Grips:** Walnut fingergroove. **Sights:** Express-style adjustable rear and barrel band front (Kodiak Hunter); none furnished most models. **Features:** Offers complete guns and barrels in the T/C Contender and Encore. Integral muzzle brake, engraved animals and model name, tuned action, high-polish or satin stainless steel or black Chromex finish. Made in U.S. by Gary Reeder Custom Guns.
Price: Kodiak Hunter (50 AE, 475 Linebaugh, 500 Linebaugh, 510 GNR, or 454 Casull, Kodiak bear and Dall sheep engravings), from **$1,195.00**
Price: Ultimate Encore (15" bbl. with muzzle brake, custom engraving), from **$1,095.00**

SSK INDUSTRIES CONTENDER AND ENCORE PISTOLS
Caliber: More than 200, including most standard pistol and rifle calibers, as well as 226 JDJ, 6mm JDJ, 257 JDJ, 6.5mm JDJ, 7mm JDJ, 6.5mm Mini- Dreadnaught, 30-06 JDJ, 280 JDJ, 375 JDJ, 6mm Whisper, 300 Whisper and 338 Whisper. **Barrel:** 10" to 26"; blued or stainless; variety of configurations. **Weight:** Varies with barrel length and features. **Length:** Varies with barrel length. **Grips:** Pachmayr, wood models available. **Features:** Offers frames, barrels and complete guns in the T/C Contender and Encore. Fluted, diamond, octagon and round barrels; flatside Contender frames; chrome-plating; muzzle brakes; trigger jobs; variety of stocks and forends; sights and optics. Made in U.S. by SSK Industries.
Price: Blued Contender frame, from **$390.00**
Price: Stainless Contender frame, from **$390.00**
Price: Blued Encore frame, from **$290.00**
Price: Stainless Encore frame, from **$318.00**
Price: Contender barrels, from **$315.00**
Price: Encore barrels, from **$340.00**

Ed Brown 702 Varmint

Ed Brown 702 Bushveld

ED BROWN CUSTOM BOLT-ACTION RIFLES

Caliber: 222, 223, 22-250, 220 Swift, 243, 243 Ackley Imp., 25-06, 270 Win., 280 Rem., 280 Ackley Imp., 6mm, 6.5/284, 7mm/08, 7mm Rem. Mag., 7STW, 30/06, 308, 300 Win. Mag., 338 Win. Mag., 375 H&H, 404 Jeffery, 416 Rem. Mag., 416 Rigby, 458 Win. Mag. **Barrel:** 21", 24", 26". **Weight:** NA. **Length:** NA. **Stock:** Fiberglass synthetic; swivel studs; recoil pad. **Sights:** Optional; Talley scope rings and base furnished; scope mounting included in price (scope extra). **Features:** Machined receiver; hand-fitted bolt with welded handle; M16-type extractor; three-position safety; trigger adjustable for pull and overtravel; match-quality, hand-lapped barrel with deep countersunk crowning. Made in U.S. by Ed Brown Custom, Inc.

Price: Model 702 Savanna short- or long-action repeater (lightweight 24" or medium-weight 26" barrel), from . **$2,800.00**
Price: Model 702 Tactical long-action repeater (heavy contour 26" barrel), from **$2,900.00**
Price: Model 702 Ozark short-action repeater (lightweight 21" barrel), from **$2,800.00**
Price: Model 702 Varmint short-action single shot (med. 26" or hvy. 24"), from **$2,800.00**
Price: Model 702 Light Tactical short-action repeater (med. 21" barrel), from **$2,800.00**
Price: Model 702 Bushveld dangerous game rifle (24" med. or heavy barrel), from **$2,900.00**
Price: Model 702 Denali mountain hunting rifle (22" super light weight bbl. or 23" light weight bbl.), from **$2,800.00**
Price: Model 702 Tactical sniper rifle (26" heavy bbl.), from **$2,900.00**
Price: Model 702 Marine Sniper (24" heavy bbl.), from **$2,900.00**

Dakota 76 Classic

Dakota 97 Hunter

DAKOTA 76 RIFLE

Caliber: All calibers from 22-250 through 458 Win. Mag. **Barrel:** 23". **Weight:** 6-1/2 lbs. **Length:** NA. **Stock:** Choice of X-grade oil-finished English, Bastogne or Claro walnut. **Features:** Short, standard short magnum or long magnum actions, hand checkered stock with 1" black recoil pad, steel grip cap and single screw stud sling swivels. Many options and upgrades available.

Price: Dakota 76 Classic, from **$4,995.00**
Price: Dakota 76 Safari (23" bbl., calibers from 257 Roberts through 458 Win. Mag. drop belly
magazine with straddle floorplate), from **$5,995.00**
Price: Dakota 76 African (24" bbl., 450 Dakota, 416 Dakota, 416 Rigby, 404 Jeffrey,
four-round magazine), from **$6,795.00**
Price: Dakota 97 Hunter (24" bbl., calibers from 25-06 to 375 Dakota, synthetic stock), from **$2,195.00**
Price: Longbow Tactical Engagement Rifle (28" bbl., 338 Lapua Mag., 330 Dakota, 300 Dakota,
McMillan fiberglass stock with full-length action bedding), from **$4,500.00**

Remington Model ABG

REMINGTON MODEL 700 CUSTOM SHOP RIFLES

Caliber: 270 Win., 280 Rem., 30-06, 7mm Rem. Mag., 7mm STW, 300 Win. Mag., 300 Wea. Mag., 338 Win. Mag., 8mm Rem. Mag., 35 Whelen, 375 H&H Mag., 416 Rem. Mag., 458 Win. Mag., 7mm RUM, 300 RUM, 338 RUM, 375 RUM. **Barrel:** 22", 24", 26". **Weight:** 6 lbs. 6 oz. to 9 lbs. **Length:** 44-1/4" to 46-1/2" overall. **Stock:** Laminated hardwood, walnut or Kevlar-reinforced fiberglass. **Sights:** Adjustable rear (Safari models); all receivers drilled and tapped for scope mounts. **Features:** Black matte, satin blue or uncolored stainless steel finish; hand-fitted action is epoxy-bedded to stock; tuned trigger; bolt-supported extractor for sure extraction; fancy wood and other options available. Made in U.S. by Remington Arms Co.

Price: Custom KS Mountain Rifle (24" barrel, synthetic stock, 6-3/4 lbs. in mag. cals.), from	**$1,314.00**
Price: Custom KS Safari Stainless (22" barrel, synthetic stock, 9 lbs.), from	**$1,697.00**
Price: Model ABG (African Big Game: 26" bbl., laminated stock, satin blue finish), from	**$1,726.00**
Price: APR (African Plains Rifle: 26" barrel, laminated stock, satin blue finish), from	**$1,716.00**
Price: AWR (Alaskan Wilderness Rifle: 24" barrel, syn. stock, black matte finish), from	**$1,593.00**
Price: Model 700 Custom C Grade, from **$1,733.00**; Custom High Grade, from	**$3,297.00**

Remington 40-XB with thumbhole stock

REMINGTON MODEL 40-X CUSTOM SHOP TARGET RIFLES

Caliber: 22 LR, 22 WMR, 22 BR Rem., 222 Rem., 223 Rem., 22-250, 220 Swift, 6mm BR Rem., 6mm Rem., 243 Win., 25-06, 260 Rem., 7.62mm NATO, 7mm BR Rem., 7mm Rem. Mag., 7mm STW, 308 Win., 30-06, 300 Win. Mag. **Barrel:** 24", 27-1/4"; various twist rates offered. **Weight:** 9-3/4 to 11 lbs. **Length:** 40" to 47" overall. **Stock:** Walnut, laminated wood or Kevlar-reinforced fiberglass. **Sights:** None; receiver drilled and tapped for scope mounts. **Features:** Single shot or 5-shot repeater; carbon steel or stainless steel receiver; externally adjustable trigger (1-1/2 to 3-1/2 lbs.); rubber butt pad. From Remington Arms Co.

Price: 40-XB Rangemaster (27-1/4" bbl., walnut stock, forend rail with hand stop), from	**$1,636.00**
Price: 40-XB (with thumbhole stock), from	**$1,848.00**
Price: 40-XB KS (27-1/4" bbl., black synthetic stock), from	**$1,876.00**
Price: 40-XRBR KS (24" bbl., Remington green synthetic stock with straight comb), from	**$1,894.00**
Price: 40-XC KS (24" bbl., gray synthetic stock with adj. comb), from	**$1,821.00**
Price: 40-XB Tactical (27-1/4" bbl., synthetic stock, matte finish), from	**$2,108.00**

Remington Model Seven Custom MS

REMINGTON MODEL SEVEN CUSTOM SHOP RIFLES

Caliber: 222 Rem., 223 Rem., 22-250 Rem., 243 Win., 6mm Rem., 250 Savage, 257 Roberts, 260 Rem., 308 Win., 7mm-08 Rem., 35 Rem., 350 Rem. Mag. **Barrel:** 20". **Weight:** 5-3/4 to 6-1/2 lbs. **Length:** 39-1/2" overall. **Stock:** Laminated hardwood or Kevlar-reinforced fiberglass. **Sights:** Adjustable ramp rear, hooded blade front. **Features:** Hand-fitted action; epoxy bedded; deep blue or non-reflective black matte finish; drilled and tapped for scope mounts. From Remington Arms Co.

Price: Model Seven Custom MS (20" bbl., Mannlicher stock, deep blue finish), from	**$1,332.00**
Price: Model Seven Custom KS (20" bbl., synthetic stock, matte finish), from	**$1,314.00**
Price: Model Seven AWR Alaskan Wilderness Rifle (22" bbl., synthetic stock, 7mm Rem. SAUM, 300 Rem. SAUM), from	**$1,546.00**

SEMI-CUSTOM RIFLES — Bolt-Action

John Rigby African Express Rifle

JOHN RIGBY CUSTOM AFRICAN EXPRESS RIFLE

Caliber: 375 H&H Magnum, 416 Rigby, 450 Rigby, 458 Winchester, 505 Gibbs. **Barrel:** To customer specs. **Weight:** NA. **Length:** To customer specs. **Stock:** Customer's choice. **Sights:** Express-type rear, hooded ramp front; scope mounts offered. **Features:** Handcrafted bolt-action rifle built to customer specifications. Variety of engraving and stock wood options available. Imported from England by John Rigby & Co.
   Price: African Express Rifle,
            from **$18,600.00**

John Rigby African Express Rifle engraving

JOHN RIGBY BOLT-ACTION RIFLES

Caliber: 300 H&H, 375 H&H, 416 Rigby, 458 Win., 500 Jeffrey (other calibers upon request) **Barrel:** NA. **Weight:** NA. **Length:** NA. **Stock:** Exhibition grade English walnut. **Sights:** Quarter rib with Express sights containing flip up night sight. **Features:** Stock custom-fitted to buyer specifications, detachable scope mounts included, Pac Nor Match grade barrel.
   Price: John Rigby Bolt Action Rifle, from **$14,500.00**

TIME PRECISION BOLT-ACTION RIFLES

Caliber: 22 LR, 222, 223, 308, 378, 300 Win. Mag., 416 Rigby, others. **Barrel:** NA. **Weight:** 10 lbs. and up. **Length:** NA. **Stock:** Fiberglass. **Sights:** None; receiver drilled and tapped for scope mount. **Features:** Thirty different action types offered, including single shots and repeaters for bench rest, varmint and big-game hunting. Machined chrome-moly action; three-position safety; Shilen match trigger (other triggers available); twin cocking cams; dual firing pin. Built to customer specifications. From Time Precision.
   Price: 22 LR Bench Rest Rifle (Shilen match-grade stainless steel bbl., fiberglass stock), from **$2,202.00**
   Price: 22 LR Target Rifle, from **$2,220.00**
   Price: 22 LR Sporter, from **$1,980.00**
   Price: 22 LR Benchrest Rifle, from **$2,202.00**
   Price: Hunting Rifle (calibers to 30-06), from **$2,202.00**
   Price: Benchrest Rifle (most calibers), from **$2,202.00**
   Price: Hunting Rifle (7mm Rem. Mag., 300 Win. Mag., 338 Win. Mag.), from **$2,322.00**

CONSULT

SHOOTER'S MARKETPLACE

Page 74, This Issue

Weatherby Safari Grade

Weatherby Crown Custom

Weatherby Custom close-up

WEATHERBY CUSTOM SHOP BOLT-ACTION RIFLES

Caliber: 257 Wby. Mag., 270 Wby. Mag., 7mm Wby. Mag., 300 Wby. Mag., 340 Wby. Mag., 375 H&H Mag., 378 Wby. Mag., 416 Wby. Mag., 460 Wby. Mag. **Barrel:** 24", 26", 28". **Weight:** NA. **Length:** NA. **Stock:** Monte Carlo, modified Monte Carlo or Classic design in Exhibition- or Exhibition Special Select grades of claro or French walnut; injection-molded synthetic in Snow Camo, Alpine Camo or Dark Timber colors. **Sights:** Quarter-rib rear with one standing and one folding leaf, hooded ramp front (Safari Grade); drilled and tapped for scope mount. Features: Rosewood or ebony pistol-grip caps with inlaid diamonds in rosewood, walnut or maple; three grades of engraving patterns for receiver, bolt and handle; gold inlays; wooden inlaid buttstock, forearm and magazine box; three grades of engraved and gold inlaid rings and bases; canvas/leather, solid leather or leather with oak trim case. From the Weatherby Custom Shop.

Price: Safari Grade (engr. floorplate, oil-finished French wal. stock w/fleur-de-lis checkering.) **$6,050.00**
Price: Crown (engr., inlaid floorplate, engr. bbl. and receiver, hand-carved walnut stock) **$7,757.00**
Price: Crown Custom (engraved barrel, receiver and triggerguard, hand-carved walnut stock, damascened bolt and follower with checkered knob), from **$7,757.00**
Price: Outfitter Krieger (Krieger stainless steel bbl.) **$3,639.00**
Price: Outfitter Custom (standard barrel, Bell and Carlson syn. camo stock), from **$2,583.00**
Price: Dangerous Game Rifle (chrome moly Criterion barrel by Krieger Monte Carlo-style composite stock, Mark V action), from **$3,095.00**

Winchester African Express

WINCHESTER MODEL 70 CLASSIC CUSTOM RIFLES

Caliber: 375 H&H Mag., 416 Rem. Mag., 458 Win. Mag., 458 Lott, 470 Capstick, 257 Roberts, 260 Rem., 7mm-08 Rem., 300 WSM, 270 WSM, 7mm WSM, 308 Win., 358 Win., 450 Marlin, 270 Win., 7mm Win., 30-06 Spfld., 25-06 Rem., 6.5x55 Swe., 264 Win. Mag., 280 Rem., 35 Whelen, 7mm Rem. Mag., 7mm Ultra Mag., 7mm STW, 300 Win. Mag., 300 Wea. Mag., 300 Ultra. Mag., 338 Ultra Mag., 375 H&H (Lwt). **Barrel:** 22", 24", 26". **Weight:** 6.5 to 9.5 lbs. **Length:** NA. **Stock:** Various grades of walnut and synthetic stocks available. **Sights:** Three-leaf express rear, adjustable front, (Express models); none furnished on other models. **Features:** Match-grade cut rifled barrels with squared, hand-honed actions. Most are available in stainless or blued, and right- or left-handed, hand-fitted actions. All utilize the pre-'64 type action with controlled round feed, receiver-mounted blade ejector and specially-tuned trigger systems. All are shipped in a hard case. Made in U.S.A. by Winchester/U.S. Repeating Arms Co.

Price: Model 70 Classic Custom African Express (22" or 24" barrel, 9.25 to 9.5 lbs), from **$4,572.00**
Price: Safari Express (24" barrel, 9 to 9.25 lbs.), from **$3,043.00**
Price: Short Action (24" barrel, 7.5 to 8.25 lbs.), from **$2,708.00**
Price: Featherweight (22" barrel, 7.25 lbs., 270 Win., 7mm Win., 30-06 Spfld.), from **$2,708.00**
Price: Carbon (24" or 26" barrel, 6.5 to 7 lbs.), from **$3,233.00**
Price: Ultimate Classic (24" or 26" barrel, 7.5 to 7.75 lbs.), from **$2,941.00**
Price: Extreme Weather (22", 24" or 26" barrel, 7.25 to 7.5 lbs.), from **$2,525.00**

Bushmaster DCM Competition Rifle

Volquartsen Grey Ghost

BROWNING SEMI-AUTO 22 LUXE

Caliber: 22 LR. **Barrel:** 19-1/4". **Weight:** 5 lbs. 3 oz. **Length:** 37". **Stock:** Polished walnut. **Sights:** Adjustable folding leaf rear, gold bead front. **Features:** The traditional John Browning-designed .22 takedown autoloader with bottom eject. Grooved receiver will accept most groove or tip-off type mounts or receiver sights. Custom shop versions are available in two grades: SA 22 Grade II and SA 22 Grade III.
   Price: From **$2,920.00**

BROWNING BAR MARK I

The original Browning BAR Mark I from the Browning Custom Shop in Belgium available in Grade IV and Grade D.
   Price: From **$7,216.00**

BUSHMASTER SEMI-AUTO RIFLES

Caliber: 223. **Barrel:** 16" regular or fluted, 20" regular, heavy or fluted, 24" heavy or fluted. **Weight:** 6.9 to 8.37 lbs. **Length:** 34.5" to 38.25" overall. **Stock:** Polymer. **Sights:** Fully adjustable dual flip-up aperture rear, blade front or Picatinny rail for scope mount. **Features:** Versions of the AR-15 style rifle. Aircraft-quality aluminum receiver; chrome-lined barrel and chamber; chrome-moly-vanadium steel barrel with 1:9" twist; manganese phosphate matte finish; forged front sight; receiver takes down without tools; serrated, finger groove pistol grip. Made in U.S.A. by Bushmaster Firearms/Quality Parts Co.
   Price: DCM Competition Rifle **$1,495.00**

LES BAER AR 223 AUTO RIFLES

Caliber: 223. **Barrel:** 16-1/4", 20", 22" or 24"; cryo-treated, stainless steel bench-rest grade. **Weight:** NA. **Length:** NA. **Stock:** Polymer. **Sights:** None; Picatinny rail for scope mount. **Features:** Forged and machined upper and lower receiver; single- or double-stage adjustable trigger; free-float handguard; Bear Coat protective finish. Made in U.S.A. by Les Baer Custom.
   Price: Ultimate Super Varmint (Jewell two-stage trigger, guar. to shoot 1/2 MOA groups), from **$1,989.00**
   Price: Ultimate M4 Flattop (16-1/4" bbl., Ultra single-stage trigger), from **$2,195.00**
   Price: Ultimate IPSC Action (20" bbl., Jewell two-stage trigger), from **$2,230.00**

SSK INDUSTRIES AR-15 RIFLES

Caliber: 223, 6mm PPC, 6.5mm PPC, Whisper and other wildcats. **Barrel:** 16-1/2" and longer (to order). **Weight:** NA. **Length:** NA. **Stock:** Black plastic. **Sights:** Blade front, adjustable rear (scopes and red-dot sights available). **Features:** Variety of designs to full match-grade guns offered. Customer's gun can be rebarreled or accurized. From SSK Industries.
   Price: Complete AR-15, from **$1,800.00**
   Price: A2 upper unit (front sight, short handguard **$1,100.00**
   Price: Match Grade upper unit (bull barrel, tubular handguard, scope mount) **$1,100.00**

VOLQUARTSEN CUSTOM 22 CALIBER AUTO RIFLES

Caliber: 22 LR, 22 Magnum. **Barrel:** 16-1/2" to 20"; stainless steel air gauge. **Weight:** 4-3/4 to 5-3/4 lbs. **Length:** NA. **Stock:** Synthetic or laminated. **Sights:** Not furnished; Weaver base provided. **Features:** Conversions of the Ruger 10/22 rifle. Tuned trigger with 2-1/2 to 3-1/2 lb. pull. Variety of configurations and features. From Volquartsen Custom.
   Price: Ultra-Light (22 LR, 16-1/2" tensioned barrel, synthetic stock, from **$670.00**
   Price: Grey Ghost (22 LR, 18-1/2" barrel, laminated wood stock), from **$690.00**
   Price: Deluxe (22 LR, 20" barrel, laminated wood or fiberglass stock), from **$850.00**
   Price: Mossad (22 LR, 20" fluted and ported barrel, fiberglass thumbhole stock), from **$970.00**
   Price: VX-2500 (22 LR, 20" fluted and ported barrel, aluminum/fiberglass stock), from **$1,044.00**
   Price: Volquartsen 22 LR (stainless steel receiver), from **$920.00**
   Price: Volquartsen 22 Mag (22 WMR, stainless steel receiver), from **$950.00**

John Rigby Boxlock

John Rigby Sidelock close-up

BERETTA EXPRESS DOUBLE RIFLES

Caliber: 9.3x74R, 375 H&H Mag., 416 Rigby, 458 Win. Mag., 470 Nitro Express, 500 Nitro Express. **Barrel:** 23" to 25". **Weight:** 11 lbs. **Length:** NA. **Stock:** Hand-finished, hand-checkered walnut with cheek rest. **Sights:** Folding-leaf, Express-type rear, blade front. **Features:** High-strength steel action with reinforced receiver sides; top tang extends to stock comb for strength; double triggers (articulated front trigger and automatic blocking device eliminate chance of simultaneous discharge); hand-cut, stepped rib; engraved receiver; trapdoor compartment in stock for extra cartridges; spare front sights stored in pistol-grip cap. Imported from Italy by Beretta USA.

Price: SSO6 o/u (optional claw mounts for scope), from **$21,000.00**
Price: SSO6 EELL o/u (engraved game scenes or color case-hardened with gold inlays), from **$23,500.00**
Price: 455 s/s (color case-hardened action), from **$36,000.00**
Price: 455 EELL s/s (receiver engraved with big-game animals), from **$47,000.00**

BROWNING EXPRESS RIFLES

Still made in Belgium in the traditional manner, two models are available, Herstal and CCS 375. Produced in five different grades of embellishment. Other specifications NA.

Price: From **$11,733.00**

JOHN RIGBY DOUBLE RIFLES

Caliber: 375 H&H, 500/416, 450 Nitro Express, 470 Nitro Express, 500 Nitro Express, 577 Nitro Express. **Barrel:** To customer specs. **Weight:** NA. **Length:** To customer specs. **Stock:** To customer specs. **Sights:** Dovetail, express-type sights; claw-foot scope mount available. **Features:** Handcrafted to customer specifications. Boxlock or sidelock action, hand-fitted; variety of engraving and other options offered. Imported from England by John Rigby & Co.

Price: Rigby Boxlock, from **$23,500.00**
Price: Rigby Sidelock, from **$41,700.00**

Ballard No. 5 Pacific

BALLARD RIFLE, LLC

Caliber: 22 LR, 32-40, 38-55, 40-65 Win., 40-70 SS, 40-90, 45-70 Gov't., 45-90, 45-110, 50-70 Gov't., 50-90 **Barrel:** 24", 26", 30", 32", 34". **Weight:** 7-1/2 to 11-1/2 lbs. **Stock:** American black walnut. **Sights:** Blade front, Rocky Mountain rear, others. **Features:** Authentic reproductions faithful to the original patent. Receivers and internal parts machined from solid 8620 steel stock, not castings. Hand finished. Many options.

Price: No. 1-1/2 Hunter's Rifle (30" round bbl., single trigger, S lever), from $2,050.00
Price: No. 1-3/4 Far West (30" round regular or heavyweight bbl., S lever), from $2,250.00
Price: No. 3 Gallery Rifle (24", 26" or 30" lightweight octagon bbl., rifle bottsrock with steel crescent buttplate, S lever), from $2,050.00
Price: No. 3F Fine Gallery Rifle (26", 28" or 30" octagon bbl., pistol grip, single or double set triggers), from . . $2,500.00
Price: No. 4 Perfection (30" or 32" octagon bbl. single or double set trigger), from $2,250.00
Price: No. 4-1/2 Mid Range (30" or 32" standard or heavyweight half octagon bbl., single or double set triggers, pistol grip shotgun buttstock), from $2,250.00
Price: No. 5 Pacific (30" or 32" standard or heavyweight octagon bbl., standard stocks in rifle or shotgun configuration), from $2,575.00
Price: No. 5-1/2 Montana Model (30" or 32" heavyweight octagon bbl., under-barrel wiping rod, set triggers, ring lever), from $2,725.00
Price: No. 6 Off Hand Rifle (30", 32" or 34" half octagon bbl., blade front sight, pistol grip receiver, double set triggers), from $2,550.00
Price: No. 7 Long Range (32" or 34" standard or heavyweight half octagon bbl., pistol grip shotgun buttstock, single or double set trigger), from $2,250.00
Price: No. 8 Union Hill Model (30" half octagon standard or heavyweight bbl., double set triggers, pistol grip stock with cheekpiece, full loop lever) from $2,500.00
Price: Standard Sporting Model 1885 High Wall (30" or 32" octagonal bbl., single trigger, small S lever), from . $2,050.00
Price: Special Sporting Model 1885 High Wall (32" bbl., shotgun buttstock with cheekpiece, shotgun buttplate, double set triggers), from $2,200.00

C. Sharps Model 1885 Highwall Classic Sporting

C. Sharps Model 1877 Custom LR Target

C. SHARPS ARMS RIFLES

Caliber: 22 RF to 50-140-3 1/4 Sharps. **Barrel:** Octagon 18" to 34". **Weight:** 9-18 lbs. **Stock:** American English walnut (premium straight grain to presentation). **Sights:** Short range to long range target. **Features:** Authentic replicas of Sharps rifles. Models 1874, 1877 & 1885 machined from solid steel. Made in U.S. by C. Sharps Arms Co. Inc.

Price: Model 1874 Hartford, from $1,775.00
Price: Model 1874 Bridgeport, from $1,495.00
Price: Model 1875 Sporting, from $1,095.00
Price: Model 1875 Classic, from $1,385.00
Price: Model 1875 Target, from $1,136.63
Price: Model 1877 Custom LR Target, from $5,500.00
Price: Model 1885 Highwall Sporting, from $1,350.00
Price: Model 1885 Highwall Classic Sporting, from $1,550.00

SEMI-CUSTOM RIFLES — Single Shot

Dakota Model 10

DAKOTA MODEL 10

Caliber: Most from 22 LR through 404 Dakota. **Barrel:** 23". **Length:** NA. **Weight:** 5-1/2 lbs. **Stock:** Walnut. **Sights:** NA. **Features:** Falling block action machined from prehardened 4140 bar stock. Many options.
Price: Dakota Model 10, from **$3,795.00**

Lone Star Silhouette

LONE STAR ROLLING BLOCK RIFLES

Caliber: 30-40 Krag, 30-30, 32-40, 38-55, 40-50 SS, 40-50 BN, 40-65, 40-70 SS, 40-70 BN, 40-82, 40-90 SBN, 40-90 SS, 44-90 Rem. Sp., 45 Colt, 45-110 (3-1/4"), 45-110 (2-7/8"), 45-100, 45-90, 45- 70, 50-70, 50-90. **Barrel:** 26" to 34". **Weight:** 6 to 11 lbs. **Length:** NA. **Stock:** American walnut. **Sights:** Buckhorn rear, blade or Beech front. **Features:** Authentic replicas of Remington rolling block rifles. Octagon barrel (except Creedmore model); bone-pack, color case-hardened action; drilled and tapped for Vernier sight; single, single-set or double-set trigger; variety of sight, finish and engraving options. Fires blackpowder or factory ammo. Made in U.S. by Lone Star Rifle Co. Inc.
Price: No. 5 Sporting Rifle (30-30 or 30-40 Krag, 26" barrel, buckhorn rear sight) **$1,595.00**
Price: Cowboy Action Rifle (28" octagonal barrel, buckhorn rear sight) **$1,595.00**
Price: Silhouette Rifle (32" or 34" octagonal barrel, drilled and tapped for Vernier sight) **$1,595.00**
Price: Sporting Rifle (straight grip, semi-crescent butt, octagonal bbl.), from **$1,995.00**
Price: Creedmoor (34" bbl. identical to original rifle) **$2,195.00**
Price: Buffalo Rifle (12 or 16 lbs., octagonal bbl.) **$2,900.00**
Price: Custer Commemorative (50-70 only, octagonal bbl.) exact replica of General George Armstrong
Custer's Remington Sporting Rifle **$2,900.00**

Meacham Low-Wall

MEACHAM HIGH-WALL SILHOUETTE RIFLE

Caliber: Any rimmed cartridge. **Barrel:** 30", 34" octagon. **Weight:** 11-1/2 to 11.9 lbs. **Length:** NA. **Stock:** Fancy eastern black walnut with cheekpiece and shadow line. **Sights:** Tang drilled for Win. base, 3/8" front dovetail. **Features:** Parts interchangeable copy of '85 Winchester. Numerous options include single trigger, single set trigger, or Schuetzen double set triggers, thick side or thin side bone charcoal color case-hardened action.
Price: Meacham High-Wall Silhouette, from **$3,299.00**
Price: Meacham Low-Wall Rifle (Calibers: 22 RF Match or 17 HMR, rimfire and centerfire pistol cartridges,
.22 Hornet or Bee), from **$3,299.00**

Remington No. 1 Mid-Range Sporter

REMINGTON CUSTOM SHOP ROLLING BLOCK RIFLES

Caliber: 45-70. **Barrel:** 30". **Weight:** NA. **Length:** NA. **Stock:** American walnut. **Sights:** Buckhorn rear and blade front (optional tang-mounted Vernier rear, globe with spirit level front). **Features:** Satin blue finish with case-colored receiver; single set trigger; steel Schnabel fore end tip; steel buttplate. From Remington Arms Co. Custom Gun Shop.
Price: No. 1 Mid-Range Sporter (round or half-octagon barrel) **$1,450.00**
Price: No. 1 Silhouette (heavy barrel with 1:18" twist; no sights) **$1,560.00**

SEMI-CUSTOM SHOTGUNS

Beretta Jubilee II 12-gauge

Beretta ASE Deluxe

Close-up of Beretta Jubilee II engraving

Close-up of Beretta ASE Deluxe engraving

BERETTA PREMIUM GRADE SHOTGUNS

Gauge: 12, 20, 410, 3" chamber; 28, 2-3/4" chamber. **Barrel:** 26", 28", 30", 32". **Weight:** 5 to 7-1/2 lbs. **Length:** NA. **Stock:** Highly figured English or American walnut; straight or pistol grip; hand-checkered. **Features:** Machined nickel-chrome-moly action, hand-fitted; cross-bolt breech lock; Boehler Antinit steel barrels with fixed chokes or Mobilchoke tubes; single selective or non-selective or double trigger; numerous stock and engraving options. From Beretta USA.

Price: Giubileo (Jubilee) o/u (engraved sideplates, trigger guard, safety and top lever), from	**$12,900.00**
Price: Giubileo II (Jubilee II) s/s (English-style stock, engraved sideplates and fixtures), from	**$12,900.00**
Price: ASE Deluxe o/u (engraved receiver and forend cap), from	**$24,000.00**
Price: SO5 Trap (single, non-selective trigger, heavy beavertail forend, fixed chokes), from	**$17,490.00**
Price: SO5 Skeet (26" or 28" bbl., heavy beavertail forend, fixed chokes), from	**$17,490.00**
Price: SO5 Sporting (single, selective trigger, Mobilchoke tubes), from	**$17,490.00**
Price: SO6 EELL o/u (engraved receiver with gold inlays, custom-fit stock), from	**$34,900.00**
Price: SO6 EL o/u (light English scroll engravings on receiver), from	**$23,900.00**
Price: SO6 EESS o/u (enamel-colored receiver in green, red or blue, arabesque engravings), from	**$34,900.00**
Price: SO9 o/u (single, non-selective trigger, engraved receiver and fixtures), from	**$44,500.00**

Beretta SO6 EELL 12-gauge

Beretta SO6 EELL engraving

Beretta SO6 EL engraving

SEMI-CUSTOM SHOTGUNS

Browning LC1

Browning LC2

BROWNING SUPERPOSED & BSL SHOTGUNS

Gauge: 20, Both the BSL side-by-side and the Superposed over-and under are still made in Belgium in the traditional, time-honored manner. The BSL is available in two grades, LC1 (blued receiver) and LC2 (silver-colored receiver). The Superposed is available in 18 grades. Custom options include: engraving of name or initials, second set of barrels, special finish or checkering, special stock dimensions, personalized engraving scenes and upgraded wood. Other specifications NA.
Price: From **$18,566.00**

DAKOTA LEGEND/PREMIER SHOTGUNS

Available in all standard gauges, features include exhibition English walnut stock, French grey finish, 50% coverage engraving, straight grip, splinter forend, double trigger, 27" barrels, game rib with gold bead, selective ejectors, choice of chokes. Various options available.
Price: Dakota Premier Grade, from **$13,950.00**
Price: Dakota Legend Shotgun (27" bbls., special selection English walnut stock,
straight grip, splinter forend), from **$18,000**

Ithaca Grade 7E

Ithaca Sousa Grade

ITHACA CLASSIC DOUBLES SIDE-BY-SIDE SHOTGUNS

Gauge: 20, 28, 2-3/4" chamber; 410, 3" chamber. **Barrel:** 26", 28", 30". **Weight:** 5 lbs. 5 oz. (410 bore) to 5 lbs. 14 oz. (20 ga.). **Length:** NA. **Stock:** Exhibition-grade American black walnut, hand-checkered with hand-rubbed oil finish. **Features:** Updated duplicates of original New Ithaca Double double-barrel shotguns. Hand-fitted box-lock action; splinter or beavertail forend; bone-charcoal color case-hardened receiver; chrome-moly steel rust-blued barrels; ejectors; gold double triggers; fixed chokes; hand-engraved game scenes. Made in U.S. by Ithaca Classic Doubles.
Price: Special Skeet Grade (plain color case-hardened receiver, feather crotch walnut stock) **$3,465.00**
Price: Grade 4E (gold-plated triggers, jeweled barrel flats, engraved game-bird scene) **$4,625.00**
Price: Grade 7E (gold-inlaid ducks, pheasants and bald eagle on scroll engraving) **$9,200.00**
Price: Sousa Grade (gold-inlaid setter, pointer, flying ducks and Sousa mermaid) **$11,550.00**

JOHN RIGBY SHOTGUNS

*John Rigby Side-by-Side
12-gauge engraving*

Gauge: 12, 16, 20, 28 and 410 bore. **Barrel:** To customer specs. **Weight:** NA. **Length:** To customer specs. **Stock:** Customer's choice. **Features:** True sidelock side-by-side and over-under shotguns made to customer's specifications. Hand-fitted actions and stocks; engraved receivers embellished with game scenes; over-under includes removable choke tubes. Imported from England by John Rigby & Co.
Price: Sidelock over-under (single selective, non-selective
or double triggers), from **$36,500.00**
Price: Sidelock side-by-side (engraved receiver,
choice of stock wood), from **$39,950.00**
Price: Hammer shotguns (manual-cocking hammers,
rebounding firing pins and hammers; extractors only),
from **$18,000.00**

SEMI-CUSTOM SHOTGUNS

Merkel 47E

Merkel 47SL

Merkel 280EL

Merkel 303EL

Merkel 2001EL

MERKEL EXHIBITION, VINTAGERS EXPO AND CUSTOM ENGRAVED SHOTGUNS

Gauge: 12, 16, 20, 28, 410. **Barrel:** 26-3/4", 28"; others optional. **Weight:** NA. **Length:** NA. **Stock:** Highly figured walnut; English (straight) or pistol grip. **Features:** Highly engraved versions of Merkel over-under and side-by-side shotguns. Imported from Germany by GSI Inc.
Price: .... **Call**

PERAZZI SCO, SCO GOLD, EXTRA AND EXTRA GOLD SHOTGUNS

Gauge: 12, 20, 28, 410. **Barrel:** 23-5/8" to 34". **Weight:** 6 lbs. 3 oz. to 8 lb. 13 oz. **Length:** NA. **Stock:** To customer specs. **Features:** Enhanced, engraved models of game and competition over-under shotguns. Customer may choose from many engraved hunting and wildlife scenes. Imported from Italy by Perazzi USA Inc.
Price: SCO Grade in competition and game o/u guns (fully engraved receiver), from **$31,275.00**
Price: SCO Gold Grade in comp. and game o/u guns (engraved w/gold inlays), from **$35,336.00**
Price: Extra Grade in competition and game o/u guns (highly detailed engraving), from **$85,140.00**
Price: Extra Gold Grade in comp. and game o/u guns (detailed engraving w/gold inlays), from **$91,684.00**
Price: SCO Grade with engraved sideplates (extends engraved area), from **$47,968.00**
Price: SCO Gold Grade with engraved sideplates, from **$54,137.00**

Perazzi MX-8

Perazzi MX-10

Perazzi SCO Grade engraving

Perazzi SCO Gold engraving

Perazzi Extra engraving

SEMI-CUSTOM SHOTGUNS

Remington 11-87 "F" Grade

REMINGTON CUSTOM SHOP AUTO SHOTGUNS

Gauge: 10, 12, 20, 28. **Barrel:** 21" to 30". **Weight:** NA. **Length:** NA. **Stock:** Two grades of American walnut. **Features:** Engraved versions of the Model 11-87 and Model 1100 shotgun. "D" or "F" grade fancy walnut, hand-checkered stock; choice of ebony, rose-wood, skeleton steel or solid steel grip cap; choice of solid steel, standard, Old English or ventilated recoil pad; optional inletted gold oval with three initials on bottom of stock. From Remington Arms. Co. Custom Gun Shop.

    Price: 11-87 and 1100 "D" Grade (English scroll engraving on receiver, breech and trig. guard) **$3,723.00**
    Price: 11-87 and 1100 "F" Grade (engraved game scene, "F" Grade walnut stock) **$7,245.00**
    Price: 11-87 and 1100 "F" Grade with gold inlay (inlaid three-panel engraved game scene) **$10,663.00**

REMINGTON CUSTOM SHOP PUMP SHOTGUNS

Gauge: 10, 12, 20, 28, 410. **Barrel:** 20" to 30". **Weight:** NA. **Length:** NA. **Stock:** Two grades of American walnut. **Features:** Engraved versions of the Model 870 shotgun. "D" or "F" grade fancy walnut hand-checkered stock; choice of ebony, rosewood, skeleton steel or solid steel grip cap; choice of solid steel, standard, Old English or ventilated recoil pad; optional inletted gold oval with three initials on bottom of stock. From Remington Arms Co. Custom Gun Shop.

    Price: 870 "D" Grade (English scroll engraving on receiver, breech and trig. guard) **$3,723.00**
    Price: 870 "F" Grade (engraved game scene, "F" grade walnut stock) **$7,245.00**
    Price: 870 "F" Grade with gold inlay (inlaid three-panel engraved game scene) **$10,663.00**

REMINGTON CUSTOM SHOP OVER/UNDER SHOTGUNS

Gauge: 12. **Barrel:** 26", 28", 30". **Weight:** 7-1/2 to 8 lbs. **Length:** 42-1/2" to 47-1/4". **Stock:** American walnut. **Features:** Barrels made of chrome-moly steel with 3" chambers, finger grooved forend, fully brazed barrel side ribs, hardened trunions, automatic ejectors. Made in U.S. by Remington Arms Co. Custom Gun Shop.

    Price: Remington Model 332 D Grade, from **$4,184.00**
    Price: Model 332 F Grade, from **$7,706.00**
    Price: Model 332 F Grade w/gold inlay, from **$11,122.00**

Tar-Hunt DSG

TAR-HUNT DSG (DESIGNATED SLUG GUN)

Gauge: 12, 16. **Barrel:** 23". **Weight:** NA. **Length:** NA. **Stock:** NA **Features:** Tar-Hunt converts the basic Remington 870 shotgun into a configuration for shooting slugs only by installation of a non-removable custom fit Shaw rifled slug barrel with muzzle brake. The 870 Wingmaster is fitted with a barrel with 2-3/4" chamber, the 870 Express Mag. and Wingmaster Mag. have a 3-inch chamber and the 870 Express Super Mag. will have a 3-1/2" chamber. Included are Leupold two-piece windage bases which will accept any standard type turn in rings.

    Price: Tar-Hunt DSG . . . . **$450.00** (with customer furnished Remington 870)
    Price: Tar-Hunt Express . . . . **$695.00** (complete gun with black synthetic stock)
    Price: Tar-Hunt Wingmaster **$950.00**

Includes models suitable for several forms of competition and other sporting purposes.

Accu-Tek HC-380

Accu-Tek XL-9

Auto-Ordnance 1911A1 Standard

Baer Custom Carry

Auto-Ordnance Deluxe

Baer Premium II

ACCU-TEK MODEL HC-380 AUTO PISTOL
Caliber: 380 ACP, 10-shot magazine. **Barrel:** 2.75". **Weight:** 26 oz. **Length:** 6" overall. **Grips:** Checkered black composition. **Sights:** Blade front, rear adjustable for windage. **Features:** External hammer; manual thumb safety with firing pin and trigger disconnect; bottom magazine release. Stainless steel construction. Introduced 1993. Price includes cleaning kit and gun lock. Made in U.S.A. by Accu-Tek.
Price: Satin stainless **$249.00**

ACCU-TEK XL-9 AUTO PISTOL
Caliber: 9mm Para., 5-shot magazine. **Barrel:** 3". **Weight:** 24 oz. **Length:** 5.6" overall. **Grips:** Black pebble composition. **Sights:** 3-dot system; rear adjustable for windage. **Features:** Stainless steel construction; double-action-only mechanism. Introduced 1999. Price includes cleaning kit and gun lock, two magazines. Made in U.S.A. by Accu-Tek.
Price: **$267.00**

AMERICAN DERRINGER LM-5 AUTOMATIC PISTOL
Caliber: 25 ACP, 5-shot magazine. **Barrel:** 2-1/4". **Weight:** 15 oz. **Length:** NA. **Grips:** Wood. **Sights:** Fixed. **Features:** Compact, stainless, semi-auto, single-action hammerless design.
Price: **$425.00**

AUTAUGA 32 AUTO PISTOL
Caliber: 32 ACP, 6-shot magazine. **Barrel:** 2". **Weight:** 11.3 oz. **Length:** 4.3" overall. **Grips:** Black polymer. **Sights:** Fixed. **Features:** Double-action-only mechanism. Stainless steel construction.
Price: . . . . **NA**

AUTO-ORDNANCE 1911A1 AUTOMATIC PISTOL
Caliber: 45 ACP, 7-shot magazine. **Barrel:** 5". **Weight:** 39 oz. **Length:** 8-1/2" overall. **Grips:** Checkered plastic with medallion. **Sights:** Blade front, rear adjustable for windage. **Features:** Same specs as 1911A1 military guns-parts interchangeable. Frame and slide blued; each radius has non-glare finish. Made in U.S.A. by Auto-Ordnance Corp.
Price: 45 ACP, blue **$511.00**
Price: 45 ACP, Parkerized **$515.00**
Price: 45 ACP Deluxe (3-dot sights, textured rubber
  wraparound grips) **$525.00**

AUTOBOND 450
Caliber: 450 Autobond (also 45 ACP). Model 1911-style. **Barrel:** 5".
Price: **$1,150.00**

BAER 1911 CUSTOM CARRY AUTO PISTOL
Caliber: 45 ACP, 7- or 10-shot magazine. **Barrel:** 5". **Weight:** 37 oz. **Length:** 8.5" overall. **Grips:** Checkered walnut. **Sights:** Baer improved ramp-style dovetailed front, Novak low-mount rear. **Features:** Baer forged NM frame, slide and barrel with stainless bushing. Baer speed trigger with 4-lb. pull. Partial listing shown. Made in U.S.A. by Les Baer Custom, Inc.
Price: Standard size, blued **$1,640.00**
Price: Standard size, stainless **$1,690.00**
Price: Comanche size, blued **$1,640.00**
Price: Comanche size, stainless **$1,690.00**
Price: Comanche size, aluminum frame, blued slide **$1,923.00**
Price: Comanche size, aluminum frame, stainless slide **$1,995.00**

BAER 1911 PREMIER II AUTO PISTOL
Caliber: 9x23, 38 Super, 400 Cor-Bon, 45 ACP, 7- or 10-shot magazine. **Barrel:** 5". **Weight:** 37 oz. **Length:** 8.5" overall. **Grips:** Checkered rosewood, double diamond pattern. **Sights:** Baer dovetailed front, low-mount Bo-Mar rear with hidden leaf. **Features:** Baer NM forged steel frame and barrel with stainless bushing, deluxe Commander hammer and sear, beavertail grip safety with pad, extended ambidextrous safety; flat mainspring housing; 30 lpi checkered front strap. Made in U.S.A. by Les Baer Custom, Inc.
Price: Blued **$1,428.00**
Price: Stainless **$1,558.00**
Price: 6" model, blued, from **$1,595.00**

BAER 1911 S.R.P. PISTOL
Caliber: 45 ACP. **Barrel:** 5". **Weight:** 37 oz. **Length:** 8.5" overall. **Grips:** Checkered walnut. **Sights:** Trijicon night sights. **Features:** Similar to the F.B.I. contract gun except uses Baer forged steel frame. Has Baer match barrel with supported chamber, Complete tactical action. Has Baer Ultra Coat finish. Introduced 1996. Made in U.S.A. by Les Baer Custom, Inc.
Price: Government or Comanche length **$2,240.00**

Beretta 96

Beretta U22 Neos

BERETTA MODEL 92FS PISTOL
Caliber: 9mm Para., 10-shot magazine. **Barrel:** 4.9". **Weight:** 34 oz. **Length:** 8.5" overall. **Grips:** Checkered black plastic. **Sights:** Blade front, rear adjustable for windage. Tritium night sights available. **Features:** Double action. Extractor acts as chamber loaded indicator, squared trigger guard, grooved front and backstraps, inertia firing pin. Matte or blued finish. Introduced 1977. Made in U.S.A. and imported from Italy by Beretta U.S.A.
Price: With plastic grips **$715.00**
Price: Vertec with access rail **$760.00**
Price: Vertec Inox **$825.00**

Beretta Model 92FS/96 Brigadier Pistols
Similar to the Model 92FS/96 except with a heavier slide to reduce felt recoil and allow mounting removable front sight. Wraparound rubber grips. 3-dot sights dovetailed to the slide, adjustable for windage. Weighs 35.3 oz. Introduced 1999.
Price: 9mm or 40 S&W, 10-shot **$795.00**
Price: Inox models (stainless steel) **$845.00**

Beretta Model 96 Pistol
Same as the Model 92FS except chambered for 40 S&W. Ambidextrous safety mechanism with passive firing pin catch, slide safety/decocking lever, trigger bar disconnect. Has 10-shot magazine. Available with 3-dot sights. Introduced 1992.
Price: Model 96, plastic grips **$795.00**
Price: Stainless, rubber grips **$845.00**
Price: Vertec with access rail **$760.00**
Price: Vertec Inox **$825.00**

BERETTA MODEL 80 CHEETAH SERIES DA PISTOLS
Caliber: 380 ACP, 10-shot magazine (M84); 8-shot (M85); 22 LR, 7-shot (M87). **Barrel:** 3.82". **Weight:** About 23 oz. (M84/85); 20.8 oz. (M87). **Length:** 6.8" overall. **Grips:** Glossy black plastic (wood optional at extra cost). **Sights:** Fixed front, drift-adjustable rear. **Features:** Double action, quick takedown, convenient magazine release. Introduced 1977. Imported from Italy by Beretta U.S.A.
Price: Model 84 Cheetah, plastic grips **$625.00**
Price: Model 85 Cheetah, plastic grips, 8-shot **$590.00**
Price: Model 87 Cheetah, wood, 22 LR, 7-shot **$625.00**
Price: Model 87 Target, plastic grips **$710.00**

BERETTA MODEL 21 BOBCAT PISTOL
Caliber: 22 LR or 25 ACP. Both double action. **Barrel:** 2.4". **Weight:** 11.5 oz.; 11.8 oz. **Length:** 4.9" overall. **Grips:** Plastic. **Features:** Available in nickel, matte, engraved or blue finish. Introduced in 1985.
Price: Bobcat, 22 or 25, blue **$275.00**
Price: Bobcat, 22, stainless **$340.00**
Price: Bobcat, 22 or 25, matte **$275.00**

BERETTA MODEL 3032 TOMCAT PISTOL
Caliber: 32 ACP, 7-shot magazine. **Barrel:** 2.45". **Weight:** 14.5 oz. **Length:** 5" overall. **Grips:** Checkered black plastic. **Sights:** Blade front, drift-adjustable rear. **Features:** Double action with exposed hammer; tip-up barrel for direct loading/unloading; thumb safety; polished or matte blue finish. Imported from Italy by Beretta U.S.A. Introduced 1996.
Price: Blue **$390.00**

Price: Matte **$370.00**
Price: Stainless **$450.00**
Price: With Tritium sights **$460.00**

BERETTA MODEL 9000S COMPACT PISTOL
Caliber: 9mm Para., 40 S&W; 10-shot magazine. **Barrel:** 3.4". **Weight:** 26.8 oz. **Length:** 6.6". **Grips:** Soft polymer. **Sights:** Windage-adjustable white-dot rear, white-dot blade front. **Features:** Glass-reinforced polymer frame; patented tilt-barrel, open-slide locking system; chrome-lined barrel; external serrated hammer; automatic firing pin and manual safeties. Introduced 2000. Imported from Italy by Beretta U.S.A.
Price: 9000S Type F
(single and double action, external hammer) **$495.00**

BERETTA MODEL U22 NEOS
Caliber: 22 LR, 10-shot magazine. **Barrel:** 4.2"; 6". **Weight:** 32 oz.; 36 oz. **Length:** 8.8"; 10.3". **Sights:** Target. **Features:** Integral rail for standard scope mounts, light, perfectly weighted, 100% American made by Beretta.
Price: **$285.00**
Price: Inox **$335.00**
Price: DLX **$355.00**
Price: Inox **$395.00**

BERSA THUNDER 45 ULTRA COMPACT PISTOL
Caliber: 45 ACP. **Barrel:** 3.6". **Weight:** 27 oz. **Length:** 6.7" overall. **Grips:** Anatomicaly designed polymer. **Sights:** White outline rear. **Features:** Double action; firing pin safeties, integral locking system. Available in matte, satin nickel, gold, or duo-tone. Introduced 2003. Imported from Argentina by Eagle Imports, Inc.
Price: Thunder 45, matte blue **$424.95**
Price: Thunder 45, duo-tone **$449.95**
Price: Thunder 45, Satin nickel **$466.95**

BLUE THUNDER/COMMODORE 1911-STYLE AUTO PISTOLS
Caliber: 45 ACP, 7-shot magazine. **Barrel:** 4-1/4", 5". **Weight:** NA. **Length:** NA. **Grips:** Checkered hardwood. **Sights:** Blade front, drift-adjustable rear. **Features:** Extended slide release and safety, spring guide rod, skeletonized hammer and trigger, magazine bumper, beavertail grip safety. Imported from the Philippines by Century International Arms, Inc.
Price: . . . . **$464.80 to $484.80**

BROWNING HI-POWER 9mm AUTOMATIC PISTOL
Caliber: 9mm Para., 10-shot magazine. **Barrel:** 4-21/32". **Weight:** 32 oz. **Length:** 7-3/4" overall. **Grips:** Walnut, hand checkered, or black Polyamide. **Sights:** 1/8" blade front; rear screw-adjustable for windage and elevation. Also available with fixed rear (drift-adjustable for windage). **Features:** External hammer with half-cock and thumb safeties. Fixed rear sight model available. Includes gun lock. Imported from Belgium by Browning.
Price: Fixed sight model, walnut grips **$628.00**
Price: Fully adjustable rear sight, walnut grips **$628.00**
Price: Mark III, standard matte black finish, fixed sight, molded grips, ambidextrous safety **$781.00**

HANDGUNS — Autoloaders, Service & Sport

Browning
Buck Mark Standard

Charles Daly M-1911-A1P

Browning Buck
Mark Challenge

Cobra FS380

Browning Hi-Power Practical Pistol

Similar to the standard Hi-Power except has silver-chromed frame with blued slide, wraparound Pachmayr rubber grips, round-style serrated hammer and removable front sight, fixed rear (drift-adjustable for windage). Available in 9mm Para. Includes gun lock. Introduced 1991.
Price: $846.00

BROWNING BUCK MARK STANDARD 22 PISTOL

Caliber: 22 LR, 10-shot magazine. **Barrel:** 5-1/2". **Weight:** 32 oz. **Length:** 9-1/2" overall. **Grips:** Black molded composite with checkering. **Sights:** Ramp front, Browning Pro Target rear adjustable for windage and elevation. **Features:** All steel, matte blue finish or nickel, gold-colored trigger. Buck Mark Plus has laminated wood grips. Includes gun lock. Made in U.S.A. Introduced 1985. From Browning.
Price: Buck Mark Standard, blue $319.00
Price: Buck Mark Stainless, nickel finish with contoured
rubber grips $345.00
Price: Buck Mark Plus, matte blue with laminated wood grips $390.00
Price: Buck Mark Plus Nickel, nickel finish, laminated wood grips . $427.00

Browning Buck Mark Camper

Similar to the Buck Mark except 5-1/2" bull barrel. Weight is 34 oz. Matte blue finish, molded composite grips. Introduced 1999. From Browning.
Price: $287.00
Price: Camper Nickel, nickel finish, molded composite grips $320.00

Browning Buck Mark Challenge

Similar to the Buck Mark except has a lightweight barrel and smaller grip diameter. Barrel length is 5-1/2", weight is 25 oz. Introduced 1999. From Browning.
Price: $356.00

Browning Buck Mark Micro

Same as the Buck Mark Standard and Buck Mark Plus except has 4" barrel. Available in blue or nickel. Has 16-click Pro Target rear sight. Introduced 1992.
Price: Micro Standard, matte blue finish $319.00
Price: Micro Nickel, nickel finish $390.00
Price: Buck Mark Micro Plus Nickel $427.00

Browning Buck Mark Bullseye

Same as the Buck Mark Standard except has 7-1/4" fluted barrel, matte blue finish. Weighs 36 oz.
Price: Bullseye Standard, molded composite grips $468.00
Price: Bullseye Target, contoured rosewood grips $604.00

Browning Buck Mark 5.5

Same as the Buck Mark Standard except has a 5-1/2" bull barrel with integral scope mount, matte blue finish.
Price: 5.5 Field, Pro-Target adj. rear sight, contoured
walnut grips $511.00
Price: 5.5 Target, hooded adj. target sights,
contoured walnut grips $511.00

BROWNING PRO-9

Caliber: 9mm Luger, 10-round magazine. **Barrel:** 4". **Weight:** 30 oz. **Overall length:** 7-1/4". **Features:** Double-action, ambidextrous decocker and safety. Fixed, 3-dot-style sights, 6" sight radius. Molded composite grips with interchangeable backstrap inserts.
Price: $628.00

BROWNING HI-POWER

Caliber: 9mm, 40 S&W. **Barrel:** 4-3/4". **Weight:** 32 to 35 oz. **Overall length:** 7-3/4". **Features:** Blued, matte, polymer or silver-chromed frame; molded, wraparound Pachmayr or walnut grips; Commander-style or spur-type hammer.
Price: Practical model, fixed sights $791.00
Price: Mark II model, epoxy finish $730.00
Price: HP Standard, blued, fixed sights, walnut grips $751.00
Price: HP Standard, blued, adj. sights $805.00

CHARLES DALY M-1911-A1P AUTOLOADING PISTOL

Caliber: 45 ACP, 7- or 10-shot magazine. **Barrel:** 5". **Weight:** 38 oz. **Length:** 8-3/4" overall. **Grips:** Checkered. **Sights:** Blade front, rear drift adjustable for windage; 3-dot system. **Features:** Skeletonized combat hammer and trigger; beavertail grip safety; extended slide release; oversize thumb safety; Parkerized finish. Introduced 1996. Imported from the Philippines by K.B.I., Inc.
Price: $469.95

COBRA ENTERPRISES FS380 AUTO PISTOL

Caliber: 380 ACP, 7-shot magazine. **Barrel:** 3.5". **Weight:** 2.1 lbs. **Length:** 6-3/8" overall. **Grips:** Black composition. **Sights:** Fixed. **Features:** Choice of bright chrome, satin nickel or black finish. Introduced 2002. Made in U.S.A. by Cobra Enterprises, Inc.
Price: $130.00

COBRA ENTERPRISES FS32 AUTO PISTOL

Caliber: 32 ACP, 8-shot magazine. **Barrel:** 3.5". **Weight:** 2.1 lbs. **Length:** 6-3/8" overall. **Grips:** Black composition. **Sights:** Fixed. **Features:** Choice of black, satin nickel or bright chrome finish. Introduced 2002. Made in U.S.A. by Cobra Enterprises, Inc.
Price: $130.00

Cobra CA32

Colt 1991 Model O

Colt 1991 Model O Commander

Colt XSE Model O Commander

Colt XSE Lightweight Commander

Colt Defender

Colt Series 70

Colt 38 Super

COBRA INDUSTRIES PATRIOT PISTOL
Caliber: 380 ACP, 9mm Luger, 10-shot magazine. **Barrel:** 3.3". **Weight:** 20 oz. **Length:** 6" overall. **Grips:** Checkered polymer. **Sights:** Fixed. **Features:** Stainless steel slide with load indicator; double-action-only trigger system. Introduced 2002. Made in U.S.A. by Cobra Enterprises, Inc.
Price: **$279.00**

COBRA INDUSTRIES CA32, CA380
Caliber: 32 ACP, 380 ACP. **Barrel:** 2.8" **Weight:** 22 oz. **Length:** 5.4". **Grips:** Laminated wood (CA32); Black molded synthetic (CA380). **Sights:** Fixed. **Features:** True pocket pistol size. Made in U.S.A. by Cobra Enterprises, Inc.
Price: . . . . **NA**

COLT MODEL 1991 MODEL O AUTO PISTOL
Caliber: 45 ACP, 7-shot magazine. **Barrel:** 5". **Weight:** 38 oz. **Length:** 8.5" overall. **Grips:** Checkered black composition. **Sights:** Ramped blade front, fixed square notch rear, high profile. **Features:** Matte finish. Continuation of serial number range used on original G.I. 1911A1 guns. Comes with one magazine and molded carrying case. Introduced 1991.
Price: **$870.00**
Price: Stainless **$920.00**

Colt Model 1991 Model O Commander Auto Pistol
Similar to the 1991 Model O except has 4-1/4" barrel. Overall length is 7-3/4". Comes with one 7-shot magazine, molded case.
Price: Blue **$870.00**
Price: Stainless steel **$920.00**

COLT XSE SERIES MODEL O AUTO PISTOLS
Caliber: 45 ACP, 8-shot magazine. **Barrel:** 4.25", 5". **Grips:** Checkered, double diamond rosewood. **Sights:** Drift-adjustable 3-dot combat. **Features:** Brushed stainless finish; adjustable, two-cut aluminum trigger; extended ambidextrous thumb safety; upswept beavertail with palm swell; elongated slot hammer. Introduced 1999. From Colt's Mfg. Co., Inc.
Price: XSE Government (5" bbl.) **$1,100.00**
Price: XSE Commander (4.25" bbl.) **$1,100.00**

COLT XSE LIGHTWEIGHT COMMANDER AUTO PISTOL
Caliber: 45 ACP, 8-shot. **Barrel:** 4-1/4". **Weight:** 26 oz. **Length:** 7-3/4" overall. **Grips:** Double diamond checkered rosewood. **Sights:** Fixed, glare-proofed blade front, square notch rear; 3-dot system. **Features:** Brushed stainless slide, nickeled aluminum frame; McCormick elongated slot enhanced hammer, McCormick two-cut adjustable aluminum hammer. Made in U.S.A. by Colt's Mfg. Co., Inc.
Price: Stainless **$1,100.00**

COLT DEFENDER
Caliber: 45 ACP, 7-shot magazine. **Barrel:** 3". **Weight:** 22-1/2 oz. **Length:** 6-3/4" overall. **Grips:** Pebble-finish rubber wraparound with finger grooves. **Sights:** White dot front, snag-free Colt competition rear. **Features:** Stainless finish; aluminum frame; combat-style hammer; Hi Ride grip safety, extended manual safety, disconnect safety. Introduced 1998. Made in U.S.A. by Colt's Mfg. Co., Inc.
Price: **$950.00**

COLT SERIES 70
Caliber: 45 ACP. **Barrel:** 5". **Weight:** NA **Length:** NA **Grips:** Rosewood with double diamond checkering pattern. **Sights:** Fixed. **Features:** Custom replica of the Original Series 70 pistol with a Series 70 firing system, original rollmarks. Introduced 2002. Made in U.S.A. by Colt's Mfg. Co., Inc.
Price: **$990.00**

COLT 38 SUPER
Caliber: 38 Super. **Barrel:** 5" **Weight:** NA. **Length:** 8-1/2" **Grips:** Checkered rubber (stainless and blue models); wood with double diamond checkering pattern (bright stainless model). **Sights:** 3-dot. **Features:** Beveled magazine well, standard thumb safety and service-style grip safety. Introduced 2003. Made in U.S.A. by Colt's Mfg. Co., Inc.
Price: . . . . (Blue) **$950.00** (Stainless steel) **$980.00**
Price: (Bright stainless steel) **$1,200.00**

Colt Gunsite

CZ 75B 9mm

CZ 75B Decocker

CZ 85

CZ 97B

CZ 75/85 Kadet

COLT GUNSITE PISTOL
Caliber: 45 ACP **Barrel:** 5". **Weight:** NA. **Length:** NA. **Grips:** Rosewood. **Sights:** Heinie front, Novak rear. **Features:** Contains most all of the Gunsite-school recommended features such as Series 70 firing system, Smith & Alexander metal grip safety w/palm swell, serrated flat mainspring housing. Available in blue or stainless steel. Introduced 2003. Made in U.S.A. by Colt's Mfg. Co., Inc.
Price: . . . . **NA**

CZ 75B AUTO PISTOL
Caliber: 9mm Para., 40 S&W, 10-shot magazine. **Barrel:** 4.7". **Weight:** 34.3 oz. **Length:** 8.1" overall. **Grips:** High impact checkered plastic. **Sights:** Square post front, rear adjustable for windage; 3-dot system. **Features:** Single action/double action design; firing pin block safety; choice of black polymer, matte or high-polish blue finishes. All-steel frame. Imported from the Czech Republic by CZ-USA.
Price: Black polymer **$529.00**
Price: Glossy blue **$559.00**
Price: Dual-tone or satin nickel **$559.00**
Price: 22 LR conversion unit **$399.00**

CZ 75B Decocker
Similar to the CZ 75B except has a decocking lever in place of the safety lever. All other specifications are the same. Introduced 1999. Imported from the Czech Republic by CZ-USA.
Price: 9mm, black polymer **$559.00**
Price: 40 S&W **$569.00**

CZ 75B Compact Auto Pistol
Similar to the CZ 75 except has 10-shot magazine, 3.9" barrel and weighs 32 oz. Has removable front sight, non-glare ribbed slide top. Trigger guard is squared and serrated; combat hammer. Introduced 1993. Imported from the Czech Republic by CZ-USA.
Price: 9mm, black polymer **$559.00**
Price: Dual tone or satin nickel **$569.00**
Price: D Compact, black polymer **$569.00**
Price: CZ2075 Sub-compact RAMI **$559.00**

CZ 75M IPSC Auto Pistol
Similar to the CZ 75B except has a longer frame and slide, slightly larger grip to accommodate new heavy-duty magazine. Ambidextrous thumb safety, safety notch on hammer; two-port in-frame compensator; slide racker; frame-mounted Firepoint red dot sight. Introduced 2001. Imported from the Czech Republic by CZ USA.
Price: 40 S&W, 10-shot mag. **$1,551.00**
Price: CZ 75 Standard IPSC (40 S&W, adj. sights) **$1,038.00**

CZ 85B Auto Pistol
Same gun as the CZ 75 except has ambidextrous slide release and safety levers; non-glare, ribbed slide top; squared, serrated trigger guard; trigger stop to prevent overtravel. Introduced 1986. Imported from the Czech Republic by CZ-USA.
Price: Black polymer **$483.00**
Price: Combat, black polymer **$540.00**
Price: Combat, dual-tone **$487.00**
Price: Combat, glossy blue **$499.00**

CZ 85 Combat
Similar to the CZ 85B (9mm only) except has an adjustable rear sight, trigger adjustable for overtravel, free-fall magazine, extended magazine catch. Does not have the firing pin block safety. Introduced 1999. Imported from the Czech Republic by CZ-USA.
Price: 9mm, black polymer **$540.00**
Price: 9mm, glossy blue **$566.00**
Price: 9mm, dual-tone or satin nickel **$586.00**

CZ 83B DOUBLE-ACTION PISTOL
Caliber: 9mm Makarov, 32 ACP, 380 ACP, 10-shot magazine. **Barrel:** 3.8". **Weight:** 26.2 oz. **Length:** 6.8" overall. **Grips:** High impact checkered plastic. **Sights:** Removable square post front, rear adjustable for windage; 3-dot system. **Features:** Single action/double action; ambidextrous magazine release and safety. Blue finish; non-glare ribbed slide top. Imported from the Czech Republic by CZ-USA.
Price: Blue **$378.00**
Price: Nickel **$397.00**

CZ 97B AUTO PISTOL
Caliber: 45 ACP, 10-shot magazine. **Barrel:** 4.85". **Weight:** 40 oz. **Length:** 8.34" overall. **Grips:** Checkered walnut. **Sights:** Fixed. **Features:** Single action/double action; full-length slide rails; screw-in barrel bushing; linkless barrel; all-steel construction; chamber loaded indicator; dual transfer bars. Introduced 1999. Imported from the Czech Republic by CZ-USA.
Price: Black polymer **$625.00**
Price: Glossy blue **$641.00**

CZ 75/85 KADET AUTO PISTOL
Caliber: 22 LR, 10-shot magazine. **Barrel:** 4.88". **Weight:** 36 oz. **Grips:** High impact checkered plastic. **Sights:** Blade front, fully adjustable rear. **Features:** Single action/double action mechanism; all-steel construction. Introduced 1999. Imported from the Czech Republic by CZ-USA.
Price: Black polymer **$486.00**

CZ 100

Dan Wesson Firearms Pointman Major

Dan Wesson Firearms Major Aussie

Dan Wesson Firearms Patriot Marksman

CZ 100 AUTO PISTOL
Caliber: 9mm Para., 40 S&W, 10-shot magazine. **Barrel:** 3.7". **Weight:** 24 oz. **Length:** 6.9" overall. **Grips:** Grooved polymer. **Sights:** Blade front with dot, white outline rear drift adjustable for windage. **Features:** Double action only with firing pin block; polymer frame, steel slide; has laser sight mount. Introduced 1996. Imported from the Czech Republic by CZ-USA.
Price: 9mm Para **$405.00**
Price: 40 S&W **$424.00**

DAN WESSON FIREARMS POINTMAN MAJOR AUTO PISTOL
Caliber: 45 ACP. **Barrel:** 5". **Grips:** Rosewood checkered. **Features:** Blued or stainless steel frame and serrated slide; Chip McCormick match-grade trigger group, sear and disconnect; match-grade barrel; high-ride beavertail safety; checkered slide release. **Sights:** High rib; interchangeable sight system; laser engraved. Introduced 2000. Made in U.S.A. by Dan Wesson Firearms.
Price: Model PM1-B (blued) **$799.00**
Price: Model PM1-S (stainless) **$699.00**

Dan Wesson Firearms Pointman Seven Auto Pistols
Similar to Pointman Major, dovetail adjustable target rear sight and dovetail target front sight. Available in blued or stainless finish. Introduced 2000. Made in U.S.A. by Dan Wesson Firearms.
Price: PM7 (blued frame and slide) **$999.00**
Price: PM7S (stainless finish) **$799.00**

Dan Wesson Firearms Pointman Guardian Auto Pistols
Similar to Pointman Major, more compact frame with 4.25" barrel. Available in blued or stainless finish with fixed or adjustable sights. Introduced 2000. Made in U.S.A. by Dan Wesson Firearms.
Price: PMG-FS, all new frame (fixed sights) **$769.00**
Price: PMG-AS (blued frame and slide, adjustable sights) **$799.00**
Price: PMGD-FS Guardian Duce, all new frame
(stainless frame and blued slide, fixed sights) **$829.00**
Price: PMGD-AS Guardian Duce
(stainless frame and blued slide, adj. sights) **$799.00**

Dan Wesson Firearms Major Tri-Ops Packs
Similar to Pointman Major. Complete frame assembly fitted to 3 match-grade complete slide assemblies (9mm, 10mm, 40 S&W). Includes recoil springs and magazines that come in hard cases fashioned after high-grade European rifle case. Brass corner protectors, dual combination locks, engraved presentation plate on the lid. Introduced 2002. Made in U.S.A. by Dan Wesson Firearms.
Price: TOP1B (blued), TOP1-S (stainless) **$2,459.00**

Dan Wesson Firearms Major Aussie
Similar to Pointman Major. Available in 45 ACP. Features Bomar-style adjustable rear target sight, low (1/16" high) sight rib 3/8" wide with lengthwise serrations. Southern Cross flag emblem laser engraved on the sides of the slide. Introduced 2002. Made in U.S.A. by Dan Wesson Firearms.
Price: PMA-B (blued) **$799.00**
Price: PMA-S (stainless) **$799.00**

Dan Wesson Firearms Pointman Minor Auto Pistol
Similar to Pointman Major. Full size (5") entry level IDPA or action pistol model with blued carbon alloy frame and round top slide, bead blast matte finish on frame and slide top and radius, satin-brushed polished finish on

sides of slide, chromed barrel, dovetail mount fixed rear target sight and tactical/target ramp front sight, match trigger, skeletonized target hammer, high ride beavertail, fitted extractor, serrations on thumb safety, slide release and magazine release, lowered and relieved ejection port, beveled magazine well, exotic hardwood grips, serrated mainspring housing, laser engraved. Introduced 2000. Made in U.S.A. by Dan Wesson Firearms.
Price: Model PM2-P **$599.00**

Dan Wesson Firearms Pointman Hi-Cap Auto Pistol
Similar to Pointman Minor. Full-size, high-capacity (10-shot) magazine with 5" chromed barrel, blued finish and dovetail fixed rear sight. Match adjustable trigger, ambidextrous extended thumb safety, beavertail safety. Introduced 2001. From Dan Wesson Firearms.
Price: PMHC (Pointman High-Cap) **$689.00**

Dan Wesson Firearms Pointman Dave Pruitt Signature Series
Similar to other full-sized Pointman models, customized by Master Pistolsmith and IDPA Grand Master Dave Pruitt. Alloy carbon-steel with black oxide bluing and bead-blast matte finish. Front and rear chevron cocking serrations, dovetail mount fixed rear target sight and tactical/target ramp front sight, ramped match barrel with fitted match bushing and link, match-grade trigger group, serrated ambidextrous tactical/carry thumb safety, high ride beavertail, serrated slide release and checkered mag release, match-grade sear and hammer, fitted extractor, lowered and relieved ejection port, beveled magazine well, full length 2-piece recoil spring guide rod, cocobolo double diamond checkered grips, serrated steel mainspring housing, special laser engraving. Introduced 2001. From Dan Wesson Firearms.
Price: PMDP (Pointman Dave Pruitt) **$899.00**

DAN WESSON FIREARMS PATRIOT 1911 PISTOL
Caliber: 45 ACP. **Grips:** Exotic exhibition grade cocobolo, double diamond hand cut checkering. **Sights:** New innovative combat/carry rear sight that completely encloses the dovetail. **Features:** The new Patriot Expert and Patriot Marksman are full-size match-grade series 70 1911s machined from steel forgings. Available in blued chome-moly steel or stainless steel. Beveled magazine well, lowered and flared ejection port, high sweep beavertail safety. Introduced June 2002.
Price: Model PTM-B (blued) **$797.00**
Price: Model PTM-S (stainless) **$898.00**
Price: Model PTE-B (blued) **$864.00**
Price: Model PTE-S (stainless) **$971.00**

Desert Eagle Mark XIX

Desert Baby Eagle

EAA Witness

Ed Brown
Commander Bobtail

Ed Brown Kobra Carry

Entréprise Elite P500

DESERT EAGLE MARK XIX PISTOL

Caliber: 357 Mag., 9-shot; 44 Mag., 8-shot; 50 AE, 7-shot. **Barrel:** 6", 10", interchangeable. **Weight:** 357 Mag.-62 oz.; 44 Mag.-69 oz.; 50 AE-72 oz. **Length:** 10-1/4" overall (6" bbl.). **Grips:** Polymer; rubber available. **Sights:** Blade on ramp front, combat-style rear. Adjustable available. **Features:** Interchangeable barrels; rotating three-lug bolt; ambidextrous safety; adjustable trigger. Military epoxy finish. Satin, bright nickel, chrome, brushed, matte or black finishes available. 10" barrel extra. Imported from Israel by Magnum Research, Inc.

Price: 357, 6" bbl., standard pistol $1,249.00
Price: 44 Mag., 6", standard pistol $1,249.00
Price: 50 Magnum, 6" bbl., standard pistol $1,249.00

DESERT BABY EAGLE PISTOLS

Caliber: 9mm Para., 40 S&W, 45 ACP, 10-round magazine. **Barrel:** 3.5", 3.7", 4.72". **Weight:** 26.8-39.8 oz. **Length:** 7.25" to 8.25" overall. **Grips:** Polymer. **Sights:** Drift-adjustable rear, blade front. **Features:** Steel frame and slide; polygonal rifling to reduce barrel wear; slide safety; decocker. Reintroduced in 1999. Imported from Israel by Magnum Research, Inc.
Price: Standard (9mm or 40 cal.; 4.72" barrel, 8.25" overall) $499.00
Price: Semi-Compact (9mm, 40 or 45 cal.; 3.7" barrel, 7.75" overall) $499.00
Price: Compact (9mm or 40 cal.; 3.5" barrel, 7.25" overall) $499.00
Price: Polymer (9mm or 40 cal; polymer frame; 3.25" barrel, 7.25" overall) $499.00

EAA WITNESS DA AUTO PISTOL

Caliber: 9mm Para., 10-shot magazine; 38 Super, 40 S&W, 10-shot magazine; 45 ACP, 10-shot magazine. **Barrel:** 4.50". **Weight:** 35.33 oz. **Length:** 8.10" overall. **Grips:** Checkered rubber. **Sights:** Undercut blade front, open rear adjustable for windage. **Features:** Double-action trigger system; round trigger guard; frame-mounted safety. Introduced 1991. Imported from Italy by European American Armory.
Price: 9mm, blue $449.00
Price: 9mm, Wonder finish $459.00
Price: 9mm Compact, blue, 10-shot $449.00
Price: As above, Wonder finish $459.00
Price: 38 Super, blue $449.00
Price: 38 Super, Wonder finish $459.00
Price: 40 S&W, blue $449.00
Price: As above, Wonder finish $459.00

Price: 40 S&W Compact, 9-shot, blue $449.00
Price: As above, Wonder finish $459.00
Price: 45 ACP, blue $449.00
Price: As above, Wonder finish $459.00
Price: 45 ACP Compact, 8-shot, blue $449.00
Price: As above, Wonder finish $459.00

ED BROWN CLASSIC CUSTOM

Caliber: 45 ACP, 7 shot. **Barrel:** 5". **Weight:** 39 oz. **Stocks:** Cocobolo wood. **Sights:** Bo-Mar adjustable rear, dovetail front. **Features:** Single-action, M1911 style, custom made to order, stainless frame and slide available.
Price: $2,895.00
Price: Stainless $3,095.00

ED BROWN KOBRA CARRY BOBTAIL

Caliber: 45 ACP, 400 Cor-Bon, 40 S&W, 357 SIG, 38 Super, 9mm Luger, 7-shot magazine. **Barrel:** 4.25". **Weight:** 34 oz. **Grips:** Hogue exotic wood. **Sights:** Customer preference front; fixed Novak low mount rear. Optional night inserts available. **Features:** Checkered forestrap and bobtailed mainspring housing.
Price: Executive Carry .... $2,195.00 to $2,370.00

ED BROWN KOBRA

Caliber: 45 ACP, 7-shot magazine. **Barrel:** 5" (Kobra); 4.25" (Kobra Carry). **Weight:** 39 oz. (Kobra); 34 oz. (Kobra Carry). **Grips:** Hogue exotic wood. **Sights:** Ramp, front; fixed Novak low-mount night sights, rear. **Features:** Has snakeskin pattern serrations on forestrap and mainspring housing, dehorned edges, beavertail grip safety.
Price: Kobra $2,095.00
Price: Kobra Carry $2,195.00

ENTRÉPRISE ELITE P500 AUTO PISTOL

Caliber: 45 ACP, 10-shot magazine. **Barrel:** 5". **Weight:** 40 oz. **Length:** 8.5" overall. **Grips:** Black ultra-slim, double diamond, checkered synthetic. **Sights:** Dovetailed blade front, rear adjustable for windage; 3-dot system. **Features:** Reinforced dust cover; lowered and flared ejection port; squared trigger guard; adjustable match trigger; bolstered front strap; high grip cut; high ride beavertail grip safety; steel flat mainspring housing; extended thumb lock; skeletonized hammer; match grade sear, disconnector; Wolff springs. Introduced 1998. Made in U.S.A. by Entréprise Arms.
Price: $739.90

Entréprise Boxer P500

Entréprise Tactical 500

Felk MTF 450

Firestorm 45 Gov't

Glock 17C

Firestorm Mini

Entréprise Medalist P500 Auto Pistol
Similar to the Elite model except has adjustable rear sight with dovetailed Patridge front; machined slide parallel rails; front and rear slide serrations; lowered and flared ejection port; full-length one-piece guide rod with plug; National Match barrel and bushing; stainless firing pin; tuned match extractor; oversize firing pin stop; slide lapped to frame. Introduced 1998. Made in U.S.A. by Entréprise Arms.
Price: 45 ACP **$979.00**
Price: 40 S&W **$1,099.00**

Entréprise Boxer P500 Auto Pistol
Similar to the Medalist model except has adjustable Competizione "melted" rear sight with dovetailed Patridge front; high mass chiseled slide with sweep cut; machined slide parallel rails; polished breech face and barrel channel. Introduced 1998. Made in U.S.A. by Entréprise Arms.
Price: **$1,399.00**

Entréprise Tactical P500 Auto Pistol
Similar to the Elite model except has Tactical2 Ghost Ring sight or Novak low-mount sight; ambidextrous thumb safety; front and rear slide serrations; full-length guide rod; throated barrel; tuned match extractor; fitted barrel and bushing; stainless firing pin; slide lapped to frame. Introduced 1998. Made in U.S.A. by Entréprise Arms.
Price: **$979.90**
Price: Tactical Plus (full-size frame, Officer's slide) **$1,049.00**

FELK MTF 450 AUTO PISTOL
Caliber: 9mm Para. (10-shot); 40 S&W (8-shot); 357 Mag, 45 ACP (9-shot magazine). **Barrel:** 3.5". **Weight:** 19.9 oz. **Length:** 6.4" overall. **Grips:** Checkered. **Sights:** Blade front; adjustable rear. **Features:** Double-action only trigger, striker fired; polymer frame; trigger safety, firing pin safety, trigger bar safety; adjustable trigger; fully interchangeable slide/barrel to change calibers. Introduced 1998. Imported by Felk Inc.
Price: **$395.00**
Price: 45 ACP pistol with 9mm and 40 S&W slide/barrel assemblies **$999.00**

FIRESTORM AUTO PISTOL
Features: 7 or 10 rd. double action pistols with matte, duo-tone or nickel finish. Distributed by SGS Importers International.
Price: 22 LR 10 rd, 380 7 rd. matte **$283.95**
Price: Duo-tone **$291.95**
Price: Mini 9mm, 40 S&W, 10 rd. matte **$399.95**
Price: Duo-tone **$408.95**
Price: Nickel **$399.95**
Price: Mini 45, seven-round matte **$408.95**
Price: Duo-tone 45 .... **$416.95**
Price: Nickel 45 .... **$433.95**
Price: 45 Government, Compact, 7-round matte **$308.95**
Price: Duo-tone **$316.95**
Price: Extra magazines .... **$29.95 to $49.95**

GLOCK 17 AUTO PISTOL
Caliber: 9mm Para., 10-shot magazine. **Barrel:** 4.49". **Weight:** 22.04 oz. (without magazine). **Length:** 7.32" overall. **Grips:** Black polymer. **Sights:** Dot on front blade, white outline rear adjustable for windage. **Features:** Polymer frame, steel slide; double-action trigger with "Safe Action" system; mechanical firing pin safety, drop safety; simple takedown without tools; locked breech, recoil operated action. Adopted by Austrian armed forces 1983. NATO approved 1984. Imported from Austria by Glock, Inc.
Price: Fixed sight, extra magazine, magazine loader, cleaning kit . **$624.00**
Price: Adjustable sight **$642.00**
Price: Model 17C, ported barrel (compensated) **$646.00**

Glock 20 10mm Auto Pistol
Similar to the Glock Model 17 except chambered for 10mm Automatic cartridge. Barrel length is 4.60", overall length is 7.59", and weight is 26.3 oz. (without magazine). Magazine capacity is 10 rds. Fixed or adjustable rear sight. Comes with an extra magazine, magazine loader, cleaning rod and brush. Introduced 1990. Imported from Austria by Glock, Inc.
Price: Fixed sight **$701.00**

Glock 21C Auto Pistol
Similar to the Glock 17 except chambered for 45 ACP, 10-shot magazine. Overall length is 7.59", weight is 25.2 oz. (without magazine). Fixed or adjustable rear sight. Introduced 1991.
Price: Fixed sight **$700.00**
Price: Adjustable sight **$730.00**

Glock 22

Glock 26

Glock 30

Glock 31

Glock 35

Glock 22 Auto Pistol

Similar to the Glock 17 except chambered for 40 S&W, 10-shot magazine. Overall length is 7.28", weight is 22.3 oz. (without magazine). Fixed or adjustable rear sight. Introduced 1990.

Price: Fixed sight **$646.00**

Glock 23 Auto Pistol

Similar to the Glock 19 except chambered for 40 S&W, 10-shot magazine. Overall length is 6.85", weight is 20.6 oz. (without magazine). Fixed or adjustable rear sight. Introduced 1990.

Price: Fixed sight **$646.00**

GLOCK 26, 27 AUTO PISTOLS

Caliber: 9mm Para. (M26), 10-shot magazine; 40 S&W (M27), 9-shot magazine. **Barrel:** 3.46". **Weight:** 21.75 oz. **Length:** 6.29" overall. **Grips:** Integral. Stippled polymer. **Sights:** Dot on front blade, fixed or fully adjustable white outline rear. **Features:** Subcompact size. Polymer frame, steel slide; double-action trigger with "Safe Action" system, three safeties. Matte black Tenifer finish. Hammer-forged barrel. Imported from Austria by Glock, Inc. Introduced 1996.

Price: Fixed sight **$624.00**
Price: Adjustable sight **$642.00**

GLOCK 29, 30 AUTO PISTOLS

Caliber: 10mm (M29), 45 ACP (M30), 10-shot magazine. **Barrel:** 3.78". **Weight:** 24 oz. **Length:** 6.7" overall. **Grips:** Integral. Stippled polymer. **Sights:** Dot on front, fixed or fully adjustable white outline rear. **Features:** Compact size. Polymer frame steel slide; double-recoil spring reduces recoil; Safe Action system with three safeties; Tenifer finish. Two magazines supplied. Introduced 1997. Imported from Austria by Glock, Inc.

Price: Fixed sight **$662.00**
Price: Adjustable sight **$680.00**

Glock 31/31C Auto Pistols

Similar to the Glock 17 except chambered for 357 Auto cartridge; 10-shot magazine. Overall length is 7.32", weight is 23.28 oz. (without magazine). Fixed or adjustable sight. Imported from Austria by Glock, Inc.

Price: Fixed sight **$646.00**

Glock 32/32C Auto Pistols

Similar to the Glock 19 except chambered for the 357 Auto cartridge; 10-shot magazine. Overall length is 6.85", weight is 21.52 oz. (without magazine). Fixed or adjustable sight. Imported from Austria by Glock, Inc.

Price: Fixed sight **$646.00**
Price: Adjustable sight **$642.00**

Glock 33 Auto Pistol

Similar to the Glock 26 except chambered for the 357 Auto cartridge; 9-shot magazine. Overall length is 6.29", weight is 19.75 oz. (without magazine). Fixed or adjustable sight. Imported from Austria by Glock, Inc.

Price: Fixed sight **$624.00**
Price: Adjustable sight **$642.00**

GLOCK 34, 35 AUTO PISTOLS

Caliber: 9mm Para. (M34), 40 S&W (M35), 10-shot magazine. **Barrel:** 5.32". **Weight:** 22.9 oz. **Length:** 8.15" overall. **Grips:** Integral. Stippled

Hammerli Trailside

polymer. **Sights:** Dot on front, fully adjustable white outline rear. **Features:** Polymer frame, steel slide; double-action trigger with "Safe Action" system; three safeties; Tenifer finish. Imported from Austria by Glock, Inc.

Price: Model 34, 9mm **$704.00**

GLOCK 36 AUTO PISTOL

Caliber: 45 ACP, 6-shot magazine. **Barrel:** 3.78". **Weight:** 20.11 oz. **Length:** 6.77" overall. **Grips:** Integral. Stippled polymer. **Sights:** Dot on front, fully adjustable white outline rear. **Features:** Polymer frame, steel slide; double-action trigger with "Safe Action" system; three safeties; Tenifer finish. Imported from Austria by Glock, Inc.

Price: Fixed sight **$662.00**
Price: Adjustable sight **$680.00**

Glock 37 Auto Pistol

Similar to the Glock 17 except 45 GAP, has a 4.49" barrel, overall length, 7.32" and weight, 25.95 oz. Magazine capacity is 10 rds. Fixed or adjustable rear sight.

Price: Fixed sight **$639.00**
Price: Adjustable sight **$657.00**
Price: Night sight **$686.00**

HAMMERLI "TRAILSIDE" TARGET PISTOL

Caliber: 22 LR. **Barrel:** 4.5", 6". **Weight:** 28 oz. **Grips:** Synthetic. **Sights:** Fixed. **Features:** 10-shot magazine. Imported from Switzerland by SIGARMS. Distributed by Hammerli U.S.A.

Price: **$579.00**

Heckler & Koch
USP Compact

Heckler & Koch USP45

Heckler & Koch
USP45 Compact

Heckler & Koch
USP45 Tactical

Heckler & Koch
Elite

Heckler & Koch
Mark 23 Special Operations

Heckler & Koch P7M8

HECKLER & KOCH USP AUTO PISTOL
Caliber: 9mm Para., 10-shot magazine, 40 S&W, 10-shot magazine, 357 Mag. **Barrel:** 4.25". **Weight:** 28 oz. (USP40). **Length:** 6.9" overall. **Grips:** Non-slip stippled black polymer. **Sights:** Blade front, rear adjustable for windage. **Features:** New HK design with polymer frame, modified Browning action with recoil reduction system, single control lever. Special "hostile environment" finish on all metal parts. Available in SA/ DA, DAO, left- and right-hand versions. Introduced 1993. Imported from Germany by Heckler & Koch, Inc.
Price: Right-hand $939.00
Price: Left-hand $794.00

Heckler & Koch USP Compact Auto Pistol
Similar to the USP except has 3.58" barrel, measures 6.81" overall, and weighs 1.60 lbs. (9mm). Available in 9mm Para. 357 SIG or 40 S&W with 10-shot magazine. Introduced 1996. Imported from Germany by Heckler & Koch, Inc.
Price: Blue $874.00

Heckler & Koch USP45 Auto Pistol
Similar to the 9mm and 40 S&W USP except chambered for 45 ACP, 10-shot magazine. Has 4.13" barrel, overall length of 7.87" and weighs 30.4 oz. Has adjustable 3-dot sight system. Available in SA/DA, DAO, left- and right-hand versions. Introduced 1995. Imported from Germany by Heckler & Koch, Inc.
Price: Right-hand $839.00

Heckler & Koch USP45 Compact
Similar to the USP45 except has stainless slide; 8-shot magazine; modified and contoured slide and frame; extended slide release; 3.80" barrel, 7.09" overall length, weighs 1.75 lbs.; adjustable 3-dot sights. Introduced 1998. Imported from Germany by Heckler & Koch, Inc.
Price: With control lever on left, stainless $874.00

HECKLER & KOCH USP45 TACTICAL PISTOL
Caliber: 45 ACP, 10-shot magazine. **Barrel:** 4.92". **Weight:** 2.24 lbs. **Length:** 8.64" overall. **Grips:** Non-slip stippled polymer. **Sights:** Blade front, fully adjustable target rear. **Features:** Has extended threaded barrel with rubber O-ring; adjustable trigger; extended magazine floorplate; adjustable trigger stop; polymer frame. Introduced 1998. Imported from Germany by Heckler & Koch, Inc.
Price: $1,115.00

HECKLER & KOCH MARK 23 SPECIAL OPERATIONS PISTOL
Caliber: 45 ACP, 10-shot magazine. **Barrel:** 5.87". **Weight:** 43 oz. **Length:** 9.65" overall. **Grips:** Integral with frame; black polymer. **Sights:** Blade front, rear drift adjustable for windage; 3-dot. **Features:** Civilian version of the SOCOM pistol. Polymer frame; double action; exposed hammer; short recoil, modified Browning action. Introduced 1996. Imported from Germany by Heckler & Koch, Inc.
Price: $2,412.00

Heckler & Koch USP Expert Pistol
Combines features of the USP Tactical and HK Mark 23 pistols with a new slide design. Chambered for 45 ACP, 40 S&W & 9mm; 10-shot magazine. Has adjustable target sights, 5.20" barrel, 8.74" overall length, weighs 1.87 lbs. Match-grade single- and double-action trigger pull with adjustable stop; ambidextrous control levers; elongated target slide; barrel O-ring seals and centers barrel. Suited to IPSC competition. Introduced 1999. Imported from Germany by Heckler & Koch, Inc.
Price: $1,356.00

Heckler & Koch Elite
A long slide version of the USP. 6.2" barrel. Available in 9mm and 45 ACP. Introduced 2003. Imported from Germany by Heckler & Koch, Inc.
Price: $1,356.00

HECKLER & KOCH P7M8 AUTO PISTOL
Caliber: 9mm Para., 8-shot magazine. **Barrel:** 4.13". **Weight:** 29 oz. **Length:** 6.73" overall. **Grips:** Stippled black plastic. **Sights:** Blade front, adjustable rear; 3-dot system. **Features:** Unique "squeeze cocker" in front strap cocks the action. Gas-retarded action. Squared combat-type trigger guard. Blue finish. Compact size. Imported from Germany by Heckler & Koch, Inc.
Price: P7M8, blued $1,515.00

Hi-Point 9MM Comp

Kahr K9

HECKLER & KOCH P2000 GPM PISTOL
Caliber: 9mmx19; 10-shot magazine. 13- or 16-round law enforcement/military magazines. **Barrel:** 3.62". **Weight:** 21.87 ozs. **Length:** 7". **Grips:** Interchangeable panels. **Sights:** Fixed Patridge style, drift adjustable for windage, standard 3-dot. **Features:** German Pistol Model incorporating features of the HK USP Compact. Introduced 2003. Imported from Germany by Heckler & Koch, Inc.
Price: **$887.00**

HECKLER & KOCK P2000SK SUBCOMPACT
Caliber: 9mm and 40 S&W. **Barrel:** 2.48". **Weight:** 1.49 lbs. (9mm) or 1.61 lbs. (40 S&W). **Sights:** Fixed Patridge style, drift adjustable. **Features:** Standard accessory rails, ambidextrous slide release, polymer frame, polygonal bore profile.
Price: **$929.00**

HI-POINT FIREARMS 9MM COMP PISTOL
Caliber: 9mm, Para., 10-shot magazine. **Barrel:** 4". **Weight:** 39 oz. **Length:** 7.72" overall. **Grips:** Textured plastic. **Sights:** Adjustable; low profile. **Features:** Single-action design. Scratch-resistant, non-glare blue finish, alloy frame. Muzzle brake/compensator. Compensator is slotted for laser or flashlight mounting. Introduced 1998. From MKS Supply, Inc.
Price: Matte black **$159.00**

HI-POINT FIREARMS MODEL 9MM COMPACT PISTOL
Caliber: 9mm Para., 8-shot magazine. **Barrel:** 3.5". **Weight:** 29 oz. **Length:** 6.7" overall. **Grips:** Textured plastic. **Sights:** Combat-style adjustable 3-dot system; low profile. **Features:** Single-action design; frame-mounted magazine release; polymer or alloy frame. Scratch-resistant matte finish. Introduced 1993. Made in U.S.A. by MKS Supply, Inc.
Price: Black, alloy frame **$149.00**
Price: With polymer frame (29 oz.), non-slip grips **$149.00**
Price: Aluminum with polymer frame **$149.00**

Hi-Point Firearms Model 380 Polymer Pistol
Similar to the 9mm Compact model except chambered for 380 ACP, 8-shot magazine, adjustable 3-dot sights. Weighs 29 oz. Polymer frame. Introduced 1998. Made in U.S.A. by MKS Supply, Inc.
Price: **$114.00**

Hi-Point Firearms 380 Comp Pistol
Similar to the 380 Polymer Pistol except has a 4" barrel with muzzle compensator; action locks open after last shot. Includes 10-shot and 8-shot magazine; trigger lock. Introduced 2001. Made in U.S.A. by MKS Supply, Inc.
Price: **$135.00**
Price: With laser sight **$229.00**

HI-POINT FIREARMS 45 POLYMER FRAME
Caliber: 45 ACP (9-shot), 40 S&W. **Barrel:** 4.5". **Weight:** 35 oz. **Sights:** Adjustable 3-dot. **Features:** Last round lock-open, grip mounted magazine release, magazine disconnect safety, integrated accessory rail. Introduced 2002. Made in U.S.A. by MKS Supply, Inc.
Price: **$179.00**

IAI M-2000 PISTOL
Caliber: 45 ACP, 8-shot. **Barrel:** 5", (Compact 4.25"). **Weight:** 36 oz. **Length:** 8.5", (6" Compact). **Grips:** Plastic or wood. **Sights:** Fixed.

Features: 1911 Government U.S. Army-style. Steel frame and slide Parkerized. GI grip safety. Beveled feed ramp barrel. By IAI, Inc.
Price: **$465.00**

KAHR K9, K40 DA AUTO PISTOLS
Caliber: 9mm Para., 7-shot, 40 S&W, 6-shot magazine. **Barrel:** 3.5". **Weight:** 25 oz. **Length:** 6" overall. **Grips:** Wraparound textured soft polymer. **Sights:** Blade front, rear drift adjustable for windage; bar-dot combat style. **Features:** Trigger-cocking double-action mechanism with passive firing pin block. Made of 4140 ordnance steel with matte black finish. Contact maker for complete price list. Introduced 1994. Made in U.S.A. by Kahr Arms.
Price: E9, black matte finish **$425.00**
Price: Matte black, night sights 9mm **$668.00**
Price: Matte stainless steel, 9mm **$638.00**
Price: 40 S&W, matte black **$580.00**
Price: 40 S&W, matte black, night sights **$668.00**
Price: 40 S&W, matte stainless **$638.00**
Price: K9 Elite 98 (high-polish stainless slide flats,
Kahr combat trigger), from **$694.00**
Price: As above, MK9 Elite 98, from **$694.00**
Price: As above, K40 Elite 98, from **$694.00**
Price: Covert, black, stainless slide, short grip **$599.00**
Price: Covert, black, Tritium nite sights **$689.00**

Kahr K9 9mm Compact Polymer Pistol
Similar to K9 steel frame pistol except has polymer frame, matte stainless steel slide. Barrel length 3.5"; overall length 6"; weighs 17.9 oz. Includes two 7-shot magazines, hard polymer case, trigger lock. Introduced 2000. Made in U.S.A. by Kahr Arms.
Price: **$599.00**

Kahr MK9/MK40 Micro Pistol
Similar to the K9/K40 except is 5.5" overall, 4" high, with a 3" barrel. Weighs 22 oz. Has snag-free bar-dot sights, polished feed ramp, dual recoil spring system, DA-only trigger. Comes with 6- and 7-shot magazines. Introduced 1998. Made in U.S.A. by Kahr Arms.
Price: Matte stainless **$638.00**
Price: Elite 98, polished stainless, Tritium night sights **$791.00**

KAHR PM9 PISTOL
Caliber: 9x19. **Barrel:** 3", 1:10 twist. **Weight:** 15.9 oz. **Length:** 5.3" overall. **Features:** Lightweight black polymer frame, polygonal rifling, stainless steel slide, DAO with passive striker block, trigger lock, hard case, 6- and 7-round mags.
Price: Matte stainless slide **$622.00**
Price: Tritium night sights **$719.00**

KEL-TEC P-11 AUTO PISTOL
Caliber: 9mm Para., 10-shot magazine. **Barrel:** 3.1". **Weight:** 14 oz. **Length:** 5.6" overall. **Grips:** Checkered black polymer. **Sights:** Blade front, rear adjustable for windage. **Features:** Ordnance steel slide, aluminum frame. Double-action-only trigger mechanism. Introduced 1995. Made in U.S.A. by Kel-Tec CNC Industries, Inc.
Price: Blue **$320.00**
Price: Hard chrome **$375.00**
Price: Parkerized **$362.00**

Kel-Tec P-32

Kel-Tec P-3AT

Kimber Pro Carry II

Kimber
Ultra Carry II

Kimber Ten II
High Capacity Polymer

Kimber Gold Match II

KEL-TEC P-32 AUTO PISTOL
Caliber: 32 ACP, 7-shot magazine. **Barrel:** 2.68". **Weight:** 6.6 oz. **Length:** 5.07" overall. **Grips:** Checkered composite. **Sights:** Fixed. **Features:** Double-action-only mechanism with 6-lb. pull; internal slide stop. Textured composite grip/frame. Now available in 380 ACP. Made in U.S.A. by Kel-Tec CNC Industries, Inc.
Price: Blue **$306.00**
Price: Hard chrome **$362.00**
Price: Parkerized **$346.00**

KEL-TEC P-3AT PISTOL
Caliber: 380 Auto; 7-rounds. **Weight:** 7.2 oz. **Length:** 5.2". **Features:** Lightest 380 auto made; aluminum frame, steel barrel.
Price: Blue **$311.00**
Price: Hard Chrome **$367.00**
Price: Parkerized **$351.00**

KIMBER CUSTOM II AUTO PISTOL
Caliber: 45 ACP, 40 S&W, 38 Super, 9mm, 10mm. **Barrel:** 5", match grade; 9mm, 10mm, 40 S&W, 38 Super barrels ramped. **Weight:** 38 oz. **Length:** 8.7" overall. **Grips:** Checkered black rubber, walnut, rosewood. **Sights:** Dovetailed front and rear, Kimber low profile adj. or fixed sights. **Features:** Slide, frame and barrel machined from steel or stainless steel. Match grade barrel, chamber and trigger group. Extended thumb safety, beveled magazine well, beveled front and rear slide serrations, high ride beavertail grip safety, checkered flat mainspring housing, kidney cut under trigger guard, high cut grip, match grade stainless steel barrel bushing, polished breech face, Commander-style hammer, lowered and flared ejection port, Wolff springs, bead blasted black oxide or matte stainless finish. Introduced in 1996. Made in U.S.A. by Kimber Mfg., Inc.
Price: Custom II **$768.00**
Price: Custom II Walnut (double-diamond walnut grips) **$775.00**
Price: Stainless II **$865.00**
Price: Stainless II 40 S&W **$884.00**
Price: Stainless II Target 45 ACP (stainless, adj. sight) **$983.00**
Price: Stainless II Target 38 Super **$1,014.00**

Kimber Compact Stainless II Auto Pistol
Similar to Pro Carry II except has stainless steel frame, 4-inch bbl., grip is .400" shorter than standard, no front serrations. Weighs 34 oz. 45 ACP only. Introduced in 1998. Made in U.S.A. by Kimber Mfg., Inc.
Price: **$907.00**

Kimber Pro Carry II Auto Pistol
Similar to Custom II, has aluminum frame, 4" bull barrel fitted directly to the slide without bushing. HD with stainless steel frame. Introduced 1998. Made in U.S.A. by Kimber Mfg., Inc.

Price: Pro Carry II **$779.00**
Price: Pro Carry II w/night sights **$902.00**
Price: Pro Carry II Stainless w/night sights **$985.00**
Price: Pro Carry HD II **$906.00**

Kimber Ultra Carry II Auto Pistol
Lightweight aluminum frame, 3" match grade bull barrel fitted to slide without bushing. Grips .4" shorter. Low effort recoil. Weighs 25 oz. Introduced in 1999. Made in U.S.A. by Kimber Mfg., Inc.
Price: **$791.00**
Price: Ultra Carry II Stainless **$875.00**
Price: Ultra Carry II Stainless 40 S&W **$921.00**

Kimber Ten II High Capacity Polymer Pistol
Similar to Custom II, Pro Carry II and Ultra Carry II depending on barrel length. Thirteen-round magazine capacity (double stack and flush fitting). Polymer grip frame molded over stainless steel or aluminum (BP Ten pistols only) frame insert. Checkered front strap and belly of trigger guard. All models have fixed sights except Gold Match Ten II, which has adjustable sight. Frame grip dimensions approximately that of the standard 1911. **Weight:** 24 to 34 oz. Improved version of the Kimber Polymer series. Made in U.S.A. by Kimber Mfg., Inc.
Price: Pro Carry Ten II **$794.00**
Price: Stainless Ten II **$786.00**

Kimber Gold Match II Auto Pistol
Similar to Custom II models. Includes stainless steel barrel with match grade chamber and barrel bushing, ambidextrous thumb safety, adjustable sight, premium aluminum trigger, hand-checkered double diamond rosewood grips. Barrel hand-fitted for target accuracy. Made in U.S.A. by Kimber Mfg., Inc.
Price: Gold Match II **$1,204.00**
Price: Gold Match Stainless II 45 ACP **$1,369.00**
Price: Gold Match Stainless II 40 S&W **$1,400.00**

Kimber Gold Combat II   Kimber CDP II   Kimber Eclipse II

Kimber Eclipse Pro II   Kimber LTP II   Llama Micromax 380

Kimber Gold Match Ten II Polymer Auto Pistol
Similar to Stainless Gold Match II. High capacity polymer frame with 13-round magazine. Thumb safety. Introduced 1999. Made in U.S.A. by Kimber Mfg., Inc.
Price: **$1,072.00**

Kimber Gold Combat II Auto Pistol
Similar to Gold Match II except designed for concealed carry. Extended and beveled magazine well, Meprolight Tritium night sights; premium aluminum trigger; 30 lpi front strap checkering; extended magazine well. Introduced 1999. Made in U.S.A. by Kimber Mfg., Inc.
Price: Gold Combat II **$1,733.00**
Price: Gold Combat Stainless II **$1,674.00**

Kimber CDP II Series Auto Pistol
Similar to Custom II, but designed for concealed carry. Aluminum frame. Standard features include stainless steel slide, fixed Meprolight tritium 3-dot (green) dovetail-mounted night sights, match grade barrel and chamber, 30 LPI front strap checkering, two-tone finish, ambidextrous thumb safety, hand-checkered double diamond rosewood grips. Introduced in 2000. Made in U.S.A. by Kimber Mfg., Inc.
Price: Ultra CDP II 40 S&W **$1,215.00**
Price: Ultra CDP II (3" barrel, short grip) **$1,177.00**
Price: Compact CDP II (4" barrel, short grip) **$1,177.00**
Price: Pro CDP II (4" barrel, full length grip) **$1,177.00**
Price: Custom CDP II (5" barrel, full length grip) **$1,177.00**

Kimber Eclipse II Series Auto Pistol
Similar to Custom II and other stainless Kimber pistols. Stainless slide and frame, black oxide, two-tone finish. Gray/black laminated grips. 30 lpi front strap checkering. All models have night sights; Target versions have Meprolight adjustable Bar/Dot version. Made in U.S.A. by Kimber Mfg., Inc.
Price: Eclipse Ultra II (3" barrel, short grip) **$1,085.00**
Price: Eclipse Pro II (4" barrel, full length grip) **$1,085.00**
Price: Eclipse Pro Target II (4" barrel, full length grip, adjustable sight) **$1,189.00**
Price: Eclipse Custom II (5" barrel, full length grip) **$1,105.00**
Price: Eclipse Target II (5" barrel, full length grip, adjustable sight) **$1,189.00**
Price: Eclipse Custom II (10mm) **$1,220.00**

Kimber LTP II Auto Pistol
Similar to Gold Match II. Built for Limited Ten competition. First Kimber pistol with new, innovative Kimber external extractor. KimPro premium finish. Stainless steel match grade barrel. Extended and beveled magazine well. Checkered front strap and trigger guard belly. Tungsten full length guide rod. Premium aluminum trigger. Ten-round single stack magazine. Wide ambidextrous thumb safety. Made in U.S.A. by Kimber Mfg., Inc.
Price: **$2,099.00**

Kimber Super Match II Auto Pistol
Similar to Gold Match II. Built for target and action shooting competition. Tested for accuracy, target included. Stainless steel barrel and chamber. KimPro finish on stainless steel slide. Stainless steel frame. 30 lpi checkered front strap, premium aluminum trigger, Kimber adjustable sight. Introduced in 1999.
Price: **$1,986.00**

KORTH PISTOL
Caliber: 40 S&W, 357 SIG (9-shot); 9mm Para, 9x21 (10-shot). **Barrel:** 4" (standard), 5" (optional). **Weight:** 3.3 lbs. (single action), 11 lbs. (double action). **Sights:** Fully adjustable. **Features:** Recoil-operated action, mechanically-locked via large pivoting bolt block. Accessories include sound suppressor for qualified buyers. Imported by Korth U.S.A.
Price: **$7,578.00**

LLAMA MICROMAX 380 AUTO PISTOL
Caliber: 32 ACP (9-shot), 380 ACP (8-shot). **Barrel:** 3-11/16". **Weight:** 23 oz. **Length:** 6-1/2" overall. **Grips:** Checkered high impact polymer. **Sights:** 3-dot combat. **Features:** Single-action. Mini custom extended slide release; mini custom extended beavertail grip safety; combat-style hammer. Introduced 1997. Distributed by Import Sports, Inc.
Price: Matte blue **$281.95**
Price: Satin chrome (380 only) **$299.95**

LLAMA MINIMAX SERIES
Caliber: 40 S&W (8-shot); 45 ACP (7-shot). **Barrel:** 3-1/2". **Weight:** 35 oz. **Length:** 7-1/3" overall. **Grips:** Checkered rubber. **Sights:** 3-dot combat. **Features:** Single action, skeletonized combat-style hammer, extended slide release, cone-style barrel, flared ejection port. Introduced 1996. Distributed by Import Sports, Inc.
Price: Blue **$308.95**
Price: Duo-tone finish (45 only) **$315.95**
Price: Satin chrome **$333.95**

Llama Minimax

Llama Max-1 Government Deluxe

North American Arms Guardian

Para-Ordnance P12.45

Para-Ordnance LDA

Para-Ordnance Carry

Para-Ordnance Limited

Llama Minimax Sub-Compact Auto Pistol
Similar to the Minimax except has 3.14" barrel, weighs 31 oz.; 6.8" overall length; has 10-shot magazine with finger extension; beavertail grip safety. Introduced 1999. Distributed by Import Sports, Inc.
Price: 45 ACP, matte blue **$315.95**
Price: As above, satin chrome **$341.95**
Price: Duo-tone finish (45 only) **$324.95**

LLAMA MAX-I AUTO PISTOLS
Caliber: 45 ACP, 7-shot. **Barrel:** 5-1/8". **Weight:** 36 oz. **Length:** 8-1/2" overall. **Grips:** Polymer. **Sights:** Blade front; 3-dot system. **Features:** Single-action trigger; skeletonized combat-style hammer; steel frame; extended manual and grip safeties, matte finish. Introduced 1995. Distributed by Import Sports, Inc.
Price: 45 ACP, 7-round, Government model **$358.95**
Price: Maxi II, 17-round model **$324.95**

NORTH AMERICAN ARMS GUARDIAN PISTOL
Caliber: 32 ACP, 380 ACP, 32NAA, 6-shot magazine. **Barrel:** 2.1". **Weight:** 13.5 oz. **Length:** 4.36" overall. **Grips:** Black polymer. **Sights:** Fixed. **Features:** Double-action only mechanism. All stainless steel construction. Introduced 1998. Made in U.S.A. by North American Arms.
Price: .... **$402.00 to $479.00**

OLYMPIC ARMS OA-93 AR PISTOL
Caliber: 5.56 NATO. **Barrel:** 6.5", chrome-moly steel. **Weight:** 5.8 lbs. **Length:** 26.5". **Sights:** None. **Features:** Black matte finish; flash suppressor; tubular handguard. Introduced 2005. Made in U.S.A. by Olympic Arms, Inc.
Price: **$1,020.00**

Olympic Arms OA-98 AR Pistol
Similar to the OA-93 except has removable 7-shot magazine, weighs 3 lbs. Introduced 1999. Made in U.S.A. by Olympic Arms, Inc.
Price: **$1,020.00**

PARA-ORDNANCE P-SERIES AUTO PISTOLS
Caliber: 9mm Para., 40 S&W, 45 ACP, 10-shot magazine. **Barrel:** 3", 3-1/2", 4-1/4", 5". **Weight:** From 24 oz. (alloy frame). **Length:** 8.5" overall. **Grips:** Textured composition. **Sights:** Blade front, rear adjustable for windage. High visibility 3-dot system. **Features:** Available with alloy, steel or stainless steel frame with black finish (silver or stainless gun). Steel and stainless steel frame guns weigh 40 oz. (P14.45), 36 oz. (P13.45), 34 oz. (P12.45). Grooved match trigger, rounded combat-style hammer. Beveled magazine well. Manual thumb, grip and firing pin lock safeties. Solid barrel bushing. Contact maker for full details. Introduced 1990. Made in Canada by Para-Ordnance.
Price: Steel frame **$855.00**
Price: Alloy frame **$840.00**
Price: Stainless steel **$988.00**

Para-Ordnance Limited Pistols
Similar to the P-Series pistols except with full-length recoil guide system; fully adjustable rear sight; tuned trigger with over-travel stop; beavertail grip safety; competition hammer; front and rear slide serrations; ambidextrous safety; lowered ejection port; ramped match-grade barrel; dove-tailed front sight. Introduced 1998. Made in Canada by Para-Ordnance.
Price: 9mm, 40 S&W, 45 ACP **$1,105.00**

Para-Ordnance LDA Auto Pistols
Similar to P-series except has double-action trigger mechanism. Steel frame with matte black finish, checkered composition grips. Available in 9mm Para., 40 S&W, 45 ACP. Introduced 1999. Made in Canada by Para-Ordnance.
Price: .... **$899.00 to $973.00**

Para-Ordnance LDA Limited Pistols
Similar to LDA, has ambidextrous safety, adjustable rear sight, front slide serrations and full-length recoil guide system. Made in Canada by Para-Ordnance.
Price: Black finish **$1,105.00**
Price: Stainless **$1,049.00**

PARA-ORDNANCE 45 LDA PARA CARRY
Caliber: 45 ACP. **Barrel:** 3", 7-shot. **Weight:** 30 oz. **Length:** 6.5". **Grips:** Double diamond checkered cocobolo. **Features:** Stainless finish and receiver. Para LDA trigger system and safeties.
Price: **$988.00**

PARA-ORDNANCE 45 LDA PARA COMPANION
Caliber: 45 ACP. **Barrel:** 3.5", 8-shot. **Weight:** 32 oz. **Length:** 7". **Grips:** Double diamond checkered cocobolo. **Features:** Para LDA trigger system with Para LDA 3 safeties (slide lock, firing pin block and grip safety). Lightning speed, full size capacity.
Price: **$899.00**

Peters Stahl High Capacity

Peters Stahl Trophy Master

Peters Stahl Millennium

Phoenix Arms HP22

Rock River Standard Match

Ruger P89

Ruger P90

PETERS STAHL AUTOLOADING PISTOLS
Caliber: 9mm Para., 45 ACP. **Barrel:** 5" or 6". **Grips:** Walnut or walnut with rubber wrap. **Sights:** Fully adjustable rear, blade front. **Features:** Stainless steel extended slide stop, safety and extended magazine release button; speed trigger with stop, approx. 3-lb. pull; polished ramp. Introduced 2000. Imported from Germany by Phillips & Rogers.
Price: High Capacity (accepts 15-shot magazines in 45 cal.; includes 10-shot magazine) **$1,695.00**
Price: Trophy Master (blued or stainless, 7-shot in 45, 8-shot in 9mm) **$1,995.00**
Price: Millennium Model (titanium coating on receiver and slide) **$2,195.00**

PHOENIX ARMS HP22, HP25 AUTO PISTOLS
Caliber: 22 LR, 10-shot (HP22), 25 ACP, 10-shot (HP25). **Barrel:** 3". **Weight:** 20 oz. **Length:** 5-1/2" overall. **Grips:** Checkered composition. **Sights:** Blade front, adjustable rear. **Features:** Single action, exposed hammer; manual hold-open; button magazine release. Available in satin nickel, polished blue finish. Introduced 1993. Made in U.S.A. by Phoenix Arms.
Price: With gun lock and cable lanyard **$130.00**
Price: HP Rangemaster kit with 5" bbl., locking case and assessories **$171.00**
Price: HP Deluxe Rangemaster kit with 3" and 5" bbls., 2 mags., case **$210.00**

ROCK RIVER ARMS STANDARD MATCH AUTO PISTOL
Caliber: 45 ACP. **Barrel:** NA. **Weight:** NA. **Length:** NA. **Grips:** Cocobolo, checkered. **Sights:** Heine fixed rear, blade front. **Features:** Chrome-moly steel frame and slide; beavertail grip safety with raised pad; checkered slide stop; ambidextrous safety; polished feed ramp and extractor; aluminum speed trigger with 3.5 lb. pull. Made in U.S.A. From Rock River Arms.
Price: **$1,025.00**

ROCKY MOUNTAIN ARMS PATRIOT PISTOL
Caliber: 223, 10-shot magazine. **Barrel:** 7", with muzzle brake. **Weight:** 5 lbs. **Length:** 20.5" overall. **Grips:** Black composition. **Sights:** None furnished. **Features:** Milled upper receiver with enhanced Weaver base; milled lower receiver from billet plate; machined aluminum National Match handguard. Finished in DuPont Teflon-S matte black or NATO green. Comes with black nylon case, one magazine. Introduced 1993. From Rocky Mountain Arms, Inc.
Price: With A-2 handle top . . . . **$2,500.00 to $2,800.00**
Price: Flat top model . . . . **$3,000.00 to $3,500.00**

RUGER P89 AUTOLOADING PISTOL
Caliber: 9mm Para., 15-shot magazine. **Barrel:** 4.50". **Weight:** 32 oz. **Length:** 7.84" overall. **Grips:** Grooved black synthetic composition. **Sights:** Square post front, square notch rear adjustable for windage, both with white dot inserts. **Features:** Double action, ambidextrous slide-mounted safety-levers. Slide 4140 chrome-moly steel or 400-series stainless steel, frame lightweight aluminum alloy. Ambidextrous magazine release. Blue, stainless steel. Introduced 1986; stainless 1990.
Price: P89, blue, extra mag and mag loader, plastic case locks . . . **$475.00**
Price: KP89, stainless, extra mag and mag loader, plastic case locks **$525.00**

Ruger P89D Decocker Autoloading Pistol
Similar to standard P89 except has ambidextrous decocking levers in place of regular slide-mounted safety. Decocking levers move firing pin inside slide where hammer cannot reach. Blue, stainless steel. Introduced 1990.
Price: P89D, blue, extra mag and mag loader, plastic case locks . . **$475.00**
Price: KP89D, stainless, extra mag and mag loader, plastic case locks **$525.00**

RUGER P90 MANUAL SAFETY MODEL AUTOLOADING PISTOL
Caliber: 45 ACP, 8-shot magazine. **Barrel:** 4.50". **Weight:** 33.5 oz. **Length:** 7.75" overall. **Grips:** Grooved black synthetic composition. **Sights:** Square post front, square notch rear adjustable for windage, both with white dot. **Features:** Double action; ambidextrous slide-mounted safety-levers. Stainless steel only. Introduced 1991.
Price: KP90 with extra mag, loader, case and gunlock **$565.00**
Price: P90 (blue) **$525.00**

Ruger KP94D

Ruger 22/45-P4

Ruger KP512

Ruger KP90 Decocker Autoloading Pistol
Similar to the P90 except has a manual decocking system. Ambidextrous decocking levers move the firing pin inside the slide where the hammer cannot reach it. Available only in stainless steel. Overall length 7.75", weighs 33.5 oz. Introduced 1991.
Price: KP90D with case, extra mag and mag loading tool **$565.00**

Ruger KP94 Autoloading Pistol
Sized midway between full-size P-Series and compact KP94. 4.25" barrel, 7.5" overall length, weighs about 33 oz. KP94 manual safety model; KP94D is decocker-only in 40-caliber with 10-shot magazine. Slide gripping grooves roll over top of slide. KP94 has ambidextrous safety-levers; KP944D has ambidextrous decocking levers. Matte finish stainless slide, barrel, alloy frame. Also blue. Includes hard case and lock. Introduced 1994. Made in U.S.A. by Sturm, Ruger & Co.
Price: P944, blue (manual safety) **$495.00**
Price: KP944 (40-caliber) (manual safety-stainless) **$575.00**
Price: KP944D (40-caliber)-decocker only **$575.00**

RUGER P95 AUTOLOADING PISTOL
Caliber: 9mm Para., 15-shot magazine. **Barrel:** 3.9". **Weight:** 27 oz. **Length:** 7.25" overall. **Grips:** Grooved; integral with frame. **Sights:** Blade front, rear drift adjustable for windage; 3-dot system. **Features:** Molded polymer grip frame, stainless steel or chrome-moly slide. Suitable for +P+ ammunition. Safety model, decocker or DAO. Introduced 1996. Made in U.S.A. by Sturm, Ruger & Co. Comes with lockable plastic case, spare magazine, loader and lock.
Price: P95D15 decocker only **$425.00**
Price: P9515 stainless steel decocker only **$475.00**
Price: KP9515 safety model, stainless steel **$475.00**
Price: P9515 safety model, blued finish **$425.00**

RUGER MARK II STANDARD AUTOLOADING PISTOL
Caliber: 22 LR, 10-shot magazine. **Barrel:** 4-3/4" or 6". **Weight:** 35 oz. (4-3/4" bbl.). **Length:** 8-5/16" (4-3/4" bbl.). **Grips:** Checkered composition grip panels. **Sights:** Fixed, wide blade front, fixed rear. **Features:** Updated design of original Standard Auto. New bolt hold-open latch. 10-shot magazine, magazine catch, safety and trigger. Introduced 1982.
Price: Blued (MKIII4, MKIII6) **$322.00**

Ruger 22/45 Mark II Pistol
Similar to other 22 Mark II autos except has grip frame of Zytel that matches angle and magazine latch of Model 1911 45 ACP pistol. Available in 4" standard, 4-3/4" and 5-1/2" bull barrels. Comes with extra magazine, plastic case, lock. Introduced 1992.
Price: P4MKIII, 4" standard barrel, adjustable sights **$307.00**
Price: KP512 (5-1/2" bull bbl.), stainless steel, adj. sights **$398.00**
Price: P512 (5-1/2" bull bbl., all blue), adj. sights **$307.00**

SAFARI ARMS ENFORCER PISTOL
Caliber: 45 ACP, 6-shot magazine. **Barrel:** 3.8", stainless. **Weight:** 36 oz. **Length:** 7.3" overall. **Grips:** Smooth walnut with etched black widow spider logo. **Sights:** Ramped blade front, LPA adjustable rear. **Features:** Extended safety, extended slide release; Commander-style hammer; beavertail grip safety; throated, polished, tuned. Parkerized matte black or satin stainless steel finishes. Made in U.S.A. by Safari Arms, Inc.
Price: **$630.00**

SAFARI ARMS GI SAFARI PISTOL
Caliber: 45 ACP, 7-shot magazine. **Barrel:** 5", 416 stainless. **Weight:** 39.9 oz. **Length:** 8.5" overall. **Grips:** Checkered walnut. **Sights:** G.I.-style blade front, drift-adjustable rear. **Features:** Beavertail grip safety; extended thumb safety and slide release; Commander-style hammer. Parkerized finish. Reintroduced 1996.
Price: **$439.00**

SAFARI ARMS CARRIER PISTOL
Caliber: 45 ACP, 7-shot magazine. **Barrel:** 6", 416 stainless steel. **Weight:** 30 oz. **Length:** 9.5" overall. **Grips:** Wood. **Sights:** Ramped blade front, LPA adjustable rear. **Features:** Beavertail grip safety; extended controls; full-length recoil spring guide; Commander-style hammer. Throated, polished and tuned. Satin stainless steel finish. Introduced 1999. Made in U.S.A. by Safari Arms, Inc.
Price: **$714.00**

SAFARI ARMS COHORT PISTOL
Caliber: 45 ACP, 7-shot magazine. **Barrel:** 3.8", 416 stainless. **Weight:** 37 oz. **Length:** 8.5" overall. **Grips:** Smooth walnut with laser-etched black widow logo. **Sights:** Ramped blade front, LPA adjustable rear. **Features:** Combines the Enforcer model, slide and MatchMaster frame. Beavertail grip safety; extended thumb safety and slide release; Commander-style hammer. Satin stainless finish. Introduced 1996. Made in U.S.A. by Safari Arms, Inc.
Price: **$654.00**

SAFARI ARMS MATCHMASTER PISTOL
Caliber: 45 ACP, 7-shot. **Barrel:** 5" or 6", 416 stainless steel. **Weight:** 38 oz. (5" barrel). **Length:** 8.5" overall. **Grips:** Smooth walnut. **Sights:** Ramped blade, LPA adjustable rear. **Features:** Beavertail grip safety; extended controls; Commander-style hammer; throated, polished, tuned. Parkerized matte-black or satin stainless steel. Made in U.S.A. by Olympic Arms, Inc.
Price: 5" barrel **$594.00**
Price: 6" bbl. **$654.00**

Safari Arms Carry Comp Pistol
Similar to the Matchmaster except has Wil Schueman-designed hybrid compensator system. Made in U.S.A. by Olympic Arms, Inc.
Price: **$1,067.00**

SEECAMP LWS 32 STAINLESS DA AUTO
Caliber: 32 ACP Win. Silvertip, 6-shot magazine. **Barrel:** 2", integral with frame. **Weight:** 10.5 oz. **Length:** 4-1/8" overall. **Grips:** Glass-filled nylon. **Sights:** Smooth, no-snag, contoured slide and barrel top. **Features:** Aircraft quality 17-4 PH stainless steel. Inertia-operated firing pin. Hammer fired double-action-only. Hammer automatically follows slide down to safety rest position after each shot, no manual safety needed. Magazine safety disconnector. Polished stainless. Introduced 1985. From L.W. Seecamp.
Price: **$425.00**

SIG-Sauer P220

SIG-Sauer P245 Compact

SIG-Sauer Pro 2009

SIG-Sauer P229 Sport

SIG-Sauer P232

SEMMERLING LM-4 SLIDE-ACTION PISTOL
Caliber: 45 ACP, 4-shot magazine. **Barrel:** 2". **Weight:** 24 oz. **Length:** NA. **Grips:** NA. **Sights:** NA. **Features:** The Semmerling LM-4 is a super compact pistol employing a thumb activated slide mechanism (the slide is manually retracted between shots). From American Derringer Corp.
Price: **$2,635.00**

SIG-SAUER P220 SERVICE AUTO PISTOL
Caliber: 45 ACP, (7- or 8-shot magazine). **Barrel:** 4-3/8". **Weight:** 27.8 oz. **Length:** 7.8" overall. **Grips:** Checkered black plastic. **Sights:** Blade front, drift adjustable rear for windage. Optional Siglite night sights. **Features:** Double action. Decocking lever permits lowering hammer onto locked firing pin. Squared combat-type trigger guard. Slide stays open after last shot. Imported from Germany by SIGARMS, Inc.
Price: Blue SA/DA or DAO **$790.00**
Price: Blue, Siglite night sights **$880.00**
Price: K-Kote or nickel slide **$830.00**
Price: K-Kote or nickel slide with Siglite night sights **$930.00**

SIG-Sauer P220 Sport Auto Pistol
Similar to the P220 except has 4.9" barrel, ported compensator, stainless steel frame and slide, adjustable sights, extended competition controls. Overall length is 9.9", weighs 43.5 oz. Introduced 1999. From SIGARMS, Inc.
Price: **$1,320.00**

SIG-Sauer P245 Compact Auto Pistol
Similar to the P220 except has 3.9" barrel, shorter grip, 6-shot magazine, 7.28" overall length, and weighs 27.5 oz. Introduced 1999. From SIGARMS, Inc.
Price: Blue **$780.00**
Price: Blue, with Siglite sights **$850.00**
Price: Two-tone **$830.00**
Price: Two-tone with Siglite sights **$930.00**
Price: With K-Kote finish **$830.00**
Price: K-Kote with Siglite sights **$930.00**

SIG-Sauer P229 DA Auto Pistol
Similar to the P228 except chambered for 9mm Para., 40 S&W, 357 SIG. Has 3.86" barrel, 7.08" overall length and 3.35" height. Weight is 30.5 oz. Introduced 1991. Frame made in Germany, stainless steel slide assembly made in U.S.; pistol assembled in U.S. From SIGARMS, Inc.

Price: **$795.00**
Price: With nickel slide **$890.00**
Price: Nickel slide Siglite night sights **$935.00**

SIG PRO AUTO PISTOL
Caliber: 9mm Para., 40 S&W, 10-shot magazine. **Barrel:** 3.86". **Weight:** 27.2 oz. **Length:** 7.36" overall. **Grips:** Composite and rubberized one-piece. **Sights:** Blade front, rear adjustable for windage. Optional Siglite night sights. **Features:** Polymer frame, stainless steel slide; integral frame accessory rail; replaceable steel frame rails; left- or right-handed magazine release. Introduced 1999. From SIGARMS, Inc.
Price: SP2340 (40 S&W) **$596.00**
Price: SP2009 (9mm Para.) **$596.00**
Price: As above with Siglite night sights **$655.00**

SIG-Sauer P226 Service Pistol
Similar to the P220 pistol except has 4.4" barrel, and weighs 28.3 oz. 357 SIG or 40 S&W. Imported from Germany by SIGARMS, Inc.
Price: Blue SA/DA or DAO **$830.00**
Price: With Siglite night sights **$930.00**
Price: Blue, SA/DA or DAO 357 SIG **$830.00**
Price: With Siglite night sights **$930.00**
Price: K-Kote finish, 40 S&W only or nickel slide **$830.00**
Price: K-Kote or nickel slide Siglite night sights **$930.00**
Price: Nickel slide 357 SIG **$875.00**
Price: Nickel slide, Siglite night sights **$930.00**

SIG-Sauer P229 Sport Auto Pistol
Similar to the P229 except in 357 SIG only; 4.8" heavy barrel; 8.6" overall length; weighs 40.6 oz.; vented compensator; adjustable target sights; rubber grips; extended slide latch and magazine release. Stainless steel. Introduced 1998. From SIGARMS, Inc.
Price: **$1,320.00**

SIG-SAUER P232 PERSONAL SIZE PISTOL
Caliber: 380 ACP, 7-shot. **Barrel:** 3-3/4". **Weight:** 16 oz. **Length:** 6-1/2" overall. **Grips:** Checkered black composite. **Sights:** Blade front, rear adjustable for windage. **Features:** Double action/single action or DAO. Blow-back operation, stationary barrel. Introduced 1997. Imported from Germany by SIGARMS, Inc.
Price: Blue SA/DA or DAO **$505.00**
Price: In stainless steel **$545.00**
Price: With stainless steel slide, blue frame **$525.00**
Price: Stainless steel, Siglite night sights, Hogue grips **$585.00**

Smith & Wesson 457 TDA

Smith & Wesson 908

Smith & Wesson 4013 TSW

Smith & Wesson 410 DA

Smith & Wesson 910 DA

Smith & Wesson 3913 LadySmith

SIG-SAUER P239 PISTOL

Caliber: 9mm Para., 8-shot, 357 SIG 40 S&W, 7-shot magazine. **Barrel:** 3.6". **Weight:** 25.2 oz. **Length:** 6.6" overall. **Grips:** Checkered black composite. **Sights:** Blade front, rear adjustable for windage. Optional Siglite night sights. **Features:** SA/DA or DAO; blackened stainless steel slide, aluminum alloy frame. Introduced 1996. Made in U.S.A. by SIGARMS, Inc.
Price: SA/DA or DAO $620.00
Price: SA/DA or DAO with Siglite night sights $720.00
Price: Two-tone finish $665.00
Price: Two-tone finish, Siglite sights $765.00

SMITH & WESSON MODEL 457 TDA AUTO PISTOL

Caliber: 45 ACP, 7-shot magazine. **Barrel:** 3-3/4". **Weight:** 29 oz. **Length:** 7-1/4" overall. **Grips:** One-piece Xenoy, wraparound with straight backstrap. **Sights:** Post front, fixed rear, 3-dot system. **Features:** Aluminum alloy frame, matte blue carbon steel slide; bobbed hammer; smooth trigger. Introduced 1996. Made in U.S.A. by Smith & Wesson.
Price: Blue finish $649.00
Price: Matte finish $676.00

SMITH & WESSON MODEL 908 AUTO PISTOL

Caliber: 9mm Para., 8-shot magazine. **Barrel:** 3-1/2". **Weight:** 24 oz. **Length:** 6-13/16". **Grips:** One-piece Xenoy, wraparound with straight backstrap. **Sights:** Post front, fixed rear, 3-dot system. **Features:** Aluminum alloy frame, matte blue carbon steel slide; bobbed hammer; smooth trigger. Introduced 1996. Made in U.S.A. by Smith & Wesson.
Price: Blue finish $587.00
Price: Matte finish $611.00

SMITH & WESSON MODEL 4013 TSW AUTO

Caliber: 40 S&W, 9-shot magazine. **Barrel:** 3-1/2". **Weight:** 26.8 oz. **Length:** 6 3/4" overall. **Grips:** Xenoy one-piece wraparound. **Sights:** Novak 3-dot system. **Features:** Traditional double-action system; stainless slide, alloy frame; fixed barrel bushing; ambidextrous decocker; reversible magazine catch, equipment rail. Introduced 1997. Made in U.S.A. by Smith & Wesson.
Price: Model 4013 TSW $973.00

SMITH & WESSON MODEL 410 DA AUTO PISTOL

Caliber: 40 S&W, 10-shot magazine. **Barrel:** 4". **Weight:** 28.5 oz. **Length:** 7.5". **Grips:** One-piece Xenoy, wraparound with straight backstrap. **Sights:** Post front, fixed rear; 3-dot system. **Features:** Aluminum alloy frame; blued carbon steel slide; traditional double action with left-side slide-mounted decocking lever. Introduced 1996. Made in U.S.A. by Smith & Wesson.
Price: Model 410 .... $649.00
Price: Model 410S, matte finish $669.00
Price: Crimson trace grips $993.00

SMITH & WESSON MODEL 910 DA AUTO PISTOL

Caliber: 9mm Para., 10-shot magazine. **Barrel:** 4". **Weight:** 28 oz. **Length:** 7-3/8" overall. **Grips:** One-piece Xenoy, wraparound with straight backstrap. **Sights:** Post front with white dot, fixed 2-dot rear. **Features:** Alloy frame, blue carbon steel slide. Slide-mounted decocking lever. Introduced 1995.
Price: Model 910 .... $587.00
Price: Model 910, matte finish $602.00

SMITH & WESSON MODEL 3913 TRADITIONAL DOUBLE ACTION

Caliber: 9mm Para., 8-shot magazine. **Barrel:** 3-1/2". **Weight:** 24.8 oz. **Length:** 6-3/4" overall. **Grips:** One-piece Delrin wraparound, textured surface. **Sights:** Post front with white dot, Novak LoMount Carry with two dots. **Features:** Aluminum alloy frame, stainless slide (M3913). Bobbed hammer with no half-cock notch; smooth .304" trigger with rounded edges. Straight backstrap. Equipment rail. Extra magazine included. Introduced 1989.
Price: $834.00

Smith & Wesson Model 3913-LS Ladysmith Auto

Similar to the standard Model 3913 except has frame that is upswept at the front, rounded trigger guard. Comes in frosted stainless steel with matching gray grips. Grips are ergonomically correct for a woman's hand. Novak LoMount Carry rear sight adjustable for windage. Extra magazine included. Introduced 1990.
Price: $858.00

SMITH & WESSON MODEL SW1911

Caliber: 45 ACP, 8 rounds. **Barrel:** 5". **Weight:** 39 oz. **Length:** 8.7". **Grips:** Wood/rubber. **Sights:** Novak Lo-Mount Carry, white dot front.
Price: Stainless steel frame $960.00
Price: Adjustable sights, stainless $1,049.00
Price: Carbon steel frame $960.00
Price: Stainless w/Crimson Trace Lasergrip $1,281.00
Price: Doug Koenig Pro Series $1,213.00

Smith & Wesson 4006

Smith & Wesson 4566 TSW

Smith & Wesson Sigma SW40V

Springfield, Inc. 1911A1 Standard

Springfield, Inc. Full-Size 1911A1

Springfield, Inc. TRP

SMITH & WESSON MODEL SW1911PD
Caliber: 45 ACP, 8 rounds. **Barrel:** 4-1/4" or 5". **Weight:** 28 oz. **Length:** 7-5/8" or 8.7". **Grips:** Wood. **Sights:** Novak Lo-Mount Carry, white dot front.
Price: 4-1/4" bbl. **$1,029.00**
Price: 5" **$1,029.00**
Price: Carbon steel frame **$960.00**
Price: Scandium alloy w/Crimson Trace Lasergrip **$1,330.00**

SMITH & WESSON MODEL 4040PD
Caliber: 40 S&W, 7 rounds. **Barrel:** 3.5". **Weight:** 25.6 oz. **Length:** 6.9". **Grips:** Rubber. **Sights:** Novak Lo-Mount Carry, white dot front.
Price: Scandium alloy frame **$840.00**

SMITH & WESSON MODEL SW990L COMPACT
Caliber: 9mm (10 rounds), 40 S&W (8 rounds). **Barrel:** 3.5". **Weight:** 23 oz. **Length:** 6.6". **Grips:** Polymer. **Sights:** Adj. rear, white dot front.
Price: **$694.00**
Price: Model 5946 DAO (as above, stainless frame and slide) **$863.00**

SMITH & WESSON ENHANCED SIGMA SERIES DAO PISTOLS
Caliber: 9mm Para., 40 S&W, 10-shot magazine. **Barrel:** 4". **Weight:** 24.7 oz. **Length:** 7-1/4" overall. **Grips:** Integral. **Sights:** White dot front, fixed rear; 3-dot system. Tritium night sights available. **Features:** Ergonomic polymer frame; low barrel centerline; internal striker firing system; corrosion-resistant slide; Teflon-filled, electroless-nickel coated magazine; equipment rail. Introduced 1994. Made in U.S.A. by Smith & Wesson.
Price: **$379.00**

SMITH & WESSON MODEL CS9 CHIEF'S SPECIAL AUTO
Caliber: 9mm Para., 7-shot magazine. **Barrel:** 3". **Weight:** 20.8 oz. **Length:** 6-1/4" overall. **Grips:** Hogue wraparound rubber. **Sights:** White dot front, fixed 2-dot rear. **Features:** Traditional double-action trigger mechanism. Alloy frame, stainless slide. Ambidextrous safety. Introduced 1999. Made in U.S.A. by Smith & Wesson.
Price: Stainless **$747.00**

SMITH & WESSON MODEL CS45 CHIEF'S SPECIAL AUTO
Caliber: 45 ACP, 6-shot magazine. **Weight:** 23.9 oz. **Features:** Introduced 1999. Made in U.S.A. by Smith & Wesson.
Price: Stainless **$787.00**

SMITH & WESSON MODEL SW990L
Caliber: 9mm Para. 4" barrel; 40 S&W 4-1/8" barrel; adj. sights. **Features:** Traditional double action satin stainless, black polymer frame, equipment rail, Saf-T-Trigger, interchangeable backstrap.
Price: 9mm, 40 S&W **$694.00**
Price: 45 ACP **$736.00**

SPRINGFIELD ARMORY FULL-SIZE 1911A1 AUTO PISTOL
Caliber: 9mm Para., 9-shot; 38 Super, 9-shot; 40 S&W, 9-shot; 45 ACP, 7-shot. **Barrel:** 5". **Weight:** 35.6 oz. **Length:** 8-5/8" overall. **Grips:** Cocobolo. **Sights:** Fixed 3-dot system. **Features:** Beveled magazine well; lowered and flared ejection port. All forged parts, including frame, barrel, slide. All new production. Introduced 1990. From Springfield Armory.
Price: Mil-Spec 45 ACP, Parkerized **$640.00**
Price: Tactical, 45 ACP, TRP Armory Kote, Novak sights **$1,560.00**
Price: Standard, 45 ACP, stainless, Novak sights **$876.00**
Price: Lightweight 45 ACP (28.6 oz., matte finish, night sights) . . . **$922.00**
Price: 40 S&W, stainless **$1,409.00**
Price: 9mm, stainless **$948.00**

Springfield Armory TRP Pistols
Similar to 1911A1 except 45 ACP only, checkered front strap and mainspring housing, Novak Night Sight combat rear sight and matching dovetailed front sight, tuned, polished extractor, oversize barrel link; lightweight speed trigger and combat action job, match barrel and bushing, extended ambidextrous thumb safety and fitted beavertail grip safety. Checkered cocobolo wood grips, comes with two Wilson 7-shot magazines. Frame is engraved "Tactical," both sides of frame with "TRP." Introduced 1998. From Springfield Armory.
Price: Standard with Armory Kote finish **$1,560.00**
Price: Standard, stainless steel **$1,409.00**
Price: Standard with Operator Light Rail Armory Kote **$1,573.00**

Springfield Armory 1911A1 High Capacity Pistol
Similar to Standard 1911A1, available in 45 ACP with 10-shot magazine. Commander-style hammer, walnut grips, beveled magazine well, plastic carrying case. Can accept higher-capacity Para-Ordnance magazines. Introduced 1993. From Springfield Armory.
Price: Mil-Spec 45 ACP **$559.00**
Price: 45 ACP Ultra Compact (3-1/2" bbl.) **$922.00**

Taurus PT-22

Taurus PT-24

Taurus PT-92

Taurus PT-100

Springfield Armory 1911A1 Champion Pistol
Similar to standard 1911A1, slide is 4". Available in 45 ACP only. Novak Night Sights. Delta hammer and cocobolo grips. Parkerized or stainless. Introduced 1989.
Price: Stainless **$886.00**

Springfield Armory Ultra Compact Pistol
Similar to 1911A1 Compact, shorter slide, 3.5" barrel, beavertail grip safety, beveled magazine well, Novak Low Mount or Novak Night Sights, Videki speed trigger, flared ejection port, stainless steel frame, blued slide, match grade barrel, rubber grips. Introduced 1996. From Springfield Armory.
Price: Stainless 45 ACP, Novak Tritium sights **$922.00**
NEW! Price: Lightweight Bi-Tone stainless **$1,184.00**

Springfield Armory Compact Lightweight Bi-Tone
Mates a Springfield Inc. Champion length slide with the shorter Ultra-Compact forged alloy frame for concealability. In 45 ACP.
Price: **$1,184.00**

Springfield Armory Trophy Match 1911A1 Pistol
Similar to Full Size model, 5" match barrel and slide, fully adjustable sights. From Springfield Armory.
Price: Trophy Match 45 ACP, stainless **$1,049.00**
Price: Trophy Match, 40 S&W, Polymer **$1,409.00**

SPRINGFIELD ARMORY MICRO-COMPACT 1911A1 PISTOL
Caliber: 45 ACP, 40 S&W 6+1 capacity. **Barrel:** 3" 1:16 LH. **Weight:** 24 oz. **Length:** 5.7". **Sights:** Novak LoMount tritium. Dovetail front. **Features:** Forged frame and slide, ambi thumb safety, extreme carry bevel treatment, lockable plastic case, 2 magazines.
Price: . . . . **$922.00 to $1,247.00**

SPRINGFIELD ARMORY DEFENDER
Caliber: 9mm, 40 S&W, 45 GAP. **Barrel:** 3". **Weight:** 23 oz. **Length:** NA **Sights:** Novak low mount. **Features:** Alloy frame, slide and barrel; adjustable trigger; Delta lightweight hammer; loaded chamber indicator.
Price: . . . . **NA**

STEYR M & S SERIES AUTO PISTOLS
Caliber: 9mm Para., 40 S&W, 357 SIG; 10-shot magazine. **Barrel:** 4" (3.58" for Model S). **Weight:** 28 oz. (22.5 oz. for Model S). **Length:** 7.05" overall (6.53" for Model S). **Grips:** Ultra-rigid polymer. **Sights:** Drift-adjustable, white-outline rear; white-triangle blade front. **Features:** Polymer frame; trigger-drop firing pin, manual and key-lock safeties; loaded chamber indicator; 5.5-lb. trigger pull; 111-degree grip. Introduced 2000. Imported from Austria by GSI Inc.
Price: Model M (full-sized frame with 4" barrel) **$609.95**
Price: Model S (compact frame with 3.58" barrel) **$609.95**
Price: Extra 10-shot magazines (Model M or S) **$39.00**

TAURUS MODEL PT-22/PT-25 AUTO PISTOLS
Caliber: 22 LR, 8-shot (PT 22); 25 ACP, 9-shot (PT 25). **Barrel:** 2.75". **Weight:** 12.3 oz. **Length:** 5.25" overall. **Grips:** Smooth rosewood or mother-of-pearl. **Sights:** Fixed. **Features:** Double action. Tip-up barrel for loading, cleaning. Blue, nickel, duo-tone or blue with gold accents. Introduced 1992. Made in U.S.A. by Taurus International.
Price: 22 LR, 25 ACP, blue, nickel or with duo-tone finish with rosewood grips **$219.00**
Price: 22 LR, 25 ACP, blue with gold trim, rosewood grips **$234.00**

Price: 22 LR, 25 ACP, blue, nickel or duo-tone finish with checkered wood grips **$219.00**
Price: 22 LR, 25 ACP, blue with gold trim, mother-of-pearl grips . . **$250.00**

TAURUS MODEL PT-24/7
Caliber: 9mm, 10+1 shot; 40 cal., 10+1 shot. **Barrel:** 4". **Weight:** 27.2 oz. **Length:** 7-18". **Grips:** RIBBER rubber-finned overlay on polymer. **Sights:** Adjustable. **Features:** Accessory rail, four safeties, blue or stainless finish. Introduced 2003. Imported from Brazil by Taurus International.
Price: 9mm **$578.00**
Price: 40 cal. **$594.00**

TAURUS MODEL PT-92 AUTO PISTOL
Caliber: 9mm Para., 10-shot mag. **Barrel:** 5". **Weight:** 34 oz. **Length:** 8.5" overall. **Grips:** Checkered rubber, rosewood, mother-of-pearl. **Sights:** Fixed notch rear. 3-dot sight system. Also offered with micrometer-click adjustable night sights. **Features:** Double action, ambidextrous 3-way hammer drop safety, allows cocked & locked carry. Blue, stainless steel, blue with gold highlights, stainless steel with gold highlights, forged aluminum frame, integral key-lock. .22 LR conversion kit available. Imported from Brazil by Taurus International.
Price: Blue . . . . **$578.00 to $672.00**

Taurus Model PT-99 Auto Pistol
Similar to PT-92, fully adjustable rear sight.
Price: Blue . . . . **$575.00 to $670.00**
Price: 22 Conversion kit for PT 92 and PT99 (includes barrel and slide) **$266.00**

TAURUS MODEL PT-100/101 AUTO PISTOL
Caliber: 40 S&W, 10-shot mag. **Barrel:** 5". **Weight:** 34 oz. **Length:** 8-1/2". **Grips:** Checkered rubber, rosewood, mother-of-pearl. **Sights:** 3-dot fixed or adjustable; night sights available. **Features:** Single/double action with three-position safety/decocker. Reintroduced in 2001. Imported by Taurus International.
Price: PT100 . . . . **$578.00 to $672.00**
Price: PT101 . . . . **$594.00 to $617.00**

TAURUS MODEL PT-111 MILLENNIUM PRO AUTO PISTOL
Caliber: 9mm Para., 10-shot mag. **Barrel:** 3.25". **Weight:** 18.7 oz. **Length:** 6-1/8" overall. **Grips:** Polymer. **Sights:** 3-dot fixed; night sights available. Low profile, 3-dot combat. **Features:** Double action only, polymer frame, matte stainless or blue steel slide, manual safety, integral key-lock. Deluxe models with wood grip inserts.
Price: . . . . **$445.00 to $539.00**

Taurus PT-132 Millennium Pro

Taurus PT-138 Millennium Pro

Taurus PT-140 Millennium Pro

Taurus PT-145 Millennium

Taurus PT-911

Taurus PT-938

Taurus PT-940

Taurus PT-945

Taurus Model PT-111 Millennium Titanium Pistol
Similar to PT-111, titanium slide, night sights.
Price: $586.00

TAURUS PT-132 MILLENNIUM PRO AUTO PISTOL
Caliber: 32 ACP, 10-shot mag. **Barrel:** 3.25". **Weight:** 18.7 oz. **Grips:** Polymer. **Sights:** 3-dot fixed; night sights available. **Features:** Double-action-only, polymer frame, matte stainless or blue steel slide, manual safety, integral key-lock action. Introduced 2001.
Price: . . . . $445.00 to $461.00

TAURUS PT-138 MILLENNIUM PRO SERIES
Caliber: 380 ACP, 10-shot mag. **Barrel:** 3.25". **Weight:** 18.7 oz. **Grips:** Polymer. **Sights:** Fixed 3-dot fixed. **Features:** Double-action-only, polymer frame, matte stainless or blue steel slide, manual safety, integral key-lock.
Price: . . . . $445.00 to $461.00

TAURUS PT-140 MILLENNIUM PRO AUTO PISTOL
Caliber: 40 S&W, 10-shot mag. **Barrel:** 3.25". **Weight:** 18.7 oz. **Grips:** Checkered polymer. **Sights:** 3-dot fixed; night sights available. **Features:** Double action only; matte stainless or blue steel slide, black polymer frame, manual safety, integral key-lock action. From Taurus International.
Price: . . . . $484.00 to $578.00

TAURUS PT-145 MILLENNIUM AUTO PISTOL
Caliber: 45 ACP, 10-shot mag. **Barrel:** 3.27". **Weight:** 23 oz. **Stock:** Checkered polymer. **Sights:** 3-dot fixed; night sights available. **Features:** Double-action only, matte stainless or blue steel slide, black polymer frame, manual safety, integral key-lock. From Taurus International.
Price: . . . . $484.00 to $578.00

TAURUS MODEL PT-911 AUTO PISTOL
Caliber: 9mm Para., 10-shot mag. **Barrel:** 4". **Weight:** 28.2 oz. **Length:** 7" overall. **Grips:** Checkered rubber, rosewood, mother-of-pearl. **Sights:** Fixed, 3-dot blue or stainless; night sights optional. **Features:** Double action, semi-auto ambidextrous 3-way hammer drop safety, allows cocked & locked carry. Blue, stainless steel, blue with gold highlights, or stainless steel with gold highlights, forged aluminum frame, integral key-lock.
Price: . . . . $523.00 to $617.00

TAURUS MODEL PT-938 AUTO PISTOL
Caliber: 380 ACP, 10-shot mag. **Barrel:** 3.72". **Weight:** 27 oz. **Length:** 6.5" overall. **Grips:** Checkered rubber. **Sights:** Fixed, 3-dot. **Features:** Double action, ambidextrous 3-way hammer drop allows cocked & locked carry. Forged aluminum frame. Integral key-lock. Imported by Taurus International.

Price: Blue $516.00
Price: Stainless $531.00

TAURUS MODEL PT-940 AUTO PISTOL
Caliber: 40 S&W, 10-shot mag. **Barrel:** 3-5/8". **Weight:** 28.2 oz. **Length:** 7" overall. **Grips:** Checkered rubber, rosewood or mother-of-pearl. **Sights:** Fixed, 3-dot blue or stainless; night sights optional. **Features:** Double action, semi-auto ambidextrous 3-way hammer drop safety, allows cocked & locked carry. Blue, stainless steel, blue with gold highlights, or stainless steel with gold highlights, forged aluminum frame, integral key-lock.
Price: . . . . $523.00 to $617.00

TAURUS MODEL PT-945 SERIES
Caliber: 45 ACP, 8-shot mag. **Barrel:** 4.25". **Weight:** 28.2/29.5 oz. **Length:** 7.48" overall. **Grips:** Checkered rubber, rosewood or mother-of-pearl. **Sights:** Fixed, 3-dot; night sights optional. **Features:** Double-action with ambidextrous 3-way hammer drop safety allows cocked & locked carry. Forged aluminum frame, PT-945C has ported barrel/slide. Blue, stainless, blue with gold highlights, stainless with gold highlights, integral key-lock. Introduced 1995. Imported by Taurus International.
Price: . . . . $563.00 to $641.00

Taurus PT-957

Walther PPK

Walther PPK/S

Walther P99

Walther P22

Wilkinson
Sherry

TAURUS MODEL PT-957 AUTO PISTOL
Caliber: 357 SIG, 10-shot mag. **Barrel:** 4". **Weight:** 28 oz. **Length:** 7" overall. **Grips:** Checkered rubber, rosewood or mother-of-pearl. **Sights:** Fixed, 3-dot blue or stainless; night sights optional. **Features:** Double-action, blue, stainless steel, blue with gold accents or stainless with gold accents, ported barrel/slide, three-position safety with decocking lever and ambidextrous safety. Forged aluminum frame, integral key-lock. Introduced 1999. Imported by Taurus International.
Price: .... **$525.00 to $620.00**
Price: Non-ported .... **$525.00 to $535.00**

TAURUS MODEL 922 SPORT PISTOL
Caliber: .22 LR, 10-shot magazine. **Barrel:** 6". **Weight:** 24.8 oz. **Length:** 9-1/8". **Grips:** Polymer. **Sights:** Adjustable. **Features:** Matte blue steel finish, machined target crown, polymer frame, single and double action, easy disassembly for cleaning.
Price: .... (blue) **$310.00**
Price: .... (stainless) **$328.00**

WALTHER PPK/S AMERICAN AUTO PISTOL
Caliber: 380 ACP, 7-shot magazine. **Barrel:** 3.27". **Weight:** 23-1/2 oz. **Length:** 6.1" overall. **Stocks:** Checkered plastic. **Sights:** Fixed, white markings. **Features:** Double action; manual safety blocks firing pin and drops hammer; chamber loaded indicator on 32 and 380; extra finger rest magazine provided. Made in the United States. Introduced 1980.
Price: 380 ACP only, blue **$563.00**
Price: As above, 32 ACP or 380 ACP, stainless **$543.00**

Walther PPK American Auto Pistol
Similar to Walther PPK/S except weighs 21 oz., has 6-shot capacity. Made in the U.S. Introduced 1986.
Price: Stainless, 32 ACP or 380 ACP **$543.00**
Price: Blue, 380 ACP only **$543.00**

WALTHER P99 AUTO PISTOL
Caliber: 9mm Para., 9x21, 40 S&W,10-shot magazine. **Barrel:** 4". **Weight:** 25 oz. **Length:** 7" overall. **Grips:** Textured polymer. **Sights:** Blade front (comes with three interchangeable blades for elevation adjustment), micrometer rear adjustable for windage. **Features:** Double-action mechanism with trigger safety, decock safety, internal striker safety; chamber loaded indicator; ambidextrous magazine release levers; polymer frame with interchangeable backstrap inserts. Comes with two magazines. Introduced 1997. Imported from Germany by Smith & Wesson U.S.A.
Price: **$665.00**

WALTHER P22 PISTOL
Caliber: 22 LR. **Barrel:** 3.4", 5". **Weight:** 19.6 oz. (3.4"), 20.3 oz. (5"). **Length:** 6.26", 7.83". **Grips:** NA. **Sights:** Interchangeable white dot, front, 2-dot adjustable, rear. **Features:** A rimfire version of the Walther P99 pistol, available in nickel slide with black frame, or green frame with black slide versions. Made in Germany and distributed in the U.S. by Smith & Wesson.
Price: From **$295.00**

WILKINSON SHERRY AUTO PISTOL
Caliber: 22 LR, 8-shot magazine. **Barrel:** 2-1/8". **Weight:** 9-1/4 oz. **Length:** 4-3/8" overall. **Grips:** Checkered black plastic. **Sights:** Fixed, groove. **Features:** Crossbolt safety locks the sear into the hammer. Available in all-blue finish or blue slide and trigger with gold frame. Introduced 1985.
Price: **$280.00**

WILKINSON LINDA AUTO PISTOL
Caliber: 9mm Para. **Barrel:** 8-5/16". **Weight:** 4 lbs., 13 oz. **Length:** 12-1/4" overall. **Grips:** Checkered black plastic pistol grip, walnut forend. **Sights:** Protected blade front, aperture rear. **Features:** Semi-auto only. Straight blowback action. Crossbolt safety. Removable barrel. From Wilkinson Arms.
Price: **$675.00**

Includes models suitable for several forms of competition and other sporting purposes.

Baer 1911 Ultimate Master

BF Ultimate

Baer 1911 Bullseye Wadcutter

Browning Buck Mark Target 5.5

Browning Buck Mark Bullseye

BAER 1911 ULTIMATE MASTER COMBAT PISTOL
Caliber: 9x23, 38 Super, 400 Cor-Bon 45 ACP (others available), 10-shot magazine. **Barrel:** 5", 6"; Baer NM. **Weight:** 37 oz. **Length:** 8.5" overall. **Grips:** Checkered rosewood. **Sights:** Baer dovetail front, low-mount Bo-Mar rear with hidden leaf. **Features:** Full-house competition gun. Baer forged NM blued steel frame and double serrated slide; Baer triple port, tapered cone compensator; fitted slide to frame; lowered, flared ejection port; Baer reverse recoil plug; full-length guide rod; recoil buff; beveled magazine well; Baer Commander hammer, sear; Baer extended ambidextrous safety, extended ejector, checkered slide stop, beavertail grip safety with pad, extended magazine release button; Baer speed trigger. Made in U.S.A. by Les Baer Custom, Inc.
Price: Compensated, open sights **$2,476.00**
Price: 6" Model 400 Cor-Bon **$2,541.00**

BAER 1911 NATIONAL MATCH HARDBALL PISTOL
Caliber: 45 ACP, 7-shot magazine. **Barrel:** 5". **Weight:** 37 oz. **Length:** 8.5" overall. **Grips:** Checkered walnut. **Sights:** Baer dovetail front with under-cut post, low-mount Bo-Mar rear with hidden leaf. **Features:** Baer NM forged steel frame, double serrated slide and barrel with stainless bushing; slide fitted to frame; Baer match trigger with 4-lb. pull; polished feed ramp, throated barrel; checkered front strap, arched mainspring housing; Baer beveled magazine well; lowered, flared ejection port; tuned extractor; Baer extended ejector, checkered slide stop; recoil buff. Made in U.S.A. by Les Baer Custom, Inc.
Price: **$1,335.00**

Baer 1911 Bullseye Wadcutter Pistol
Similar to National Match Hardball except designed for wadcutter loads only. Polished feed ramp and barrel throat; Bo-Mar rib on slide; full length recoil rod; Baer speed trigger with 3-1/2-lb. pull; Baer deluxe hammer and sear; Baer beavertail grip safety with pad; flat mainspring housing checkered 20 lpi. Blue finish; checkered walnut grips. Made in U.S.A. by Les Baer Custom, Inc.
Price: From **$1,495.00**
Price: With 6" barrel, from **$1,690.00**

BF ULTIMATE SILHOUETTE HB SINGLE SHOT PISTOL
Caliber: 7mm U.S., 22 LR Match and 100 other chamberings. **Barrel:** 10.75" Heavy Match Grade with 11-degree target crown. **Weight:** 3 lbs., 15 oz. **Length:** 16" overall. **Grips:** Thumbrest target style. **Sights:** Bo-Mar/Bond ScopeRib I Combo with hooded post front adjustable for height and width, rear notch available in .032", .062", .080" and .100" widths; 1/2-MOA clicks. **Features:** Designed to meet maximum rules for IHMSA Production Gun. Hand fitted and headspaced. Etched receiver; gold-colored trigger. Introduced 1988. Made in U.S.A. by E. Arthur Brown Co. Inc.
Price: **$669.00**

BF Classic Hunting Pistol
Similar to BF Ultimate Silhouette HB Single Shot Pistol, except no sights; drilled and tapped for scope mount. Barrels from 8" to 15". Variety of options offered. Made in U.S.A. by E. Arthur Brown Co. Inc.
Price: **$599.00**

BROWNING BUCK MARK TARGET 5.5
Caliber: 22 LR, 10-shot magazine. **Barrel:** 5-1/2" barrel with .900" diameter. **Weight:** 35-1/2 oz. **Length:** 9-5/8" overall. **Grips:** Contoured walnut grips with thumbrest, or finger-groove walnut. **Sights:** Hooded sights mounted on scope base that accepts optical or reflex sight. Rear sight is Browning fully adjustable Pro Target, front sight is adjustable post that customizes to different widths, can be adjusted for height. **Features:** Matte blue finish. Introduced 1990. From Browning.
Price: **$496.00**

Browning Buck Mark Field 5.5
Same as Target 5.5, hoodless ramp-style front sight and low profile rear sight. Matte blue finish, contoured or finger-groove walnut stocks. Introduced 1991.
Price: **$496.00**

Browning Buck Mark Bullseye
Similar to Buck Mark Silhouette, 7-1/4" heavy barrel with three flutes per side; trigger adjusts from 2-1/2 to 5 lbs.; specially designed rosewood target or three-finger-groove stocks with competition-style heel rest, or with contoured rubber grip. Overall length 11-5/16", weighs 36 oz. Introduced 1996. Made in U.S.A. From Browning.
Price: With ambidextrous moulded composite stocks **$468.00**
Price: With rosewood stocks, or wraparound finger groove **$604.00**

Colt Special Combat

Competitor Single Shot

EAA Witness Gold Team

COLT DEFENDER XSE
Caliber: 45 ACP. **Barrel:** 3", 4.25" and 5". **Weight:** 23-40 oz. **Sights:** Fixed. **Features:** Rubber wraparound or rosewood grips; single-action; carbon or stainless steel; blue or stainless finish, 7- or 8-round magazines.
Price: Blue **$9500.00**
Price: Stainless **$1,100.00**

COLT GOLD CUP
Caliber: 45 ACP. **Barrel:** 5". **Weight:** 39 oz. **Sights:** Dovetail front, BoMar-style rear; or Colt adjustable staked front. **Features:** Stainless or blue finish; adjustable trigger; furnished with 7- and 8-round magazines.
Price: Blued **$1,300.00**
Price: Stainless **$1,400.00**

COLT GUNSITE PISTOL
Caliber: 45 ACP. **Barrel:** 5", 4.5". **Weight:** 38 to 36 oz. **Sights:** Heinie front, Novak rear. **Features:** Brushed stainless or blue finish; short trigger; Wilson safety; grip safety. Furnished with two 6- and 8-round magazines.
Price: **$1,400.00**

COLT COMBAT GOVERNMENT
Caliber: 45 ACP, 38 Super. **Barrel:** 5". **Weight:** 39 oz. **Sights:** Dovetail front, Bo-Mar-style rear. **Features:** Chromed or blued slide; ambidextrous thumb safety; 8-round standard with bumper magazines.
Price: **$2,000.00**

COLT MODEL 1991/2991
Caliber: 45 ACP, 28 Super. **Barrel:** 5". **Weight:** 39 oz. **Sight:** Fixed white dot style. **Features:** Stainless or blue finish; furnished with 7-round magazines.
Price: . . . . **$870.00 to $980.00**

COLT GOLD CUP MODEL O PISTOL
Caliber: 45 ACP, 8-shot magazine. **Barrel:** 5", with new design bushing. **Weight:** 39 oz. **Length:** 8-1/2". **Grips:** Checkered rubber composite with silver-plated medallion. **Sights:** Patridge-style front, Bo-Mar-style rear adjustable for windage and elevation, sight radius 6-3/4". **Features:** Arched or flat housing; wide, grooved trigger with adjustable stop; ribbed-top slide, hand fitted, with improved ejection port.
Price: Blue **$1,300.00**
Price: Stainless **$1,400.00**

COLT SPECIAL COMBAT GOVERNMENT
Caliber: 45 ACP. **Barrel:** 5". **Weight:** NA. **Length:** 8-1/2". **Grips:** Rosewood w/double diamond checkering pattern. **Sights:** Clark dovetail, front; Bo-Mar adjustable, rear. **Features:** A competition-ready pistol with enhancements such as skeletonized trigger, upswept grip safety, custom tuned action, polished feed ramp. Blue or satin nickel finish. Introduced 2003. Made in U.S.A. by Colt's Mfg. Co.
Price: **$2,000.00**

COMPETITOR SINGLE SHOT PISTOL
Caliber: 22 LR through 50 Action Express, including belted magnums. **Barrel:** 14" standard; 10.5" silhouette; 16" optional. **Weight:** About 59 oz. (14" bbl.). **Length:** 15.12" overall. **Grips:** Ambidextrous; synthetic (standard) or laminated or natural wood. **Sights:** Ramp front, adjustable rear. **Features:** Rotary canon-type action cocks on opening; cammed ejector; interchangeable barrels, ejectors. Adjustable single stage trigger, sliding thumb safety and trigger safety. Matte blue finish. Introduced 1988. From Competitor Corp., Inc.
Price: 14", standard calibers, synthetic grip **$414.95**
Price: Extra barrels . . . . **From $159.95**

CZ 75 CHAMPION COMPETITION PISTOL
Caliber: 9mm Para., 9x21, 40 S&W, 10-shot mag. **Barrel:** 4.49". **Weight:** 35 oz. **Length:** 9.44" overall. **Grips:** Black rubber. **Sights:** Blade front, fully adjustable rear. **Features:** Single-action trigger mechanism; three-port compensator (40 S&W, 9mm have two port) full-length guide rod; extended magazine release; ambidextrous safety; flared magazine well; fully adjustable match trigger. Introduced 1999. Imported from the Czech Republic by CZ-USA.
Price: 9mm Para., 9x21, 40 S&W, dual-tone finish **$1,551.00**

CZ 75 ST IPSC AUTO PISTOL
Caliber: 40 S&W, 10-shot magazine. **Barrel:** 5.12". **Weight:** 2.9 lbs. **Length:** 8.86" overall. **Grips:** Checkered walnut. **Sights:** Fully adjustable rear. **Features:** Single-action mechanism; extended slide release and ambidextrous safety; full-length slide rail; double slide serrations. Introduced 1999. Imported from the Czech Republic by CZ-USA.
Price: Dual-tone finish **$1,038.00**

EAA/BAIKAL IZH-35 AUTO PISTOL
Caliber: 22 LR, 5-shot mag. **Barrel:** 6". **Grips:** Walnut; fully adjustable right-hand target-style. **Sights:** Fully adjustable rear, blade front; detachable scope mount. **Features:** Hammer-forged target barrel; machined steel receiver; adjustable trigger; manual slide hold back, grip and manual trigger-bar disconnect safeties; cocking indicator. Introduced 2000. Imported from Russia by European American Armory.
Price: Blued finish **$489.00**

EAA WITNESS GOLD TEAM AUTO
Caliber: 9mm Para., 9x21, 38 Super, 40 S&W, 45 ACP. **Barrel:** 5.1". **Weight:** 44 oz. **Length:** 10.5" overall. **Grips:** Checkered walnut, competition-style. **Sights:** Square post front, fully adjustable rear. **Features:** Triple-chamber cone compensator; competition SA trigger; extended safety and magazine release; competition hammer; beveled magazine well; beavertail grip. Hand-fitted major components. Hard chrome finish. Match-grade barrel. From E.A.A. Custom Shop. Introduced 1992. From European American Armory.
Price: **$1,699.00**

EAA Witness Silver Team Auto
Similar to Witness Gold Team with double-chamber compensator, oval magazine release, black rubber grips, double-dip blue finish. Super Sight and drilled and tapped for scope mount. Introduced 1992. From European American Armory Custom Shop.
Price: 9mm Para., 9x21, 38 Super, 40 S&W, 45 ACP **$968.00**

Freedom Arms 83 22 Silhouette Class

Hammerli SP 20

High Standard Trophy

ED BROWN CLASSIC CUSTOM PISTOL
Caliber: 45 ACP. **Barrel:** 5". **Weight:** 39 oz. **Grips:** Hogue exotic wood. **Sights:** Modified ramp or post, front; fully-adjustable Bo-Mar, rear. **Features:** Highly-polished slide, two-piece guide rod, oversize mag release, ambidextrous safety.
Price: **$2,895.00**

ED BROWN CLASS A LIMITED
Caliber: 45 ACP, 400 Cor-Bon, 10mm, 40 S&W, 357 SIG, 38 Super, 9x23, 9mm Luger, 7-shot magazine. **Barrel:** 4.25", 5". **Weight:** 34 to 39 oz. **Grips:** Hogue exotic wood. **Sights:** Customer preference, front; fixed Novak low-mount or fully-adjustable Bo-Mar, rear. **Features:** Checkered forestrap and mainspring housing, matte finished top sighting surface. Many options available.
Price: **$2,250.00**

ENTRÉPRISE TOURNAMENT SHOOTER MODEL I
Caliber: 45 ACP, 10-shot mag. **Barrel:** 6". **Weight:** 40 oz. **Length:** 8.5" overall. **Grips:** Black ultra-slim double diamond checkered synthetic. **Sights:** Dovetailed Patridge front, adjustable rear. **Features:** Oversized magazine release button; flared magazine well; fully machined parallel slide rails; front and rear slide serrations; serrated top of slide; stainless ramped bull barrel with fully supported chamber; full-length guide rod with plug; stainless firing pin; match extractor; polished ramp; tuned match extractor; black oxide. Introduced 1998. Made in U.S.A. by Entréprise Arms.
Price: **$2,300.00**
Price: TSMIII (Satin chrome finish, two-piece guide rod) **$2,700.00**

EXCEL INDUSTRIES CP-45, XP-45 AUTO PISTOL
Caliber: 45 ACP, 6-shot & 10-shot mags. **Barrel:** 3-1/4". **Weight:** 31 oz. & 25 oz. **Length:** 6-3/8" overall. **Grips:** Checkered black nylon. **Sights:** Fully adjustable rear. **Features:** Stainless steel frame and slide; single action with external hammer and firing pin block, manual thumb safety; last-shot hold open. Includes gun lock and cleaning kit. Introduced 2001. Made in U.S.A. by Excel Industries Inc.
Price: CP-45 .... **$425.00**
Price: XP-45 .... **$465.00**

FEINWERKEBAU AW93 TARGET PISTOL
Caliber: 22. **Barrel:** 6". **Grips:** Fully adjustable orthopaedic. **Sights:** Fully adjustable micrometer. **Features:** Advanced Russian design with German craftmanship. Imported from Germany by Nygord Precision Products.
Price: **$1,495.00**

FREEDOM ARMS MODEL 83 22 FIELD GRADE SILHOUETTE CLASS
Caliber: 22 LR, 5-shot cylinder. **Barrel:** 10". **Weight:** 63 oz. **Length:** 15.5" overall. **Grips:** Black Micarta. **Sights:** Removable Patridge front blade; Iron Sight Gun Works rear, click adjustable for windage and elevation (optional adj. front sight and hood). **Features:** Stainless steel, matte finish, manual sliding-bar safety system; dual firing pins, lightened hammer for fast lock time, pre-set trigger stop. Introduced 1991. Made in U.S.A. by Freedom Arms.
Price: Silhouette Class **$1,901.75**
Price: Extra fitted 22 WMR cylinder **$264.00**

FREEDOM ARMS MODEL 83 CENTERFIRE SILHOUETTE MODELS
Caliber: 357 Mag., 41 Mag., 44 Mag.; 5-shot cylinder. **Barrel:** 10", 9" (357 Mag. only). **Weight:** 63 oz. (41 Mag.). **Length:** 15.5", 14-1/2" (357 only). **Grips:** Pachmayr Presentation. **Sights:** Iron Sight Gun Works silhouette rear sight, replaceable adjustable front sight blade with hood. **Features:** Stainless steel, matte finish, manual sliding-bar safety system. Made in U.S.A. by Freedom Arms.
Price: Silhouette Models **$1,634.85**

GAUCHER GP SILHOUETTE PISTOL
Caliber: 22 LR, single shot. **Barrel:** 10". **Weight:** 42.3 oz. **Length:** 15.5" overall. **Grips:** Stained hardwood. **Sights:** Hooded post on ramp front, open rear adjustable for windage and elevation. **Features:** Matte chrome barrel, blued bolt and sights. Other barrel lengths available on special order. Introduced 1991. Imported by Mandall Shooting Supplies.
Price: **$425.00**

HAMMERLI SP 20 TARGET PISTOL
Caliber: 22 LR, 32 S&W. **Barrel:** 4.6". **Weight:** 34.6-41.8 oz. **Length:** 11.8" overall. **Grips:** Anatomically shaped synthetic Hi-Grip available in five sizes. **Sights:** Integral front in three widths, adjustable rear with changeable notch widths. **Features:** Extremely low-level sight line; anatomically shaped trigger; adjustable JPS buffer system for different recoil characteristics. Receiver available in red, blue, gold, violet or black. Introduced 1998. Imported from Switzerland by SIGARMS, Inc and Hammerli Pistols USA.
Price: Hammerli 22 LR **$1,668.00**
Price: Hammerli 32 S&W **$1,743.00**

HAMMERLI X-ESSE SPORT PISTOL
An all-steel .22 LR target pistol with a Hi-Grip in a new anatomical shape and an adjustable hand rest. Made in Switzerland. Introduced 2003.
Price: **$710.00**

HARRIS GUNWORKS SIGNATURE JR. LONG RANGE PISTOL
Caliber: Any suitable caliber. **Barrel:** To customer specs. **Weight:** 5 lbs. **Stock:** Gunworks fiberglass. **Sights:** None furnished; comes with scope rings. **Features:** Right- or left-hand benchrest action of titanium or stainless steel; single shot or repeater. Comes with bipod. Introduced 1992. Made in U.S.A. by Harris Gunworks, Inc.
Price: **$2,700.00**

HIGH STANDARD TROPHY TARGET PISTOL
Caliber: 22 LR, 10-shot mag. **Barrel:** 5-1/2" bull or 7-1/4" fluted. **Weight:** 44 oz. **Length:** 9.5" overall. **Stock:** Checkered hardwood with thumbrest. **Sights:** Undercut ramp front, frame-mounted micro-click rear adjustable for windage and elevation; drilled and tapped for scope mounting. **Features:** Gold-plated trigger, slide lock, safety-lever and magazine release; stippled front grip and backstrap; adjustable trigger and sear. Barrel weights optional. From High Standard Manufacturing Co., Inc.
Price: 5-1/2", scope base **$540.00**
Price: 7.25" **$689.00**
Price: 7.25", scope base **$625.00**

High Standard Victor

Kimber Super Match II

HIGH STANDARD VICTOR TARGET PISTOL
Caliber: 22 LR, 10-shot magazine. **Barrel:** 4-1/2" or 5-1/2"; push-button takedown. **Weight:** 46 oz. **Length:** 9.5" overall. **Stock:** Checkered hardwood with thumbrest. **Sights:** Undercut ramp front, micro-click rear adjustable for windage and elevation. Also available with scope mount, rings, no sights. **Features:** Stainless steel construction. Full-length vent rib. Gold-plated trigger, slide lock, safety-lever and magazine release; stippled front grip and backstrap; polished slide; adjustable trigger and sear. Comes with barrel weight. From High Standard Manufacturing Co., Inc.
Price: 4-1/2" scope base **$564.00**
Price: 5-1/2", sights **$625.00**
Price: 5-1/2" scope base **$564.00**

KIMBER SUPER MATCH II
Caliber: 45 ACP, 7-shot magazine. **Barrel:** 5". **Weight:** 38 oz. **Length:** 18.7" overall. **Sights:** Blade front, Kimber fully adjustable rear. **Features:** Guaranteed shoot 1" group at 25 yards. Stainless steel frame, black KimPro slide; two-piece magazine well; premium aluminum match-grade trigger; 30 lpi front strap checkering; stainless match-grade barrel; ambidextrous safety; special Custom Shop markings. Introduced 1999. Made in U.S.A. by Kimber Mfg., Inc.
Price: **$1,986.00**

KORTH MATCH REVOLVER
Caliber: 357 Mag., 38 Special, 32 S&W Long, 9mm Para., 22 WMR, 22 LR. **Barrel:** 5-1/4", 6". **Grips:** Adjustable match of oiled walnut with matte finish. **Sights:** Fully adjustable rear sight leaves (width of sight notch: 3.4mm, 3.5mm, 3.6mm); undercut Patridge, front. **Trigger:** Equipped with machined trigger shoe. Interchangeable caliber cylinders available as well as a variety of finishes. Made in Germany.
Price: From **$7,619.00**

MORINI MODEL 84E FREE PISTOL
Caliber: 22 LR, single shot. **Barrel:** 11.4". **Weight:** 43.7 oz. **Length:** 19.4" overall. **Grips:** Adjustable match type with stippled surfaces. **Sights:** Interchangeable blade front, match-type fully adjustable rear. **Features:** Fully adjustable electronic trigger. Introduced 1995. Imported from Switzerland by Nygord Precision Products.
Price: **$1,450.00**

PARDINI MODEL SP, HP TARGET PISTOLS
Caliber: 22 LR, 32 S&W, 5-shot magazine. **Barrel:** 4.7". **Weight:** 38.9 oz. **Length:** 11.6" overall. **Grips:** Adjustable; stippled walnut; match type. **Sights:** Interchangeable blade front, interchangeable, fully adjustable rear. **Features:** Fully adjustable match trigger. Introduced 1995. Imported from Italy by Nygord Precision Products.
Price: Model SP (22 LR) **$995.00**
Price: Model HP (32 S&W) **$1,095.00**

PARDINI GP RAPID FIRE MATCH PISTOL
Caliber: 22 Short, 5-shot magazine. **Barrel:** 4.6". **Weight:** 43.3 oz. **Length:** 11.6" overall. **Grips:** Wraparound stippled walnut. **Sights:** Interchangeable post front, fully adjustable match rear. Introduced 1995. Imported from Italy by Nygord Precision Products.
Price: Model GP **$1,095.00**
Price: Model GP-E Electronic, has special parts **$1,595.00**

PARDINI K22 FREE PISTOL
Caliber: 22 LR, single shot. **Barrel:** 9.8". **Weight:** 34.6 oz. **Length:** 18.7" overall. **Grips:** Wrap-around walnut; adjustable match type. **Sights:**

Interchangeable post front, fully adjustable match open rear. **Features:** Removable, adjustable match trigger. Barrel weights mount above the barrel. Upgraded model introduced in 2002. Imported from Italy by Nygord Precision Products.
Price: **$1,295.00**

PARDINI GT45 TARGET PISTOL
Caliber: 45, 9mm, 40 S&W. **Barrel:** 5", 6". **Grips:** Checkered forestrap. **Sights:** Interchangeable post front, fully adjustable match open rear. **Features:** Ambi-safeties, trigger pull adjustable. Fits Helweg Glock holsters for defense shooters. Imported from Italy by Nygord Precision Products.
Price: 5" **$1,050.00**
Price: 6" **$1,125.00**
Price: Frame mount available .... **$75.00 extra**
Price: Slide mount available .... **$35.00 extra**

PARDINI/NYGORD "MASTER" TARGET PISTOL
Caliber: 22 cal. **Barrel:** 5-1/2". **Grips:** Semi-wraparound. **Sights:** Micrometer rear and red dot. **Features:** Reciprocating internal weight barrel shroud. Imported from Italy by Nygord Precision Products.
Price: **$1,145.00**

RUGER MARK III TARGET MODEL AUTOLOADING PISTOL
Caliber: 22 LR, 10-shot magazine. **Barrel:** 6-7/8". **Weight:** 42 oz. **Length:** 11-1/8" overall. **Grips:** Checkered composition grip panels. **Sights:** .125" blade front, micro-click rear, adjustable for windage and elevation, loaded chamber indicator; integral lock, magazine disconnect. Sight radius 9-3/8". Plastic case with lock included. **Features:** Introduced 1982.
Price: Blued (MK-678) **$382.00**
Price: Stainless models .... **$483.00 to $567.00**

Ruger Mark III Government Target Model
Same gun as Mark III Target Model except has 6-7/8" barrel, higher sights and is roll marked "Government Target Model" on right side of receiver below rear sight. Identical in all aspects to military model except markings. Comes with factory test target, also lockable plastic case. Introduced 1987.
Price: Blued (MK-678G) **$425.00**
Price: Stainless (KMK-678G) **$509.00**

Ruger Stainless Competition Model Pistol
Similar to Mark III Government Target Model stainless pistol, 6-7/8" slab-sided barrel; receiver top is fitted with Ruger scope base of blued, chrome-moly steel; has Ruger 1" stainless scope rings for mounting variety of optical sights; checkered laminated grip panels with right-hand thumbrest. Blued open sights with 9-1/4" radius. Overall length 11-1/8", weight 45 oz. Case and lock included. Introduced 1991.
Price: KMK III 678 and 678 GC .... **$382.00 to $555.00**

Ruger Mark III Bull Barrel
Same gun as Target Model except has 5-1/2" or 10" heavy barrel. Weight with 5-1/2" barrel is 42 oz. Case with lock included.
Price: Blued (MKIII-512) **$382.00**
Price: Stainless (KMKIII-512) **$483.00**

Smith & Wesson Model 41

Smith & Wesson Model 22A

Smith & Wesson Model 22S

Springfield, Inc. 1911A1
Bullseye Wadcutter

SAFARI ARMS BIG DEUCE PISTOL
Caliber: 45 ACP, 7-shot magazine. **Barrel:** 6", 416 stainless steel. **Weight:** 40.3 oz. **Length:** 9.5" overall. **Grips:** Smooth walnut. **Sights:** Ramped blade front, LPA adjustable rear. **Features:** Beavertail grip safety; extended thumb safety and slide release; Commander-style hammer. Throated, polished and tuned. Parkerized matte black slide with satin stainless steel frame. Introduced 1995. Made in U.S.A. by Safari Arms, Inc.
Price: $714.00

SMITH & WESSON MODEL 41 TARGET
Caliber: 22 LR, 10-shot clip. **Barrel:** 5-1/2", 7". **Weight:** 41 oz. (5-1/2" barrel). **Length:** 10-1/2" overall (5-1/2" barrel). **Grips:** Checkered walnut with modified thumbrest, usable with either hand. **Sights:** 1/8" Patridge on ramp base; micro-click rear adjustable for windage and elevation. **Features:** 3/8" wide, grooved trigger; adjustable trigger stop drilled and tapped.
Price: S&W Bright Blue, either barrel $1,062.00

SMITH & WESSON MODEL 22A TARGET PISTOL
Caliber: 22 LR, 10-shot magazine. **Barrel:** 5-1/2" bull. **Weight:** 39 oz. **Length:** 9-1/2" overall. **Grips:** Dymondwood® with ambidextrous thumbrests and flared bottom or rubber soft touch with thumbrest. **Sights:** Patridge front, fully adjustable rear. **Features:** Sight bridge with Weaver-style integral optics mount; alloy frame, stainless barrel and slide; blue finish. Introduced 1997. Made in U.S.A. by Smith & Wesson.
Price: $407.00
Price: HiViz front sight $429.00
Price: Camo model $367.00
Price: Two-tone model $401.00
Price: Light barrel model $324.00
Price: 4" bbl. $293.00
Price: 7" bbl. $367.00

Smith & Wesson Model 22S Target Pistol
Similar to the Model 22A except has stainless steel frame. Introduced 1997. Made in U.S.A. by Smith & Wesson.
Price: $434.00
Price: HiViz front sight $453.00

SPRINGFIELD ARMORY 1911A1 BULLSEYE WADCUTTER PISTOL
Caliber: 38 Super, 45 ACP. **Barrel:** 5". **Weight:** 45 oz. **Length:** 8.59" overall (5" barrel). **Grips:** Checkered walnut. **Sights:** Bo-Mar rib with undercut blade front, fully adjustable rear. **Features:** Built for wadcutter loads only. Has full-length recoil spring guide rod, fitted Videki speed trigger with 3.5-lb. pull; match Commander hammer and sear; beavertail grip safety; lowered and flared ejection port; tuned extractor; fitted slide to frame; recoil buffer system; beveled and polished magazine well; checkered front strap and steel mainspring housing (flat housing standard); polished and throated National Match barrel and bushing. Comes with two magazines, plastic carrying case, test target. Introduced 1992. From Springfield Armory.
Price: $1,499.00
Price: Adj. Target $1,049.00
Price: M1911SC, Commander-style $1,029.00

Springfield Armory Basic Competition Pistol
Has low-mounted Bo-Mar adjustable rear sight, undercut blade front; match throated barrel and bushing; polished feed ramp; lowered and flared ejection port; fitted Videki speed trigger with tuned 3.5-lb. pull; fitted slide to frame; recoil buffer system; checkered walnut grips; serrated, arched mainspring housing. Comes with two magazines with slam pads, plastic carrying case. Introduced 1992. From Springfield Armory.
Price: 45 ACP, blue, 5" only $1,295.00

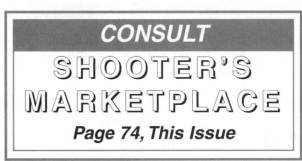

CONSULT

SHOOTER'S

MARKETPLACE

Page 74, This Issue

Springfield, Inc. Expert

Springfield, Inc. 1911A1 Trophy Match

Springfield, Inc. Distinguished

Springfield, Inc. N.M. Hardball

Springfield Armory Expert Pistol

Similar to the Competition Pistol except has triple-chamber tapered cone compensator on match barrel with dovetailed front sight; lowered and flared ejection port; fully tuned for reliability; fitted slide to frame; extended ambidextrous thumb safety, extended magazine release button; beavertail grip safety; Pachmayr wraparound grips. Comes with two magazines, plastic carrying case. Introduced 1992. From Springfield Armory.

Price: 45 ACP, Duo-tone finish **$1,724.00**
Price: Expert Ltd. (non-compensated) **$1,624.00**

Springfield Armory Distinguished Pistol

Has all the features of the 1911A1 Expert except is full-house pistol with deluxe Bo-Mar low-mounted adjustable rear sight; full-length recoil spring guide rod and recoil spring retainer; checkered frontstrap; S&A magazine well; walnut grips. Hard chrome finish. Comes with two magazines, plastic carrying case. From Springfield Armory.

Price: 45 ACP **$2,445.00**
Price: Distinguished Limited (non-compensated) **$2,345.00**

Springfield Armory 1911A1 N.M. Hardball Pistol

Has Bo-Mar adjustable rear sight with undercut front blade; fitted match Videki trigger with 4-lb. pull; fitted slide to frame; throated National Match barrel and bushing; recoil buffer system; tuned extractor; Herrett walnut grips. Comes with two magazines, plastic carrying case, test target. Introduced 1992. From Springfield Armory

Price: 45 ACP, blue **$1,336.00**

Springfield Armory Leatham Legend TGO Series Pistols

Three models of 5" barrel, 45 ACP 1911 pistols built for serious competition. TGO 1 has deluxe low mount Bo-Mar rear sight, Dawson fiber optics front sight, 3.5 lb. trigger pull. TGO 2 has Bo-Mar low mount adjustable rear sight, Dawson fiber optic front sight, 4.5 to 5 lb. trigger pull. TGO 3 has Springfield Armory fully adjustable rear sight with low mount BoMar cut Dawson fiber optic front sight, 4.5 to 5 lb. trigger.

Price: TGO 1 . . . . **$2,999.00**
Price: TGO 2 . . . . **$1,899.00**
Price: TGO 3 . . . . **$1,295.00**

Springfield Armory Trophy Match Pistol

Similar to Springfield Armory's Full Size model, but designed for bullseye and action shooting competition. Available with a Service Model 5" frame with matching slide and barrel in 5" and 6" lengths. Fully adjustable sights, checkered frame front strap, match barrel and bushing. In 45 ACP only. From Springfield Inc.

Price: **$1,248.00**

STI EAGLE 5.0, 6.0 PISTOL

Caliber: 9mm, 9x21, 38 & 40 Super, 40 S&W, 10mm, 45 ACP, 10-shot magazine. **Barrel:** 5", 6" bull. **Weight:** 34.5 oz. **Length:** 8.62" overall. **Grips:** Checkered polymer. **Sights:** STI front, Novak or Heine rear. **Features:** Standard frames plus 7 others; adjustable match trigger; skeletonized hammer; extended grip safety with locator pad. Introduced 1994. Made in U.S.A. by STI International.

Price: . . . . (5.0 Eagle) **$1,794.00**, (6.0 Eagle) **$1,894.00**

STI EXECUTIVE PISTOL

Caliber: 40 S&W. **Barrel:** 5" bull. **Weight:** 39 oz. **Length:** 8-5/8". **Grips:** Gray polymer. **Sights:** Dawson fiber optic, front; STI adjustable rear. **Features:** Stainless mag. well, front and rear serrations on slide. Made in U.S.A. by STI.

Price: **$2,389.00**

STI TROJAN

Caliber: 9mm, 38 Super, 40S&W, 45 ACP. **Barrel:** 5", 6". **Weight:** 36 oz. **Length:** 8.5". **Grips:** Rosewood. **Sights:** STI front with STI adjustable rear. **Features:** Stippled front strap, flat top slide, one-piece steel guide rod.

Price: (Trojan 5") **$1,024.00**
Price: (Trojan 6", not available in 38 Super) **$1,232.50**

WALTHER GSP MATCH PISTOL

Caliber: 22 LR, 32 S&W Long (GSP-C), 5-shot magazine. **Barrel:** 4.22". **Weight:** 44.8 oz. (22 LR), 49.4 oz. (32). **Length:** 11.8" overall. **Grips:** Walnut. **Sights:** Post front, match rear adjustable for windage and elevation. **Features:** Available with either 2.2-lb. (1000 gm) or 3-lb. (1360 gm) trigger. Spare magazine, barrel weight, tools supplied. Imported from Germany by Nygord Precision Products.

Price: GSP, with case **$1,495.00**
Price: GSP-C, with case **$1,595.00**

Includes models suitable for hunting and competitive courses of fire, both police and international.

Comanche III

Dan Wesson Firearms
Model 445 Supermag

ARMSPORT MODEL 4540 REVOLVER
Caliber: 38 Special. **Barrel:** 4". **Weight:** 32 oz. **Length:** 9" overall. **Sights:** Fixed rear, blade front. **Features:** Ventilated rib; blued finish. Imported from Argentina by Armsport Inc.
Price: **$140.00**

COLT SINGLE-ACTION ARMY
Caliber: 32-20, 38 Special, 357 Magnum, 38-40, 44-4-, 44 Special, 45 Long Colt. **Barrel:** 4.7 5", 5.5", 7.5". **Weight:** 40-44 oz. **Sights:** Blade front, notch rear. **Features:** Available in black powder and sheriff's models; nickel, blued or case-hardened frame; 6-round cylinder.
Price: . . . . (Blued) **$1,380.00**; (Stainless) **$1,530.00**

COMANCHE I, II, III DA REVOLVERS
Features: Adjustable sights. Blue or stainless finish. Distributed by SGS Importers.
Price: I 22 LR, 6" bbl., 9-shot, blue **$236.95**
Price: I 22LR, 6" bbl., 9-shot, stainless **$258.95**
Price: II 38 Special, 3", 4" bbl., 6-shot, blue **$219.95**
Price: II 38 Special, 4" bbl., 6-shot, stainless **$236.95**
Price: III 357 Mag, 3", 4", 6" bbl., 6-shot, blue **$253.95**
Price: III 357 Mag, 3", 4", 6" bbl., 6-shot, stainless **$274.95**
Price: II 38 Special, 3" bbl., 6-shot, stainless steel **$236.95**

DAN WESSON FIREARMS MODEL 722 SILHOUETTE REVOLVER
Caliber: 22 LR, 6-shot. **Barrel:** 10" vented heavy. **Weight:** 53 oz. **Grips:** Combat style. **Sights:** Patridge-style front, .080" narrow notch rear. **Features:** Single action only. Satin brushed stainless finish. Reintroduced 1997. Made in U.S.A. by Dan Wesson Firearms.
Price: 722 VH10 (vent heavy 10" bbl.) **$888.00**
Price: 722 VH10 SRS1 (Super Ram Silhouette, Bo-Mar sights, front hood, trigger job) **$1,164.00**

DAN WESSON FIREARMS MODEL 3220/73220 TARGET REVOLVER
Caliber: 32-20, 6-shot. **Barrel:** 2.5", 4", 6", 8", 10" standard vent, vent heavy. **Weight:** 47 oz. (6" VH). **Length:** 11.25" overall. **Grips:** Hogue Gripper rubber (walnut, exotic hardwoods optional). **Sights:** Red ramp interchangeable front, fully adjustable rear. **Features:** Bright blue (3220) or stainless (73220). Reintroduced 1997. Made in U.S.A. by Dan Wesson Firearms.
Price: 3220 VH2.5 (blued, 2.5" vent heavy bbl.) **$643.00**
Price: 73220 VH10 (stainless 10" vent heavy bbl.) **$873.00**

DAN WESSON FIREARMS MODEL 40/740 REVOLVERS
Caliber: 357 Maximum, 6-shot. **Barrel:** 4", 6", 8", 10". **Weight:** 72 oz. (8" bbl.). **Length:** 14.3" overall (8" bbl.). **Grips:** Hogue Gripper rubber (walnut or exotic hardwood optional). **Sights:** 1/8" serrated front, fully adjustable rear. **Features:** Blue or stainless steel. Made in U.S.A. by Dan Wesson Firearms.
Price: Blue, 4" **$702.00**
Price: Blue, 6" **$749.00**
Price: Blue, 8" **$795.00**
Price: Blue, 10" **$858.00**
Price: Stainless, 4" **$834.00**
Price: Stainless, 6" **$892.00**
Price: Stainless, 8" slotted **$1,024.00**
Price: Stainless, 10" **$998.00**
Price: 4", 6", 8" Compensated, blue . . . . **$749.00 to $885.00**
Price: As above, stainless . . . . **$893.00 to $1,061.00**

Dan Wesson Firearms Model 414/7414 and 445/7445 SuperMag Revolvers
Similar size and weight as Model 40 revolvers. Chambered for 414 SuperMag or 445 SuperMag cartridge. Barrel lengths of 4", 6", 8", 10". Contact maker for complete price list. Reintroduced 1997. Made in the U.S.A. by Dan Wesson Firearms.
Price: 4", vent heavy, blue or stainless **$904.00**
Price: 8", vent heavy, blue or stainless **$1,026.00**
Price: 10", vent heavy, blue or stainless **$1,103.00**
Price: Compensated models . . . . **$965.00 to $1,149.00**

DAN WESSON FIREARMS MODEL 22/722 REVOLVERS
Caliber: 22 LR, 22 WMR, 6-shot. **Barrel:** 2-1/2", 4", 6", 8" or 10"; interchangeable. **Weight:** 36 oz. (2-1/2"), 44 oz. (6"). **Length:** 9-1/4" overall (4" barrel). **Grips:** Hogue Gripper rubber (walnut, exotic woods optional). **Sights:** 1/8" serrated, interchangeable front, white outline rear adjustable for windage and elevation. **Features:** Built on the same frame as the Wesson 357; wide trigger with over-travel adjustment, wide spur hammer, with short double-action travel. Available in blue or stainless steel. Reintroduced 1997.
Price: 22 VH2.5/722 VH2.5 (blued or stainless 2-1/2" bbl.) **$551.00**
Price: 22VH10/722 VH10 (blued or stainless 10" bbl.) **$750.00**

Dan Wesson 722M Small Frame Revolver
Similar to Model 22/722 except chambered for 22 WMR. Blued or stainless finish, 2-1/2", 4", 6", 8" or 10" barrels.
Price: Blued or stainless finish . . . . **$643.00 to $873.00**

DAN WESSON FIREARMS MODEL 15/715 and 32/732 REVOLVERS
Caliber: 32-20, 32 H&R Mag. (Model 32), 357 Mag. (Model 15). **Barrel:** 2-1/2", 4", 6", 8" (M32), 2-1/2", 4", 6", 8", 10" (M15); vented heavy. **Weight:** 36 oz. (2-1/2" barrel). **Length:** 9-1/4" overall (4" barrel). **Grips:** Checkered, interchangeable. **Sights:** 1/8" serrated front, fully adjustable rear. **Fea-tures:** New Generation Series. Interchangeable barrels; wide, smooth trigger, wide hammer spur; short double-action travel. Available in blue or stainless. Reintroduced 1997. Made in U.S.A. by Dan Wesson Firearms.
Price: Model 15/715, 2-1/2" (blue or stainless) **$551.00**
Price: Model 15/715, 8" (blue or stainless) **$612.00**
Price: Model 15/715, compensated . . . . **$704.00 to $827.00**
Price: Model 32/732, 4" (blue or stainless) **$674.00**
Price: Model 32/732, 8" (blue or stainless) **$766.00**

DAN WESSON FIREARMS MODEL 41/741, 44/744 and 45/745 REVOLVERS
Caliber: 41 Mag., 44 Mag., 45 Colt, 6-shot. **Barrel:** 4", 6", 8", 10"; interchangeable; 4", 6", 8" compensated. **Weight:** 48 oz. (4"). **Length:** 12" overall (6" bbl.) **Grips:** Smooth. **Sights:** 1/8" serrated front, white outline rear adjustable for windage and elevation. **Features:** Available in blue or stainless steel. Smooth, wide trigger with adjustable over-travel, wide hammer spur. Available in Pistol Pac set also. Reintroduced 1997. Made in U.S.A. by Dan Wesson Firearms.
Price: 41 Mag., 4", vent heavy (blue or stainless) **$643.00**
Price: 44 Mag., 6", vent heavy (blue or stainless) **$689.00**
Price: 45 Colt, 8", vent heavy (blue or stainless) **$766.00**
Price: Compensated models (all calibers) . . . . **$812.00 to $934.00**

Dan Wesson Firearms
Super Ram Silhouette

Dan Wesson Firearms
Alaskan Guide Special

EAA Windicator

DAN WESSON FIREARMS LARGE FRAME SERIES REVOLVERS
Caliber: 41, 741/41 Magnum; 44, 744/44 Magnum; 45, 745/45 Long Colt; 360, 7360/357; 460, 7460/45. **Barrel:** 2"-10". **Weight:** 49 oz.-69 oz. **Grips:** Standard, Hogue rubber Gripper Grips. **Sights:** Standard front, serrated ramp with color insert. Standard rear, adustable wide notch. Other sight options available. **Features:** Available in blue or stainless steel. Smooth, wide trigger with overtravel, wide hammer spur. Double and single action.
Price: .... $769.00 to $889.00

DAN WESSON FIREARMS MODEL 360/7360 REVOLVERS
Caliber: 357 Mag. **Barrel:** 4", 6", 8", 10"; vent heavy. **Weight:** 64 oz. (8" barrel). **Grips:** Hogue rubber finger groove. **Sights:** Interchangeable ramp or Patridge front, fully adjustable rear. **Features:** New Generation Large Frame Series. Interchangeable barrels and grips; smooth trigger, wide hammer spur. Blue (360) or stainless (7360). Introduced 1999. Made in U.S.A. by Dan Wesson Firearms.
Price: 4" bbl., blue or stainless $735.00
Price: 10" bbl., blue or stainless $873.00
Price: Compensated models .... $858.00 to $980.00

DAN WESSON FIREARMS MODEL 460/7460 REVOLVERS
Caliber: 45 ACP, 45 Auto Rim, 45 Super, 45 Winchester Magnum and 460 Rowland. **Barrel:** 4", 6", 8", 10"; vent heavy. **Weight:** 49 oz. (4" barrel). **Grips:** Hogue rubber finger groove; interchangeable. **Sights:** Interchangeable ramp or Patridge front, fully adjustable rear. **Features:** New Generation Large Frame Series. Shoots five cartridges (45 ACP, 45 Auto Rim, 45 Super, 45 Winchester Magnum and 460 Rowland; six half-moon clips for auto cartridges included). Interchangeable barrels and grips. Available with non-fluted cylinder and slotted lightweight barrel shroud. Introduced 1999. Made in U.S.A. by Dan Wesson Firearms.
Price: 4" bbl., blue or stainless $735.00
Price: 10" bbl., blue or stainless $888.00
Price: Compensated models .... $919.00 to $1,042.00

DAN WESSON FIREARMS STANDARD SILHOUETTE REVOLVERS
Caliber: 357 SuperMag/Maxi, 41 Mag., 414 SuperMag, 445 SuperMag. **Barrel:** 8", 10". **Weight:** 64 oz. (8" barrel). **Length:** 14.3" overall (8" barrel). **Grips:** Hogue rubber finger groove; interchangeable. **Sights:** Patridge front, fully adjustable rear. **Features:** Interchangeable barrels and grips, fluted or non-fluted cylinder, satin brushed stainless finish. Introduced 1999. Made in U.S.A. by Dan Wesson Firearms.
Price: 357 SuperMag/Maxi, 8" $1,057.00
Price: 41 Mag., 10" $888.00
Price: 414 SuperMag., 8" $1,057.00
Price: 445 SuperMag., 8" $1,057.00

Dan Wesson Firearms Super Ram Silhouette Revolver
Similar to Standard Silhouette except has 10 land and groove Laser Coat barrel, Bo-Mar target sights with hooded front, special laser engraving. Fluted or non-fluted cylinder. Introduced 1999. Made in U.S.A. by Dan Wesson Firearms.
Price: 357 SuperMag/Maxi, 414 SuperMag., 445 SuperMag., 8", blue or stainless $1,364.00
Price: 41 Magnum, 44 Magnum, 8", blue or stainless $1,241.00
Price: 41 Magnum, 44 Magnum, 10", blue or stainless $1,333.00

DAN WESSON FIREARMS ALASKAN GUIDE SPECIAL
Caliber: 445 SuperMag, 44 Magnum. **Barrel:** Compensated 4" vent heavy barrel assembly. **Features:** Stainless steel with baked on, non-glare, matte black coating, special laser engraving.
Price: Model 7445 VH4C AGS $995.00
Price: Model 744 VH4C AGS $855.00

EAA WINDICATOR REVOLVERS
Caliber: 38 Spec., 6-shot; 357 magnum, 6-shot. **Barrel:** 2", 4". **Weight:** 38 oz. (22 rimfire, 4"). **Length:** 8.5" overall (4" bbl.). **Grips:** Rubber with finger grooves. **Sights:** Blade front, fixed or adjustable on rimfires; fixed only on 32, 38. **Features:** Swing-out cylinder; hammer block safety; blue finish. Introduced 1991. Imported from Germany by European American Armory.
Price: 38 Special 2" $249.00
Price: 38 Special, 4" $259.00
Price: 357 Magnum, 2" $259.00
Price: 357 Magnum, 4" $279.00

KORTH COMBAT REVOLVER
Caliber: 357 Mag., 32 S&W Long, 9mm Para., 22 WMR, 22 LR. **Barrel:** 3", 4", 5-1/4", 6", 8". **Sights:** Fully adjustable, rear; Baughman ramp, front. **Grips:** Walnut (checkered or smooth). Also available as a Target model in 22 LR, 38 Spl., 32 S&W Long, 357 Mag. with undercut Patridge front sight; fully adjustable rear. Made in Germany. Imported by Korth USA.
Price: From $7,203.00

KORTH TROJA REVOLVER
Caliber: .357 Mag. **Barrel:** 6". **Finish:** Matte blue. **Grips:** Smooth, over-sized finger contoured walnut. Introduced 2003. Imported from Germany by Korth USA.
Price: From $5,593.00

CONSULT
SHOOTER'S
MARKETPLACE
Page 74, This Issue

Medusa Model 47

Rossi Model 971

Rossi Model 972

Rossi Model 851

Ruger GP-161

Ruger KGP-141

MEDUSA MODEL 47 REVOLVER
Caliber: Most 9mm, 38 and 357 caliber cartridges; 6-shot cylinder. **Barrel:** 2-1/2", 3", 4", 5", 6"; fluted. **Weight:** 39 oz. **Length:** 10" overall (4" barrel). **Grips:** Gripper-style rubber. **Sights:** Changeable front blades, fully adjustable rear. **Features:** Patented extractor allows gun to chamber, fire and extract over 25 different cartridges in the 355 to 357 range without half-moon clips. Steel frame and cylinder; match quality barrel. Matte blue finish. Introduced 1996. Made in U.S.A. by Phillips & Rogers, Inc.
Price: **$899.00**

ROSSI MODEL 351/352 REVOLVERS
Caliber: 38 Special +P, 5-shot. **Barrel:** 2". **Weight:** 24 oz. **Length:** 6-1/2" overall. **Grips:** Rubber. **Sights:** Blade front, fixed rear. **Features:** Patented key-lock Taurus Security System; forged steel frame. Introduced 2001. Imported by BrazTech/Taurus.
Price: Model 351 (blued finish) **$298.00**
Price: Model 352 (stainless finish) **$345.00**

ROSSI MODEL 461/462 REVOLVERS
Caliber: 357 Magnum +P, 6-shot. **Barrel:** 2". **Weight:** 26 oz. **Length:** 6-1/2" overall. **Grips:** Rubber. **Sights:** Fixed. **Features:** Single/double action. Patented key-lock Taurus Security System; forged steel frame. Introduced 2001. Imported by BrazTech/Taurus.
Price: Model 461 (blued finish) **$298.00**
Price: Model 462 (stainless finish) **$345.00**

ROSSI MODEL 971/972 REVOLVERS
Caliber: 357 Magnum +P, 6-shot. **Barrel:** 4", 6". **Weight:** 40-44 oz. **Length:** 8-1/2" or 10-1/2" overall. **Grips:** Rubber. **Sights:** Fully adjustable. **Features:** Single/double action. Patented key-lock Taurus Security System; forged steel frame. Introduced 2001. Imported by BrazTech/Taurus.
Price: Model 971 (blued finish, 4" bbl.) **$345.00**
Price: Model 972 (stainless steel finish, 6" bbl.) **$391.00**

Rossi Model 851
Similar to Model 971/972, chambered for 38 Special +P. Blued finish, 4" barrel. Introduced 2001. From BrazTech/Taurus.
Price: **$298.00**

RUGER GP-100 REVOLVERS
Caliber: 38 Spec., 357 Mag., 6-shot. **Barrel:** 3", 3" full shroud, 4", 4" full shroud, 6", 6" full shroud. **Weight:** 3" barrel-35 oz., 3" full shroud-36 oz., 4" barrel-37 oz., 4" full shroud-38 oz. **Sights:** Fixed; adjustable on 4" full shroud, all 6" barrels. **Grips:** Ruger Santoprene Cushioned Grip with Goncalo Alves inserts. **Features:** Uses action, frame features of both the Security-Six and Redhawk revolvers. Full length, short ejector shroud. Satin blue and stainless steel.
Price: GP-141 (357, 4" full shroud, adj. sights, blue) **$499.00**
Price: GP-160 (357, 6", adj. sights, blue) **$499.00**
Price: GP-161 (357, 6" full shroud, adj. sights, blue), 46 oz. **$499.00**
Price: GPF-331 (357, 3" full shroud) **$495.00**
Price: GPF-340 (357, 4") **$495.00**
Price: GPF-341 (357, 4" full shroud) **$495.00**
Price: KGP-141 (357, 4" full shroud, adj. sights, stainless) **$555.00**
Price: KGP-160 (357, 6", adj. sights, stainless), 43 oz. **$555.00**
Price: KGP-161 (357, 6" full shroud, adj. sights, stainless) 46 oz. . . **$555.00**
Price: KGPF-330 (357, 3", stainless) **$555.00**
Price: KGPF-331 (357, 3" full shroud, stainless) **$555.00**
Price: KGPF-340 (357, 4", stainless), KGPF-840 (38 Special) **$555.00**
Price: KGPF-341 (357, 4" full shroud, stainless) **$555.00**
Price: KGPF-840 (38 Special, 4", stainless) **$555.00**

Ruger SP101 Double-Action-Only Revolver
Similar to standard SP101 except double-action-only with no single-action sear notch. Spurless hammer, floating firing pin and transfer bar safety system. Available with 2-1/4" barrel in 357 Magnum. Weighs 25 oz., overall length 7.06". Natural brushed satin, high-polish stainless steel. Introduced 1993.
Price: KSP321XL (357 Mag.) **$495.00**

RUGER SP101 REVOLVERS
Caliber: 22 LR, 32 H&R Mag., 6-shot; 38 Spec. +P, 357 Mag., 5-shot. **Barrel:** 2-1/4", 3-1/16", 4". **Weight:** (38 & 357 mag models) 2-1/4"-25 oz.; 3-1/16"-27 oz. **Sights:** Adjustable on 22, 32, fixed on others. **Grips:** Ruger Cushioned Grip with inserts. **Features:** Compact, small frame, double-action revolver. Full-length ejector shroud. Stainless steel only. Introduced 1988.
Price: KSP-821X (2-1/4", 38 Spec.) **$495.00**
Price: KSP-831X (3-1/16", 38 Spec.) **$495.00**
Price: KSP-241X (4" heavy bbl., 22 LR), 34 oz. **$495.00**
Price: KSP-3231X (3-1/16", 32 H&R), 30 oz. **$495.00**
Price: KSP-321X (2-1/4", 357 Mag.) **$495.00**
Price: KSP-331X (3-1/16", 357 Mag.) **$495.00**
Price: KSP-3241X (32 Mag., 4" bbl.) **$495.00**

Ruger Redhawk

Smith & Wesson
Model 10

Ruger Super Redhawk

Smith & Wesson Model 386

Smith & Wesson Model 629 Classic DX

Smith & Wesson
Model 36LS

RUGER REDHAWK
Caliber: 44 Rem. Mag., 45 Colt, 6-shot. **Barrel:** 5-1/2", 7-1/2". **Weight:** About 54 oz. (7-1/2" bbl.). **Length:** 13" overall (7-1/2" barrel). **Grips:** Square butt cushioned grip panels. **Sights:** Interchangeable Patridge-type front, rear adjustable for windage and elevation. **Features:** Stainless steel, brushed satin finish, blued ordnance steel. 9-1/2" sight radius. Introduced 1979.
Price: Blued, 44 Mag., 5-1/2" RH-445, 7-1/2" RH-44 . . . . **$585.00**
Price: Blued, 44 Mag., 7-1/2" RH44R, with scope mount, rings . . . **$625.00**
Price: Stainless, 44 Mag., KRH445, 5-1/2", 7-1/2" KRH-44 . . . . . . **$645.00**
Price: Stainless, 44 Mag., 7-1/2", with scope mount,
rings KRH-44R **$685.00**
Price: Stainless, 45 Colt, KRH455, 5-1/2", 7-1/2" KRH-45 . . . . **$645.00**
Price: Stainless, 45 Colt, 7-1/2", with scope mount and rings
KRH-45R **$685.00**

Ruger Super Redhawk Revolver
Similar to standard Redhawk except has heavy extended frame with Ruger Integral Scope Mounting System on wide topstrap. Also available in 454 Casull and 480 Ruger. Wide hammer spur lowered for better scope clearance. Incorporates mechanical design features and improvements of GP-100. Choice of 7-1/2" or 9-1/2" barrel, both ramp front sight base with Redhawk-style Interchangeable Insert sight blades, adjustable rear sight. Target gray stainless steel. Introduced 1987.
Price: KSRH-7 (7-1/2"), KSRH-9 (9-1/2"), 44 Mag **$685.00**
Price: KSRH-7454 (7-1/2") 454 Casull, 9-1/2 KSRH-9454 . . . . **$775.00**
Price: KSRH-7480 (7-1/2") 480 Ruger **$775.00**
Price: KSRH-9480 (9-1/2") 480 Ruger **$775.00**

SMITH & WESSON MODEL 10 M&P HB REVOLVER
Caliber: 38 Spec., 6-shot. **Barrel:** 4". **Weight:** 36 oz. **Length:** 8-7/8" overall. **Grips:** Uncle Mike's Combat soft rubber; square butt. **Sights:** Fixed; ramp front, square notch rear.
Price: Blue **$544.00**

SMITH & WESSON MODEL 325PD
Caliber: 45 ACP, 6-round. **Barrel:** 2-1/2". **Weight:** 21.5 oz. **Length:** 7-1/4". **Grips:** Wood. **Sights:** Adj. rear, HiViz front. **Features:** Alloy large frame, titanium cylinder.
Price: **$939.00**

SMITH & WESSON MODEL 329PD
Caliber: 44 Mag., 44 Spec., 6-round. **Barrel:** 4". **Weight:** 26 oz. **Length:** 9-1/2". **Grips:** Wood. **Sights:** Adj. rear, HiViz front. **Features:** Alloy large frame, titanium cylinder.
Price: **$960.00**

SMITH & WESSON MODEL 386
Caliber: 357 Mag., 38 Spec., 7-round. **Barrel:** 3-1/8". **Weight:** 18.5 oz. **Length:** 8-1/8". **Grips:** Hogue Bantam. **Sights:** Adj. rear, HiViz front. **Features:** Alloy large frame, titanium cylinder.
Price: **$876.00**

SMITH & WESSON MODEL 629 REVOLVERS
Caliber: 44 Magnum, 44 S&W Special, 6-shot. **Barrel:** 4". **Weight:** 45 oz. (6" bbl.). **Length:** 11-5/8" overall (6" bbl.). **Grips:** Soft rubber; wood optional. **Sights:** 1/8" red ramp front, white outline rear, internal lock, adjustable for windage and elevation.
Price: Model 629, 4" **$787.00**
Price: Model 629, 6" **$810.00**

Smith & Wesson Model 629 Classic Revolver
Similar to standard Model 629 with full-lug 5", 6-1/2" or 8-3/8" barrel, chamfered front of cylinder, interchangeable red ramp front sight with adjustable white outline rear, Hogue grips with S&W monogram, drilled and tapped for scope mounting. Factory accurizing and endurance packages. Overall length with 5" barrel is 10-1/2"; weighs 45.5 oz. Introduced 1990.
Price: Model 629 Classic (stainless), 5", 6-1/2" **$843.00**
Price: As above, 8-3/8" **$871.00**
Price: Model 629 Classic with HiViz front sight **$894.00**

SMITH & WESSON MODEL 37 AIRWEIGHT
Caliber: 38 Spec. +P, 5-shot. **Barrel:** 1-7/8". **Weight:** 15.0 oz. **Length:** 6-5/16" (round butt). **Grips:** Round butt soft rubber. **Sights:** Fixed, serrated ramp front, square notch rear. Glass beaded finish.
Price: Model 37 . . . . **$573.00**

Smith & Wesson Model 637 Airweight Revolver
Similar to the Model 37 Airweight except has alloy frame, stainless steel barrel, cylinder and yoke; rated for 38 Spec. +P; Uncle Mike's Boot Grip. Weighs 15 oz. Introduced 1996. Made in U.S.A. by Smith & Wesson.
Price: **$450.00**

SMITH & WESSON MODEL 36LS, 60LS LADYSMITH
Caliber: .38 S&W Special +P (M36), 357 Mag. (M60LS), 5-shot. **Barrel:** 1-7/8, 2-1/8". **Weight:** 20 oz. **Length:** 6-3/16 overall (1-7/8" barrel). **Grips:** Combat Dymondwood® grips with S&W monogram. **Sights:** Serrated ramp front, fixed notch rear. **Features:** Speedloader cutout. Comes in a fitted carry/storage case. Introduced 1989.
Price: Model 36LS **$568.00**
Price: Model 60LS, 2-1/8" bbl. stainless, 357 Magnum **$621.00**
Price: Model 36LS, 38 Spec **$450.00**

Smith & Wesson
Model 60 Chief's Special

Smith & Wesson
Model 317 AirLite

Smith & Wesson Model 625

Smith & Wesson
Model 340 PD Airlite Sc

SMITH & WESSON MODEL 60 CHIEF'S SPECIAL
Caliber: 357 Magnum, 38 Spec., 5-shot. **Barrel:** 2-1/8", 3" or 5". **Weight:** 24 oz. **Length:** 7-1/2 overall (3" barrel). **Grips:** Rounded butt synthetic grips. **Sights:** Fixed, serrated ramp front, square notch rear. **Features:** Stainless steel construction. 3" full lug barrel, adjustable sights, internal lock. Made in U.S.A. by Smith & Wesson.
Price: 2-1/8" barrel $594.00
Price: 3" bbl. $630.00
Price: 5" bbl. $671.00

SMITH & WESSON MODEL 65
Caliber: 357 Mag. and 38 Spec., 6-shot. **Barrel:** 4". **Weight:** 34 oz. **Length:** 9-5/16" overall (4" bbl.). **Grips:** Uncle Mike's Combat. **Sights:** 1/8" serrated ramp front, fixed square notch rear. **Features:** Heavy barrel. Stainless steel construction. Internal lock.
Price: $531.00

SMITH & WESSON MODEL 317 AIRLITE, 317 KIT GUN REVOLVERS
Caliber: 22 LR, 8-shot. **Barrel:** 1-7/8", 3". **Weight:** 10.05 oz. **Length:** 6-3/16" overall. **Grips:** Dymondwood® Boot or Uncle Mike's Boot. **Sights:** Serrated ramp front, fixed notch rear. **Features:** Aluminum alloy, carbon and stainless steels, and titanium construction. Short spur hammer, smooth combat trigger. Clear Cote finish. Introduced 1997. Made in U.S.A. by Smith & Wesson.
Price: With Uncle Mike's Boot grip $603.00
Price: With Boot grip, 3" barrel, HiViz front sight, internal lock $658.00

SMITH & WESSON MODEL 351PD
Caliber: 22 Mag. **Barrel:** 2". **Features:** Seven-shot, Scandium alloy.
Price: $625.00

SMITH & WESSON MODEL 64 STAINLESS M&P
Caliber: 38 Spec. +P, 6-shot. **Barrel:** 3", 4". **Weight:** 36 oz. **Length:** 8-7/16" overall. **Grips:** Soft rubber. **Sights:** Fixed, 1/8" serrated ramp front, square notch rear. **Features:** Satin finished stainless steel, square butt.
Price: 3", 4" bbl. $583.00

SMITH & WESSON MODEL 648
Caliber: 22 Mag., 6-round. **Barrel:** 6". **Weight:** 45 oz. **Length:** 11-1/8". **Grips:** Rubber. **Sights:** Adj. rear, Patridge front. **Features:** Stainless steel frame, satin finish.
Price: $703.00

SMITH & WESSON MODEL 619
Caliber: 38 S&W Special; 7 rounds. **Barrel:** 4". **Weight:** 37.5 oz. **Length:** 9-1/2". **Grips:** Rubber. **Sights:** White outline rear, red ramp front. **Features:** Stainless frame and cylinder.
Price: $615.00

SMITH & WESSON MODEL 620
Caliber: 38 S&W Special; 7 rounds. **Barrel:** 4". **Weight:** 37.5 oz. **Length:** 9-1/2". **Grips:** Rubber. **Sights:** White outline rear, red ramp front. **Features:** Stainles frame and cylinder.
Price: $669.00

SMITH & WESSON MODEL 686
Caliber: 357 Mag., 38 S&W Special; 6 rounds. **Barrel:** 2-1/2", 4", 6". **Weight:** 40 oz. (4"). **Length:** 9-9/16". **Grips:** Rubber. **Sights:** White outline rear, red ramp front. **Features:** Stainless frame and cylinder.
Price: 2-1/2" bbl. $667.00
Price: 4" bbl. $694.00
Price: 6" bbl. $700.00

SMITH & WESSON MODEL 686 POWERPORT
Caliber: 357 Mag., 38 S&W Special; 6 rounds. **Barrel:** 6". **Weight:** 44 oz. **Length:** 11-3/8". **Grips:** Rubber. **Sights:** Adj. rear, Patridge front. **Features:** Stainless frame and cylinder.
Price: $747.00

Smith & Wesson Model 686 Magnum PLUS Revolver
Similar to the Model 686 except has 7-shot cylinder, 2-1/2", 4" or 6" barrel. Weighs 34-1/2 oz., overall length 7-1/2" (2-1/2" barrel). Hogue rubber grips. Internal lock. Introduced 1996. Made in U.S.A. by Smith & Wesson.
Price: 2-1/2" bbl. $692.00
Price: 4" bbl. $716.00
Price: 6" bbl. $727.00

SMITH & WESSON MODEL 625 REVOLVER
Caliber: 45 ACP, 6-shot. **Barrel:** 4", 5". **Weight:** 45 oz. **Length:** 10-3/8" overall. **Grips:** Soft rubber; wood optional. **Sights:** Patridge front on ramp, S&W micrometer click rear adjustable for windage and elevation. **Features:** Stainless steel construction with .400" semi-target hammer, .312" smooth combat trigger; full lug barrel. Glass beaded finish. Introduced 1989.
Price: 5" $817.00
Price: 4" with internal lock $817.00
Price: 5" Jerry Miculek Pro series $845.00

SMITH & WESSON MODEL 640 CENTENNIAL DA ONLY
Caliber: 357 Mag., 38 Spec. +P, 5-shot. **Barrel:** 2-1/8". **Weight:** 23 oz. **Length:** 6-3/4" overall. **Grips:** Uncle Mike's Boot grip. **Sights:** Serrated ramp front, fixed notch rear. **Features:** Stainless steel. Fully concealed hammer, snag-proof smooth edges. Internal lock. Introduced 1995 in 357 Magnum.
Price: $658.00

SMITH & WESSON MODEL 617 K-22 MASTERPIECE
Caliber: 22 LR, 6- or 10-shot. **Barrel:** 4", 6". **Weight:** 41 oz. (4" barrel). **Length:** NA. **Grips:** Soft rubber. **Sights:** Patridge front, adjustable rear. Drilled and tapped for scope mount. **Features:** Stainless steel with satin finish; 4" has .312" smooth trigger, .375" semi-target hammer; 6" has either .312" combat or .400" serrated trigger, .375" semi-target or .500" target hammer; 8-3/8" with .400" serrated trigger, .500" target hammer. Introduced 1990.
Price: 4" $707.00
Price: 6", target hammer, target trigger $686.00
Price: 6", 10-shot $734.00

SMITH & WESSON MODEL 340PD AIRLITE Sc CENTENNIAL
Caliber: 357 Magnum, 38 Spec. +P, 5-shot. **Barrel:** 1-7/8". **Grips:** Rounded butt grip. **Sights:** HiViz front. **Features:** Synthetic grip, internal lock. Blue.
Price: HiViz front $877.00
Price: Red ramp front $862.00

Smith & Wesson Model 360 PD
Airlite SC Chief's Special

Smith & Wesson Model
386 PD Airlite SC

Smith & Wesson Model 340

Smith & Wesson Model
360 Kit Gun

Smith & Wesson Model 67

Smith & Wesson Model 442

Smith & Wesson Model 638

SMITH & WESSON MODEL 360PD AIRLITE Sc CHIEF'S SPECIAL
Caliber: 357 Magnum, 38 Spec. +P, 5-shot. **Barrel:** 1-7/8". **Grips:** Rounded butt grip. **Sights:** Fixed. **Features:** Synthetic grip, internal lock. Stainless.
Price: Red ramp front **$834.00**
Price: HiViz front **$858.00**

SMITH & WESSON MODEL 386PD AIRLITE Sc
Caliber: 357 Magnum, 38 Spec. +P, 7-shot. **Barrel:** 2-1/2". **Grips:** Rounded butt grip. **Sights:** Adjustable, HiViz front. **Features:** Synthetic grip, internal lock.
Price: Blue **$873.00**

SMITH & WESSON MODEL 340
Caliber: 357 Mag., 38 Spec., 5-shot. **Barrel:** 1-7/8". **Weight:** 12 oz. **Length:** 6-5/16" overall. **Grips:** Rubber. **Sights:** Black blade ramp front, fixed rear. **Features:** Alloy frame; titanium cylinder; stainless steel barrel liner. Matte finish. Made in U.S.A. by Smith & Wesson.
Price: Model 340 . . . . **$838.00**

Smith & Wesson Model 360 and 260 Kit Gun
Same as Model 340 except with 3" barrel option.
Price: M 360 . . . . **$818.00**
Price: Kit Gun **$865.00**

SMITH & WESSON MODEL 337 CHIEF'S SPECIAL AIRLITE Ti
Caliber: 38 Spec. +P, 5-shot. **Barrel:** 1-7/8". **Weight:** 11.2 oz. (Dymondwood® grips). **Length:** 6-5/16" overall. **Grips:** Uncle Mike's Boot or Dymondwood® Boot. **Sights:** Black serrated front, fixed notch rear. **Features:** Aluminum alloy frame, barrel shroud and yoke; titanium cylinder; stainless steel barrel liner. Matte finish. Introduced 1999. Made in U.S.A. by Smith & Wesson.
Price: **$716.00**

SMITH & WESSON MODEL 431PD/432PD
Caliber: 32 H&R, 6-shot. **Barrel:** 2". **Weight:** 15 oz. **Length:** 6-5/16" overall. **Grips:** Rubber. **Sights:** Black blade front, fixed rear. **Features:** Alloy black frame and cylinder; black finish.
Price: Chief's Special **$450.00**
Price: Centennial frame **$469.00**

SMITH & WESSON MODEL 67
Caliber: 38 S&W Special, 6-shot. **Barrel:** 4". **Weight:** 36 oz. **Length:** 8-7/8". **Grips:** Rubber. **Sights:** Adj. rear, red ramp front. **Features:** Stainless steel frame and cylinder.
Price: **$642.00**

Smith & Wesson Model 442 Centennial Airweight
Similar to Model 640 Centennial, alloy frame, weighs 15 oz. Chambered for 38 Special +P, 1-7/8" carbon steel barrel; carbon steel cylinder; concealed hammer; Uncle Mike's Boot grip. Fixed square notch rear sight, serrated ramp front. DA only, glass beaded finish. Introduced 1993.
Price: Blue **$600.00**

SMITH & WESSON MODEL 638 AIRWEIGHT BODYGUARD
Caliber: 38 Spec. +P, 5-shot. **Barrel:** 1-7/8". **Weight:** 15 oz. **Length:** 6-15/16" overall. **Grips:** Uncle Mike's Boot grip. **Sights:** Serrated ramp front, fixed notch rear. **Features:** Alloy frame, stainless cylinder and barrel; shrouded hammer. Glass beaded finish. Introduced 1997. Made in U.S.A. by Smith & Wesson.
Price: With Uncle Mike's Boot grip **$620.00**

Smith & Wesson Model 642 Airweight Revolver
Similar to Model 442 Centennial Airweight, stainless steel barrel, cylinder and yoke with matte finish; Uncle Mike's Boot grip; DA only; weighs 15 oz. Introduced 1996. Made in U.S.A. by Smith & Wesson.
Price: **$469.00**

Smith & Wesson Model 642LS Ladysmith Revolver
Same as Model 642 except has smooth combat wood grips, comes with deluxe soft case; Dymondwood® grip; aluminum alloy frame, stainless cylinder, barrel and yoke; frosted matte finish. Weighs 14.5 oz. Introduced 1996. Made in U.S.A. by Smith & Wesson.
Price: 1-7/8" **$633.00**

SMITH & WESSON MODEL 649 BODYGUARD REVOLVER
Caliber: 357 Mag., 38 Spec. +P, 5-shot. **Barrel:** 2-1/8". **Weight:** 23 oz. **Length:** 6-5/16" overall. **Grips:** Uncle Mike's Combat. **Sights:** Black pinned ramp front, fixed notch rear. **Features:** Stainless steel construction; shrouded hammer; smooth combat trigger. Internal lock. Made in U.S.A. by Smith & Wesson.
Price: **$651.00**

Smith & Wesson Model 657

Smith & Wesson Model 500

Taurus Model 17 Tracker

Taurus Model 65

Taurus Model 82

Taurus Model 85

SMITH & WESSON MODEL 657 REVOLVER
Caliber: 41 Mag., 6-shot. **Barrel:** 7-1/2" full lug. **Weight:** 52 oz. **Grips:** Soft rubber. **Sights:** Pinned 1/8" red ramp front, micro-click rear adjustable for windage and elevation. Target hammer, drilled and tapped, unfluted cylinder. **Features:** Stainless steel construction.
Price: $774.00

SMITH & WESSON MODEL 460 XVR
Caliber: 460 S&W Mag., 5-shot. **Barrel:** 8-3/8". **Weight:** 72.5 oz. **Length:** 15". **Grips:** Rubber. **Sights:** Adj. rear, blade front. **Features:** Stainless steel frame and cylinder, interchangeable compensator.
Price: **$1,253.00**

SMITH & WESSON MODEL 500
Caliber: 50 S&W Mag. **Barrel:** 4" and 8-3/8". **Weight:** 72.5 oz. **Length:** NA. **Grips:** Rubber. **Sights:** Interchangeable blade, front, adjustable rear. **Features:** Built on the massive, new X-Frame, recoil compensator, ball detent cylinder latch. Made in U.S.A. by Smith & Wesson.
Price: 4" bbl. **$1,196.00**
Price: 8-3/8" bbl. **$1,130.00**

TAURUS SILHOUETTE REVOLVERS
Available in calibers from 22 LR through 454 Casull, 12" vent rib barrel. An optional arm support that wraps around the forearm is available.
Price: . . . . **$414.00 to $859.00**

TAURUS MODEL 17 "TRACKER"
Caliber: 17 HMR, 7-shot. **Barrel:** 6-1/2". **Weight:** 45.8 oz. **Grips:** Rubber. **Sights:** Adjustable. **Features:** Double action, matte stainless, integral key-lock.
Price: . . . . **$430.00 to $438.00**

TAURUS MODEL 17-12 TARGET "SILHOUETTE"
Caliber: 17 HMR, 7-shot. **Barrel:** 12". **Weight:** 57.8 oz. **Grips:** Rubber. **Sights:** Adjustable. **Features:** Vent rib, double action, adjustable main spring and trigger stop. Matte stainless, integral key-lock.
Price: **$430.00**

Taurus Model 17-C Series
Similar to the Models 17 Tracker and Silhouette series but 8-shot cylinder, 2", 4" or 5" barrel, blue or stainless finish and regular (24 oz.) or UltraLite (18.5 oz.) versions available.
Price: . . . . **$359.00 to $391.00**

TAURUS MODEL 63
Caliber: 22 LR, 10 + 1 shot. **Barrel:** 23". **Weight:** 97.9 oz. **Grips:** Premium hardwood. **Sights:** Adjustable. **Features:** Auto loading action, round

barrel, manual firing pin block, integral security system lock, trigger guard mounted safety, blue or stainless finish.
Price: . . . . **$295.00 to $310.00**

TAURUS MODEL 65 REVOLVER
Caliber: 357 Mag., 6-shot. **Barrel:** 4". **Weight:** 38 oz. **Length:** 10-1/2" overall. **Grips:** Soft rubber. **Sights:** Fixed. **Features:** Double action, integral key-lock. Imported by Taurus International.
Price: Blue or matte stainless . . . . **$375.00 to $422.00**

Taurus Model 66 Revolver
Similar to Model 65, 4" or 6" barrel, 7-shot cylinder, adjustable rear sight. Integral key-lock action. Imported by Taurus International.
Price: Blue or matte stainless . . . . **$422.00 to $469.00**

Taurus Model 66 Silhouette Revolver
Similar to Model 66, 12" barrel, 7-shot cylinder, adjustable sight. Integral key-lock action, blue or matte stainless steel finish, rubber grips. Introduced 2001. Imported by Taurus International.
Price: . . . . **$414.00 to $461.00**

TAURUS MODEL 82 HEAVY BARREL REVOLVER
Caliber: 38 Spec., 6-shot. **Barrel:** 4", heavy. **Weight:** 36.5 oz. **Length:** 9-1/4" overall (4" bbl.). **Grips:** Soft black rubber. **Sights:** Serrated ramp front, square notch rear. **Features:** Double action, solid rib, integral key-lock. Imported by Taurus International.
Price: Blue or matte stainless . . . . **$352.00 to $398.00**

TAURUS MODEL 85 REVOLVER
Caliber: 38 Spec., 5-shot. **Barrel:** 2". **Weight:** 17-24.5 oz., titanium 13.5-15.4 oz. **Grips:** Rubber, rosewood or mother-of-pearl. **Sights:** Ramp front, square notch rear. **Features:** Blue, matte stainless, blue with gold accents, stainless with gold accents; rated for +P ammo. Integral keylock. Introduced 1980. Imported by Taurus International.
Price: . . . . **$375.00 to $547.00**
Price: Total Titanium **$531.00**

Taurus Model 94 UL

Taurus Model 22H Raging Hornet

Taurus Model 44

Taurus Model 30C Raging Thirty

Taurus Model 218 Raging Bee

Taurus Model 415

Taurus Model 425
Total Titanium

Taurus Model 445

TAURUS MODEL 94 REVOLVER
Caliber: 22 LR, 9-shot cylinder. **Barrel:** 2", 4", 5". **Weight:** 18.5-27.5 oz. **Grips:** Soft black rubber. **Sights:** Serrated ramp front, click-adjustable rear. **Features:** Double action, integral key-lock. Introduced 1989. Imported by Taurus International.
Price: Blue $325.00
Price: Matte stainless $375.00
Price: Model 94 UL, forged aluminum alloy, 18-18.5 oz. $365.00
Price: As above, stainless $410.00

TAURUS MODEL 22H RAGING HORNET REVOLVER
Caliber: 22 Hornet, 8-shot. **Barrel:** 10". **Weight:** 50 oz. **Length:** 6.5" overall. **Grips:** Soft black rubber. **Sights:** Fully adjustable, scope mount base included. **Features:** Ventilated rib, stainless steel construction with matte finish. Double-action, integral key-lock. Introduced 1999. Imported by Taurus International.
Price: $898.00

TAURUS MODEL 30C RAGING THIRTY
Caliber: 30 Carbine, 8-shot. **Barrel:** 10". **Weight:** 72.3 oz. **Grips:** Soft black rubber. **Sights:** Adjustable. **Features:** Double-action, ventilated rib, matte stainless, comes with five "Stellar" full-moon clips, integral key-lock.
Price: $898.00

TAURUS MODEL 44 REVOLVER
Caliber: 44 Mag., 6-shot. **Barrel:** 4", 6-1/2", 8-3/8". **Weight:** 44-3/4 oz. **Grips:** Rubber. **Sights:** Adjustable. **Features:** Double-action. Integral key-lock. Introduced 1994. New Model 44S12 has 12" vent rib barrel. Imported from Brazil by Taurus International Manufacturing, Inc.
Price: Blue or stainless steel .... **$445.00 to $602.00**

TAURUS MODEL 217 TARGET "SILHOUETTE"
Caliber: 218 Bee, 8-shot. **Barrel:** 12". **Weight:** 52.3 oz. **Grips:** Rubber. **Sights:** Adjustable. **Features:** Double-action, ventilated rib, adjustable mainspring and trigger stop, matte stainless, integral key-lock.
Price: $461.00

TAURUS MODEL 218 RAGING BEE
Caliber: 218 Bee, 7-shot. **Barrel:** 10". **Weight:** 74.9 oz. **Grips:** Rubber. **Sights:** Adjustable rear. **Features:** Ventilated rib, adjustable action, matte stainless, integral key-lock. Also available as Model 218SS6 Tracker with 6-1/2" vent rib barrel.
Price: (Raging Bee) $898.00
Price: (Tracker) $406.00

TAURUS MODEL 415 REVOLVER
Caliber: 41 Mag., 5-shot. **Barrel:** 2-1/2". **Weight:** 30 oz. **Length:** 7-1/8" overall. **Grips:** Rubber. **Sights:** Fixed. **Features:** Stainless steel construction; matte finish; ported barrel. Double action. Integral key-lock. Introduced 1999. Imported by Taurus International.
Price: $508.00
Price: Total Titanium $602.00

TAURUS MODEL 425/627 TRACKER REVOLVERS
Caliber: 357 Mag., 7-shot; 41 Mag., 5-shot. **Barrel:** 4" and 6". **Weight:** 28.8-40 oz. (titanium) 24.3-28. (6"). **Grips:** Rubber. **Sights:** Fixed front, adjustable rear. **Features:** Double-action stainless steel, Shadow Gray or Total Titanium; vent rib (steel models only); integral key-lock action. Imported by Taurus International.
Price: .... **$508.00 to $516.00**
Price: Total Titanium $688.00

TAURUS MODEL 445
Caliber: 44 Special, 5-shot. **Barrel:** 2". **Weight:** 20.3-28.25 oz. **Length:** 6-3/4" overall. **Grips:** Rubber. **Sights:** Ramp front, notch rear. **Features:** Blue or stainless steel. Standard or DAO concealed hammer, optional porting. Introduced 1997. Imported by Taurus International.
Price: .... **$345.00 to $500.00**
Price: Total Titanium 19.8 oz. $600.00

HANDGUNS — Double-Action Revolvers, Service & Sport

Taurus Model 460 Tracker

Taurus Model 605

Taurus Model 731

Taurus Model 454 Raging Bull

Taurus Model 608

Taurus Model 450

Taurus Raging Bull Model 416

TAURUS MODEL 455 "STELLAR TRACKER"
Caliber: 45 ACP, 5-shot. **Barrel:** 2", 4", 6". **Weight:** 28/33/38.4 oz. **Grips:** Rubber. **Sights:** Adjustable. **Features:** Double-action, matte stainless, includes five "Stellar" full-moon clips, integral key-lock.
Price: **$523.00**

TAURUS MODEL 460 "TRACKER"
Caliber: 45 Colt, 5-shot. **Barrel:** 4" or 6". **Weight:** 33/38.4 oz. **Grips:** Rubber. **Sights:** Adjustable. **Features:** Double-action, ventilated rib, matte stainless steel, comes with five "Stellar" full-moon clips.
Price: **$516.00**
Price: (Shadow Gray, Total Titanium) **$688.00**

TAURUS MODEL 605 REVOLVER
Caliber: 357 Mag., 5-shot. **Barrel:** 2". **Weight:** 24 oz. **Grips:** Rubber. **Sights:** Fixed. **Features:** Double-action, blue or stainless, concealed hammer models DAO, porting optional, integral key-lock. Introduced 1995. Imported by Taurus International.
Price: . . . . **$375.00 to $438.00**

Taurus Model 731 Revolver
Similar to the Taurus Model 605, except in .32 Magnum.
Price: . . . . **$438.00 to $531.00**

TAURUS MODEL 608 REVOLVER
Caliber: 357 Mag. 38 Spec., 8-shot. **Barrel:** 4", 6-1/2", 8-3/8". **Weight:** 44-57 oz. **Length:** 9-3/8" overall. **Grips:** Soft black rubber. **Sights:** Adjustable. **Features:** Double-action, integral key-lock action. Available in blue or stainless. Introduced 1995. Imported by Taurus International.
Price: . . . . **$469.00 to $547.00**

Taurus Model 44 Series Revolver
Similar to Taurus Model 60 series, but in .44 Rem. Mag. With six-shot cylinder, blue and matte stainless finishes.
Price: . . . . **$500.00 to $578.00**

TAURUS MODEL 650CIA REVOLVER
Caliber: 357 Magnum, 5-shot. **Barrel:** 2". **Weight:** 24.5 oz. **Grips:** Rubber. **Sights:** Ramp front, square notch rear. **Features:** Double-action only, blue or matte stainless steel, integral key-lock, internal hammer. Introduced 2001. From Taurus International.
Price: . . . . **$406.00 to $453.00**

TAURUS MODEL 651CIA REVOLVER
Caliber: 357 Magnum, 5-shot. **Barrel:** 2". **Weight:** 17-24.5 oz. **Grips:** Rubber. **Sights:** Fixed. **Features:** Concealed single-action/double-action design. Shrouded cockable hammer, blue, matte stainless, Shadow Gray, Total Titanium, integral key-lock. Made in Brazil. Imported by Taurus International Manufacturing, Inc.
Price: . . . . **$406.00 to $578.00**

TAURUS MODEL 450 REVOLVER
Caliber: 45 Colt, 5-shot. **Barrel:** 2". **Weight:** 21.2-22.3 oz. **Length:** 6-5/8" overall. **Grips:** Rubber. **Sights:** Ramp front, notch rear. **Features:** Double-action, blue or stainless, ported, integral key-lock. Introduced 1999. Imported from Brazil by Taurus International.
Price: **$492.00**
Price: Ultra-Lite (alloy frame) **$523.00**
Price: Total Titanium, 19.2 oz. **$600.00**

TAURUS MODEL 444/454/480 RAGING BULL REVOLVERS
Caliber: 44 Mag., 45 LC, 454 Casull, 480 Ruger, 5-shot. **Barrel:** 5", 6-1/2", 8-3/8". **Weight:** 53-63 oz. **Length:** 12" overall (6-1/2" barrel). **Grips:** Soft black rubber. **Sights:** Patridge front, adjustable rear. **Features:** Double-action, ventilated rib, ported, integral key-lock. Introduced 1997. Imported by Taurus International.
Price: Blue . . . . **$578.00 to $797.00**
Price: Matte stainless . . . . **$641.00 to $859.00**

TAURUS RAGING BULL MODEL 416
Caliber: 41 Magnum, 6-shot. **Barrel:** 6-1/2". **Weight:** 61.9 oz. **Grips:** Rubber. **Sights:** Adjustable. **Features:** Double-action, ported, ventilated rib, matte stainless, integral key-lock.
Price: **$641.00**

Taurus Model 617

Taurus Model 817

Taurus Model 941 Ultra Lite

Taurus Model 850 Titanium

Taurus Model 970 Tracker

Taurus Model 980 Silhouette

Taurus Model 905

TAURUS MODEL 617 REVOLVER
Caliber: 357 Magnum, 7-shot. **Barrel:** 2". **Weight:** 28.3 oz. **Length:** 6-3/4" overall. **Grips:** Soft black rubber. **Sights:** Fixed. **Features:** Double-action, blue, Shadow Gray, bright spectrum blue or matte stainless steel, integral key-lock. Available with porting, concealed hammer. Introduced 1998. Imported by Taurus International.
Price: . . . . **$391.00 to $453.00**
Price: Total Titanium, 19.9 oz. **$602.00**

Taurus Model 445 Series Revolver
Similar to Taurus Model 617 series except in 44 Spl. with 5-shot cylinder.
Price: . . . . **$389.00 to $422.00**

Taurus Model 617ULT Revolver
Similar to Model 617 except aluminum alloy and titanium components, matte stainless finish, integral key-lock action. Weighs 18.5 oz. Available ported or non-ported. Introduced 2001. Imported by Taurus International.
Price: (5-shot cylinder) . . . . **$530.00 to $545.00**

TAURUS MODEL 817 ULTRA-LITE REVOLVER
Caliber: 38 Spec., 7-shot. **Barrel:** 2". **Weight:** 21 oz. **Length:** 6-1/2" overall. **Grips:** Soft rubber. **Sights:** Fixed. **Features:** Double-action, integral key-lock. Rated for +P ammo. Introduced 1999. Imported from Brazil by Taurus International.
Price: Blue **$375.00**
Price: Blue, ported **$395.00**
Price: Matte, stainless **$420.00**
Price: Matte, stainless, ported **$440.00**

TAURUS MODEL 850CIA REVOLVER
Caliber: 38 Special, 5-shot. **Barrel:** 2". **Weight:** 17-24.5 oz. **Grips:** Rubber, mother-of-pearl. **Sights:** Ramp front, square notch rear. **Features:** Double-action only, blue or matte stainless steel, rated for +P ammo, integral key-lock, internal hammer. Introduced 2001. From Taurus International.
Price: . . . . **$406.00 to $453.00**
Price: Total Titanium **$578.00**

TAURUS MODEL 851CIA REVOLVER
Caliber: 38 Spec., 5-shot. **Barrel:** 2". **Weight:** 17-24.5 oz. **Grips:** Rubber. **Sights:** Fixed-UL/ULT adjustable. **Features:** Concealed single-action/double-action design. Shrouded cockable hammer, blue, matte stainless, Total Titanium, blue or stainless UL and ULT, integral key-lock. Rated for +P ammo.
Price: . . . . **$406.00 to $578.00**

TAURUS MODEL 94, 941 REVOLVER
Caliber: 22 LR (Mod. 94), 22 WMR (Mod. 941), 8-shot. **Barrel:** 2", 4", 5". **Weight:** 27.5 oz. (4" barrel). **Grips:** Soft black rubber. **Sights:** Serrated ramp front, rear adjustable. **Features:** Double-action, integral key-lock. Introduced 1992. Imported by Taurus International.
Price: Blue . . . . **$328.00 to $344.00**
Price: Stainless (matte) . . . . **$375.00 to $391.00**
Price: Model 941 Ultra Lite, forged aluminum alloy, 2" . **$359.00 to $375.00**
Price: As above, stainless . . . . **$406.00 to $422.00**

TAURUS MODEL 970/971 TRACKER REVOLVERS
Caliber: 22 LR (Model 970), 22 Magnum (Model 971); 7-shot. **Barrel:** 6". **Weight:** 53.6 oz. **Grips:** Rubber. **Sights:** Double barrel, heavy barrel with ventilated rib; matte stainless finish, integral key-lock. Introduced 2001. From Taurus International.
Price: . . . . **$391.00 to $406.00**

TAURUS MODEL 980/981 SILHOUETTE REVOLVERS
Caliber: 22 LR (Model 980), 22 Magnum (Model 981); 7-shot. **Barrel:** 12". **Weight:** 68 oz. **Grips:** Rubber. **Sights:** Adjustable. **Features:** Double-action, heavy barrel with ventilated rib and scope mount, matte stainless finish, integral key-lock. Introduced 2001. From Taurus International.
Price: (Model 980) **$398.00**
Price: (Model 981) **$414.00**

TAURUS MODEL 905, 405, 455 PISTOL CALIBER REVOLVERS
Caliber: 9mm, .40, .45 ACP, 5-shot. **Barrel:** 2", 4", 6-1/2". **Weight:** 21 oz. to 40.8 oz. **Grips:** Rubber. **Sights:** Fixed, adjustable on Model 455SS6 in .45 ACP. **Features:** Produced as a backup gun for law enforcement officers. Introduced 2003. Imported from Brazil by Taurus International.
Price: . . . . **$383.00 to $523.00**

Both classic six-shooters and modern adaptations for hunting and sport.

Century Model 100

Cimarron Lightning

Cimarron Model P
New Sheriff

Cimarron Bisley

Cimarron Model P Jr.

Cimarron USV

Cimarron Open Top

CENTURY GUN DIST. MODEL 100 SINGLE-ACTION
Caliber: 30-30, 375 Win., 444 Marlin, 45-70, 50-70. **Barrel:** 6-1/2" (standard), 8", 10". **Weight:** 6 lbs. (loaded). **Length:** 15" overall (8" bbl.). **Grips:** Smooth walnut. **Sights:** Ramp front, Millett adjustable square notch rear. **Features:** Highly polished high tensile strength manganese bronze frame, blue cylinder and barrel; coil spring trigger mechanism. Introduced 1975. Made in U.S.A. From Century Gun Dist., Inc.
Price: 6-1/2" barrel, 45-70 . . . . **$2,000.00**

CIMARRON LIGHTNING SA
Caliber: 32-20, 32 H&R, 38 Colt, 38 Special. **Barrel:** 3-1/2", 4-3/4", 5-1/2". **Grips:** Smooth or checkered walnut. **Sights:** Blade front. **Features:** Replica of the Colt 1877 Lightning DA. Similar to Cimarron Thunderer™, except smaller grip frame to fit smaller hands. Standard blue, charcoal blue or nickel finish with forged, old model, or color case hardened frame. Introduced 2001. From Cimarron F.A. Co.
Price: . . . . **$499.00 to $559.00**

CIMARRON MODEL P
Caliber: 32 WCF, 38 WCF, 357 Mag., 44 WCF, 44 Spec., 45 Colt, 45LC and 45 ACP. **Barrel:** 4-3/4", 5-1/2", 7-1/2". **Weight:** 39 oz. **Length:** 10" overall (4" barrel). **Grips:** Walnut. **Sights:** Blade front, fixed or adjustable rear. **Features:** Uses "old model" black powder frame with "Bullseye" ejector or New Model frame. Imported by Cimarron F.A. Co.
Price: . . . . **$499.00 to $559.00**
Price: New Sheriff . . . . **$499.00 to $559.00**

Cimarron Bisley Model Single-Action Revolvers
Similar to 1873 Model P, special grip frame and trigger guard, knurled wide-spur hammer, curved trigger. Available in 357 Mag., 44 WCF, 44 Spl., 45 Colt. Introduced 1999. Imported by Cimarron F.A. Co.
Price: **$525.00**

CIMARRON MODEL "P" JR.
Caliber: 32-20, 32 H&R, 38 Special. **Barrel:** 3-1/2", 4-3/4", 5-1/2". **Grips:** Checkered walnut. **Sights:** Blade front. **Features:** Styled after 1873 Colt Peacemaker, except 20 percent smaller. Blue finish with color case-

hardened frame; Cowboy Comp® action. Introduced 2001. From Cimarron F.A. Co.
Price: . . . . **$489.00 to $529.00**

CIMARRON U. S. VOLUNTEER ARTILLERY MODEL SINGLE-ACTION
Caliber: 45 Colt. **Barrel:** 5-1/2". **Weight:** 39 oz. **Length:** 11-1/2" overall. **Grips:** Walnut. **Sights:** Fixed. **Features:** U.S. markings and cartouche, case-hardened frame and hammer; 45 Colt only. Imported by Cimarron F.A. Co.
Price: . . . . **$549.00 to $599.00**

CIMARRON 1872 OPEN TOP REVOLVER
Caliber: 38, 44 Special, 44 Colt, 44 Russian, 45LC, 45 S&W Schofield. **Barrel:** 5-1/2" and 7-1/2". **Grips:** Walnut. **Sights:** Blade front, fixed rear. **Features:** Replica of first cartridge-firing revolver. Blue, charcoal blue, nickel or Original® finish; Navy-style brass or steel Army-style frame. Introduced 2001 by Cimarron F.A. Co.
Price: . . . . **$529.00 to $599.00**

Cimarron Thunderer

Colt Single-Action Army

EAA Bounty Hunter

EMF Hartford

EMF 1894 Bisley

CIMARRON THUNDERER REVOLVER

Caliber: 357 Mag., 44 WCF, 44 Spl, 45 Colt, 6-shot. **Barrel:** 3-1/2", 4-3/4", 5-1/2", 7-1/2", with ejector. **Weight:** 38 oz. (3-1/2" barrel). **Grips:** Smooth or checkered walnut. **Sights:** Blade front, notch rear. **Features:** Thunderer grip; color case-hardened frame with balance blued. Introduced 1993. Imported by Cimarron F.A. Co.

Price: 3-1/2", 4-3/4", smooth grips . . . . **$519.00 to $549.00**
Price: As above, checkered grips . . . . **$564.00 to $584.00**
Price: 5-1/2", 7-1/2", smooth grips . . . . **$519.00 to $549.00**
Price: As above, checkered grips . . . . **$564.00 to $584.00**

COLT SINGLE-ACTION ARMY REVOLVER

Caliber: 357 Mag., 38 Special, .32/20, 44-40, 45 Colt, 6-shot. **Barrel:** 4-3/4", 5-1/2", 7-1/2". **Weight:** 40 oz. (4-3/4" barrel). **Length:** 10-1/4" overall (4-3/4" barrel). **Grips:** Black Eagle composite. **Sights:** Blade front, notch rear. **Features:** Available in full nickel finish with nickel grip medallions, or Royal Blue with color case-hardened frame. Reintroduced 1992.

Price: . . . . **$1,380.00 to $1,500.00**

EAA BOUNTY HUNTER SA REVOLVERS

Caliber: 22 LR/22 WMR, 357 Mag., 44 Mag., 45 Colt, 6-shot. **Barrel:** 4-1/2", 7-1/2". **Weight:** 2.5 lbs. **Length:** 11" overall (4-5/8" barrel). **Grips:** Smooth walnut. **Sights:** Blade front, grooved topstrap rear. **Features:** Transfer bar safety; 3-position hammer; hammer forged barrel. Introduced 1992. Imported by European American Armory.

Price: Blue or case-hardened **$369.00**
Price: Nickel **$399.00**
Price: 22LR/22WMR, blue **$269.00**
Price: As above, nickel **$299.00**

EMF MODEL 1873 FRONTIER MARSHAL

Caliber: 357 Mag., 45 Colt. **Barrel:** 4-3/4", 5-1/2, 7-1/2". **Weight:** 39 oz. **Length:** 10-1/2" overall. **Grips:** One-piece walnut. **Sights:** Blade front, notch rear. **Features:** Bright brass trigger guard and backstrap, color case-hardened frame, blued barrel and cylinder. Introduced 1998. Imported from Italy by IAR, Inc.

Price: **$395.00**

EMF HARTFORD SINGLE-ACTION REVOLVERS

Caliber: 357 Mag., 32-20, 38-40, 44-40, 44 Spec., 45 Colt. **Barrel:** 4-3/4", 5-1/2", 7-1/2". **Weight:** 45 oz. **Length:** 13" overall (7-1/2" barrel). **Grips:** Smooth walnut. **Sights:** Blade front, fixed rear. **Features:** Identical to the original Colts with inspector cartouche on left grip, original patent dates and U.S. markings. All major parts serial numbered using original Colt-style lettering, numbering. Bullseye ejector head and color case-hardening on frame and hammer. Introduced 1990. From E.M.F.

Price: **$500.00**
Price: Cavalry or Artillery **$390.00**
Price: Nickel plated, add **$125.00**
Price: Case-hardened New Model frame **$365.00**

EMF 1894 Bisley Revolver

Similar to the Hartford single-action revolver except has special grip frame and trigger guard, wide spur hammer; available in 38-40 or 45 Colt, 4-3/4", 5-1/2" or 7-1/2" barrel. Introduced 1995. Imported by E.M.F.

Price: Case-hardened/blue **$400.00**
Price: Nickel **$525.00**

EMF Hartford Pinkerton Single-Action Revolver

Same as the regular Hartford except has 4" barrel with ejector tube and bird's-head grip. Calibers: 357 Mag., 45 Colt. Introduced 1997. Imported by E.M.F.

Price: **$375.00**

EMF Hartford Express Single-Action Revolver

Same as the regular Hartford model except uses grip of the Colt Lightning revolver. Barrel lengths of 4", 4-3/4", 5-1/2". Introduced 1997. Imported by E.M.F.

Price: **$375.00**

EMF 1875 Outlaw

EMF 1890 Police

Freedom Arms Model 83 Premier Grade

Freedom Arms Model 83 Field Grade

Freedom Arms Model 83 475 Linebaugh

Freedom Arms Model 83 Varmint Class

EMF 1875 OUTLAW REVOLVER
Caliber: 357 Mag., 44-40, 45 Colt. **Barrel:** 7-1/2". **Weight:** 46 oz. **Length:** 13-1/2" overall. **Grips:** Smooth walnut. **Sights:** Blade front, fixed groove rear. **Features:** Authentic copy of 1875 Remington with firing pin in hammer; color case-hardened frame, blue cylinder, barrel, steel backstrap and brass trigger guard. Also available in nickel, factory engraved. Imported by E.M.F.
Price: All calibers $575.00
Price: Nickel $735.00

EMF 1890 Police Revolver
Similar to the 1875 Outlaw except has 5-1/2" barrel, weighs 40 oz., with 12-1/2" overall length. Has lanyard ring in butt. No web under barrel. Calibers 357, 44-40, 45 Colt. Imported by E.M.F.
Price: All calibers $590.00
Price: Nickel $750.00

FREEDOM ARMS MODEL 83 PREMIER GRADE REVOLVER
Caliber: 357 Mag., 41 Mag., 44 Mag., 454 Casull, 475 Linebaugh, 50 AE, 5-shot. **Barrel:** 4-3/4", 6", 7-1/2", 9" (357 Mag. only), 10". **Weight:** 52.8 oz. **Length:** 13" (7-1/2" bbl.). **Grips:** Impregnated hardwood. **Sights:** Blade front, notch or adjustable rear. **Features:** All stainless steel construction; sliding bar safety system. Lifetime warranty. Made in U.S.A. by Freedom Arms, Inc.
Price: 454 Casull, 475 Linebaugh, 50 AE. $2,058.00
Price: 454 Casull, fixed sight $1,979.00

Price: 357 Mag., 41 Mag., 44 Mag. $1,976.00
Price: 44 Mag., fixed sight $1,911.00

Freedom Arms Model 83 Field Grade Revolver
Model 83 frame. Weighs 52-56 oz. Adjustable rear sight, replaceable front blade, matte finish, Pachmayr grips. All stainless steel. Introduced 1988. Made in U.S.A. by Freedom Arms Inc.
Price: 454 Casull, 475 Linebaugh, 50 AE, adj. sights $1,591.00
Price: 454 Casull, fixed sights $1,553.00
Price: 357 Mag., 41 Mag., 44 Mag. $1,527.00

FREEDOM ARMS MODEL 83 VARMINT CLASS REVOLVERS
Caliber: 22 LR, 5-shot. **Barrel:** 5-1/8, 7-1/2". **Weight:** 58 oz. (7-1/2" bbl.). **Length:** 11-1/2" (7-1/2" bbl.). **Grips:** Impregnated hardwood. **Sights:** Steel base adjustable "V" notch rear sight and replaceable brass bead front sight. **Features:** Stainless steel, matte finish, manual sliding bar system, dual firing pins, pre-set trigger stop. Made in U.S.A. by Freedom Arms, Inc.
Price: Varmint Class $1,828.00
Price: Extra fitted 22 WMR cylinder $264.00

Freedom Arms Model 97 Premier Grade

Heritage Rough Rider

Magnum Research Long Cylinder BFR

Navy Arms Flat Top

Navy Arms Bisley

FREEDOM ARMS MODEL 97 PREMIER GRADE REVOLVER
Caliber: 22 LR, 357 Mag., 41 Mag., 44 Special, 45 Colt, 5-shot. **Barrel:** 4-1/2", 5-1/2", 7-1/2", 10". **Weight:** 37 oz. (45 Colt 5-1/2"). **Length:** 10-3/4" (5-1/2" bbl.). **Grips:** Impregnated hardwood. **Sights:** Adjustable rear, replaceable blade front. **Features:** Stainless steel, brushed finish, automatic transfer bar safety system. Introduced in 1997. Made in U.S.A. by Freedom Arms.
Price: 357 Mag., 41 Mag., 45 Colt **$1,668.00**
Price: 357 Mag., 45 Colt, fixed sight **$1,576.00**
Price: Extra fitted cylinders 38 Special, 45 ACP **$264.00**
Price: 22 LR with sporting chambers **$1,732.00**
Price: Extra fitted 22 WMR cylinder **$264.00**
Price: Extra fitted 22 LR match grade cylinder **$476.00**
Price: 22 match grade chamber instead of 22 LR sport chamber . . **$214.00**

HERITAGE ROUGH RIDER REVOLVER
Caliber: 17HMR, 17LR, 32 H&R, 32 S&W, 32 S&W Long, .45LC, 22 LR, 22 LR/22 WMR combo, 6-shot. **Barrel:** 2-3/4", 3-1/2", 4-3/4", 6-1/2", 9". **Weight:** 31 to 38 oz. **Length:** NA. **Grips:** Exotic hardwood, laminated wood or mother-of-pearl; bird's-head models offered. **Sights:** Blade front, fixed rear. Adjustable sight on 4", 6" and 9" models. **Features:** Hammer block safety. High polish blue, black satin, silver satin, case-hardened and nickel finish. Introduced 1993. Made in U.S.A. by Heritage Mfg., Inc.
Price: . . . . **$159.95 to $389.95**

MAGNUM RESEARCH BFR SINGLE-ACTION REVOLVER
(Long cylinder) Caliber: 30/30, 45/70 Government, 444 Marlin, 45 LC/410, 450 Marlin, .500 S&W. **Barrel:** 7.5", 10". **Weight:** 4 lbs., 4.36 lbs. **Length:** 15", 17.5".
(Short cylinder) Caliber: 50AE, 454 Casull, 22 Hornet, BFR 480/475. **Barrel:** 6.5", 7.5", 10". **Weight:** 3.2 lbs., 3.5 lbs., 4.36 lbs. (10"). **Length:** 12.75 (6"), 13.75", 16.25".
Sights: All have fully adjustable rear, black blade ramp front. **Features:** Stainless steel construction, rubber grips, all 5-shot capacity. Barrels are stress-relieved and cut rifled. Made in U.S.A. From Magnum Research, Inc.
Price: **$899.00**

NAVY ARMS FLAT TOP TARGET MODEL REVOLVER
Caliber: 45 Colt, 6-shot cylinder. **Barrel:** 7-1/2". **Weight:** 40 oz. **Length:** 13-1/4" overall. **Grips:** Smooth walnut. **Sights:** Spring-loaded German silver front, rear adjustable for windage. **Features:** Replica of Colt's Flat Top Frontier target revolver made from 1888 to 1896. Blue with color case-hardened frame. Introduced 1997. Imported by Navy Arms.
Price: **$450.00**

NAVY ARMS BISLEY MODEL SINGLE-ACTION REVOLVER
Caliber: 44-40 or 45 Colt, 6-shot cylinder. **Barrel:** 4-3/4", 5-1/2", 7-1/2". **Weight:** 40 oz. **Length:** 12-1/2" overall (7-1/2" barrel). **Grips:** Smooth walnut. **Sights:** Blade front, notch rear. **Features:** Replica of Colt's Bisley Model. Polished blue finish, color case-hardened frame. Introduced 1997. Imported by Navy Arms.
Price: . . . . **$425.00 to $460.00**

Navy Arms 1873

Navy Arms 1875 Schofield

North American Mini

North American Mini-Master

Navy Arms New Model Russian

North American Black Widow

NAVY ARMS 1873 SINGLE-ACTION REVOLVER

Caliber: 357 Mag., 44-40, 45 Colt, 6-shot cylinder. **Barrel:** 4-3/4", 5-1/2", 7-1/2". **Weight:** 36 oz. **Length:** 10-3/4" overall (5-1/2" barrel). **Grips:** Smooth walnut. **Sights:** Blade front, notch rear. **Features:** Blue with color case-hardened frame. Introduced 1991. Imported by Navy Arms.
Price: **$405.00**

NAVY ARMS 1875 SCHOFIELD REVOLVER

Caliber: 44-40, 45 Colt, 6-shot cylinder. **Barrel:** 3-1/2", 5", 7". **Weight:** 39 oz. **Length:** 10-3/4" overall (5" barrel). **Grips:** Smooth walnut. **Sights:** Blade front, notch rear. **Features:** Replica of Smith & Wesson Model 3 Schofield. Single-action, top-break with automatic ejection. Polished blue finish. Introduced 1994. Imported by Navy Arms.
Price: Hideout Model, 3-1/2" barrel **$695.00**
Price: Wells Fargo, 5" barrel **$695.00**
Price: U.S. Cavalry model, 7" barrel, military markings **$695.00**

NAVY ARMS NEW MODEL RUSSIAN REVOLVER

Caliber: 44 Russian, 6-shot cylinder. **Barrel:** 6-1/2". **Weight:** 40 oz. **Length:** 12" overall. **Grips:** Smooth walnut. **Sights:** Blade front, rear. **Features:** Replica of the S&W Model 3 Russian Third Model revolver. Spur trigger guard, polished blue finish. Introduced 1999. Imported by Navy Arms.
Price: **$769.00**

NAVY ARMS 1851 NAVY CONVERSION REVOLVER

Caliber: 38 Spec., 38 Long Colt. **Barrel:** 5-1/2", 7-1/2". **Weight:** 44 oz. **Length:** 14" overall (7-1/2" barrel). **Grips:** Smooth walnut. **Sights:** Bead front, notch rear. **Features:** Replica of Colt's cartridge conversion revolver. Polished blue finish with color case-hardened frame, silver plated trigger guard and backstrap. Introduced 1999. Imported by Navy Arms.
Price: **$165.00**

NAVY ARMS 1860 ARMY CONVERSION REVOLVER

Caliber: 38 Spec., 38 Long Colt. **Barrel:** 5-1/2", 7-1/2". **Weight:** 44 oz. **Length:** 13-1/2" overall (7-1/2" barrel). **Grips:** Smooth walnut. **Sights:** Blade front, notch rear. **Features:** Replica of Colt's conversion revolver.

Polished blue finish with color case-hardened frame, full-size 1860 Army grip with blued steel backstrap. Introduced 1999. Imported by Navy Arms.
Price: **$190.00**

NORTH AMERICAN MINI REVOLVERS

Caliber: 22 Short, 22 LR, 22 WMR, 5-shot. **Barrel:** 1-1/8", 1-5/8". **Weight:** 4 to 6.6 oz. **Length:** 3-5/8" to 6-1/8" overall. **Grips:** Laminated wood. **Sights:** Blade front, notch fixed rear. **Features:** All stainless steel construction. Polished satin and matte finish. Engraved models available. From North American Arms.
Price: 22 Short, 22 LR **$193.00**
Price: 22 WMR, 1-1/8" or 1-5/8" bbl. **$193.00**
Price: 22 WMR, 1-1/8" or 1-5/8" bbl. with extra 22 LR cylinder **$193.00**

NORTH AMERICAN MINI-MASTER

Caliber: 22 LR, 22 WMR, 17 HMR, 5-shot cylinder. **Barrel:** 4". **Weight:** 10.7 oz. **Length:** 7.75" overall. **Grips:** Checkered hard black rubber. **Sights:** Blade front, white outline rear adjustable for elevation, or fixed. **Features:** Heavy vented barrel; full-size grips. Non-fluted cylinder. Introduced 1989.
Price: Adjustable sight, 22 WMR, 17 HMR or 22 LR **$301.00**
Price: As above with extra WMR/LR cylinder **$330.00**
Price: Fixed sight, 22 WMR, 17 HMR or 22 LR **$272.00**
Price: As above with extra WMR/LR cylinder **$330.00**

North American Black Widow Revolver

Similar to Mini-Master, 2" heavy vent barrel. Built on 22 WMR frame. Non-fluted cylinder, black rubber grips. Available with Millett Low Profile fixed sights or Millett sight adjustable for elevation only. Overall length 5-7/8", weighs 8.8 oz. From North American Arms.
Price: Adjustable sight, 22 LR, 17 HMR or 22 WMR **$287.00**
Price: As above with extra WMR/LR cylinder **$316.00**
Price: Fixed sight, 22 LR, 17 HMR or 22 WMR **$287.00**
Price: As above with extra WMR/LR cylinder **$287.00**

Ruger "Bird's-Head" Single Six

Ruger SSMBH-4F

Ruger Blackhawk

Ruger Bisley Single-Action

Ruger Super Blackhawk Hunter

Ruger Vaquero

RUGER NEW MODEL SINGLE SIX REVOLVER
Caliber: 32 H&R. **Barrel:** 4-5/8", 6-shot. **Grips:** Black Micarta "bird's-head", rosewood with color case. **Sights:** Fixed. **Features:** High impact case, gun lock standard.
Price: Stainless, KSSMBH-4F, bird's-head **$576.00**
Price: Color case, SSMBH-4F, bird's-head **$576.00**
Price: Color case, SSM-4F-S, rosewood **$576.00**

RUGER NEW MODEL BLACKHAWK AND BLACKHAWK CONVERTIBLE
Caliber: 30 Carbine, 357 Mag./38 Spec., 41 Mag., 45 Colt, 6-shot. **Barrel:** 4-5/8" or 5-1/2", either caliber; 7-1/2" (30 carbine and 45 Colt). **Weight:** 42 oz. (6-1/2" bbl.). **Length:** 12-1/4" overall (5-1/2" bbl.). **Grips:** American walnut. **Sights:** 1/8" ramp front, micro-click rear adjustable for windage and elevation. **Features:** Ruger transfer bar safety system, independent firing pin, hardened chrome-moly steel frame, music wire springs throughout. Case and lock included.
Price: Blue 30 Carbine, 7-1/2" (BN31) **$435.00**
Price: Blue, 357 Mag., 4-5/8", 6-1/2" (BN34, BN36) **$435.00**
Price: As above, stainless (KBN34, KBN36) **$530.00**
Price: Blue, 357 Mag./9mm Convertible, 4-5/8", 6-1/2"
(BN34X, BN36X) includes extra cylinder **$489.00**
Price: Blue, 41 Mag., 4-5/8", 6-1/2" (BN41, BN42) **$435.00**
Price: Blue, 45 Colt, 4-5/8", 5-1/2", 7-1/2" (BN44, BN455, BN45) . . **$435.00**
Price: Stainless, 45 Colt, 4-5/8", 7-1/2" (KBN44, KBN45) **$530.00**
Price: Blue, 45 Colt/45 ACP Convertible, 4-5/8", 5-1/2"
(BN44X, BN455X) includes extra cylinder **$489.00**

Ruger Bisley Single-Action Revolver
Similar to standard Blackhawk, hammer is lower with smoothly curved, deeply checkered wide spur. The trigger is strongly curved with wide smooth surface. Longer grip frame. Adjustable rear sight, ramp-style front. Unfluted cylinder and roll engraving, adjustable sights. Chambered for 357, 44 Mags. and 45 Colt; 7-1/2" barrel; overall length of 13"; weighs 48 oz. Plastic lockable case. Introduced 1985.
Price: RB-35W, 357Mag, RBD-44W, 44Mag, RB-45W, 45 Colt . . . **$535.00**

RUGER NEW MODEL SUPER BLACKHAWK
Caliber: 44 Mag., 6-shot. Also fires 44 Spec. **Barrel:** 4-5/8", 5-1/2", 7-1/2", 10-1/2" bull. **Weight:** 48 oz. (7-1/2" bbl.), 51 oz. (10-1/2" bbl.). **Length:** 13-3/8" overall (7-1/2" bbl.). **Grips:** American walnut. **Sights:** 1/8" ramp front, micro-click rear adjustable for windage and elevation. **Features:** Ruger transfer bar safety system, fluted or unfluted cylinder, steel grip and

cylinder frame, round or square back trigger guard, wide serrated trigger, wide spur hammer. With case and lock.
Price: Blue, 4-5/8", 5-1/2", 7-1/2" (S458N, S45N, S47N) **$519.00**
Price: Blue, 10-1/2" bull barrel (S411N) **$529.00**
Price: Stainless, 4-5/8", 5-1/2", 7-1/2" (KS458N, KS45N, KS47N) . **$535.00**
Price: Stainless, 10-1/2" bull barrel (KS411N) **$545.00**

RUGER NEW MODEL SUPER BLACKHAWK HUNTER
Caliber: 44 Mag., 6-shot. **Barrel:** 7-1/2", full-length solid rib, unfluted cylinder. **Weight:** 52 oz. **Length:** 13-5/8". **Grips:** Black laminated wood. **Sights:** Adjustable rear, replaceable front blade. **Features:** Reintroduced Ultimate SA revolver. Includes instruction manual, high-impact case, set 1" medium scope rings, gun lock, ejector rod as standard.
Price: **$639.00**

RUGER VAQUERO SINGLE-ACTION REVOLVER
Caliber: 357 Mag., 44-40, 44 Mag., 45 LC, 6-shot. **Barrel:** 4-5/8", 5-1/2", 7-1/2". **Weight:** 38-41 oz. **Length:** 13-1/8" overall (7-1/2" barrel). **Grips:** Smooth rosewood with Ruger medallion. **Sights:** Blade front, fixed notch rear. **Features:** Transfer bar safety system and loading gate interlock. Blued model color case-hardened finish on frame, rest polished and blued. Stainless has high-gloss. Introduced 1993. From Sturm, Ruger & Co.
Price: 357 Mag. BNV34, KBNV34 (4-5/8"),
BNV35, KBNV35 (5-1/2") **$535.00**
Price: 44-40 BNV40, KBNV40 (4-5/8"). BNV405,
KBNV405 (5-1/2"). BNV407, KBNV407 (7-1/2") **$535.00**
Price: 44 Mag., BNV474, KBNV474 (4-5/8"). BNV475,
KBNV475 (5-1/2"). BNV477, KBNV477 (7-1/2") **$535.00**
Price: 45 LC, BN444, KBNV44 (4-5/8"). BNV455,
KBNV455 (5-1/2"). BNV45, KBNV45 (7-1/2") **$535.00**
Price: 45 LC, BNVBH453, KBNVBH453 3-3/4" with
"bird's-head" grip **$576.00**
Price: 357 Mag., RBNV35 (5-1/2") **$535.00**; KRBNV35 (5-1/2") . . . **$555.00**
Price: 45 LC, RBNV44 (4-5/8"), RBNV455 (5-1/2") **$535.00**
Price: 45 LC, KRBNV44 (4-5/8"), KRBNV455 (5-1/2") **$555.00**

Ruger Bisley-Vaquero

Ruger New Bearcat

Ruger Single-Six

Ruger Super Single-Six

Ruger Bisley

Tristar Regulator

Ruger Bisley-Vaquero Single-Action Revolver

Similar to Vaquero model with Bisley-style hammer, grip and trigger, available in 357 Magnum, 44 Magnum and 45 LC only; 4-5/8" or 5-1/2" barrel. Smooth rosewood grips with Ruger medallion. Roll-engraved, unfluted cylinder. Introduced 1997. From Sturm, Ruger & Co.
Price: Color case-hardened frame, blue grip frame, barrel and cylinder,
RBNV-475, RBNV-474, 44 Mag. $535.00
Price: High-gloss stainless steel, KRBNV-475, KRBNV-474 . . . . . . $555.00
Price: For simulated ivory grips, add . . . . $41.00 to $44.00

RUGER NEW BEARCAT SINGLE-ACTION

Caliber: 22 LR, 6-shot. **Barrel:** 4". **Weight:** 24 oz. **Length:** 8-7/8" overall. **Grips:** Smooth rosewood with Ruger medallion. **Sights:** Blade front, fixed notch rear. **Features:** Reintroduction of the Ruger Bearcat with slightly lengthened frame, Ruger patented transfer bar safety system. Available in blue only. Introduced 1993. With case and lock. From Sturm, Ruger & Co.
Price: SBC4, blue $379.00
Price: KSBC-4, ss $429.00

RUGER MODEL SINGLE-SIX REVOLVER

Caliber: 32 H&R Magnum. **Barrel:** 4-5/8", 6-shot. **Weight:** 33 oz. **Length:** 10-1/8". **Grips:** Blue, rosewood, stainless, simulated ivory. **Sights:** Blade front, notch rear fixed. **Features:** Transfer bar and loading gate interlock safety, instruction manual, high impact case and gun lock.
Price: $576.00
Price: Blue, SSM4FS $576.00
Price: SS, KSSM4FSI $576.00

RUGER SINGLE-SIX AND SUPER SINGLE-SIX CONVERTIBLE

Caliber: 22 LR, 6-shot; 22 WMR in extra cylinder; 17 HMR. **Barrel:** 4-5/8", 5-1/2", 6-1/2", 9-1/2" (6-groove). **Weight:** 35 oz. (6-1/2" bbl.). **Length:** 11-13/16" overall (6-1/2" bbl.). **Grips:** Smooth American walnut. **Sights:** Improved Patridge front on ramp, fully adjustable rear protected by integral frame ribs (super single-six); or fixed sight (single six). **Features:** Transfer bar safety system, loading gate interlock, hardened chrome-moly steel frame, wide trigger, music wire springs throughout, independent firing pin.
Price: 4-5/8", 5-1/2", 6-1/2", 9-1/2" barrel, blue,
adjustable sight NR4, NR5, NR6, NR9 . . . . $399.00
Price: 5-1/2", 6-1/2" bbl. only, stainless steel, adjustable sight
KNR5, KNR6 . . . . $485.00
Price: 5-1/2", 6-1/2" barrel, blue fixed sights $399.00
Price: 6-1/2" barrel, NR 617, 17 HMR $399.00
Price: Ruger 50th Anniversary Single Six with 4-5/8" barrel and a
gold-colored rollmark, "50 years of Single Six 1953 to 2003," blued
steel finish, cocobolo wood grips with red Ruger medallions and
both 22 LR and 22 WMR cylinders $599.00
Price: Stainless Hunter $650.00

Ruger Bisley Small Frame Revolver

Similar to Single-Six, frame is styled after classic Bisley "flat-top." Hammer is lower and smoothly curved with deeply checkered spur. Trigger is strongly curved with wide smooth surface. Longer grip frame design, and trigger guard is a large oval. Adjustable dovetail rear sight; front sight base accepts interchangeable square blades. Unfluted cylinder and roll engraving. Weighs 41 oz. Chambered for 22 LR, 6-1/2" barrel only. Plastic lockable case. Introduced 1985.
Price: RB-22AW $422.00

TRISTAR/UBERTI REGULATOR REVOLVER

Caliber: 45 Colt. **Barrel:** 4-3/4", 5-1/2". **Weight:** 32-38 oz. **Length:** 8-1/4" overall (4-3/4" bbl.) **Grips:** One-piece walnut. **Sights:** Blade front, notch rear. **Features:** Uberti replica of 1873 Colt Model "P" revolver. Color-case hardened steel frame, brass backstrap and trigger guard, hammer-block safety. Imported from Italy by Tristar Sporting Arms.
Price: Regulator $335.00
Price: Regulator Deluxe (blued backstrap, trigger guard) $367.00

Uberti 1873 Cattleman

Uberti Russian

Uberti 1870 Schofield

Uberti Bisley

U.S. Firearms Single Action Army Revolver

U.S. Firearms United States Pre-War

UBERTI 1873 CATTLEMAN SINGLE-ACTION
Caliber: 357 Mag., 44-40, 45 Colt; 6-shot. **Barrel:** 4-3/4", 5-1/2", 7-1/2"; 44-40, 45 Colt also with 3", 3-1/2", 4". **Weight:** 38 oz. (5-1/2" bbl.). **Length:** 10-3/4" overall (5-1/2" bbl.). **Grips:** One-piece smooth walnut. **Sights:** Blade front, groove rear. **Features:** Steel or brass backstrap, trigger guard; color case-hardened frame, blued barrel, cylinder. Imported from Italy by Uberti U.S.A.
Price: Steel backstrap, trigger guard, fixed sights **$410.00**
Price: Brass backstrap, trigger guard, fixed sights **$359.00**

UBERTI NEW MODEL RUSSIAN REVOLVER
Caliber: 44 Russian, 6-shot cylinder. **Barrel:** 6-1/2". **Weight:** 40 oz. **Length:** 12" overall. **Grips:** Smooth walnut. **Sights:** Blade front, notch rear. **Features:** Replica of the S&W Model 3 Russian Third Model revolver. Spur trigger guard, polished blue finish. Introduced 1999. Imported by Uberti U.S.A.
Price: **$825.00**

UBERTI 1870 SCHOFIELD-STYLE BREAK-TOP REVOLVER
Caliber: 44-40, 45 Colt, 6-shot cylinder. **Barrel:** 5", 7". **Weight:** 39 oz. **Length:** 10-3/4" overall (5" barrel). **Grips:** Smooth walnut. **Sights:** Blade front, notch rear. **Features:** Replica of Smith & Wesson Model 3 Schofield. Single-action, top-break with automatic ejection. Polished blue finish (first model). Introduced 1994. Imported by Uberti U.S.A.
Price: **$775.00**

UBERTI BISLEY MODEL SINGLE-ACTION REVOLVER
Caliber: 357 Mag., 45 Colt, 6-shot cylinder. **Barrel:** 4-3/4", 5-1/2", 7-1/2". **Weight:** 40 oz. **Length:** 12-1/2" overall (7-1/2" barrel). **Grips:** Smooth walnut. **Sights:** Blade front, notch rear. **Features:** Replica of Colt's Bisley Model. Polished blue finish, color case-hardened frame. Introduced 1997. Imported by Uberti U.S.A.
Price: **$460.00**

U.S. FIRE ARMS SINGLE ACTION ARMY REVOLVER
Caliber: 45 Colt (standard); 32 WCF, 38 WCF, 38 S&W, 41 Colt, 44WCF, 44 S&W (optional, additional charge), 6-shot cylinder. **Barrel:** 4-3/4", 5-1/2", 7-1/2". **Weight:** 37 oz. **Length:** NA. **Grips:** Hard rubber. **Sights:** Blade front, notch rear. **Features:** Recreation of original guns; 3" and 4" have no ejector. Available with all-blue, blue with color case-hardening, or full nickel-plate finish. Made in U.S.A. by United States Fire Arms Mfg. Co.
Price: Blue/cased-colors **$949.00**
Price: Nickel **$1,220.00**

U.S. FIRE ARMS NETTLETON CAVALRY
Caliber: 45 Colt, 6-shot cylinder. **Barrel:** 5-1/2" (artillery model), 7-1/2". **Grips:** One-piece walnut. **Features:** Military armory blue and bone case finish. Made in U.S.A. by Fire Arms Mfg. Co.
Price: Blued finish **$1,485.00**
Price: Nickel finish **$1,619.00**

U.S. FIRE ARMS RODEO COWBOY ACTION REVOLVER
Caliber: 45 Colt. **Barrel:** 4-3/4", 5-1/2". **Grips:** Rubber. **Features:** Historically correct Armory bone case hammer, blue satin finish, transfer bar safety system, correct solid firing pin. Entry level basic cowboy SASS gun.
Price: **$649.00**

U.S. FIRE ARMS UNITED STATES PRE-WAR
Caliber: 45 Colt, other caliber available. **Barrel:** 4-3/4", 5-1/2", 7-1/2". **Grips:** Hard rubber. **Features:** Armory bone case/Armory blue finish standard, cross-pin or black powder frame. Introduced 2002. Made in U.S.A. by United States Firearms Mfg. Co.
Price: **$1,345.00**

Specially adapted single-shot and multi-barrel arms.

American Derringer Model 1

American Derringer Model 4

American Derringer Model 6

American Derringer Model 7

American Derringer Lady Derringer

American Derringer DA 38

AMERICAN DERRINGER MODEL 1

Caliber: 22 LR, 22 WMR, 30 Carbine, 30 Luger, 30-30 Win., 32 H&R Mag., 32-20, 380 ACP, 38 Super, 38 Spec., 38 Spec. shotshell, 38 Spec. +P, 9mm Para., 357 Mag., 357 Mag./45/410, 357 Maximum, 10mm, 40 S&W, 41 Mag., 38-40, 44-40 Win., 44 Spec., 44 Mag., 45 Colt, 45 Win. Mag., 45 ACP, 45 Colt/410, 45-70 single shot. **Barrel:** 3". **Weight:** 15-1/2 oz. (38 Spec.). **Length:** 4.82" overall. **Grips:** Rosewood, Zebra wood. **Sights:** Blade front. **Features:** Made of stainless steel with high-polish or satin finish. Two-shot capacity. Manual hammer block safety. Introduced 1980. Available in most pistol calibers. From American Derringer Corp.

Price: 22 LR . . . . **CALL**
Price: 38 Spec. . . . . **CALL**
Price: 357 Maximum . . . . **CALL**
Price: 357 Mag. . . . . **CALL**
Price: 9mm, 380 . . . . **CALL**
Price: 40 S&W . . . . **CALL**
Price: 44 Spec. . . . . **CALL**
Price: 44-40 Win. . . . . **CALL**
Price: 45 Colt . . . . **CALL**
Price: 30-30, 45 Win. Mag. . . . . **CALL**
Price: 41, 44 Mags. . . . . **CALL**
Price: 45-70, single shot . . . . **CALL**
Price: 45 Colt, 410, 2-1/2" . . . . **CALL**
Price: 45 ACP, 10mm Auto . . . . **CALL**

American Derringer Model 4

Similar to the Model 1 except has 4.1" barrel, overall length of 6", and weighs 16-1/2 oz.; chambered for 357 Mag., 357 Maximum, 45-70, 3" 410-bore shotshells or 45 Colt or 44 Mag. Made of stainless steel. Manual hammer block safety. Introduced 1980.

Price: 3" 410/45 Colt **$425.00**
Price: 45-70 . . . . **$560.00**
Price: 44 Mag. with oversize grips **$515.00**
Price: Alaskan Survival model
(45-70 upper barrel, 410 or 45 Colt lower) **$475.00**

American Derringer Model 6

Similar to the Model 1 except has 6" barrel chambered for 3" 410 shotshells or 22 WMR, 357 Mag., 45 ACP, 45 Colt; rosewood stocks. 8.2" o.a.l. and weighs 21 oz. Manual hammer block safety. Introduced 1980.

Price: 22 WMR **$440.00**
Price: 357 Mag. **$440.00**
Price: 45 Colt/410 . . . . **$450.00**
Price: 45 ACP **$440.00**

American Derringer Model 7 Ultra Lightweight

Similar to Model 1 except made of high strength aircraft aluminum. Weighs 7-1/2 oz., 4.82" o.a.l., rosewood stocks. Available in 22 LR, 22 WMR, 32 H&R Mag., 380 ACP, 38 Spec., 44 Spec. Introduced 1980.

Price: 22 LR, WMR **$325.00**
Price: 38 Spec. **$325.00**
Price: 380 ACP **$325.00**
Price: 32 H&R Mag/32 S&W Long **$325.00**
Price: 44 Spec. **$565.00**

American Derringer Model 10 Ultra Lightweight

Similar to the Model 1 except frame is aluminum, giving weight of 10 oz. Stainless barrels. Available in 38 Spec., 45 Colt or 45 ACP only. Matte gray finish. Introduced 1980.

Price: 45 Colt **$385.00**
Price: 45 ACP **$330.00**
Price: 38 Spec. **$305.00**

American Derringer Lady Derringer

Same as the Model 1 except has tuned action, is fitted with scrimshawed synthetic ivory grips; chambered for 32 H&R Mag. and 38 Spec.; 357 Mag., 45 Colt, 45/410. Deluxe Grade is highly polished; Deluxe Engraved is engraved in a pattern similar to that used on 1880s derringers. All models come in a French-fitted jewelry box. Introduced 1989.

Price: 32 H&R Mag. **$375.00**
Price: 357 Mag. **$405.00**
Price: 38 Spec. **$360.00**
Price: 45 Colt, 45/410 . . . . **$435.00**

American Derringer Texas Commemorative

Model 1 Derringer with solid brass frame, stainless steel barrel and rosewood grips. Available in 38 Spec., 44-40 Win., or 45 Colt. Introduced 1980.

Price: 38 Spec. **$365.00**
Price: 44-40 . . . . **$420.00**
Price: Brass frame, 45 Colt **$450.00**

AMERICAN DERRINGER DA 38 MODEL

Caliber: 22 LR, 9mm Para., 38 Spec., 357 Mag., 40 S&W. **Barrel:** 3". **Weight:** 14.5 oz. **Length:** 4.8" overall. **Grips:** Rosewood or other hardwoods. **Sights:** Fixed. **Features:** Double-action only; two shots. Manual safety. Made of satin-finished stainless steel and aluminum. Introduced 1989. From American Derringer Corp.

Price: 22 LR **$435.00**
Price: 38 Spec. **$460.00**
Price: 9mm Para. **$445.00**
Price: 357 Mag. **$450.00**
Price: 40 S&W **$475.00**

ANSCHUTZ MODEL 64P SPORT/TARGET PISTOL

Caliber: 22 LR, 22 WMR, 5-shot magazine. **Barrel:** 10". **Weight:** 3 lbs. 8 oz. **Length:** 18-1/2" overall. **Stock:** Choate Rynite. **Sights:** None furnished; grooved for scope mounting. **Features:** Right-hand bolt; polished blue finish. Introduced 1998. Imported from Germany by AcuSport.

Price: 22 LR **$455.95**
Price: 22 WMR **$479.95**

Bond Arms Texas Defender

Bond Arms Century 2000 Defender

Cobra Big Bore

Cobra D-Series

Comanche Super Single Shot

Gaucher GN1 Silhouette

Downsizer WSP Single Shot

BOND ARMS DEFENDER DERRINGER
Caliber: From 22 LR to 45 LC/410 shotshells **Barrel:** 3". **Weight:** 19-20 oz. **Grips:** Rosewood. **Sights:** Blade front, fixed rear. **Features:** Interchangeable barrels, stainless steel firing pins, cross-bolt safety, automatic extractor for rimmed calibers. Stainless steel construction. Right or left hand.
Price: Texas (with removable trigger guard) 3" bbl. $379.00

BOND ARMS CENTURY 200
Caliber: 45LC/410 shotshells. **Barrel:** 3.5". **Weight:** 21 oz. **Features:** Similar to Defender series.
Price: $394.00

BOND ARMS SNAKE SLAYER
Caliber: 45 LC/410 shotshell (2-1/2" or 3"). **Barrel:** 3.5". **Weight:** 21 oz. Grips: Extended rosewood. **Sights:** Blade front, fixed rear. **Features:** Single-action; interchangeable barrels; stainless steel firing pin. Introduced 2005.
Price: $445.00

BROWN CLASSIC SINGLE SHOT PISTOL
Caliber: 17 Ackley Hornet through 375x444. **Barrel:** 15" air-gauged match grade. **Weight:** About 3 lbs. 7 oz. **Grips:** Walnut; thumb rest target-style. **Sights:** None furnished; drilled and tapped for scope mounting. **Features:** Falling block action gives rigid barrel-receiver mating; hand fitted and headspaced. Introduced 1998. Made in U.S.A. by E.A. Brown Mfg.
Price: $589.00

COBRA BIG BORE DERRINGERS
Caliber: 22 WMR, 32 H&R Mag., 38 Spec., 9mm Para. **Barrel:** 2.75". **Weight:** 11.5 oz. **Length:** 4.65" overall. **Grips:** Textured black synthetic. **Sights:** Blade front, fixed notch rear. **Features:** Alloy frame, steel-lined barrels, steel breech block. Plunger-type safety with integral hammer block. Chrome or black Teflon finish. Introduced 2002. Made in U.S.A. by Cobra Enterprises.
Price: $98.00
Price: 9mm Para $136.00

COBRA LONG-BORE DERRINGERS
Caliber: 22 WMR, 38 Spec., 9mm Para. **Barrel:** 3.5". **Weight:** 13 oz. **Length:** 5.65" overall. **Grips:** Textured black synthetic. **Sights:** Fixed. **Features:** Chrome or black Teflon finish. Larger than Davis D-Series models. Introduced 2002. Made in U.S.A. by Cobra Enterprises.
Price: $136.00
Price: 9mm Para. $136.00
Price: Big-Bore models (same calibers, 3/4" shorter barrels) $136.00

COBRA STARBIRD-SERIES DERRINGERS
Caliber: 22 LR, 22 WMR, 25 ACP, 32 ACP. **Barrel:** 2.4". **Weight:** 9.5 oz. **Length:** 4" overall. **Grips:** Laminated wood or pearl. **Sights:** Blade front, fixed notch rear. **Features:** Choice of black powder coat, satin nickel or chrome finish; spur trigger. Introduced 2002. Made in U.S.A. by Cobra Enterprises.
Price: $112.00

COMANCHE SUPER SINGLE SHOT PISTOL
Caliber: 45 LC, 410 ga. **Barrel:** 10". **Sights:** Adjustable. **Features:** Blue finish, not available for sale in CA, MA. Distributed by SGS Importers International, Inc.
Price: $174.95
Price: Satin nickel $191.95
Price: Duo-tone $185.95

DOWNSIZER WSP SINGLE SHOT PISTOL
Caliber: 357 Magnum, 45 ACP, 38 Special. **Barrel:** 2.10". **Weight:** 11 oz. **Length:** 3.25" overall. **Grips:** Black polymer. **Sights:** None. **Features:** Single shot, tip-up barrel. Double action only. Stainless steel construction. Measures .900" thick. Introduced 1997. From Downsizer Corp.
Price: $499.00

GAUCHER GN1 SILHOUETTE PISTOL
Caliber: 22 LR, single shot. **Barrel:** 10". **Weight:** 2.4 lbs. **Length:** 15.5" overall. **Grips:** European hardwood. **Sights:** Blade front, open adjustable rear. **Features:** Bolt action, adjustable trigger. Introduced 1990. Imported from France by Mandall Shooting Supplies.
Price: About $525.00
Price: Model GP Silhouette $425.00

Maximum Single Shot

RPM XL Pistol

Thompson/Center G2 Contender

MAXIMUM SINGLE SHOT PISTOL
Caliber: 22 LR, 22 Hornet, 22 BR, 22 PPC, 223 Rem., 22-250, 6mm BR, 6mm PPC, 243, 250 Savage, 6.5mm-35M, 270 MAX, 270 Win., 7mm TCU, 7mm BR, 7mm-35, 7mm INT-R, 7mm-08, 7mm Rocket, 7mm Super-Mag., 30 Herrett, 30 Carbine, 30-30, 308 Win., 30x39, 32-20, 350 Rem. Mag., 357 Mag., 357 Maximum, 358 Win., 375 H&H, 44 Mag., 454 Casull. **Barrel:** 8-3/4", 10-1/2", 14". **Weight:** 61 oz. (10-1/2" bbl.); 78 oz. (14" bbl.). **Length:** 15", 18-1/2" overall (with 10-1/2" and 14" bbl., respectively). **Grips:** Smooth walnut stocks and forend. Also available with 17" finger groove grip. **Sights:** Ramp front, fully adjustable open rear. **Features:** Falling block action; drilled and tapped for M.O.A. scope mounts; integral grip frame/receiver; adjustable trigger; Douglas barrel (interchangeable). Introduced 1983. Made in U.S.A. by M.O.A. Corp.
Price: Stainless receiver, blue barrel **$799.00**
Price: Stainless receiver, stainless barrel **$883.00**
Price: Extra blued barrel **$254.00**
Price: Extra stainless barrel **$317.00**
Price: Scope mount **$60.00**

RPM XL SINGLE SHOT PISTOL
Caliber: 22 LR through 45-70. **Barrel:** 8", 10-3/4", 12", 14". **Weight:** About 60 oz. **Grips:** Smooth Goncalo Alves with thumb and heel rests. **Sights:** Hooded front with interchangeable post, or Patridge; ISGW rear adjustable for windage and elevation. **Features:** Barrel drilled and tapped for scope mount. Visible cocking indicator. Spring-loaded barrel lock, positive hammer-block safety. Trigger adjustable for weight of pull and over-travel. Contact maker for complete price list. Made in U.S.A. by RPM.
Price: XL Hunter model (action only) **$1,045.00**
Price: Extra barrel, 8" through 10-3/4" **$407.50**
Price: Extra barrel, 12" through 14" **$547.50**
Price: Muzzle brake **$160.00**
Price: Left-hand action, add **$50.00**

SAVAGE STRIKER BOLT-ACTION HUNTING HANDGUN
Caliber: 223, 243, 7mm-08, 308, 300 WSM 2-shot mag. **Barrel:** 14". **Weight:** About 5 lbs. **Length:** 22-1/2" overall. **Stock:** Black composite ambidextrous mid-grip; grooved forend; "Dual Pillar" bedding. **Sights:** None furnished; drilled and tapped for scope mounting. **Features:** Short left-hand bolt with right-hand ejection; free-floated barrel; uses Savage Model 110 rifle scope rings/bases. Introduced 1998. Made in U.S.A. by Savage Arms, Inc.
Price: Model 503 (blued barrel and action) **$285.00**
Price: Model 503 R17FSS (stainless barrel and action) **$281.00**
Price: Model 516FSAK black stock (ss, aMB, 300 WSM) **$260.00**

Savage Sport Striker Bolt-Action Hunting Handgun
Similar to Striker, but chambered in 22 LR and 22 WMR. Detachable 10-shot magazine (5-shot magazine for 22 WMR). Overall length 19", weighs 4 lbs. Ambidextrous fiberglass/graphite composite rear grip. Drilled and tapped, scope mount installed. Introduced 2000. Made in U.S.A. by Savage Arms Inc.
Price: Model 501F (blue finish, 22 LR) **$236.00**
Price: Model 501FXP with soft case, 1.25-4x28 scope **$258.00**
Price: Model 502F (blue finish, 22 WMR) **$238.00**

SPRINGFIELD M6 SCOUT PISTOL
Caliber: 22 LR/45 LC/410, 22 Hornet, 45 LC/410. **Barrel:** 10". **Weight:** NA. **Length:** NA. **Grips:** NA. **Sights:** NA. **Features:** Adapted from the U.S. Air Force M6 Survival Rifle, also available as a carbine with 16" barrel.
Price: . . . . **$169.00 to $197.00**
Price: Pistol/Carbine . . . . **$183.00 to $209.00**

THOMPSON/CENTER ENCORE PISTOL
Caliber: 22-250, 223, 204 Ruger, 6.8 Rem., 260 Rem., 7mm-08, 243, 308, 270, 30-06, 375 JDJ, 204 Ruger, 44 Mag., 454 Casull, 480 Ruger, 444 Marlin single shot, 450 Marlin with muzzle tamer, no sights. **Barrel:** 12", 15", tapered round. **Weight:** NA. **Length:** 21" overall with 12" barrel. **Grips:** American walnut with finger grooves, walnut forend. **Sights:** Blade on ramp front, adjustable rear, or none. **Features:** Interchangeable barrels; action opens by squeezing the trigger guard; drilled and tapped for scope mounting; blue finish. Announced 1996. Made in U.S.A. by Thompson/Center Arms.
Price: . . . . **$589.00 to $592.00**
Price: Extra 12" barrels **$262.00**
Price: Extra 15" barrels **$270.00**
Price: 45 Colt/410 barrel, 12" **$292.00**
Price: 45 Colt/410 barrel, 15" **$299.00**

Thompson/Center Stainless Encore Pistol
Similar to blued Encore, made of stainless steel, available with 15" barrel in 223, 22-250, 243 Win., 7mm-08, 308, 30/06 Sprgfld., 45/70 Gov't., 45/410 VR. With black rubber grip and forend. Made in U.S.A. by Thompson/Center Arms.
Price: . . . . **$636.00 to $644.00**

Thompson/Center G2 Contender Pistol
A second generation Contender pistol maintaining the same barrel interchangeability with older Contender barrels and their corresponding forends (except Herrett forend). The G2 frame will not accept old-style grips due to the change in grip angle. Incorporates an automatic hammer block safety with built-in interlock. Features include trigger adjustable for overtravel, adjustable rear sight; ramp front sight blade, blued steel finish.
Price: **$570.00**

UBERTI ROLLING BLOCK TARGET PISTOL
Caliber: 22 LR, 22 WMR, 22 Hornet, 357 Mag., 45 Colt, single shot. **Barrel:** 9-7/8", half-round, half-octagon. **Weight:** 44 oz. **Length:** 14" overall. **Stock:** Walnut grip and forend. **Sights:** Blade front, fully adjustable rear. **Features:** Replica of the 1871 rolling block target pistol. Brass trigger guard, color case-hardened frame, blue barrel. Imported by Uberti U.S.A.
Price: **$410.00**

Both classic arms and recent designs in American-style repeaters for sport and field shooting.

Armalite M15A2

Armalite AR-10A4

Armalite AR-180B

ARMALITE M15A2 CARBINE
Caliber: 223, 30-round magazine. **Barrel:** 16" heavy chrome lined; 1:9" twist. **Weight:** 7 lbs. **Length:** 35-11/16" overall. **Stock:** Green or black composition. **Sights:** Standard A2. **Features:** Upper and lower receivers have push-type pivot pin; hard coat anodized; A2-style forward assist; M16A2-type raised fence around magazine release button. Made in U.S.A. by ArmaLite, Inc.
Price: Green $1,100.00
Price: Black $1,100.00

ARMALITE AR-10A4 SPECIAL PURPOSE RIFLE
Caliber: 308 Win., 10- and 20-round magazine. **Barrel:** 20" chrome-lined, 1:11.25" twist. **Weight:** 9.6 lbs. **Length:** 41" overall. **Stock:** Green or black composition. **Sights:** Detachable handle, front sight, or scope mount available; comes with international style flattop receiver with Picatinny rail. **Features:** Forged upper receiver with case deflector. Receivers are hard-coat anodized. Introduced 1995. Made in U.S.A. by ArmaLite, Inc.
Price: Green. $1,506.00
Price: Black $1,506.00
Price: Green or black with match trigger $1,606.00

ArmaLite AR-10(T)
Similar to the ArmaLite AR-10A4 but with stainless steel, barrel, machined tool steel, two-stage National Match trigger group and other features.
Price: AR-10(T) rifle $2,126.00
Price: AR-10(T) carbine. $2,126.00

ArmaLite AR-10A2
Utilizing the same 20" double-lapped, heavy barrel as the ArmaLite AR-10A4 Special Purpose Rifle. Offered in 308 caliber only. Made in U.S.A. by ArmaLite, Inc.
Price: AR-10A2 rifle or carbine $1,506.00
Price: AR-10A2 rifle or carbine with match trigger $1,606.00

ARMALITE AR-180B RIFLE
Caliber: 223, 10-shot magazine. **Barrel:** 19.8". **Weight:** 6 lbs. **Length:** 38". **Stock:** Synthetic. **Sights:** Rear sight adjustable for windage, small and large apertures. **Features:** Lower receiver made of polymer, upper formed of sheet metal. Uses standard AR-15 magazines. Made in U.S.A. by Armalite.
Price: $750.00

ARSENAL USA SSR-56
Caliber: 7.62x39mm. **Barrel:** 16.25". **Weight:** 7.4 lbs. **Length:** 35.5". **Stock:** Black polymer. **Sights:** Adjustable rear. **Features:** An AK-47-style rifle built on a hardened Hungarian FEG receiver with the required six U.S.-made parts to make it legal for use with all extra-capacity magazines. From Arsenal I, LLC.
Price: $565.00

ARSENAL USA SSR-74-2
Caliber: 5.45x39mm **Barrel:** 16.25" **Weight:** 7 lbs. **Length:** 36.75" **Stock:** Polymer or wood. **Sights:** Adjustable. **Features:** Built with parts from an unissued Bulgarian AK-47 rifle, it has a Buffer Technologies recoil buffer, enough U.S.-made parts to allow pistol grip stock and use with all extra-capacity magazines. Assembled in U.S.A. From Arsenal I, LLC.
Price: $499.00

ARSENAL USA SSR-85C-2
Caliber: 7.62x39mm. **Barrel:** 16.25". **Weight:** 7.1 lbs. **Length:** 35.5". **Stock:** Polymer or wood. **Sights:** Adjustable rear calibrated to 800 meters. **Features:** Built from parts obtained from unissued Polish AK-47 rifles, the gas tube is vented and the receiver cover is plain. Rifle contains enough U.S.-sourced parts to allow pistol grip stock and use with all extra-capacity magazines. Assembled in U.S.A. by Arsenal I, LLC.
Price: $499.00

CENTERFIRE RIFLES — Autoloaders

Auto-Ordnance 1927 A-1 Thompson

Barrett Model 82A-1

Browning Mark II Safari

None. **Features:** Auto-regulating gas-operated system, three-lug rotary bolt, interchangeable barrels. Introduced 2003. Imported from Italy by Benelli USA.
Price: **$1,080.00**

BROWNING BAR MARK II SAFARI SEMI-AUTO RIFLE
Caliber: 243, 25-06, 270, 30-06, 308, 270 WSM, 7mm WSM. **Barrel:** 22" round tapered. **Weight:** 7-3/8 lbs. **Length:** 43" overall. **Stock:** French walnut pistol grip stock and forend, hand checkered. **Sights:** Gold bead on hooded ramp front, click adjustable rear, or no sights. **Features:** Has new bolt release lever; removable trigger assembly with larger trigger guard; redesigned gas and buffer systems. Detachable 4-round box magazine. Scroll-engraved receiver is tapped for scope mounting. BOSS barrel vibration modulator and muzzle brake system available only on models without sights. Mark II Safari introduced 1993. Imported from Belgium by Browning.
Price: Safari, with sights **$833.00**
Price: Safari, no sights **$815.00**
Price: Safari, 270 and 30-06, no sights, BOSS **$891.00**

Browning BAR Mark II Safari Rifle (Magnum)
Same as the standard caliber model, except weighs 8-3/8 lbs., 45" overall, 24" bbl., 3-round mag. Cals. 7mm Mag., 300 Win. Mag., 338 Win. Mag. BOSS barrel vibration modulator and muzzle brake system available only on models without sights. Introduced 1993.
Price: Safari, no sights **$908.00**
Price: Safari, no sights, BOSS **$1,007.00**

BROWNING BAR SHORT TRAC/LONG TRAC AUTO RIFLES
Caliber: (Short Trac models) 270 WSM, 7mm WSM, 300 WSM, 243 Win., 308 WIn.; (Long Trac models) 270 Win., 30-06 Sprfld., 7mm Rem. Mag., 300 Win. Mag. **Barrel:** 23". **Weight:** 6 lbs. 10 oz. to 7 lbs. 4 oz. **Length:** 41-1/2" to 44". **Stock:** Satin-finish walnut, pistol-grip, fluted forend. **Sights:** Adj. rear, bead front standard, no sights on BOSS models (optional). **Features:** Designed to handle new WSM chamberings. Gas-operated, blued finish, rotary bolt design (Long Trac models).
Price: Short Trac, WSM calibers **$885.00**
Price: Short Trac, 243, 308 . . . . **$885.00**
Price: Long Trac calibers **$965.00**

AUTO-ORDNANCE 1927 A-1 THOMPSON
Caliber: 45 ACP. **Barrel:** 16-1/2". **Weight:** 13 lbs. **Length:** About 41" overall (Deluxe). **Stock:** Walnut stock and vertical forend. **Sights:** Blade front, open rear adjustable for windage. **Features:** Recreation of Thompson Model 1927. Semi-auto only. Deluxe model has finned barrel, adjustable rear sight and compensator; Standard model has plain barrel and military sight. From Auto-Ordnance Corp.
Price: Deluxe **$950.00**
Price: 1927A1C lightweight model (9-1/2 lbs.) **$950.00**

Auto-Ordnance Thompson M1/M1-C
Similar to the 1927 A-1 except is in the M-1 configuration with side cocking knob, horizontal forend, smooth unfinned barrel, sling swivels on butt and forend. Matte black finish. Introduced 1985.
Price: M1 semi-auto carbin **$950.00**
Price: M1-C lightweight semi-auto **$925.00**

Auto-Ordnance 1927 A-1 Commando
Similar to the 1927 A-1 except has Parkerized finish, black-finish wood butt, pistol grip, horizontal forend. Comes with black nylon sling. Introduced 1998. Made in U.S.A. by Auto-Ordnance Corp.
Price: **$950.00**

BARRETT MODEL 82A-1 SEMI-AUTOMATIC RIFLE
Caliber: 50 BMG, 10-shot detachable box magazine. **Barrel:** 29". **Weight:** 28.5 lbs. **Length:** 57" overall. **Stock:** Composition with energy-absorbing recoil pad. **Sights:** Scope optional. **Features:** Semi-automatic, recoil operated with recoiling barrel. Three-lug locking bolt; muzzle brake. Adjustable bipod. Introduced 1985. Made in U.S.A. by Barrett Firearms.
Price: From **$7,200.00**

BENELLI RI RIFLE
Caliber: 300 Win. Mag., 30-06, 308, 300 WSM, 270 WSM. **Barrel:** 20", 22", 24". **Weight:** 7.1 lbs. **Length:** 43.75" **Stock:** Select satin walnut. **Sights:**

Bushmaster M17S Bullpup

Bushmaster XM15 E2S Carbine

Bushmaster Varminter

Colt Match Target Lightweight

BROWNING BAR STALKER AUTO RIFLES
Caliber: 243, 308, 270, 30-06, 7mm Rem. Mag., 300 Win. Mag., 338 Win. Mag., 270 WSM, 7mm WSM. **Barrel:** 20", 22" and 24". **Weight:** 6 lbs., 12 oz. (243) to 8 lbs., 2 oz. (magnum cals.) **Length:** 41" to 45" overall. **Stock:** Black composite stock and forearm. **Sights:** Hooded front and adjustable rear or none. **Features:** Optional BOSS (no sights); gas-operated action with seven-lug rotary bolt; dual action bars; 3- or 4-shot magazine (depending on caliber). Introduced 2001. Imported by Browning.
Price: BAR Stalker, open sights (243, 308, 270, 30-06) **$883.00**
Price: BAR Stalker, open sights (7mm, 300 Win. Mag.,
338 Win. Mag.) **$964.00**

BUSHMASTER M17S BULLPUP RIFLE
Caliber: 223, 10-shot magazine. **Barrel:** 21.5", chrome lined; 1:9" twist. **Weight:** 8.2 lbs. **Length:** 30" overall. **Stock:** Fiberglass-filled nylon. **Sights:** Designed for optics-carrying handle incorporates scope mount rail for Weaver-type rings; also includes 25-meter open iron sights. **Features:** Gas-operated, short-stroke piston system; ambidextrous magazine release. Introduced 1993. Made in U.S.A. by Bushmaster Firearms, Inc./Quality Parts Co.
Price: **$765.00**

BUSHMASTER SHORTY XM15 E2S CARBINE
Caliber: 223, 10-shot magazine. **Barrel:** 16", heavy; 1:9" twist. **Weight:** 7.2 lbs. **Length:** 34.75" overall. **Stock:** A2 type; fixed black composition. **Sights:** Fully adjustable M16A2 sight system. **Features:** Patterned after Colt M-16A2. Chrome-lined barrel with manganese phosphate finish. "Shorty" handguards. Has forged aluminum receivers with pushpin. Made in U.S.A. by Bushmaster Firearms, Inc.
Price: (A2) **$985.00**
Price: (A3) **$1,085.00**

Bushmaster XM15 E2S Dissipator Carbine
Similar to the XM15 E2S Shorty carbine except has full-length "Dissipator" handguards. Weighs 7.6 lbs.; 34.75" overall; forged aluminum receivers with push-pin style takedown. Made in U.S.A. by Bushmaster Firearms, Inc.

Price: (A2 type) **$995.00**
Price: (A3 type) **$1,095.00**

Bushmaster XM15 E25 AK Shorty Carbine
Similar to the XM15 E2S Shorty except has 14.5" barrel with an AK muzzle brake permanently attached giving 16" barrel length. Weighs 7.3 lbs. Introduced 1999. Made in U.S.A. by Bushmaster Firearms, Inc.
Price: (A2 type) **$1,005.00**
Price: (A3 type) **$1,105.00**

Bushmaster M4/M4A3 Post-Ban Carbine
Similar to the XM15 E2S except has 14.5" barrel with Mini Y compensator, and fixed telestock. MR configuration has fixed carry handle; M4A3 has removeable carry handle.
Price: (M4) **$1,065.00**
Price: (M4A3) **$1,165.00**

BUSHMASTER VARMINTER RIFLE
Caliber: 223 Rem., 5-shot. **Barrel:** 24", 1:9" twist, fluted, heavy, stainless. **Weight:** 8-3/4 lbs. **Length:** 42-1/4". **Stock:** Rubberized pistol grip. **Sights:** 1/2" scope risers. **Features:** Gas-operated, semi-auto, two-stage trigger, slotted free floater forend, lockable hard case.
Price: **$1,245.00**

COLT MATCH TARGET MODEL RIFLE
Caliber: 223 Rem., 5-shot magazine. **Barrel:** 16.1" or 20". **Weight:** 7.1 to 8-1/2 lbs. **Length:** 34-1/2" to 39" overall. **Stock:** Composition stock, grip, forend. **Sights:** Post front, rear adjustable for windage and elevation. **Features:** 5-round detachable box magazine, flash suppressor, sling swivels. Forward bolt assist included. Introduced 1991. Made in U.S.A. by Colt's Mfg. Co., Inc.
Price: Match Target HBAR, from **$1,300.00**

DSA SA58 Standard

DSA SA58 Carbine

DSA SA58 Medium Contour Tactical

DSA SA58 Medium Contour

DPMS PANTHER ARMS A-15 RIFLES
Caliber: 223 Rem., 7.62x39. **Barrel:** 16" to 24". **Weight:** 7-3/4 to 11-3/4 lbs. **Length:** 34-1/2" to 42-1/4" overall. **Stock:** Black Zytel® composite. **Sights:** Square front post, adjustable A2 rear. **Features:** Steel or stainless steel heavy or bull barrel; hardcoat anodized receiver; aluminum free-float tube handguard; many options. From DPMS Panther Arms.
Price: Panther Bull A-15 (20" stainless bull bbl.) **$915.00**
Price: Panther Bull Twenty-Four (24" stainless bull bbl.) **$945.00**
Price: Bulldog (20" stainless fluted bbl., flattop receiver) **$1,219.00**
Price: Panther Bull Sweet Sixteen (16" stainless bull bbl.) **$885.00**
Price: DCM Panther (20" stainless heavy bbl., n.m. sights) **$1,099.00**
Price: Panther 7.62x39 (20" steel heavy bbl.) **$849.00**

DSA SA58 CONGO, PARA CONGO
Caliber: 308 Win. **Barrel:** 18" w/short muzzle brake. **Weight:** 8.6 lbs. (Congo); 9.85 lbs. (Para Congo). **Length:** 39.75" **Stock:** Synthetic w/military grade furniture (Congo); Synthetic with non-folding steel para stock (Para Congo). **Sights:** Post, front, windage adjustable peep, rear (Congo); Belgian-style para flip peep, rear (Para Congo). **Features:** Fully-adjustable gas system, high-grade steel upper receiver with carry handle. Made in U.S.A. by DSA, Inc.
Price: . . . . (Congo) **$1,695.00**; (Para Congo) **$1,995.00**

DSA SA58 GRAY WOLF
Caliber: 308 Win., 300 WSM. **Barrel:** 21" match-grade bull w/target crown. **Weight:** 13 lbs. **Length:** 41.75". **Stock:** Synthetic. **Sights:** Elevation adjustable post, front; windage adjustable match peep, rear. **Features:** Fully-adjustable gas system, high-grade steel upper receiver, Picatinny scope mount, DuraCoat finish. Made in U.S.A. by DSA, Inc.
Price: **$2,120.00**

DSA SA58 PREDATOR
Caliber: 260 Rem., 243 Win., 308 Win. **Barrel:** 16" and 19" w/target crown. **Weight:** 9 to 9.3 lbs. **Length:** 36.25" to 39.25". **Stock:** Synthetic. **Sights:** Elevation adjustable post, front; windage adjustable match peep, rear. **Features:** Fully-adjustable gas system, high-grade steel upper receiver, Picatinny scope mount, DuraCoat solid and camo finishes.
Price: . . . . (308 Win.) **$1,595.00**; (243 Win., 260 Rem.) **$1,695.00**

DSA SA58 T48
Caliber: 308 Win. **Barrel:** 16.25" with Browning replica flash hider. **Weight:** 9.3 lbs. **Length:** 44.5". **Stock:** European walnut. **Sights:** Adjustable post front, adjustable rear peep. **Features:** Gas-operated semi-auto with fully adjustable gas system, high grade steel upper receiver. DuraCoat finishes. Made in U.S.A. by DSA, Inc.
Price: **$1,795.00**

DSA SA58 GI
Similar to the SA58 T48 except has steel bipod cut handguard with hardwood stock and synthetic pistol grip, original GI steel lower receiver with GI bipod. Made in U.S.A. by DSA, Inc.
Price: **$1,695.00**

DSA SA58 TACTICAL CARBINE, CARBINE
Caliber: 308 Win., limited 243 and 260. **Barrel:** 16.25" with integrally machined muzzle brake. **Weight:** 8.75 lbs. **Length:** 38.25". **Stock:** Fiberglass reinforced synthetic handguard. **Sights:** Adjustable post front, adjustable rear peep. **Features:** Gas-operated semi-auto with fully adjustable gas system, high grade steel or 416 stainless upper receiver. In variety of camo finishes. Made in U.S.A. by DSA, Inc.
Price: Tactical fluted bbl. **$1,475.00**
Price: Carbine stainless steel bbl. **$1,645.00**
Price: Carbine high-grade steel bbl. **$1,395.00**

DSA SA58 MEDIUM CONTOUR
Caliber: 308 Win., limited 243 and 260. **Barrel:** 21" with integrally machined muzzle brake. **Weight:** 9.75 lbs. **Length:** 43". **Stock:** Fiberglass reinforced synthetic handguard. **Sights:** Adjustable post front with match rear peep. **Features:** Gas-operated semi-auto with fully adjustable gas system, high grade steel or 416 stainless upper receiver. In variety of camo finishes. Made in U.S.A. by DSA, Inc.
Price: Chrome-moly **$1,475.00**
Price: Stainless steel. **$1,725.00**

DSA SA58 Bull

Heckler & Koch USC

DSA SA58 OSW

Hi-Point Carbine

DSA SA58 21" OR 24" BULL BARREL RIFLE
Caliber: 308 Win., 300 WSM. **Barrel:** 21" or 24". **Weight:** 11.1 and 11.5 lbs. **Length:** 41.5" and 44.5". **Stock:** Synthetic, free floating handguard. **Sights:** Elevation adjustable protected post front, match rear peep. **Features:** Gas-operated semi-auto with fully adjustable gas system, high grade steel or stainless upper receiver. Made in U.S.A. by DSA, Inc.
Price: 21", 24" **$1,745.00**
Price: 24" fluted bbl.. . . . . **$1,795.00**

DSA SA58 MINI OSW
Caliber: 7.62 NATO. **Barrel:** 11" or 13" with muzzle brake. **Weight:** 9 to 9.35 lbs. **Length:** 33". **Stock:** Synthetic. **Features:** Gas-operated semi-auto or select fire with fully adjustable short gas system, optional FAL Rail Interface Handguard, SureFire Vertical Foregrip System, EOTech HOLOgraphic Sight and ITC cheekrest. Made in U.S.A. by DSA, Inc.
Price: **$1,525.00**

EAA/SAIGA SEMI-AUTO RIFLE
Caliber: 7.62x39, 308, 223. **Barrel:** 20.5", 22", 16.3". **Weight:** 7 to 8-1/2 lbs. **Length:** 43". **Stock:** Synthetic or wood. **Sights:** Adjustable, sight base. **Features:** Based on AK Combat rifle by Kalashnikov. Imported from Russia by EAA Corp.
Price: 7.62x39 (syn.) **$239.00**
Price: 308 (syn. or wood). **$429.00**
Price: 223 (syn.). **$389.00**

EAGLE ARMS AR-10 RIFLE
Caliber: 308. **Barrel:** 20", 24". **Weight:** NA. **Length:** NA. **Stock:** Synthetic. **Sights:** Adjustable A2, front, Std. A2, rear; Flattop and Match Rifle have no sights but adjustable Picatinny rail furnished. **Features:** Introduced 2003. Made in U.S.A. by Eagle Arms.
Price: AR-10 Service rifle **$1,055.00**
Price: AR-10 Flattop rifle **$999.95**
Price: AR-10 Match rifle **$1,480.00**

EAGLE ARMS M15 RIFLE
Caliber: 223. **Barrel:** 16", 20". **Weight:** NA. **Length:** NA. **Stock:** Synthetic. **Sights:** Adjustable A2, front; Std. A2, rear; flattop rifle and carbine

versions, no sights furnished. **Features:** Available in 4 different configurations. Introduced 2003. Made in U.S.A. by Eagle Arms.
Price: A2 Rifle **$795.00**
Price: A2 carbine. **$795.00**
Price: Flattop rifle **$835.00**
Price: Flattop carbine **$835.00**

HECKLER & KOCH USC CARBINE
Caliber: 45 ACP, 10-shot magazine. **Barrel:** 16". **Weight:** 8.6 lb. **Length:** 35.4" overall. **Stock:** Skeletonized polymer thumbhole. **Sights:** Blade front with integral hood, fully adjustable diopter. **Features:** Based on German UMP submachine gun. Blowback operation; almost entirely constructed of carbon fiber-reinforced polymer. Free-floating heavy target barrel. Introduced 2000. From H&K.
Price: **$1,249.00**

HI-POINT 9MM CARBINE
Caliber: 9mm Para., 40 S&W, 10-shot magazine. **Barrel:** 16-1/2" (17-1/2" for 40 S&W). **Weight:** 4-1/2 lbs. **Length:** 31-1/2" overall. **Stock:** Black polymer, camouflage. **Sights:** Protected post front, aperture rear. Integral scope mount. **Features:** Grip-mounted magazine release. Black or chrome finish. Sling swivels. Available with laser or red dot sights. Introduced 1996. Made in U.S.A. by MKS Supply, Inc.
Price: Black or chrome, 9mm **$199.00**
Price: 40 S&W. **$225.00**
Price: Camo stock. **$210.00**

IAI M-333 M1 GARAND
Caliber: 30-06, 8-shot clip. **Barrel:** 24". **Weight:** 9-1/2 lbs. **Length:** 43.6" overall. **Stock:** Hardwood. **Sights:** Blade front, aperture adjustable rear. **Features:** Parkerized finish; gas-operated semi-automatic; remanufactured to military specifications. From Intrac Arms International, Inc.
Price: **$971.75**

Les Baer Flattop

Les Baer IPSC

IAI M-888 M1 CARBINE SEMI-AUTOMATIC RIFLE
Caliber: 22, 30 carbine. **Barrel:** 18"-20". **Weight:** 5-1/2 lbs. **Length:** 35"-37" overall. **Stock:** Laminate, walnut or birch. **Sights:** Blade front, adjustable rear. **Features:** Gas-operated, air cooled, manufactured to military specifications. 10/15/30 rnd. mag. scope available. From Intrac Arms International, Inc..
Price: 30 cal. . . . . **$556.00 to $604.00**
Price: 22 cal. . . . . **$567.00 to $654.00**

IAI-65 Rifle
A civilian-legal version of the original HKM rifle manufactured in Hungary. Manufactured by Gordon Technologies using an original AMD-65 matching parts kit built on an AKM receiver. The original wire stock is present, but it is welded in the open position as per BATF regulations. Furnished with a 12.6" barrel with large weld-in-place muzzle brake to bring its length over the 16" federal minimum. This rifle accepts all 7.62x39mm magazines and drums. Introduced 2002. From Intrac Arms International, Inc.
Price: **$799.00**

LES BAER CUSTOM ULTIMATE AR 223 RIFLES
Caliber: 223. **Barrel:** 18", 20", 22", 24". **Weight:** 7-3/4 to 9-3/4 lb. **Length:** NA. **Stock:** Black synthetic. **Sights:** None furnished; Picatinny-style flattop rail for scope mounting. **Features:** Forged receiver; Ultra single-stage trigger (Jewell two-stage trigger optional); titanium firing pin; Versa-Pod bipod; chromed National Match carrier; stainless steel, hand-lapped and cryo-treated barrel; guaranteed to shoot 1/2 or 3/4 MOA, depending on model. Made in U.S.A. by Les Baer Custom Inc.
Price: Super Varmint Model. **$1,989.00**
Price: M4 flattop model **$2,195.00**
Price: IPSC action model **$2,195.00**

LR 300 SR LIGHT SPORT RIFLE
Caliber: 223. **Barrel:** 16-1/4"; 1:9" twist. **Weight:** 7.2 lbs. **Length:** 36" overall (extended stock), 26-1/4" (stock folded). **Stock:** Folding, tubular steel, with thumbhole-type grip. **Sights:** Trijicon post front, Trijicon rear. **Features:** Uses AR-15 type upper and lower receivers; flattop receiver

with weaver base. Accepts all AR-15/M-16 magazines. Introduced 1996. Made in U.S.A. from Z-M Weapons.
Price: **$2,550.00**

OLYMPIC ARMS CAR-97 RIFLES
Caliber: 223, 7-shot; 9mm Para., 45 ACP, 40 S&W, 10mm, 10-shot. **Barrel:** 16". **Weight:** 7 lbs. **Length:** 34.75" overall. **Stock:** A2 stowaway grip, telescoping-look butt. **Sights:** Post front, fully adjustable aperature rear. **Features:** Based on AR-15 rifle. Post-ban version of the CAR-15. Made in U.S.A. by Olympic Arms, Inc.
Price: 223 . . . . **$780.00**
Price: 9mm Para., 45 ACP, 40 S&W, 10mm **$840.00**
Price: PCR Eliminator (223, full-length handguards) **$803.00**

OLYMPIC ARMS PCR-4 RIFLE
Caliber: 223, 10-shot magazine. **Barrel:** 20". **Weight:** 8 lbs., 5 oz. **Length:** 38.25" overall. **Stock:** A2 stowaway grip, trapdoor buttstock. **Sights:** Post front, A1 rear adjustable for windage. **Features:** Based on the AR-15 rifle. Barrel is button rifled with 1:9" twist. No bayonet lug. Introduced 1994. Made in U.S.A. by Olympic Arms, Inc.
Price: **$803.00**

OLYMPIC ARMS K-3B RIFLE
Caliber: 5.56 NATO, 10-shot magazine. **Barrel:** Match grade, 16". **Weight:** 7 lbs. **Length:** 34" overall. **Stock:** Collapsible. **Sights:** Adj. front and rear. **Features:** Black matte anodized, flash suppressor and bayonet lug. Carbine or Featherweight models. Introduced In 2005. Made in U.S.A. by Olympic Arms, Inc.
Price: Rifle. **$1,012.00**
Price: Carbine **$810.00**

PANTHER ARMS CLASSIC AUTO RIFLE
Caliber: 5.56x45mm. **Barrel:** Heavy 16" to 20" w/flash hider. **Weight:** 7 to 9 lbs. **Length:** 34-11/16" to 38-7/16". **Sights:** Adj. rear and front. **Stock:** Black Zytel w/trap door assembly. **Features:** Gas operated rotating bolt, mil spec or Teflon black finish.
Price: **$809.00**
Price: Stainless, match sights. **$1,099.00**
Price: Southpaw **$875.00**
Price: 16" bbl. **$799.00**
Price: Panther Lite, 16" bbl. **$720.00**
Price: Panther carbine. . . . . **$799.00 to $989.00**
Price: Panther bull bbl. **$885.00 to $1,199.00**

Remington Model 7400

Ruger Deerfield 99/44 Carbine

Ruger PC4 Carbine

Ruger Ranch Mini 14/5R

REMINGTON MODEL 7400 AUTO RIFLE
Caliber: 243 Win., 270 Win., 308 Win., 30-06, 4-shot magazine. **Barrel:** 22" round tapered. **Weight:** 7-1/2 lbs. **Length:** 42-5/8" overall. **Stock:** Walnut, deluxe cut checkered pistol grip and forend. Satin or high-gloss finish. **Sights:** Gold bead front sight on ramp; step rear sight with windage adjustable. **Features:** Redesigned and improved version of the Model 742. Positive cross-bolt safety. Receiver tapped for scope mount. Introduced 1981.
Price: $624.00
Price: Carbine (18-1/2" bbl., 30-06 only) $624.00
Price: With black synthetic stock, matte black metal,
rifle or carbine $520.00
Price: Weathermaster, nickel-plated w/synthetic stock and forend,
270, 30-06 . . . . $624.00

ROCK RIVER ARMS STANDARD A2 RIFLE
Caliber: 45 ACP. **Barrel:** NA. **Weight:** 8.2 lbs. **Length:** NA. **Stock:** Thermoplastic. **Sights:** Standard AR-15 style sights. **Features:** Two-stage, national match trigger; optional muzzle brake. Made in U.S.A. From River Rock Arms.
Price: $925.00

RUGER DEERFIELD 99/44 CARBINE
Caliber: 44 Mag., 4-shot rotary magazine. **Barrel:** 18-1/2". **Weight:** 6-1/4 lbs. **Length:** 36-7/8" overall. **Stock:** Hardwood. **Sights:** Gold bead front, folding adjustable aperture rear. **Features:** Semi-automatic action; dual front-locking lugs lock directly into receiver; integral scope mount; push-button safety; includes 1" rings and gun lock. Introduced 2000. Made in U.S.A. by Sturm, Ruger & Co.
Price: $675.00

RUGER PC4, PC9 CARBINES
Caliber: 9mm Para., 40 cal., 10-shot magazine. **Barrel:** 16.25". **Weight:** 6 lbs., 4 oz. **Length:** 34.75" overall. **Stock:** Black high impact synthetic checkered grip and forend. **Sights:** Blade front, open adjustable rear; integral Ruger scope mounts. **Features:** Delayed blowback action; manual push-button cross bolt safety and internal firing pin block safety automatic slide lock. Introduced 1997. Made in U.S.A. by Sturm, Ruger & Co.
Price: PC9, PC4, (9mm, 40 cal.) $605.00
Price: PC4GR, PC9GR, (40 auto, 9mm, post sights, ghost ring). . . $628.00

RUGER MINI-14/5 AUTOLOADING RIFLE
Caliber: 223 Rem., 5-shot detachable box magazine. **Barrel:** 18-1/2". Rifling twist 1:9". **Weight:** 6.4 lbs. **Length:** 37-1/4" overall. **Stock:** American hardwood, steel reinforced. **Sights:** Ramp front, fully adjustable rear. **Features:** Fixed piston gas-operated, positive primary extraction. New buffer system, redesigned ejector system. Ruger S100RM scope rings included on Ranch Rifle.
Price: Mini-14/5R, Ranch Rifle, blued, scope rings $695.00
Price: K-Mini-14/5R, Ranch Rifle, stainless, scope rings $770.00
Price: Mini-14/5, blued $655.00
Price: K-Mini-14/5, stainless $715.00
Price: K-Mini-14/5P, stainless, synthetic stock $715.00
Price: K-Mini-14/5RP, Ranch Rifle, stainless, synthetic stock $770.00

Ruger Mini Thirty Rifle
Similar to the Mini-14 Ranch Rifle except modified to chamber the 7.62x39 Russian service round. Weight is about 6-7/8 lbs. Has 6-groove barrel with 1:10" twist, Ruger Integral Scope Mount bases and folding peep rear sight. Detachable 5-shot staggered box magazine. Blued finish. Introduced 1987.
Price: Blue, scope rings $695.00
Price: Stainless, scope rings $770.00

Springfield M1A

Springfield National Match M1A

Springfield Super Match with Camo M1A

SPRINGFIELD ARMORY M1A RIFLE
Caliber: 7.62mm NATO (308), 5- or 10-shot box magazine. **Barrel:** 25-1/16" with flash suppressor, 22" without suppressor. **Weight:** 9-3/4 lbs. **Length:** 44-1/4" overall. **Stock:** American walnut with walnut-colored heat-resistant fiberglass handguard. Matching walnut handguard available. Also available with fiberglass stock. **Sights:** Military, square blade front, full click-adjustable aperture rear. **Features:** Commercial equivalent of the U.S. M-14 service rifle with no provision for automatic firing. From Springfield Armory

Price: Standard M1A, black fiberglass stock.................. $1,498.00
Price: Standard M1A, black fiberglass stock, stainless......... $1,727.00
Price: Standard M1A, black stock, carbon barrel $1,379.00
Price: Standard M1A, Mossy Oak stock, carbon barrel $1,507.00
Price: Scout Squad M1A..................... $1,653.00 to $1,727.00
Price: National Match .... $2,049.00 to $2,098.00
Price: Super Match (heavy premium barrel), about $3,149.00
Price: M1A SOCOM II rifle, about......................... $1,948.00
Price: M25 White Feather Tactical rifle $4,648.00

SPRINGFIELD M1 GARAND RIFLE
Caliber: 308, 30-06. **Barrel:** 24". **Weight:** 9.5 lbs. **Length:** 43-3/5". **Stock:** Walnut. **Sights:** Military aperture with MOA adjustments for both windage and elevation, rear; military square post, front. **Features:** Original U.S. government-issue parts on a new walnut stock.
Price:.................................... $1,348.00 to $1,378.00

STONER SR-15 M-5 RIFLE
Caliber: 223. **Barrel:** 20". **Weight:** 7.6 lbs. **Length:** 38" overall. **Stock:** Black synthetic. **Sights:** Post front, fully adjustable rear (300-meter sight).

Features: Modular weapon system; two-stage trigger. Black finish. Introduced 1998. Made in U.S.A. by Knight's Mfg.
Price: $1,650.00
Price: M-4 Carbine (16" barrel, 6.8 lbs) $1,555.00

STONER SR-25 CARBINE
Caliber: 7.62 NATO, 10-shot steel magazine. **Barrel:** 16" free-floating **Weight:** 7-3/4 lbs. **Length:** 35.75" overall. **Stock:** Black synthetic. **Sights:** Integral Weaver-style rail. Scope rings, iron sights optional. **Features:** Shortened, non-slip handguard; removable carrying handle. Matte black finish. Introduced 1995. Made in U.S.A. by Knight's Mfg. Co.
Price: $3,345.00

WILKINSON LINDA CARBINE
Caliber: 9mm Para. **Barrel:** 16-3/16". **Weight:** 7 lbs. **Stocks:** Fixed tubular with wood pad. **Sights:** Aperture rear sight. **Features:** Aluminum receiver, pre-ban configuration (limited supplies), vent. barrel shroud, small wooden forearm, 18 or 31 shot mag. Many accessories.
Price: $1,800.00

Wilkinson Linda L2 Limited Edition
Manufactured from the last 600 of the original 2,200 pre-ban Linda carbines, includes many upgrades and accessories. New in 2002.
Price: $4,800.00

WILKINSON TERRY CARBINE
Caliber: 9mm Para. **Barrel:** 16-3/16". **Weight:** 7 lbs. **Stocks:** Black or maple. **Sights:** Adjustable. **Features:** Blowback semi-auto action, 31-shot mag., closed breech.
Price:... NA

Both classic arms and recent designs in American-style repeaters for sport and field shooting.

Browning Lightning

Cimarron 1866 Winchester Replica

Cimarron 1873 Long Range

Dixie 1873

BROWNING MODEL '81 LIGHTNING LEVER-ACTION RIFLE
Caliber: 22-250, 243, 7mm-08, 308 Win., 270 WSM, 7mm WSM, 300 WSM, 358 Win., 450 Marlin, 270 Win., 30-06 Sprg., 7mm Rem. Mag., 300 Win. Mag. 4-shot detachable magazine. **Barrel:** 20" round tapered. **Weight:** 6 lbs., 8 oz. **Length:** 39-1/2" overall. **Stock:** Walnut. Checkered grip and forend, high-gloss finish. **Sights:** Gold bead on ramp front; low profile square notch adjustable rear. **Features:** Wide, grooved trigger; half-cock hammer safety; fold-down hammer. Receiver tapped for scope mount. Recoil pad installed. Introduced 1996. Imported from Japan by Browning.
Price: **$710.00**

Browning Model '81 Lightning Long Action
Similar to the standard Lightning BLR except has long action to accept 30-06, 270, 7mm Rem. Mag. and 300 Win. Mag. Barrel lengths are 22" for 30-06 and 270, 24" for 7mm Rem. Mag. and 300 Win. Mag. Has six-lug rotary bolt; bolt and receiver are full-length fluted. Fold-down hammer at half-cock. Weighs about 7 lbs., overall length 42-7/8" (22" barrel). Introduced 1996.
Price: **$686.00**

CIMARRON 1860 HENRY REPLICA
Caliber: 44 WCF, 45LC; 13-shot magazine. **Barrel:** 24-1/4" (rifle), 22" (carbine). **Weight:** 9-1/2 lbs. **Length:** 43" overall (rifle). **Stock:** European walnut. **Sights:** Bead front, open adjustable rear. **Features:** Brass receiver and buttplate. Uses original Henry loading system. Copy of the original rifle. Introduced 1991. Imported by Cimarron F.A. Co.
Price: **$1,199.00**

CIMARRON 1866 WINCHESTER REPLICAS
Caliber: 38 Spec., 357, 45LC, 32 WCF, 38 WCF, 44 WCF. **Barrel:** 24-1/4" (rifle), 19" (carbine). **Weight:** 9 lbs. **Length:** 43" overall (rifle). **Stock:**
European walnut. **Sights:** Bead front, open adjustable rear. **Features:** Solid brass receiver, buttplate, forend cap. Octagonal barrel. Copy of the original Winchester '66 rifle. Introduced 1991. Imported by Cimarron F.A. Co.
Price: Rifle **$965.00**
Price: Carbine **$950.00**

CIMARRON 1873 SHORT RIFLE
Caliber: 357 Mag., 38 Spec., 32 WCF, 38 WCF, 44 Spec., 44 WCF, 45 Colt. **Barrel:** 20" tapered octagon. **Weight:** 7.5 lbs. **Length:** 39" overall. **Stock:** Walnut. **Sights:** Bead front, adjustable semi-buckhorn rear. **Features:** Has half "button" magazine. Original-type markings, including caliber, on barrel and elevator and "Kings" patent. From Cimarron F.A. Co.
Price: **$1,149.00**

Cimarron 1873 Sporting Rifle
Similar to the 1873 Short Rifle except has 24" barrel with half-magazine.
Price: **$1,149.00**

CIMARRON 1873 LONG RANGE RIFLE
Caliber: 44 WCF, 45 Colt. **Barrel:** 30", octagonal. **Weight:** 8-1/2 lbs. **Length:** 48" overall. **Stock:** Walnut. **Sights:** Blade front, semi-buckhorn ramp rear. Tang sight optional. **Features:** Color case-hardened frame; choice of modern blue-black or charcoal blue for other parts. Barrel marked "Kings Improvement." From Cimarron F.A. Co.
Price: **$1,199.00**

DIXIE ENGRAVED 1873 RIFLE
Caliber: 44-40, 11-shot magazine. **Barrel:** 20", round. **Weight:** 7-3/4 lbs. **Length:** 39" overall. **Stock:** Walnut. **Sights:** Blade front, adjustable rear. **Features:** Engraved and case-hardened frame. Replica of Winchester 1873. Made in Italy. From 21 Gun Works.
Price: **$1,350.00**
Price: Plain, blued carbine **$850.00**

Marlin 336C

Marlin 336Y Spikehorn

E.M.F. 1860 HENRY RIFLE
Caliber: 44-40 or 45 Colt. **Barrel:** 24.25". **Weight:** About 9 lbs. **Length:** About 43.75" overall. **Stock:** Oil-stained American walnut. **Sights:** Blade front, rear adjustable for elevation. **Features:** Reproduction of the original Henry rifle with brass frame and buttplate, rest blued. From E.M.F.
Price: Brass frame $850.00
Price: Steel frame $950.00

E.M.F. 1866 YELLOWBOY LEVER ACTIONS
Caliber: 38 Spec., 44-40. **Barrel:** 19" (carbine), 24" (rifle). **Weight:** 9 lbs. **Length:** 43" overall (rifle). **Stock:** European walnut. **Sights:** Bead front, open adjustable rear. **Features:** Solid brass frame, blued barrel, lever, hammer, buttplate. Imported from Italy by E.M.F.
Price: Rifle $690.00
Price: Carbine $675.00

E.M.F. HARTFORD MODEL 1892 LEVER-ACTION RIFLE
Caliber: 45 Colt. **Barrel:** 24", octagonal. **Weight:** 7-1/2 lbs. **Length:** 43" overall. **Stock:** European walnut. **Sights:** Blade front, open adjustable rear. **Features:** Color case-hardened frame, lever, trigger and hammer with blued barrel, or overall blue finish. Introduced 1998. Imported by E.M.F.
Price: Standard $590.00

E.M.F. MODEL 1873 LEVER-ACTION RIFLE
Caliber: 32/20, 357 Mag., 38/40, 44-40, 44 Spec., 45 Colt. **Barrel:** 24". **Weight:** 8 lbs. **Length:** 43-1/4" overall. **Stock:** European walnut. **Sights:** Bead front, rear adjustable for windage and elevation. **Features:** Color case-hardened frame (blue on carbine). Imported by E.M.F.
Price: Rifle $865.00
Price: Carbine, 19" barrel $865.00

E.M.F. MODEL 1873 REVOLVER CARBINE
Caliber: 357 Mag., 45 Colt. **Barrel:** 18". **Weight:** 4 lbs., 8 oz. **Length:** 34" overall. **Stock:** One-piece walnut. **Sights:** Blade front, notch rear. **Features:** Color case-hardened frame, blue barrel, backstrap and trigger guard. Introduced 1998. Imported from Italy by IAR, Inc.
Price: Standard $490.00

MARLIN MODEL 336C LEVER-ACTION CARBINE
Caliber: 30-30 or 35 Rem., 6-shot tubular magazine. **Barrel:** 20" Micro-Groove®. **Weight:** 7 lbs. **Length:** 38-1/2" overall. **Stock:** Checkered American black walnut, capped pistol grip. Mar-Shield® finish; rubber buttpad; swivel studs. **Sights:** Ramp front with Wide-Scan hood, semi-buckhorn folding rear adjustable for windage and elevation. **Features:** Hammer-block safety. Receiver tapped for scope mount, offset hammer spur; top of receiver sandblasted to prevent glare. Includes safety lock.
Price: $558.00

Marlin Model 336A Lever-Action Carbine
Same as the Marlin 336C except has cut-checkered, walnut-finished hardwood pistol grip stock with swivel studs, 30-30 only, 6-shot. Hammer-block safety. Adjustable rear sight, brass bead front. Includes safety lock.
Price: $477.00
Price: With 4x scope and mount $527.00

Marlin Model 336SS Lever-Action Carbine
Same as the 336C except receiver, barrel and other major parts are machined from stainless steel. 30-30 only, 6-shot; receiver tapped for scope. Includes safety lock.
Price: $692.00

Marlin Model 336W Lever-Action Rifle
Similar to the Model 336C except has walnut-finished, cut-checkered Maine birch stock; blued steel barrel band has integral sling swivel; no front sight hood; comes with padded nylon sling; hard rubber buttplate. Introduced 1998. Includes safety lock. Made in U.S.A. by Marlin.
Price: $482.00
Price: With 4x scope and mount $535.00

Marlin Model 336Y "Spikehorn"
Similar to the models in the 336 series except in a compact format with 16-1/2" barrel measuring only 34" in overall length. Weight is 6-1/2 lbs., length of pull 12-1/2". Blued steel barrel and receiver. Chambered for 30/30 cartridge. Introduced 2003.
Price: $586.00

MARLIN MODEL 444 LEVER-ACTION SPORTER
Caliber: 444 Marlin, 5-shot tubular magazine. **Barrel:** 22" deep cut Ballard rifling. **Weight:** 7-1/2 lbs. **Length:** 40-1/2" overall. **Stock:** Checkered American black walnut, capped pistol grip, rubber rifle buttpad. Mar-Shield® finish; swivel studs. **Sights:** Hooded ramp front, folding semi-buckhorn rear adjustable for windage and elevation. **Features:** Hammer-block safety. Receiver tapped for scope mount; offset hammer spur. Includes safety lock.
Price: $654.00

MARLIN MODEL 1894 LEVER-ACTION CARBINE
Caliber: 44 Spec./44 Mag., 10-shot tubular magazine. **Barrel:** 20" Ballard-type rifling. **Weight:** 6 lbs. **Length:** 37-1/2" overall. **Stock:** Checkered American black walnut, straight grip and forend. Mar-Shield® finish. Rubber rifle buttpad; swivel studs. **Sights:** Wide-Scan hooded ramp front, semi-buckhorn folding rear adjustable for windage and elevation. **Features:** Hammer-block safety. Receiver tapped for scope mount, offset hammer spur, solid top receiver sand blasted to prevent glare. Includes safety lock.
Price: $591.00

Marlin Model 1894C Carbine
Similar to the standard Model 1894 except chambered for 38 Spec./357 Mag. with full-length 9-shot magazine, 18-1/2" barrel, hammer-block safety, hooded front sight. Introduced 1983. Includes safety lock.
Price: $591.00

Marlin 1894 Cowboy

Marlin 1894SS

Marlin 1895

Marlin 1895GS

Marlin 1895M

studs. **Sights:** Bead front with Wide-Scan hood, semi-buckhorn folding rear adjustable for windage and elevation. **Features:** Hammer-block safety. Solid receiver tapped for scope mounts or receiver sights; offset hammer spur. Includes safety lock.
Price: **$719.00**

Marlin Model 1895G Guide Gun Lever-Action Rifle
Similar to Model 1895 with deep-cut Ballard-type rifling; straight-grip walnut stock. Overall length is 37", weighs 7 lbs. Introduced 1998. Includes safety lock. Made in U.S.A. by Marlin.
Price: **$668.00**

Marlin Model 1895GS Guide Gun
Similar to Model 1895G except receiver, barrel and most metal parts are machined from stainless steel. Chambered for 45-70, 4-shot, 18-1/2" barrel. Overall length is 37", weighs 7 lbs. Introduced 2001. Includes safety lock. Made in U.S.A. by Marlin.
Price: **$805.00**

Marlin Model 1895 Cowboy Lever-Action Rifle
Similar to Model 1895 except has 26" tapered octagon barrel with Ballard-type rifling, Marble carbine front sight and Marble adjustable semi-buckhorn rear sight. Receiver tapped for scope or receiver sight. Overall length is 44-1/2", weighs about 8 lbs. Introduced 2001. Includes safety lock. Made in U.S.A. by Marlin.
Price: **$849.00**

Marlin Model 1895M Lever-Action Rifle
Similar to Model 1895 except has an 18-1/2" barrel with Ballard-type cut rifling. New Model 1895MR variant has 22" barrel, pistol grip. Chambered for 450 Marlin. Includes safety lock.
Price: (Model 1895M) **$719.00**

MARLIN MODEL 1894 COWBOY
Caliber: 357 Mag., 44 Mag., 45 Colt, 10-shot magazine. **Barrel:** 20" except .45 Colt which has a 24" tapered octagon, deep cut rifling. **Weight:** 7-1/2 lbs. **Length:** 41-1/2" overall. **Stock:** Straight grip American black walnut, hard rubber buttplate, Mar-Shield® finish. **Sights:** Marble carbine front, adjustable Marble semi-buckhorn rear. **Features:** Squared finger lever; straight grip stock; blued steel forend tip. Designed for Cowboy Shooting events. Introduced 1996. Includes safety lock. Made in U.S.A. by Marlin.
Price: **$849.00**

Marlin Model 1894 Cowboy Competition Rifle
Similar to Model 1894 except 20" barrel, 37-1/2" long, weighs 6 lbs., antique finish on receiver, lever and bolt. Factory-tuned for competitive cowboy action shooting. Available in .38 Spl. and .45 Colt.
Price: **$986.00**

Marlin Model 1894SS
Similar to Model 1894 except has stainless steel barrel, receiver, lever, guard plate, magazine tube and loading plate. Nickel-plated swivel studs.
Price: **$716.00**

MARLIN MODEL 1895 LEVER-ACTION RIFLE
Caliber: 45-70, 4-shot tubular magazine. **Barrel:** 22" round. **Weight:** 7-1/2 lbs. **Length:** 40-1/2" overall. **Stock:** Checkered American black walnut, full pistol grip. Mar-Shield® finish; rubber buttpad; quick detachable swivel

Navy Arms Henry Trapper

Navy Arms Iron Frame Henry

Navy Arms 1866 Yellow Boy

Navy Arms 1873 Winchester-Style

Navy Arms 1892 Rifle

NAVY ARMS MILITARY HENRY RIFLE
Caliber: 44-40 or 45 Colt, 12-shot magazine. **Barrel:** 24-1/4". **Weight:** 9 lbs., 4 oz. **Stock:** European walnut. **Sights:** Blade front, adjustable ladder-type rear. **Features:** Brass frame, buttplate, rest blued. Replica of the model used by cavalry units in the Civil War. Has full-length magazine tube, sling swivels; no forend. Imported from Italy by Navy Arms.
Price: $989.00

Navy Arms Iron Frame Henry
Similar to the Military Henry Rifle except receiver is blued or color case-hardened steel. Imported by Navy Arms.
Price: $1,035.00

NAVY ARMS 1860 HENRY RIFLES
Caliber: 45 Colt. **Barrel:** 24-1/4" octagonal; 1:16" twist. **Weight:** 9.26 lbs. **Length:** 43-3/4" overall. **Stock:** Walnut. **Sights:** Blade front, adjustable folding rear. **Features:** Steel color case-hardened or brass receiver; 13-shot magazine. Introduced 2001. Imported from Uberti by Navy Arms.
Price: (Steel color case-hardened receiver) $984.00
Price: (Brass receiver) $1,035.00

NAVY ARMS 1866 YELLOW BOY RIFLE
Caliber: 38 Spec., 44-40, 45 Colt, 12-shot magazine. **Barrel:** 20" or 24", full octagon. **Weight:** 8-1/2 lbs. **Length:** 42-1/2" overall. **Stock:** Walnut. **Sights:** Blade front, adjustable ladder-type rear. **Features:** Brass frame,

forend tip, buttplate, blued barrel, lever, hammer. Introduced 1991. Imported from Italy by Navy Arms.
Price: $761.00
Price: Carbine, 19" barrel $746.00

NAVY ARMS 1866 SPORTING YELLOW BOY RIFLES
Caliber: 45 Colt. **Barrel:** 24-1/4" octagonal; 1:16" twist. **Weight:** 8.16 lbs. **Length:** 43-3/4" overall. **Stock:** Walnut. **Sights:** Blade front, adjustable folding rear. **Features:** Brass receiver; blued or white barrel; 13-shot magazine. Introduced 2001. Imported from Uberti by Navy Arms.
Price: (blued barrel) $761.00

NAVY ARMS 1873 WINCHESTER-STYLE RIFLE
Caliber: 357 Mag., 44-40, 45 Colt, 12-shot magazine. **Barrel:** 24-1/4". **Weight:** 8-1/4 lbs. **Length:** 43" overall. **Stock:** European walnut. **Sights:** Blade front, buckhorn rear. **Features:** Color case-hardened frame, rest blued. Full-octagon barrel. Imported by Navy Arms.
Price: $890.00
Price: 1873 Carbine, 19" barrel $869.00
Price: 1873 Sporting Rifle (full oct. bbl., checkered walnut stock
and forend) $1,005.00
Price: 1873 Border Model, 20" octagon barrel $890.00
Price: 1873 Deluxe Border Model. $1,005.00

NAVY ARMS 1892 RIFLE
Caliber: 357 Mag., 44-40, 45 Colt. **Barrel:** 24-1/4" octagonal. **Weight:** 7 lbs. **Length:** 42" overall. **Stock:** American walnut. **Sights:** Blade front, semi-buckhorn rear. **Features:** Replica of Winchester's early Model 1892 with octagonal barrel, forend cap and crescent buttplate. Blued or color case-hardened receiver. Introduced 1998. Imported by Navy Arms.
Price: $545.00

CENTERFIRE RIFLES — Lever & Slide

Navy Arms 1892 Short Rifle

Puma Model 92

Remington 7600 Rifle

Ruger Model 96/44

Tristar 1873 Sporting Rifle

Navy Arms 1892 Stainless Carbine
Similar to the 1892 Rifle except stainless steel, has 20" round barrel, weighs 5-3/4 lbs., and is 37-1/2" overall. Introduced 1998. Imported by Navy Arms.
Price: **$585.00**

Navy Arms 1892 Short Rifle
Similar to the 1892 Rifle except has 20" octagonal barrel, weighs 6-1/4 lbs., and is 37-3/4" overall. Replica of the rare, special order 1892 Winchester nicknamed the "Texas Special." Blued or color case-hardened receiver and furniture. Introduced 1998. Imported by Navy Arms.
Price: **$545.00**
Price: (stainless steel, 20" octagon barrel) **$585.00**

NAVY ARMS 1892 STAINLESS RIFLE
Caliber: 357 Mag., 44-40, 45 Colt. **Barrel:** 24-1/4" octagonal. **Weight:** 7 lbs. **Length:** 42". **Stock:** American walnut. **Sights:** Brass bead front, semi-buckhorn rear. **Features:** Designed for the Cowboy Action Shooter. Stainless steel barrel, receiver and furniture. Introduced 2000. Imported by Navy Arms.
Price: **$585.00**

PUMA MODEL 92 RIFLES & CARBINES
Caliber: 38 Spec./357 Mag., 44 Mag., 45 Colt, 454 Casull (20" carbine only), 480 Ruger. **Barrel:** 16". 18", 20" round, 24" octagonal; porting available. **Weight:** 6.1 to 7.7 lbs. **Stock:** Walnut-stained hardwood. **Sights:** Open, buckhorn front & rear; HiViz also available. **Features:** Blue, case-hardened, stainless steel and brass receivers, matching buttplates.

Blued, stainless steel barrels, full-length magazines. Thumb safety. 45 Colt and 454 Casull carbine introduced in 2002. The 480 Ruger version introduced in 2003. Imported from Brazil by Legacy Sports International.
Price: . . . . **$257.00 to $603.00**

REMINGTON MODEL 7600 PUMP ACTION
Caliber: 243, 270, 30-06, 308. **Barrel:** 22" round tapered. **Weight:** 7-1/2 lbs. **Length:** 42-5/8" overall. **Stock:** Cut-checkered walnut pistol grip and forend, Monte Carlo with full cheekpiece. Satin or high-gloss finish. **Sights:** Gold bead front sight on matted ramp, open step adjustable sporting rear. **Features:** Redesigned and improved version of the Model 760. Detachable 4-shot clip. Cross-bolt safety. Receiver tapped for scope mount. Introduced 1981.
Price: **$588.00**
Price: Carbine (18-1/2" bbl., 30-06 only) **$588.00**
Price: With black synthetic stock, matte black metal, rifle or carbine. **$484.00**

RUGER MODEL 96/44 LEVER-ACTION RIFLE
Caliber: 44 Mag., 4-shot rotary magazine. **Barrel:** 18-1/2". **Weight:** 5-7/8 lbs. **Length:** 37-5/16" overall. **Stock:** American hardwood. **Sights:** Gold bead front, folding leaf rear. **Features:** Solid chrome-moly steel receiver. Manual cross-bolt safety, visible cocking indicator; short-throw lever action; integral scope mount; blued finish; color case-hardened lever. Introduced 1996. Made In U.S. by Sturm, Ruger & Co.
Price: 96/44M, 44 Mag **$546.00**

TRISTAR/UBERTI 1873 SPORTING RIFLE
Caliber: 44-40, 45 Colt. **Barrel:** 24-1/4", 30", octagonal. **Weight:** 8.1 lbs. **Length:** 43-1/4" overall. **Stock:** Walnut. **Sights:** Blade front adjustable for windage, open rear adjustable for elevation. **Features:** Color case-hardened frame, blued barrel, hammer, lever, buttplate, brass elevator. Imported from Italy by Tristar Sporting Arms Ltd.
Price: 24-1/4" barrel **$925.00**
Price: 30" barrel **$969.00**

Tristar 1866 Yellowboy Carbine

Tristar 1860 Henry

Winchester 94 Traditional

Winchester Model 94 Trapper

TRISTAR/UBERTI 1866 SPORTING RIFLE, CARBINE
Caliber: 22 LR, 22 WMR, 38 Spec., 44-40, 45 Colt. **Barrel:** 24-1/4", octagonal. **Weight:** 8.1 lbs. **Length:** 43-1/4" overall. **Stock:** Walnut. **Sights:** Blade front adjustable for windage, rear adjustable for elevation. **Features:** Frame, buttplate, forend cap of polished brass, balance charcoal blued. Imported by Tristar Sporting Arms Ltd.
Price: **$779.00**
Price: Yellowboy carbine (19" round bbl.) **$739.00**

TRISTAR/UBERTI 1860 HENRY RIFLE
Caliber: 44-40, 45 Colt. **Barrel:** 24-1/4", half-octagon. **Weight:** 9.2 lbs. **Length:** 43-3/4" overall. **Stock:** American walnut. **Sights:** Blade front, rear adjustable for elevation. **Features:** Frame, elevator, magazine follower, buttplate are brass, balance blue. Imported by Tristar Sporting Arms Ltd. Arms, Inc.
Price: **$989.00**

Tristar/Uberti 1860 Henry Trapper Carbine
Similar to the 1860 Henry Rifle except has 18-1/2" barrel, measures 37-3/4" overall, and weighs 8 lbs. Introduced 1999. Imported from Italy by Tristar Sporting Arms Ltd.
Price: Brass frame, blued barrel **$989.00**

U.S. FIRE ARMS LIGHTNING MAGAZINE RIFLE
Caliber: 45 Colt, 44 WCF, 44 Spl., 38 WCF, 32 WCF, 15-shot. **Barrel:** 26" (rifle); 20" carbine, round or octagonal. **Stock:** Oiled walnut. **Finish:** Dome

blue. Introduced 2002. Made in U.S.A. by United States Fire-Arms Manufacturing Co.
Price: **$1,480.00**

WINCHESTER TIMBER CARBINE
Caliber: Chambered for 450 Marlin. **Barrel:** 18" barrel, ported. **Weight:** 6 lbs. **Length:** 36-1/4" overall. **Stock:** Half-pistol grip stock with buttpad; checkered grip and forend. **Sights:** XS ghost-ring sight. **Features:** Introduced 1999. Made in U.S.A. by U.S. Repeating Arms Co., Inc.
Price: **$610.00**

WINCHESTER MODEL 94 TRADITIONAL-CW
Caliber: 30-30 Win., 6-shot; 44 Mag., 11-shot tubular magazine. **Barrel:** 20". **Weight:** 6-1/2 lbs. **Length:** 37-3/4" overall. **Stock:** Straight grip checkered walnut stock and forend. **Sights:** Hooded blade front, semi-buckhorn rear. Drilled and tapped for scope mount. Post front sight on Trapper model. **Features:** Solid frame, forged steel receiver; side ejection, exposed rebounding hammer with automatic trigger-activated transfer bar. Introduced 1984.
Price: 30-30 . . . . **$469.00**
Price: 44 Mag. **$492.00**
Price: Traditional (no checkering, 30-30 only) **$435.00**

Winchester Model 94 Trapper
Similar to Model 94 Traditional except has 16" barrel, 5-shot magazine in 30-30, 9-shot in 357 Mag., 44 Magnum/44 Special, 45 Colt. Has stainless steel claw extractor, saddle ring, hammer spur extension, smooth walnut stocks.
Price: 30-30 . . . . **$459.00**
Price: 44 Mag., 357 Mag., 45 Colt **$459.00**

Winchester Model 94 Trails End

Winchester Model 94 Legacy

Winchester Model 94 Ranger

Winchester Model 94 Ranger Compact

Winchester Model 94 Trail's End
Similar to the Model 94 Traditional except octagon-barrel version available, chambered only for 357 Mag., 44-40, 44 Mag., 45 Colt; 11-shot magazine. Available with standard lever loop. Introduced 1997. From U.S. Repeating Arms Co., Inc.
Price: With standard lever loop **$474.00**

Winchester Model 94 Legacy
Similar to the Model 94 Traditional except has half-pistol grip walnut stock, checkered grip and forend. Chambered for 30-30, 357 Mag., 44 Mag., 45 Colt; 24" barrel. Introduced 1995. Made in U.S.A. by U.S. Repeating Arms Co., Inc.
Price: With 24" barrel. **$487.00**

Winchester Model 94 Ranger
Similar to the Model 94 Traditional except has a hardwood stock, post-style front sight and hammer-spur extension.
Price: (20" barrel). **$379.00**
Price: Trail's End octagon **$757.00**
Price: Trail's End octagon, case color **$815.00**

Winchester Model 94 Ranger Compact
Similar to the Model 94 Ranger except 357, 30-30 calibers, has 16" barrel and 12-1/2" length of pull, rubber recoil pad, post front sight. Introduced 1998. Made in U.S.A. by U.S. Repeating Arms Co., Inc.
Price: **$402.00**

WINCHESTER MODEL 1895 LEVER-ACTION RIFLE
Caliber: 405 Win, 4-shot magazine. **Barrel:** 24", round. **Weight:** 8 lbs. **Length:** 42" overall. **Stock:** American walnut. **Sights:** Gold bead front, buckhorn rear adjustable for elevation. **Features:** Re-creation of the original Model 1895. Polished blue finish. Two-piece cocking lever, Schnabel forend, straight-grip stock. Introduced 1995. From U.S. Repeating Arms Co., Inc.
Price: Grade I **$1,116.00**

CONSULT

SHOOTER'S MARKETPLACE

Page 74, This Issue

Includes models for a wide variety of sporting and competitive purposes and uses.

Anschutz 1733D

Barrett Model 95

Blaser R93 Classic

ANSCHUTZ 1743D BOLT-ACTION RIFLE

Caliber: 222 Rem., 3-shot magazine. **Barrel:** 19.7". **Weight:** 6.4 lbs. **Length:** 39" overall. **Stock:** European walnut. **Sights:** Hooded blade front, folding leaf rear. **Features:** Receiver grooved for scope mounting; single stage trigger; claw extractor; sling safety; sling swivels. Imported from Germany by AcuSport Corp.

Price: **$1,588.95**

ANSCHUTZ 1740 MONTE CARLO RIFLE

Caliber: 22 Hornet, 5-shot clip; 222 Rem., 3-shot clip. **Barrel:** 24". **Weight:** 6-1/2 lbs. **Length:** 43.25" overall. **Stock:** Select European walnut. **Sights:** Hooded ramp front, folding leaf rear; drilled and tapped for scope mounting. **Features:** Uses Match 54 action. Adjustable single stage trigger. Stock has roll-over Monte Carlo cheekpiece, slim forend with Schnabel tip, Wundhammer palm swell on grip, rosewood gripcap with white diamond insert. Skip-line checkering on grip and forend. Introduced 1997. Imported from Germany by AcuSport Corp.

Price: From **$1,439.00**
Price: Model 1730 Monte Carlo, as above except in
22 Hornet **$1,439.00**

Anschutz 1733D Rifle

Similar to the 1740 Monte Carlo except has full-length, walnut, Mannlicher-style stock with skip-line checkering, rosewood Schnabel tip, and is chambered for 22 Hornet. Weighs 6.4 lbs., overall length 39", barrel length 19.7". Imported from Germany by AcuSport Corp.

Price: **$1,588.95**

BARRETT MODEL 95 BOLT-ACTION RIFLE

Caliber: 50 BMG, 5-shot magazine. **Barrel:** 29". **Weight:** 22 lbs. **Length:** 45" overall. **Stock:** Energy-absorbing recoil pad. **Sights:** Scope optional. **Features:** Bolt-action, bullpup design. Disassembles without tools; extendable bipod legs; match-grade barrel; muzzle brake. Introduced 1995. Made in U.S.A. by Barrett Firearms Mfg., Inc.

Price: From **$4,950.00**

BLASER R93 BOLT-ACTION RIFLE

Caliber: 22-250, 243, 6.5x55, 270, 7x57, 7mm-08, 308, 30-06, 257 Wby. Mag., 7mm Rem. Mag., 300 Win. Mag., 300 Wby. Mag., 338 Win Mag., 375 H&H, 416 Rem. Mag. **Barrel:** 22" (standard calibers), 26" (magnum).

Weight: 7 lbs. **Length:** 40" overall (22" barrel). **Stock:** Two-piece European walnut. **Sights:** None furnished; drilled and tapped for scope mounting. **Features:** Straight pull-back bolt action with thumb-activated safety slide/cocking mechanism; interchangeable barrels and bolt heads. Introduced 1994. Imported from Germany by SIGARMS.

Price: R93 Classic. **$3,680.00**
Price: R93 LX **$1,895.00**
Price: R93 Synthetic (black synthetic stock). **$1,595.00**
Price: R93 Safari Synthetic (416 Rem. Mag. only) **$1,855.00**
Price: R93 Grand Lux **$4,915.00**
Price: R93 Attaché **$5,390.00**

BRNO 98 BOLT-ACTION RIFLE

Caliber: 7x64, 243, 270, 308, 30-06, 300 Win. Mag., 9.3x62. **Barrel:** 23.6". **Weight:** 7.2 lbs. **Length:** 40.9" overall. **Stock:** European walnut. **Sights:** Blade on ramp front, open adjustable rear. **Features:** Uses Mauser 98-type action; polished blue. Announced 1998. Imported from the Czech Republic by Euro-Imports.

Price: Standard calibers **$507.00**
Price: Magnum calibers **$547.00**
Price: With set trigger, standard calibers **$615.00**
Price: As above, magnum calibers **$655.00**
Price: With full stock, set trigger, standard calibers **$703.00**
Price: As above, magnum calibers **$743.00**
Price: 300 Win. Mag., with BOSS **$933.00**

BROWNING A-BOLT RIFLES

Caliber: 223, 22-250, 243, 7mm-08, 308, 25-06, 260, 270, 30-06, 260 Rem., 7mm Rem. Mag., 300 Win. Short Mag., 300 Win. Mag., 338 Win. Mag., 375 H&H Mag, 223 WSSM, 243 WSSM, 270 WSM, 7mm WSM, 300 WSM. **Barrel:** 22" medium sporter weight with recessed muzzle; 26" on mag. cals. **Weight:** 6-1/2 to 7-1/2 lbs. **Length:** 44-3/4" overall (magnum and standard); 41-3/4" (short action). **Stock:** Classic style American walnut; recoil pad standard on magnum calibers. **Features:** Short-throw (60°) fluted bolt, three locking lugs, plunger-type ejector; adjustable trigger is grooved and gold-plated. Hinged floorplate, detachable box magazine (4 rounds std. cals., 3 for magnums). Slide tang safety. BOSS barrel vibration modulator and muzzle brake system not available in 375 H&H. Introduced 1985. Imported from Japan by Browning.

Price: Hunter, no sights. **$705.00**
Price: Hunter, no sights, magnum calibers **$734.00**
Price: For BOSS add **$80.00**

Browning A-Bolt Medallion

Browning A-Bolt White Gold Medallion

Browning A-Bolt Eclipse M-1000

Browning A-Bolt Medallion
Similar to standard A-Bolt except has glossy stock finish, rosewood grip and forend caps, engraved receiver, high-polish blue, no sights. New calibers include 223 WSSM, 243 WSSM, 270 WSM, 7mm WSM.
Price: Short-action calibers **$805.00**
Price: Long-action calibers **$805.00**
Price: Medallion, 375 H&H Mag., open sights **$835.00**
Price: 300 Win. Short Magnum **$835.00**
Price: For BOSS, add **$80.00**

Browning A-Bolt Medallion Left-Hand
Same as the Medallion model A-Bolt except has left-hand action and is available in 270, 30-06, 7mm Rem. Mag., 300 Win. Mag. Introduced 1987.
Price: 270, 30-06 (no sights) **$837.00**
Price: 7mm Mag., 300 Win. Mag. (no sights) **$865.00**
Price: For BOSS, add **$80.00**

Browning A-Bolt White Gold Medallion
Similar to the standard A-Bolt except has select walnut stock with brass spacers between rubber recoil pad and between the rosewood gripcap and forend tip; gold-filled barrel inscription; palm-swell pistol grip, Monte Carlo comb, 22 lpi checkering with double borders; engraved receiver flats. In 270, 30-06, 7mm Rem. Mag. and 300 Win. Mag. Introduced 1988.
Price: 270, 30-06 . . . . **$1,183.00**
Price: 7mm Rem. Mag, 300 Win. Mag. **$1,155.00**
Price: For BOSS, add **$80.00**

BROWNING A-BOLT WHITE GOLD RMEF
Caliber: 7mm Rem. Mag. Similar to the A-Bolt Medallion except has select walnut stock with rosewood forend cap, RMEF-engraved gripcap;

continental cheekpiece; gold engraved, stainless receiver and bbl. Introduced 2004. Imported from Japan by Browning.
Price: **$1,261.00**

Browning A-Bolt Eclipse Hunter
Similar to the A-Bolt except has gray/black laminated, thumbhole stock, BOSS barrel vibration modulator and muzzle brake. Available in long and short action with heavy barrel. In 270 Win., 30-06, 7mm Rem. Mag. Introduced 1996. Imported from Japan by Browning.
Price: 270, 30-06, with BOSS **$1,134.00**
Price: 7mm Rem. Mag., with BOSS **$1,162.00**

Browning A-Bolt Eclipse M-1000
Similar to the A-Bolt Eclipse except has long action and heavy target barrel. Chambered only for 300 Win. Mag. Adjustable trigger, bench-style forend, 3-shot magazine; laminated thumbhole stock; BOSS system standard. Introduced 1997. Imported for Japan by Browning.
Price: **$1,292.00**

Browning A-Bolt Micro Hunter
Similar to the A-Bolt Hunter except has 13-5/16" length of pull, 20" barrel, and comes in 260 Rem., 243, 308, 7mm-08, 223, 22-250, 22 Hornet, 270 WSM, 7mm WSM, 300 WSM. Weighs 6 lbs., 1 oz. Introduced 1999. Imported by Browning. Also available in left-hand version.
Price: (no sights) **$714.00**

Browning A-Bolt Mountain TI
Similar to the A-Bolt Hunter except has low-luster bluing and walnut stock with Monte Carlo comb, pistol grip palm swell, double-border checkering. Available in 223 WSSM, 243 WSSM. Introduced 1999. Imported by Browning.
Price: WSM **$1,690.00**
Price: WSSM **$1,669.00**

Browning A-Bolt Stalker

Charles Daly Field Mauser

CZ 527 Lux

CZ 550 Lux

Browning A-Bolt Stainless Stalker
Similar to the A-Bolt Hunter model except receiver and barrel are made of stainless steel; other exposed metal surfaces are finished silver-gray matte. Graphite-fiberglass composite textured stock. No sights are furnished. Available in 260, 243, 308, 7mm-08, 270, 280,30-06, 7mm Rem. Mag., 300 WSM, 300 Rem. Ultra Mag., 338 Win. Mag., 338 Rem. Ultra Mag., 375 H&H, 223 WSSM, 243 WSSM, 270 WSM, 7mm WSM. Introduced 1987.

Price: Short-action calibers **$897.00**
Price: Magnum calibers **$926.00**
Price: 300 Win. Short Magnum **$926.00**
Price: For BOSS, add **$80.00**
Price: Left-hand, 270, 30-06 . . . . **$1,005.00**
Price: Left-hand, 7mm, 300 Win. Mag., 338 Win. Mag. **$1,034.00**
Price: Left-hand, 375 H&H, with sights **$1,034.00**
Price: Left-hand, for BOSS, add **$80.00**

Browning A-Bolt Composite Stalker
Similar to the A-Bolt Hunter except has black graphite-fiberglass stock with textured finish. Matte blue finish on all exposed metal surfaces. Available in 223, 22-250, 243, 7mm-08, 308, 30-06, 270, 280, 25-06, 7mm Rem. Mag., 300 WSM, 300 Win. Mag., 338 Win. Mag, 223 WSSM, 243 WSSM, 270 WSM, 7mm WSM. BOSS barrel vibration modulator and muzzle brake system offered in all calibers. Introduced 1994.

Price: Standard calibers, no sights **$705.00**
Price: WSSM **$755.00**
Price: Magnum calibers, no sights **$734.00**
Price: For BOSS, add **$80.00**

CARBON ONE BOLT-ACTION RIFLE
Caliber: 22-250 to 375 H&H. **Barrel:** Up to 28". **Weight:** 5-1/2 to 7-1/4 lbs. **Length:** Varies. **Stock:** Synthetic or wood. **Sights:** None furnished. **Features:** Choice of Remington, Browning or Winchester action with free-floated Christensen graphite/epoxy/steel barrel, trigger pull tuned to 3 to 3-1/2 lbs. Made in U.S.A. by Christensen Arms.

Price: Carbon One Hunter Rifle, 6-1/2 to 7 lbs. **$1,499.00**
Price: Carbon One Custom, 5-1/2 to 6-1/2 lbs., Shilen trigger. . . . **$2,750.00**
Price: Carbon Ranger, 50 BMG, 5-shot repeater **$4,750.00**
Price: Carbon Ranger, 50 BMG, single shot **$3,950.00**

CHARLES DALY FIELD MAUSER RIFLE
Caliber: 22-250, 243, 25-06, 270, 308, 30-06 (in 22" barrels); 7mm Rem. Mag. and 300 Win. Mag. in 24" barrels. **Weight:** NA **Sights:** None; drilled and tapped for scope mounts. **Features:** Mauser Model 98-type action; carbon or stainless steel barrels; slide safety; polymer stock; fully adjustable trigger.

Price: Field Grade Mauser **$459.00**
Price: Mauser SS **$549.00**
Price: Magnum calibers **$579.00**

CZ 527 LUX BOLT-ACTION RIFLE
Caliber: 22 Hornet, 222 Rem., 223 Rem., detachable 5-shot magazine. **Barrel:** 23-1/2"; standard or heavy barrel. **Weight:** 6 lbs., 1 oz. **Length:** 42-1/2" overall. **Stock:** European walnut with Monte Carlo. **Sights:** Hooded front, open adjustable rear. **Features:** Improved mini-Mauser action with non-rotating claw extractor; single set trigger; grooved receiver. Imported from the Czech Republic by CZ-USA.

Price: **$566.00**
Price: Model FS, full-length stock, cheekpiece **$658.00**

CZ 527 American Classic Bolt-Action Rifle
Similar to the CZ 527 Lux except has classic-style stock with 18 lpi checkering; free-floating barrel; recessed target crown on barrel. No sights furnished. Introduced 1999. Imported from the Czech Republic by CZ-USA.
Price: 22 Hornet, 222 Rem., 223 Rem. . . . . **$586.00 to $609.00**

CZ 550 LUX BOLT-ACTION RIFLE
Caliber: 22-250, 243, 6.5x55, 7x57, 7x64, 308 Win., 9.3x62, 270 Win., 30-06. **Barrel:** 20.47". **Weight:** 7.5 lbs. **Length:** 44.68" overall. **Stock:** Turkish walnut in Bavarian style or FS (Mannlicher). **Sights:** Hooded front, adjustable rear. **Features:** Improved Mauser-style action with claw extractor, fixed ejector, square bridge dovetailed receiver; single set trigger. Imported from the Czech Republic by CZ-USA.

Price: Lux . . . . **$566.00 to $609.00**
Price: FS (full stock) **$706.00**

CZ 550 American Classic

CZ 550 Magnum

Dakota 76 Classic

Dakota 76 Safari

CZ 550 American Classic Bolt-Action Rifle

Similar to CZ 550 Lux except has American classic-style stock with 18 lpi checkering; free-floating barrel; recessed target crown. Has 25.6" barrel; weighs 7.48 lbs. No sights furnished. Introduced 1999. Imported from the Czech Republic by CZ-USA.

Price: . . . . **$586.00 to $609.00**

CZ 550 Medium Magnum Bolt-Action Rifle

Similar to the CZ 550 Lux except chambered for the 300 Win. Mag. and 7mm Rem. Mag.; 5-shot magazine. Adjustable iron sights, hammer-forged barrel, single-set trigger, Turkish walnut stock. Weighs 7.5 lbs. Introduced 2001. Imported from the Czech Republic by CZ-USA.

Price: **$621.00**

CZ 550 Magnum Bolt-Action Rifle

Similar to CZ 550 Lux except has long action for 300 Win. Mag., 375 H&H, 416 Rigby, 458 Win. Mag. Overall length is 46.45"; barrel length 25"; weighs 9.24 lbs. Hooded front sight, express rear with one standing, two folding leaves. Imported from the Czech Republic by CZ-USA.

Price: 300 Win. Mag. **$717.00**
Price: 375 H&H **$756.00**
Price: 416 Rigby **$809.00**
Price: 458 Win. Mag. **$744.00**

CZ 700 M1 SNIPER RIFLE

Caliber: 308 Winchester, 10-shot magazine. **Barrel:** 25.6". **Weight:** 11.9 lbs. **Length:** 45" overall. **Stock:** Laminated wood thumbhole with adjustable buttplate and cheekpiece. **Sights:** None furnished; permanently attached Weaver rail for scope mounting. **Features:** 60-degree bolt throw; oversized trigger guard and bolt handle for use with gloves; full-length equipment rail on forend; fully adjustable trigger. Introduced 2001. Imported from the Czech Republic by CZ-USA.

Price: **$2,097.00**

DAKOTA 76 TRAVELER TAKEDOWN RIFLE

Caliber: 257 Roberts, 25-06, 7x57, 270, 280, 30-06, 338-06, 35 Whelen (standard length); 7mm Rem. Mag., 300 Win. Mag., 338 Win. Mag., 416 Taylor, 458 Win. Mag. (short magnums); 7mm, 300, 330, 375 Dakota Magnums. **Barrel:** 23". **Weight:** 7-1/2 lbs. **Length:** 43-1/2" overall. **Stock:** Medium fancy-grade walnut in classic style. Checkered grip and forend; solid buttpad. **Sights:** None furnished; drilled and tapped for scope mounts. **Features:** Threadless disassembly. Uses modified Model 76 design with many features of the Model 70 Winchester. Left-hand model also available. Introduced 1989. Made in U.S.A. by Dakota Arms, Inc.

Price: Classic **$4,495.00**
Price: Safari **$5,495.00**
Price: Extra barrels . . . . **$1,650.00 to $1,950.00**

DAKOTA 76 CLASSIC BOLT-ACTION RIFLE

Caliber: 257 Roberts, 270, 280, 30-06, 7mm Rem. Mag., 338 Win. Mag., 300 Win. Mag., 375 H&H, 458 Win. Mag. **Barrel:** 23". **Weight:** 7-1/2 lbs. **Length:** 43-1/2" overall. **Stock:** Medium fancy grade walnut in classic style. Checkered pistol grip and forend; solid buttpad. **Sights:** None furnished; drilled and tapped for scope mounts. **Features:** Has many features of the original Winchester Model 70. One-piece rail trigger guard assembly; steel gripcap. Model 70-style trigger. Many options available. Left-hand rifle available at same price. Introduced 1988. From Dakota Arms, Inc.

Price: **$3,595.00**

DAKOTA 76 SAFARI BOLT-ACTION RIFLE

Caliber: 270 Win., 7x57, 280, 30-06, 7mm Dakota, 7mm Rem. Mag., 300 Dakota, 300 Win. Mag., 330 Dakota, 338 Win. Mag., 375 Dakota, 458 Win. Mag., 300 H&H, 375 H&H, 416 Rem. **Barrel:** 23". **Weight:** 8-1/2 lbs. **Length:** 43-1/2" overall. **Stock:** XXX fancy walnut with ebony forend tip; point-pattern with wraparound forend checkering. **Sights:** Ramp front, standing leaf rear. **Features:** Has many features of the original Winchester Model 70. Barrel band front swivel, inletted rear. Cheekpiece with shadow line. Steel gripcap. Introduced 1988. From Dakota Arms, Inc.

Price: Wood stock **$4,595.00**

Dakota Longbow

Dakota 97 Lightweight Hunter

Dakota Hunter

Ed Brown 702 Savanna

Dakota African Grade
Similar to 76 Safari except chambered for 338 Lapua Mag., 404 Jeffery, 416 Rigby, 416 Dakota, 450 Dakota, 4-round magazine, select wood, two stock cross-bolts. 24" barrel, weighs 9-10 lbs. Ramp front sight, standing leaf rear. Introduced 1989.
Price: **$4,995.00**

DAKOTA LONGBOW TACTICAL E.R. RIFLE
Caliber: 300 Dakota Magnum, 330 Dakota Magnum, 338 Lapua Magnum.
Barrel: 28", .950" at muzzle **Weight:** 13.7 lbs. **Length:** 50" to 52" overall.
Stock: Ambidextrous McMillan A-2 fiberglass, black or olive green color; adjustable cheekpiece and buttplate. **Sights:** None furnished. Comes with Picatinny one-piece optical rail. **Features:** Uses the Dakota 76 action with controlled-round feed; three-position firing pin block safety, claw extractor; Model 70-style trigger. Comes with bipod, case tool kit. Introduced 1997. Made in U.S.A. by Dakota Arms, Inc.
Price: **$4,250.00**

DAKOTA 97 LIGHTWEIGHT HUNTER
Caliber: 22-250 to 330. **Barrel:** 22" to 24". **Weight:** 6.1 to 6.5 lbs. **Length:** 43" overall. **Stock:** Fiberglass. **Sights:** Optional. **Features:** Matte blue finish, black stock. Right-hand action only. Introduced 1998. Made in U.S.A. by Dakota Arms, Inc.
Price: **$1,995.00**

DAKOTA LONG RANGE HUNTER RIFLE
Caliber: 25-06, 257 Roberts, 270 Win., 280 Rem., 7mm Rem. Mag., 7mm Dakota Mag., 30-06, 300 Win. Mag., 300 Dakota Mag., 338 Win. Mag., 330 Dakota Mag., 375 H&H Mag., 375 Dakota Mag. **Barrel:** 24", 26", match-quality; free-floating. **Weight:** 7.7 lbs. **Length:** 45" to 47" overall. **Stock:** H-S Precision black synthetic, with one-piece bedding block system. **Sights:** None furnished. Drilled and tapped for scope mounting. **Features:** Cylindrical machined receiver controlled round feed; Mauser-style extractor; three-position striker blocking safety; fully adjustable match trigger. Right-hand action only. Introduced 1997. Made in U.S.A. by Dakota Arms, Inc.
Price: **$1,995.00**

ED BROWN SAVANNA RIFLE
Caliber: 30-06, 300 Win. Mag., 300 Weatherby, 338 Win. Mag. **Barrel:** 22", 23", 24". **Weight:** 8 to 8-1/2 lbs. **Stock:** Fully glass-bedded McMillan fiberglass sporter. **Sights:** None furnished. Talley scope mounts utilizing heavy duty 8-40 screws. **Features:** Custom action with machined steel trigger guard and hinged floor plate. Available in left-hand version.
Price: From .... **$2,795.00 to $2,895.00**

Ed Brown 702 Ozark

Ed Brown 702 Bushveld

Ed Brown 702 Varmint

Harris Gunworks Alaskan

Ed Brown Model 702 Denali, Ozark
Similar to the Ed Brown Model 702 Savanna but lighter weight, designed specifically for mountain hunting, especially suited to the 270 and 280 calibers. Right-hand only. Weighs about 7.75 lbs. The Model 702 Ozark is made on a short action with a lightweight stock. Ozark calibers are 223, 243, 6mm, 260 Rem., 7mm-08, 308. Weight 6.5 lbs.
Price: From **$2,800.00**

ED BROWN MODEL 702 BUSHVELD
Caliber: 338 Win. Mag., 375 H&H, 416 Rem. Mag., 458 Win. Mag., 458 Lott and all Ed Brown Savanna long action calibers. **Barrel:** 24" medium or heavy weight. **Weight:** 8.25 lbs. **Stock:** Fully bedded McMillan fiberglass with Monte Carlo style cheekpiece, Pachmayr Decelerator recoil pad. **Sights:** None furnished. Talley scope mounts utilizing heavy duty 8-40 screws. **Features:** Options include left-hand action, stainless steel barrel, additional calibers, iron sights.
Price: From . . . . **$2,895.00 to $3,195.00**

ED BROWN MODEL 702 VARMINT
Caliber: 223, 22-250, 220 Swift, 243, 6mm, 308. **Barrel:** Medium weight #5 contour 24"; heavyweight #17 contour 24"; 26" optional. **Weight:** 9 lbs. **Stock:** Fully glass-bedded McMillan fiberglass with recoil pad. **Sights:** None furnished. Talley scope mounts with heavy duty 8-40 screws. **Features:** Fully-adjustable trigger, steel trigger guard and floor plate, many options available.
Price: From **$2,495.00**

HARRIS GUNWORKS SIGNATURE CLASSIC SPORTER
Caliber: 22-250, 243, 6mm Rem., 7mm-08, 284, 308 (short action); 25-06, 270, 280 Rem., 30-06, 7mm Rem. Mag., 300 Win. Mag., 300 Wby. (long action); 338 Win. Mag., 340 Wby., 375 H&H (magnum action). **Barrel:** 22", 24", 26". **Weight:** 7 lbs. (short action). **Stock:** Fiberglass in green, beige, brown or black. Recoil pad and 1" swivels installed. Length of pull up to 14-1/4". **Sights:** None furnished. Comes with 1" rings and bases. **Features:** Uses right- or left-hand action with matte black finish. Trigger pull set at 3 lbs. Four-round magazine for standard calibers; three for magnums. Aluminum floorplate. Wood stock optional. Introduced 1987. From Harris Gunworks, Inc.
Price: **$2,700.00**

Harris Gunworks Signature Classic Stainless Sporter
Similar to Signature Classic Sporter except action is made of stainless steel. Same calibers, in addition to 416 Rem. Mag. Fiberglass stock, right- or left-hand action in natural stainless, glass bead or black chrome sulfide finishes. Introduced 1990. From Harris Gunworks, Inc.
Price: **$2,900.00**

Harris Gunworks Signature Alaskan
Similar to Classic Sporter except match-grade barrel with single leaf rear sight, barrel band front, 1" detachable rings and mounts, steel floorplate, electroless nickel finish. Wood Monte Carlo stock with cheekpiece, palm-swell grip, solid buttpad. Chambered for 270, 280 Rem., 30-06, 7mm Rem. Mag., 300 Win. Mag., 300 Wby., 358 Win., 340 Wby., 375 H&H. Introduced 1989.
Price: **$3,800.00**

Harris Gunworks Signature Titanium Mountain

Harris Gunworks Signature Super Varminter

Harris Gunworks Talon Safari

Howa Lightning

Harris Gunworks Signature Titanium Mountain Rifle
Similar to Classic Sporter except action made of titanium alloy, barrel of chrome-moly steel. Stock is graphite reinforced fiberglass. Weight is 5-1/2 lbs. Chambered for 270, 280 Rem., 30-06, 7mm Rem. Mag., 300 Win. Mag. Fiberglass stock optional. Introduced 1989.
Price: **$3,300.00**
Price: With graphite-steel composite lightweight barrel **$3,700.00**

Harris Gunworks Signature Varminter
Similar to Signature Classic Sporter except has heavy contoured barrel, adjustable trigger, field bipod and special hand-bedded fiberglass stock. Chambered for 223, 22-250, 220 Swift, 243, 6mm Rem., 25-06, 7mm-08, 7mm BR, 308, 350 Rem. Mag. Comes with 1" rings and bases. Introduced 1989.
Price: **$2,700.00**

HARRIS GUNWORKS TALON SAFARI RIFLE
Caliber: 300 Win. Mag., 300 Wby. Mag., 300 Phoenix, 338 Win. Mag., 30/378, 338 Lapua, 300 H&H, 340 Wby. Mag., 375 H&H, 404 Jeffery, 416 Rem. Mag., 458 Win. Mag. (Safari Magnum); 378 Wby. Mag., 416 Rigby, 416 Wby. Mag., 460 Wby. Mag. (Safari Super Magnum). **Barrel:** 24". **Weight:** About 9-10 lbs. **Length:** 43" overall. **Stock:** Gunworks fiberglass Safari. **Sights:** Barrel band front ramp, multi-leaf express rear. **Features:** Uses Harris Gunworks Safari action. Has quick detachable 1" scope mounts, positive locking steel floorplate, barrel band sling swivel. Match-grade barrel. Matte black finish standard. Introduced 1989. From Harris Gunworks, Inc.

Price: Talon Safari Magnum **$3,900.00**
Price: Talon Safari Super Magnum **$4,200.00**

HARRIS GUNWORKS TALON SPORTER RIFLE
Caliber: 22-250, 243, 6mm Rem., 6mm BR, 7mm BR, 7mm-08, 25-06, 270, 280 Rem., 284, 308, 30-06, 350 Rem. Mag. (long action); 7mm Rem. Mag., 7mm STW, 300 Win. Mag., 300 Wby. Mag., 300 H&H, 338 Win. Mag., 340 Wby. Mag., 375 H&H, 416 Rem. Mag. **Barrel:** 24" (standard). **Weight:** About 7-1/2 lbs. **Length:** NA. **Stock:** Choice of walnut or fiberglass. **Sights:** None furnished; comes with rings and bases. Open sights optional. **Features:** Uses pre-'64 Model 70-type action with cone breech, controlled feed, claw extractor and three-position safety. Barrel and action are of stainless steel; chrome-moly optional. Introduced 1991. From Harris Gunworks, Inc.
Price: **$2,900.00**

HOWA LIGHTNING BOLT-ACTION RIFLE
Caliber: 223, 22-250, 243, 6.5x55, 270, 308, 30-06, 7mm Rem. Mag., 300 Win. Mag., 338 Win. Mag, 300 WSM, 7mm WSM, 270 WSM. **Barrel:** 22", 24" magnum calibers. **Weight:** 7-1/2 lbs. **Length:** 42" overall (22" barrel). **Stock:** Black Bell & Carlson Carbelite composite with Monte Carlo comb; checkered grip and forend; also Realtree camo available. **Sights:** None furnished. Drilled and tapped for scope mounting. **Features:** Three-position thumb safety; hinged floorplate; polished blue/black finish. Introduced 1993. From Legacy Sports International.
Price: Blue, standard calibers **$508.00**
Price: Blue, magnum calibers **$531.00**
Price: Stainless, standard calibers **$620.00**
Price: Stainless, magnum calibers **$649.00**

Howa M-1500 Hunter

Howa M-1500 Ultralight

Howa M-1500 Varmint Supreme

Kimber 84M Classic

Howa M-1500 Hunter Bolt-Action Rifle

Similar to Lightning Model except has walnut-finished hardwood stock, three-position safety. Polished blue finish or stainless steel. Introduced 1999. From Legacy Sports International.

Price: Blue, standard calibers	**$574.00**
Price: Stainless, standard calibers	**$682.00**
Price: Blue, magnum calibers	**$595.00**
Price: Stainless, magnum calibers	**$704.00**
Price: Blued, camo stock	**$545.00**
Price: Blued, camo, magnum cal.	**$568.00**
Price: Stainless, camo, standard cal.	**$661.00**
Price: Stainless, camo, magnum cal.	**$690.00**

Howa M-1500 Supreme Rifles

Similar to Howa M-1500 Lightning except stocked with JRS Classic or Thumbhole Sporter laminated wood stocks in Nutmeg (brown/black) or Pepper (gray/black) colors. Barrel: 22"; 24" magnum calibers. Weights are JRS stock 8 lbs., THS stock 8.3 lbs. Three-position safety. Introduced 2001. Imported from Japan by Legacy Sports International.

Price: Blue, standard calibers, JRS stock	**$646.00**
Price: Blue, standard calibers, THS stock	**$704.00**
Price: Blue, magnum calibers, JRS stock	**$675.00**
Price: Blue, magnum calibers, THS stock	**$733.00**
Price: Stainless, standard calibers, JRS stock	**$755.00**
Price: Stainless, standard calibers, THS stock	**$813.00**
Price: Stainless, magnum calibers, JRS stock	**$784.00**
Price: Stainless, magnum calibers, THS stock	**$842.00**

Howa M-1500 Ultralight

Similar to Howa M-1500 Lightning except receiver milled to reduce weight; three-position safety; tapered 22" barrel; 1-10" twist. Chambered for 243 Win. Stocks are black texture-finished hardwood. Weighs 6.4 lbs. Length 40" overall.

Price: Blued	**$539.00**
Price: Stainless model	**$658.00**

Howa M-1500 Varmint and Varmint Supreme Rifles

Similar to M-1500 Lightning except has heavy 24" hammer-forged barrel. Chambered for 223, 22-250, 308. Weighs 9.3 lbs.; overall length 44.5". Introduced 1999. Imported from Japan by Interarms/Howa. Varminter Supreme has heavy barrel, target crown muzzle; three-position safety. Heavy 24" barrel, laminated wood with raised comb stocks, rollover cheekpiece, vented beavertail forearm; available in 223 Rem., 22-250 Rem., 308 Win. Weighs 9.9 lbs. Introduced 2001. Imported from Japan by Legacy Sports International.

Price: Varminter, blue, polymer stock	**$546.00**
Price: Varminter, stainless, polymer stock	**$664.00**
Price: Varminter, blue, wood stock	**$610.00**
Price: Varminter, stainless, wood stock	**$719.00**
Price: Varminter Supreme, blued	**$711.00 to $733.00**
Price: Varminter Supreme, stainless	**$820.00 to $842.00**
Price: Varminter, blued, camo stock	**$582.00**
Price: Varminter, stainless, camo stock	**$704.00**

KIMBER MODEL 8400 BOLT-ACTION RIFLE

Caliber: 270, 7mm, 300 or 325 WSM, 4 shot. **Barrel:** 24". **Weight:** 6 lbs. 3 oz. to 6 lbs 10 oz. **Length:** 43.25". **Stock:** Claro walnut or Kevlar-reinforced fiberglass. **Sights:** None; drilled and tapped for bases. **Features:** Mauser claw extractor, two-position wing safety, action bedded on aluminum pillars and fiberglass, free-floated barrel, match grade adjustable trigger set at 4 lbs., matte or polished blue or matte stainless finish. Introduced 2003. Made in U.S.A. by Kimber Mfg. Inc.

Price: Classic	**$1,080.00 to $2,030.00**

KIMBER MODEL 84M BOLT-ACTION RIFLE

Caliber: 22-250, 204 Ruger, 223, 243, 260 Rem., 7mm-08, 308, 5-shot. **Barrel:** 22", 24", 26". **Weight:** 5 lbs., 10 oz. to 10 lbs. **Length:** 41" to 45". **Stock:** Claro walnut, checkered with steel gripcap; synthetic or gray laminate. **Sights:** None; drilled and tapped for bases. **Features:** Mauser claw extractor, three-position wing safety, action bedded on aluminum pillars, free-floated barrel, match-grade trigger set at 4 lbs., matte blue finish. Includes cable lock. Introduced 2001. Made in U.S.A. by Kimber Mfg. Inc.

Price: Classic (243, 260, 7mm-08, 308)	**$945.00 to $1,828.00**
Price: Varmint (22-250)	**$1,038.00**

Kimber 84M Varmint

L.A.R. Grizzly

Magnum Research Tactical

Raptor Bolt-Action

Remington 673 Guide

L.A.R. GRIZZLY 50 BIG BOAR RIFLE
Caliber: 50 BMG, single shot. **Barrel:** 36". **Weight:** 30.4 lbs. **Length:** 45.5" overall. **Stock:** Integral. Ventilated rubber recoil pad. **Sights:** None furnished; scope mount. **Features:** Bolt-action bullpup design, thumb and bolt stop safety. All-steel construction. Introduced 1994. Made in U.S.A. by L.A.R. Mfg., Inc.
Price: **$2,295.00**

MAGNUM RESEARCH MAGNUM LITE TACTICAL RIFLE
Caliber: 223 Rem., 22-250, 308 Win., 300 Win. Mag., 300 WSM. **Barrel:** 26" Magnum Lite™ graphite. **Weight:** 8.3 lbs. **Length:** NA. **Stock:** H-S Precision™ tactical black synthetic. **Sights:** None furnished; drilled and tapped for scope mount. **Features:** Accurized Remington 700 action; adjustable trigger; adjustable comb height. Tuned to shoot 1/2" MOA or better. Introduced 2001. From Magnum Research Inc.
Price: **$2,400.00**

MOUNTAIN EAGLE MAGNUM LITE RIFLE
Caliber: 22-250, 223 Rem. (Varmint); 280, 30-06 (long action); 7mm Rem. Mag., 300 Win. Mag., (magnum action). **Barrel:** 24", 26", free floating.

Weight: 7 lbs., 13 oz. **Length:** 44" overall (24" barrel). **Stock:** Kevlar-graphite with aluminum bedding block, high comb, recoil pad, swivel studs; made by H-S Precision. **Sights:** None furnished; accepts any Remington 700-type base. **Features:** Special Sako action with one-piece forged bolt, hinged steel floorplate, lengthened receiver ring; adjustable trigger. Krieger cut-rifled benchrest barrel. Introduced 1996. From Magnum Research, Inc.
Price: Magnum Lite (graphite barrel) **$2,295.00**

RAPTOR BOLT-ACTION RIFLE
Caliber: 270, 30-06, 243, 25-06, 308; 4-shot magazine. **Barrel:** 22". **Weight:** 7 lbs., 6 oz. **Length:** 42.5" overall. **Stock:** Black synthetic, fiberglass reinforced; checkered grip and forend; vented recoil pad; Monte Carlo cheekpiece. **Sights:** None furnished; drilled and tapped for scope mounts. **Features:** Rust-resistant "Taloncote" treated barreled action; pillar bedded; stainless bolt with three locking lugs; adjustable trigger. Introduced 1997. Made in U.S.A. by Raptor Arms Co., Inc.
Price: **$249.00**

REMINGTON MODEL 673 GUIDE RIFLE
Caliber: 65mm Rem. Mag., 308 Win., 300 Rem. SA Ultra Mag., 350 Rem. Mag. **Barrel:** 22". **Weight:** 7-1/2 lbs. **Length:** 41-3/16". **Stock:** Two-tone wide striped, laminated, weather resistant. **Features:** Magnum contour barrel with machined steel ventilated rib, iron sights.
Price: **$825.00**

Remington 700 Classic

Remington 700 ADL Synthetic

Remington 700 BDL

Remington 700 BDL Left-Hand

REMINGTON MODEL 700 CLASSIC RIFLE
Caliber: 300 Savage. **Barrel:** 24". **Weight:** About 7-1/4 lbs. **Length:** 44-1/2" overall. **Stock:** American walnut, 20 lpi checkering on pistol grip and forend. Classic styling. Satin finish. **Sights:** None furnished. Receiver drilled and tapped for scope mounting. **Features:** A "classic" version of the BDL with straight comb stock. Fitted with rubber recoil pad. Sling swivel studs installed. Hinged floorplate. Limited production in 2003 only.
Price: $683.00
Price: Left-hand model . . . . $769.00 to $796.00

REMINGTON MODEL 700 ADL DELUXE RIFLE
Caliber: 270, 30-06. **Barrel:** 22" round tapered. **Weight:** 7-1/4 lbs. **Length:** 41-5/8" overall. **Stock:** Walnut. Satin-finished pistol grip stock with fine-line cut checkering, Monte Carlo. **Sights:** Gold bead ramp front; removable, step-adjustable rear with windage screw. **Features:** Side safety, receiver tapped for scope mounts.
Price: $580.00

Remington Model 700 ADL Synthetic
Similar to the 700 ADL except has a fiberglass-reinforced synthetic stock with straight comb, raised cheekpiece, positive checkering, and black rubber buttpad. Metal has matte finish. Available in 22-250, 223, 243, 270, 308, 30-06 with 22" barrel, 300 Win. Mag., 7mm Rem. Mag. with 24" barrel. Introduced 1996.
Price: From . . . . $500.00 to $527.00

Remington Model 700 ADL Synthetic Youth
Similar to the Model 700 ADL Synthetic except has 1" shorter stock, 20" barrel. Chambered for 243, 308. Introduced 1998.
Price: $500.00

Remington Model 700 BDL Custom Deluxe Rifle
Same as 700 ADL except chambered for 222, 223 (short action, 24" barrel), 7mm-08, 280, 22-250, 25-06, (short action, 22" barrel), 243, 270, 30-06, skip-line checkering, black forend tip and gripcap with white line spacers. Matted receiver top, quick-release floorplate. Hooded ramp front sight, quick detachable swivels.
Price: $683.00
Also available in 17 Rem., 7mm Rem. Mag., 7mm Rem. Ultra Mag., 300 Win. Mag. (long action, 24" barrel); 300 Rem. Ultra Mag. (26" barrel). Overall length 44-1/2", weight about 7-1/2 lbs.
Price: . . . . $709.00 to $723.00

Remington Model 700 BDL Left-Hand Custom Deluxe
Same as 700 BDL except mirror-image left-hand action, stock. Available in 270, 30-06, 7mm Rem. Mag., 300 Rem. Ultra Mag, 338 Rem. Ultra Mag., 7mm Rem. Ultra Mag.
Price: . . . . $709.00 to $749.00

Remington Model 700 BDL DM Rifle
Same as 700 BDL except detachable box magazine (4-shot, standard calibers, 3-shot for magnums). Glossy stock finish, open sights, recoil pad, sling swivels. Available in 270, 30-06, 7mm Rem. Mag., 300 Win. Mag. Introduced 1995.
Price: From . . . . $749.00 to $776.00

Remington 700 BDL SS

Remington 700 BDL SS DM

Remington 700 LSS Mountain

Remington 700 Safari KS

Remington 700 APR African Plains

Remington Model 700 BDL SS Rifle
Similar to 700 BDL rifle except hinged floorplate, 24" standard weight barrel in all calibers; magnum calibers have magnum-contour barrel. No sights supplied, but comes drilled and tapped. Corrosion-resistant follower and fire control, stainless BDL-style barreled action with fine matte finish. Synthetic stock has straight comb and cheekpiece, textured finish, positive checkering, plated swivel studs. Calibers: 270, 30-06; magnums:7mm Rem. Mag., 7mm Rem. UltraMag., 300 Rem. Ultra Mag. (26" barrel) 300 Win. Mag., 338 Rem. Ultra Mag., 7mm Rem. SAUM, 300 Rem. SAUM. Weight: 7-3/8 to 7-1/2 lbs. Introduced 1993.
Price: From . . . . **$735.00 to $775.00**

Remington Model 700 BDL SS DM Rifle
Same as 700 BDL SS except detachable box magazine. Barrel, receiver and bolt made of #416 stainless steel; black synthetic stock, fine-line engraving. Available in 270, 30-06, 7mm Rem. Mag., 300 Win. Mag. Introduced 1995.
Price: From . . . . **$801.00 to $828.00**

Remington Model 700 Custom KS Mountain Rifle
Similar to 700 BDL except custom finished with aramid fiber reinforced resin synthetic stock. Available in left- and right-hand versions. Chambered 270 Win., 280 Rem., 30-06, 7mm Rem. Mag., 7mm STW, 300 Rem. Ultra Mag., 338 Rem. Ultra Mag., 300 Win. Mag., 300 Wby. Mag., 35 Whelen, 338 Win. Mag., 8mm Rem. Mag., 375 H&H, with 24" barrel (except 300 Rem. Ultra Mag., 26"), 7mm RUM, 375 RUM. Weighs 6 lbs., 6 oz. Introduced 1986.
Price: Right-hand. **$1,314.00**

Price: Left-hand. **$1,393.00**
Price: Stainless . . . . **$1,500.00 to $1,580.00**

Remington Model 700 LSS Mountain Rifle
Similar to Model 700 Custom KS Mountain Rifle except stainless steel 22" barrel and two-tone laminated stock. Chambered in 260 Rem., 7mm-08, 270 Winchester and 30-06. Overall length 42-1/2", weighs 6-5/8 oz. Introduced 1999.
Price: **$800.00**

Remington Model 700 Safari Grade
Similar to 700 BDL aramid fiber reinforced fiberglass stock, blued carbon steel bbl. and action, or stainless, w/cheekpiece, custom finished and tuned. In 8mm Rem. Mag., 375 H&H, 416 Rem. Mag. or 458 Win. Mag. calibers only with heavy barrel. Right- and left-hand versions.
Price: Safari KS. . . . . **$1,520.00 to $1,601.00**
Price: Safari KS (stainless right-hand only) **$1,697.00**

Remington Model 700 AWR Alaskan Wilderness Rifle
Similar to the 700 BDL except has stainless barreled action and black Teflon 24" bbl. 26" Ultra Mag raised cheekpiece, magnum-grade black rubber recoil pad. Chambered for 7mm RUM., 375 RUM, 7mm STW, 300 Rem. Ultra Mag., 300 Win. Mag., 300 Wby. Mag., 338 Rem. Ultra Mag., 338 Win. Mag., 375 H&H. Aramid fiber reinforced fiberglass stock. Introduced 1994.
Price: . . . . (right-hand) **$1,593.00**; (left-hand) **$1,673.00**

Remington Model 700 APR African Plains Rifle
Similar to Model 700 BDL except magnum receiver and specially contoured 26" Custom Shop barrel with satin blued finish, laminated wood stock with raised cheekpiece, satin finish, black buttpad, 20 lpi cut checkering. Chambered for 7mm Rem. Mag., 7mm RUM, 375 RUM, 300 Rem. Ultra Mag., 300 Win. Mag., 300 Wby. Mag., 338 Win. Mag., 338 Rem. Ultra Mag., 375 H&H. Introduced 1994.
Price: **$1,716.00**

Remington 700 Titanium

Remington 700 VLS

Remington 700 VS

Remington 700 VS SF

Remington 700 Sendero SF

Remington Model 700 LSS Rifle

Similar to 700 BDL except stainless steel barreled action, gray laminated wood stock with Monte Carlo comb and cheekpiece. No sights furnished. Available in (RH) 7mm Rem. Mag., 300 Win. Mag., 300 RUM, 338 RUM, 7mm Rem. Ultra Mag., 375 Rem. Ultra Mag., (LH) 7mm Rem. Ultra Mag., 300 Rem. Ultra Mag., and 338 RUM. Introduced 1996.
Price: From . . . . (Right-hand) **$820.00 to $840.00**; (left-hand) **$867.00**

Remington Model 700 MTN DM Rifle

Similar to 700 BDL except weighs 6-1/2 to 6-5/8 lbs., 22" tapered barrel. Redesigned pistol grip, straight comb, contoured cheekpiece, hand-rubbed oil stock finish, deep cut checkering, hinged floorplate and magazine follower, two-position thumb safety. Chambered for 260 Rem., 270 Win., 7mm-08, 25-06, 280 Rem., 30-06, 4-shot detachable box magazine. Overall length is 41-5/8" to 42-1/2". Introduced 1995.
Price: **$728.00**

Remington Model 700 Titanium

Similar to 700 BDL except has titanium receiver, spiral-cut fluted bolt, skeletonized bolt handle and carbon-fiber and aramid fiber reinforced stock with sling swivel studs. Barrel 22"; weighs 5-1/4 lbs. (short action) or 5-1/2 lbs. (long action). Satin stainless finish. 260 Rem., 270 Win., 7mm-08, 30-06, 308 Win. Introduced 2001.
Price: **$1,239.00**

Remington Model 700 VLS Varmint Laminated Stock

Similar to 700 BDL except 26" heavy barrel without sights, brown laminated stock with beavertail forend, gripcap, rubber buttpad. Available in 223 Rem., 22-250, 6mm, 243, 308. Polished blue finish. Introduced 1995.
Price: From **$705.00**

Remington Model 700 VS Varmint Synthetic Rifles

Similar to 700 BDL Varmint Laminated except composite stock reinforced with aramid fiber reinforced, fiberglass and graphite. Aluminum bedding block that runs full length of receiver. Free-floating 26" barrel. Metal has black matte finish; stock has textured black and gray finish and swivel studs. Available in 223, 22-250, 308. Right- and left-hand. Introduced 1992.
Price: . . . . **$811.00 to $837.00**

Remington Model 700 VS SF Rifle

Similar to Model 700 Varmint Synthetic except satin-finish stainless barreled action with 26" fluted barrel, spherical concave muzzle crown. Chambered for 223, 220 Swift, 22-250 and 204 Ruger. Introduced 1994.
Price: **$1,025.00**

Remington Model 700 EtronX VSSF Rifle

Similar to Model 700 VS SF except features battery-powered ignition system for near-zero lock time and electronic trigger mechanism. Requires ammunition with EtronX electrically fired primers. Aluminum-bedded 26" heavy, stainless steel, fluted barrel; overall length 45-7/8"; weight 8 lbs., 14 oz. Black, Kevlar-reinforced composite stock. Light-emitting diode display on grip top indicates fire or safe mode, loaded or unloaded chamber, battery condition. Introduced 2000.
Price: 220 Swift, 22-250 or 243 Win. **$1,332.00**

Remington Model 700 XCR Rifle

Similar to standard Model 700 except 24" or 26" barrel; black matte finish; stainless steel barrel and receiver; comes in standard, magnum and short/long magnum calibers.
Price: . . . . **$867.00 to $893.00**

REMINGTON MODEL 700 SENDERO SF RIFLE

Caliber: 7mm Rem. SAUM, 300 Rem. SAUM, 7mm Rem. Mag., 7mm STW, 300 Rem. Ultra Mag., 338 Rem. Ultra Mag., 300 Win. Mag., 7mm Rem. Ultra Mag. **Barrel:** 26". **Weight:** 8-1/2 lbs. **Length:** 45-3/4" to 46-5/8" overall. **Stock:** Aramid fiber refinforced fiberglass. **Sights:** NA **Features:** Stainless steel action and fluted stainless barrel. Introduced 1996.
Price: . . . . **$1,003.00 to $1,016.00**

CENTERFIRE RIFLES — Bolt-Action

Remington Seven LS

Remington Model Seven LS Mag

Remington Model Seven SS Mag

Remington Model Seven Custom MS

Remington Seven Custom KS

REMINGTON MODEL 710 BOLT-ACTION RIFLE
Caliber: 270 Win., 30-06. **Barrel:** 22". **Weight:** 7-1/8 lbs. **Length:** 42-1/2" overall. **Stock:** Gray synthetic. **Sights:** Bushnell Sharpshooter 3-9x scope mounted and bore-sighted. **Features:** Unique action locks bolt directly into barrel; 60-degree bolt throw; 4-shot dual-stack magazine; key-operated Integrated Security System locks bolt open. Introduced 2001. Made in U.S.A. by Remington Arms Co.
Price: **$425.00**

REMINGTON MODEL SEVEN LS
Caliber: 223 Rem., 243 Win., 7mm-08 Rem., 308 Win. **Barrel:** 20". **Weight:** 6-1/2 lbs. **Length:** 39-1/4" overall. **Stock:** Brown laminated, satin finished. **Features:** Satin finished carbon steel barrel and action, 4-round magazine, hinged magazine floorplate. Furnished with iron sights and sling swivel studs, drilled and tapped for scope mounts.
Price: **$701.00**
Price: 7mmRSAUM, 300RSAUM, LS Magnum, 22" bbl. **$741.00**
Price: AWR model **$1,547.00**

Remington Model Seven SS
Similar to Model Seven LS except stainless steel barreled action and black synthetic stock, 20" barrel. Chambered for 243, 260 Rem., 7mm-08, 308. Introduced 1994.

Price: **$729.00**
Price: 7mmRSAUM, 300RSAUM, Model Seven SS
Magnum, 22" bbl. **$769.00**

Remington Model Seven Custom MS Rifle
Similar to Model Seven LS except full-length Mannlicher-style stock of laminated wood with straight comb, solid black recoil pad, black steel forend tip, cut checkering, gloss finish. Barrel length 20", weighs 6-3/4 lbs. Available in 222 Rem., 223, 22-250, 243, 6mm Rem., 260 Rem., 7mm-08 Rem., 308, 350 Rem. Mag., 250 Savage, 257 Roberts, 35 Rem. Polished blue finish. Introduced 1993. From Remington Custom Shop.
Price: From **$1,332.00**

Remington Model Seven Youth Rifle
Similar to Model Seven LS except hardwood stock, 1" shorter length of pull, chambered for 223, 243, 260 Rem., 7mm-08. Introduced 1993.
Price: **$547.00**

Remington Model Seven Custom KS
Similar to Model Seven LS except gray aramid fiber reinforced stock with 1" black rubber recoil pad and swivel studs. Blued satin carbon steel barreled action. No sights on 223, 260 Rem., 7mm-08, 308; 35 Rem. and 350 Rem. have iron sights.
Price: **$1,314.00**

Ruger Magnum

Ruger 77/22 Hornet Varmint

Ruger M77 Mark II

Ruger KM77RLFP MKII

Ruger KM77RFP MKII

RUGER MAGNUM RIFLE
Caliber: 375 H&H, 416 Rigby, 458 Lott. **Barrel:** 23". **Weight:** 9-1/2 to 10-1/4 lbs. **Length:** 44". **Stock:** AAA Premium Grade Circassian walnut with live-rubber recoil pad, metal gripcap, and studs for mounting sling swivels. **Sights:** Blade, front; V-notch rear express sights (one stationary, two folding) drift-adjustable for windage. **Features:** Floorplate latch secures the hinged floorplate against accidental dumping of cartridges; one-piece bolt has a non-rotating Mauser-type controlled-feed extractor; fixed-blade ejector.
Price: M77RSMMKII **$1,975.00**

RUGER 77/22 HORNET BOLT-ACTION RIFLE
Caliber: 22 Hornet, 6-shot rotary magazine. **Barrel:** 20". **Weight:** About 6 lbs. **Length:** 39-3/4" overall. **Stock:** Checkered American walnut, black rubber buttpad. **Sights:** Brass bead front, open adjustable rear; also available without sights. **Features:** Same basic features as rimfire model except slightly lengthened receiver. Uses Ruger rotary magazine. Three-position safety. Comes with 1" Ruger scope rings. Introduced 1994.
Price: 77/22RH (rings only) **$649.00**
Price: K77/22VHZ Varmint, laminated stock, no sights. **$685.00**

RUGER M77 MARK II RIFLE
Caliber: 223, 220 Swift, 22-250, 204 Ruger, 243, 6mm Rem., 257 Roberts, 25-06, 6.5x55 Swedish, 270, 260 Rem., 280 Rem., 308, 30-06, 7mm Rem. Mag., 7mm WSM, 7mm/08, 7mm Rem. Short Ultra Mag., 300 Rem. Short Ultra Mag., 300 WSM, 300 Win. Mag., 338 Win. Mag., 4-shot magazine. **Barrel:** 20", 22"; 24" (magnums). **Weight:** About 7 lbs. **Length:** 39-3/4" overall. **Stock:** Synthetic American walnut; swivel studs, rubber buttpad. **Sights:** None furnished. Receiver has Ruger integral scope mount base, Ruger 1" rings. Some with iron sights. **Features:** Short action with new trigger, 3-position safety. Steel trigger guard. Left-hand available. Introduced 1989.

Price: M77RMKII (no sights). **$716.00**
Price: M77LRMKII (left-hand, 25/06, 270, 30-06, 7mm Rem.
Mag.,300 Win. Mag.) **$716.00**

Ruger M77RSI International Carbine
Same as standard Model 77 except 18" barrel, full-length International-style stock, steel forend cap, loop-type steel sling swivels. Integral base receiver, open sights, Ruger 1" steel rings. Improved front sight. Available in 243, 270, 308, 30-06. Weighs 7 lbs. Length overall is 38-3/8".
Price: M77RSIMKII **$819.00**

Ruger M77 Mark II All-Weather and Sporter Model Stainless Rifle
Similar to wood-stock M77 Mark II except all metal parts are stainless steel, has an injection-molded, glass-fiber-reinforced polymer stock. Laminated wood stock. Chambered for 223, 22/250, 25/06, 260 Rem., 7mm WSM, 7mm/08, 7mm SWM, 280 Rem., 300 WSM, 204 Ruger, 243, 270, 308, 30-06, 7mm Rem. Mag., 300 Win. Mag., 338 Win. Mag. Fixed-blade-type ejector, three-position safety, new trigger guard with patented floorplate latch. Integral Scope Base Receiver, 1" Ruger scope rings, built-in sling swivel loops. Introduced 1990.
Price: K77RFPMKII. **$716.00**
Price: K77RLFPMKII Ultra-Light, synthetic stock, rings, no sights. . **$716.00**
Price: K77LRBBZMKII, left-hand bolt, rings, no sights, laminated
stock **$773.00**
Price: K77RBZMKII, no sights, laminated wood stock, 223,
22/250, 243, 270, 280 Rem., 7mm Rem. Mag., 30-06,
308, 300 Win. Mag., 338 Win. Mag. **$773.00**
Price: KM77RFPMKII, M77RMKII **$773.00**

Ruger M77RL Ultra Light
Similar to standard M77 except weighs 6 lbs., chambered for 223, 243, 308, 270, 30-06, 257 Roberts, barrel tapped for target scope blocks, 20" Ultra Light barrel. Overall length 40". Ruger's steel 1" scope rings supplied. Introduced 1983.
Price: M77RLMKII. **$729.00**

Ruger M77VT Target

Ruger Frontier

Sako TRG-S

Sako 75 Hunter

Sako 75 Stainless Hunter

Ruger M77 Mark II Compact Rifles
Similar to standard M77 except reduced 16-1/2" barrel, weighs 5-3/4 lbs. Chambered for 223, 243, 260 Rem., 308, and 7mm-08.
Price: M77CR MKII (blued finish, walnut stock) **$675.00**
Price: KM77CRBBZ MkII (stainless finish, black laminated stock) . . **$729.00**

RUGER M77VT TARGET RIFLE
Caliber: 22-250, 220 Swift, 223, 204 Ruger, 243, 25-06, 308. **Barrel:** 26" heavy stainless steel with target gray finish. **Weight:** 9-3/4 lbs. **Length:** Approx. 44" overall. **Stock:** Laminated American hardwood with beavertail forend, steel swivel studs; no checkering or gripcap. **Sights:** Integral scope mount bases in receiver. **Features:** Ruger diagonal bedding system. Ruger steel 1" scope rings supplied. Fully adjustable trigger. Steel floorplate and trigger guard. New version introduced 1992.
Price: K77VTMKII **$870.00**

RUGER FRONTIER RIFLE
Caliber: 243, 7mm/08, 308, 300WSM. **Barrel:** 16-1/2". **Weight:** 6-1/4 lbs. **Stock:** Black laminate. **Features:** Front scope mounting rib, blued finish; overall length 35-1/2". Introduced 2005.
Price: **$799.00**

SAKO TRG-42 BOLT-ACTION RIFLE
Caliber: 338 Lapua Mag. and 300 Win. Mag. **Barrel:** 27-1/8". **Weight:** 11-1/4 lbs. **Length:** NA. **Stock:** NA. **Sights:** NA. **Features:** 5-shot magazine, fully adjustable stock and competition trigger. Imported from Finland by Beretta USA.
Price: **$3,589.00**

SAKO 75 HUNTER BOLT-ACTION RIFLE
Caliber: 17 Rem., 222, 223, 22-250, 243, 7mm-08, 308 Win., 25-06, 270, 280, 30-06; 270 Wby. Mag., 7mm Rem. Mag., 7mm STW, 7mm Wby. Mag., 300 Win. Mag., 300 Wby. Mag., 338 Win. Mag., 340 Wby. Mag., 375 H&H, 416 Rem. Mag. **Barrel:** 22", standard calibers; 24", 26" magnum calibers. **Weight:** About 6 lbs. **Length:** NA. **Stock:** European walnut with matte lacquer finish. **Sights:** None furnished; dovetail scope mount rails. **Features:** New design with three locking lugs and a mechanical ejector, key locks firing pin and bolt, cold hammer-forged barrel is free-floating, two-position safety, hinged floorplate or detachable magazine that can be loaded from the top, short 70-degree bolt lift. Five action lengths. Introduced 1997. Imported from Finland by Beretta USA.
Price: Standard calibers **$1,419.00**
Price: Magnum calibers **$1,499.00**

Sako 75 Stainless Synthetic Rifle
Similar to 75 Hunter except all metal is stainless steel, synthetic stock has soft composite panels molded into forend and pistol grip. Available in 22-250, 243, 308 Win., 25-06, 270, 30-06 with 22" barrel, 7mm Rem. Mag., 7mm STW, 300 Win. Mag., 338 Win. Mag. and 375 H&H Mag. with 24" barrel and 300 Wby. Mag., 300 Rem. Ultra Mag. with 26" barrel. Introduced 1997. Imported from Finland by Beretta USA.
Price: Standard calibers **$1,499.00**
Price: Magnum calibers **$1,499.00**

Sako 75 Deluxe

Sako 75 Varmint

Savage 110GXP3

Savage 11FXP3

Sako 75 Deluxe Rifle
Similar to 75 Hunter except select wood rosewood gripcap and forend tip. Available in 17 Rem., 222, 223, 25-06, 243, 7mm-08, 308, 25-06, 270, 280, 30-06; 270 Wby. Mag., 7mm Rem. Mag., 7mm STW, 7mm Wby. Mag., 300 Win. Mag., 300 Wby. Mag., 338 Win. Mag., 340 Wby. Mag., 375 H&H, 416 Rem. Mag. Introduced 1997. Imported from Finland by Beretta USA.
Price: Standard calibers **$2,044.00**
Price: Magnum calibers **$2,044.00**

Sako 75 Varmint Stainless Laminated Rifle
Similar to Sako 75 Hunter except chambered only for 222, 223, 22-250, 22 PPC USA, 6mm PPC, heavy 24" barrel with recessed crown; set trigger; all metal is stainless steel, laminated wood stock with beavertail forend. Introduced 1999. Imported from Finland by Beretta USA.
Price: **$1,959.00**

Sako 75 Varmint Rifle
Similar to Model 75 Hunter except chambered only for 17 Rem., 222 Rem., 223 Rem., 22-250 Rem., 22 PPC and 6mm PPC, 24" heavy barrel with recessed crown; set trigger; beavertail forend. Introduced 1998. Imported from Finland by Beretta USA.
Price: **$1,684.00**

SAUER 202 BOLT-ACTION RIFLE
Caliber: Standard 243, 6.5x55, 270 Win., 308 Win., 30-06; magnum 7mm Rem. Mag., 300 Win. Mag., 300 Wby. Mag., 375 H&H. **Barrel:** 23.6" (standard), 26" (magnum). **Weight:** 7.7 lbs. (standard). **Length:** 44.3" overall (23.6" barrel). **Stock:** Select American Claro walnut with high-gloss epoxy finish, rosewood grip and forend caps; 22 lpi checkering. Synthetic also available. **Sights:** None furnished; drilled and tapped for scope mounting. **Features:** Short 60" bolt throw; detachable box magazine; six-lug bolt; quick-change barrel; tapered bore; adjustable two-stage trigger; firing pin cocking indicator. Introduced 1994. Imported from Germany by SIGARMS, Inc.
Price: Standard calibers, right-hand **$1,035.00**
Price: Magnum calibers, right-hand **$1,106.00**
Price: Standard calibers, synthetic stock **$985.00**
Price: Magnum calibers, synthetic stock **$1,056.00**

SAVAGE MODEL 10GXP3, 110GXP3 PACKAGE GUNS
Caliber: 223 Rem., 22-250 Rem., 243 Win., 7mm-08 Rem., 308 Win., 300 WSM (10GXP3). 25-06 Rem., 270 Win., 30-06 Spfld., 7mm Rem. Mag., 300 Win. Mag., 300 Rem. Ultra Mag. (110GXP3). **Barrel:** 22" 24", 26". **Weight:** 7.5 lbs. average. **Length:** 43" to 47". **Stock:** Walnut Monte Carlo with checkering. **Sights:** 3-9x40mm scope, mounted & bore sighted. **Features:** Blued, free floating and button rifled, internal box magazines, swivel studs, leather sling. Left-hand available.
Price: Accu-trigger **$539.00**

SAVAGE MODEL 11FXP3, 111FXP3, 111FCXP3, 11FYXP3 (Youth) PACKAGE GUNS
Caliber: 223 Rem., 22-250 Rem., 243 Win., 308 Win., 300 WSM (11FXP3). 270 Win., 30-06 Spfld., 25-06 Rem., 7mm Rem. Mag., 300 Win. Mag., 338 Win. Mag., 300 Rem. Ultra Mag. (11FCXPE & 111FXP3). **Barrel:** 22" to 26". **Weight:** 6.5 lbs. **Length:** 41" to 47". **Stock:** Synthetic checkering, dual pillar bed. **Sights:** 3-9X40mm scope, mounted & bore sighted. **Features:** Blued, free floating and button rifled, Top loading internal box mag (except 111FXCP3 has detachable box mag.). Nylon sling and swivel studs. Some left-hand available.
Price: Model 11FXP3 . . . . **$516.00**
Price: Model 111FCXP3 . . . . **$411.00**
Price: Model 11FYXP3, 243 Win., 12.5" pull (youth) **$501.00**

Savage 111FCXP3

Savage Model 10FP

Savage Model 10FPLE1

Savage Model 10FPXP-LE

SAVAGE MODEL 16FXP3, 116FXP3 SS ACTION PACKAGE GUNS
Caliber: 223 Rem., 243 Win., 308 Win., 300 WSM, 270 Win., 30-06 Spfld., 7mm Rem. Mag., 300 Win. Mag., 338 Win. Mag., 375 H&H, 7mm S&W, 7mm Rem. Ultra Mag., 300 Rem. Ultra Mag. **Barrel:** 22", 24", 26". **Weight:** 6.75 lbs. average. **Length:** 41" to 46". **Stock:** Synthetic checkering, dual pillar bed. **Sights:** 3-9X40mm scope, mounted & bore sighted. **Features:** Free floating and button rifled. Internal box mag., nylon sling and swivel studs.
Price: $601.00

SAVAGE MODEL 10FM SIERRA ULTRA LIGHT RIFLE
Caliber: 223, 243, 308. **Barrel:** 20". **Weight:** 6 lbs. **Length:** 41-1/2". **Stock:** "Dual Pillar" bedding in black synthetic stock with silver medallion in gripcap. **Sights:** None furnished; drilled and tapped for scope mounting. **Features:** True short action. Model 10FCM has detachable box magazine. Comes with sling and quick-detachable swivels. Introduced 1998. Made in U.S.A. by Savage Arms, Inc.
Price: $552.00

SAVAGE MODEL 10/110FP LONG RANGE RIFLE
Caliber: 223, 25-06, 308, 30-06, 300 Win. Mag., 7mm Rem. Mag., 4-shot magazine. **Barrel:** 24", heavy; recessed target muzzle. **Weight:** 8-1/2 lbs.

Length: 45.5" overall. **Stock:** Black graphite/fiberglass composition; positive checkering. **Sights:** None furnished. Receiver drilled and tapped for scope mounting. **Features:** Pillar-bedded stock. Black matte finish on all metal parts. Double swivel studs on the forend for sling and/or bipod mount. Right- or left-hand. Introduced 1990. From Savage Arms, Inc.
Price: Right- or left-hand $601.00

Savage Model 10FP Tactical Rifle
Similar to the Model 110FP except has true short action, chambered for 223, 308; black synthetic stock with "Dual Pillar" bedding. Introduced 1998. Made in U.S.A. by Savage Arms, Inc.
Price: $601.00
Price: Model 10FLP (left-hand) $601.00
Price: Model 10FP-LE1 (20"), 10FPLE2 (26") $601.00
Price: Model 10FPXP-LE w/Burris 3.5-10x50 scope,
Harris bipod package $1,805.00

Savage Model 10FP-LE1A Tactical Rifle
Similar to the Model 110FP except weighs 10.75 lbs. and has overall length of 39.75". Chambered for 223 Rem., 308 Win. Black synthetic Choate™ adjustable stock with accessory rail and swivel studs.
Price: $729.00

Savage Model 111F

Savage Model 11FCNS

Savage Model 11G

Savage Model 10GY

Savage Model 12FV

SAVAGE MODEL 111 CLASSIC HUNTER RIFLES
Caliber: 25-06 Rem., 270 Win., 30-06 Spfld., 7mm Rem. Mag., 300 Win. Mag., 7mm RUM, 300 RUM. **Barrel:** 22", 24", 26" (magnum calibers). **Weight:** 6.5 to 7.5 lbs. **Length:** 42.75" to 47.25". **Stock:** Walnut-finished hardwood (M111G, GC); graphite/fiberglass filled composite. **Sights:** Ramp front, open fully adjustable rear; drilled and tapped for scope mounting. **Features:** Three-position top tang safety, double front locking lugs, free-floated button-rifled barrel. Comes with trigger lock, target, ear puffs. Introduced 1994. Made in U.S.A. by Savage Arms, Inc.
Price: Model 111F (270 Win., 30-06 Spfld., 7mm Rem. Mag., 300 Win. Mag.) **$486.00**
Price: Model 111F (25-06 Rem., 338 Win. Mag., 7mm Rem. Ultra Mag, 300 Rem. Ultra Mag.) **$486.00**
Price: Model 111G
(wood stock, top-loading magazine, right- or left-hand) **$436.00**
Price: Model 111GNS (wood stock, detachable box magazine, no sights, right-hand only) **$518.00**

Savage Model 11 Classic Hunter Rifles, Short Action
Similar to the Model 111F except has true short action, chambered for 22-250, Rem., 243 Win., 7mm-08 Rem., 308 Win.; black synthetic stock with "Dual Pillar" bedding, positive checkering. Introduced 1998. Made in U.S.A. by Savage Arms, Inc.
Price: Model 11F **$486.00**
Price: Model 11FL (left-hand) **$486.00**
Price: Model 11FCNS (right-hand, no sights) **$507.00**
Price: Model 11G (wood stock) **$496.00**
Price: Model 11GL (as above, left-hand) **$496.00**

Savage Model 10GY
Similar to the Model 111G except weighs 6.3 lbs., is 42-1/2" overall, and the stock is scaled for ladies, small-framed adults and youths. Chambered for 223, 243, 308. Ramp front sight, open adjustable rear; drilled and tapped for scope mounts. Made in U.S.A. by Savage Arms, Inc.
Price: Model 10GY (short action, calibers 223, 243, 308) **$496.00**

SAVAGE MODEL 112 LONG RANGE RIFLES
Caliber: 5-shot magazine. **Barrel:** 26" heavy. **Weight:** 8.8 lbs. **Length:** 47.5" overall. **Stock:** Black graphite/fiberglass filled composite with positive checkering. **Sights:** None furnished; drilled and tapped for scope mounting. **Features:** Pillar-bedded stock. Blued barrel with recessed target-style muzzle. Double front swivel studs for attaching bipod. Introduced 1991. Made in U.S.A. by Savage Arms, Inc.
Price: Model 112BVSS (heavy-prone laminated stock with high comb, Wundhammer swell, fluted stainless barrel, bolt handle, trigger guard) **$675.00**

Savage Model 12 Long Range Rifles
Similar to the Model 112 Long Range except with true short action, chambered for 223, 22-250, 308. Models 12FV, 12FVSS have black synthetic stocks with "Dual Pillar" bedding, positive checkering, swivel studs; Model 12BVSS has brown laminated stock with beavertail forend, fluted stainless barrel. Introduced 1998. Made in U.S.A. by Savage Arms, Inc.
Price: Model 12FV (223, 22-250, 243 Win., 308 Win., blue) **$549.00**
Price: Model 12FVSS (blue action, fluted stainless barrel) **$667.00**
Price: Model 12FLV (as above, left-hand) **$549.00**
Price: Model 12FVS (blue action, fluted stainless barrel, single shot) **$667.00**
Price: Model 12BVSS (laminated stock) **$721.00**
Price: Model 12BVSS-S (as above, single shot) **$721.00**

Savage Model 12VSS

Savage Model 16FCSS

Savage Model 116FSAK

Sigarms SHR 970

Steyr Mannlicher SBS

Savage Model 12VSS Varminter Rifle
Similar to other Model 12s except blue/stainless steel action, fluted stainless barrel, Choate full pistol grip, adjustable synthetic stock, Sharp Shooter trigger. Overall length 47-1/2", weighs appx. 15 lbs. No sights; drilled and tapped for scope mounts. Chambered in 223, 22-250, 308 Win. Made in U.S.A. by Savage Arms, Inc.
Price: **$934.00**

SAVAGE MODEL 116 WEATHER WARRIORS
Caliber: 375 H&H, 300 Rem. Ultra Mag., 308 Win., 300 Rem. Ultra Mag., 300 WSM, 7mm Rem. Ultra Mag., 7mm Rem. Short Ultra Mag., 7mm S&W, 7mm-08 Rem. **Barrel:** 22", 24" for 7mm Rem. Mag., 300 Win. Mag., 338 Win. Mag. (M116FSS only). **Weight:** 6.25 to 6.5 lbs. **Length:** 41" to 47". **Stock:** Graphite/fiberglass filled composite. **Sights:** None furnished; drilled and tapped for scope mounting. **Features:** Stainless steel with matte finish; free-floated barrel; quick-detachable swivel studs; laser-etched bolt; scope bases and rings. Left-hand models available in all models, calibers at same price. Model 116FSS introduced 1991; 116FSAK introduced 1994. Made in U.S.A. by Savage Arms, Inc.
Price: Model 116FSS (top-loading magazine) **$520.00**
Price: Model 116FSAK (top-loading magazine,
Savage adjustable muzzle brake system) **$601.00**
Price: Model 16BSS (brown laminate, 24") **$668.00**
Price: Model 116BSS (brown laminate, 26") **$668.00**

Savage Model 16FCSS Rifle
Similar to Model 116FSS except true short action, chambered for 223, 243, 22" free-floated barrel; black graphite/fiberglass stock, "Dual Pillar" bedding. Also left-hand version available. Introduced 1998. Made in U.S.A. by Savage Arms, Inc.
Price: **$552.00**

SIGARMS SHR 970 SYNTHETIC RIFLE
Caliber: 270, 30-06. **Barrel:** 22". **Weight:** 7.2 lbs. **Length:** 41.9" overall. **Stock:** Textured black fiberglass or walnut. **Sights:** None furnished; drilled and tapped for scope mounting. **Features:** Quick takedown; interchangeable barrels; removable box magazine; cocking indicator; three-position safety. Introduced 1998. Imported by SIGARMS, Inc.
Price: Synthetic stock **$499.00**
Price: Walnut stock **$550.00**

STEYR CLASSIC MANNLICHER SBS RIFLE
Caliber: 243, 25-06, 308, 6.5x55, 6.5x57, 270, 7x64 Brenneke, 7mm-08, 7.5x55, 30-06, 9.3x62, 6.5x68, 7mm Rem. Mag., 300 Win. Mag., 8x68S, 4-shot magazine. **Barrel:** 23.6" standard; 26" magnum; 20" full stock standard calibers. **Weight:** 7 lbs. **Length:** 40.1" overall. **Stock:** Hand-checkered fancy European oiled walnut with standard forend. **Sights:** Ramp front adjustable for elevation, V-notch rear adjustable for windage. **Features:** Single adjustable trigger; 3-position roller safety with "safe-bolt" setting; drilled and tapped for Steyr factory scope mounts. Introduced 1997. Imported from Austria by GSI, Inc.
Price: Full-stock, standard calibers. **$1,749.00**

Steyr SBS Forester

Steyr SBS Prohunter

Steyr Scout Rifle

Tikka T-3 Hunter

STEYR SBS FORESTER RIFLE

Caliber: 243, 25-06, 270, 7mm-08, 308 Win., 30-06, 7mm Rem. Mag., 300 Win. Mag. Detachable 4-shot magazine. **Barrel:** 23.6", standard calibers; 25.6", magnum calibers. **Weight:** 7.5 lbs. **Length:** 44.5" overall (23.6" barrel). **Stock:** Oil-finished American walnut with Monte Carlo cheekpiece. Pachmayr 1" swivels. **Sights:** None furnished. Drilled and tapped for Browning A-Bolt mounts. **Features:** Three-position ambidextrous roller tang safety. Matte finish on barrel and receiver; adjustable trigger. Rotary cold-hammer forged barrel. Introduced 1997. Imported by GSI, Inc.

Price: Standard calibers **$799.00**
Price: Magnum calibers **$829.00**

Steyr SBS Prohunter Rifle

Similar to the SBS Forester except has ABS synthetic stock with adjustable butt spacers, straight comb without cheekpiece, palm swell, Pachmayr 1" swivels. Special 10-round magazine conversion kit available. Introduced 1997. Imported by GSI.

Price: Standard calibers **$769.00**
Price: Magnum calibers **$799.00**

STEYR SCOUT BOLT-ACTION RIFLE

Caliber: 308 Win., 5-shot magazine. **Barrel:** 19", fluted. **Weight:** NA. **Length:** NA. **Stock:** Gray Zytel. **Sights:** Pop-up front & rear, Leupold M8 2.5x28 IER scope on Picatinny optic rail with Steyr mounts. **Features:** luggage case, scout sling, two stock spacers, two magazines. Introduced 1998. From GSI.

Price: From **$1,969.00**

STEYR SSG BOLT-ACTION RIFLE

Caliber: 308 Win., detachable 5-shot rotary magazine. **Barrel:** 26". **Weight:** 8.5 lbs. **Length:** 44.5" overall. **Stock:** Black ABS Cycolac with spacers for length of pull adjustment. **Sights:** Hooded ramp front adjustable for elevation, V-notch rear adjustable for windage. **Features:** Sliding safety; NATO rail for bipod; 1" swivels; Parkerized finish; single or double-set triggers. Imported from Austria by GSI, Inc.

Price: SSG-PI, iron sights **$1,699.00**
Price: SSG-PII, heavy barrel, no sights **$1,699.00**
Price: SSG-PIIK, 20" heavy barrel, no sights **$1,699.00**
Price: SSG-PIV, 16.75" threaded heavy barrel with flash hider . . . **$2,659.00**

TIKKA T-3 BIG BOAR SYNTHETIC BOLT-ACTION RIFLE

Caliber: 308, 30-06, 300 WSM. **Barrel:** 19". **Weight:** 6 lbs. **Length:** 39.5" overall. **Stock:** Laminated. **Sights:** None furnished. **Features:** Detachable, 3-round. Receiver dove-tailed for scope mounting. Reintroduced 1996. Imported from Finland by Beretta USA.

Price: Left-hand. **$719.00**

Tikka T-3 Varmint Rifle

Similar to the standard T-3 rifle except has 23-3/8" heavy stainless or blued barrel. Chambered for 22-250, 223, 308. Reintroduced 2005. Made in Finland by Sako. Imported by Beretta USA.

Price: . . . . **$839.00 to $908.00**

TIKKA T-3 HUNTER

Caliber: 223, 22-250, 243, 308, 25-06, 270, 30-06, 300 Win. Mag., 338 Win. Mag., 270 WSM, 300 WSM, 6.5x55 Swedish Mauser, 7mm Rem. Mag. **Stock:** Walnut. **Sight:** None furnished. **Barrel:** 22-7/16", 24-3/8". **Features:** Detachable magazine, aluminum scope rings. Introduced 2005. Imported from Finland by Beretta USA.

Price: Standard cal.. . . . . **$759.00**
Price: Magnum calibers **$798.00**
Price: T-3 Lite (synthetic stock) . . . . **$674.00 to $709.00**

Weatherby Mark V Lazermark

Weatherby Mark V Sporter

Weatherby Mark V Stainless

Weatherby Mark V Synthetic

Tikka T-3 Stainless Synthetic
  Similar to the T-3 Hunter except stainless steel, synthetic stock. Available in 243, 25-06, 270, 308, 30-06, 270 WSM, 300 WSM, 7mm Rem. Mag., 300 Win. Mag., 338 Win. Mag. Introduced 2005. Imported from Finland by Beretta USA.
Price: Standard calibers **$908.00**
Price: Magnum calibers **$944.00**

ULTRA LIGHT ARMS BOLT-ACTION RIFLES
Caliber: 17 Rem. to 416 Rigby. **Barrel:** Douglas, length to order. **Weight:** 4-3/4 to 7-1/2 lbs. **Length:** Varies. **Stock:** Kevlar® graphite composite, variety of finishes. **Sights:** None furnished; drilled and tapped for scope mounts. **Features:** Timney trigger, hand-lapped action, button-rifled barrel, hand-bedded action, recoil pad, sling-swivel studs, optional Jewell trigger. Made in U.S.A. by New Ultra Light Arms.
Price: Model 20 (short action) **$2,800.00**
Price: Model 24 (long action) **$2,900.00**
Price: Model 28 (magnum action) **$3,200.00**
Price: Model 40 (300 Wby. Mag., 416 Rigby) **$3,200.00**
Price: Left-hand models, add **$100.00**

WEATHERBY MARK V DELUXE BOLT-ACTION RIFLE
Caliber: All Weatherby calibers plus 22-250, 243, 25-06, 270 Win., 280 Rem., 7mm-08, 30-06, 308 Win. **Barrel:** 24" barrel on standard calibers. **Weight:** 8-1/2 to 10-1/2 lbs. **Length:** 46-5/8" to 46-3/4" overall. **Stock:** Walnut, Monte Carlo with cheekpiece; high luster finish; checkered pistol grip and forend; recoil pad. **Sights:** None furnished. **Features:** Cocking indicator; adjustable trigger; hinged floorplate, thumb safety; quick detachable sling swivels. Made in U.S.A. From Weatherby.
Price: 257, 270, 7mm. 300, 340 Wby. Mags., 26" barrel **$1,767.00**
Price: 416 Wby. Mag. with Accubrake, 28" barrel **$2,079.00**
Price: 460 Wby. Mag. with Accubrake, 28" barrel **$2,443.00**
Price: 24" barrel **$1,715.00**

Weatherby Mark V Lazermark Rifle
  Same as Mark V Deluxe except stock has extensive oak leaf pattern laser carving on pistol grip and forend. Introduced 1981.

Price: 257, 270, 7mm Wby. Mag., 300, 340, 26" **$1,923.00**
Price: 378 Wby. Mag., 28" **$2,266.00**
Price: 416 Wby. Mag., 28", Accubrake **$2,266.00**
Price: 460 Wby. Mag., 28", Accubrake **$2,661.00**

Weatherby Mark V Sporter Rifle
  Same as the Mark V Deluxe without the embellishments. Metal has low-luster blue, stock is Claro walnut with matte finish, Monte Carlo comb, recoil pad. Introduced 1993. From Weatherby.
Price: 22-250, 243, 240 Wby. Mag., 25-06, 7mm-08,
  270 WCF, 280, 30-06, 308; 24" **$1,091.00**
Price: 257 Wby., 270, 7 mm Wby., 7mm Rem., 300 Wby.,
  300 Win., 340 Wby., 338 Win. Mag., 26" barrel for Wby. calibers;
  24" for non-Wby. calibers **$1,143.00**

Weatherby Mark V Stainless Rifle
  Similar to the Mark V Deluxe except made of 410-series stainless steel. Also available in 30-378 Wby. Mag. Has lightweight injection-molded synthetic stock with raised Monte Carlo comb, checkered grip and forend, custom floorplate release. Right-hand only. Introduced 1995. Made in U.S.A. From Weatherby.
Price: 22-250 Rem., 243 Win., 240 Wby. Mag., 25-06 Rem.,
  270 Win., 280 Rem., 7mm-08 Rem., 30-06 Spfld., 308 Win.,
  24" barrel **$1,018.00**
Price: 257, 270, 7mm, 300, 340 Wby. Mag., 26" barrel **$1,070.00**
Price: 7mm Rem. Mag., 300 Win. Mag., 338 Win. Mag.,
  375 H&H Mag., 24" barrel **$1,070.00**

Weatherby Mark V Synthetic
  Similar to the Mark V Stainless except made of matte finished blued steel. Injection molded synthetic stock. Weighs 6-1/2 lbs., 24" barrel. Available in 22-250, 240 Wby. Mag., 243, 25-06, 270, 7mm-08, 280, 30-06, 308. Introduced 1997. Made in U.S.A. From Weatherby.
Price: **$923.00**
Price: 257, 270, 7mm, 300, 340 Wby. Mags., 26" barrel **$975.00**
Price: 7mm STW, 7mm Rem. Mag., 300, 338 Win. Mags **$975.00**
Price: 375 H&H, 24" barrel **$975.00**
Price: 30-378 Wby. Mag., 338-378 Wby. 28" barrel **$1,151.00**

Weatherby Mark V Accumark

Weatherby Mark V SVR

Weatherby Mark V Fibermark

Weatherby Mark V Dangerous Game Rifle

WEATHERBY MARK V ACCUMARK RIFLE
Caliber: 257, 270, 7mm, 300, 340 Wby. Mags., 338-378 Wby. Mag., 30-378 Wby. Mag., 7mm STW, 7mm Rem. Mag., 300 Win. Mag. **Barrel:** 26", 28". **Weight:** 8-1/2 lbs. **Length:** 46-5/8" overall. **Stock:** Bell & Carlson with full length aluminum bedding block. **Sights:** None furnished. Drilled and tapped for scope mounting. **Features:** Uses Mark V action with heavy-contour stainless barrel with black oxidized flutes, muzzle diameter of .705". Introduced 1996. Made in U.S.A. From Weatherby.
Price: 26" **$1,507.00**
Price: 30-378 Wby. Mag., 338-378 Wby. Mag., 28",
  Accubrake **$1,724.00**
Price: 223, 22-250, 243, 240 Wby. Mag., 25-06, 270,
  280 Rem., 7mm-08, 30-06, 308; 24" **$1,455.00**
Price: Accumark left-hand 257, 270, 7mm, 300, 340 Wby.
  Mag., 7mm Rem. Mag., 7mm STW, 300 Win. Mag. **$1,559.00**
Price: Accumark left-hand 30-378, 333-378 Wby. Mags. **$1,788.00**

Weatherby Mark V Accumark Ultra Lightweight Rifles
Similar to the Mark V Accumark except weighs 5-3/4 lbs., 6-3/4 lbs. in Mag. calibers.; 24", 26" fluted barrel with recessed target crown; hand-laminated stock with CNC-machined aluminum bedding plate and faint gray "spider web" finish. Available in 257, 270, 7mm, 300 Wby. Mags., (26"); 243, 240 Wby. Mag., 25-06, 270 Win., 280 Rem., 7mm-08, 7mm Rem. Mag., 30-06, 338-06 A-Square, 308, 300 Win. Mag. (24"). Introduced 1998. Made in U.S.A. by Weatherby.
Price: . . . . **$1,459.00 to $1,517.00**
Price: Left-hand models. **$1,559.00**

Weatherby Mark V SVM/SPM Rifles
Similar to the Mark V Accumark except has 26" fluted (SVM) or 24" fluted Krieger barrel, spiderweb-pattern tan laminated synthetic stock. SVM has a fully adjustable trigger. Chambered for 223, 22-250, 220 Swift (SVM only), 243, 7mm-08 and 308. Made in U.S.A. by Weatherby.
Price: SVM (Super VarmintMaster), repeater or single-shot **$1,517.00**
New! Price: SPM (Super Predator Master) **$1,459.00**

Weatherby Mark V Special Varmint Rifle (SVR)
Similar to the Super VarmintMaster and Accumark with 22", #3 contour chrome-moly 4140 steel Krieger Criterion button-rifled barrel with one-degree target crown and hand-laminated composite stock. Available in .223 Rem. (5+1 magazine capacity) and .22-250 Rem. (4+1 magazine capacity) in right-hand models only.
Price: **$999.00**

Weatherby Mark V Fibermark Rifles
Similar to other Mark V models except has black Kevlar® and fiberglass composite stock and bead-blast blue or stainless finish. Chambered for 19 standard and magnum calibers. Introduced 1983; reintroduced 2001. Made in U.S.A. by Weatherby.
Price: Fibermark . . . . **$1,070.00 to $1,347.00**
Price: Fibermark stainless . . . . **$1,165.00 to $1,390.00**

WEATHERBY MARK V DANGEROUS GAME RIFLE
Caliber: 375 H&H, 375 Wby. Mag., 378 Wby. Mag., 416 Rem. Mag., 416 Wby. Mag., 458 Win. Mag., .458 Lott, 460 Wby. Mag. 300 Win. Mag., 300 Wby., Mag., 338 Win. Mag., 340 Wby. Mag., 24" only **Barrel:** 24" or 26". **Weight:** 8-3/4 to 9-1/2 lbs. **Length:** 44-5/8" to 46-5/8" overall. **Stock:** Kevlar® and fiberglass composite. **Sights:** Barrel-band hooded front with large gold bead, adjustable ramp/shallow "V" rear. **Features:** Designed for dangerous game hunting. Black oxide matte finish on all metalwork; Pachmayr Decelerator™ recoil pad, short-throw Mark V action. Introduced 2001. Made in U.S.A. by Weatherby.
Price: . . . . **$2,703.00 to $2,935.00**

Wilderness Explorer

Winchester Model 70 Classic

Winchester Model 70 Classic Stainless

Winchester Model 70 Classic Featherweight

WEATHERBY MARK V SUPER BIG GAMEMASTER DEER RIFLE
Caliber: 240 Wby. Mag., 25-06 Rem., 270 Win., 280 Rem., 30-06 Spfld., 257 Wby. Mag., 270 Wby. Mag., 7mm Rem., Mag., 7mm Wby. Mag., 338-06 A-Square, 300 Win. Mag., 300 Wby. Mag. **Barrel:** 26", target crown. **Weight:** 5-3/4 lbs., (6-3/4 lbs. Magnum). **Stock:** Raised comb Monte Carlo composite. **Features:** Fluted barrel, aluminum bedding block, Pachmayr decelerator, 54-degree bolt lift, adj. trigger.
Price: **$1,459.00**
Price: Magnum **$1,517.00**

WEATHERBY MARK V ROYAL CUSTOM RIFLE
Caliber: 257, 270, 7mm, 300, 340 all Wby. Mags. Other calibers available upon request. **Barrel:** 26". **Stock:** Monte Carlo hand-checkered Claro walnut with high gloss finish. **Features:** Bolt and follower are damascened with checkered knob. Engraved receiver, bolt sleeve and floorplate sport scroll pattern. Animal images on floorplate optional. High gloss blue, 24-karat gold and nickel-plating. Made in U.S.A. From Weatherby.
Price: **$5,831.00**

WEATHERBY THREAT RESPONSE RIFLES (TRR) SERIES
Caliber: TRR 223 Rem., 300 Win. TRR Magnum and Magnum Custom 300 Win. Mag., 300 Wby. Mag., 30-378 Wby. Mag., 328-378 Wby. Mag. **Barrel:** 22", 26", target crown. **Stock:** Hand-laminated composite. TTR & TRR Magnum have raised comb Monte Carlo style. TRR Magnum Custom adjustable ergonomic stock. **Features:** Adjustable trigger, aluminum bedding block, beavertail forearms dual tapered, flat-bottomed. "Rocker Arm" lockdown scope mounting. 54 degree bolt. Pachmayr decelerator pad. Made in U.S.A.
Price: TRR Magnum Custom 300 . . . . **$2,699.00**
Price: 30-378, 338-378 with accubrake. **$2,861.00**

WILDERNESS EXPLORER MULTI-CALIBER CARBINE
Caliber: 22 Hornet, 218 Bee, 44 Magnum, 50 A.E. (interchangeable). **Barrel:** 18", match grade. **Weight:** 5.5 lbs **Length:** 38-1/2" overall. **Stock:** Synthetic or wood. **Sights:** None furnished; comes with Weaver-style mount on barrel. **Features:** Quick-change barrel and bolt face for caliber switch. Removable box magazine; adjustable trigger with side safety; detachable swivel studs. Introduced 1997. Made in U.S.A. by Phillips & Rogers, Inc.
Price: **$995.00**

WINCHESTER MODEL 70 CLASSIC SPORTER III
Caliber: 25-06, 270 Win., 30-06, 7mm STW, 7mm Rem. Mag., 300 Win. Mag., 338 Win. Mag., 3-shot magazine; 5-shot in 25-06, 270 Win., 30-06. **Barrel:** 24", 26" for magnums. **Weight:** 7-3/4 to 8 lbs. **Length:** 46-3/4" overall (26" bbl.). **Stock:** American walnut with cut checkering and satin finish. Classic style with straight comb. **Sights:** None furnished. Drilled and tapped for scope mounting. **Features:** Uses pre-64-type action with controlled round feeding. Three-position safety, stainless steel magazine follower; rubber buttpad; epoxy bedded receiver recoil lug. From U.S. Repeating Arms Co.
Price: 25-06, 270, 30-06 . . . . **$742.00**
Price: Other calibers **$810.00**
Price: Left-hand, 270 or 30-06 . . . . **$778.00**
Price: Left-hand, 7mm Rem. Mag or 300 Win. Mag. **$810.00**

Winchester Model 70 Classic Stainless Rifle
Same as Model 70 Classic Sporter except stainless steel barrel and pre-64-style action with controlled round feeding and matte gray finish, black composite stock impregnated with fiberglass and graphite, contoured rubber recoil pad. No sights (except in 375 H&H). Available in 270 Win., 30-06, 7mm STW, 7mm Rem. Mag., 300 Win. Mag., 300 Ultra Mag., 338 Win. Mag., 375 H&H Mag. (24" barrel), 3- or 5-shot magazine. Weighs 7-1/2 lbs. Introduced 1994.
Price: 270, 30-06. . . . . **$817.00**
Price: 375 H&H Mag., with sights. **$943.00**
Price: Other calibers **$847.00**

Winchester Model 70 Classic Featherweight
Same as Model 70 Classic except action bedded in standard-grade walnut stock. Available in 22-250, 243, 6.5x55, 308, 7mm-08, 270 Win., 30-06. Drilled and tapped for scope mounts. Weighs 7 lbs. Introduced 1992.
Price: **$814.00**

Winchester Model 70 Classic Compact

Winchester Model 70 Coyote

Winchester Model 70 Stealth

Winchester Model 70 Classic Super Grade

Winchester Model 70 WSM

Winchester Model 70 Classic Compact
Similar to Model 70 Classic Featherweight except scaled down for smaller shooters. 20" barrel, 12-1/2" length of pull. Pre-'64-type action. Available in 243, 308 or 7mm-08. Introduced 1998. Made in U.S.A. by U. S. Repeating Arms Co.
Price: **$762.00**

Winchester Model 70 Coyote
Similar to Model 70 Classic except laminated wood stock, 24" medium-heavy stainless steel barrel. Available in 223 Rem., 22-250 Rem., 243 Win., or 308 Win.
Price: **$742.00**

WINCHESTER MODEL 70 STEALTH RIFLE
Caliber: 223, 22-250, 308 Win. **Barrel:** 26". **Weight:** 10-3/4 lbs. **Length:** 46" overall. **Stock:** Kevlar/fiberglass/graphite Pillar Plus Accu-Block with full-length aluminum bedding block. **Sights:** None furnished. **Features:** Push-feed bolt design; matte finish. Introduced 1999. Made in U.S.A. by U.S. Repeating Arms Co.
Price: **$886.00**

WINCHESTER MODEL 70 CLASSIC SUPER GRADE
Caliber: 25-06, 270, 30-06, 5-shot magazine; 7mm Rem. Mag., 300 Win. Mag., 338 Win. Mag., 3-shot magazine. **Barrel:** 24", 26" for magnums. **Weight:** 7-3/4 lbs. to 8 lbs. **Length:** 44-1/2" overall (24" bbl.) **Stock:** Walnut with straight comb, sculptured cheekpiece, wraparound cut

checkering, tapered forend, solid rubber buttpad. **Sights:** None furnished; comes with scope bases and rings. **Features:** Controlled round feeding with stainless steel claw extractor, bolt guide rail, 3-position safety; all steel bottom metal, hinged floorplate, stainless magazine follower. Introduced 1994. From U.S. Repeating Arms Co.
Price: 25-06, 270, 30-06 . . . . **$1,036.00**
Price: Other calibers **$1,024.00**

WINCHESTER MODEL 70 CLASSIC SAFARI EXPRESS
Caliber: 375 H&H Mag., 416 Rem. Mag., 458 Win. Mag., 3-shot magazine. **Barrel:** 24". **Weight:** 8-1/4 to 8-1/2 lbs. **Stock:** American walnut with Monte Carlo cheekpiece. Wrap-around checkering and finish. **Sights:** Hooded ramp front, open rear. **Features:** Controlled round feeding. Two steel cross bolts in stock for added strength. Front sling swivel stud mounted on barrel. Contoured rubber buttpad. From U.S. Repeating Arms Co.
Price: **$1,189.00**
Price: Left-hand, 375 H&H only **$1,163.00**

WINCHESTER MODEL 70 WSM RIFLES
Caliber: 300 WSM, 3-shot magazine. **Barrel:** 24". **Weight:** 7-1/4 to 7-3/4 lbs. **Length:** 44" overall. **Stock:** Checkered walnut, black synthetic or laminated wood. **Sights:** None. **Features:** Model 70 designed for the new 300 Winchester Short Magnum cartridge. Short-action receiver, 3-position safety, knurled bolt handle. Introduced 2001. From U.S. Repeating Arms Co.
Price: Classic Featherweight WSM
(checkered walnut stockand forearm) **$892.00**
Price: Classic stainless WSM (black syn. stock, stainless steel bbl.) **$859.00**
Price: Classic laminated WSM (laminated wood stock) **$810.00**

Ballard No. 5 Pacific

Ballard No. 7

ARMALITE AR-50 RIFLE
Caliber: 50 BMG **Barrel:** 31". **Weight:** 33.2 lbs. **Length:** 59.5" **Stock:** Synthetic. **Sights:** None furnished. **Features:** A single-shot bolt action rifle designed for long range shooting. Available in left-hand model. Made in U.S.A. by Armalite.
Price: $2,885.00

ARMSPORT 1866 SHARPS RIFLE, CARBINE
Caliber: 45-70. **Barrel:** 28", round or octagonal. **Weight:** 8.10 lbs. **Length:** 46" overall. **Stock:** Walnut. **Sights:** Blade front, folding adjustable rear. Tang sight set optionally available. **Features:** Replica of the 1866 Sharps. Color case-hardened frame, rest blued. Imported by Armsport.
Price: $865.00
Price: With octagonal barrel $900.00
Price: Carbine, 22" round barrel $850.00

BALLARD NO. 1 3/4 FAR WEST RIFLE
Caliber: 22 LR, 32-40, 38-55, 40-65, 40-70, 45-70, 45-110, 50-70, 50-90. **Barrel:** 30" std. or heavyweight. **Weight:** 10-1/2 lbs. (std.) or 11-3/4 lbs. (heavyweight bbl.) **Length:** NA. **Stock:** Walnut. **Sights:** Blade front, Rocky Mountain rear. **Features:** Single or double-set triggers, S-lever or ring-style lever; color case-hardened finish; hand polished and lapped Badger barrel. Made in U.S.A. by Ballard Rifle & Cartridge Co.
Price: $2,250.00

BALLARD NO. 4 PERFECTION RIFLE
Caliber: 22 LR, 32-40, 38-55, 40-65, 40-70, 45-70, 45-90, 45-110, 50-70, 50-90. **Barrel:** 30" or 32" octagon, standard or heavyweight. **Weight:** 10-1/2 lbs. (standard) or 11-3/4 lbs. (heavyweight bbl.). **Length:** NA. **Stock:** Smooth walnut. **Sights:** Blade front, Rocky Mountain rear. **Features:** Rifle or shotgun-style buttstock, straight grip action, single or double-set trigger, "S" or right lever, hand polished and lapped Badger barrel. Made in U.S.A. by Ballard Rifle & Cartridge Co.
Price: $2,250.00

BALLARD NO. 5 PACIFIC SINGLE-SHOT RIFLE
Caliber: 32-40, 38-55, 40-65, 40-90, 40-70 SS, 45-70 Govt., 45-110 SS, 50-70 Govt., 50-90 SS. **Barrel:** 30", or 32" octagonal. **Weight:** 10-1/2 lbs. **Length:** NA. **Stock:** High-grade walnut; rifle or shotgun style. **Sights:** Blade front, Rocky Mountain rear. **Features:** Standard or heavy barrel; double-set triggers; under-barrel wiping rod; ring lever. Introduced 1999. Made in U.S.A. by Ballard Rifle & Cartridge Co.
Price: $2,575.00

BALLARD NO. 7 LONG RANGE RIFLE
Caliber: 32-40, 38-55, 40-65, 40-70 SS, 45-70 Govt., 45-90, 45-110. **Barrel:** 32", 34" half-octagon. **Weight:** 11-3/4 lbs. **Length:** NA. **Stock:** Walnut; checkered pistol grip shotgun butt, ebony forend cap. **Sights:** Globe front. **Features:** Designed for shooting up to 1000 yards. Standard or heavy barrel; single or double-set trigger; hard rubber or steel buttplate. Introduced 1999. Made in U.S.A. by Ballard Rifle & Cartridge Co.
Price: From $2,475.00

BALLARD NO. 8 UNION HILL RIFLE
Caliber: 22 LR, 32-40, 38-55, 40-65 Win., 40-70 SS. **Barrel:** 30" half-octagon. **Weight:** About 10-1/2 lbs. **Length:** NA. **Stock:** Walnut; pistol grip butt with cheekpiece. **Sights:** Globe front. **Features:** Designed for 200-yard offhand shooting. Standard or heavy barrel; double-set triggers; full loop lever; hook Schuetzen buttplate. Introduced 1999. Made in U.S.A. by Ballard Rifle & Cartridge Co.
Price: From $2,500.00

BALLARD MODEL 1885 HIGH WALL SINGLE SHOT RIFLE
Caliber: 17 Bee, 22 Hornet, 218 Bee, 219 Don Wasp, 219 Zipper, 22 Hi-Power, 225 Win., 25-20 WCF, 25-35 WCF, 25 Krag, 7mmx57R, 30-30, 30-40 Krag, 303 British, 33 WCF, 348 WCF, 35 WCF, 35-30/30, 9.3x74R, 405 WCF, 50-110 WCF, 500 Express, 577 Express. **Barrel:** Lengths to 34". **Weight:** NA. **Length:** NA. **Stock:** Straight-grain American walnut. **Sights:** buckhorn or flattop rear, blade front. **Features:** Faithful copy of original Model 1885 High Wall; parts interchange with original rifles; variety of options available. Introduced 2000. Made in U.S.A. by Ballard Rifle & Cartridge LLC.
Price: From $2,313.00
Price: With single set trigger from $2,355.00

BARRETT MODEL 99 SINGLE SHOT RIFLE
Caliber: 50 BMG. **Barrel:** 33". **Weight:** 25 lbs. **Length:** 50.4" overall. **Stock:** Anodized aluminum with energy-absorbing recoil pad. **Sights:** None furnished; integral M1913 scope rail. **Features:** Bolt action; detachable bipod; match-grade barrel with high-efficiency muzzle brake. Introduced 1999. Made in U.S.A. by Barrett Firearms.
Price: From $3,000.00

BROWN MODEL 97D SINGLE SHOT RIFLE
Caliber: 17 Ackley Hornet through 45-70 Govt. **Barrel:** Up to 26", air gauged match grade. **Weight:** About 5 lbs., 11 oz. **Stock:** Sporter style with pistol grip, cheekpiece and Schnabel forend. **Sights:** None furnished; drilled and tapped for scope mounting. **Features:** Falling block action gives rigid barrel-receiver matting; polished blue/black finish. Hand-fitted action. Many options. Made in U.S.A. by E. Arthur Brown Co., Inc.
Price: From $699.00

C. Sharps New Model 1875 Old Reliable

C. Sharps New Model 1874

C. Sharps New Model 1885

Cabela's Sharps

BROWNING MODEL 1885 HIGH WALL SINGLE SHOT RIFLE
Caliber: 22-250, 30-06, 270, 7mm Rem. Mag., 454 Casull, 45-70. **Barrel:** 28". **Weight:** 8 lbs., 12 oz. **Length:** 43-1/2" overall. **Stock:** Walnut with straight grip, Schnabel forend. **Sights:** None furnished; drilled and tapped for scope mounting. **Features:** Replica of J.M. Browning's high-wall falling block rifle. Octagon barrel with recessed muzzle. Imported from Japan by Browning. Introduced 1985.
Price: **$1,027.00**

BRNO ZBK 110 SINGLE SHOT RIFLE
Caliber: 222 Rem., 5.6x52R, 22 Hornet, 5.6x50 Mag., 6.5x57R, 7x57R, 8x57JRS. **Barrel:** 23.6". **Weight:** 5.9 lbs. **Length:** 40.1" overall. **Stock:** European walnut. **Sights:** None furnished; drilled and tapped for scope mounting. **Features:** Top tang opening lever; cross-bolt safety; polished blue finish. Announced 1998. Imported from The Czech Republic by Euro-Imports.
Price: Standard calibers **$223.00**
Price: 7x57R, 8x57JRS **$245.00**
Price: Lux model, standard calibers **$311.00**
Price: Lux model, 7x57R, 8x57JRS **$333.00**

C. SHARPS ARMS NEW MODEL 1875 OLD RELIABLE RIFLE
Caliber: 22LR, 32-40 & 38-55 Ballard, 38-56 WCF, 40-65 WCF, 40-90 3-1/4", 40-90 2-5/8", 40-70 2-1/10", 40-70 2-1/4", 40-70 2-1/2", 40-50 1-11/16", 40-50 1-7/8", 45-90, 45-70, 45-100, 45-110, 45-120. Also available on special order only in 50-70, 50-90, 50-140. **Barrel:** 24", 26", 30" (standard), 32", 34" optional. **Weight:** 8-12 lbs. **Stock:** Walnut, straight grip, shotgun butt with checkered steel buttplate. **Sights:** Silver blade front, Rocky Mountain buckhorn rear. **Features:** Recreation of the 1875 Sharps rifle. Production guns will have case-colored receiver. Available in Custom Sporting and Target versions upon request. Announced 1986. From C. Sharps Arms Co.
Price: 1875 Sporting Rifle (30" tapered oct. bbl.) **$1,185.00**

C. Sharps Arms 1875 Classic Sharps
Similar to New Model 1875 Sporting Rifle except 26", 28" or 30" full octagon barrel, crescent buttplate with toe plate, Hartford-style forend with cast German silver nose cap. Blade front sight, Rocky Mountain buckhorn rear. Weighs 10 lbs. Introduced 1987. From C. Sharps Arms Co.
Price: **$1,470.00**

C. Sharps Arms New Model 1875 Target & Long Range
Similar to New Model 1875 in all listed calibers except 22 LR; 34" tapered octagon barrel; globe with post front sight, Long Range Vernier tang sight with windage adjustments. Pistol grip stock with cheek rest; checkered steel buttplate. Introduced 1991. From C. Sharps Arms Co.
Price: **$1,549.50**

C. SHARPS ARMS NEW MODEL 1874 OLD RELIABLE
Caliber: 40-50, 40-70, 40-90, 45-70, 45-90, 45-100, 45-110, 45-120, 50-70, 50-90, 50-140. **Barrel:** 26", 28", 30" tapered octagon. **Weight:** About 10 lbs. **Length:** NA. **Stock:** American black walnut; shotgun butt with checkered steel buttplate; straight grip, heavy forend with Schnabel tip. **Sights:** Blade front, buckhorn rear. Drilled and tapped for tang sight. **Features:** Recreation of the Model 1874 Old Reliable Sharps Sporting Rifle. Double-set triggers. Reintroduced 1991. Made in U.S.A. by C. Sharps Arms.
Price: **$1,584.00**

C. SHARPS ARMS NEW MODEL 1885 HIGHWALL RIFLE
Caliber: 22 LR, 22 Hornet, 219 Zipper, 25-35 WCF, 32-40 WCF, 38-55 WCF, 40-65, 30-40 Krag, 40-50 ST or BN, 40-70 ST or BN, 40-90 ST or BN, 45-70 2-1/10" ST, 45-90 2-4/10" ST, 45-100 2-6/10" ST, 45-110 2-7/8" ST, 45-120 3-1/4" ST. **Barrel:** 26", 28", 30", tapered full octagon. **Weight:** About 9 lbs., 4 oz. **Length:** 47" overall. **Stock:** Oil-finished American walnut; Schnabel-style forend. **Sights:** Blade front, buckhorn rear. Drilled and tapped for optional tang sight. **Features:** Single trigger; octagonal receiver top; checkered steel buttplate; color case-hardened receiver and buttplate, blued barrel. Many options available. Made in U.S.A. by C. Sharps Arms Co
Price: From **$1,439.00**

C. SHARPS ARMS CUSTOM NEW MODEL 1877 LONG RANGE TARGET RIFLE
Caliber: 44-90 Sharps/Rem., 45-70, 45-90, 45-100 Sharps. **Barrel:** 32", 34" tapered round with Rigby flat. **Weight:** Appx. 10 lbs. **Stock:** Walnut checkered. Pistol grip/forend. **Sights:** Classic long range with windage. **Features:** Custom production only.
Price: . . . . **$5,550.00 and up**

CABELA'S SHARPS SPORTING RIFLE
Caliber: 45-70, 45-120, 45-110, 50-70. **Barrel:** 32", tapered octagon. **Weight:** 9 lbs. **Length:** 47-1/4" overall. **Stock:** Checkered walnut. **Sights:** Blade front, open adjustable rear. **Features:** Color case-hardened receiver and hammer, rest blued. Introduced 1995. Imported by Cabela's.
Price: **$999.99**
Price: (Heavy target Sharps, 45-70, 45-120, 50-70) **$1,199.99**
Price: (Quigley Sharps, 45-70, 45-120, 45-110) **$1,499.99**
Price: Sharps Competition 45/70 . . . . **$1,299.99**

Cimarron Billy Dixon

Cimarron Quigley

Cimarron 1885 High Wall

Cumberland Mountain Plateau

Dakota Single Shot

CIMARRON BILLY DIXON 1874 SHARPS SPORTING RIFLE
Caliber: 40-40, 50-90, 50-70, 45-70. **Barrel:** 32" tapered octagonal. **Weight:** NA. **Length:** NA. **Stock:** European walnut. **Sights:** Blade front, Creedmoor rear. **Features:** Color case-hardened frame, blued barrel. Hand-checkered grip and forend; hand-rubbed oil finish. Introduced 1999. Imported by Cimarron F.A. Co.
Price: **$1,670.00**

CIMARRON QUIGLEY MODEL 1874 SHARPS SPORTING RIFLE
Caliber: 45-110, 50-70, 50-40, 45-70, 45-90, 45-120. **Barrel:** 34" octagonal. **Weight:** NA. **Length:** NA. **Stock:** Checkered walnut. **Sights:** Blade front, adjustable rear. **Features:** Blued finish; double-set triggers. From Cimarron F.A. Co.
Price: **$1,805.00**

CIMARRON SILHOUETTE MODEL 1874 SHARPS SPORTING RIFLE
Caliber: 45-70, 50-70. **Barrel:** 32" octagonal. **Weight:** NA. **Length:** NA. **Stock:** Walnut. **Sights:** Blade front, adjustable rear. **Features:** Pistol-grip stock with shotgun-style buttplate; cut-rifled barrel. From Cimarron F.A. Co.
Price: **$1,620.00**

CIMARRON MODEL 1885 HIGH WALL RIFLE
Caliber: 38-55, 40-65, 45-70, 45-90, 45-120, 30-40 Krag, 348 Winchester. **Barrel:** 30" octagonal. **Weight:** NA. **Length:** NA. **Stock:** European walnut. **Sights:** Bead front, semi-buckhorn rear. **Features:** Replica of the

Winchester 1885 High Wall rifle. Color case-hardened receiver and lever, blued barrel. Curved buttplate. Optional double-set triggers. Introduced 1999. Imported by Cimarron F.A. Co.
Price: **$995.00**
Price: With pistol grip **$1,175.00**

CUMBERLAND MOUNTAIN PLATEAU RIFLE
Caliber: 40-65, 45-70. **Barrel:** Up to 32"; round. **Weight:** About 10-1/2 lbs. (32" barrel). **Length:** 48" overall (32" barrel). **Stock:** American walnut. **Sights:** Marble's bead front, Marble's open rear. **Features:** Falling block action with underlever. Blued barrel and receiver. Stock has lacquer finish, crescent buttplate. Introduced 1995. Made in U.S.A. by Cumberland Mountain Arms, Inc.
Price: **$1,085.00**

DAKOTA MODEL 10 SINGLE SHOT RIFLE
Caliber: Most rimmed and rimless commercial calibers. **Barrel:** 23". **Weight:** 6 lbs. **Length:** 39-1/2" overall. **Stock:** Medium fancy grade walnut in classic style. Checkered grip and forend. **Sights:** None furnished. Drilled and tapped for scope mounting. **Features:** Falling block action with underlever. Top tang safety. Removable trigger plate for conversion to single set trigger. Introduced 1990. Made in U.S.A. by Dakota Arms.
Price: **$3,595.00**
Price: Barreled action **$2,095.00**
Price: Action only **$1,850.00**
Price: Magnum calibers **$3,595.00**
Price: Magnum barreled action. **$2,050.00**
Price: Magnum action only **$1,675.00**

Dixie 1874 Sharps Silhouette

H&R Ultra Varmint

H&R Ultra Hunter

H&R Buffalo

DIXIE 1874 SHARPS BLACK POWDER SILHOUETTE RIFLE
Caliber: 45-70. **Barrel:** 30"; tapered octagon; blued; 1:18" twist. **Weight:** 10 lbs., 3 oz. **Length:** 47-1/2" overall. **Stock:** Oiled walnut. **Sights:** Blade front, ladder-type hunting rear. **Features:** Replica of the Sharps #1 Sporter. Shotgun-style butt with checkered metal buttplate; color case-hardened receiver, hammer, lever and buttplate. Tang is drilled and tapped for tang sight. Double-set triggers. Meets standards for NRA blackpowder cartridge matches. Introduced 1995. Imported from Italy by Dixie Gun Works.
Price: **$1,075.00**

Dixie 1874 Sharps Lightweight Hunter/Target Rifle
Same as the Dixie 1874 Sharps Black Powder Silhouette model except has a straight-grip buttstock with military-style buttplate. Based on the 1874 military model. Introduced 1995. Imported from Italy by Dixie Gun Works.
Price: **$1,025.00**

E.M.F. 1874 METALLIC CARTRIDGE SHARPS RIFLE
Caliber: 45-70, 45/120. **Barrel:** 28", octagon. **Weight:** 10-3/4 lbs. **Length:** NA. **Stock:** Oiled walnut. **Sights:** Blade front, flip-up open rear. **Features:** Replica of the 1874 Sharps Sporting rifle. Color case-hardened lock; double-set trigger; blue finish. Imported by E.M.F.
Price: From **$700.00**
Price: With browned finish............................ **$1,000.00**
Price: Military Carbine **$650.00**

HARRINGTON & RICHARDSON ULTRA VARMINT RIFLE
Caliber: 223, 243. **Barrel:** 24", heavy. **Weight:** About 7.5 lbs. **Stock:** Hand-checkered laminated birch with Monte Carlo comb. **Sights:** None furnished. Drilled and tapped for scope mounting. **Features:** Break-open action with side-lever release, positive ejection. Scope mount. Blued receiver and barrel. Swivel studs. Introduced 1993. From H&R 1871, Inc.
Price: **$332.00**

Harrington & Richardson Ultra Hunter Rifle
Similar to Ultra Varmint rifle except chambered for 25-06 with 26" barrel, or 308 Win., 450 Marlin with 22" barrel. Stock and forend are of cinnamon-colored laminate; hand-checkered grip and forend. Introduced 1995. Made in U.S.A. by H&R 1871, LLC.
Price: **$332.00**

HARRINGTON & RICHARDSON BUFFALO CLASSIC RIFLE
Caliber: 45-70. **Barrel:** 32" heavy. **Weight:** 8 lbs. **Length:** 52" overall. **Stock:** American black walnut. **Sights:** Williams receiver sight; Lyman target front sight with 8 aperture inserts. **Features:** Color case-hardened Handi-Rifle action with exposed hammer; color case-hardened crescent buttplate; 19th century checkering pattern. Introduced 1995. Made in U.S.A. by H&R 1871, LLC.
Price: About **$418.00**

Harrington & Richardson 38-55 Target Rifle
Similar to the Buffalo Classic rifle except chambered for 38-55 Win., has 28" barrel. The barrel, steel trigger guard and forend spacer, are highly polished and blued. Color case-hardened receiver and buttplate. Williams receiver sight; Lyman target front sight with 8 aperture inserts. Introduced 1998. Made in U.S.A. by H&R 1871, LLC.
Price: **$418.00**

HARRIS GUNWORKS ANTIETAM SHARPS RIFLE
Caliber: 40-65, 45-75. **Barrel:** 30", 32", octagon or round, hand-lapped stainless or chrome-moly. **Weight:** 11.25 lbs. **Length:** 47" overall. **Stock:** Choice of straight grip, pistol grip or Creedmoor with Schnabel forend; pewter tip optional. Standard wood is A Fancy; higher grades available. **Sights:** Montana Vintage Arms #111 Low Profile Spirit Level front, #108 mid-range tang rear with windage adjustments. **Features:** Recreation of the 1874 Sharps sidehammer. Action is color case-hardened, barrel satin black. Chrome-moly barrel optionally blued. Optional sights include #112 Spirit Level Globe front with windage, #107 Long Range rear with windage. Introduced 1994. Made in U.S.A. by Harris Gunworks.
Price: **$2,400.00**

Lonestar Silhouette

Model 1885 High Wall

Mossberg SSi-One Sporter

Mossberg SSi-One Varminter

KRIEGHOFF HUBERTUS SINGLE-SHOT RIFLE
Caliber: 222, 243, 270, 308, 30-06, 5.6x50R Mag., 5.6x52R, 6x62R Freres, 6.5x57R, 6.5x65R, 7x57R, 7x65R, 8x57JRS, 8x75RS, 7mm Rem. Mag., 300 Win. Mag. **Barrel:** 23-1/2". **Weight:** 6-1/2 lbs. **Length:** NA. **Stock:** High-grade walnut. **Sights:** Blade front, open rear. **Features:** Break-open loading with manual cocking lever on top tang; takedown; extractor; Schnabel forearm; many options. Imported from Germany by Krieghoff International Inc.
Price: Hubertus single shot, from **$5,950.00**
Price: Hubertus, magnum calibers **$6,950.00**

LONE STAR NO. 5 REMINGTON PATTERN ROLLING BLOCK RIFLE
Caliber: 25-35, 30-30, 30-40 Krag. **Barrel:** 26" to 34". **Weight:** NA. **Length:** NA **Stock:** American walnut. **Sights:** Beech style, Marble bead, Rocky Mountain-style, front; Buckhorn, early or late combination, rear. **Features:** Round, tapered round, octagon, tapered octagon, half octagon-half round barrels; bone-pack color case-hardened actions; single, single set, or double-set triggers. Made in U.S.A. by Lone Star Rifle Co., Inc.
Price: **$1,595.00**

Lone Star Cowboy Action Rifle
Similar to the Lone Star No. 5 rifle, but designed for cowboy action shooting with 28-33" barrel, buckhorn rear sight.
Price: **$1,595.00**

Lone Star Custom Silhouette Rifle
Similar to the Lone Star No. 5 rifle but custom made in any caliber or barrel length.
Price: **$1,995.00**

MEACHAM HIGHWALL SILHOUETTE RIFLE
Caliber: 40-65 Match, 45-70 Match. **Barrel:** 30", 34" octagon. **Stock:** Black walnut with cheekpiece. **Weight:** 11.5 to 11.9 lbs. **Sights:** None. Tang drilled for Win. base, 3/8" dovetail notch, front. **Length of pull:** 13-5/8". **Features:** Parts interchangeable copy of '85 Winchester. Available with single trigger, single set trigger, or Schuetzen-style double-set triggers. Color case-hardened action. Introduced 2002. From Meacham T&H, Inc.
Price: **$2,999.00**

MERKEL K-1 MODEL LIGHTWEIGHT STALKING RIFLE
Caliber: 243 Win., 270 Win., 7x57R, 308 Win., 30-06, 7mm Rem. Mag., 300 Win. Mag., 9.3x74R. **Barrel:** 23.6". **Weight:** 5.6 lbs. unscoped. **Stock:** Satin-finished walnut, fluted and checkered; sling-swivel studs. **Sights:** None (scope base furnished). **Features:** Franz Jager single-shot break-open action, cocking/uncocking slide-type safety, matte silver receiver, selectable trigger pull weights, integrated, quick detach 1" or 30mm optic mounts (optic not included). Imported from Germany by GSI.
Price: Standard, simple border engraving **$3,795.00**
Price: Premium, light arabesque scroll. **$3,795.00**
Price: Jagd, fine engraved hunting scenes. **$4,395.00**

MODEL 1885 HIGH WALL RIFLE
Caliber: 30-40 Krag, 32-40, 38-55, 40-65 WCF, 45-70. **Barrel:** 26" (30-40), 28" to 30" all others. Douglas Premium #3 tapered octagon. **Weight:** 9 lbs, 4 oz. **Length:** 47" overall. **Stock:** Premium American black walnut. **Sights:** Marble's standard ivory bead front, #66 long blade top rear with reversible notch and elevator. **Features:** Receiver with octagon top, thick-wall High Wall with coil spring action. Tang drilled, tapped for High Wall tang sight. Receiver, lever, hammer and breechblock color case-hardened. Available from Montana Armory, Inc.
Price: **$1,350.00**

MOSSBERG SSi-ONE SINGLE SHOT RIFLE
Caliber: 223 Rem., 22-250 Rem., 243 Win., 270 Win., 308 Rem., 30-06. **Barrel:** 24". **Weight:** 8 lbs. **Length:** 40". **Stock:** Satin-finished walnut, fluted and checkered; sling-swivel studs. **Sights:** None (scope base furnished). **Features:** Frame accepts interchangeable barrels including 12 gauge, fully rifled slug barrel and 12 ga., 3-1/2" chambered barrel with Ulti-Full Turkey choke tube. Lever-opening, break-action design; single-stage trigger; ambidextrous, top-tang safety; internal eject/extract selector. Introduced 2000. From Mossberg.
Price: SSi-One Sporter (standard barrel) or 12 ga., 3-1/2" chamber . **$459.00**
Price: SSi-One Varmint (bull barrel, 22-250 Rem. only;
weighs 10 lbs.) **$480.00**
Price: SSi-One 12 gauge Slug (fully rifled barrel, no sights,
scope base). **$480.00**

Navy Arms #2 Creedmoor

Navy Arms 1874 Sharps Cavalry Carbine

Navy Arms 1874 Sharps Plains

Navy Arms 1874 Sharps Sporting

Navy Arms 1873 Springfield

NAVY ARMS 1873 SHARPS "QUIGLEY" RIFLE
Caliber: 45/70. **Barrel:** 34" heavy octagonal. **Stock:** Walnut. **Features:** Case-hardened receiver and military patchbox. Exact reproduction from "Quigley Down Under."
Price: **$1,390.00**

NAVY ARMS 1873 SHARPS NO. 2 CREEDMOOR RIFLE
Caliber: 45/70. **Barrel:** 30" tapered round. **Stock:** Walnut. **Sights:** Front globe, "soule" tang rear. **Features:** Nickel receiver and action. Lightweight sporting rifle.
Price: **$1,300.00**

NAVY ARMS 1874 SHARPS CAVALRY CARBINE
Caliber: 45-70. **Barrel:** 22". **Weight:** 7 lbs., 12 oz. **Length:** 39" overall. **Stock:** Walnut. **Sights:** Blade front, military ladder-type rear. **Features:** Replica of the 1874 Sharps miltary carbine. Color case-hardened receiver and furniture. Imported by Navy Arms.
Price: **$1,000.00**

NAVY ARMS 1874 SHARPS BUFFALO RIFLE
Caliber: 45-70, 45-90. **Barrel:** 28" heavy octagon. **Weight:** 10 lbs., 10 oz. **Length:** 46" overall. **Stock:** Walnut; checkered grip and forend. **Sights:** Blade front, ladder rear; tang sight optional. **Features:** Color case-hardened receiver, blued barrel; double-set triggers. Imported by Navy Arms.
Price: **$1,160.00**

Navy Arms Sharps Plains Rifle
Similar to Sharps Buffalo rifle except 45-70 only, 32" medium-weight barrel, weighs 9 lbs., 8 oz., and is 49" overall. Imported by Navy Arms.
Price: **$1,125.00**

Navy Arms Sharps Sporting Rifle
Same as the Navy Arms Sharps Plains Rifle except has pistol grip stock. Introduced 1997. Imported by Navy Arms.
Price: 45-70 only **$1,160.00**

NAVY ARMS 1885 HIGH WALL RIFLE
Caliber: 45-70; others available on special order. **Barrel:** 28" round, 30" octagonal. **Weight:** 9.5 lbs. **Length:** 45-1/2" overall (30" barrel). **Stock:** Walnut. **Sights:** Blade front, vernier tang-mounted peep rear. **Features:** Replica of Winchester's High Wall designed by Browning. Color case-hardened receiver, blued barrel. Introduced 1998. Imported by Navy Arms.
Price: 28", round barrel, target sights **$920.00**
Price: 30" octagonal barrel, target sights **$995.00**

NAVY ARMS 1873 SPRINGFIELD CAVALRY CARBINE
Caliber: 45-70. **Barrel:** 22". **Weight:** 7 lbs. **Length:** 40-1/2" overall. **Stock:** Walnut. **Sights:** Blade front, military ladder rear. **Features:** Blued lockplate and barrel; color case-hardened breechblock; saddle ring with bar. Replica of 7th Cavalry gun. Imported by Navy Arms.
Price: **$930.00**

Navy Arms Rolling Block Buffalo

New England Firearms Handi-Rifle

New England Firearms Super Light

New England Firearms Survivor

NAVY ARMS ROLLING BLOCK RIFLE
Caliber: 45-70. **Barrel:** 26", 30". **Stock:** Walnut. **Sights:** Blade front, adjustable rear. **Features:** Reproduction of classic rolling block action. Available with full-octagon or half-octagon/half-round barrel. Color case-hardened action, steel fittings. From Navy Arms.
Price: Buffalo $825.00
Price: Special Sporting, 26" half round bbl. $730.00

NAVY ARMS "JOHN BODINE" ROLLING BLOCK RIFLE
Caliber: 45-70. **Barrel:** 30" heavy octagonal. **Stock:** Walnut. **Sights:** Globe front, "soule" tang rear. **Features:** Double-set triggers.
Price: $1,385.00

NAVY ARMS SHARPS NO. 3 LONG RANGE RIFLE
Caliber: 45-70, 45-90. **Barrel:** 34" octagon. **Weight:** 10 lbs., 12 oz. **Length:** 51-1/2". **Stock:** Deluxe walnut. **Sights:** Globe target front and match grade rear tang. **Features:** Shotgun buttplate, German silver forend cap, color case hardenend receiver. Imported by Navy Arms.
Price: $1,885.00

NEW ENGLAND FIREARMS HANDI-RIFLE
Caliber: 22 Hornet, 223, 243, 30-30, 270, 280 Rem., 308, 30-06, 357 Mag., 44 Mag., 45-70. **Barrel:** 22", 24"; 26" for 280 Rem. **Weight:** 7 lbs. **Stock:** Walnut-finished hardwood; black rubber recoil pad. **Sights:** Ramp front, folding rear (22 Hornet, 30-30, 45-70). Drilled and tapped for scope mount; 223, 243, 270, 280, 30-06 have no open sights, come with scope mounts.

Features: Break-open action with side-lever release. The 223, 243, 270 and 30-06 have recoil pad and Monte Carlo stock for shooting with scope. Swivel studs on all models. Blue finish. Introduced 1989. From New England Firearms.
Price: $270.00
Price: 280 Rem., 26" barrel. $270.00
Price: Synthetic Handi-Rifle (black polymer stock and forend, swivels, recoil pad) $281.00
Price: Handi-Rifle Youth (223, 243). $270.00
Price: Stainless Handi-Rifle (223 Rem., 243 Rem.). $337.00

New England Firearms Super Light Rifle
Similar to Handi-Rifle except new barrel taper, shorter 20" barrel with recessed muzzle, special lightweight synthetic stock and forend. No sights furnished on 223 and 243 versions, which have factory-mounted scope base and offset hammer spur; Monte Carlo stock; 22 Hornet has ramp front, fully adjustable open rear. Overall length 36", weight is 5.5 lbs. Introduced 1997. Made in U.S.A. by New England Firearms.
Price: 22 Hornet, 223 Rem. or 243 Win. $281.00

NEW ENGLAND FIREARMS SURVIVOR RIFLE
Caliber: 223, 308 Win., single shot. **Barrel:** 22". **Weight:** 6 lbs. **Length:** 36" overall. **Stock:** Black polymer, thumbhole design. **Sights:** None furnished; scope mount provided. **Features:** Receiver drilled and tapped for scope mounting. Stock and forend have storage compartments for ammo, etc.; comes with integral swivels and black nylon sling. Introduced 1996. Made in U.S.A. by New England Firearms.
Price: Blue finish $284.00

Remington No. 1 Mid-Range

Ruger No. 1B

Ruger K1-B-BBZ

Ruger No. 1A Light Sporter

Ruger No. 1V Varminter

REMINGTON NO. 1 ROLLING BLOCK MID-RANGE SPORTER
Caliber: 45-70. **Barrel:** 30" round. **Weight:** 8-3/4 lbs. **Length:** 46-1/2" overall. **Stock:** American walnut with checkered pistol grip and forend. **Sights:** Beaded blade front, adjustable center-notch buckhorn rear. **Features:** Recreation of the original. Polished blue metal finish. Many options available. Introduced 1998. Made in U.S.A. by Remington.
Price: **$1,450.00**
Price: Silhouette model with single-set trigger, heavy barrel **$1,560.00**

ROSSI SINGLE SHOT CENTERFIRE RIFLE
Caliber: 308 Win., 270 Win., 30-06 Spfld., 223 Rem., 243 Win. **Barrel:** 23". **Weight:** 6 to 6.5 lbs. **Stock:** Monte Carlo, exotic woods, walnut finish & swivels with white line space and recoil pad. **Sights:** None, scope rails and hammer extension included. **Features:** Break-open, positive ejection, internal transfer bar mechanism and manual external safety. Trigger block system included.
Price: **$179.95**

ROSSI CENTERFIRE/SHOTGUN "MATCHED PAIRS"
Caliber: 12 ga./223 Rem., full size, 20 ga./223 Rem. full & youth, 12 ga./342 Win. full, 20 ga./243 Win., full & youth, 12 ga./308 Win. full, 20 ga./308 Win. full & youth, 12 ga./30-06 Spfld. full, 20 ga./30-06 Spfld. full, 12 ga./270 Win. full, 20 ga./270 Win. full. **Barrel:** 28"/23" full, 22"/22" youth. **Weight:** 5 to 7 lbs. **Stock:** Straight, exotic woods, walnut finish and swivels with white line spacer and recoil pad. **Sights:** Bead front shotgun, fully adjustable rifle, drilled and tapped. **Features:** Break-open, positive

ejection, internal transfer bar mechanism and manual external safety. Trigger block system included.
Price: **$350.00**

RUGER NO. 1B SINGLE SHOT
Caliber: 218 Bee, 22 Hornet, 220 Swift, 22-250, 223, 204 Ruger, 243, 25-06, 270, 30-06, 7mm Rem. Mag., 300 Win. Mag., 308 Win., 338 Win. Mag., 270 Wby., 300 Wby. **Barrel:** 26" round tapered with quarter-rib; with Ruger 1" rings. **Weight:** 8 lbs. **Length:** 42-1/4" overall. **Stock:** Walnut, two-piece, checkered pistol grip and semi-beavertail forend. **Sights:** None, 1" scope rings supplied for integral mounts. **Features:** Under-lever, hammerless falling block design has auto ejector, top tang safety.
Price: 1B **$966.00**
Price: K1-B-BBZ stainless steel, laminated stock 25-06, 7MM mag, 7MM STW, 300 Win Mag., 243 Win., 30-06, 308 Win. **$910.00**

Ruger No. 1A Light Sporter
Calibers: 204 Ruger, 243, 30-06, 270 and 7x57. **Weight:** About 7-1/4 lbs. Similar to the No. 1B Standard Rifle except has lightweight 22" barrel, Alexander Henry-style forend, adjustable folding leaf rear sight on quarter-rib, dovetailed ramp front with gold bead.
Price: No. 1A **$966.00**

Ruger No. 1V Varminter
Similar to the No. 1B Standard Rifle except has 24" heavy barrel. Semi-beavertail forend, barrel ribbed for target scope block, with 1" Ruger scope rings. Calibers 22-250, 220 Swift (w/26" bbl.), 223, 25-06, 6mm Rem. Weight about 9 lbs.
Price: No. 1V **$966.00**
Price: K1-V-BBZ stainless steel, laminated stock 22-250 .... **$998.00**

Ruger No. 1 RSI

Ruger No. 1H Tropical

Ruger No. 1S Medium Sporter

Shiloh 1874 Long Range Express

Shiloh 1874 Quigley

Ruger No. 1 RSI International
Similar to the No. 1B Standard Rifle except has lightweight 20" barrel, full-length International-style forend with loop sling swivel, adjustable folding leaf rear sight on quarter-rib, ramp front with gold bead. Calibers 243, 30-06, 270 and 7x57. Weight is about 7-1/4 lbs.
Price: No. 1 RSI **$998.00**

Ruger No. 1H Tropical Rifle
Similar to the No. 1B Standard Rifle except has Alexander Henry forend, adjustable folding leaf rear sight on quarter-rib, ramp front with dovetail gold bead, 24" heavy barrel. Calibers 375 H&H, 416 Rigby, 458 Lott, 405 Win. and 458 Win. Mag. (weighs about 9 lbs.).
Price: No. 1H **$966.00**
Price: K1-H-BBZ, S/S, 375 H&H, 416 Rigby **$998.00**

Ruger No. 1S Medium Sporter
Similar to the No. 1B Standard Rifle except has Alexander Henry-style forend, adjustable folding leaf rear sight on quarter-rib, ramp front sight base and dovetail-type gold bead front sight. Calibers 218 Bee, 45-70 with 22" barrel. Weighs about 7-1/2 lbs. In 45-70.
Price: No. 1S **$966.00**
Price: K1-S-BBZ, S/S, 45-70 . . . . **$998.00**

SHILOH RIFLE CO. SHARPS 1874 LONG RANGE EXPRESS
Caliber: 40-50 BN, 40-70 BN, 40-90 BN, 45-70 ST, 45-90 ST, 45-110 ST, 50-70 ST, 50-90 ST, 38-55, 40-70 ST, 40-90 ST. **Barrel:** 34" tapered octagon. **Weight:** 10-1/2 lbs. **Length:** 51" overall. **Stock:** Oil-finished walnut (upgrades available) with pistol grip, shotgun-style butt, traditional cheek rest, Schnabel forend. **Sights:** Customer's choice. **Features:** Re-creation of the Model 1874 Sharps rifle. Double-set triggers. Made in U.S.A. by Shiloh Rifle Mfg. Co.
Price: **$1,638.00**
Price: Sporting Rifle No. 1 (similar to above except with 30" bbl., blade front, buckhorn rear sight) **$1,638.00**
Price: Sporting Rifle No. 3 (similar to No. 1 except straight-grip stock, standard wood) **$1,547.00**

SHILOH RIFLE CO. SHARPS 1874 QUIGLEY
Caliber: 45-70, 45-110. **Barrel:** 34" heavy octagon. **Stock:** Military-style with patch box, standard grade American walnut. **Sights:** Semi buckhorn, interchangeable front and midrange vernier tang sight with windage. **Features:** Gold inlay initials, pewter tip, Hartford collar, case color or antique finish. Double-set triggers.
Price: **$2,903.00**

Shiloh 1874 Saddle

Shiloh 1874 Montana Roughrider

Shiloh 1874 Creedmoor

Thompson/Center Encore

Thompson/Center Encore "Katahdin"

SHILOH RIFLE CO. SHARPS 1874 SADDLE RIFLE
Caliber: 38-55, 40-50 BN, 40-65 Win., 40-70 BN, 40-70 ST, 40-90 BN, 40-90 ST, 44-77 BN, 44-90 BN, 45-70 ST, 45-90 ST, 45-100 ST, 45-110 ST, 45-120 ST, 50-70 ST, 50-90 ST. **Barrel:** 26" full or half octagon. **Stock:** Semi fancy American walnut. Shotgun style with cheekrest. **Sights:** Buckhorn and blade. **Features:** Double-set trigger, numerous custom features can be added.
Price: **$1,594.00**

SHILOH RIFLE CO. SHARPS 1874 MONTANA ROUGHRIDER
Caliber: 38-55, 40-50 BN, 40-65 Win., 40-70 BN, 40-70 ST, 40-90 BN, 40-90 ST, 44-77 BN, 44-90 BN, 45-70 ST, 45-90 ST, 45-100 ST, 45-110 ST, 45-120 ST, 50-70 ST, 50-90 ST. **Barrel:** 30" full or half octagon. **Stock:** American walnut in shotgun or military style. **Sights:** Buckhorn and blade. **Features:** Double-set triggers, numerous custom features can be added.
Price: **$1,638.00**

SHILOH RIFLE CO. SHARPS CREEDMOOR TARGET
Caliber: 38-55, 40-50 BN, 40-65 Win., 40-70 BN, 40-70 ST, 40-90 BN, 40-90 ST, 44-77 BN, 44-90 BN, 45-70 ST, 45-90 ST, 45-100 ST, 45-110 ST, 45-120 ST, 50-70 ST, 50-90 ST. **Barrel:** 32", half round-half octagon. **Stock:** Extra fancy American walnut. Shotgun style with pistol grip. **Sights:** Customer's choice. **Features:** Single trigger, AA finish on stock, polished barrel and screws, pewter tip.
Price: **$2,485.00**

THOMPSON/CENTER ENCORE RIFLE
Caliber: 22-250, 223, 243, 204 Ruger, 6.8 Rem. Spec., 25-06, 270, 7mm-08, 308, 30-06, 7mm Rem. Mag., 300 Win. Mag. **Barrel:** 24", 26". **Weight:** 6 lbs., 12 oz. (24" barrel). **Length:** 38-1/2" (24" barrel). **Stock:** American walnut. Monte Carlo style; Schnabel forend or black composite. **Sights:** Ramp-style white bead front, fully adjustable leaf-type rear. **Features:** Interchangeable barrels; action opens by squeezing trigger guard; drilled and tapped for T/C scope mounts; polished blue finish. Introduced 1996. Made in U.S.A. by Thompson/Center Arms.
Price: . . . . **$604.00 to $663.00**
Price: Extra barrels **$277.00**

Thompson/Center Stainless Encore Rifle
Similar to blued Encore except stainless steel with blued sights, black composite stock and forend. Available in 22-250, 223, 7mm-08, 30-06, 308. Introduced 1999. Made in U.S.A. by Thompson/Center Arms.
Price: . . . . **$680.00 to $738.00**

THOMPSON/CENTER ENCORE "KATAHDIN" CARBINE
Caliber: 45-70 Gov't., 450 Marlin. **Barrel:** 18" with muzzle tamer. **Stock:** Composite.
Price: **$619.00**

Thompson/Center G2 Contender Rifle
Similar to the G2 Contender pistol, but in a compact rifle format. Weighs 5-1/2 lbs. Features interchangeable 23" barrels, chambered for 17 HMR, 22LR, 223 Rem. and 45/70 Gov't; plus a 45 Cal. Muzzleloading barrel. All of the 16-1/4" and 21" barrels made for the old-style Contender will fit. Introduced 2003. Made in U.S.A. by Thompson/Center Arms.
Price: . . . . **$622.00 to $637.00**

Traditions 1874 Sharps Deluxe

Traditions 1874 Sharps Sporting Deluxe

**Tristar/Uberti
1885 Single Shot**

TRADITIONS 1874 SHARPS DELUXE RIFLE
Caliber: 45-70. **Barrel:** 32" octagonal; 1:18" twist. **Weight:** 11.67 lbs. **Length:** 48.8" overall. **Stock:** Checkered walnut with German silver nose cap and steel buttplate. **Sights:** Globe front, adjustable Creedmore rear with 12 inserts. **Features:** Color case-hardened receiver; double-set triggers. Introduced 2001. Imported from Pedersoli by Traditions.
Price: **$999.00**

Traditions 1874 Sharps Sporting Deluxe Rifle
Similar to Sharps Deluxe but custom silver engraved receiver, European walnut stock and forend, satin finish, set trigger, fully adjustable.
Price: **$1,999.00**

Traditions 1874 Sharps Standard Rifle
Similar to 1874 Sharps Deluxe except has blade front and adjustable buckhorn-style rear sight. Weighs 10.67 pounds. Introduced 2001. Imported from Pedersoli by Traditions.
Price: **$769.00**

TRADITIONS ROLLING BLOCK SPORTING RIFLE
Caliber: 45-70. **Barrel:** 30" octagonal; 1:18" twist. **Weight:** 11.67 lbs. **Length:** 46.7" overall. **Stock:** Walnut. **Sights:** Blade front, adjustable rear. **Features:** Antique silver, color case-hardened receiver, drilled and tapped for tang/globe sights; brass buttplate and trigger guard. Introduced 2001. Imported from Pedersoli by Traditions.
Price: **$769.00**

TRADITIONS ROLLING BLOCK SPORTING RIFLE IN 30-30 WINCHESTER
Caliber: 30-30. **Barrel:** 28" round, blued. **Weight:** 8.25 lbs. **Stock:** Walnut. **Sights:** Fixed front, adjustable rear. **Features:** Steel buttplate, trigger guard, barrel band.
Price: **$769.00**

TRISTAR/SHARPS 1874 SPORTING RIFLE
Caliber: 45-70. **Barrel:** 28", 32", 34" octagonal. **Weight:** 9.75 lbs. **Length:** 44.5" overall. **Stock:** Walnut. **Sights:** Dovetail front, adjustable rear. **Features:** Cut checkering, case colored frame finish.
Price: **$795.00**

TRISTAR/UBERTI 1885 SINGLE SHOT
Caliber: 45-70. **Barrel:** 28". **Weight:** 8.75 lbs. **Length:** 44.5" overall. **Stock:** European walnut. **Sights:** Bead on blade front, open step-adjustable rear. **Features:** Recreation of the 1885 Winchester. Color case-hardened receiver and lever, blued barrel. Introduced 1998. Imported from Italy by Tristar Sporting Arms Ltd.
Price: . . . . **$850.00 to $1,050.00**

UBERTI BABY ROLLING BLOCK CARBINE
Caliber: 22 LR, 22 WMR, 22 Hornet, 357 Mag., single shot. **Barrel:** 22". **Weight:** 4.8 lbs. **Length:** 35-1/2" overall. **Stock:** Walnut stock and forend. **Sights:** Blade front, fully adjustable open rear. **Features:** Resembles Remington New Model No. 4 carbine. Brass trigger guard and buttplate; color case-hardened frame, blued barrel. Imported by Uberti USA Inc.
Price: **$535.00**
Price: Rolling Block Rifle, 26" bbl. **$600.00**

WINCHESTER MODEL 1885 HIGH WALL WSM
Caliber: 17 HMR, 17 Mach 2. **Barrel:** 28". **Weight:** 8.5 lbs. **Length:** 44". **Stock:** Walnut. **Features:** Single-shot, Pachmayr recoil pad.
. . . . **$1,085.00**

Designs for sporting and utility purposes worldwide.

Beretta Express SSO

Beretta Model 455 SxS

Charles Daly Superior

Charles Daly Empire Combo

BERETTA EXPRESS SSO O/U DOUBLE RIFLES
Caliber: 375 H&H, 458 Win. Mag., 9.3x74R. **Barrel:** 25.5". **Weight:** 11 lbs. **Stock:** European walnut with hand-checkered grip and forend. **Sights:** Blade front on ramp, open V-notch rear. **Features:** Sidelock action with color case-hardened receiver (gold inlays on SSO6 Gold). Ejectors, double triggers, recoil pad. Introduced 1990. Imported from Italy by Beretta U.S.A.
Price: SSO6 . . . . **$21,000.00**
Price: SSO6 Gold **$23,500.00**

BERETTA MODEL 455 SxS EXPRESS RIFLE
Caliber: 375 H&H, 458 Win. Mag., 470 NE, 500 NE 3", 416 Rigby. **Barrel:** 23-1/2" or 25-1/2". **Weight:** 11 lbs. **Stock:** European walnut with hand-checkered grip and forend. **Sights:** Blade front, folding leaf V-notch rear. **Features:** Sidelock action with easily removable sideplates; color case-hardened finish (455), custom big game or floral motif engraving (455EELL). Double triggers, recoil pad. Introduced 1990. Imported from Italy by Beretta U.S.A.
Price: Model 455 . . . . **$36,000.00**
Price: Model 455EELL. **$47,000.00**

BRNO 500 COMBINATION GUNS
Caliber/Gauge: 12 (2-3/4" chamber) over 5.6x52R, 5.6x50R, 222 Rem., 243, 6.x55, 308, 7x57R, 7x65R, 30-06. **Barrel:** 23.6". **Weight:** 7.6 lbs. **Length:** 40.5" overall. **Stock:** European walnut. **Sights:** Bead front, V-notch rear; grooved for scope mounting. **Features:** Boxlock action; double-set trigger; blue finish with etched engraving. Announced 1998. Imported from The Czech Republic by Euro-Imports.
Price: **$1,023.00**
Price: O/U double rifle, 7x57R, 7x65R, 8x57JRS **$1,125.00**

BRNO ZH 300 COMBINATION GUN
Caliber/Gauge: 22 Hornet, 5.6x50R Mag., 5.6x52R, 7x57R, 7x65R, 8x57JRS over 12, 16 (2-3/4" chamber). **Barrel:** 23.6". **Weight:** 7.9 lbs. **Length:** 40.5" overall. **Stock:** European walnut. **Sights:** Blade front, open adjustable rear. **Features:** Boxlock action; double triggers; automatic safety. Announced 1998. Imported from The Czech Republic by Euro-Imports.
Price: **$724.00**

BRNO ZH Double Rifles
Similar to ZH 300 Combination guns except double rifle barrels. Available in 7x65R, 7x57R and 8x57JRS. Announced 1998. Imported from The Czech Republic by Euro-Imports.
Price: **$1,125.00**

CHARLES DALY SUPERIOR COMBINATION GUN
Caliber/Gauge: 12 ga. over 22 Hornet, 223 Rem., 22-250, 243 Win., 270 Win., 308 Win., 30-06. **Barrel:** 23.5", shotgun choked Imp. Cyl. **Weight:** About 7.5 lbs. **Stock:** Checkered walnut pistol grip buttstock and semi-beavertail forend. **Features:** Silvered, engraved receiver; chrome-moly steel barrels; double triggers; extractors; sling swivels; gold bead front sight. Introduced 1997. Imported from Italy by K.B.I. Inc.
Price: **$1,479.00**

Charles Daly Empire Combination Gun
Same as the Superior grade except has deluxe wood with European-style comb and cheekpiece; slim forend. Introduced 1997. Imported from Italy by K.B.I., Inc.
Price: **$2,189.00**

CZ 584 SOLO COMBINATION GUN
Caliber/Gauge: 7x57R; 12, 2-3/4" chamber. **Barrel:** 24.4". **Weight:** 7.37 lbs. **Length:** 45.25" overall. **Stock:** Circassian walnut. **Sights:** Blade front, open rear adjustable for windage. **Features:** Kersten-style double lump locking system; double-trigger Blitz-type mechanism with drop safety and adjustable set trigger for the rifle barrel; auto safety, dual extractors; receiver dovetailed for scope mounting. Imported from the Czech Republic by CZ-USA.
Price: **$851.00**

CZ 584 Solo

Hoenig Rotary Round Action Double Rifle

Hoenig Rotary Round Action Combination

Krieghoff Classic Double Rifle

CZ 589 STOPPER OVER/UNDER GUN
Caliber: 458 Win. Magnum. **Barrels:** 21.7". **Weight:** 9.3 lbs. **Length:** 37.7" overall. **Stock:** Turkish walnut with sling swivels. **Sights:** Blade front, fixed rear. **Features:** Kersten-style action; Blitz-type double trigger; hammer-forged, blued barrels; satin-nickel, engraved receiver. Introduced 2001. Imported from the Czech Republic by CZ USA.
Price: **$2,999.00**
Price: Fully engraved model **$3,999.00**

DAKOTA DOUBLE RIFLE
Caliber: 470 Nitro Express, 500 Nitro Express. **Barrel:** 25". **Stock:** Exhibition-grade walnut. **Sights:** Express-style. **Features:** Round action; selective ejectors; recoil pad; Americase. From Dakota Arms Inc.
Price: **$25,000.00**

EAA/BAIKAL IZH-94 COMBINATION GUN
Caliber/Gauge: 12, 3" chamber; 222 Rem., 223, 5.6x50R, 5.6x55E, 7x57R, 7x65R, 7.62x39, 7.62x51, 308, 7.62x53R, 7.62x54R, 30-06. **Barrel:** 24", 26"; imp., mod. and full choke tubes. **Weight:** 7.28 lbs. **Stock:** Walnut; rubber buttpad. **Sights:** Express-style. **Features:** Hammer-forged barrels with chrome-lined bores; machined receiver; single-selective or double triggers. Imported by European American Armory.
Price: Blued finish **$549.00**
Price: 20 ga./22 LR, 20/22 Mag., 3" **$629.00**

GARBI EXPRESS DOUBLE RIFLE
Caliber: 7x65R, 9.3x74R, 375 H&H. **Barrel:** 24-3/4". **Weight:** 7-3/4 to 8-1/2 lbs. **Length:** 41-1/2" overall. **Stock:** Turkish walnut. **Sights:** Quarter-rib with express sight. **Features:** Side-by-side double; H&H-pattern sidelock ejector with reinforced action, chopper lump barrels of Boehler steel; double triggers; fine scroll and rosette engraving, or full coverage ornamental; coin-finished action. Introduced 1997. Imported from Spain by Wm. Larkin Moore.
Price: **$19,900.00**

HOENIG ROTARY ROUND ACTION DOUBLE RIFLE
Caliber: Most popular calibers from 225 Win. to 9.3x74R. **Barrel:** 22" to 26". **Stock:** English Walnut; to customer specs. **Sights:** Swivel hood front with button release (extra bead stored in trap door gripcap), express-style rear on quarter-rib adjustable for windage and elevation; scope mount. **Features:** Round action opens by rotating barrels, pulling forward. Inertia extractor system, rotary safety blocks strikers. Single lever quick-detachable scope mount. Simple takedown without removing forend. Introduced 1997. Made in U.S.A. by George Hoenig.
Price: **$24,975.00**

HOENIG ROTARY ROUND ACTION COMBINATION
Caliber: 28 ga. **Barrel:** 26". **Weight:** 7 lbs. **Stock:** English Walnut to customer specs. **Sights:** Front ramp with button release blades. Foldable aperture tang sight windage and elevation adjustable. Quarter-rib with scope mount. **Features:** Round action opens by rotating barrels, pulling forward. Inertia extractor; rotary safety blocks strikers. Simple takedown without removing forend. Made in U.S.A. by George Hoenig.
Price: **$24,975.00**

KRIEGHOFF CLASSIC DOUBLE RIFLE
Caliber: 7x57R, 7x65R, 308 Win., 30-06, 8x57 JRS, 8x75RS, 9.3x74R, 375NE, 500/416NE, 470NE, 500NE. **Barrel:** 23.5". **Weight:** 7.3 to 8 lbs. **Stock:** High grade European walnut. Standard model has conventional rounded cheekpiece, Bavaria model has Bavarian-style cheekpiece. **Sights:** Bead front with removable, adjustable wedge (375 H&H and below), standing leaf rear on quarter-rib. **Features:** Boxlock action; double triggers; short opening angle for fast loading; quiet extractors; sliding, self-adjusting wedge for secure bolting; Purdey-style barrel extension; horizontal firing pin placement. Many options available. Introduced 1997. Imported from Germany by Krieghoff International.
Price: With small Arabesque engraving **$8,475.00**
Price: With engraved sideplates **$11,725.00**
Price: For extra barrels **$4,950.00**
Price: Extra 20-ga., 28" shotshell barrels **$3,750.00**

Krieghoff Classic Big Five Double Rifle
Similar to the standard Classic except available in 375 Flanged Mag. N.E., 500/416 N.E., 470 N.E., 500 N.E. Has hinged front trigger, non-removable muzzle wedge (models larger than 375 caliber), Universal Trigger System, Combi Cocking Device, steel trigger guard, specially weighted stock bolt for weight and balance. Many options available. Introduced 1997. Imported from Germany by Krieghoff International.
Price: **$10,975.00**
Price: With engraved sideplates **$14,225.00**

LEBEAU-COURALLY EXPRESS RIFLE SxS
Caliber: 7x65R, 8x57JRS, 9.3x74R, 375 H&H, 470 N.E. **Barrel:** 24" to 26". **Weight:** 7-3/4 to 10-1/2 lbs. **Stock:** Fancy French walnut with cheekpiece. **Sights:** Bead on ramp front, standing left express rear on quarter-rib. **Features:** Holland & Holland-type sidelock with automatic ejectors; double triggers. Built to order only. Imported from Belgium by Wm. Larkin Moore.
Price: **$41,000.00**

Merkel 96K Engraved

Merkel 140-1

Rizzini Express

Savage 24F Combination

Springfield M6 Scout

MERKEL DRILLINGS
Caliber/Gauge: 12, 20, 3" chambers, 16, 2-3/4" chambers; 22 Hornet, 5.6x50R Mag., 5.6x52R, 222 Rem., 243 Win., 6.5x55, 6.5x57R, 7x57R, 7x65R, 308, 30-06, 8x57JRS, 9.3x74R, 375 H&H. **Barrel:** 25.6". **Weight:** 7.9 to 8.4 lbs. depending upon caliber. **Stock:** Oil-finished walnut with pistol grip; cheekpiece on 12-, 16-gauge. **Sights:** Blade front, fixed rear. **Features:** Double barrel locking lug with Greener cross bolt; scroll-engraved, case-hardened receiver; automatic trigger safety; Blitz action; double triggers. Imported from Germany by GSI.
Price: Model 96K (manually cocked rifle system), from $7,495.00
Price: Model 96K Engraved (hunting series on receiver) $8,595.00

MERKEL BOXLOCK DOUBLE RIFLES
Caliber: 5.6x52R, 243 Winchester, 6.5x55, 6.5x57R, 7x57R, 7x65R, 308 Winchester, 30-06 Springfield, 8x57 IRS, 9.3x74R. **Barrel:** 23.6". **Weight:** 7.7 oz. **Length:** NA. **Stock:** Walnut, oil finished, pistol grip. **Sights:** Fixed 100 meter. **Features:** Anson & Deely boxlock action with cocking indicators, double triggers, engraved color case-hardened receiver. Introduced 1995. Imported from Germany by GSI.
Price: Model 140-1, from $6,695.00
Price: Model 140-1.1 (engraved silver-gray receiver), from $7,795.00

RIZZINI EXPRESS 90L DOUBLE RIFLE
Caliber: 30-06, 7x65R, 9.3x74R. **Barrel:** 24". **Weight:** 7-1/2 lbs. **Length:** 40" overall. **Stock:** Select European walnut with satin oil finish; English-style cheekpiece. **Sights:** Ramp front, quarter-rib with express sight. **Features:** Color case-hardened boxlock action; automatic ejectors; single selective trigger; polished blue barrels. Extra 20 gauge shotgun barrels available. Imported for Italy by Wm. Larkin Moore.
Price: With case $3,850.00

SAVAGE 24F PREDATOR O/U COMBINATION GUN
Caliber/Gauge: 22 Hornet, 223, 30-30 over 12 (24F-12) or 22 LR, 22 Hornet, 223, 30-30 over 20 ga. (24F-20); 3" chambers. **Action:** Takedown, low rebounding visible hammer. Single trigger, barrel selector spur on hammer. **Barrel:** 24" separated barrels; 12 ga. has mod. choke tubes, 20 ga. has fixed Mod. choke. **Weight:** 8 lbs. **Length:** 40-1/2" overall. **Stock:** Black Rynite composition. **Sights:** Blade front, rear open adjustable for elevation. **Features:** Introduced 1989.
Price: 24F-12 . . . . $661.00
Price: 24F-20 . . . . $628.00

SPRINGFIELD ARMORY M6 SCOUT RIFLE/SHOTGUN
Caliber/Gauge: 22 LR or 22 Hornet over 410 bore. **Barrel:** 18.25". **Weight:** 4 lbs. **Length:** 32" overall. **Stock:** Folding detachable with storage for 15 22 LR, four 410 shells. **Sights:** Blade front, military aperture for 22; V-notch for 410. **Features:** All metal construction. Designed for quick disassembly and minimum maintenance. Folds for compact storage. Introduced 1982; reintroduced 1996. Imported from the Czech Republic by Springfield Armory.
Price: Parkerized. $185.00
Price: Stainless steel. $219.00

Designs for hunting, utility and sporting purposes, including training for competition.

Browning Buck Mark Target

Browning Semi-Auto 22

CZ 511 Auto

Henry U.S. Survival

Marlin Model 60

AR-7 EXPLORER CARBINE
Caliber: 22 LR, 8-shot magazine. **Barrel:** 16". **Weight:** 2-1/2 lbs. **Length:** 34-1/2", 16-1/2" stowed. **Stock:** Molded Cycolac; snap-on rubber buttpad. **Sights:** Square blade front, aperture rear. **Features:** Takedown design stores barrel and action in hollow stock. Light enough to float. Reintroduced 1999. From AR-7 Industries, LLC.
Price: Black matte finish **$150.00**
Price: AR-20 Sporter (tubular stock, barrel shroud) **$200.00**
New! Price: AR-7 camo- or walnut-finish stock. **$164.95**

BROWNING BUCK MARK SEMI-AUTO RIFLES
Caliber: 22 LR, 10-shot magazine. **Barrel:** 18" tapered (Sporter), heavy bull (Target), or carbon composite barrel (Classic Carbon). **Weight:** 4 lbs., 2 oz. (Sporter) or 5 lbs., 4 oz. (Target). **Length:** 34" overall. **Stock:** Walnut stock and forearm with full pistol grip. **Sights:** HiViz adjustable (Sporter). **Features:** A rifle version of the Buck Mark Pistol; straight blowback action; machined aluminum receiver with integral rail scope mount; recessed muzzle crown; manual thumb safety. Introduced 2001. From Browning.
Price: Sporter (adj. sights) **$518.00**
Price: Target (heavy bbl., no sights) **$518.00**

BROWNING SEMI-AUTO 22 RIFLE
Caliber: 22 LR, 11-shot. **Barrel:** 19-1/4". **Weight:** 5 lbs., 3 oz. **Length:** 37" overall. **Stock:** Checkered select walnut with pistol grip and semi-beavertail forend. **Sights:** Gold bead front, folding leaf rear. **Features:** Engraved receiver with polished blue finish; cross-bolt safety; tubular magazine in buttstock; easy takedown for carrying or storage. Imported from Japan by Browning.
Price: Grade I. **$479.00**

Browning Semi-Auto 22, Grade VI
Same as the Grade I Auto-22 except available with either grayed or blued receiver with extensive engraving with gold-plated animals: right side pictures a fox and squirrel in a woodland scene; left side shows a beagle chasing a rabbit. On top is a portrait of the beagle. Stock and forend are of high-grade walnut with a double-bordered cut checkering design. Introduced 1987.
Price: Grade VI, blue or gray receiver. **$1,028.00**

BRNO ZKM 611 AUTO RIFLE
Caliber: 22 WMR, 6- or 10-shot magazine. **Barrel:** 20.4". **Weight:** 5.9 lbs. **Length:** 38.9" overall. **Stock:** European walnut. **Sights:** Hooded blade front, open adjustable rear. **Features:** Removable box magazine; polished blue finish; cross-bolt safety; grooved receiver for scope mounting; easy takedown for storage. Imported from The Czech Republic by Euro-Imports.
Price: **$475.00**

CZ 511 AUTO RIFLE
Caliber: 22 LR, 8-shot magazine. **Barrel:** 22.2". **Weight:** 5.39 lbs. **Length:** 38.6" overall. **Stock:** Walnut with checkered pistol grip. **Sights:** Hooded front, adjustable rear. **Features:** Polished blue finish; detachable magazine; sling swivel studs. Imported from the Czech Republic by CZ-USA.
Price: **$351.00**

HENRY U.S. SURVIVAL RIFLE .22
Caliber: 22 LR, 8-shot magazine. **Barrel:** 16" steel lined. **Weight:** 2.5 lbs. **Stock:** ABS plastic. **Sights:** Blade front on ramp, aperture rear. **Features:** Takedown design stores barrel and action in hollow stock. Light enough to float. Silver, black or camo finish. Comes with two magazines. Introduced 1998. From Henry Repeating Arms Co.
Price: **$205.00**

MARLIN MODEL 60 AUTO RIFLE
Caliber: 22 LR, 14-shot tubular magazine. **Barrel:** 19" round tapered. **Weight:** About 5-1/2 lbs. **Length:** 37-1/2" overall. **Stock:** Press-checkered, walnut-finished Maine birch with Monte Carlo, full pistol grip; Mar-Shield® finish. **Sights:** Ramp front, open adjustable rear. **Features:** Matted receiver is grooved for scope mount. Manual bolt hold-open; automatic last-shot bolt hold-open. Model 60C is similar except has hardwood Monte Carlo stock with Mossy Oak Break-Up camouflage pattern. From Marlin.
Price: **$185.00**
Price: With 4x scope **$193.00**
Price: (Model 60C) **$220.00**

Marlin Model 60SSK

Marlin Model 70PSS

Marlin 795

Remington 552 BDL Speedmaster

Remington 597

Marlin Model 60SS Self-Loading Rifle
Same as the Model 60 except breech bolt, barrel and outer magazine tube are made of stainless steel; most other parts are either nickel-plated or coated to match the stainless finish. Monte Carlo stock is of black/gray Maine birch laminate, and has nickel-plated swivel studs, rubber buttpad. Introduced 1993. From Marlin.
Price: **$297.00**
Price: Model 60SSK (black fiberglass-filled stock) **$257.00**
Price: Model 60SB (walnut-finished birch stock) **$235.00**
Price: Model 60SB with 4x scope **$251.00**

MARLIN 70PSS PAPOOSE STAINLESS RIFLE
Caliber: 22 LR, 7-shot magazine. **Barrel:** 16-1/4" stainless steel, Micro-Groove® rifling. **Weight:** 3-1/4 lbs. **Length:** 35-1/4" overall. **Stock:** Black fiberglass-filled synthetic with abbreviated forend, nickel-plated swivel studs, molded-in checkering. **Sights:** Ramp front with orange post, cut-away Wide Scan™ hood; adjustable open rear. Receiver grooved for scope mounting. **Features:** Takedown barrel; cross-bolt safety; manual bolt hold-open; last shot bolt hold-open; comes with padded carrying case. Introduced 1986. Made in U.S.A. by Marlin.
Price: **$304.00**

MARLIN MODEL 7000 AUTO RIFLE
Caliber: 22 LR, 10-shot magazine **Barrel:** 18" heavy target with 12-groove Micro-Groove® rifling, recessed muzzle. **Weight:** 5-1/2 lbs. **Length:** 37" overall. **Stock:** Black fiberglass-filled synthetic with Monte Carlo combo, swivel studs, molded-in checkering. **Sights:** None furnished; comes with ring mounts. **Features:** Automatic last-shot bolt hold-open, manual bolt hold-open; cross-bolt safety; steel charging handle; blue finish, nickel-plated magazine. Introduced 1997. Made in U.S.A. by Marlin Firearms Co.
Price: **$249.00**

MARLIN MODEL 795 AUTO RIFLE
Caliber: 22. **Barrel:** 18" with 16-groove Micro-Groove® rifling. Ramp front sight, adjustable rear. Receiver grooved for scope mount. **Stock:** Black synthetic. **Features:** 10-round magazine, last shot hold-open feature. Introduced 1997. Made in U.S.A. by Marlin Firearms Co.
Price: **$176.00**

Marlin Model 795SS Auto Rifle
Similar to Model 795 except stainless steel barrel. Most other parts nickel-plated. Adjustable folding semi-buckhorn rear sights, ramp front high-visibility post and removeable cutaway wide scan hood.
Price: **$235.00**

REMINGTON MODEL 552 BDL DELUXE SPEEDMASTER RIFLE
Caliber: 22 S (20), L (17) or LR (15) tubular mag. **Barrel:** 21" round tapered. **Weight:** 5-3/4 lbs. **Length:** 40" overall. **Stock:** Walnut. Checkered grip and forend. **Sights:** Big game. **Features:** Positive cross-bolt safety, receiver grooved for tip-off mount.
Price: **$393.00**

REMINGTON 597 AUTO RIFLE
Caliber: 22 LR, 10-shot clip. **Barrel:** 20". **Weight:** 5-1/2 lbs. **Length:** 40" overall. **Stock:** Black synthetic. **Sights:** Big game. **Features:** Matte black finish, nickel-plated bolt. Receiver is grooved and drilled and tapped for scope mounts. Introduced 1997. Made in U.S.A. by Remington.
Price: **$169.00**
Price: Model 597 Magnum, 22 WMR, 8-shot clip **$335.00**
Price: Model 597 LSS (laminated stock, stainless) **$279.00**
Price: Model 597 SS
(22 LR, stainless steel, black synthetic stock) **$224.00**
Price: Model 597 LS heavy barrel (22 LR, laminated stock) **$265.00**
Price: Model 597 Magnum LS heavy barrel
(22 WMR, lam. stock) **$399.00**
Price: Model 597 Magnum 17 HMR, 8-shot clip **$361.00**

Ruger 10/22 Deluxe Sporter

Ruger 10/22 Target

Savage Model 64FV

RUGER 10/22 AUTOLOADING CARBINE
Caliber: 22 LR, 10-shot rotary magazine. **Barrel:** 18-1/2" round tapered. **Weight:** 5 lbs. **Length:** 37-1/4" overall. **Stock:** American hardwood with pistol grip and barrel band or synthetic. **Sights:** Brass bead front, folding leaf rear adjustable for elevation. **Features:** Detachable rotary magazine fits flush into stock, cross-bolt safety, receiver tapped and grooved for scope blocks or tip-off mount. Scope base adaptor furnished with each rifle.
Price: Model 10/22 RB (blue) $258.00
Price: Model K10/22RB (bright finish stainless barrel) $304.00
Price: Model 10/22RPF (blue, synthetic stock) $258.00

Ruger 10/22 Deluxe Sporter
Same as 10/22 Carbine except walnut stock with hand checkered pistol grip and forend; straight buttplate, no barrel band, has sling swivels.
Price: Model 10/22 DSP $324.00

Ruger 10/22T Target Rifle
Similar to the 10/22 except has 20" heavy, hammer-forged barrel with tight chamber dimensions, improved trigger pull, laminated hardwood stock dimensioned for optical sights. No iron sights supplied. Introduced 1996. Made in U.S.A. by Sturm, Ruger & Co.
Price: 10/22T $445.00
Price: K10/22T, stainless steel $495.00
Price: K10/22R, 20" bbl. $275.00

Ruger K10/22RPF All-Weather Rifle
Similar to the stainless K10/22/RB except has black composite stock of thermoplastic polyester resin reinforced with fiberglass; checkered grip and forend. Brushed satin, natural metal finish with clear hardcoat finish. Weighs 5 lbs., measures 36-3/4" overall. Introduced 1997. From Sturm, Ruger & Co.
Price: $304.00

RUGER 10/22 MAGNUM AUTOLOADING CARBINE
Caliber: 22 WMR, 9-shot rotary magazine. **Barrel:** 18-1/2". **Weight:** 6 lbs. **Length:** 37-1/4" overall. **Stock:** Birch. **Sights:** Gold bead front, folding rear. **Features:** All-steel receiver has integral Ruger scope bases for the included 1" rings. Introduced 1999. Made in U.S.A. by Sturm, Ruger & Co.
Price: 10/22RBM $536.00

SAVAGE MODEL 64G AUTO RIFLE
Caliber: 22 LR, 10-shot magazine. **Barrel:** 20", 21". **Weight:** 5-1/2 lbs. **Length:** 40", 41". **Stock:** Walnut-finished hardwood with Monte Carlo-type comb, checkered grip and forend. **Sights:** Bead front, open adjustable rear. Receiver grooved for scope mounting. **Features:** Thumb-operated rotating safety. Blue finish. Side ejection, bolt hold-open device. Introduced 1990. Made in Canada, from Savage Arms.
Price: $162.00
Price: Model 64FSS, stainless $202.00
Price: Model 64F, black synthetic stock $135.00
Price: Model 64GXP package gun includes
4x15 scope and mounts $171.00
Price: Model 64FXP (black stock, 4x15 scope) $142.00
Price: Model 64F Camo $135.00

Savage Model 64FV Auto Rifle
Similar to the Model 64F except has heavy 21" barrel with recessed crown; no sights provided, comes with Weaver-style bases. Introduced 1998. Imported from Canada by Savage Arms, Inc.
Price: $135.00
Price: Model 64FSS, stainless $202.00

TAURUS MODEL 63 RIFLE
Caliber: 22 LR, 10-shot tube-fed magazine. **Barrel:** 23". **Weight:** 72 oz. **Length:** 32-1/2". **Stock:** Hand-fitted walnut-finished hardwood. **Sights:** Adjustable rear, fixed front. **Features:** Manual safety, metal buttplate, can accept Taurus tang sight. Charged and cocked with operating plunger at front of forend. Available in blue or polished stainless steel.
Price: 63 . . . . $295.00
Price: 63SS $311.00

THOMPSON/CENTER 22 LR CLASSIC RIFLE
Caliber: 22 LR, 8-shot magazine. **Barrel:** 22" match-grade. **Weight:** 5-1/2 pounds. **Length:** 39-1/2" overall. **Stock:** Satin-finished American walnut with Monte Carlo-type comb and pistol gripcap, swivel studs. **Sights:** Ramp-style front and fully adjustable rear, both with fiber optics. **Features:** All-steel receiver drilled and tapped for scope mounting; barrel threaded to receiver; thumb-operated safety; trigger guard safety lock included. New .22 Classic Benchmark TGT target rifle variant has 18" heavy barrel, brown laminated target stock, blued with matte finish, 10-shot magazine and no sights; drilled and tapped.
Price: T/C 22 LR Classic (blue). $396.00
Price: T/C 22 LR Classic Benchmark $505.00

Classic and modern models for sport and utility, including training.

Browning BL-22

Henry Lever-Action 22

Henry Golden Boy 22

Henry Pump-Action 22

Marlin Model 39A

BROWNING BL-22 LEVER-ACTION RIFLE
Caliber: 22 S (22), L (17) or LR (15), tubular magazine. **Barrel:** 20" round tapered. **Weight:** 5 lbs. **Length:** 36-3/4" overall. **Stock:** Walnut, two-piece straight grip Western style. **Sights:** Bead post front, folding-leaf rear. **Features:** Short throw lever, half-cock safety, receiver grooved for tip-off scope mounts, gold-colored trigger. Imported from Japan by Browning.
Price: Grade I. **$415.00**
Price: Grade II (engraved receiver, checkered grip and forend) **$471.00**
Price: Classic, Grade I (blued trigger, no checkering) **$415.00**
Price: Classic, Grade II (cut checkering, satin wood finish,
polished bluing) **$471.00**

HENRY LEVER-ACTION 22
Caliber: 22 Long Rifle (15-shot). **Barrel:** 18-1/4" round. **Weight:** 5-1/2 lbs. **Length:** 34" overall. **Stock:** Walnut. **Sights:** Hooded blade front, open adjustable rear. **Features:** Polished blue finish; full-length tubular magazine; side ejection; receiver grooved for scope mounting. Introduced 1997. Made in U.S.A. by Henry Repeating Arms Co.
Price: **$279.95**
Price: Youth model (33" overall, 11-round 22 LR) **$279.95**

HENRY GOLDEN BOY 22 LEVER-ACTION RIFLE
Caliber: 22 LR, 22 Magnum, 16-shot. **Barrel:** 20" octagonal. **Weight:** 6.25 lbs. **Length:** 38" overall. **Stock:** American walnut. **Sights:** Blade front, open rear. **Features:** Brasslite receiver, brass buttplate, blued barrel and lever. Introduced 1998. Made in U.S.A. from Henry Repeating Arms Co.
Price: **$409.95**
Price: Magnum **$485.00**

HENRY PUMP-ACTION 22 PUMP RIFLE
Caliber: 22 LR, 15-shot. **Barrel:** 18.25". **Weight:** 5.5 lbs. **Length:** NA. **Stock:** American walnut. **Sights:** Bead on ramp front, open adjustable rear. **Features:** Polished blue finish; receiver groved for scope mount; grooved slide handle; two barrel bands. Introduced 1998. Made in U.S.A. from Henry Repeating Arms Co.
Price: **$309.95**

MARLIN MODEL 39A GOLDEN LEVER-ACTION RIFLE
Caliber: 22, S (26), L (21), LR (19), tubular mag. **Barrel:** 24" Micro-Groove®. **Weight:** 6-1/2 lbs. **Length:** 40" overall. **Stock:** Checkered American black walnut; Mar-Shield® finish. Swivel studs; rubber buttpad. **Sights:** Bead ramp front with detachable Wide-Scan™ hood, folding rear semi-buckhorn adjustable for windage and elevation. **Features:** Hammer block safety; rebounding hammer. Takedown action, receiver tapped for scope mount (supplied), offset hammer spur, gold-plated steel trigger. From Marlin Firearms.
Price: **$552.00**

Remington Model 572 BDL Deluxe Fieldmaster

Ruger Model 96/22

Ruger Model 96/17

Taurus 62R

Taurus 72C-SS

Winchester 9422 Legacy

REMINGTON 572 BDL DELUXE FIELDMASTER PUMP RIFLE
Caliber: 22 S (20), L (17) or LR (15), tubular mag. **Barrel:** 21" round tapered. **Weight:** 5-1/2 lbs. **Length:** 40" overall. **Stock:** Walnut with checkered pistol grip and slide handle. **Sights:** Big game. **Features:** Cross-bolt safety; removing inner magazine tube converts rifle to single shot; receiver grooved for tip-off scope mount.
Price: **$407.00**

RUGER MODEL 96 LEVER-ACTION RIFLE
Caliber: 22 WMR, 9 rounds; 44 Magnum, 4 rounds; 17 HMR 9 rounds. **Barrel:** 18-1/2". **Weight:** 5-1/4 lbs. **Length:** 37-1/4" overall. **Stock:** Hardwood. **Sights:** Gold bead front, folding leaf rear. **Features:** Sliding cross button safety, visible cocking indicator; short-throw lever action. Introduced 1996. Made in U.S.A. by Sturm, Ruger & Co.
Price: 96/22M (22 WMR)..................................... **$390.00**
Price: 96/22M (44 Mag.) **$546.00**
Price: 96/17M (17 HMR) **$390.00**

TAURUS MODEL 62 PUMP RIFLE
Caliber: 22 LR, 12- or 13-shot. **Barrel:** 16-1/2" or 23" round. **Weight:** 72 oz. to 80 oz. **Length:** 39" overall. **Stock:** Premium hardwood. **Sights:** Adjustable rear, bead blade front, optional tang. **Features:** Blue, case hardened or stainless, bolt-mounted safety, pump action, manual firing pin block, integral security lock system. Imported from Brazil by Taurus International.
Price: M62C (blue).. **$280.00**
Price: M62C-CH (case-hardened, blue) **$280.00**
Price: M62CCH-T (case-hardened, blue)..................... **$358.00**
Price: M62C-SS (stainless steel)........................... **$295.00**
Price: M62CSS-T (stainless steel) **$373.00**
Price: M62C-SS-Y (stainless steel)......................... **$327.00**

Price: M62C-T (blue)...................................... **$358.00**
Price: M62C-Y (blue) **$311.00**
Price: M62R (blue) **$280.00**
Price: M62R-CH (case-hardened, blue)..................... **$280.00**
Price: M62RCH-T (case-hardened, blue)..................... **$358.00**
Price: M62R-SS (stainless steel) **$295.00**
Price: M62RSS-T (stainless steel) **$373.00**
Price: M62R-T (blue)...................................... **$358.00**

Taurus Model 72 Pump Rifle
Same as Model 62 except chambered in 22 Magnum or .17 HMR; 16-1/2" bbl. holds 10-12 shots, 23" bbl. holds 11-13 shots. Weighs 72 oz. to 80 oz. Introduced 2001. Imported from Brazil by Taurus International.
Price: M72C (blue) **$295.00**
Price: M72C-CH (case-hardened, blue)..................... **$295.00**
Price: M72CCH-T (case-hardened, blue)..................... **$373.00**
Price: M72C-SS (stainless steel) **$311.00**
Price: M72CSS-T (stainless steel) **$389.00**
Price: M72C-T (blue)...................................... **$373.00**
Price: M72R (blue) **$295.00**
Price: M72R-CH (case-hardened, blue)..................... **$295.00**
Price: M72RCH-T (case-hardened, blue)..................... **$373.00**
Price: M72R-SS (stainless steel) **$311.00**
Price: M72RSS-T (stainless steel) **$389.00**
Price: M72R-T (blue)...................................... **$373.00**

WINCHESTER MODEL 9422 LEVER-ACTION RIFLES
Caliber: 22 LR, 22 WMR, tubular magazine. **Barrel:** 20-1/2". **Weight:** 6-1/4 lbs. **Length:** 37-1/8" overall. **Stock:** American walnut, two-piece, straight grip (Traditional) or semi-pistol grip (Legacy). **Sights:** Hooded ramp front, adjustable semi-buckhorn rear. **Features:** Side ejection, receiver grooved for scope mounting, takedown action. From U.S. Repeating Arms Co.
Price: Traditional, 22 LR 15-shot.......................... **$465.00**
Price: Traditional, 22WMR, 11-shot **$487.00**
Price: Legacy, 22 LR 15-shot **$498.00**
Price: Legacy 22 WMR, 11-shot............................ **$521.00**

Includes models for a variety of sports, utility and competitive shooting.

Anschutz 1710D

Chipmunk Deluxe

CZ 452 Lux

ANSCHUTZ 1416D/1516D CLASSIC RIFLES
Caliber: 22 LR (1416D), 5-shot clip; 22 WMR (1516D), 4-shot clip. **Barrel:** 22-1/2". **Weight:** 6 lbs. **Length:** 41" overall. **Stock:** European hardwood with walnut finish; classic style with straight comb, checkered pistol grip and forend. **Sights:** Hooded ramp front, folding leaf rear. **Features:** Uses Match 64 action. Adjustable single stage trigger. Receiver grooved for scope mounting. Imported from Germany by AcuSport Corp.
Price: 1416D, 22 LR $755.95
Price: 1516D, 22 WMR $779.95
Price: 1416D Classic left-hand $679.95

Anschutz 1416D/1516D Walnut Luxus Rifles
Similar to the Classic models except have European walnut stocks with Monte Carlo cheekpiece, slim forend with Schnabel tip, cut checkering on grip and forend. Introduced 1997. Imported from Germany by AcuSport Corp.
Price: 1416D (22 LR) $755.95
Price: 1516D (22 WMR) $779.95

ANSCHUTZ 1518D LUXUS BOLT-ACTION RIFLE
Caliber: 22 WMR, 4-shot magazine. **Barrel:** 19-3/4". **Weight:** 5-1/2 lbs. **Length:** 37-1/2" overall. **Stock:** European walnut. **Sights:** Blade on ramp front, folding leaf rear. **Features:** Receiver grooved for scope mounting; single stage trigger; skip-line checkering; rosewood forend tip; sling swivels. Imported from Germany by AcuSport Corp.
Price: $1,186.95

ANSCHUTZ 1710D CUSTOM RIFLE
Caliber: 22 LR, 5-shot clip. **Barrel:** 24-1/4". **Weight:** 7-3/8 lbs. **Length:** 42-1/2" overall. **Stock:** Select European walnut. **Sights:** Hooded ramp front, folding leaf rear; drilled and tapped for scope mounting. **Features:** Match 54 action with adjustable single-stage trigger; roll-over Monte Carlo cheekpiece, slim forend with Schnabel tip, Wundhammer palm swell on pistol grip, rosewood gripcap with white diamond insert; skip-line checkering on grip and forend. Introduced 1988. Imported from Germany by AcuSport Corp.
Price: $1,289.95

CHARLES DALY SUPERIOR II RIMFIRE RIFLE
Caliber: 22LR, 22MRF, 17HRM. **Barrel:** 22". **Weight:** 6 pounds. **Sights:** None. Drilled and tapped for scope mounts. **Features:** Manufactured by Zastava. Walnut stock, two-position safety; 5-round magazine capacity. Introduced 2005.

Price: 22LR $259.00
Price: 22WMR $299.00
Price: 17HMR $334.00

CHIPMUNK SINGLE SHOT RIFLE
Caliber: 22 LR, 22 WMR, single shot. **Barrel:** 16-1/8". **Weight:** About 2-1/2 lbs. **Length:** 30" overall. **Stocks:** American walnut. **Sights:** Post on ramp front, peep rear adjustable for windage and elevation. **Features:** Drilled and tapped for scope mounting using special Chipmunk base ($13.95). Engraved model also available. Made in U.S.A. Introduced 1982. From Rogue Rifle Co., Inc.
Price: Standard $194.25
Price: Standard 22 WMR $209.95
Price: Deluxe (better wood, checkering) $246.95
Price: Deluxe 22 WMR $262.95
Price: Laminated stock $209.95
Price: Laminated stock, 22 WMR $225.95
Price: Bull barrel models of above, add $16.00

CHIPMUNK TM (TARGET MODEL)
Caliber: 22 S, L, or LR. **Barrel:** 18" blue. **Weight:** 5 lbs. **Length:** 33". Stocks: Walnut with accessory rail. **Sights:** 1/4 minute micrometer adjustable. **Features:** Manually cocking single shot bolt action, blue receiver, adjustable buttplate and buttpad.
Price: $329.95

COOPER MODEL 57-M BOLT-ACTION RIFLE
Caliber: 22 LR, 22 WMR, 17 HMR. **Barrel:** 23-3/4" stainless steel or 41-40 match grade. **Weight:** 6.6 lbs. **Stock:** Claro walnut, 22 lpi hand checkering. **Sights:** None furnished. **Features:** Three rear locking lug, repeating bolt-action with 5-shot mag. Fully adjustable trigger. Many options. Made 100% in the U.S.A. by Cooper Firearms of Montana, Inc.
Price: Classic $1,295.00
Price: LVT $1,395.00
Price: Custom Classic. $1,995.00
Price: Western Classic $2,595.00

CZ 452 LUX BOLT-ACTION RIFLE
Caliber: 22 LR, 22 WMR, 5-shot detachable magazine. **Barrel:** 24.8". **Weight:** 6.6 lbs. **Length:** 42.63" overall. **Stock:** Walnut with checkered pistol grip. **Sights:** Hooded front, fully adjustable tangent rear. **Features:** All-steel construction, adjustable trigger, polished blue finish. Imported from the Czech Republic by CZ-USA.
Price: 22 LR, 22 WMR $378.00

CZ 452 Varmint

CZ 452 American Classic

Henry "Mini" Bolt 22

Kimber 22 Classic

Kimber 22 SuperAmerica

CZ 452 Varmint Rifle
Similar to the Lux model except has heavy 20.8" barrel; stock has beavertail forend; weighs 7 lbs.; no sights furnished. Available only in 22 LR. Imported from the Czech Republic by CZ-USA.
Price: **$407.00**

CZ 452 American Classic Bolt-Action Rifle
Similar to the CZ 452 M 2E Lux except has classic-style stock of Circassian walnut; 22.5" free-floating barrel with recessed target crown; receiver dovetail for scope mounting. No open sights furnished. Introduced 1999. Imported from the Czech Republic by CZ-USA.
Price: 22 LR, 22 WMR. **$420.00**

HARRINGTON & RICHARDSON
ULTRA HEAVY BARREL 22 MAG RIFLE
Caliber: 22 WMR, single shot. **Barrel:** 22" bull. **Stock:** Cinnamon laminated wood with Monte Carlo cheekpiece. **Sights:** None furnished; scope mount rail included. **Features:** Hand-checkered stock and forend; deep-crown rifling; tuned trigger; trigger locking system; hammer extension. Introduced 2001. From H&R 1871 LLC.
Price: **$193.00**

HENRY ACU-BOLT RIFLE
Caliber: 22, 22 Mag., 17HMR; single shot. **Barrel:** 20". **Weight:** 4.15 lbs. **Length:** 36". **Stock:** One-piece fiberglass synthetic. **Sights:** Scope mount and 4x scope included. **Features:** Stainless barrel and receiver, bolt-action.
Price: **$325.00**

HENRY "MINI" BOLT ACTION 22 RIFLE
Caliber: 22 LR, single shot youth gun. **Barrel:** 16" stainless, 8-groove rifling. **Weight:** 3.25 lbs. **Length:** 30", LOP 11-1/2". **Stock:** Synthetic, pistol grip, wraparound checkering and beavertail forearm. **Sights:** William Fire sights. **Features:** One-piece bolt configuration manually operated safety.
Price: **$169.95**

KIMBER 22 CLASSIC BOLT-ACTION RIFLE
Caliber: 22 LR and 17 Mach 2, 5-shot magazine. **Barrel:** 18", 22", 24" match grade; 11-degree target crown. **Weight:** 5 to 8 lbs. **Length:** 35" to 43". **Stock:** Classic Claro walnut, hand-checkering, steel gripcap, swivel studs. **Sights:** None, drilled and tapped. **Features:** All-new action with Mauser-style full-length claw extractor, two-position wing safety, match trigger, pillar-bedded action with recoil lug. Introduced 1999. Made in U.S.A. by Kimber Mfg., Inc.
Price: Classic 22 . . . . **$1,147.00**
Price: Classic Varmint (22 or17M2) **$1,055.00**
Price: Hunter (22) **$809.00**
Price: Hunter (17M2) **$846.00**

Kimber 22 SuperAmerica Bolt-Action Rifle
Similar to 22 Classic except has AAA Claro walnut stock with wraparound 22 lpi hand-cut checkering, ebony forend tip, beaded cheekpiece. Introduced 1999. Made in U.S.A. by Kimber Mfg., Inc.
Price: **$1,865.00**

Kimber 22 SVT

Kimber 22 HS

Marlin 917V

Marlin Model 15YN "Little Buckaroo"

Marlin Model 980S

Kimber 22 SVT Bolt-Action Rifle
Similar to 22 Classic except has 18" stainless steel, fluted bull barrel, gray laminated, high-comb target-style stock with deep pistol grip, high comb, beavertail forend with bipod stud. Weighs 7.5 lbs., overall length 36.5". Matte finish on action. Introduced 1999. Made in U.S.A. by Kimber Mfg., Inc.

Price: 22 model **$1,007.00**
Price: 17M2 model. **$1,055.00**

Kimber 22 HS (Hunter Silhouette) Bolt-Action Rifle
Similar to 22 Classic except 24" medium sporter match-grade barrel with half-fluting; high comb, walnut, Monte Carlo target stock with 18 lpi checkering; matte blue metal finish. Introduced 1999. Made in U.S.A. by Kimber Mfg., Inc.

Price: **$915.00**

MARLIN MODEL 917V MAGNUM
Caliber: 17 Magnum, 7-shot. **Barrel:** 22. **Weight:** 6 lbs., stainless 7 lbs. **Length:** 41". **Stock:** Checkered walnut Monte Carlo SS, laminated black/grey. **Sights:** No sights but receiver grooved. **Features:** Swivel studs, positive thumb safety, red cocking indicator, safety lock, SS 1" brushed aluminum scope rings.

Price: **$284.00**
Price: W/fire control system **$450.00**

MARLIN MODEL 15YN "LITTLE BUCKAROO"
Caliber: 22 S, L, LR, single shot. **Barrel:** 16-1/4" Micro-Groove®. **Weight:** 4-1/4 lbs. **Length:** 33-1/4" overall. **Stock:** One-piece walnut-finished, press-checkered Maine birch with Monte Carlo; Mar-Shield® finish. **Sights:** Ramp front, adjustable open rear. **Features:** Beginner's rifle with thumb safety, easy-load feed throat, red cocking indicator. Receiver grooved for scope mounting. Introduced 1989.

Price: **$221.00**
Price: Stainless steel with fire sights **$233.00**

MARLIN MODEL 980S BOLT-ACTION RIFLE
Caliber: 22 LR, 7-shot clip magazine. **Barrel:** 22" Micro-Groove®. **Weight:** 6 lbs. **Length:** 41" overall. **Stock:** Black fiberglass-filled synthetic with nickel-plated swivel studs and molded-in checkering. **Sights:** Ramp front with orange post and cutaway Wide-Scan™ hood, adjustable semi-buckhorn folding rear. **Features:** Stainless steel barrel, receiver, front breech bolt and striker; receiver grooved for scope mounting. Introduced 1994. Model 880SQ (Squirrel Rifle) is similar but has heavy 22" barrel. Made in U.S.A. by Marlin.

Price: (Model 980S) **$333.00**

Marlin Model 981T Bolt-Action Rifle
Same as Marlin 980S except blued steel, tubular magazine, holds 17 Long Rifle cartridges. Weighs 6 lbs.

Price: **$225.00**

Marlin 880V

Marlin 925

Marlin 925C

Marlin 883S

Marlin 983T

Marlin Model 980V
Similar to Model 980S except uses heavy target barrel. Black synthetic stock with molded-in checkering, double bedding screws, matte blue finish. Without sights, no dovetail or filler screws; receiver grooved for scope mount. Weighs 7 lbs. Introduced 2005. Made in U.S.A. by Marlin.
Price: **$349.00**

Marlin Model 925 Bolt-Action Repeater
Similar to Marlin 980S, except walnut-finished hardwood stock, adjustable open rear sight, ramp front. Weighs 5.5 lbs.
Price: **$223.00**
Price: With 4x scope and mount **$232.00**

Marlin Model 925C Bolt-Action Repeater
Same as Model 980S except Mossy Oak® Break-Up camouflage stock. Made in U.S.A. by Marlin. Weighs 5.5 lbs.
Price: **$263.00**

MARLIN MODEL 982 BOLT-ACTION RIFLE
Caliber: 22 WMR. **Barrel:** 22" Micro-Groove®. **Weight:** 6 lbs. **Length:** 41" overall. **Stock:** Walnut Monte Carlo genuine American black walnut with swivel studs; full pistol grip; classic cut checkering; rubber rifle butt pad; tough Mar-Shield® finish. **Sights:** Adjustable semi-buckhorn folding rear, ramp front sight with brass bead and Wide-Scan™ front sight hood. **Features:** 7-shot clip, thumb safety, red cocking indicator, receiver grooved for scope mount. Made in U.S.A. by Marlin Firearms Co.
Price: **$341.00**
Price: Model 982L (laminated hardwood stock; weighs 6-1/4 lbs.). . **$342.00**

Marlin Model 982S Bolt-Action Rifle
Same as the Marlin Model 982 except has stainless steel front breech bolt, barrel, receiver and bolt knob. All other parts are either stainless steel or nickel-plated. Has black Monte Carlo stock of fiberglass-filled polycarbonate with molded-in checkering, nickel-plated swivel studs. Introduced 2005. Made in U.S.A. by Marlin Firearms Co.
Price: **$364.00**

Marlin Model 982VS Bolt-Action Rifle
Similar to the Model 982S except has selected heavy 22" stainless steel barrel with recessed muzzle, and comes without sights; receiver is grooved for scope mount and 1" ring mounts are included. Weighs 7 lbs. Introduced 1997. Made in U.S.A. by Marlin Firearms Co.
Price: **$357.00**

Marlin Model 925M/925MC Bolt-Action Rifles
Similar to the Model 982 except chambered for 22 WMR. Has 7-shot clip magazine, 22" Micro-Groove® barrel, checkered walnut-finished Maine birch stock. Introduced 1989.
Price: 25M. **$255.00**
New! Price: 25MC (Mossy Oak® Break-Up camouflage stock) . . . **$294.00**

MARLIN MODEL 983 BOLT-ACTION RIFLE
Caliber: 22 WMR. **Barrel:** 22"; 1:16" twist. **Weight:** 6 lbs. **Length:** 41" overall. **Stock:** Walnut Monte Carlo with sling swivel studs, rubber buttpad. **Sights:** Ramp front with brass bead, removable hood; adjustable semi-buckhorn folding rear. **Features:** Thumb safety, red cocking indicator, receiver grooved for scope mount. Made in U.S.A. by Marlin Firearms Co.
Price: **$356.00**

Marlin Model 983S Bolt-Action Rifle
Same as the Model 983 except front breech bolt, striker knob, trigger stud, cartridge lifter stud and outer magazine tube are of stainless steel; other parts are nickel-plated. Has two-tone brown laminated Monte Carlo stock with swivel studs, rubber buttpad. Introduced 1993.
Price: **$377.00**

Marlin Model 983T Bolt-Action Rifle
Same as the Model 983 except has a black Monte Carlo fiberglass-filled synthetic stock with sling swivel studs. Weighs 6 lbs., length 41" overall. Introduced 2001. Made in U.S.A. by Marlin Firearms Co.
Price: **$273.00**

Ruger K77/22 Varmint

Ruger 77/22R

Savage Mark I-G

Savage Mark II-BV

Price: K77/22VBZ, 22 LR **$685.00**
Price: K77/22VMBZ, 22 WMR **$685.00**

MEACHAM LOW-WALL RIFLE
Caliber: 22 RF Match, 17 HMR. **Barrel:** 28". **Weight:** 10 lbs. **Sights:** None. Tang drilled for Win. base, 3/8" dovetail slot, front. **Stock:** Fancy eastern black walnut with cheekpiece; ebony insert in forend. **Features:** Available with single trigger, single set trigger, or Schuetzen-style double-set triggers. Introduced 2002. From Meacham T&H, Inc.
Price: **$2,999.00**

NEW ENGLAND FIREARMS SPORTSTER™ SINGLE-SHOT RIFLES
Caliber: 22 LR, 22 WMR, 17 HMR, single-shot. **Barrel:** 20". **Weight:** 5-1/2 lbs. **Length:** 36-1/4" overall. **Stock:** Black polymer. **Sights:** None furnished; scope mount included. **Features:** Break open, side-lever release; automatic ejection; recoil pad; sling swivel studs; trigger locking system. Introduced 2001. Made in U.S.A. by New England Firearms.
Price: **$149.00**
Price: Youth model (20" bbl., 33" overall, weighs 5-1/3 lbs.) **$149.00**
Price: Sportster 17 HMR **$180.00**

NEW ULTRA LIGHT ARMS 20RF BOLT-ACTION RIFLE
Caliber: 22 LR, single shot or repeater. **Barrel:** Douglas, length to order. **Weight:** 5-1/4 lbs. **Length:** Varies. **Stock:** Kevlar®/graphite composite, variety of finishes. **Sights:** None furnished; drilled and tapped for scope mount. **Features:** Timney trigger, hand-lapped action, button-rifled barrel, hand-bedded action, recoil pad, sling-swivel studs, optional Jewell trigger. Made in U.S.A. by New Ultra Light Arms.
Price: 20 RF single shot **$800.00**
Price: 20 RF repeater **$850.00**

ROSSI MATCHED PAIR SINGLE-SHOT RIFLE/SHOTGUN
Caliber: 22 LR or 22 Mag. **Barrel:** 18-1/2" or 23". **Weight:** 6 lbs. **Stock:** Hardwood (brown or black finish). **Sights:** Fully adjustable front and rear. **Features:** Break-open breech, transfer-bar manual safety, includes matched 410-, 20 or 12 gauge shotgun barrel with bead front sight. Introduced 2001. Imported by BrazTech/Taurus.
Price: Blue **$139.95**
Price: Stainless steel **$169.95**

RUGER K77/22 VARMINT RIFLE
Caliber: 22 LR, 10-shot, 22 WMR, 9-shot detachable rotary magazine. **Barrel:** 24", heavy. **Weight:** 6-7/8 lbs. **Length:** 43.25" overall. **Stock:** Laminated hardwood with rubber buttpad, quick-detachable swivel studs. **Sights:** None furnished. Comes with Ruger 1" scope rings. **Features:** Stainless steel or blued finish. Three-position safety, dual extractors. Stock has wide, flat forend. Introduced 1993.

RUGER 77/22 RIMFIRE BOLT-ACTION RIFLE
Caliber: 22 LR, 10-shot rotary magazine; 22 WMR, 9-shot rotary magazine. **Barrel:** 20". **Weight:** About 6 lbs. **Length:** 39-3/4" overall. **Stock:** Checkered American walnut, laminated hardwood, or synthetic stocks, stainless sling swivels. **Sights:** Plain barrel with 1" Ruger rings. **Features:** Mauser-type action uses Ruger's rotary magazine. Three-position safety, simplified bolt stop, patented bolt locking system. Uses the dual-screw barrel attachment system of the 10/22 rifle. Integral scope mounting system with 1" Ruger rings. Blued model introduced 1983. Stainless steel and blued with synthetic stock introduced 1989.
Price: 77/22R (no sights, rings, walnut stock) **$613.00**
Price: K77/22RP (stainless, no sights, rings, synthetic stock) **$613.00**
Price: 77/22RM (22 WMR, blue, walnut stock) **$613.00**
Price: K77/22RMP (22 WMR, stainless, synthetic stock) **$613.00**
Price: K77/17RM, 17RMP, 17VMBBZ (17 HMR, walnut, synthetic or laminate stocks, no sights, rings, blued or stainless) .. **$613.00 to $746.00**

SAVAGE MARK I-G BOLT-ACTION RIFLE
Caliber: 22 LR, single shot. **Barrel:** 20-3/4". **Weight:** 5-1/2 lbs. **Length:** 39-1/2" overall. **Stock:** Walnut-finished hardwood with Monte Carlo-type comb, checkered grip and forend. **Sights:** Bead front, open adjustable rear. Receiver grooved for scope mounting. **Features:** Thumb-operated rotating safety. Blue finish. Rifled or smooth bore. Introduced 1990. Made in Canada, from Savage Arms Inc.
Price: Mark IG, rifled or smooth bore, right- or left-handed **$152.00**
Price: Mark I-GY (Youth), 19" bbl., 37" overall, 5 lbs............ **$152.00**
Price: Mark I-LY (Youth), 19" bbl., color laminate **$187.00**
Price: Mark I-GSB (22 LR shot cartridge) **$152.00**

SAVAGE MARK II BOLT-ACTION RIFLE
Caliber: 22 LR, 10-shot magazine. **Barrel:** 20-1/2". **Weight:** 5-1/2 lbs. **Length:** 39-1/2" overall. **Stock:** Walnut-finished hardwood with Monte Carlo-type comb, checkered grip and forend. **Sights:** Bead front, open adjustable rear. Receiver grooved for scope mounting. **Features:** Thumb-operated rotating safety. Blue finish. Introduced 1990. Made in Canada, from Savage Arms, Inc.
Price: Mark II-BV............................... **$264.00**
Price: Mark II Camo **$184.00**
Price: Mark II-GY (youth), 19" barrel, 37" overall, 5 lbs......... **$169.00**
Price: Mark II-GL, left-hand. **$169.00**
Price: Mark II-GLY (youth) left-hand **$169.00**
Price: Mark II-FXP (as above with black synthetic stock)........ **$158.00**
Price: Mark II-F (as above, no scope)..................... **$151.00**

Savage Mark II-FXP

Savage Mark II-FSS

Savage Model 93G

Savage Model 93FSS

Savage Model 93FVSS

Savage Mark II-FSS Stainless Rifle
Similar to the Mark II except has stainless steel barreled action and black synthetic stock with positive checkering, swivel studs, and 20.75" free-floating and button-rifled barrel with detacheable magazine. Weighs 5.5 lbs. Introduced 1997. Imported from Canada by Savage Arms, Inc.
Price: **$213.00**

SAVAGE MODEL 93G MAGNUM BOLT-ACTION RIFLE
Caliber: 22 WMR, 5-shot magazine. **Barrel:** 20-3/4". **Weight:** 5-3/4 lbs. **Length:** 39-1/2" overall. **Stock:** Walnut-finished hardwood with Monte Carlo-type comb, checkered grip and forend. **Sights:** Bead front, adjustable open rear. Receiver grooved for scope mount. **Features:**

Thumb-operated rotary safety. Blue finish. Introduced 1994. Made in Canada, from Savage Arms.
Price: **$195.00**
Price: Model 93F (as above with black graphite/fiberglass stock) . . **$187.00**

Savage Model 93FSS Magnum Rifle
Similar to Model 93G except stainless steel barreled action and black synthetic stock with positive checkering. Weighs 5-1/2 lbs. Introduced 1997. Imported from Canada by Savage Arms, Inc.
Price: **$236.00**

Savage Model 93FVSS Magnum Rifle
Similar to Model 93FSS Magnum except 21" heavy barrel with recessed target-style crown, satin-finished stainless barreled action, black graphite/fiberglass stock. Drilled and tapped for scope mounting; comes with Weaver-style bases. Introduced 1998. Imported from Canada by Savage Arms, Inc.
Price: **$267.00**
Price: With scope **$305.00**

Savage Model 30G Stevens "Favorite"

Savage Cub G Youth

Winchester Model 52B

Winchester Model 1885 Low Wall

SAVAGE MODEL 30G STEVENS "FAVORITE"
Caliber: 22 LR, 22WMR Model 30GM, 17 HMR Model 30R17. **Barrel:** 21".
Weight: 4.25 lbs. **Length:** 36.75". **Stock:** Walnut, straight grip, Schnabel
forend. **Sights:** Adjustable rear, bead post front. **Features:** Lever action
falling block, inertia firing pin system, Model 30G half octagonal bbl. Model
30GM full octagonal bbl.
Price: Model 30G. **$228.00**
Price: Model 30GM **$266.00**
Price: Model 30R17. . . . . **$292.00**

SAVAGE CUB G YOUTH
Caliber: 22 S, L, LR; 17 Mach 2. **Barrel:** 16.125" **Weight:** 3.3 lbs. **Length:**
33" **Stock:** Walnut finished hardwood. **Sights:** Bead post, front; peep,
rear. **Features:** Mini single shot bolt action, free-floating button-rifled
barrel, blued finish. From Savage Arms.

Price: 22 S, L, LR **$156.00**
Price: 17 Mach 2. . . . . **$165.00**

WINCHESTER MODEL 52B BOLT-ACTION RIFLE
Caliber: 22 Long Rifle, 5-shot magazine. **Barrel:** 24". **Weight:** 7 lbs.
Length: 41-3/4" overall. **Stock:** Walnut with checkered grip and forend.
Sights: None furnished; grooved receiver and drilled and tapped for
scope mounting. **Features:** Adjustable trigger; match chamber;
detachable magazine. Reintroduced 1997. From U.S. Repeating Arms
Co.
Price: **$662.00**

WINCHESTER MODEL 1885 LOW WALL RIMFIRE
Caliber: 17 HMR, single-shot. **Barrel:** 24-1/2"; half-octagon. **Weight:** 8 lbs.
Length: 41" overall. **Stock:** Walnut. **Sights:** Blade front, semi-buckhorn
rear. **Features:** Drilled and tapped for scope mount or tang sight; target
chamber. From U.S. Repeating Arms Co.
Price: Grade I **$1,014.00**

Includes models for classic American and ISU target competition and other sporting and competitive shooting.

Anschutz 1451 Target

Anschutz 2013

ANSCHUTZ 1451R SPORTER TARGET RIFLE
Caliber: 22 LR, 5-shot magazine. **Barrel:** 22" heavy match. **Weight:** 6.4 lbs. **Length:** 39.75" overall. **Stock:** European hardwood with walnut finish. **Sights:** None furnished. Grooved receiver for scope mounting or Anschutz micrometer rear sight. **Features:** Sliding safety, two-stage trigger. Adjustable buttplate; forend slide rail to accept Anschutz accessories. Imported from Germany by AcuSport Corp.
Price: **$549.00**

ANSCHUTZ 1451 TARGET RIFLE
Caliber: 22 LR. **Barrel:** 22". **Weight:** About 6.5 lbs. **Length:** 40". **Sights:** Optional. Receiver grooved for scope mounting. **Features:** Designed for the beginning junior shooter with adjustable length of pull from 13.25" to 14.25" via removable butt spacers. Two-stage trigger factory set at 2.6 lbs. Introduced 1999. Imported from Germany by Gunsmithing, Inc.
Price: **$347.00**
Price: #6834 Match Sight Set **$227.10**

ANSCHUTZ 1808D-RT SUPER RUNNING TARGET RIFLE
Caliber: 22 LR, single shot. **Barrel:** 32-1/2". **Weight:** 9 lbs. **Length:** 50" overall. **Stock:** European walnut. Heavy beavertail forend; adjustable cheekpiece and buttplate. Stippled grip and forend. **Sights:** None furnished. Grooved for scope mounting. **Features:** Designed for Running Target competition. Nine-way adjustable single-stage trigger, slide safety. Introduced 1991. Imported from Germany by Accuracy International, Gunsmithing, Inc.
Price: Right-hand. **$1,364.10**

ANSCHUTZ 1903 MATCH RIFLE
Caliber: 22 LR, single shot. **Barrel:** 25.5", .75" diameter. **Weight:** 10.1 lbs. **Length:** 43.75" overall. **Stock:** Walnut-finished hardwood with adjustable cheekpiece; stippled grip and forend. **Sights:** None furnished. **Features:** Uses Anschutz Match 64 action and #5098 two-stage trigger. A medium weight rifle for intermediate and advanced Junior Match competition. Introduced 1987. Imported from Germany by Accuracy International, Gunsmithing, Inc.
Price: Right-hand. **$720.40**
Price: Left-hand **$757.90**

ANSCHUTZ 64-MS R SILHOUETTE RIFLE
Caliber: 22 LR, 5-shot magazine. **Barrel:** 21-1/2", medium heavy; 7/8" diameter. **Weight:** 8 lbs. **Length:** 39.5" overall. **Stock:** Walnut-finished hardwood, silhouette-type. **Sights:** None furnished. **Features:** Uses Match 64 action. Designed for metallic silhouette competition. Stock has stippled checkering, contoured thumb groove with Wundhammer swell. Two-stage #5098 trigger. Slide safety locks sear and bolt. Introduced 1980. Imported from Germany by AcuSport Corp., Accuracy International, Gunsmithing, Inc.
Price: 64-MS R **$704.30**

ANSCHUTZ 2013 BENCHREST RIFLE
Caliber: 22 LR, single shot. **Barrel:** 19.6". **Weight:** About 10.3 lbs. **Length:** 37.75" to 42.5" overall. **Stock:** Benchrest style of European hardwood. Stock length adjustable via spacers and buttplate. **Sights:** None furnished. Receiver grooved for mounts. **Features:** Uses the Anschutz 2013 target action; two-stage adjustable target trigger factory set at 3.9 oz. Introduced 1994. Imported from Germany by Accuracy International, Gunsmithing, Inc.
Price: **$1,757.20**

Anschutz 2007 Match Rifle
Uses same action as the Model 2013, but has a lighter barrel. European walnut stock in right-hand, true left-hand or extra-short models. Sights optional. Available with 19.6" barrel with extension tube, or 26", both in stainless or blue. Introduced 1998. Imported from Germany by Gunsmithing, Inc., Accuracy International.
Price: Right-hand, blue, no sights. **$1,766.60**
Price: Right-hand, blue, no sights, extra-short stock **$1,756.60**
Price: Left-hand, blue, no sights **$1,856.80**

ANSCHUTZ 1827 BIATHLON RIFLE
Caliber: 22 LR, 5-shot magazine. **Barrel:** 21-1/2". **Weight:** 8-1/2 lbs. with sights. **Length:** 42-1/2" overall. **Stock:** European walnut with cheekpiece, stippled pistol grip and forend. **Sights:** Optional globe front specially designed for Biathlon shooting, micrometer rear with hinged snow cap. **Features:** Uses Super Match 54 action and nine-way adjustable trigger; adjustable wooden buttplate, biathlon butthook, adjustable hand-stop rail. Introduced 1982. Imported from Germany by Accuracy International, Gunsmithing, Inc.
Price: Right-hand, with sights, about . . . . **$1,500.50 to $1,555.00**

Anschutz 1827BT Fortner Biathlon Rifle
Similar to the Anschutz 1827 Biathlon rifle except uses Anschutz/Fortner system straight-pull bolt action, blued or stainless steel barrel. Introduced 1982. Imported from Germany by Accuracy International, Gunsmithing, Inc.
Price: Right-hand, with sights . . . . **$1,908.00 to $2,210.00**
Price: Left-hand, with sights . . . . **$2,099.20 to $2,395.00**
Price: Right-hand, sights, stainless barrel **$2,045.20**

Anschutz 2012

Anschutz 54.18MS REP

ANSCHUTZ SUPER MATCH SPECIAL MODEL 2013 RIFLE
Caliber: 22 LR, single shot. **Barrel:** 25.9". **Weight:** 13 lbs. **Length:** 41.7" to 42.9". **Stock:** A thumbhole version made of European walnut, both the cheekpiece and buttplate are highly adjustable. **Sights:** None furnished. **Features:** Developed by Anschütz for women to shoot in the sport rifle category. Stainless or blue. Introduced in 1997.
Price: Right-hand, blue, no sights, walnut **$2,219.30**
Price: Right-hand, stainless, no sights, walnut **$2,345.30**
Price: Left-hand, blue, no sights, walnut **$2,319.50**

ANSCHUTZ 2012 SPORT RIFLE
Caliber: 22 LR, 5-shot magazine. **Barrel:** 22.4" match; detachable muzzle tube. **Weight:** 7.9 lbs. **Length:** 40.9" overall. **Stock:** European walnut, thumbhole design. **Sights:** None furnished. **Features:** Uses Anschutz 54.18 barreled action with two-stage match trigger. Introduced 1997. Imported from Germany by Accuracy International, AcuSport Corp.
Price: . . . . **$1,425.00 to $2,219.95**

ANSCHUTZ 1911 PRONE MATCH RIFLE
Caliber: 22 LR, single shot. **Barrel:** 27-1/4". **Weight:** 11 lbs. **Length:** 46" overall. **Stock:** Walnut-finished European hardwood; American prone-style with adjustable cheekpiece, textured pistol grip, forend with swivel rail and adjustable rubber buttplate. **Sights:** None furnished. Receiver grooved for Anschutz sights (extra). **Features:** Two-stage trigger adjustable from 2.1 to 8.6 oz. Extremely fast lock time. Stainless or blue barrel. Imported from Germany by Accuracy International, Gunsmithing, Inc.
Price: Right-hand, no sights **$1,714.20**

ANSCHUTZ 1912 SPORT RIFLE
Caliber: 22 LR, single shot. **Barrel:** 25.9". **Weight:** About 11.4 lbs. **Length:** 41.7 to 42.9". **Stock:** European walnut or aluminum. **Sights:** None furnished. **Features:** Lightweight sport rifle version of the 1913 but weighs 1.5 pounds less. Stainless or blue barrel. Introduced 1997.
Price: Right-hand, blue, no sights, walnut **$1,789.50**
Price: Right-hand, blue, no sights, aluminum **$2,129.80**
Price: Right-hand, stainless, no sights, walnut **$1,910.30**
Price: Left-hand, blue, no sights, walnut **$1,879.00**

ANSCHUTZ 1913 SUPER MATCH RIFLE
Caliber: 22 LR, single shot. **Barrel:** 27.1". **Weight:** About 14.3 lbs. **Length:** 44.8 to 46". **Stock:** European walnut, color laminate, or aluminum. **Sights:** None furnished. **Features:** Two-stage #5018 trigger. Extremely fast lock time. Stainless or blue barrel.

Price: Right-hand, blue, no sights, walnut stock **$2,262.90**
Price: Right-hand, blue, no sights, color laminate stock **$2,275.10**
Price: Right-hand, blue, no sights, aluminum stock **$2,262.90**
Price: Left-hand, blue, no sights, walnut stock **$2,382.20**

Anschutz 1913 Super Match Rifle
Same as the Model 1911 except European walnut International-type stock with adjustable cheekpiece, or color laminate, both available with straight or lowered forend, adjustable aluminum hook buttplate, adjustable hand stop, weighs 15.5 lbs., 46" overall. Stainless or blue barrel. Imported from Germany by Accuracy International, Gunsmithing, Inc.
Price: Right-hand, blue, no sights, walnut stock . . . . **$2,139.00 to $2,175.00**
Price: Right-hand, blue, no sights, color laminate stock **$2,199.40**
Price: Right-hand, blue, no sights, walnut, lowered forend **$2,181.80**
Price: Right-hand, blue, no sights, color laminate,
lowered forend **$2,242.20**
Price: Left-hand, blue, no sights, walnut stock . . . . . **$2,233.10 to $2,275.00**

Anschutz 54.18MS REP Deluxe Silhouette Rifle
Same basic action and trigger specifications as the Anschutz 1913 Super Match but with removable 5-shot clip magazine, 22.4" barrel extendable to 30" using optional extension and weight set. Weight is 8.1 lbs. Receiver drilled and tapped for scope mounting. Stock is thumbhole silhouette version or standard silhouette version, both are European walnut. Introduced 1990. Imported from Germany by Accuracy International, Gunsmithing, Inc.
Price: Thumbhole stock **$1,461.40**
Price: Standard stock **$1,212.10**

Anschutz 1907 Standard Match Rifle
Same action as Model 1913 but with 7/8" diameter 26" barrel (stainless or blue). Length is 44.5" overall, weighs 10.5 lbs. Choice of stock configurations. Vented forend. Designed for prone and position shooting ISU requirements; suitable for NRA matches. Also available with walnut flat-forend stock for benchrest shooting. Imported from Germany by Accuracy International, Gunsmithing, Inc.
Price: Right-hand, blue, no sights,
hardwood stock . . . . **$1,253.40 to $1,299.00**
Price: Right-hand, blue, no sights, colored laminated
stock . . . . **$1,316.10 to $1,375.00**
Price: Right-hand, blue, no sights, walnut stock **$1,521.10**
Price: Left-hand, blue barrel, no sights, walnut stock **$1,584.60**

Anschutz 1907

Armalite
AR-10(T)

Bushmaster A2

Bushmaster DCM

ARMALITE AR-10(T) RIFLE
Caliber: 308, 10-shot magazine. **Barrel:** 24" target-weight Rock 5R custom. **Weight:** 10.4 lbs. **Length:** 43.5" overall. **Stock:** Green or black compostion; N.M. fiberglass handguard tube. **Sights:** Detachable handle, front sight, or scope mount available. Comes with international-style flattop receiver with Picatinny rail. **Features:** National Match two-stage trigger. Forged upper receiver. Receivers hard-coat anodized. Introduced 1995. Made in U.S.A. by ArmaLite, Inc.
Price: Green. **$2,126.00**
Price: Black **$2,126.00**

ARMALITE M15A4(T) EAGLE EYE RIFLE
Caliber: 223, 10-round magazine. **Barrel:** 24" heavy stainless; 1:8" twist. **Weight:** 9.2 lbs. **Length:** 42-3/8" overall. **Stock:** Green or black butt, N.M. fiberglass handguard tube. **Sights:** One-piece international-style flattop receiver with Weaver-type rail, including case deflector. **Features:** Detachable carry handle, front sight and scope mount (30mm or 1") available. Upper and lower receivers have push-type pivot pin, hard coat anodized. Made in U.S.A. by ArmaLite, Inc.
Price: Green. **$1,378.00**
Price: Black **$1,393.00**

BLASER R93 LONG RANGE RIFLE
Caliber: 308 Win., 10-shot detachable box magazine. **Barrel:** 24". **Weight:** 10.4 lbs. **Length:** 44" overall. **Stock:** Aluminum with synthetic lining. **Sights:** None furnished; accepts detachable scope mount. **Features:** Straight-pull bolt action with adjustable trigger; fully adjustable stock; quick takedown; corrosion resistant finish. Introduced 1998. Imported from Germany by SIGARMS.
Price: **$2,360.00**

BUSHMASTER A2 RIFLE
Caliber: 308, 5.56mm. **Barrel:** 16", 20". **Weight:** 8.3 lbs. **Length:** 38.25" overall (20" barrel). **Stock:** Black composition; A2 type. **Sights:** Adjustable post front, adjustable aperture rear. **Features:** Patterned after Colt M-16A2. Chrome-lined barrel with manganese phosphate exterior. Forged aluminum receivers with push-pin takedown. Available in stainless barrel and camo stock versions. Made in U.S.A. by Bushmaster Firearms Co.
Price: 20" match heavy barrel (A2 type). . . . . **$1,025.00 to $1,185.00**
Price: (A3 type) **$1,135.00**

BUSHMASTER DCM COMPETITION RIFLE
Caliber: 223. **Barrel:** 20" extra-heavy (1" diameter) barrel with 1.8" twist for heavier competition bullets. **Weight:** Appx. 12 lbs. with balance weights. **Length:** NA. **Stock:** NA. **Sights:** A2 rear sight. **Features:** Has special competition rear sight with interchangeable apertures, extra-fine 1/2- or 1/4-MOA windage and elevation adjustments; specially ground front sight post in choice of three widths. Full-length handguards over free-floater barrel tube. Introduced 1998. Made in U.S.A. by Bushmaster Firearms, Inc.
Price: **$1,395.00**

Colt Accurized

Colt Match Target HBAR

Colt Match Target HBAR II

EAA/IZHMASH URAL 5.1

BUSHMASTER VARMINTER RIFLE
Caliber: 5.56mm. **Barrel:** 24", fluted. **Weight:** 8.4 lbs. **Length:** 42.25" overall. **Stock:** Black composition, A2 type. **Sights:** None furnished; upper receiver has integral scope mount base. **Features:** Chrome-lined .950" extra heavy barrel with counter-bored crown, manganese phosphate finish, free-floating aluminum handguard, forged aluminum receivers with push-pin takedown, hard anodized mil-spec finish. Competition trigger optional. Made in U.S.A. by Bushmaster Firearms, Inc.
Price: 20" Match heavy barrel **$1,265.00**
Price: Stainless barrel **$1,265.00**

COLT MATCH TARGET MODEL RIFLE
Caliber: 223 Rem., 8-shot magazine. **Barrel:** 20". **Weight:** 7.5 lbs. **Length:** 39" overall. **Stock:** Composition stock, grip, forend. **Sights:** Post front, aperture rear adjustable for windage and elevation. **Features:** Five-round detachable box magazine, standard-weight barrel, sling swivels. Has forward bolt assist. Military matte black finish. Introduced 1991.
Price: **$1,144.00**
Price: With compensator **$1,150.00**

Colt Accurized Rifle
Similar to the Match Target Model except has 24" barrel. Features flat-top receiver for scope mounting, stainless steel heavy barrel, tubular handguard, and free-floating barrel. Matte black finish. Weighs 9.25 lbs. Made in U.S.A. by Colt's Mfg. Co., Inc.
Price: Model CR6724 . . . . **$1,290.00 to $1,470.00**

Colt Match Target HBAR Rifle
Similar to the Target Model except has heavy barrel, 800-meter rear sight adjustable for windage and elevation, 9-round capacity. Weighs 8 lbs. Introduced 1991.
Price: Model MT6601, MT6601C **$1,300.00**

Colt Match Target Competition HBAR Rifle
Similar to the Match Target except has removeable carry handle for scope mounting, 1:9" rifling twist, 9-round magazine. Weighs 8.5 lbs. Introduced 1991.
Price: Model MT6700, MT6700C **$1,315.00**

Colt Match Target Competition HBAR II Rifle
Similar to the Match Target Competition HBAR except has 16:1" barrel, overall length 34.5", and weighs 7.1 lbs. Introduced 1995.
Price: Model MT6731 . . . . **$1,290.00**

EAA/HW 660 MATCH RIFLE
Caliber: 22 LR. **Barrel:** 26". **Weight:** 10.7 lbs. **Length:** 45.3" overall. **Stock:** Match-type walnut with adjustable cheekpiece and buttplate. **Sights:** Globe front, match aperture rear. **Features:** Adjustable match trigger; stippled pistol grip and forend; forend accessory rail. Introduced 1991. Imported from Germany by European American Armory.
Price: About. **$999.00**
Price: With laminate stock. **$1,159.00**

EAA/IZHMASH URAL 5.1 TARGET RIFLE
Caliber: 22 LR. **Barrel:** 26.5". **Weight:** 11.3 lbs. **Length:** 44.5". **Stock:** Wood, international style. **Sights:** Adjustable click rear, hooded front with inserts. **Features:** Forged barrel with rifling, adjustable trigger, aluminum rail for accessories, hooked adjustable buttplate. Adjustable comb, adjustable large palm rest. Hand stippling on grip area.
Price: . . . . **NA**

EAA/IZHMASH Biathlon

EAA/IZHMASH Biathlon Target

Ed Brown Model 702 Light Tactical

Ed Brown Model 702 Tactical

Ed Brown 702

EAA/Izhmash Biathlon Target Rifle
Similar to URAL with addition of snow covers for barrel and sights, stock holding extra mags, round trigger block. Unique bolt utilizes toggle action. Designed to compete in 40 meter biathlon event. 22 LR, 19.5" bbl.
Price: $979.00

EAA/Izhmash Biathalon Basic Target Rifle
Same action as Biathlon but designed for plinking or fun. Beech stock, heavy barrel with Weaver rail for scope mount. 22 LR, 19.5" bbl.
Price: $339.00

ED BROWN MODEL 702 LIGHT TACTICAL
Caliber: 223, 308. **Barrel:** 21". **Weight:** 8.75 lbs. **Stock:** Fully glass-bedded fiberglass with recoil pad. Wide varmint-style forend. **Sights:** None furnished. Talley scope mounts utilizing heavy duty screws.
Price: From $2,800.00

ED BROWN MODEL 702 TACTICAL
Caliber: 308, 300 Win. Mag. **Barrel:** 26". **Weight:** 11.25 lbs. **Stock:** Hand bedded McMillan A-3 fiberglass tactical stock with recoil pad. **Sights:**
None furnished. Leupold Mark 4 30mm scope mounts utilizing heavy-duty screws. **Features:** Custom short or long action, steel trigger guard, hinged floor plate, additional calibers available.
Price: From $2,900.00

ED BROWN MODEL 702, M40A2 MARINE SNIPER
Caliber: 308 Win., 30-06 Springfield. **Barrel:** Match-grade 24". **Weight:** 9.25 lbs. **Stock:** Hand bedded McMillan GP fiberglass tactical stock with recoil pad in special Woodland Camo molded-in colors. **Sights:** None furnished. Leupold Mark 4 30mm scope mounts with heavy-duty screws. **Features:** Steel trigger guard, hinged floor plate, three position safety. Left-hand model available.
Price: From $2,900.00

HARRIS GUNWORKS NATIONAL MATCH RIFLE
Caliber: 7mm-08, 308, 5-shot magazine. **Barrel:** 24", stainless steel. **Weight:** About 11 lbs. (std. bbl.). **Length:** 43" overall. **Stock:** Fiberglass with adjustable buttplate. **Sights:** Barrel band and Tompkins front; no rear sight furnished. **Features:** Gunworks repeating action with clip slot, Canjar trigger. Match-grade barrel. Available in right-hand only. Fiberglass stock, sight installation, special machining and triggers optional. Introduced 1989. From Harris Gunworks, Inc.
Price: $3,500.00

Harris Gunworks Long Range

Harris Gunworks M-86

Remington 40-XB Rangemaster

HARRIS GUNWORKS LONG RANGE RIFLE
Caliber: 300 Win. Mag., 7mm Rem. Mag., 300 Phoenix, 338 Lapua, single shot. **Barrel:** 26", stainless steel, match-grade. **Weight:** 14 lbs. **Length:** 46-1/2" overall. **Stock:** Fiberglass with adjustable buttplate and cheekpiece. Adjustable for length of pull, drop, cant and cast-off. **Sights:** Barrel band and Tompkins front; no rear sight furnished. **Features:** Uses Gunworks solid bottom single shot action and Canjar trigger. Barrel twist 1:12". Introduced 1989. From Harris Gunworks, Inc.
Price: **$3,620.00**

HARRIS GUNWORKS M-86 SNIPER RIFLE
Caliber: 308, 30-06, 4-shot magazine; 300 Win. Mag., 3-shot magazine. **Barrel:** 24", Gunworks match-grade in heavy contour. **Weight:** 11-1/4 lbs. (308), 11-1/2 lbs. (30-06, 300). **Length:** 43-1/2" overall. **Stock:** Specially designed McHale fiberglass stock with textured grip and forend, recoil pad. **Sights:** None furnished. **Features:** Uses Gunworks repeating action. Comes with bipod. Matte black finish. Sling swivels. Introduced 1989. From Harris Gunworks, Inc.
Price: **$2,700.00**

HARRIS GUNWORKS M-89 SNIPER RIFLE
Caliber: 308 Win., 5-shot magazine. **Barrel:** 28" (with suppressor). **Weight:** 15 lbs., 4 oz. **Stock:** Fiberglass; adjustable for length; recoil pad. **Sights:** None furnished. Drilled and tapped for scope mounting. **Features:** Uses Gunworks repeating action. Comes with bipod. Introduced 1990. From Harris Gunworks, Inc.
Price: Standard (non-suppressed) **$3,200.00**

HARRIS GUNWORKS COMBO M-87 SERIES 50-CALIBER RIFLES
Caliber: 50 BMG, single shot. **Barrel:** 29, with muzzle brake. **Weight:** About 21-1/2 lbs. **Length:** 53" overall. **Stock:** Gunworks fiberglass. **Sights:** None furnished. **Features:** Right-handed Gunworks stainless steel receiver, chrome-moly barrel with 1:15" twist. Introduced 1987. From Harris Gunworks, Inc.
Price: **$3,885.00**
Price: M87R 5-shot repeater **$4,000.00**
Price: M-87 (5-shot repeater) "Combo" **$4,300.00**
Price: M-92 Bullpup (shortened M-87 single shot with bullpup stock) **$4,770.00**
Price: M-93 (10-shot repeater with folding stock, detachable magazine) **$4,150.00**

OLYMPIC ARMS PCR-SERVICEMATCH RIFLE
Caliber: 223, 10-shot magazine. **Barrel:** 20", broach-cut 416 stainless steel. **Weight:** About 10 lbs. **Length:** 39.5" overall. **Stock:** A2 stowaway grip and trapdoor buttstock. **Sights:** Post front, E2-NM fully adjustable aperture rear. **Features:** Based on the AR-15. Conforms to all DCM standards. Free-floating 1:8.5" or 1:10" barrel; crowned barrel; no bayonet lug. Introduced 1996. Made in U.S.A. by Olympic Arms, Inc.
Price: **$1,062.00**

OLYMPIC ARMS PCR-1 RIFLE
Caliber: 223, 10-shot magazine. **Barrel:** 20", 24"; 416 stainless steel. **Weight:** 10 lbs., 3 oz. **Length:** 38.25" overall with 20" barrel. **Stock:** A2 stowaway grip and trapdoor butt. **Sights:** None supplied; flattop upper receiver, cut-down front sight base. **Features:** Based on the AR-15 rifle. Broach-cut, free-floating barrel with 1:8.5" or 1:10" twist. No bayonet lug. Crowned barrel; fluting available. Introduced 1994. Made in U.S.A. by Olympic Arms, Inc.
Price: **$1,038.00**

Olympic Arms PCR-2, PCR-3 Rifles
Similar to the PCR-1 except has 16" barrel, weighs 8 lbs., 2 oz.; has post front sight, fully adjustable aperture rear. Model PCR-3 has flattop upper receiver, cut-down front sight base. Introduced 1994. Made in U.S.A. by Olympic Arms, Inc.
Price: **$958.00**

REMINGTON 40-XB RANGEMASTER TARGET CENTERFIRE
Caliber: 15 calibers from 220 Swift to 300 Win. Mag. **Barrel:** 27-1/4". **Weight:** 11-1/4 lbs. **Length:** 47" overall. **Stock:** American walnut, laminated thumbhole or Kevlar with high comb and beavertail forend stop. Rubber non-slip buttplate. **Sights:** None. Scope blocks installed. **Features:** Adjustable trigger. Stainless barrel and action. Receiver drilled and tapped for sights.
Price: Standard single shot . . (right-hand) **$1,636.00**; (left-hand) **$1,761.00**
Price: Repeater **$1,734.00**

REMINGTON 40-XBBR KS
Caliber: Five calibers from 22 BR to 308 Win. **Barrel:** 20" (light varmint class), 24" (heavy varmint class). **Weight:** 7-1/4 lbs. (light varmint class); 12 lbs. (heavy varmint class). **Length:** 38" (20" bbl.), 42" (24" bbl.). **Stock:** Aramid fiber. **Sights:** None. Supplied with scope blocks. **Features:** Unblued benchrest with stainless steel barrel, trigger adjustable from 1-1/2 lbs. to 3-1/2 lbs. Special two-oz. trigger extra cost. Scope and mounts extra.
Price: Single shot **$1,876.00**

Remington 40-XC KS

Springfield, Inc. M1A Super Match

Springfield, Inc. M1A/M-21

Stoner SR-25

REMINGTON 40-XC KS TARGET RIFLE
Caliber: 7.62 NATO, 5-shot. **Barrel:** 24", stainless steel. **Weight:** 11 lbs. without sights. **Length:** 43-1/2" overall. **Stock:** Aramid fiber. **Sights:** None furnished. **Features:** Designed to meet the needs of competitive shooters. Stainless steel barrel and action.
Price: $1,821.00

REMINGTON 40-XR CUSTOM SPORTER
Caliber: 22 LR, 22 WM. **Features:** Model XR-40 Target rifle action. Many options available.
Price: Single shot.................................. $3,383.00

SAKO TRG-22 BOLT-ACTION RIFLE
Caliber: 308 Win., 10-shot magazine. **Barrel:** 26". **Weight:** 10-1/4 lbs. **Length:** 45-1/4" overall. **Stock:** Reinforced polyurethane with fully adjustable cheekpiece and buttplate. **Sights:** None furnished. Optional quick-detachable, one-piece scope mount base, 1" or 30mm rings. **Features:** Resistance-free bolt, free-floating heavy stainless barrel, 60-degree bolt lift. Two-stage trigger is adjustable for length, pull, horizontal or vertical pitch. Introduced 2000. Imported from Finland by Beretta USA.
Price: Green.. $2,898.00
Price: Model TRG-42, as above except in 338 Lapua Mag or 300
Win. Mag... $2,829.00
Price: Green (new) $3,243.00

SPRINGFIELD ARMORY M1A SUPER MATCH
Caliber: 308 Win. **Barrel:** 22", heavy Douglas Premium. **Weight:** About 11 lbs. **Length:** 44.31" overall. **Stock:** Heavy walnut competition stock with longer pistol grip, contoured area behind the rear sight, thicker butt and forend, glass bedded. **Sights:** National Match front and rear. **Features:** Has figure-eight-style operating rod guide. Introduced 1987. From Springfield Armory.
Price: About....................................... $2,479.00

Springfield Armory M1A/M-21 Tactical Model Rifle
Similar to M1A Super Match except special sniper stock with adjustable cheekpiece and rubber recoil pad. Weighs 11.6 lbs. From Springfield Armory.
Price: $2,975.00

SPRINGFIELD ARMORY M-1 GARAND AMERICAN COMBAT RIFLES
Caliber: 30-06, 308 Win., 8-shot. **Barrel:** 24". **Weight:** 9.5 lbs. **Length:** 43.6". **Stock:** American walnut. **Sights:** Military square post front, military aperture, MOA adjustable rear. **Features:** Limited production, certificate of authenticity, all new receiver, barrel and stock with remaining parts USGI mil-spec. Two-stage military trigger.
Price: About.. $2,479.00

STONER SR-15 MATCH RIFLE
Caliber: 223. **Barrel:** 20". **Weight:** 7.9 lbs. **Length:** 38" overall. **Stock:** Black synthetic. **Sights:** None furnished; flattop upper receiver for scope mounting. **Features:** Short Picatinny rail, two-stage match trigger. Introduced 1998. Made in U.S.A. by Knight's Mfg.Co.
Price: $1,650.00

STONER SR-25 MATCH RIFLE
Caliber: 7.62 NATO, 10-shot steel magazine, 5-shot optional. **Barrel:** 24" heavy match; 1:11.25" twist. **Weight:** 10.75 lbs. **Length:** 44" overall. **Stock:** Black synthetic AR-15A2 design. Full floating forend of mil-spec synthetic attaches to upper receiver at a single point. **Sights:** None furnished. Has integral Weaver-style rail. Rings and iron sights optional. **Features:** Improved AR-15 trigger, AR-15-style seven-lug rotating bolt. Introduced 1993. Made in U.S.A. by Knight's Mfg. Co.
Price: $3,345.00
Price: SR-25 Lightweight Match (20" medium match target
contour barrel, 9.5 lbs., 40" overall) $3,345.00

Includes a wide variety of sporting guns and guns suitable for various competitions.

Benelli Legacy

**Beretta AL391
Urika Gold Sporting**

AYA MODEL 4/53 SHOTGUNS
Gauge: 12, 16, 20, 28, 410. **Barrel:** 27" (28 and 410) or 28". **Weight:** To customer specifications. **Length:** To customer specifications. **Features:** Hammerless boxlock action; double triggers; light scroll engraving; automatic safety; straight grip oil finish walnut stock; checkered butt.
Price: **$2,795.00**

BENELLI LEGACY SHOTGUN
Gauge: 12, 20, 2-3/4" and 3" chamber. **Barrel:** 24", 26", 28" (Full, Mod., Imp. Cyl., Imp. Mod., cylinder choke tubes). Mid-bead sight. **Weight:** 5.8 to 7.4 lbs. **Length:** 49-5/8" overall (28" barrel). **Stock:** Select European walnut with satin finish. **Features:** Uses the rotating bolt inertia recoil operating system with a two-piece steel/aluminum etched receiver (bright on lower, blue upper). Drop adjustment kit allows the stock to be custom fitted without modifying the stock. Introduced 1998. Imported from Italy by Benelli USA, Corp.
Price: **$1,435.00**

Benelli Sport II Shotgun
Similar to the Legacy model except has dual tone blue/silver receiver, two carbon fiber interchangeable vent ribs, adjustable butt pad, adjustable buttstock, and functions with ultra-light target loads. Walnut stock with satin finish. Introduced 1997. Imported from Italy by Benelli USA.
Price: **$1,470.00**

BENELLI M2 FIELD SHOTGUNS
Gauge: 12 ga. **Barrel:** 21", 24", 26", 28". **Weight:** 6 lbs., 9 oz. to 7 lbs., 2 oz. **Length:** 14-3/8" overall. **Stock:** Synthetic, Advantage® Max-4 HD™, Advantage® Timber HD™. **Sights:** Red bar. **Features:** Uses the Inertia Driven™ bolt mechanism. Vent rib. Comes with set of five choke tubes. Imported from Italy by Benelli USA.
Price: Timber HD **$1,165.00**
Price: 24" rifled barrel Synthetic **$1,165.00**
Price: 24" rifled barrel Timber HD **$1,165.00**

BENELLI MONTEFELTRO SHOTGUNS
Gauge: 12 and 20 ga. Full, Imp. Mod, Mod., Imp. Cyl. choke tubes. **Barrel:** 24", 26", 28". **Weight:** 6.8 to 7.1 lbs. **Stock:** Checkered walnut with satin finish. **Length:** 14-3/8" overall. **Features:** Uses the Montefeltro rotating bolt system with a simple inertia recoil design. Finish is blue. Introduced 1987.
Price: 24", 26", 28" **$1,070.00**
Price: Left-hand, 26" **$1,080.00**
Price: Grade I, 26" **$1,070.00**
Price: Short stock model **$1,080.00**

BENELLI SUPER BLACK EAGLE II SHOTGUNS
Gauge: 12, 3-1/2" chamber. **Barrel:** 24", 26", 28" (Cyl. Imp. Cyl., Mod., Imp. Mod., Full choke tubes). **Weight:** 7 lbs., 5 oz. **Length:** 49-5/8" overall (28" barrel). **Stock:** European walnut with satin finish, or polymer. Adjustable for drop. **Sights:** Red bar front. **Features:** Uses Montefeltro inertia recoil bolt system. Fires all 12 gauge shells from 2-3/4" to 3-1/2" magnums, vent rib. Introduced 1991. Imported from Italy by Benelli USA.

Price: With 26" and 28" barrel, wood stock. **$1,400.00**
Price: Timber HD Camo 24", 26", 28" barrel **$1,455.00**
Price: With 24", 26" and 28" barrel, polymer stock **$1,335.00**
Price: Left-hand, 24", 26", 28", polymer stock **$1,455.00**
Price: Steadygrip Turkey Gun **$1,535.00**

Benelli Super Black Eagle Slug Guns
Similar to the Benelli Super Black Eagle except has 24" rifled barrel with 2-3/4" and 3" chamber, drilled and tapped for scope. Uses the inertia recoil bolt system. Matte finish receiver. Weight is 7.5 lbs., overall length 45.5". Wood or polymer stocks available. Introduced 1992. Imported from Italy by Benelli USA.
Price: With polymer stock **$1,465.00**
Price: 24" barrel, Timber HD camo **$1,585.00**
Price: W/ComforTech stock **$1,035.00**

BENELLI CORDOBA HIGH-VOLUME SHOTGUN
Gauge: 12; 5-round magazine. **Barrel:** 28" and 30", ported, 10mm sporting rib. **Weight:** 7.2 lbs. **Length:** 49.6". **Features:** Designed for high-volume sporting clays and Argentina dove shooting. Inertia-driven action, CrioChokes, ComfortTech stock reduces felt recoil by 49 percent.
Price: **$1,600.00**

BERETTA AL391 TEKNYS SHOTGUNS
Gauge: 12, 20 gauge; 3" chamber, semi-auto. **Barrel:** 26", 28". **Weight:** 5.9 lbs. (20 ga.), 7.3 lbs. (12 ga.). **Length:** NA. **Stock:** X-tra wood (special process wood enhancement). **Features:** Flat 1/4 rib, TruGlo Tru-Bead sight, recoil reducer, stock spacers, overbored bbls., flush choke tubes. Comes with fitted, lined case.
Price: **$1,295.00**
Price: Teknys Gold (green enamel inlays, oil-finished walnut) . . . **$1,595.00**
Price: Teknys Gold Sporting (blue inlays, select walnut) **$1,995.00**

BERETTA AL391 URIKA AUTO SHOTGUNS
Gauge: 12, 20 gauge; 3" chamber. **Barrel:** 22", 24", 26", 28", 30"; five Mobilchoke choke tubes. **Weight:** 5.95 to 7.28 lbs. **Length:** Varies by model. **Stock:** Walnut, black or camo synthetic; shims, spacers and interchangeable recoil pads allow custom fit. **Features:** Self-compensating gas operation handles full range of loads; recoil reducer in receiver; enlarged trigger guard; reduced-weight receiver, barrel and forend; hard-chromed bore. Introduced 2000. Imported from Italy by Beretta USA.
Price: AL391 Urika (12 ga., 26", 28", 30" barrels) **$1,095.00**
Price: AL391 Urika (20 ga., 24", 26", 28" barrels) **$1,095.00**
Price: AL391 Urika Synthetic
(12 ga., 24", 26", 28", 30" barrels) **$1,095.00**
Price: AL391 Urika Camo. (12 ga., Realtree Hardwoods
or Max 4-HD) **$1,195.00**

Beretta AL391 Urika Gold and Gold Sporting Auto Shotguns
Similar to AL391 Urika except features deluxe wood, jewelled bolt and carrier, gold-inlaid receiver with black or silver finish. Introduced 2000. Imported from Italy by Beretta USA.
Price: AL391 Urika Gold Sporting
(12 or 20, black receiver, engraving) **$1,395.00**
Price: AL391 Urika Gold Sporting
(12 ga., silver receiver, engraving **$1,395.00**

Beretta AL391 Urika Sporting

Beretta A391 Xtrema2 3.5

Browning
Gold Deer Hunter

Browning Gold Fusion

Beretta AL391 Urika Sporting Auto Shotguns
Similar to AL391 Urika except has competition sporting stock with rounded rubber recoil pad, wide vent rib with white front and mid-rib beads, satin-black receiver with silver markings. Available in 12 and 20 gauge. Introduced 2000. Imported from Italy by Beretta USA.
Price: AL391 Urika Sporting. $1,195.00

Beretta AL391 Urika Trap Auto Shotguns
Similar to AL391 Urika except in 12 ga. only, has wide vent rib with white front and mid-rib beads, Monte Carlo stock and special trap recoil pad. Gold Trap features highly figured walnut stock and forend, gold-filled Beretta logo and signature on receiver. Optima bore and Optima choke tubes. Introduced 2000. Imported from Italy by Beretta USA.
Price: AL391 Urika Trap $1,195.00

Beretta AL391 Urika Parallel Target RL and SL Auto Shotguns
Similar to AL391 Urika except has parallel comb, Monte Carlo stock with tighter grip radius and stepped vent rib. SL model has same features but with 13.5" length of pull stock. Introduced 2000. Imported from Italy by Beretta USA.
Price: AL391 Urika Parallel Target RL $1,195.00
Price: AL391 Urika Parallel Target SL $1,195.00

Beretta AL391 Urika Youth Shotgun
Similar to AL391 Urika except has a 24" or 26" barrel with 13.5" stock for youths and smaller shooters. Introduced 2000. From Beretta USA.
Price: $1,035.00

BERETTA A391 XTREMA2 3.5 AUTO SHOTGUNS
Gauge: 12 ga. 3-1/2" chamber. **Barrel:** 24", 26", 28". **Weight:** 7.8 lbs. **Stock:** Synthetic. **Features:** Semi-auto goes with two-lug rotating bolt and self-compensating gas valve, extended tang, cross bolt safety, self-cleaning, with case.
Price: Synthetic. $1,295.00
Price: Realtree Hardwood HD Camo and Max 4-HD $1,495.00

BROWNING GOLD HUNTER AUTO SHOTGUN
Gauge: 12, 3" or 3-1/2" chamber; 20, 3" chamber. **Barrel:** 12 ga.-26", 28", 30", Invector Plus choke tubes; 20 ga.-26", 30", Invector choke tubes. **Weight:** 7 lbs., 9 oz. (12 ga.), 6 lbs., 12 oz. (20 ga.). **Length:** 46-1/4" overall (20 ga., 26" barrel). **Stock:** 14"x1-1/2"x2-1/3"; select walnut with gloss finish; palm swell grip. **Features:** Self-regulating, self-cleaning gas system shoots all loads; lightweight receiver with special non-glare deep black finish; large reversible safety button; large rounded trigger guard, gold trigger. The 20 gauge has slightly smaller dimensions; 12 gauge have back-bored barrels, Invector Plus tube system. Introduced 1994. Imported by Browning.
Price: 12 or 20 gauge, 3" chamber. $894.00
Price: 12 ga., 3-1/2" chamber $1,038.00
Price: Extra barrels . . . . $336.00 to $415.00

Browning Gold Rifled Deer Hunter Auto Shotgun
Similar to the Gold Hunter except 12 or 20 gauge, 22" rifled barrel with cantilever scope mount, walnut stock with extra-thick recoil pad. Weighs 7 lbs., 12 oz., overall length 42-1/2". Sling swivel studs fitted on the magazine cap and butt. Introduced 1997. Imported by Browning.
Price: 12 gauge. $1,131.00
Price: With Mossy Oak® Break-up camouflage $1,218.00
Price: 20 ga. (satin-finish walnut stock, 3" chamber) $1,131.00

Browning Gold Deer Stalker Shotgun
Similar to the Gold Deer Hunter except has black composite stock and forend, fully rifled barrel, cantilever scope mount. Introduced 1999. Imported by Browning.
Price: 12 gauge $1,131.00

Browning Gold Fusion Auto Shotgun
Similar to the Gold Hunter, 12 and 20 gauge with 26", 28" or 30" barrel; front HiViz Pro-Comp and center bead on tapered vent rib; ported and back-bored Invector Plus barrel; 2-3/4" chamber; satin-finished stock with solid, radiused recoil pad with hard heel insert; non-glare black alloy receiver, shim-adj. stock. Introduced 1996. Imported from Japan by Browning.
Price: $2,095.00

Browning NWTF Mossy Oak® Break-Up™

Browning Gold Light 10 Gauge

Browning Gold Micro Auto Shotgun
Similar to the Gold Hunter except has a 26" barrel, 13-7/8" pull length and smaller pistol grip for youths and other small shooters. Weighs 6 lbs., 10 oz. Introduced 2001. From Browning.
Price: $1,329.00

Browning Gold Stalker Auto Shotgun
Similar to the Gold Hunter except has black composite stock and forend. Choice of 3" or 3-1/2" chamber.
Price: 12 ga. with 3" chamber $941.00
Price: With 3-1/2" chamber $1,148.00

Browning Gold Mossy Oak® Shadow Grass Shotgun
Similar to the Gold Hunter except 12 gauge only, completely covered with Mossy Oak® Shadow Grass camouflage. Choice of 3" or 3-1/2" chamber and 26" or 28" barrel. Introduced 1999. Imported by Browning.
Price: 12 ga. 3" chamber $1,127.00
Price: 12 ga., 3-1/2" chamber $1,332.00

Browning Gold Mossy Oak® Break-Up™ Shotguns
Similar to the Gold Hunter except 12 gauge only, completely covered with Mossy Oak® Break-Up™ camouflage. Imported by Browning.
Price: 3" chamber $1,202.00
Price: 3-1/2" chamber $1,332.00
Price: NWTF model, 3" chamber, 24" bbl. with HiViz sight $1,202.00
Price: NWTF model, 3-1/2" chamber, 24" bbl. with HiViz sight .. $1,440.00
Price: Gold Rifled Deer (22" rifled bbl., Cantilever scope mount) $1,218.00

Browning Gold Field Hunter Auto Shotgun
Similar to the Gold Hunter 3" except has semi-hump back receiver, magazine cut-off, adjustable comb, and satin-finish wood. Introduced 1999. Imported by Browning.
Price: 12 or 20 gauge $1,025.00

Browning Gold NWTF Turkey Series Camo Shotgun
Similar to the Gold Hunter except 10- or 12-gauge (3" or 3-1/2" chamber), 24" barrel with extra-full choke tube, HiViz fiber-optic sights and complete gun coverage in Mossy Oak® Break-Up™ camouflage with National Wild Turkey Federation logo on stock. Introduced 2001. From Browning.
Price: 10 gauge $738.00
Price: 12 gauge, 3-1/2" chamber Ultimate $1,440.00
Price: 12 gauge, 3" chamber $1,202.00

Browning Gold Upland Special Auto Shotgun
Similar to the Gold Hunter except has straight-grip walnut stock, 12 or 20 gauge, 3" chamber. Introduced 2001. From Browning
Price: 12-gauge model (24" bbl., weighs 7 lbs.) $1,025.00
Price: 20-gauge model (26" bbl., weighs 6 lbs., 12 oz.) $1,025.00

Browning Gold Light 10 Gauge Auto Shotgun
Similar to the Gold Hunter except has an alloy receiver that is 1 lb. lighter than standard model. Offered in 26" or 28" bbls. With Mossy Oak® Break-Up™ or Shadow Grass coverage; 5-shot magazine. Weighs 9 lbs., 10 oz. (28" bbl.). Introduced 2001. Imported by Browning.
Price: Camo model only $1,336.00

Browning Gold Evolve Shotgun
Similar to Gold Auto shotguns with new rib design, HiViz sights, three bbl. lengths (12 ga. only, 26", 28" or 30").
Price: $1,196.00

CHARLES DALY FIELD SEMI-AUTO SHOTGUNS
Gauge: 12, 20, 28. **Barrel:** 22", 24", 26", 28" or 30". **Stock:** Synthetic black, Realtree Hardwoods or Advantage Timber. **Features:** Interchangeable barrels handle all loads including steel shot. Slug model has adjustable sights.
Price: Field Hunter $389.00
Price: Field Hunter Advantage $459.00
Price: Field Hunter TImber $459.00
Price: Field Advantage Max $559.00

CHARLES DALY SUPERIOR II SEMI-AUTO SHOTGUNS
Gauge: 12, 20, 28. **Barrel:** 26", 28" or 30". **Stock:** Select Turkish walnut. **Features:** Factory ported interchangeable barrels; wide vent rib on Trap and Sport models; fluorescent red sights.
Price: Superior Hunter VR-MC $539.00
Price: Superior Sport $569.00
Price: Superior Trap $589.00

DIAMOND SEMI-AUTO SHOTGUNS
Gauge: 12 ga., 2-3/4" and 3" chambers. **Barrel:** 20" to 30". **Stock:** Walnut, synthetic. **Features:** One-piece receiver, rotary butt, gas ejection, high strength steel. Gold, Silver Marine, Elite and Panther series with vented barrels and all but Silver have 3 chokes. Slug guns available, all but Panther with sights. Imported from Istanbul by Adco Sales, Inc.
Price: Gold, 28", walnut................................. $549.00
Price: Gold, 28", synthetic $499.00
Price: Gold Slug, 24", w/sights walnut $549.00
Price: Gold Slug, 24", w/sights, synthetic $499.00
Price: Silver Mariner, 22", synthetic $499.00
Price: Silver Mariner, 20" slug w/sights, synthetic $479.00
Price: Elite, 22" Slug, 24"-28", walnut .... $429.00 to $449.00
Price: Panther, 22" slug; 26", 28", vent rib w/3 chokes,
synthetic .... $379.00 to $399.00
Price: Imperial 12, 20 ga., 24" slug w/sights, 26",
28" vent rib w/3 chokes, walnut .... $479.00 to $499.00
Price: Imperial, 12 ga., 28" vent rib w/3 chokes,
3.5" chamber, walnut $499.00

EAA/Baikal MP-153

Escort Model AS

Fabarm Gold Lion Mark III

Fabarm Sporting Clays Extra

EAA BAIKAL MP-153 AUTO SHOTGUNS
Gauge: 12, 3-1/2" chamber. **Barrel:** 24", 26", 28"; Imp., Mod. and Full choke tubes. **Weight:** 7.8 lbs. **Stock:** Walnut. **Features:** Gas-operated action with automatic gas-adjustment valve allows use of light and heavy loads interchangeably; 4-round magazine; rubber recoil pad. Introduced 2000. Imported by European American Armory.
Price: MP-153 (blued finish, walnut stock and forend) $459.00
Price: MP-153 (field grade, synthetic stock) $349.00

EAA SAIGA AUTO SHOTGUN
Gauge: 12, 20, .410, 3" chamber. **Barrel:** 19", 21", 24". **Weight:** 6.6 to 7.6 lbs. **Length:** 40" to 45". **Stock:** Synthetic. **Features:** Retains best features of the AK Rifle by Kalashnikov as the semi-auto shotgun. Magazine fed. Imported from Russia by EAA Corp.
Price: .410 ga. $299.00
Price: 20 ga. $389.00
Price: 12 ga. . . . . $409.00 to $439.00

ESCORT SEMI-AUTO SHOTGUNS
Gauge: 12, 20. **Barrel:** 22", 24", 26", 18" (AimGuard model); 3" chambers. **Weight:** 6 lbs, 4 0. to 7 lbs., 6 oz. **Stock:** Polymer, black, or camo finish; also Turkish walnut. **Features:** Black chrome finish; top of receiver dovetailed for sight mounting. Gold-plated trigger, trigger guard safety, magazine cut-off. Three choke tubes (IC, M, F — except AimGuard); 24" bbl. model comes with turkey choke tube. **Sights:** Optional HiViz Spark and TriViz fiber-optic sights. Introduced 2002. Camo model introduced 2003. Youth, Slug, Obsession Camo models introduced 2005. Imported from Turkey by Legacy Sports International.
Price: Model AS, walnut stock. $421.00
Price: Model PS, black polymer stock $399.00
Price: Camo polymer stock, Spark sight $443.00
Price: Camo, 24" bbl; 3.5 mag.; TriViz sight, turkey choke $523.00
Price: AimGuard, 18" bbl., black stock, cyl bore $392.00
Price: Waterfowl/turkey combo, camo, 2 bbls $574.00

FABARM GOLD LION MARK III AUTO SHOTGUN
Gauge: 12, 3" chamber. **Barrel:** 24", 26", 28", choke tubes. **Weight:** 7 lbs. **Length:** 45.5" overall. **Stock:** European walnut with gloss finish; olive wood grip cap. **Features:** TriBore barrel, reversible safety; gold-plated trigger and carrier release button; leather-covered rubber recoil pad. Introduced 1998. Imported from Italy by Heckler & Koch, Inc.
Price: $939.00

Fabarm Sporting Clays Extra Auto Shotgun
Similar to Gold Lion except 28" TriBore ported barrel with interchangeable colored front-sight beads, mid-rib bead, 10mm channeled vent rib, carbon-fiber finish, oil-finished walnut stock and forend with olive wood gripcap. Stock dimensions are 14.58"x1.58"x2.44". Distinctive gold-colored receiver logo. Available in 12 gauge only, 3" chamber. Introduced 1999. Imported from Italy by Heckler & Koch, Inc.
Price: $1,249.00

FRANCHI 48AL SHOTGUN
Gauge: 20 or 28, 2-3/4" chamber. **Barrel:** 24", 26", 28" (Full, Cyl., Mod., choke tubes). **Weight:** 5.5 lbs. (20 gauge). **Length:** 44" to 48". **Stock:** 14-1/4"x1-5/8"x2-1/2". Walnut with checkered grip and forend. **Features:** Long recoil-operated action. Chrome-lined bore; cross-bolt safety. Imported from Italy by Benelli USA.
Price: 20 ga. $735.00
Price: 28 ga. $1,020.00

Franchi 48AL Deluxe Shotgun
Similar to 48AL but with select walnut stock and forend and high-polish blue finish with gold trigger. Introduced 2000.
Price: (20 gauge, 26" barrel) $970.00
Price: (28 gauge, 26" barrel) $990.00

Franchi 48AL English Shotgun
Similar to 48AL Deluxe but with straight grip English-style stock. 20 ga., 28 ga., 26" bbl, ICMF tubes.
Price: 20 gauge $970.00
Price: 28 gauge $1,020.00

Franchi 48AL Short Stock Shotgun
Similar to 48AL but with stock shortened to 12-1/2" length of pull.
Price: (20 gauge, 26" barrel) $735.00

FRANCHI MODEL 912 SHOTGUNS
Gauge: 12. **Barrel:** 24", 26", 28", 30". **Weight:** 7.5 to 7.8 lbs. **Length:** 46" to 52". **Stock:** Satin walnut; synthetic. **Sights:** White bead front. **Features:** Chambered for 3-1/2" magnum shells with Dual-Recoil-Reduction-System, multi-lugged rotary bolt. Made in Italy and imported by Benelli USA.
Price: Walnut $850.00
Price: Synthetic $790.00
Price: Timber HD & Max-4 . . . . $900.00
Price: Steadygrip Timber HD $850.00

Remington Model 11-87 Premier

Remington Model 11-87 Dale Earnhardt Tribute

Remington Model 11-87 Special Purpose Magnum

Remington Model 11-87 SPS Camo

Remington Model 11-87 SPS-T Turkey Camo

FRANCHI RAPTOR SPORTING CLAYS SHOTGUN
Gauge: 12 and 20; 6-round capacity. **Barrel:** 30" (12 ga.) or 28" (20 ga.); ported; tapered target rib and bead front sight. **Weight:** 7.1 lbs. (Model 712) or 6.2 lbs. (Model 720). **Stock:** Walnut with WeatherCoat (impervious to weather). **Features:** Gas-operated, satin nickel receiver.
Price: **$850.00**

REMINGTON MODEL 11-87 PREMIER SHOTGUNS
Gauge: 12, 20, 3" chamber. **Barrel:** 26", 28", 30" RemChoke tubes. Light Contour barrel. **Weight:** About 7-3/4 lbs. **Length:** 46" overall (26" bbl.). **Stock:** Walnut with satin or high-gloss finish; cut checkering; solid brown buttpad; no white spacers. **Sights:** Bradley-type white-faced front, metal bead middle. **Features:** Pressure compensating gas system allows shooting 2-3/4" or 3" loads interchangeably with no adjustments. Stainless magazine tube; redesigned feed latch, barrel support ring on operating bars; pinned forend. Introduced 1987.
Price: Light contour barrel **$777.00**
Price: Left-hand, 28" barrel **$831.00**
Price: Premier cantilever deer barrel, fully-rifled, 21" sling, swivels,
Monte Carlo stock **$859.00**
Price: 3-1/2" Super Magnum, 28" barrel **$865.00**
Price: Dale Earnhardt Tribute, 12 ga., 28" barrel **$972.00**

Remington Model 11-87 Special Purpose Magnum
Similar to the 11-87 Premier except has dull stock finish, Parkerized exposed metal surfaces. Bolt and carrier have dull blackened coloring. Comes with 26" or 28" barrel with RemChokes, padded Cordura nylon sling and quick detachable swivels. Introduced 1987.
Price: With synthetic stock and forend (SPS) **$791.00**

Remington Model 11-87 SPS Special Purpose Synthetic Camo
Similar to the 11-87 Special Purpose Magnum except has synthetic stock and all metal (except bolt and trigger guard) and stock covered with Mossy Oak® Break-Up™ camo finish. In 12 gauge only, 26", RemChoke. Comes with camo sling, swivels. Introduced 1992.
Price: **$925.00**

Remington Model 11-87 SPS-T Turkey Camo
Similar to the 11-87 Special Purpose Magnum except with synthetic stock, 21" vent rib barrel with RemChoke tube. Completely covered with Mossy Oak® Break-Up™ Brown camouflage. Bolt body, trigger guard and recoil pad are non-reflective black.
Price: **$905.00**
Price: Model 11-87 SPS-T Camo CL cantilever **$907.00**

Remington Model 11-87
SPS-T Synthetic Camo

Remington Model 11-87 SPS-Deer

Remington Model 11-87 SPS Cantilever

Remington Model 11-87 SP

Remington Model 11-87 SPS-T Super Magnum Synthetic Camo Shotguns
Similar to the 11-87 SPS-T Turkey Camo except has 23" vent rib barrel with Turkey Super full choke tube, chambered for 12 ga., 3-1/2", TruGlo rifle sights. Version available without TruGlo sights. Introduced 2001.
Price: **$963.00**

Remington Model 11-87 SPS-Deer Shotgun
Similar to the 11-87 Special Purpose Camo except has fully-rifled 21" barrel with rifle sights, black non-reflective, synthetic stock and forend, black carrying sling. Introduced 1993.
Price: **$824.00**
Price: With wood stock (Model 11-87 SP Deer Gun) RemChoke, 21" barrel w/rifle sights **$756.00**

Remington Model 11-87 SPS Cantilever Shotgun
Similar to the 11-87 SPS except has fully rifled barrel; synthetic stock with Monte Carlo comb; cantilever scope mount deer barrel. Comes with sling and swivels. Introduced 1994.
Price: **$872.00**

Remington Model 11-87 SP and SPS Super Magnum Shotguns
Similar to Model 11-87 Special Purpose Magnum except has 3-1/2" chamber. Available in flat finish American walnut or black synthetic stock,

26" or 28" black matte finished barrel and receiver; Imp. Cyl., Modified and Full RemChoke tubes. Overall length 45-3/4", weighs 8 lbs., 2 oz. Introduced 2000. From Remington Arms Co.
Price: 11-87 SP Super Magnum (walnut stock) **$865.00**
Price: 11-87 SPS Super Magnum (synthetic stock) **$879.00**
Price: 11-87 SPS Super Magnum, 28" (camo) **$963.00**

Remington Model 11-87 Upland Special Shotgun
Similar to 11-87 Premier except has 23" vent rib barrel with straight grip, English-style walnut stock. Available in 12 or 20 gauge. Overall length 43-1/2", weighs 7-1/4 lbs. (6-1/2 lbs. in 20 ga.). Comes with Imp. Cyl., Modified and Full choke tubes. Introduced 2000.
Price: 12 or 20 gauge **$777.00**

REMINGTON MODEL 1100 SYNTHETIC LT-20 SHOTGUN
Gauge: 20. **Barrel:** 26" RemChokes. **Weight:** 6-3/4 lbs. **Stock:** 14"x1-1/2"x2-1/2". Black synthetic, checkered pistol grip and forend. **Features:** Matted receiver top with scroll work on both sides of receiver.
Price: **$549.00**
Price: Youth Gun LT-20 (21" RemChoke) **$549.00**
Price: Remington Model 1100 Synthetic, 12 gauge, black synthetic stock; vent rib 28" barrel, Mod. RemChoke tube. Weighs about 7-1/2 lbs. Introduced 1996 . . . . **$549.00**

Remington Model 1100 Youth Turkey Camo

Remington 1100 LT-20 Deer

Remington Model 1100 Sporting 28

Remington Model 1100 Classic Trap

Remington Model 1100 Sporting 12

Remington Model SP-10

Remington Model 1100 Youth Synthetic Turkey Camo Shotgun
Similar to the Model 1100 LT-20 except has 1" shorter stock, 21" vent rib barrel with Full RemChoke tube; 3" chamber; synthetic stock and forend are covered with Skyline Excel camo, and barrel and receiver have non-reflective, black matte finish. Introduced 2003.
Price: **$612.00**

Remington Model 1100 LT-20 Synthetic Deer Shotgun
Similar to the Model 1100 LT-20 except has 21" fully rifled barrel with rifle sights, 2-3/4" chamber, and fiberglass reinforced synthetic stock. Introduced 1997. Made in U.S. by Remington.
Price: **$583.00**

Remington Model 1100 Sporting 28 Shotgun
Similar to the 1100 LT-20 except in 28 gauge with 25" barrel; comes with skeet, Imp. Cyl., Light Mod., Mod. RemChoke tube. Semi-fancy walnut with gloss finish, Sporting rubber butt pad. Made in U.S. by Remington. Introduced 1996.
Price: **$901.00**

Remington Model 1100 Sporting 20 Shotgun
Similar to Model 1100 LT-20 except tournament-grade American walnut stock with gloss finish and sporting style recoil pad, 28" RemChoke barrel for skeet, Imp. Cyl., Light Modified and Modified. Introduced 1998.
Price: **$868.00**

Remington Model 1100 Classic Trap Shotgun
Similar to Standard Model 1100 except 12 gauge with 30", low-profile barrel, semi-fancy American walnut stock, high-polish blued receiver with engraving and gold eagle inlay. Singles, mid handicap and long handicap choke tubes. Overall length 50-1/2", weighs 8 lbs., 4 oz. Introduced 2000. From Remington Arms Co.
Price: **$895.00**

Remington Model 1100 Sporting 12 Shotgun
Similar to Model 1100 Sporting 20 Shotgun except in 12 gauge, 28" ventilated barrel with semi-fancy American walnut stock, gold-plated trigger. Overall length 49", weighs 8 lbs. Introduced 2000. From Remington Arms Co.
Price: **$901.00**

Remington Model SP-10 Camo

Stoeger Model 2000

Tristar CD Diana

Traditions ALS 2100

Remington Model 1100 Synthetic Deer Shotgun

Similar to Model 1100 LT-20 except 12 gauge, 21" fully rifled barrel with cantilever scope mount and fiberglass-reinforced synthetic stock with Monte Carlo comb. Introduced 1997. Made in U.S. by Remington Arms Co.

Price: **$629.00**

REMINGTON MODEL SP-10 MAGNUM SHOTGUN

Gauge: 10, 3-1/2" chamber, 2-shot magazine. **Barrel:** 26", 30" (full and mod. RemChokes). **Weight:** 10-3/4 to 11 lbs. **Length:** 47-1/2" overall (26" barrel). **Stock:** Walnut with satin finish or black synthetic with 26" barrel. Checkered grip and forend. **Sights:** Twin bead. **Features:** Stainless steel gas system with moving cylinder; 3/8" vent rib. Receiver and barrel have matte finish. Brown recoil pad. Comes with padded Cordura nylon sling. Introduced 1989.

Price: **$1,317.00**

Remington Model SP-10 Magnum Camo Shotgun

Similar to SP-10 Magnum except buttstock, forend, receiver, barrel and magazine cap are covered with Mossy Oak® Break-Up™ camo finish; bolt body and trigger guard have matte black finish. RemChoke tube, 26" vent rib barrel with mid-rib bead and Bradley-style front sight, swivel studs and quick-detachable swivels, non-slip Cordura carrying sling in same camo pattern. Introduced 1993.

Price: **$1,453.00**

SARSILMAZ SEMI-AUTOMATIC SHOTGUN

Gauge: 12, 3" chamber. **Barrel:** 26" or 28"; fixed chokes. **Stock:** Walnut or synthetic. **Features:** Handles 2-3/4" or 3" magnum loads. Introduced 2000. Imported from Turkey by Armsport Inc.

Price: With walnut stock. **$969.95**
Price: With synthetic stock **$919.95**

STOEGER MODEL 2000 SHOTGUNS

Gauge: 12, 3" chamber, set of five choke tubes. **Barrel:** 24", 26", 28", 30". **Stock:** Walnut, deluxe, synthetic, and Timber HD. **Sights:** White bar.

Features: Inertia-recoil for light target to turkey loads. Single trigger combo 26"/24" pack with optional 24" slug barrel.

Price: Walnut, 26", 28", 30" bbl. **$475.00**
Price: Synthetic, 24", 26", 28" bbl. **$400.00**
Price: Timber HD, 24", 26", 28" bbl. **$475.00**
Price: Slug model **$589.00**

STOEGER P-350 PUMP SHOTGUN

Gauge: 12. **Barrel:** 18.5" to 28". **Weight:** 6.4 to 6.9 lbs. **Features:** Synthethic, Timber HD or Max-4 stock; extended turkey choke available.

Price: . . . . **$269.00 to $329.00**

TRADITIONS ALS 2100 SERIES SEMI-AUTOMATIC SHOTGUNS

Gauge: 12, 3" chamber; 20, 3" chamber. **Barrel:** 24", 26", 28" (Imp. Cyl., Mod. and Full choke tubes). **Weight:** 5 lbs., 10 oz. to 6 lbs., 5 oz. **Length:** 44" to 48" overall. **Stock:** Walnut or black composite. **Features:** Gas-operated; vent rib barrel with Beretta-style threaded muzzle. Introduced 2001 by Traditions.

Price: Field Model (12 or 20 ga., 26" or 28" bbl., walnut stock) **$479.00**
Price: Youth Model (12 or 20 ga., 24" bbl., walnut stock) **$479.00**
Price: (12 or 20 ga., 26" or 28" barrel, composite stock) **$459.00**

Traditions ALS 2100 Turkey Semi-Automatic Shotgun

Similar to ALS 2100 Field Model except chambered in 12 gauge, 3" only with 26" barrel and Mossy Oak® Break Up™ camo finish. Weighs 6 lbs.; 46" overall.

Price: **$519.00**

Traditions ALS 2100 Waterfowl Semi-Automatic Shotgun

Similar to ALS 2100 Field Model except chambered in 12 gauge, 3" only with 28" barrel and Advantage® Wetlands™ camo finish. Weighs 6.25 lbs.; 48" overall. Multi chokes.

Price: **$529.00**

Traditions ALS 2100 Hunter Combo

Similar to ALS 2100 Field Model except 2 barrels, 28" vent rib and 24" fully rifled deer. Weighs 6 to 6.5 lbs.; 48" overall. Choice TruGlo adj. sights or fixed cantilever mount on rifled barrel. Multi chokes.

Price: Walnut, rifle barrel **$609.00**
Price: Walnut, cantilever **$629.00**
Price: Synthetic **$579.00**

Weatherby SAS Field

Weatherby SAS Slug

Winchester X2 NWTF Turkey

Winchester Super X2 Sporting Clays

Winchester Super X2 Field

Traditions ALS 2100 Slug Hunter Shotgun

Similar to ALS 2100 Field Model, 12 ga., 24" barrel, overall length 44"; weighs 6.25 lbs. Designed specifically for the deer hunter. Rifled barrel has 1 in 36" twist. Fully adjustable fiber-optic sights.

Price: Walnut, rifle barrel **$529.00**
Price: Synthetic, rifle barrel **$499.00**
Price: Walnut, cantilever **$549.00**
Price: Synthetic, cantilever **$529.00**

Traditions ALS 2100 Home Security Shotgun

Similar to ALS 2100 Field Model, 12 ga., 20" barrel, overall length 40", weighs 6 lbs. Can be reloaded with one hand while shouldered and on-target. Swivel studs installed in stock.

Price: **$399.00**

TRISTAR CD DIANA AUTO SHOTGUNS

Gauge: 12, shoots 2-3/4" or 3" interchangeably. **Barrel:** 24", 26", 28" (Imp. Cyl., Mod., Full choke tubes). **Stock:** European walnut or black synthetic. **Features:** Gas-operated action; blued barrel; checkered pistol grip and forend; vent rib barrel. Available with synthetic and camo stock and in slug model. First introduced 1999 under the name "Tristar Phantom." Imported by Tristar Sporting Arms Ltd.

Price: . . . . **$399.00 to $535.00**

VERONA MODEL SX400 SEMI AUTO SHOTGUNS

Gauge: 12. **Barrel:** 26", 30". **Weight:** 6-1/2 lbs. **Stock:** Walnut, black composite. **Sights:** Red dot. **Features:** Aluminum receivers, gas-operated, 2-3/4" or 3" Magnum shells without adj. or Mod., 4 screw-in chokes and wrench included. Sling swivels, gold trigger. Blued barrel. Imported from Italy by B.C. Outdoors.

Price: 401S, 12 ga. **$398.40**
Price: 405SDS, 12 ga. **$610.00**
Price: 405L, 12 ga. **$331.20**

WEATHERBY SAS (SEMI-AUTOMATIC SHOTGUNS)

Gauge: 12 ga. **Barrel:** Vent ribbed, 24" to 30". **Weight:** 7 lbs. to 7-3/4 lbs. **Stock:** SAS field and sporting clays, walnut. SAS Shadow Grass, Break-Up™, Synthetic, composite. **Sights:** SAS sporting clays, brass front and mid-point rear. SAS Shadow Grass and Break-Up™, HiViz front and brass mid. Synthetic has brass front. **Features:** Easy to shoot, load, clean; lightweight, reduced recoil, IMC system includes 3 chrome-moly screw-in choke tubes. Slug gun has 22" rifled barrel with matte blue finish and cantilever base for scope mounting.

Price: Field, Sporting Clays, Shadow Grass, Break-Up™,
Synthetic, Slug Gun . . . . **$699.00 to $849.00**

WINCHESTER SUPER X2 AUTO SHOTGUNS

Gauge: 12, 3", 3-1/2" chamber. **Barrel:** Belgian, 24", 26", 28"; Invector Plus choke tubes. **Weight:** 7-1/4 to 7-1/2 lbs. **Stock:** 14-1/4"x1-3/4"x2". Walnut or black synthetic. **Features:** Gas-operated action shoots all loads without adjustment; vent rib barrels; 4-shot magazine. Introduced 1999. Assembled in Portugal by U.S. Repeating Arms Co.

Price: Magnum, 3-1/2", synthetic stock, 26" or 28" bbl. **$1,185.00**
Price: Camo Waterfowl, 3-1/2", Mossy Oak® Shadow Grass **$1,185.00**
Price: NWTF Turkey, 3-1/2", Mossy Oak® Break-Up™ camo **$1,236.00**
Price: Universal Hunter Model **$1,252.00**

Winchester Super X2 Sporting Clays Auto Shotguns

Similar to the Super X2 except has two gas pistons (one for target loads, one for heavy 3" loads), adjustable comb system and high-post rib. Back-bored barrel with Invector Plus choke tubes. Offered in 28" and 30" barrels. Introduced 2001. From U.S. Repeating Arms Co.

Price: Super X2 sporting clays **$1,015.00**
Price: Signature red stock **$976.00**

Winchester Super X2 Field 3" Auto Shotgun

Similar to the Super X2 except 3" chamber, walnut stock and forearm and high-profile rib. Back-bored barrel and Invector Plus choke tubes. Introduced 2001. From U.S. Repeating Arms Co.

Price: Super X2 Field 3", 26" or 28" bbl. **$1,015.00**

Includes a wide variety of sporting guns and guns suitable for competitive shooting.

Benelli Nova Pump

Benelli Nova Pump Slug

Browning BPS 10 gauge

Browning BPS 10 gauge Mossy Oak® Shadow Grass

BENELLI NOVA PUMP SHOTGUNS
Gauge: 12, 20. **Barrel:** 24", 26", 28". **Stock:** Synthetic, Max-4 and Timber H-D (12 ga. and 20 ga). **Sights:** Red bar. **Features:** 2-3/4", 3" chamber (3-1/2" 12 ga. only). Montefeltro rotating bolt design with dual action bars, magazine cut-off, synthetic trigger assembly, 4-shot magazine. Introduced 1999. Imported from Italy by Benelli USA.
Price: Synthetic **$350.00**
Price: Timber HD **$435.00**
Price: Max-4 . . . . **$425.00**
Price: Youth Model **$440.00**

Benelli Nova Pump Tactical Shotgun
Similar to the Nova except has 18.5" barrel with adjustable rifle-type or ghost ring sights; weighs 7.2 lbs.; black synthetic stock. Introduced 1999. Imported from Italy by Benelli USA.
Price: With rifle sights **$315.00**
Price: With ghost-ring sights **$350.00**

Benelli Nova Pump Rifled Slug Gun
Similar to Nova Pump Slug Gun except has 24" barrel and rifled bore; open rifle sights; synthetic stock; weighs 8.1 lbs.
Price: Synthetic **$525.00**
Price: Timber HD **$600.00**
Price: Field/Slug combo, synthetic **$545.00**

BROWNING BPS PUMP SHOTGUNS
Gauge: 10, 12, 3-1/2" chamber; 12 or 20, 3" chamber (2-3/4" in target guns), 28, 2-3/4" chamber, 5-shot magazine, .410, 3" chamber. **Barrel:** 10 ga.-24" Buck Special, 28", 30", 32" Invector, 12, 20 ga.-22", 24", 26", 28", 30", 32" (Imp. Cyl., Mod. or Full), .410-26" barrel. (Imp. Cyl., Mod. and Full choke tubes.) Also available with Invector choke tubes, 12 or 20 ga.; Upland Special has 22" barrel with Invector tubes. BPS 3" and 3-1/2" have back-bored barrel. **Weight:** 7 lbs., 8 oz. (28" barrel). **Length:** 48-3/4" overall (28" barrel). **Stock:** 14-1/4"x1-1/2"x2-1/2". Select walnut, semi-beavertail forend, full pistol grip stock. **Features:** All 12 gauge 3" guns except Buck Special and game guns have back-bored barrels with Invector Plus choke tubes. Bottom feeding and ejection, receiver top safety, high post vent rib. Double action bars eliminate binding. Vent rib barrels only. All 12 and 20 gauge guns with 3" chamber available with fully engraved receiver flats at no extra cost. Each gauge has its own unique game scene. Introduced 1977. Imported from Japan by Browning.
Price: 12 ga., 3-1/2" Magnum Stalker (black syn. stock) **$688.00**
Price: 12, 20 ga., Hunter, Invector Plus **$509.00**
Price: 12 ga. Deer Hunter (22" rifled bbl., cantilever mount) **$624.00**
Price: 28 ga., Hunter, Invector **$544.00**
Price: .410, Hunter, Invector **$544.00**

Browning BPS 10 Gauge Camo Pump Shotgun
Similar to the standard BPS except completely covered with Mossy Oak® Shadow Grass camouflage. Available with 24", 26", 28" barrel. Introduced 1999. Imported by Browning.
Price: **$688.00**

Browning BPS Waterfowl Camo Pump Shotgun
Similar to the standard BPS except completely covered with Mossy Oak® Shadow Grass camouflage. Available in 12 gauge, with 24", 26" or 28" barrel, 3" chamber. Introduced 1999. Imported by Browning.
Price: **$688.00**

Browning BPS Game Gun Deer Hunter
Similar to the standard BPS except has newly designed receiver/magazine tube/barrel mounting system to eliminate play, heavy 20.5" barrel with rifle-type sights with adjustable rear, solid receiver scope mount, "rifle" stock dimensions for scope or open sights, sling swivel studs. Gloss or matte finished wood with checkering, polished blue metal. Introduced 1992.
Price: **$624.00**

Browning BPS Game Gun Turkey Special
Similar to the standard BPS except has satin-finished walnut stock and dull-finished barrel and receiver. Receiver is drilled and tapped for scope mounting. Rifle-style stock dimensions and swivel studs. Has Extra-Full Turkey choke tube. Introduced 1992.
Price: **$605.00**

EAA Baikal MP-133

Escort AimGuard

Escort Field Hunter

Price: Field Hunter **$469.00**
Price: Field Hunter Advantage **$539.00**
Price: Field Hunter Hardwoods **$539.00**
Price: Field Hunter Turkey **$609.00**

Browning BPS Stalker Pump Shotgun
Same gun as the standard BPS except all exposed metal parts have a matte blued finish and the stock has a durable black finish with a black recoil pad. Available in 10 ga. (3-1/2") and 12 ga. with 3" or 3-1/2" chamber, 22", 28", 30" barrel with Invector choke system. Introduced 1987.
Price: 12 ga., 3" chamber, Invector Plus $492.00
Price: 10, 12 ga., 3-1/2" chamber $579.00

Browning BPS NWTF Turkey Series Pump Shotgun
Similar to the BPS Stalker except has full coverage Mossy Oak® Break-Up™ camo finish on synthetic stock, forearm and exposed metal parts. Offered in 10 and 12 gauge, 3" or 3-1/2" chamber; 24" bbl. has extra-full choke tube and HiViz fiber-optic sights. Introduced 2001. From Browning.
Price: 10 ga., 3-1/2" chamber **$738.00**
Price: 12 ga., 3-1/2" chamber **$674.00**
Price: 12 ga., 3" chamber **$738.00**

Browning BPS Micro Pump Shotgun
Similar to the BPS Stalker except 20 ga. only, 22" Invector barrel, stock has pistol grip with recoil pad. Length of pull is 13-1/4"; weighs 6 lbs., 12 oz. Introduced 1986.
Price: **$509.00**

CHARLES DALY FIELD PUMP SHOTGUNS
Gauge: 12, 20. **Barrel:** Interchangeable 18-1/2", 24", 26", 28", 30" multi-choked. **Weight:** NA. **Stock:** Synthetic, various finishes, recoil pad. **Receiver:** Machined aluminum. **Features:** Field Tactical and Slug models come with adustable sights; Youth models may be upgraded to full size. Imported from Akkar, Turkey.
Price: Field Tactical $199.00
Price: Field Hunter $289.00
Price: Field Hunter, Realtree Hardwood $289.00
Price: Field Hunter Advantage $289.00

CHARLES DALY MAXI-MAG PUMP SHOTGUNS
Gauge: 12 gauge, 3-1/2". **Barrel:** 24", 26", 28"; multi-choke system. **Weight:** NA. **Stock:** Synthetic black, Realtree Hardwoods, or Advantage Timber receiver, aluminum alloy. **Features:** Handles 2-3/4", 3" and 3-1/2" loads. Interchangeable ported barrels; Turkey package includes sling, HiViz sights, XX Full choke. Imported from Akkar, Turkey.

DIAMOND 12 GA. PUMP SHOTGUNS
Gauge: 12, 2-3/4" and 3" chambers. **Barrel:** 18"-30". **Weight:** 7 lbs. **Stock:** Walnut, synthetic. **Features:** Aluminum one-piece receiver sculpted for lighter weight. Double locking on fixed bolt. Gold, Elite and Panther series with vented barrels and 3 chokes. All series slug guns available (Gold and Elite with sights). Imported from Istanbul by ADCO Sales.
Price: Gold, 28" vent rib w/3 chokes, walnut **$359.00**
Price: Gold, 28", synthetic **$329.00**
Price: Gold Slug, 24" w/sights, walnut or synthetic . . . **$329.00 to $359.00**
Price: Silver Mariner 18.5" Slug, synthetic **$399.00**
Price: Silver Mariner 22" vent rib w/3 chokes **$419.00**
Price: Elite, 22" slug w/sights; 24", 28" vent rib w/3 chokes,
walnut . . . . $329.00 to $349.00
Price: Panther, 28", 30" vent rib w/3 chokes, synthetic **$279.00**
Price: Panther,18.5", 22" Slug, synthetic . . . . **$209.00 to $265.00**
Price: Imperial 12 ga., 28" vent rib w/3 chokes, 3.5" chamber,
walnut **$399.00**

EAA BAIKAL MP-133 PUMP SHOTGUN
Gauge: 12, 3-1/2" chamber. **Barrel:** 18-1/2", 20", 24", 26", 28"; Imp., Mod. and Full choke tubes. **Weight:** NA. **Stock:** Walnut; checkered grip and grooved forearm. **Features:** Hammer-forged, chrome-lined barrel with vent rib; machined steel parts; dual action bars; trigger-block safety; 4-shot magazine tube; handles 2-3/4" through 3-1/2" shells. Introduced 2000. Imported by European American Armory.
Price: MP-133 (blued finish, walnut stock and forend) **$359.00**

ESCORT PUMP SHOTGUNS
Gauge: 12, 20; 3" chamber. **Barrel:** 18" (AimGuard model); 22" (FH Slug model), 24", 26" and 28" (Field Hunter models), choke tubes (M, IC, F); turkey choke w/24" bbl. **Weight:** 6.4 to 7 lbs. **Stock:** Polymer, black chrome or camo finish. **Features:** Alloy receiver w/dovetail for sight mounting. Two stock adjusting spacers included. Introduced 2003. From Legacy Sports International.
Price: Field Hunter, black stock **$247.00**
Price: Field Hunter, camo stock **$812.00**
Price: Camo, 24" bbl. **$363.00**
Price: AimGuard, 20" bbl., black stock **$211.00**
Price: MarineGuard, nickel finish **$254.00**
Price: Combo (2 bbls.) **$270.00**

Fabarm Field Pump

Ithaca Model 37 Waterfowl

Ithaca Model 37 Deerslayer II

Mossberg Model 835 Mossy Oak Camo

FABARM FIELD PUMP SHOTGUN
Gauge: 12, 3" chamber. **Barrel:** 28" (24" rifled slug barrel available). **Weight:** 76.6 lbs. **Length:** 48.25" overall. **Stock:** Polymer. **Features:** Similar to Fabarm FP6 Pump Shotgun. Alloy receiver; twin action bars; available in black or Mossy Oak® Break-Up™ camo finish. Includes Cyl., Mod. and Full choke tubes. Introduced 2001. Imported from Italy by Heckler & Koch Inc.
Price: Matte black finish... $399.00
Price: Mossy Oak® Break-Up™ finish $469.00

ITHACA MODEL 37 DELUXE PUMP SHOTGUNS
Gauge: 12, 16, 20, 3" chamber. **Barrel:** 26", 28", 30" (12 gauge), 26", 28" (16 and 20 gauge), choke tubes. **Weight:** 7 lbs. **Stock:** Walnut with cut-checkered grip and forend. **Features:** Steel receiver; bottom ejection; brushed blue finish, vent rib barrels. Reintroduced 1996. Made in U.S. by Ithaca Gun Co.
Price:... $633.00
Price: With straight English-style stock $803.00
Price: Model 37 New Classic (ringtail forend, sunburst recoil pad, hand-finished walnut stock, 26" or 28" barrel) $803.00

Ithaca Model 37 Waterfowl Shotgun
Similar to Model 37 Deluxe except in 12 gauge only with 24", 26", or 30" barrel, special extended steel shot choke tube system. Complete coverage in Advantage Wetlands or Hardwoods camouflage. Storm models have synthetic stock. Introduced 1999. Made in U.S. by Ithaca Gun Co.
Price:....................................... $499.00 to $549.00

ITHACA MODEL 37 ULTRALIGHT DELUXE SHOTGUNS
Gauge: 16 ga. 2-3/4" chamber. **Barrel:** 24", 26", 28". **Weight:** 5.25 lbs. **Stock:** Standard deluxe. **Sights:** Raybar. **Features:** Vent rib, drilled and tapped, interchangeable barrel. F, M, IC choke tubes.
Price: Deluxe $649.00
Price: Classic/English $824.00
Price: Classic/Pistol $824.00

ITHACA MODEL 37 DEERSLAYER II PUMP SHOTGUNS
Gauge: 12, 16, 20; 3" chamber. **Barrel:** 24", 26", fully rifled. **Weight:** 11 lbs. **Stock:** Cut-checkered American walnut with Monte Carlo comb. **Sights:** Rifle-type. **Features:** Integral barrel and receiver. Bottom ejection. Brushed blue finish. Introduced 1999. Made in U.S. by Ithaca Gun Co. Reintroduced 1997. Made in U.S. by Ithaca Gun Co.
Price:... $633.00
Price: Smooth Bore Deluxe $582.00

Price: Rifled Deluxe $582.00
Price: Storm $399.00

ITHACA MODEL 37 DEERSLAYER III PUMP SHOTGUN
Gauge: 12, 20, 2-3/4" and 3" chambers. **Barrel:** 26" free floated. **Weight:** 9 lbs. **Stock:** Monte Carlo laminate. **Sights:** Rifled. **Features:** Barrel length gives increased velocity. Trigger and sear set hand filed and stoned for creep-free operation. Weaver-style scope base. Swivel studs. Matte blue. Made in U.S. by Ithaca Gun Co.
Price:.................................... **Custom order only**

ITHACA MODEL 37 RUFFED GROUSE SPECIAL EDITION SHOTGUN
Gauge: 20 ga. **Barrel:** 22", 24", interchangeable choke tubes. **Weight:** 5.25 lbs. **Stock:** American black walnut. **Features:** Laser engraved stock with line art drawing. Bottom eject. Vent rib and English style. Right- or left-hand through simple safety change. Aluminum receiver. Made in U.S.A. by Ithaca Gun Co.
Price:... $840.00

ITHACA TURKEYSLAYER STORM SHOTGUN
Gauge: 12 or 20 ga., 3" chamber. **Barrel:** 24" ported. **Stock:** Composite. **Sights:** TruGlo front and rear. **Features:** IthaChoke full turkey choke tube. Matte metal, Realtree Hardwoods pattern, swivel studs.
Price: Storm $459.00

MARLIN PARDNER PUMP SHOTGUN
Gauge: 12 ga., 3". **Barrel:** 28" vent rib, screw-in Modified choke tube. **Weight:** 7-1/2 lbs. **Length:** 48-1/2". **Stock:** American walnut, grooved forend, ventilated recoil pad. **Sights:** Bead front. **Features:** Machined steel receiver, double action bars, five-shot magazine.
Price: $200.00

MOSSBERG MODEL 835 ULTI-MAG PUMP SHOTGUNS
Gauge: 12, 3-1/2" chamber. **Barrel:** Ported 24" rifled bore, 24", 28", Accu-Mag choke tubes for steel or lead shot. **Weight:** 7-3/4 lbs. **Length:** 48-1/2" overall. **Stock:** 14"x1-1/2"x2-1/2". Dual Comb. Cut-checkered hardwood or camo synthetic; both have recoil pad. **Sights:** White bead front, brass mid-bead; fiber-optic rear. **Features:** Shoots 2-3/4", 3" or 3-1/2" shells. Back-bored and ported barrel to reduce recoil, improve patterns. Ambidextrous thumb safety, twin extractors, dual slide bars. Mossberg Cablelock included. Introduced 1988.
Price: 28" vent rib, hardwood stock $394.00
Price: Combos, 24" rifled or smooth bore, rifle sights, 24" vent rib Accu-Mag Ulti-Full choke tube, Mossy Oak® camo finish $556.00
Price: RealTree Camo Turkey, 24" vent rib, Accu-Mag extra-full tube, synthetic stock $460.00
Price: Mossy Oak® Camo, 28" vent rib, Accu-Mag tubes, synthetic stock $460.00
Price: OFM Camo, 28" vent rib, Accu-Mag Mod. tube, synthetic stock $438.00

Mossberg Model 500 Sporting

Mossberg Model 500 Bantam

Mossberg Model 500 Trophy Slugster

Remington 870 Wingmaster

Mossberg Model 835 Synthetic Stock Shotgun
Similar to the Model 835, except with 28" ported barrel with Accu-Mag Mod. choke tube, Parkerized finish, black synthetic stock and forend. Introduced 1998. Made in U.S. by Mossberg.
Price: **$394.00**

MOSSBERG MODEL 500 SPORTING PUMP SHOTGUNS
Gauge: 12, 20, .410, 3" chamber. **Barrel:** 18-1/2" to 28" with fixed or Accu-Choke, plain or vent rib. **Weight:** 6-1/4 lbs. (.410), 7-1/4 lbs. (12). **Length:** 48" overall (28" barrel). **Stock:** 14"x1-1/2"x2-1/2". Walnut-stained hardwood. Cut-checkered grip and forend. **Sights:** White bead front, brass mid-bead; fiber-optic. **Features:** Ambidextrous thumb safety, twin extractors, disconnecting safety, dual action bars. Quiet Carry forend. Many barrels are ported. From Mossberg.
Price: From about **$316.00**
Price: Sporting Combos (field barrel and Slugster barrel). From ... **$381.00**

Mossberg Model 500 Bantam Pump Shotgun
Same as the Model 500 Sporting Pump except 12 or 20 gauge, 22" vent rib Accu-Choke barrel with choke tube set; has 1" shorter stock, reduced length from pistol grip to trigger, reduced forend reach. Introduced 1992.
Price: **$316.00**
Price: With Realtree Hardwoods camouflage finish (20 ga. only) .. **$364.00**

Mossberg Model 500 Camo Pump Shotgun
Same as the Model 500 Sporting Pump except 12 gauge only and entire gun is covered with Mossy Oak® Advantage camouflage finish. Receiver drilled and tapped for scope mounting. Comes with quick detachable swivel studs, swivels, camouflage sling, Mossberg Cablelock.
Price: From about **$364.00**

MOSSBERG MODEL 500 PERSUADER/CRUISER SHOTGUNS
Similar to Mossberg Model 500 except has 18-1/2" or 20" barrel with cylinder bore choke, synthetic stock and blue or Parkerized finish.

Available in 12, 20 and .410 with bead or ghost ring sights, 6- or 8-shot magazines. From Mossberg.
Price: 12 gauge, 20" barrel, 8-shot, bead sight. **$391.00**
Price: 20 gauge or .410, 18-1/2" barrel, 6-shot, bead sight **$353.00**
Price: 12 gauge, Parkerized finish, 6-shot, 18-1/2" barrel,
ghost ring sights **$468.00**
Price: Home Security 410 (.410, 18-1/2" barrel
with spreader choke) **$335.00**

Mossberg Model 590 Special Purpose Shotgun
Similar to Model 500 except has Parkerized or Marinecote finish, 9-shot magazine and black synthetic stock (some models feature Speed Feed). Available in 12 gauge only with 20", cylinder bore barrel. Weighs 7-1/4 lbs. From Mossberg.
Price: Bead sight, heat shield over barrel **$417.00**
Price: Ghost ring sight, Speed Feed stock **$586.00**

MOSSBERG MODEL 500 SLUGSTER SHOTGUN
Gauge: 12, 20, 3" chamber. **Barrel:** 24", ported rifled bore. Integral scope mount. **Weight:** 7-1/4 lbs. **Length:** 44" overall. **Stock:** 14" pull, 1-3/8" drop at heel. Walnut. Dual Comb design for proper eye positioning with or without scoped barrels. Recoil pad and swivel studs. **Features:** Ambidextrous thumb safety, twin extractors, dual slide bars. Comes with scope mount. Mossberg Cablelock included. Introduced 1988.
Price: Rifled bore, integral scope mount, 12 or 20 ga. **$361.00**
Price: Fiber-optic, rifle sights **$361.00**
Price: Rifled bore, rifle sights **$338.00**
Price: 20 ga., Standard or Bantam. From **$338.00**

REMINGTON MODEL 870 WINGMASTER SHOTGUNS
Gauge: 12 ga., 16 ga., 3" chamber. **Barrel:** 26", 28", 30" (RemChokes). **Weight:** 7-1/4 lbs. **Length:** 46", 48". **Stock:** Walnut, hardwood, synthetic. **Sights:** Single bead (Twin bead Wingmaster). **Features:** Light contour barrel. Double action bars, cross-bolt safety, blue finish.
Price: Wingmaster, walnut, blued, 26", 28", 30" **$584.00**
Price: 870 Wingmaster Super Magnum, 3-1/2" chamber, 28" **$665.00**

SHOTGUNS — Slide & Lever Actions

Remington Model 870 50th Anniversary Classic Trap

Remington Model 870 Marine Magnum

Remington Model 870 Wingmaster LW

Remington Model 870 Express Super Magnum

Remington Model 870 50th Anniversary Classic Trap Shotgun
Similar to Model 870 Wingmaster except has 30" vent rib, light contour barrel, singles, mid- and long-handicap choke tubes, semi-fancy American walnut stock, high-polish blued receiver with engraving. Chamber 2-1/2". From Remington Arms Co.
Price: **$792.00**

Remington Model 870 Marine Magnum Shotgun
Similar to 870 Wingmaster except all metal plated with electroless nickel, black synthetic stock and forend. Has 18" plain barrel (cyl.), bead front sight, 7-shot magazine. Introduced 1992.
Price: **$573.00**

Remington Model 870 Wingmaster LW Shotgun
Similar to Model 870 Wingmaster except in 20, 28 gauges and .410-bore only, 25" vent rib barrel with RemChoke tubes, high-gloss wood finish. 26" & 28" barrels 20 ga.
Price: 20 gauge **$584.00**
Price: .410-bore **$612.00**
Price: 28 gauge **$665.00**

Remington Model 870 Express Shotguns
Similar to Model 870 Wingmaster except walnut-toned hardwood stock with solid, black recoil pad and pressed checkering on grip and forend. Outside metal surfaces have black oxide finish. Comes with 26" or 28" vent rib barrel with mod. RemChoke tube.
Price: 12 ga., 20 ga., 16 ga. (28") **$332.00**
Price: Express Combo, 12 ga., 26" vent rib with mod. RemChoke and 20" fully rifled barrel with rifle sights, or RemChoke . . . . . **$443.00 to $476.00**
Price: Express L-H (left-hand), 12 ga., 28" vent rib with mod. RemChoke tube **$359.00**
Price: Express synthetic, 12-ga., 26" or 28" **$332.00**
Price: Express combo (20 ga.) with extra deer rifled barrel, fully rifled or RemChoke . . . . **$443.00 to $476.00**
Price: Express small bore 28 ga., 25" **$359.00**
Price: Express small bore .410, 25" **$359.00**

Remington Model 870 Express Super Magnum Shotgun
Similar to Model 870 Express except 28" vent rib barrel with 3-1/2" chamber, vented recoil pad. Introduced 1998.
Price: **$376.00**
Price: Super Magnum synthetic, 26" **$376.00**
Price: Super Magnum turkey camo (full-coverage RealTree Advantage camo), 23" **$500.00**
Price: Super Magnum combo (26" with Mod. RemChoke and 20" fully rifled deer barrel with 3" chamber and rifle sights; wood stock) **$523.00**
Price: Super Magnum synthetic turkey, 23" (black) **$389.00**

Remington Model 870 Wingmaster Super Magnum Shotgun
Similar to Model 870 Express Super Magnum except high-polish blued finish, 28" ventilated barrel with Imp. Cyl., Modified and Full choke tubes, checkered high-gloss walnut stock. Overall length 48", weighs 7-1/2 lbs. Introduced 2000.
Price: 3-1/2" chamber **$665.00**

Remington Model 870 SPS Super Slug Deer Gun Shotgun
Similar to the Model 870 Express synthetic except has 23" rifled, modified contour barrel with cantilever scope mount. Comes with black synthetic stock and forend with swivel studs, black Cordura nylon sling. Fully rifled cantilever barrel. Introduced 1999.
Price: **$580.00**

Remington Model 870 SPS-T Synthetic Camo Shotguns
Similar to the Model 870 Express synthetic, chambered for 12 ga., 3" shells, has Mossy Oak® Break-Up™ synthetic stock and metal treatment, TruGlo fiber-optic sights. Introduced 2001.
Price: 20" RS, Rem. choke **$595.00**
Price: Youth version **$595.00**
Price: Super Magnum Camo, 23", CL Rem. Choke **$609.00**
Price: Super Magnum Camo 23", VT Rem. Choke **$591.00**
Price: 20 ga., Truglo sights, Rem. Choke, Mossy Oak® Break-Up™ Camo **$595.00**

Remington Model 870 Express Deer Gun

Remington Model 870 Express Turkey

Remington Model 870 SPS Super Slug Deer Gun

Remington Model 870 SPS-T Camo

Winchester 1300 Walnut Field Pump

Remington Model 870 Express Youth Gun Shotgun
Same as Model 870 Express except 13" length of pull, 21" barrel with mod. RemChoke tube. Weighs 6.25 lbs. Hardwood stock with low-luster finish. Introduced 1991.
Price: 20 ga. Express Youth (1" shorter stock), from **$332.00**
Price: 20 ga. Youth Deer 20" FR/RS **$365.00**
Price: 16 ga. Youth Synthetic **$332.00**

Remington Model 870 Express Rifle-Sighted Deer Gun Shotguns
Same as Model 870 Express except 20" barrel with fixed imp. cyl. choke, open iron sights, Monte Carlo stock. Introduced 1991.
Price: **$332.00**
Price: With fully rifled barrel **$365.00**
Price: Express Synthetic Deer
(black synthetic stock, black matte metal) **$372.00**

Remington Model 870 Express Turkey Shotguns
Same as Model 870 Express except 3" chamber, 21" vent rib turkey barrel and extra-full Rem. choke turkey tube; 12 ga. only. Introduced 1991.
Price: **$345.00**
Price: Express Turkey Camo stock has Skyline Excel
camo, matte black metal **$399.00**
Price: Express Youth Turkey camo (as above with 1" shorter
length of pull), 20 ga., Skyline Excel camo **$399.00**

Remington Model 870 Express Synthetic 18" Shotgun
Similar to Model 870 Express with 18" barrel except synthetic stock and forend; 7-shot. Introduced 1994.
Price: **$319.00**

REMINGTON MODEL 870 SPS SUPER MAGNUM CAMO SHOTGUN
Gauge: 12, 3-1/2" chamber. **Barrel:** 26", 28", vent rib, with Full, Mod., Imp. Cyl. RemChoke. **Weight:** 7-1/4 lbs. to 7-1/2 lbs. **Length:** 46" to 481/2" overall. **Stock:** Mossy Oak® Break-Up™ camo finish. **Sights:** Metal bead front. **Features:** Synthetic stock and all metal (except bolt and trigger guard) and stock covered with Mossy Oak® Break-Up™ camo finish. Comes with camo sling, swivels.
Price: **$637.00**

SARSILMAZ PUMP SHOTGUN
Gauge: 12, 3" chamber. **Barrel:** 26" or 28". **Stocks:** Oil-finished hardwood. **Features:** Includes extra pistol-grip stock. Introduced 2000. Imported from Turkey by Armsport Inc.
Price: With pistol-grip stock. **$299.95**
Price: With metal stock **$349.95**

WINCHESTER MODEL 1300 WALNUT SPORTING/FIELD PUMP SHOTGUN
Gauge: 12, 20, 3" chamber, 5-shot capacity. **Barrel:** 26", 28", vent rib, with Full, Mod., Imp. Cyl. Winchoke tubes. **Weight:** 6-3/8 lbs. **Length:** 42-5/8" overall. **Stock:** American walnut with deep cut checkering on pistol grip, traditional ribbed forend; high luster finish. **Sights:** Metal bead front. **Features:** Twin action slide bars; front-locking rotary bolt; roll-engraved receiver; blued, highly polished metal; cross-bolt safety with red indicator. Introduced 1984. From U.S. Repeating Arms Co., Inc.
Price: **$439.00**

Winchester 1300 Black Shadow Field Gun

Winchester 1300 Deer Black Shadow Gun

Winchester 1300 Ranger Compact

Winchester 9410

Winchester Model 1300 Upland Pump Shotgun
Similar to Model 1300 Walnut except straight-grip stock, 24" barrel. Introduced 1999. Made in U.S. by U.S. Repeating Arms Co.
Price: **$438.00**

Winchester Model 1300 Black Shadow Field Shotgun
Similar to Model 1300 Walnut except black composite stock and forend, matte black finish. Has vent rib 26" or 28" barrel, 3" chamber, Mod. Winchoke tube. Introduced 1995. From U.S. Repeating Arms Co., Inc.
Price: 12 or 20 gauge **$351.00**

Winchester Model 1300 Deer Black Shadow Shotguns
Similar to Model 1300 Black Shadow Turkey Gun except ramp-type front sight, fully adjustable rear, drilled and tapped for scope mounting. Black composite stock and forend, matte black metal. Smoothbore 22" barrel with one Imp. Cyl. Winchoke tube; 12 gauge only, 3" chamber. Weighs 6-3/4 lbs. Introduced 1994. From U.S. Repeating Arms Co., Inc.
Price: With rifled barrel **$453.00**
Price: Combo (22" rifled and 28" smoothbore bbls.) **$453.00**

WINCHESTER MODEL 1300 RANGER PUMP SHOTGUNS
Gauge: 12, 20, 3" chamber, 5-shot magazine. **Barrel:** 28" vent rib with Full, Mod., Imp. Cyl. Winchoke tubes. **Weight:** 7 to 7-1/4 lbs. **Length:** 48-5/8" to 50-5/8" overall. **Stock:** Walnut-finished hardwood with ribbed forend. **Sights:** Metal bead front. **Features:** Cross-bolt safety, black rubber recoil pad, twin action slide bars, front-locking rotating bolt. From U.S. Repeating Arms Co., Inc.

Price: Vent rib barrel, Winchoke **$366.00**
Price: Model 1300 Compact, 24" vent rib **$366.00**
Price: Compact wood model, 20 ga. **$366.00**

WINCHESTER MODEL 1300 UNIVERSAL HUNTER TURKEY SHOTGUN
Gauge: 12, 3". **Barrel:** 26" vent rib with Extra Long, Extra Full Extended, Full, Mod., Imp. Cyl. Winchoke tubes. **Weight:** 7 lbs. **Length:** 47" overall. **Stock:** Composite. **Sights:** Red dot. **Features:** Rotary bolt action. Durable Mossy Oak® break-up finish. TruGlo® 3-dot sights and stock sling studs also included. From U.S. Repeating Arms Co., Inc.
Price: Universal Hunter **$509.00**

WINCHESTER MODEL 9410 LEVER-ACTION SHOTGUN
Gauge: .410, 2-1/2" chamber. **Barrel:** 24" cyl. bore, also Invector choke system. **Weight:** 6-3/4 lbs. **Length:** 42-1/8" overall. **Stock:** Checkered walnut straight-grip; checkered walnut forearm. **Sights:** Adjustable "V" rear, TruGlo® front. **Features:** Model 94 rifle action (smoothbore) chambered for .410 shotgun. Angle Controlled Eject extractor/ejector; choke tubes; 9-shot tubular magazine; 13-1/2" length of pull. Introduced 2001. From U.S. Repeating Arms Co.
Price: 9410 fixed choke. **$626.00**
Price: 9410 Packer w/chokes **$647.00**
Price: 9410 w/Invector, traditional model **$626.00**
Price: 9410 w/Invector, Packer model **$647.00**
Price: 9410 w/Invector, semi-fancy traditional **$626.00**

Includes a variety of game guns and guns for competitive shooting.

Beretta S687 EELL Combo

Beretta 686 Onyx

Beretta S686 Silver Pigeon

BERETTA DT10 TRIDENT SHOTGUNS
Gauge: 12, 2-3/4", 3" chambers. **Barrel:** 28", 30", 32", 34"; competition-style vent rib; fixed or Optima choke tubes. **Weight:** 7.9 to 9 lbs. **Stock:** High-grade walnut stock with oil finish; hand-checkered grip and forend, adjustable stocks available. **Features:** Detachable, adjustable trigger group, raised and thickened receiver, forend iron has adjustment nut to guarantee wood-to-metal fit. Introduced 2000. Imported from Italy by Beretta USA.

Price: DT10 Trident Trap (selective, lockable single trigger,
adjustable stock). **$6,995.00**
Price: DT10 Trident Top Single **$6,995.00**
Price: DT10 Trident X Trap Combo
(single and o/u barrels) **$8,995.00**
Price: DT10 Trident skeet (skeet stock with rounded recoil
pad, tapered rib) **$6,995.00**
Price: DT10 Trident Sporting (sporting clays stock with
rounded recoil pad) **$6,495.00**
Price: DT10L Sporting **$7,995.00**

BERETTA SERIES 682 GOLD E SKEET, TRAP, SPORTING O/U SHOTGUNS
Gauge: 12, 2-3/4" chambers. **Barrel:** skeet-28"; trap-30" and 32", Imp. Mod. & Full and Mobilchoke; trap mono shotguns-32" and 34" Mobilchoke; trap top single guns-32" and 34" Full and Mobilchoke; trap combo sets-from 30" O/U, to 32" O/U, 34" top single. **Stock:** Close-grained walnut, hand checkered. **Sights:** White Bradley bead front sight and center bead. **Features:** Receiver has Greystone gunmetal gray finish with gold accents. Trap Monte Carlo stock has deluxe trap recoil pad. Various grades available. Imported from Italy by Beretta USA.

Price: 682 Gold E Trap with adjustable stock **$4,125.00**
Price: 682 Gold E Trap Top Combo **$5,295.00**
Price: 682 Gold E Sporting **$3,595.00**
Price: 682 Gold E skeet, adjustable stock **$3,905.00**
Price: 687 EELL Diamond Pigeon Sporting **$6,495.00**

BERETTA 686 ONYX O/U SHOTGUNS
Gauge: 12, 3" chambers. **Barrel:** 28", 30" (Mobilchoke tubes). **Weight:** 7.7 lbs. **Stock:** Checkered American walnut. **Features:** Intended for the beginning sporting clays shooter. Has wide, vented target rib, radiused recoil pad. Polished black finish on receiver and barrels. Introduced 1993. Imported from Italy by Beretta U.S.A.

Price: White Onyx **$1,795.00**
Price: Onyx Pro **$1,895.00**
Price: Onyx Pro 3.5 . . . . **$2,795.00**

Beretta S686 Silver Pigeon

BERETTA 686 SILVER PIGEON O/U SHOTGUNS
Gauge: 12, 20, 28, 3" chambers (2-3/4" 28 ga.). **Barrel:** 26", 28". **Weight:** 6.8 lbs. **Stock:** Checkered walnut. **Features:** Interchangeable barrels (20 and 28 ga.), single selective gold-plated trigger, boxlock action, auto safety, Schnabel forend.

Price: Silver Pigeon S **$1,995.00**
Price: Silver Pigeon S Combo **$2,795.00**

BERETTA ULTRALIGHT O/U SHOTGUNS
Gauge: 12, 2-3/4" chambers. **Barrel:** 26", 28", Mobilchoke tubes. **Weight:** About 5 lbs., 13 oz. **Stock:** Select American walnut with checkered grip and forend. **Features:** Low-profile aluminum alloy receiver with titanium breech face insert. Electroless nickel receiver with game scene engraving. Single selective trigger; automatic safety. Introduced 1992. Imported from Italy by Beretta U.S.A.

Price: **$1,995.00**
Price: Silver Pigeon II **$2,395.00**
Price: Silver Pigeon II Combo **$3.295.00**
Price: Silver Pigeon III. **$2,495.00**
Price: Silver Pigeon IV **$2,795.00**
Price: Silver Pigeon V **$3,295.00**
Price: Ultralight Deluxe **$2,495.00**

Beretta Over/Under Field Shotgun

Beretta SO9

Browning Citori
White Lightning

Beretta Ultralight Deluxe O/U Shotgun
Similar to the Ultralight except has matte electroless nickel finish receiver with gold game scene engraving; matte oil-finished, select walnut stock and forend. Imported from Italy by Beretta U.S.A.
Price: **$2,495.00**

BERETTA COMPETITION SHOTGUNS
Gauge: 12, 20, 28, and .410 bore, 2-3/4", 3" and 3-1/2" chambers. **Barrel:** 26" and 28" (Mobilchoke tubes). **Stock:** Close-grained walnut. **Features:** Highly-figured, American walnut stocks and forends, and a unique, weather-resistant finish on barrels. Silver designates standard 686, 687 models with silver receivers; 686 Silver Pigeon has enhanced engraving pattern, Schnabel forend; Gold indicates higher grade 686EL, 687EL models with full sideplates; Diamond is for 687EELL models with highest grade wood, engraving. Case provided with Gold and Diamond grades. Imported from Italy by Beretta U.S.A.
Price: S687 EL Gold Pigeon II (deep relief engraving) **$4,795.00**
Price: S687 EEU Gold Pigeon Sporting (D.R. engraving) **$6,495.00**
Price: Gold Sporting Pigeon **$4,971.00**
Price: 28 and 410 combo **$5,520.00**

BERETTA MODEL SO5, SO6, SO9 SHOTGUNS
Gauge: 12, 2-3/4" chambers. **Barrel:** To customer specs. **Stock:** To customer specs. **Features:** SO5-trap, skeet and sporting clays models SO5; SO6-SO6 and SO6 EELL are field models. SO6 has a case-hardened or silver receiver with contour hand engraving. SO6 EELL has hand-engraved receiver in a fine floral or "fine English" pattern or game scene, with bas-relief chisel work and gold inlays. SO6 and SO6 EELL are available with sidelocks removable by hand. Imported from Italy by Beretta U.S.A.
Price: SO5 Trap, skeet, Sporting **$13,000.00**
Price: SO6 Trap, skeet, Sporting **$17,500.00**
Price: SO6 EELL Field, custom specs **$28,000.00**
Price: SO9 (12, 20, 28, .410, 26", 28", 30", any choke) **$31,000.00**

BRNO ZH 300 O/U SHOTGUNS
Gauge: 12, 2-3/4" chambers. **Barrel:** 26", 27-1/2", 29" (skeet, Imp. Cyl., Mod., Full). **Weight:** 7 lbs. **Length:** 44.4" overall. **Stock:** European walnut. **Features:** Double triggers; automatic safety; polished blue finish, engraved receiver. Announced 1998. Imported from the Czech Republic by Euro-Imports.
Price: ZH 301, field **$594.00**
Price: ZH 302, skeet **$608.00**

Price: ZH 303, 12 ga. trap **$608.00**
Price: ZH 321, 16 ga. **$595.00**

BRNO 501.2 O/U SHOTGUN
Gauge: 12, 2-3/4" chambers. **Barrel:** 27.5" (Full & Mod.). **Weight:** 7 lbs. **Length:** 44" overall. **Stock:** European walnut. **Features:** Boxlock action with double triggers, ejectors; automatic safety; hand-cut checkering. Announced 1998. Imported from the Czech Republic by Euro-Imports.
Price: **$850.00**

BROWNING CYNERGY O/U SHOTGUNS
Gauge: 12, 20, 28. **Barrel:** 26", 28", 30", 32". **Stock:** Walnut or composite. **Features:** Mono-Lock hinge, recoil-reducing Inflex recoil pad, silver nitride receiver; ported barrel option.
Price: Cynergy Field, 20 and 28 gauge **$2,062.00**
Price: Cynergy Sporting, 20 and 28 gauge **$3,080.00**
Price: Cynergy Field, 12 gauge **$2,048.00**
Price: Cynergy Field, composite stock **$1,890.00**
Price: Cynergy Sporting, 12 gauge **$3,046.00**
Price: Cynergy Sporting, composite stock **$2,846.00**

BROWNING CITORI O/U SHOTGUNS
Gauge: 12, 20, 28 and .410. **Barrel:** 26", 28" in 28 and .410. Offered with Invector choke tubes. All 12 and 20 gauge models have back-bored barrels and Invector Plus choke system. **Weight:** 6 lbs., 8 oz. (26" .410) to 7 lbs., 13 oz. (30" 12 ga.). **Length:** 43" overall (26" bbl.). **Stock:** Dense walnut, hand checkered, full pistol grip, beavertail forend. Field-type recoil pad on 12 ga. field guns and trap and skeet models. **Sights:** Medium raised beads, German nickel silver. **Features:** Barrel selector integral with safety, automatic ejectors, three-piece takedown. Imported from Japan by Browning.
Price: Lightning, 12 and 20 gauge **$1,645.00**
Price: Lightning, 28 and .410 .... **$1,709.00**
Price: White Lightning, 12 and 20 gauge **$1,714.00**
Price: White Lightning, 28 and .410 Lightning **$1,790.00**
Price: Lightning, 525 Field, 12, 20 .... **$1,981.00**
Price: Lightning, 525 Field, 28 and 410 .... **$2,010.00**
Price: Superlight Feather, 12, 20 .... **$1,938.00**
Price: Super Lightning, Grade I, 12 and 20 gauge **$1,866.00**
Price: Classic Lightning, Grade I, 12 and 20 gauge **$1,891.00**
Price: Classic Lightning Feather, Grade I, 12 and 20 gauge ... **$1,952.00**

Browning Citori High Grade Shotguns
Similar to standard Citori except has engraved hunting scenes and gold inlays, high-grade, hand-oiled walnut stock and forearm. Introduced 2000. From Browning.
Price: Citori VI Lightning blue or gray
(gold inlays of ducks and pheasants) From **$2,608.00**

Browning Citori XS Special

Browning Citori 525 Sporting Clays

Browning Citori XT Trap

Browning Lightning Feather

Charles Daly Superior II Trap AE-MC

Charles Daly Field Hunter

Browning Citori XS Sporting O/U Shotguns

Similar to the standard Citori except available in 12, 20, 28 or .410 with, 26" or 28" barrels choked skeet, Cylinder, Imp. Cyl., Mod. and Imp. Mod. Has pistol grip stock, rounded or Schnabel forend. Weighs 7 lbs. 1 oz. to 8 lbs. 10 oz., 15 oz. Introduced 2005.

Price: Citori XS Special, 12 gauge **$2,727.00**
Price: Citori XS Sporting, 12 or 20 gauge **$2,472.00**
Price: Citori XS Skeet, 12 or 20 gauge **$2,434.00**
Price: Citori 525 Sporting, Grade I, 12 gauge **$2,319.00**
Price: Citori 525 Golden Clays, 12 or 20 gauge **$3,058.00**
Price: Citori 525 Golden Clays, 28 or .410 .... **$4,653.00**

Browning Citori XT Trap O/U Shotgun

Similar to the Citori XS Special except has engraved silver nitride receiver with gold highlights, vented side barrel rib. Available in 12 gauge with 30" or 32" barrels, Invector-Plus choke tubes, adjustable comb and buttplate. Introduced 1999. Imported by Browning.

Price: .... **$2,275.00 to $4,221.00**
Price: With adjustable-comb stock **$2,549.00**

Browning Citori Lightning Feather O/U Shotgun

Similar to the 12 gauge Citori Grade I except has 2-3/4" chambers, rounded pistol grip, lightning-style forend, and lightweight alloy receiver. Weighs 6 lbs. 15 oz. with 26" barrels (12 ga.); 6 lbs., 2 oz. (20 ga., 26" bbl.), silvered, engraved receiver. Introduced 1999. Imported by Browning.

Price: 12 or 20 ga., 26" or 28" barrels **$1,693.00**
Price: Lightning Feather Combo
(20 and 28 ga. bbls., 27" each) **$2,751.00**

BROWNING BT-99 TRAP O/U SHOTGUNS

GAUGE: 12. **Barrel:** 30", 32", 34". **Stock:** Walnut; standard or adjustable. **Weight:** 7 lbs. 11 oz. to 9 lbs. **Features:** Back-bored single barrel; interchangeable chokes; beavertail forearm; extractor only; high rib.

Price: BT-99, adj. comb **$1,329.00**
Price: BT-99, Golden Clays **$3,509.00**
Price: BT-99 Micro **$1,329.00**

CHARLES DALY SUPERIOR II TRAP AE-MC O/U SHOTGUN

Gauge: 12, 2-3/4" chambers. **Barrel:** 30" choke tubes. **Weight:** About 7 lbs. **Length:** 47-3/8". **Stock:** Checkered walnut; pistol grip, semi-beavertail forend. **Features:** Silver engraved receiver, chrome-moly steel barrels; gold single selective trigger; automatic safety, automatic ejectors; red bead front sight, metal bead center; recoil pad. Introduced 1997. Imported from Italy by K.B.I., Inc.

Price: **$1,699.00**

CHARLES DALY FIELD II HUNTER O/U SHOTGUN

Gauge: 12, 20, 28 and .410 bore (3" chambers, 28 ga. has 2-3/4"). **Barrel:** 28" Mod & Full, 26" Imp. Cyl. & Mod (.410 is Full & Full). **Weight:** About 7 lbs. **Length:** 42-3/4" to 44-3/4". **Stock:** Checkered walnut pistol grip and forend. **Features:** Blued engraved receiver, chrome-moly steel barrels; gold single selective trigger; automatic safety; extractors; gold bead front sight. Introduced 1997. Imported from Italy by K.B.I., Inc.

Price: 12 or 20 ga. **$1,029.00**
Price: 28 ga., .410 bore **$1,129.00**

Charles Daly Superior Hunter

Charles Daly Empire II Mono Trap

Charles Daly Empire II EDL Hunter

Charles Daly Empire Sporting O/U

Charles Daly Superior II Hunter AE O/U Shotgun
Similar to the Field Hunter AE except has silvered, engraved receiver. Introduced 1997. Imported from Italy by F.B.I., Inc.
Price: 28 ga., .410 bore **$1,449.00**

Charles Daly Field Hunter AE-MC O/U Shotgun
Similar to the Field Hunter except in 12 or 20 only, 26" or 28" barrels with five multi-choke tubes; automatic ejectors. Introduced 1997. Imported from Italy by K.B.I., Inc.
Price: 12 or 20 ga. **$1,279.00**

Charles Daly Superior II Sporting O/U Shotgun
Similar to the Field Hunter AE-MC except 28" or 30" barrels; silvered, engraved receiver; five choke tubes; ported barrels; red bead front sight. Introduced 1997. Imported from Italy by K.B.I., Inc.
Price: **$1,659.00**

CHARLES DALY EMPIRE II EDL HUNTER AE, AE-MC O/U SHOTGUNS
Gauge: 12, 20, .410, 3" chambers, 28 ga., 2-3/4". **Barrel:** 26", 28" (12, 20, choke tubes), 26" (Imp. Cyl. & Mod., 28 ga.), 26" (Full & Full, .410). **Weight:** About 7 lbs. **Stocks:** Checkered walnut pistol grip buttstock, semi-beavertail forend; recoil pad. **Features:** Silvered, engraved receiver; chrome-moly barrels; gold single selective trigger; automatic safety; automatic ejectors; red bead front sight, metal bead middle sight. Introduced 1997. Imported from Italy by K.B.I., Inc.
Price: Empire II EDL AE-MC (dummy sideplates) 12 or 20 . . . . . **$2,029.00**
Price: Empire II EDL AE, 28 . . . . **$2,019.00**
Price: Empire II EDL AE, .410 . . . . **$2,019.00**

Charles Daly Empire II Sporting AE-MC O/U Shotgun
Similar to the Empire II EDL Hunter except 12 or 20 gauge only, 28", 30" barrels with choke tubes; ported barrels; special stock dimensions. Introduced 1997. Imported from Italy by K.B.I., Inc.
Price: **$2,049.00**

CHARLES DALY EMPIRE II TRAP AE-MC O/U SHOTGUNS
Gauge: 12, 2-3/4" chambers. **Barrel:** 30" choke tubes. **Weight:** About 7 lbs. **Stock:** Checkered walnut; pistol grip, semi-beavertail forend. **Features:** Silvered, engraved, reinforced receiver; chrome-moly steel barrels; gold single selective trigger; automatic safety, automatic ejector; red bead front sight, metal bead center; recoil pad. Imported from Italy by K.B.I., Inc.
Price: **$2,099.00**
Price: Mono AE-MC, adj. comb **$2,999.00**
Price: AE-MC combo set, adj. comb **$3,919.00**

CHARLES DALY DIAMOND REGENT GTX DL HUNTER O/U SHOTGUNS
Gauge: 12, 20, .410, 3" chambers, 28, 2-3/4" chambers. **Barrel:** 26", 28", 30" (choke tubes), 26" (Imp. Cyl. & Mod. in 28, 26" (Full & Full) in .410. **Weight:** About 7 lbs. **Stock:** Extra select fancy European walnut with 24" hand checkering, hand rubbed oil finish. **Features:** Boss-type action with internal side lumps. Deep cut hand-engraved scrollwork and game scene set in full sideplates. GTX detachable single selective trigger system with coil springs; chrome-moly steel barrels; automatic safety; automatic ejectors, white bead front sight, metal bead center sight. Introduced 1997. Imported from Italy by K.B.I., Inc.
Price: 12 or 20. . . . . **Special order only**
Price: 28 . . . . **Special order only**
Price: .410 bore . . . . **Special order only**
Price: Diamond Regent GTX EDL Hunter (as above with engraved scroll and birds, 10 gold inlays), 12 or 20 . . **Special order only**
Price: As above, 28 . . . . **Special order only**
Price: As above, .410 . . . . **Special order only**

CHARLES DALY DIAMOND GTX SPORTING O/U SHOTGUN
Gauge: 12, 20, 3" chambers. **Barrel:** 28", 30" with choke tubes. **Weight:** About 8.5 lbs. **Stock:** Checkered deluxe walnut; sporting clays dimensions. Pistol grip; semi-beavertail forend; hand rubbed oil finish. **Features:** Chromed, hand-engraved receiver; chrome-moly steel barrels; GTX detachable single selective trigger system with coil springs, automatic safety; automatic ejectors; red bead front sight; ported barrels. Introduced 1997. Imported from Italy by K.B.I., Inc.
Price: . . . . **Price on request**

CHARLES DALY DIAMOND GTX TRAP AE-MC O/U SHOTGUN
Gauge: 12, 2-3/4" chambers. **Barrel:** 30" (Full & Full). **Weight:** About 8.5 lbs. **Stock:** Checkered deluxe walnut; pistol grip; trap dimensions; semi-beavertail forend; hand-rubbed oil finish. **Features:** Silvered, hand-engraved receiver; chrome-moly steel barrels; GTX detachable single selective trigger system with coil springs, automatic safety, automatic ejectors, red bead front sight, metal bead middle; recoil pad. Imported from Italy by K.B.I., Inc.
Price: . . . . **Price on request**

CZ 581 Solo

EAA Baikal IZH27

Fabarm Max Lion

Fabarm Silver Lion Youth

CHARLES DALY DIAMOND GTX DL HUNTER O/U SHOTGUN
Gauge: 12, 20, .410, 3" chambers, 28, 2-3/4" chambers. **Barrel:** 26, 28", choke tubes in 12 and 20 ga., 26" (Imp. Cyl. & Mod.), 26" (Full & Full) in .410-bore. **Weight:** About 8.5 lbs. **Stock:** Select fancy European walnut stock, with 24 lpi hand checkering; hand-rubbed oil finish. **Features:** Boss-type action with internal side lugs, hand-engraved scrollwork and game scene. GTX detachable single selective trigger system with coil springs; chrome-moly steel barrels, automatic safety, automatic ejectors, red bead front sight, recoil pad. Introduced 1997. Imported from Italy by K.B.I., Inc.
Price: . . . . **Special order only**

CZ 581 SOL O/U SHOTGUN
Gauge: 12, 2-3/4" chambers. **Barrel:** 27.6" (Mod. & Full). **Weight:** 7.37 lbs. **Length:** 44.5" overall. **Stock:** Circassian walnut. **Features:** Automatic ejectors; double triggers; Kersten-style double lump locking system. Imported from the Czech Republic by CZ-USA.
Price: **$799.00**

EAA BAIKAL IZH27 O/U SHOTGUN
Gauge: 12 (3" chambers), 16 (2-3/4" chambers), 20 (3" chambers), 28 (2-3/4" chambers), .410 (3"). **Barrel:** 26-1/2", 28-1/2" (imp., mod. and full choke tubes for 12 and 20 gauges; improved cylinder and modified for 16 and 28 gauges; Improved Modified and Full for .410; 16 also offered in Mod. and Full). **Weight:** NA. **Stock:** Walnut, checkered forearm and grip. Imported by European American Armory.
Price: IZH27 (12, 16 and 20 gauge) **$509.00**
Price: IZH27 (28 gauge and .410) **$569.00**

EAA Baikal IZH27 O/U Shotgun
Basic IZH27 with barrel porting, wide vent rib with double sight beads, engraved nickel receiver, checkered walnut stock and forend with palm swell and semi beavertail, 3 screw-in chokes, SS trigger, selectable ejectors, auto tang safety.
Price: 12 ga., 29" bbl. **$589.00**

EAA Baikal Nickel O/U Shotgun
Same as IZH27 but with polished nickel receiver.
Price: **$529.00**

FABARM MAX LION O/U SHOTGUN
Gauge: 12, 3" chambers, 20, 3" chambers. **Barrel:** 26", 28", 30" (12 ga.); 26", 28" (20 ga.), choke tubes. **Weight:** 7.4 lbs. **Length:** 47.5" overall (26"

barrel). **Stock:** European walnut; leather-covered recoil pad. **Features:** TriBore barrel, boxlock action with single selective trigger, manual safety, automatic ejectors; chrome-lined barrels; adjustable trigger. Silvered, engraved receiver. Comes with locking, fitted luggage case. Introduced 1998. Imported from Italy by Heckler & Koch, Inc.
Price: 12 or 20 . . . . **$1,799.00**

FABARM ULTRA CAMO MAG LION O/U SHOTGUN
Gauge: 12, 3-1/2" chambers. **Barrel:** 28" (Cyl., Imp. Cyl., Mod., Imp. Mod., Full, SS-mod., SS-full choke tubes). **Weight:** 7.9 lbs. **Length:** 50" overall. **Stock:** Camo-colored walnut. **Features:** TriBore barrel, Wetlands Camo finished metal surfaces, single selective trigger, non-auto ejectors, leather-covered recoil pad. Locking hard plastic case. Introduced 1998. Imported from Italy by Heckler & Koch, Inc.
Price: **$1,229.00**

FABARM MAX LION PARADOX O/U SHOTGUN
Gauge: 12, 20, 3" chambers. **Barrel:** 24". **Weight:** 7.6 lbs. **Length:** 44.5" overall. **Stock:** Walnut with special enhancing finish. **Features:** TriBore upper barrel, both wood and receiver are enhanced with special finishes, color case-hardened type finish.
Price: 12 or 20 . . . . **$1,129.00**

FABARM SILVER LION O/U SHOTGUN
Gauge: 12, 3" chambers, 20, 3" chambers. **Barrel:** 26", 28", 30" (12 ga.); 26", 28" (20 ga.), choke tubes. **Weight:** 7.2 lbs. **Length:** 47.5" overall (26" barrels). **Stock:** Walnut; leather-covered recoil pad. **Features:** TriBore barrel, boxlock action with single selective trigger; silvered receiver with engraving; automatic ejectors. Comes with locking hard plastic case. Introduced 1998. Imported from Italy by Heckler & Koch, Inc.
Price: 12 or 20 . . . . **$1,229.00**

Fabarm Silver Lion Youth Model O/U Shotgun
Similar to the Silver Lion except has 12.5" length of pull, 12 gauge only, comes with 24" TriBore barrel system. Weight is 6 lbs. Introduced 1999. Imported from Italy by Heckler & Koch, Inc.
Price: **$1,229.00**

Franchi Alcione

Hoenig Rotary Game

Kimber Augusta Sport

FABARM CAMO TURKEY MAG O/U SHOTGUN
Gauge: 12, 3-1/2" chambers. **Barrel:** 20" TriBore (Ultra-Full ported tubes). **Weight:** 7.5 lbs. **Length:** 46" overall. **Stock:** 14.5"x1.5"x2.29". Walnut. **Sights:** Front bar, Picatinny rail scope base. **Features:** Completely covered with Xtra Brown camouflage finish. Unported barrels. Introduced 1999. Imported from Italy by Heckler & Koch, Inc.
Price: **$1,199.00**

FABARM SPORTING CLAYS COMPETITION EXTRA O/U SHOTGUN
Gauge: 12, 20, 3" chambers. **Barrel:** 12 ga. has 30", 20 ga. has 28"; ported TriBore barrel system with five tubes. **Weight:** 7 to 7.8 lbs. **Length:** 49.6" overall (20 ga.). **Stock:** 14.50"x1.38"x2.17" (20 ga.); deluxe walnut; leather-covered recoil pad. **Features:** Single selective trigger, auto ejectors; 10mm channeled rib; carbon fiber finish. Introduced 1999. Imported from Italy by Heckler & Koch, Inc.
Price: **$1,749.00**

FRANCHI ALCIONE FIELD O/U SHOTGUN
Gauge: 12, 20, 3" chambers. **Barrel:** 26", 28"; IC, M, F tubes. **Weight:** 7.5 lbs. **Length:** 43" overall with 26" barrels. **Stock:** European walnut. **Features:** Boxlock action with ejectors, barrel selector mounted on trigger; silvered, engraved receiver, vent center rib, automatic safety, interchangeable 20 ga. bbls., left-hand available. Imported from Italy by Benelli USA. Hard case included.
Price: **$1,310.00**
Price: (12 or 20 gauge barrel set) **$490.00**

Franchi Alcione SX O/U Shotgun
Similar to Alcione Field model with high grade walnut stock and forend. Gold engraved removeable sideplates, interchangeable barrels.
Price: **$1,855.00**
Price: (12 gauge barrel set) .... **$490.00 to $560.00**
Price: (20 gauge barrel set) **$490.00**

Franchi Alcione Sport SL O/U Shotgun
Similar to Alcione Field except 2-3/4" chambers, elongated forcing cones and porting for sporting clays shooting. 10mm vent rib, tightly curved pistol grip, manual safety, removeable sideplates. Imported from Italy by Benelli USA.
Price: **$1,700.00**

FRANCHI ALCIONE TITANIUM O/U SHOTGUN
Gauge: 12, 20, 3" chambers. **Barrel:** 26", 28"; IC, M, F tubes. **Weight:** 6.8 lbs. **Length:** 43", 45". **Stock:** Select walnut. **Sights:** Front/mid. **Features:** Receiver (titanium inserts) made of aluminum alloy. 7mm vent rib. Fast locking triggers. Left-hand available.

Price: **$1,470.00**
Price: Two-barrel set (12 and 20 ga.) **$1,930.00**

FRANCHI 912 O/U SHOTGUNS
Gauge: 12 ga., 2-3/4", 3", 3-1/2" chambers. **Barrel:** 24" to 30". **Weight:** Appx. 7.6 lbs. **Length:** 46" to 52". **Stock:** Walnut, synthetic, Timber HD, Max-4. **Sights:** White bead front. **Features:** Based on 612 design, magazine cut-off, stepped vent rib, dual-recoil-reduction system.
Price: Satin walnut **$850.00**
Price: Synthetic **$790.00**
Price: Timber HD & Max-4 .... **$900.00**
Price: Steadygrip Timber HD **$850.00**

FRANCHI VELOCE O/U SHOTGUN
Gauge: 20, 28. **Barrel:** 26", 28"; IC, M, F tubes. **Weight:** 5.5 to 5.8 lbs. **Length:** 43" to 45". **Stock:** High grade walnut. **Features:** Aluminum receiver with steel reinforcement scaled to 20 gauge for light weight. Pistol grip stock with slip recoil pad. Imported by Benelli USA. Hard case included.
Price: **$1,470.00**
Price: 28 ga. **$1,545.00**

Franchi Veloce English O/U Shotgun
Similar to Veloce standard model with straight grip English-style stock. Available with 26" barrels in 20 and 28 gauge. Hard case included.
Price: **$1,470.00**
Price: 28 ga. **$1,545.00**

HOENIG ROTARY ROUND ACTION GAME GUN O/U SHOTGUN
Gauge: 20, 28. **Barrel:** 26", 28", solid tapered rib. **Weight:** 6 lbs. and 6-1/4 lbs. **Stock:** English walnut to customer specifications. **Features:** Round action opens by rotating barrels, pulling forward. Inertia extraction system, rotary wing safety blocks strikers. Simple takedown without removing forend. Introduced 1997. Made in U.S.A. by George Hoenig.
Price: **$19,980.00**

KHAN ARTEMIS O/U SHOTGUN
Gauge: 12, 20, 28, 410. **Barrel:** 26", 28". **Stock:** Walnut. **Features:** Engraved receiver, single selective trigger, vent rib; choke tubes and extractors (Fixed IC, M choke on 410 models). Introduced 2005. Imported by Legacy Sports Int.
Price: .... **$617.00 to $791.00**
Price: Sporting clays model **$1,104.00**

KIMBER AUGUSTA O/U SHOTGUNS
Gauge: 12, 3". **Barrel:** 26" to 27-1/2". **Weight:** 7 lbs., 2 oz. **Length:** NA. **Stock:** Checkered AAA-grade European walnut. **Features:** Premium over/under, Boss-type action. Tri-alloy barrel with choke tubes. Back bored, long forcing cones. HiViz sight with center bead on vent rib. Satin or high gloss finish. Imported from Italy by Kimber Mfg., Inc.
Price: Field, Skeet, Sporting, Trap **$6,000.00**

Kolar Sporting Clays

Krieghoff K-80 Sporting Clays

Ljutic LM-6 Super Deluxe

KOLAR SPORTING CLAYS O/U SHOTGUNS
Gauge: 12, 2-3/4" chambers. **Barrel:** 30", 32", 34"; extended choke tubes. **Stock:** 14-5/8"x2-1/2"x1-7/8"x1-3/8". French walnut. Four stock versions available. **Features:** Single selective trigger, detachable, adjustable for length; overbored barrels with long forcing cones; flat tramline rib; matte blue finish. Made in U.S. by Kolar.
Price: Standard **$7,995.00**
Price: Elite **$10,990.00**
Price: Elite Gold **$12,990.00**
Price: Legend **$13,990.00**
Price: Select **$15,990.00**
Price: Custom . . . . **Price on request**

Kolar AAA Competition Trap O/U Shotgun
Similar to the Sporting Clays gun except has 32" O/U /34" Unsingle or 30" O/U /34" Unsingle barrels as an over/under, unsingle, or combination set. Stock dimensions are 14-1/2"x2-1/2"x1-1/2"; American or French walnut; step parallel rib standard. Contact maker for full listings. Made in U.S.A. by Kolar.
Price: Over/under, choke tubes, standard. **$8,220.00**
Price: Unsingle, choke tubes, standard **$8,600.00**
Price: Combo (30"/34", 32"/34"), standard **$10,995.00**

Kolar AAA Competition Skeet O/U Shotgun
Similar to the Sporting Clays gun except has 28" or 30" barrels with Kolarite AAA sub gauge tubes; stock of American or French walnut with matte finish; flat tramline rib; under barrel adjustable for point of impact. Many options available. Contact maker for complete listing. Made in U.S.A. by Kolar.
Price: Standard, choke tubes **$8,645.00**
Price: Standard, choke tubes, two-barrel set **$10,995.00**

KRIEGHOFF K-80 SPORTING CLAYS O/U SHOTGUN
Gauge: 12. **Barrel:** 28", 30" or 32" with choke tubes. **Weight:** About 8 lbs. **Stock:** #3 Sporting stock designed for gun-down shooting. **Features:** Standard receiver with satin nickel finish and classic scroll engraving. Selective mechanical trigger adjustable for position. Choice of tapered flat or 8mm parallel flat barrel rib. Free-floating barrels. Aluminum case. Imported from Germany by Krieghoff International, Inc.
Price: Standard grade with five choke tubes, from **$9,395.00**

KRIEGHOFF K-80 SKEET O/U SHOTGUNS
Gauge: 12, 2-3/4" chambers. **Barrel:** 28", 30", (skeet & skeet), optional choke tubes). **Weight:** About 7-3/4 lbs. **Stock:** American skeet or straight skeet stocks, with palm-swell grips. Walnut. **Features:** Satin gray receiver finish. Selective mechanical trigger adjustable for position. Choice of

ventilated 8mm parallel flat rib or ventilated 8-12mm tapered flat rib. Introduced 1980. Imported from Germany by Krieghoff International, Inc.
Price: Standard, skeet chokes **$8,220.00**
Price: Skeet Special (28" or 30", tapered flat rib,
skeet & skeet choke tubes) **$8,920.00**

KRIEGHOFF K-80 TRAP O/U SHOTGUNS
Gauge: 12, 2-3/4" chambers. **Barrel:** 30", 32" (Imp. Mod. & Full or choke tubes). **Weight:** About 8-1/2 lbs. **Stock:** Four stock dimensions or adjustable stock available; all have palm-swell grips. Checkered European walnut. **Features:** Satin nickel receiver. Selective mechanical trigger, adjustable for position. Ventilated step rib. Introduced 1980. Imported from Germany by Krieghoff International, Inc.
Price: K-80 O/U (30", 32", Imp. Mod. & Full), from **$8,695.00**
Price: K-80 Unsingle (32", 34", Full), standard, from **$9,675.00**
Price: K-80 Combo (two-barrel set), standard, from **$13,990.00**

Krieghoff K-20 O/U Shotgun
Similar to the K-80 except built on a 20-gauge frame. Designed for skeet, sporting clays and field use. Offered in 20, 28 and .410; 28", 30" and 32" barrels. Imported from Germany by Krieghoff International Inc.
Price: K-20, 20 gauge, from **$9,395.00**
Price: K-20, 28 gauge, from **$9,545.00**
Price: K-20, .410, from **$9,545.00**

L. C. SMITH O/U SHOTGUN
Gauge: 12, 20. **Barrel:** 26", 28". **Stock:** Checkered walnut w/recoil pad. **Features:** 3" chambers; single selective trigger, selective automatic ejectors; vent rib; bead front sight. Imported from Italy by Marlin. Introduced 2005.
Price: **$1,394.00**

LEBEAU-COURALLY BOSS-VEREES O/U SHOTGUN
Gauge: 12, 20, 2-3/4" chambers. **Barrel:** 25" to 32". **Weight:** To customer specifications. **Stock:** Exhibition-quality French walnut. **Features:** Boss-type sidelock with automatic ejectors; single or double triggers; chopper lump barrels. A custom gun built to customer specifications. Imported from Belgium by Wm. Larkin Moore.
Price: From **$96,000.00**

LJUTIC LM-6 SUPER DELUXE O/U SHOTGUNS
Gauge: 12. **Barrel:** 28" to 34", choked to customer specs for live birds, trap, international trap. **Weight:** To customer specs. **Stock:** To customer specs. Oil finish, hand checkered. **Features:** Custom-made gun. Hollow-milled rib, pull or release trigger, push-button opener in front of trigger guard. From Ljutic Industries.
Price: Super Deluxe LM-6 O/U. **$19,995.00**
Price: Over/Under combo (interchangeable single barrel,
two trigger guards, one for single trigger, one for doubles) **$27,995.00**
Price: Extra over/under barrel sets, 29"-32" **$6,995.00**

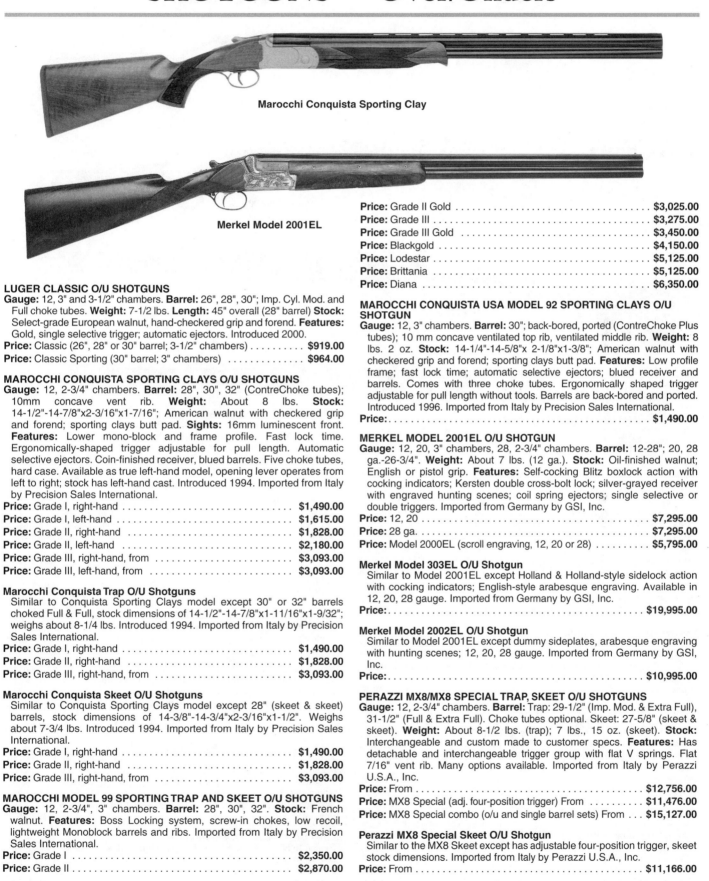

Marocchi Conquista Sporting Clay

Merkel Model 2001EL

LUGER CLASSIC O/U SHOTGUNS
Gauge: 12, 3" and 3-1/2" chambers. **Barrel:** 26", 28", 30"; Imp. Cyl. Mod. and Full choke tubes. **Weight:** 7-1/2 lbs. **Length:** 45" overall (28" barrel) **Stock:** Select-grade European walnut, hand-checkered grip and forend. **Features:** Gold, single selective trigger; automatic ejectors. Introduced 2000.
Price: Classic (26", 28" or 30" barrel; 3-1/2" chambers) **$919.00**
Price: Classic Sporting (30" barrel; 3" chambers) **$964.00**

MAROCCHI CONQUISTA SPORTING CLAYS O/U SHOTGUNS
Gauge: 12, 2-3/4" chambers. **Barrel:** 28", 30", 32" (ContreChoke tubes); 10mm concave vent rib. **Weight:** About 8 lbs. **Stock:** 14-1/2"-14-7/8"x2-3/16"x1-7/16"; American walnut with checkered grip and forend; sporting clays butt pad. **Sights:** 16mm luminescent front. **Features:** Lower mono-block and frame profile. Fast lock time. Ergonomically-shaped trigger adjustable for pull length. Automatic selective ejectors. Coin-finished receiver, blued barrels. Five choke tubes, hard case. Available as true left-hand model, opening lever operates from left to right; stock has left-hand cast. Introduced 1994. Imported from Italy by Precision Sales International.
Price: Grade I, right-hand **$1,490.00**
Price: Grade I, left-hand **$1,615.00**
Price: Grade II, right-hand **$1,828.00**
Price: Grade II, left-hand **$2,180.00**
Price: Grade III, right-hand, from **$3,093.00**
Price: Grade III, left-hand, from **$3,093.00**

Marocchi Conquista Trap O/U Shotguns
Similar to Conquista Sporting Clays model except 30" or 32" barrels choked Full & Full, stock dimensions of 14-1/2"-14-7/8"x1-11/16"x1-9/32"; weighs about 8-1/4 lbs. Introduced 1994. Imported from Italy by Precision Sales International.
Price: Grade I, right-hand **$1,490.00**
Price: Grade II, right-hand **$1,828.00**
Price: Grade III, right-hand, from **$3,093.00**

Marocchi Conquista Skeet O/U Shotguns
Similar to Conquista Sporting Clays model except 28" (skeet & skeet) barrels, stock dimensions of 14-3/8"-14-3/4"x2-3/16"x1-1/2". Weighs about 7-3/4 lbs. Introduced 1994. Imported from Italy by Precision Sales International.
Price: Grade I, right-hand **$1,490.00**
Price: Grade II, right-hand **$1,828.00**
Price: Grade III, right-hand, from **$3,093.00**

MAROCCHI MODEL 99 SPORTING TRAP AND SKEET O/U SHOTGUNS
Gauge: 12, 2-3/4", 3" chambers. **Barrel:** 28", 30", 32". **Stock:** French walnut. **Features:** Boss Locking system, screw-in chokes, low recoil, lightweight Monoblock barrels and ribs. Imported from Italy by Precision Sales International.
Price: Grade I **$2,350.00**
Price: Grade II **$2,870.00**

Price: Grade II Gold **$3,025.00**
Price: Grade III **$3,275.00**
Price: Grade III Gold **$3,450.00**
Price: Blackgold **$4,150.00**
Price: Lodestar **$5,125.00**
Price: Brittania **$5,125.00**
Price: Diana **$6,350.00**

MAROCCHI CONQUISTA USA MODEL 92 SPORTING CLAYS O/U SHOTGUN
Gauge: 12, 3" chambers. **Barrel:** 30"; back-bored, ported (ContreChoke Plus tubes); 10 mm concave ventilated top rib, ventilated middle rib. **Weight:** 8 lbs. 2 oz. **Stock:** 14-1/4"-14-5/8"x 2-1/8"x1-3/8"; American walnut with checkered grip and forend; sporting clays butt pad. **Features:** Low profile frame; fast lock time; automatic selective ejectors; blued receiver and barrels. Comes with three choke tubes. Ergonomically shaped trigger adjustable for pull length without tools. Barrels are back-bored and ported. Introduced 1996. Imported from Italy by Precision Sales International.
Price: **$1,490.00**

MERKEL MODEL 2001EL O/U SHOTGUN
Gauge: 12, 20, 3" chambers, 28, 2-3/4" chambers. **Barrel:** 12-28"; 20, 28 ga.-26-3/4". **Weight:** About 7 lbs. (12 ga.). **Stock:** Oil-finished walnut; English or pistol grip. **Features:** Self-cocking Blitz boxlock action with cocking indicators; Kersten double cross-bolt lock; silver-grayed receiver with engraved hunting scenes; coil spring ejectors; single selective or double triggers. Imported from Germany by GSI, Inc.
Price: 12, 20 . . . . **$7,295.00**
Price: 28 ga. **$7,295.00**
Price: Model 2000EL (scroll engraving, 12, 20 or 28) **$5,795.00**

Merkel Model 303EL O/U Shotgun
Similar to Model 2001EL except Holland & Holland-style sidelock action with cocking indicators; English-style arabesque engraving. Available in 12, 20, 28 gauge. Imported from Germany by GSI, Inc.
Price: **$19,995.00**

Merkel Model 2002EL O/U Shotgun
Similar to Model 2001EL except dummy sideplates, arabesque engraving with hunting scenes; 12, 20, 28 gauge. Imported from Germany by GSI, Inc.
Price: **$10,995.00**

PERAZZI MX8/MX8 SPECIAL TRAP, SKEET O/U SHOTGUNS
Gauge: 12, 2-3/4" chambers. **Barrel:** Trap: 29-1/2" (Imp. Mod. & Extra Full), 31-1/2" (Full & Extra Full). Choke tubes optional. Skeet: 27-5/8" (skeet & skeet). **Weight:** About 8-1/2 lbs. (trap); 7 lbs., 15 oz. (skeet). **Stock:** Interchangeable and custom made to customer specs. **Features:** Has detachable and interchangeable trigger group with flat V springs. Flat 7/16" vent rib. Many options available. Imported from Italy by Perazzi U.S.A., Inc.
Price: From **$12,756.00**
Price: MX8 Special (adj. four-position trigger) From **$11,476.00**
Price: MX8 Special combo (o/u and single barrel sets) From . . . **$15,127.00**

Perazzi MX8 Special Skeet O/U Shotgun
Similar to the MX8 Skeet except has adjustable four-position trigger, skeet stock dimensions. Imported from Italy by Perazzi U.S.A., Inc.
Price: From **$11,166.00**

Perazzi MX8

Perazzi MX28

Piotti Boss

Rizzini S790 Emel

PERAZZI MX8 O/U SHOTGUNS
Gauge: 12, 2-3/4" chambers. **Barrel:** 28-3/8" (Imp. Mod. & Extra Full), 29-1/2" (choke tubes). **Weight:** 7 lbs., 12 oz. **Stock:** Special specifications. **Features:** Has single selective trigger; flat 7/16" x 5/16" vent rib. Many options available. Imported from Italy by Perazzi U.S.A., Inc.
Price: Standard **$12,532.00**
Price: Sporting **$11,166.00**
Price: Trap Double Trap (removable trigger group) **$15,581.00**
Price: Skeet **$12,756.00**
Price: SC3 grade (variety of engraving patterns) . . . . **$23,000.00+**
Price: SCO grade (more intricate engraving, gold inlays) . . . . **$39,199.00+**

Perazzi MX8/20 O/U Shotgun
Similar to the MX8 except has smaller frame and has a removable trigger mechanism. Available in trap, skeet, sporting or game models with fixed chokes or choke tubes. Stock is made to customer specifications. Introduced 1993. Imported from Italy by Perazzi U.S.A., Inc.
Price: From **$11,166.00**

PERAZZI MX12 HUNTING O/U SHOTGUNS
Gauge: 12, 2-3/4" chambers. **Barrel:** 26-3/4", 27-1/2", 28-3/8", 29-1/2" (Mod. & Full); choke tubes available in 27-5/8", 29-1/2" only (MX12C). **Weight:** 7 lbs., 4 oz. **Stock:** To customer specs; interchangeable. **Features:** Single selective trigger; coil springs used in action; Schnabel forend tip. Imported from Italy by Perazzi U.S.A., Inc.
Price: From **$11,166.00**
Price: MX12C (with choke tubes) From **$11,960.00**

Perazzi MX20 Hunting O/U Shotguns
Similar to the MX12 except 20 ga. frame size. Non-removable trigger group. Available in 20, 28, .410 with 2-3/4" or 3" chambers. 26" standard, and choked Mod. & Full. Weight is 6 lbs., 6 oz. Imported from Italy by Perazzi U.S.A., Inc.
Price: From **$11,166.00**
Price: MX20C (as above, 20 ga. only, choke tubes) From **$11,960.00**

PERAZZI MX10 O/U SHOTGUN
Gauge: 12, 2-3/4" chambers. **Barrel:** 29.5", 31.5" (fixed chokes). **Weight:** NA. **Stock:** Walnut; cheekpiece adjustable for elevation and cast. **Features:** Adjustable rib; vent side rib. Externally selective trigger. Available in single barrel, combo, over/under trap, skeet, pigeon and sporting models. Introduced 1993. Imported from Italy by Perazzi U.S.A., Inc.
Price: MX200410 . . . . **$18,007.00**

PERAZZI MX28, MX410 GAME O/U SHOTGUN
Gauge: 28, 2-3/4" chambers, .410, 3" chambers. **Barrel:** 26" (Imp. Cyl. & Full). **Weight:** NA. **Stock:** To customer specifications. **Features:** Made on scaled-down frames proportioned to the gauge. Introduced 1993. Imported from Italy by Perazzi U.S.A., Inc.
Price: From **$22,332.00**

PIOTTI BOSS O/U SHOTGUN
Gauge: 12, 20. **Barrel:** 26" to 32", chokes as specified. **Weight:** 6.5 to 8 lbs. **Stock:** Dimensions to customer specs. Best quality figured walnut. **Features:** Essentially a custom-made gun with many options. Introduced 1993. Imported from Italy by Wm. Larkin Moore.
Price: From **$48,000.00**

REMINGTON MODEL 332 O/U SHOTGUN
Gauge: 12, 3" chambers. **Barrel:** 26", 28", 30". **Weight:** 7.75 lbs. **Length:** 42" to 47". **Stock:** Satin-finished American walnut. **Sights:** Twin bead. **Features:** Light-contour, vent rib, RemChoke barrel, blued, traditional M-32 experience with M-300 Ideal performance, standard auto ejectors, set trigger. Proven boxlock action.
Price: **$1,624.00**

RIZZINI S790 EMEL O/U SHOTGUN
Gauge: 20, 28, .410. **Barrel:** 26", 27.5" (Imp. Cyl. & Imp. Mod.). **Weight:** About 6 lbs. **Stock:** 14"x1-1/2"x2-1/8". Extra fancy select walnut. **Features:** Boxlock action with profuse engraving; automatic ejectors; single selective trigger; silvered receiver. Comes with Nizzoli leather case. Introduced 1996. Imported from Italy by Wm. Larkin Moore & Co.
Price: From **$9,725.00**

Rizzini S792 EMEL O/U Shotgun
Similar to S790 EMEL except dummy sideplates with extensive engraving coverage. Nizzoli leather case. Introduced 1996. Imported from Italy by Wm. Larkin Moore & Co.
Price: From **$9,075.00**

Ruger Red Label

Sigarms SA5 Field

Silma 70EJ Deluxe

RIZZINI UPLAND EL O/U SHOTGUN
Gauge: 12, 16, 20, 28, .410. **Barrel:** 26", 27-1/2", Mod. & Full, Imp. Cyl. & Imp. Mod. choke tubes. **Weight:** About 6.6 lbs. **Stock:** 14-1/2"x1-1/2"x2-1/4". **Features:** Boxlock action; single selective trigger; ejectors; profuse engraving on silvered receiver. Comes with fitted case. Introduced 1996. Imported from Italy by Wm. Larkin Moore & Co.
Price: From **$3,350.00**

Rizzini Artemis O/U Shotgun
Same as Upland EL model except dummy sideplates with extensive game scene engraving. Fancy European walnut stock. Fitted case. Introduced 1996. Imported from Italy by Wm. Larkin Moore & Co.
Price: From **$2,100.00**

RIZZINI S782 EMEL O/U SHOTGUN
Gauge: 12, 2-3/4" chambers. **Barrel:** 26", 27.5" (Imp. Cyl. & Imp. Mod.). **Weight:** About 6.75 lbs. **Stock:** 14-1/2"x1-1/2"x2-1/4". Extra fancy select walnut. **Features:** Boxlock action with dummy sideplates, extensive engraving with gold inlaid game birds, silvered receiver, automatic ejectors, single selective trigger. Nizzoli leather case. Introduced 1996. Imported from Italy by Wm. Larkin Moore & Co.
Price: From **$11,450.00**

RUGER RED LABEL O/U SHOTGUNS
Gauge: 12, 20, 3" chambers; 28 2-3/4" chambers. **Barrel:** 26", 28" (skeet [two], Imp. Cyl., Full, Mod. screw-in choke tubes). Proved for steel shot. **Weight:** About 7 lbs. (20 ga.); 7-1/2 lbs. (12 ga.). **Length:** 43" overall (26" barrels). **Stock:** 14"x1-1/2"x2-1/2". Straight grain American walnut or black synthetic. Checkered pistol grip and forend, rubber butt pad. **Features:** Stainless steel receiver. Single selective mechanical trigger, selective automatic ejectors; serrated free-floating vent rib. Comes with two skeet, one Imp. Cyl., one Mod., one Full choke tube and wrench. Made in U.S. by Sturm, Ruger & Co.
Price: Red Label with pistol grip stock. **$1,622.00**
Price: English Field with straight-grip stock **$1,622.00**
Price: All-Weather Red Label with black synthetic stock **$1,622.00**
Price: Sporting clays (30" bbl.) **$1,622.00**

Ruger Engraved Red Label O/U Shotgun
Similar to Red Label except scroll engraved receiver with 24-carat gold game bird (pheasant in 12 gauge, grouse in 20 gauge, woodcock in 28 gauge, duck on All-Weather 12 gauge). Introduced 2000.
Price: Engraved Red Label
(12, 20 and 28 gauge in 26" and 28" barrels) **$1,811.00**

SARSILMAZ O/U SHOTGUNS
Gauge: 12, 3" chambers. **Barrel:** 26", 28"; fixed chokes or choke tubes. **Weight:** NA. **Length:** NA. **Stock:** Oil-finished hardwood. **Features:** Double or single selective trigger, wide vent rib, chrome-plated parts, blued finish. Introduced 2000. Imported from Turkey by Armsport Inc.
Price: Double triggers; mod. and full or imp. cyl.
and mod. fixed chokes **$499.95**
Price: Single selective trigger; imp. cyl. and mod. or mod.
and full fixed chokes **$575.00**
Price: Single selective trigger; five choke tubes and wrench **$695.00**

SIGARMS SA5 O/U SHOTGUNS
Gauge: 12, 20, 3" chamber. **Barrel:** 26-1/2", 27" (Full, Imp. Mod., Mod., Imp. Cyl., Cyl. choke tubes). **Weight:** 6.9 lbs. (12 gauge), 5.9 lbs. (20 gauge). **Stock:** 14-1/2" x 1-1/2" x 2-1/2". Select grade walnut; checkered 20 lpi at grip and forend. **Features:** Single selective trigger, automatic ejectors; hand engraved detachable side plate; matte nickel receiver, rest blued; tapered bolt lock-up. Introduced 1997. Imported by SIGARMS, Inc.
Price: Field, 12 gauge **$2,670.00**
Price: Sporting clays **$2,800.00**
Price: Field 20 gauge **$2,670.00**

SILMA MODEL 70EJ DELUXE O/U SHOTGUNS
Gauge: 12 (3-1/2" chambers), 20, .410 (3" chambers), 28 (2-3/4" chambers). **Barrel:** 28" (12 and 20 gauge, fixed and tubed, 28 and .410 fixed), 26" (12 and 20 fixed). **Weight:** 7.6 lbs 12 gauge, 6.9 lbs, 20, 28 and .410. **Stock:** Checkered select European walnut, pistol grip, solid rubber recoil pad. **Features:** Monobloc construction, chrome-moly blued steel barrels, raised vent rib, automatic safety and ejectors, single selective trigger, gold plated, bead front sight. Brushed, engraved receiver. Introduced 2002. Clays models introduced 2003. Imported from Italy by Legacy Sports International.
Price: 12 gauge. **$1,089.00**
Price: 20 gauge **$1,016.00**
Price: 28, .410 . . . . **$1,140.00**
Price: Sporting clays **$1,387.00**

Silma Model 70EJ Superlight O/U Shotgun
Similar to Silma 70EJ Deluxe except 12 gauge, 3" chambers, alloy receiver, weighs 5.6 lbs.
Price: 12, 20 multi-chokes (IC, M, F) **$1,191.00**

Silma Model 70EJ Standard O/U Shotgun
Similar to Silma 70EJ Deluxe except 12 and 20 gauge only, standard walnut stock, light engraving, silver-plated trigger.
Price: 12 gauge. **$1,016.00**
Price: 20 gauge **$944.00**

Stoeger Condor

Tristar Silver Sporting

SKB MODEL 85TSS O/U SHOTGUNS
Gauge: 12, 20, .410: 3"; 28, 2-3/4". **Barrel:** Chrome lined 26", 28", 30", 32" (w/choke tubes). **Weight:** 7 lbs., 7 oz. to 8 lbs., 14 oz. **Stock:** Hand-checkered American walnut with matte finish, Schnabel or grooved forend. Target stocks available in various styles. **Sights:** Metal bead front or HiViz competition sights. **Features:** Low profile boxlock action with Greener-style cross bolt; single selective trigger; manual safety. Back-bored barrels with lengthened forcing cones. Introduced 2004. Imported from Japan by G.U. Inc.
Price: Sporting clays, 12 or 20 . . . . **$1,949.00**
Price: Sporting clays, 28 . . . . **$1,949.00**
Price: Sporting clays set, 12 and 20 . . . . **$3,149.00**
Price: Skeet, 12 or 20 . . . . **$1,949.00**
Price: Skeet, 28 or .410 . . . . **$2,129.00 to $2,179.00**
Price: Skeet, three-barrel set, 20, 28, .410 . . . . **$4,679.00**
Price: Trap, standard or Monte Carlo **$1,499.00**
Price: Trap adjustable comb **$2,129.00**

SKB MODEL 585 O/U SHOTGUNS
Gauge: 12 or 20, 3"; 28, 2-3/4"; .410, 3". **Barrel:** 12 ga.-26", 28", 30", 32", 34" (InterChoke tubes); 20 ga.-26", 28" (InterChoke tubes); 28-26", 28" (InterChoke tubes); .410-26", 28" (InterChoke tubes). Ventilated side ribs. **Weight:** 6.6 to 8.5 lbs. **Length:** 43" to 51-3/8" overall. **Stock:** 14-1/8"x1-1/2"x2-3/16". Hand checkered walnut with high-gloss finish. Target stocks available in standard and Monte Carlo. **Sights:** Metal bead front (field), target style on skeet, trap, sporting clays. **Features:** Boxlock action; silver nitride finish with field or target pattern engraving; manual safety, automatic ejectors, single selective trigger. All 12 gauge barrels are back-bored, have lengthened forcing cones and longer choke tube system. Sporting clays models in 12 gauge with 28" or 30" barrels available with optional 3/8" step-up target-style rib, matte finish, nickel center bead, white front bead. Introduced 1992. Imported from Japan by G.U., Inc.
Price: Field **$1,499.00**
Price: Two-barrel field set, 12 & 20 . . . . **$2,399.00**
Price: Two-barrel field set, 20 & 28 or 28 & .410 . . . . **$2,469.00**

SKB Model 585 Gold Package
Similar to Model 585 Field except gold-plated trigger, two gold-plated game inlays, Schnabel forend. Silver or blue receiver. Introduced 1998. Imported from Japan by G.U. Inc.
Price: 12, 20 ga. **$1,689.00**
Price: 28, .410 . . . . **$1,749.00**

SKB Model 505 O/U Shotgun
Similar to Model 585 except blued receiver, standard bore diameter, standard InterChoke system on 12, 20, 28, different receiver engraving. Imported from Japan by G.U. Inc.
Price: Field, 12 (26", 28"), 20 (26", 28") **$1,229.00**

STOEGER CONDOR SPECIAL O/U SHOTGUNS
Gauge: 12, 20, 2-3/4" 3" chambers. **Barrel:** 26", 28". **Weight:** 7.7 lbs. **Sights:** Brass bead. **Features:** IC and M screw-in choke tubes with each gun. Oil finished hardwood with pistol grip and forend. Auto safety, single trigger, automatic extractors.

Price: **$350.00**
Price: Condor Special **$415.00**
Price: Supreme Deluxe w/SS and red bar sights **$500.00**
Price: Youth Model **$350.00**
Price: Competition Model (w/ported bbls.) **$579.00**

TRADITIONS CLASSIC SERIES O/U SHOTGUNS
Gauge: 12, 3"; 20, 3"; 16, 2-3/4"; 28, 2-3/4"; .410, 3". **Barrel:** 26" and 28". **Weight:** 6 lbs., 5 oz. to 7 lbs., 6 oz. **Length:** 43" to 45" overall. **Stock:** Walnut. **Features:** Single-selective trigger; chrome-lined barrels with screw-in choke tubes; extractors (Field Hunter and Field I models) or automatic ejectors (Field II and Field III models); rubber butt pad; top tang safety. Imported from Fausti of Italy by Traditions.
Price: Field Hunter: Blued receiver; 12 or 20 ga.; 26" bbl. has IC and Mod. tubes, 28" has mod. and full tubes **$669.00**
Price: Field I: Blued receiver; 12, 20, 28 ga. or .410; fixed chokes (26" has I.C. and mod., 28" has mod. and full) **$619.00**
Price: Field II: Coin-finish receiver; 12, 16, 20, 28 ga. or .410; gold trigger; choke tubes **$789.00**
Price: Field III: Coin-finish receiver; gold engraving and trigger; 12 ga.; 26" or 28" bbl.; choke tubes **$999.00**
Price: Upland II: Blued receiver; 12 or 20 ga.; English-style straight walnut stock; choke tubes **$839.00**
Price: Upland III: Blued receiver, gold engraving; 20 ga.; high-grade pistol grip walnut stock; choke tubes **$1,059.00**
Price: Upland III: Blued, gold engraved receiver, 12 ga. Round pistol grip stock, choke tubes **$1,059.00**
Price: Sporting Clay II: Silver receiver; 12 ga.; ported barrels with skeet, i.c., mod. and full extended tubes **$959.00**
Price: Sporting Clay III: Engraved receivers, 12 and 20 ga., walnut stock, vent rib, extended choke tubes **$1,189.00**

TRADITIONS MAG 350 SERIES O/U SHOTGUNS
Gauge: 12, 3-1/2". **Barrel:** 24", 26" and 28". **Weight:** 7 lbs. to 7 lbs., 4 oz. **Length:** 41" to 45" overall. **Stock:** Walnut or composite with Mossy Oak® Break-Up™ or Advantage® Wetlands ™ camouflage. **Features:** Black matte, engraved receiver; vent rib; automatic ejectors; single-selective trigger; three screw-in choke tubes; rubber recoil pad; top tang safety. Imported from Fausti of Italy by Traditions.
Price: (Mag Hunter II: 28" black matte barrels, walnut stock, includes I.C., Mod. and Full tubes) **$799.00**
Price: (Turkey II: 24" or 26" camo barrels, Break-Up™ camo stock, includes Mod., Full and X-Full tubes) **$889.00**
Price: (Waterfowl II: 28" camo barrels, Advantage Wetlands camo stock, includes IC, Mod. and Full tubes) **$899.00**

TRISTAR SILVER SPORTING O/U SHOTGUN
Gauge: 12, 2-3/4" chambers, 20 3" chambers. **Barrel:** 28", 30" (skeet, Imp. Cyl., Mod., Full choke tubes). **Weight:** 7-3/8 lbs. **Length:** 45-1/2" overall. **Stock:** 14-3/8"x1-1/2"x2-3/8". Figured walnut, cut checkering; sporting clays quick-mount buttpad. **Sights:** Target bead front. **Features:** Boxlock action with single selective trigger, automatic selective ejectors; special broadway channeled rib; vented barrel rib; chrome bores. Chrome-nickel finish on frame, with engraving. Introduced 1990. Imported from Italy by Tristar Sporting Arms Ltd.
Price: **$799.00**

Tristar Silver II

Tristar TR-SC "Emilio Rizzini"

Tristar TR Royal "Emilio Rizzini"

Tristar TR-Mag "Emilio Rizzini"

Tristar TR-Mag "Emilio Rizzini"
Mossy Oak® Shadow Grass Camo

Tristar Silver II O/U Shotgun
Similar to the Silver except 26" barrel (Imp. Cyl., Mod., Full choke tubes, 12 and 20 ga.), 28" (Imp. Cyl., Mod., Full choke tubes, 12 ga. only), 26" (Imp. Cyl. & Mod. fixed chokes, 28 and .410), automatic selective ejectors. Weight is about 6 lbs., 15 oz. (12 ga., 26").
Price: **$669.00**

TRISTAR TR-SC "EMILIO RIZZINI" O/U SHOTGUN
Gauge: 12, 20, 3" chambers. **Barrel:** 28", 30" (Imp. Cyl., Mod., Full choke tubes). **Weight:** 7-1/2 lbs. **Length:** 46" overall (28" barrel). **Stock:** 1-1/2"x2-3/8"x14-3/8". Semi-fancy walnut; pistol grip with palm swell; semi-beavertail forend; black sporting clays recoil pad. **Features:** Silvered boxlock action with Four Locks locking system, auto ejectors, single selective (inertia) trigger, auto safety. Hard chrome bores. Vent 10mm rib with target-style front and mid-rib beads. Introduced 1998. Imported from Italy by Tristar Sporting Arms, Ltd.
Price: Sporting clay model. **$1,047.00**
Price: 20 ga. **$1,127.00**

Tristar TR-Royal "Emilio Rizzini" O/U Shotgun
Similar to the TR-SC except has special parallel stock dimensions (1-1/2"x1-5/8"x14-3/8") to give low felt recoil; Rhino ported, extended choke tubes; solid barrel spacer; has "TR-Royal" gold engraved on the silvered receiver. Available in 12 gauge (28", 30") 20 and 28 gauge (28" only). Introduced 1999. Imported from Italy by Tristar Sporting Arms, Ltd.
Price: 12, 20, 28 ga. **$1,319.00**

Tristar TR-L "Emilio Rizzini" O/U Shotgun
Similar to the TR-SC except has stock dimensions designed for female shooters (1-1/2"x3"x13-1/2"). Standard grade walnut. Introduced 1998. Imported from Italy by Tristar Sporting Arms, Ltd.
Price: **$1,063.00**

TRISTAR TR-I, II "EMILIO RIZZINI" O/U SHOTGUNS
Gauge: 12, 20, 3" chambers (TR-I); 12, 16, 20, 28, .410 3" chambers. **Barrel:** 12 ga., 26" (Imp. Cyl. & Mod.), 28" (Mod. & Full); 20 ga., 26" (Imp. Cyl. & Mod.), fixed chokes. **Weight:** 7-1/2 lbs. **Stock:** 1-1/2"x2-3/8"x14-3/8". Walnut with palm swell pistol grip, hand checkering, semi-beavertail forend, black recoil pad. **Features:** Boxlock action with blued finish, Four Locks locking system, gold single selective (inertia) trigger system, automatic ejectors, extractors. Introduced 1998. Imported from Italy by Tristar Sporting Arms, Ltd.
Price: TR-I. **$779.00**
Price: TR-II (automatic ejectors, choke tubes) 12, 16 ga. **$919.00**
Price: 20, 28 ga., .410 . . . . **$969.00**

Tristar TR-Mag "Emilio Rizzini" O/U Shotguns
Similar to TR-I, 3-1/2" chambers; choke tubes; 24" or 28" barrels with three choke tubes; extractors; auto safety. Matte blue finish on all metal, non-reflective wood finish. Introduced 1998. Imported from Italy by Tristar Sporting Arms, Ltd.
Price: **$799.00**
Price: Mossy Oak® Break-Up™ camo **$969.00**
Price: Mossy Oak® Shadow Grass camo **$969.00**
Price: 10 ga., Mossy Oak® camo patterns **$1,132.10**

Tristar TR-Class SL "Emilio Rizzini"

Verona LX501 Hunting Combo

Verona LX692G

Verona LX680TC

TRISTAR TR-CLASS SL "EMILIO RIZZINI" O/U SHOTGUN
Gauge: 12, 2-3/4" chambers. **Barrel:** 28", 30". **Weight:** 7-3/4 lbs. **Stock:** Fancy walnut, hand checkering, semi-beavertail forend, black recoil pad, gloss finish. **Features:** Hand-fitted gun. Boxlock action with silvered, engraved sideplates; Four Lock locking system; automatic ejectors; hard chrome bores; vent tapered 7mm rib with target-style front bead. Introduced 1999. Imported from Italy by Tristar Sporting Arms, Ltd.
Price: **$1,775.00**

TRISTAR WS/OU 12 O/U SHOTGUN
Gauge: 12, 3-1/2" chambers. **Barrel:** 28" or 30" (Imp. Cyl., Mod., Full choke tubes). **Weight:** 6 lbs., 15 oz. **Length:** 46" overall. **Stock:** 14-1/8"x1-1/8"x2-3/8". European walnut with cut checkering, black vented recoil pad, matte finish. **Features:** Boxlock action with single selective trigger, automatic selective ejectors; chrome bores. Matte metal finish. Imported by Tristar Sporting Arms Ltd.
Price: **$645.00**

VERONA LX501 HUNTING O/U SHOTGUNS
Gauge: 12, 20, 28, .410 (2-3/4", 3" chambers). **Barrel:** 28"; 12, 20 ga. have Interchoke tubes, 28 ga. and .410 have fixed Full & Mod. **Weight:** 6-7 lbs. **Stock:** Matte-finished walnut with machine-cut checkering. **Features:** Gold-plated single-selective trigger; ejectors; engraved, blued receiver, non-automatic safety; coil spring-operated firing pins. Introduced 1999. Imported from Italy by B.C. Outdoors.
Price: 12 and 20 ga. **$878.08**
Price: 28 ga. and .410 . . . . **$926.72**
Price: .410 . . . . **$907.01**
Price: Combos 20/28, 28/.410 . . . . **$1,459.20**

Verona LX692 Gold Hunting O/U Shotguns
Similar to Verona LX501 except engraved, silvered receiver with false sideplates showing gold inlaid bird hunting scenes on three sides;

Schnabel forend tip; hand-cut checkering; black rubber butt pad. Available in 12 and 20 gauge only, five Interchoke tubes. Introduced 1999. Imported from Italy by B.C. Outdoors.
Price: **$1,295.00**
Price: LX692G Combo 28/.410 . . . . **$2,192.40**

Verona LX680 Sporting O/U Shotgun
Similar to Verona LX501 except engraved, silvered receiver; ventilated middle rib; beavertail forend; hand-cut checkering; available in 12 or 20 gauge only with 2-3/4" chambers. Introduced 1999. Imported from Italy by B.C. Outdoors.
Price: **$1,159.68**

Verona LX680 Skeet/Sporting/Trap O/U Shotgun
Similar to Verona LX501 except skeet or trap stock dimensions; beavertail forend, palm swell on pistol grip; ventilated center barrel rib. Introduced 1999. Imported from Italy by B.C. Outdoors.
Price: **$1,736.96**

Verona LX692 Gold Sporting O/U Shotgun
Similar to Verona LX680 except false sideplates have gold-inlaid bird hunting scenes on three sides; red high-visibility front sight. Introduced 1999. Imported from Italy by B.C. Outdoors.
Price: Skeet/sporting **$1,765.12**
Price: Trap (32" barrel, 7-7/8 lbs.) **$1,594.80**

VERONA LX680 COMPETITION TRAP O/U SHOTGUNS
Gauge: 12. **Barrel:** 30" O/U, 32" single bbl. **Weight:** 8-3/8 lbs. combo, 7 lbs. single. **Stock:** Walnut. **Sights:** White front, mid-rib bead. **Features:** Interchangeable barrels switch from o/u to single configurations. 5 Briley chokes in combo, 4 in single bbl. extended forcing cones, ported barrels 32" with raised rib. By B.C. Outdoors.
Price: Trap Single (LX680TGTSB) **$1,736.96**
Price: Trap Combo (LX680TC) **$2,553.60**

SHOTGUNS — Over/Unders

Verona LX702GCT

Weatherby Athena Grade V Classic Field

Weatherby Orion Grade III Field

Weatherby Orion Upland

Winchester Supreme Sporting

VERONA LX702 GOLD TRAP COMBO O/U SHOTGUNS
Gauge: 20/28, 2-3/4" chamber. **Barrel:** 30". **Weight:** 7 lbs. **Stock:** Turkish walnut with beavertail forearm. **Sights:** White front bead. **Features:** 2-barrel competition gun. Color case-hardened side plates and receiver with gold inlaid pheasant. Vent rib between barrels. 5 Interchokes. Imported from Italy by B.C. Outdoors.
Price: Combo **$2,467.84**
Price: 20 ga. **$1,829.12**

Verona LX702 Skeet/Trap O/U Shotguns
Similar to Verona LX702. Both are 12 gauge and 2-3/4" chamber. Skeet has 28" barrel and weighs 7-3/4 lbs. Trap has 32" barrel and weighs 7-7/8 lbs. By B.C. Outdoors.
Price: Skeet **$1,829.12**
Price: Trap **$1,829.12**

WEATHERBY ATHENA GRADE V CLASSIC FIELD O/U SHOTGUN
Gauge: 12, 20, 3" chambers. **Barrel:** 26", 28", IMC multi-choke tubes. **Weight:** 12 ga., 7-1/4 to 8 lbs.; 20 ga. 6-1/2 to 7-1/4 lbs. **Stock:** Oil-finished American Claro walnut with fine-line checkering, rounded pistol grip and slender forend. **Features:** Old English recoil pad. Sideplate receiver has rose and scroll engraving.
Price: **$3,037.00**

Weatherby Athena Grade III Classic Field O/U Shotgun
Similar to Athena Grade V, has Grade III Claro walnut with oil finish, rounded pistol grip, slender forend; silver nitride/gray receiver has rose and scroll engraving with gold-overlay upland game scenes. Introduced 1999. Imported from Japan by Weatherby.
Price: 12, 20, 28 ga. **$2,173.00**

WEATHERBY ORION GRADE III FIELD O/U SHOTGUNS
Gauge: 12, 20, 3" chambers. **Barrel:** 26", 28", IMC multi-choke tubes. **Weight:** 6-1/2 to 8 lbs. **Stock:** 14-1/4"x1-1/2"x2-1/2". American walnut, checkered grip and forend. Rubber recoil pad. **Features:** Selective automatic ejectors, single selective inertia trigger. Top tang safety,

Greener cross bolt. Has silver-gray receiver with engraving and gold duck/pheasant. Imported from Japan by Weatherby.
Price: Orion III, Field, 12, IMC, 26", 28" **$1,955.00**
Price: Orion III, Field, 20, IMC, 26", 28" **$1,955.00**

Weatherby Orion Grade II Classic Field O/U Shotgun
Similar to Orion Grade III Field except stock has high-gloss finish, and bird on receiver is not gold. Available in 12 gauge, 26", 28", 30" barrels, 20 gauge, 26" 28", both with 3" chambers, 28 gauge, 26", 2-3/4" chambers. All have IMC choke tubes. Imported from Japan by Weatherby.
Price: **$1,622.00**

Weatherby Orion Upland O/U Shotgun
Similar to Orion Grade III Field. Plain blued receiver, gold W on trigger guard; rounded pistol grip, slender forend of Claro walnut with high-gloss finish; black butt pad. Available in 12 and 20 gauge with 26" and 28" barrels. Introduced 1999. Imported from Japan by Weatherby.
Price: **$1,299.00**

WEATHERBY ORION SSC O/U SHOTGUN
Gauge: 12, 3" chambers. **Barrel:** 28", 30", 32" (skeet, SC1, Imp. Cyl., SC2, Mod. IMC choke tubes). **Weight:** About 8 lbs. **Stock:** 14-3/4"x2-1/4"x1-1/2". Claro walnut with satin oil finish; Schnabel forend tip; sporter-style pistol grip; Pachmayr Decelerator recoil pad. **Features:** Designed for sporting clays competition. Has lengthened forcing cones and back-boring; ported barrels with 12mm grooved rib with mid-bead sight; mechanical trigger is adjustable for length of pull. Introduced 1998. Imported from Japan by Weatherby.
Price: SSC (Super Sporting Clays). **$2,059.00**

WINCHESTER SELECT O/U SHOTGUNS
Gauge: 12, 2-3/4", 3" chambers. **Barrel:** 28", 30", Invector Plus choke tubes. **Weight:** 7 lbs. 6 oz. to 7 lbs. 12. oz. **Length:** 45" overall (28" barrel). **Stock:** Checkered walnut stock. **Features:** Chrome-plated chambers; back-bored barrels; tang barrel selector/safety; deep-blued finish. Introduced 2000. From U.S. Repeating Arms. Co.
Price: Select Field (26" or 28" barrel, 6mm vent rib) **$1,498.00**
Price: Select Energy **$1,950.00**
Price: Select Elegance **$2,320.00**
Price: Select Energy Trap **$1,871.00**
Price: Select Energy Trap adjustable **$2,115.00**
Price: Select Energy Sporting adjustable **$2,115.00**

Variety of models for utility and sporting use, including some competitive shooting.

Charles Daly Superior Hunter

Charles Daly Empire Hunter AE-MC

Charles Daly Diamond DL

Charles Daly Diamond Regent DL

ARRIETA SIDELOCK DOUBLE SHOTGUNS
Gauge: 12, 16, 20, 28, .410. **Barrel:** Length and chokes to customer specs. **Weight:** To customer specs. **Stock:** To customer specs. Straight English with checkered butt (standard), or pistol grip. Select European walnut with oil finish. **Features:** Essentially custom gun with myriad options. H&H pattern hand-detachable sidelocks, selective automatic ejectors, double triggers (hinged front) standard. Some have self-opening action. Finish and engraving to customer specs. Imported from Spain by Wingshooting Adventures.

Price: Model 557, auto ejectors. From **$3,250.00**
Price: Model 570, auto ejectors. From **$3,950.00**
Price: Model 578, auto ejectors. From **$4,350.00**
Price: Model 600 Imperial, self-opening. From **$6,050.00**
Price: Model 601 Imperial Tiro, self-opening. From **$6,950.00**
Price: Model 801. From **$9,135.00**
Price: Model 802. From **$9,135.00**
Price: Model 803. From **$6,930.00**
Price: Model 871, auto ejectors. From **$5,060.00**
Price: Model 872, self-opening. From **$12,375.00**
Price: Model 873, self-opening. From **$8,200.00**
Price: Model 874, self-opening. From **$9,250.00**
Price: Model 875, self-opening. From **$14,900.00**

CHARLES DALY SUPERIOR HUNTER AND SUPERIOR MC DOUBLE SHOTGUNS
Gauge: 12, 20, 3" chambers, 28, 2-3/4" chambers. **Barrel:** 28" (Mod. & Full) 26" (Imp. Cyl. & Mod.). **Weight:** About 7 lbs. **Stock:** Checkered walnut pistol grip buttstock, splinter forend. **Features:** Silvered, engraved receiver; chrome-lined barrels; gold single trigger; automatic safety; extractors; gold bead front sight. Introduced 1997. Imported from Italy by K.B.I., Inc.

Price: Superior Hunter, 28 gauge and .410 . . . . **$1,659.00**
Price: Superior Hunter MC 26"-28" **$1,629.00**

CHARLES DALY EMPIRE HUNTER AE-MC Double Shotgun
Similar to Superior Hunter except deluxe wood English-style stock, game scene engraving, automatic ejectors. Introduced 1997. Imported from Italy by K.B.I., Inc.

Price: 12 or 20 . . . . **$2,119.00**

CHARLES DALY DIAMOND DL DOUBLE SHOTGUN
Gauge: 12, 20, .410, 3" chambers, 28, 2-3/4" chambers. **Barrel:** 28" (Mod. & Full), 26" (Imp. Cyl. & Mod.), 26" (Full & Full, .410). **Weight:** From 5 lbs. to 7 lbs. **Stock:** Select fancy European walnut, English-style butt, beavertail forend; hand-checkered, hand-rubbed oil finish. **Features:** Drop-forged action with gas escape valves; demi-block barrels with concave rib; selective automatic ejectors; hand-detachable double safety sidelocks with hand-engraved rose and scrollwork. Hinged front trigger. Color case-hardened receiver. Introduced 1997. Imported from Spain by K.B.I., Inc.

Price: . . . . **Special order only**

CHARLES DALY DIAMOND REGENT DL DOUBLE SHOTGUN
Gauge: 12, 20, .410, 3" chambers, 28, 2-3/4" chambers. **Barrel:** 28" (Mod. & Full), 26" (Imp. Cyl. & Mod.), 26" (Full & Full, .410). **Weight:** About 5-7 lbs. **Stock:** Special select fancy European walnut, English-style butt, splinter forend; hand-checkered; hand-rubbed oil finish. **Features:** Drop-forged action with gas escape valves; demi-block barrels of chrome-nickel steel with concave rib; selective automatic-ejectors; hand-detachable, double-safety H&H sidelocks with demi-relief hand engraving; H&H pattern easy-opening feature; hinged trigger; coin finished action. Introduced 1997. Imported from Spain by K.B.I., Inc.

Price: Special Custom Order . . . . **NA**

CHARLES DALY FIELD II, AE-MC HUNTER DOUBLE SHOTGUN
Gauge: 12, 20, 28, .410 (3" chambers; 28 has 2-3/4"). **Barrel:** 32" (Mod. & Mod.), 28, 30" (Mod. & Full), 26" (Imp. Cyl. & Mod.) .410 (Full & Full). **Weight:** 6 lbs. to 11.4 lbs. **Stock:** Checkered walnut pistol grip and forend. **Features:** Silvered, engraved receiver; gold single selective trigger in 10, 12, and 20 ga.; double triggers in 28 and .410; automatic safety; extractors; gold bead front sight. Introduced 1997. Imported from Spain by K.B.I., Inc.

Price: 28 ga., .410-bore **$1,189.00**
Price: 12 or 20 AE-MC **$1,099.00**

Charles Daly Field II Hunter

EAA Baikal IZH43K Bounty Hunter

EAA Baikal MP-213

Fabarm Classic Lion

Fabarm Classic Lion Elite

DAKOTA PREMIER GRADE SHOTGUN
Gauge: 12, 16, 20, 28, .410. **Barrel:** 27". **Weight:** NA. **Length:** NA. **Stock:** Exhibition-grade English walnut, hand-rubbed oil finish with straight grip and splinter forend. **Features:** French grey finish; 50 percent coverage engraving; double triggers; selective ejectors. Finished to customer specifications. Made in U.S. by Dakota Arms.
Price: 12, 16, 20 gauge **$13,950.00**
Price: 28 gauge and .410 .... **$15,345.00**

Dakota Legend Shotgun
Similar to Premier Grade except has special selection English walnut, full-coverage scroll engraving, oak and leather case. Made in U.S. by Dakota Arms.
Price: 12, 16, 20 gauge **$18,000.00**
Price: 28 gauge and .410 .... **$19,800.00**

EAA BAIKAL BOUNTY HUNTER IZH43K SHOTGUN
Gauge: 12, 3" chambers. **Barrel:** 18-1/2", 20", 24", 26", 28", three choke tubes. **Weight:** 7.28 lbs. Overall **length:** NA. **Stock:** Walnut, checkered forearm and grip. **Features:** Machined receiver; hammer-forged barrels with chrome-lined bores; external hammers; double triggers (single, selective trigger available); rifle barrel inserts optional. Imported by European American Armory.
Price: .... **$379.00 to 399.00**

EAA BAIKAL IZH43 BOUNTY HUNTER SHOTGUN
Gauge: 12, 3" chambers. **Barrel:** 20", 24", 26", 28"; imp., mod. and full choke tubes. **Stock:** Hardwood or walnut; checkered forend and grip.

Features: Hammer forged barrel; internal hammers; extractors; engraved receiver; automatic tang safety; non-glare rib. Imported by European American Armory.
Price: IZH43 Bounty Hunter (12 gauge, 2-3/4" chambers, 20" brl.,
dbl. triggers, hardwood stock) **$329.00**
Price: IZH43 Bounty Hunter (20 gauge, 3" chambers,
20" bbl., dbl. triggers, walnut stock) **$359.00**

E.M.F. HARTFORD MODEL COWBOY SHOTGUN
Gauge: 12. **Barrel:** 20". **Weight:** NA. **Length:** NA. **Stock:** Checkered walnut. **Sights:** Center bead. **Features:** Exposed hammers; color case-hardened receiver; blued barrel. Introduced 2001. Imported from Spain by E.M.F. Co. Inc.
Price: **$625.00**

FABARM CLASSIC LION DOUBLE SHOTGUNS
Gauge: 12, 3" chambers. **Barrel:** 26", 28", 30" (Cyl., Imp. Cyl., Mod., Imp. Mod., Full choke tubes). **Weight:** 7.2 lbs. **Length:** 44.5"-48.5. **Stock:** English-style or pistol grip oil-finished European walnut. **Features:** Boxlock action with double triggers, automatic ejectors, automatic safety. Introduced 1998. Imported from Italy by Heckler & Koch, Inc.
Price: Grade I **$1,499.00**
Price: Grade II **$2,099.00**
Price: Elite (color case-hardened type finish, 44.5") **$1,689.00**

A.H. Fox DE Grade

Garbi Model 100

Bill Hanus Birdgun

FOX, A.H., SIDE-BY-SIDE SHOTGUNS
Gauge: 16, 20, 28, .410. **Barrel:** Length and chokes to customer specifications. Rust-blued Chromox or Krupp steel. **Weight:** 5-1/2 to 6-3/4 lbs. **Stock:** Dimensions to customer specifications. Hand-checkered Turkish Circassian walnut with hand-rubbed oil finish. Straight, semi or full pistol grip; splinter, Schnabel or beavertail forend; traditional pad, hard rubber buttplate or skeleton butt. **Features:** Boxlock action with automatic ejectors; double or Fox single selective trigger. Scalloped, rebated and color case-hardened receiver; hand finished and hand-engraved. Grades differ in engraving, inlays, grade of wood, amount of hand finishing. Introduced 1993. Made in U.S. by Connecticut Shotgun Mfg.

Price: CE Grade	$11,000.00
Price: XE Grade	$12,500.00
Price: DE Grade	$15,000.00
Price: FE Grade	$20,000.00
Price: Exhibition Grade	$30,000.00
Price: 28/.410 CE Grade	$12,500.00
Price: 28/.410 XE Grade	$14,000.00
Price: 28/.410 DE Grade	$16,500.00
Price: 28/.410 FE Grade	$21,500.00
Price: 28/.410 Exhibition Grade	$30,000.00
Price: 28 or .410-bore	$1,500.00

GARBI MODEL 100 DOUBLE SHOTGUN
Gauge: 12, 16, 20, 28. **Barrel:** 26", 28", choked to customer specs. **Weight:** 5-1/2 to 7-1/2 lbs. **Stock:** 14-1/2"x2-1/4"x1-1/2". European walnut. Straight grip, checkered butt, classic forend. **Features:** Sidelock action, automatic ejectors, double triggers standard. Color case-hardened action, coin finish optional. Single trigger; beavertail forend; etc. optional. Five additional models available. Imported from Spain by Wm. Larkin Moore.
Price: From $4,850.00

Garbi Model 101 Side-by-Side Shotgun
Similar to the Garbi Model 100 except hand engraved with scroll engraving; select walnut stock; better overall quality than the Model 100. Imported from Spain by Wm. Larkin Moore.
Price: From $6,250.00

Garbi Model 103 A & B Side-by-Side Shotguns
Similar to the Garbi Model 100 except has Purdey-type fine scroll and rosette engraving. Better overall quality than the Model 101. Model 103B has nickel-chrome steel barrels, H&H-type easy opening mechanism; other mechanical details remain the same. Imported from Spain by Wm. Larkin Moore.
Price: Model 103A. From $8,000.00
Price: Model 103B. From $11,800.00

Garbi Model 200 Side-by-Side Shotgun
Similar to the Garbi Model 100 except has heavy-duty locks, magnum proofed. Very fine Continental-style floral and scroll engraving, well figured walnut stock. Other mechanical features remain the same. Imported from Spain by Wm. Larkin Moore.
Price: $11,200.00

HANUS BIRDGUN SHOTGUN
Gauge: 16, 20, 28. **Barrel:** 27", 20 and 28 ga.; 28", 16 ga. (skeet 1 & skeet 2). **Weight:** 5 lbs., 4 oz. to 6 lbs., 4 oz. **Stock:** 14-3/8"x1-1/2"x2-3/8", with 1/4" cast-off. Select walnut. **Features:** Boxlock action with ejectors; splinter forend, straight English grip; checkered butt; English leather-covered handguard and AyA snap caps included. Made by AyA. Introduced 1998. Imported from Spain by Bill Hanus Birdguns.
Price: $2,795.00

ITHACA CLASSIC DOUBLES SKEET GRADE SxS SHOTGUN
Gauge: 20, 28, 2-3/4" chambers, .410, 3". **Barrel:** 26", 28", 30", fixed chokes. **Weight:** 5 lbs., 14 oz. (20 gauge). **Stock:** 14-1/2"x2-1/4"x1-3/8". High-grade American black walnut, hand-rubbed oil finish; splinter or beavertail forend, straight or pistol grip. **Features:** Double triggers, ejectors; color case-hardened, engraved action body with matted top surfaces. Introduced 1999. Made in U.S. by Ithaca Classic Doubles.
Price: From $5,999.00

ITHACA CLASSIC DOUBLES GRADE 4E CLASSIC SXS SHOTGUN
Gauge: 10, 12, 16, 20, 28, .410 bore, 2-3/4" and 3" chambers. **Barrels:** 26", 28", 30". **Weight:** 5 lbs., 5 oz. to 6 lbs., 6 oz. **Features:** Gold-plated triggers, jewelled barrel flats and hand-turned locks. Feather crotch and flame-grained black walnut hand-checkered 28 lpi with fleur-de-lis pattern. Action body engraved with three game scenes and bank note scroll, color case-hardened. Introduced 1999. Made in U.S.A. by Ithaca Classic Doubles.
Price: From $7,500.00

ITHACA CLASSIC DOUBLES GRADE 5E SXS SHOTGUN
Gauge: 10, 12, 16, 20, 28, .410 bore, 2-3/4" and 3" chambers. **Barrels:** 26", 28", 30". **Weight:** 5 lbs., 5 oz. to 6 lbs., 6 oz. **Stock:** High-grade Turkish and American walnut and are hand-checkered. **Features:** Completely handmade, based on the early Ithaca engraving patterns of master engraver William McGraw. The hand engraving is at 90% coverage in deep chiseled floral scroll with game scenes in 24kt gold inlays. Available in 12, 16, 20, 28 gauges and .410 bore including two-barrel combination sets in 16/20 ga. and 28/.410 bore. Introduced 2003. Made in U.S.A. by Ithaca Classic Doubles.
Price: From $8,500.00

Merkel Model 47E

Merkel Model 47SL

Merkel Model 280EL/360EL Two-Barrel Set

ITHACA CLASSIC DOUBLES GRADE 6E SIDE-BY-SIDE SHOTGUN

Gauge: 10, 12, 16, 20, 28, .410 bore, 2-3/4" and 3" chambers. **Barrels:** 26", 28", 30". **Weight:** 5 lbs., 5 oz. to 6 lbs., 6 oz. **Stock:** Handmade of best quality American, Turkish or English walnut with hand checkering. **Features:** Features hand engraving of fine English scroll coupled with game scenes and 24kt gold inlays. All metal work is finished in traditional bone and charcoal color case-hardening and deep rust blue. Available in 12, 16, 20, 28 gauges and .410 bore. Introduced 2003. Made in U.S.A. by Ithaca Classic Doubles.
Price: From **$10,000.00**

ITHACA CLASSIC DOUBLES GRADE 7E CLASSIC SXS SHOTGUN

Gauge: 10, 12, 16, 20, 28, .410 bore, 2-3/4" and 3" chambers. **Barrels:** 26", 28", 30". **Weight:** 5 lbs., 5 oz. to 6 lbs., 6 oz. **Stock:** Exhibition grade American black walnut stock and forend with eight-panel fleur-de-lis borders. **Features:** Engraved with banknote scroll and flat 24k gold game scenes; gold setter and gold pointer on opposite action sides, American bald eagle inlaid on bottom plate. Hand polished, jewelled ejectors and locks. Introduced 1999. Made in U.S.A. by Ithaca Classic Doubles.
Price: From **$11,000.00**

ITHACA CLASSIC DOUBLES SOUSA GRADE SIDE-BY-SIDE SHOTGUN

Gauge: 10, 12, 16, 20, 28, .410 bore, 3" chambers. **Barrels:** 26", 28", 30". **Weight:** 5 lbs., 5 oz. to 6 lbs., 6 oz. **Stock:** American black walnut, hand-carved and checkered. **Features:** Presentation grade hand-engraving with 24-karat gold inlays; tuned action and hand-applied finishes. Made in U.S.A. by Ithaca Classic Doubles.
Price: From **$18,000.00**

KIMBER VALIER GRADE I and II SHOTGUN

Gauge: 20, 3" chambers. **Barrels:** 26" or 28", IC and M. **Weight:** 6 lbs. 8 oz. **Stock:** Turkish walnut, English style. **Features:** Sidelock design, double triggers, 50-percent engraving; 24 lpi checkering; auto-ejectors (extractors only on Grade I). Color case-hardened sidelocks, rust blue barrels. Imported from Turkey by Kimber Mfg., Inc.
Price: Grade I **$3,879.00**
Price: Grade II **$4,480.00**

LEBEAU — COURALLY BOXLOCK SIDE-BY-SIDE SHOTGUN

Gauge: 12, 16, 20, 28, .410-bore. **Barrel:** 25" to 32". **Weight:** To customer specifications. **Stock:** French walnut. **Features:** Anson & Deely-type action with automatic ejectors; single or double triggers. Custom gun built to customer specifications. Imported from Belgium by Wm. Larkin Moore.
Price: From **$25,500.00**

L. C. SMITH SIDE-BY-SIDE SHOTGUN

Gauge: 12, 20. **Barrel:** 26", 28". **Weight:** 6 or 6-1/4 lbs. **Stock:** Checkered walnut w/recoil pad. **Features:** 3" chambers, single trigger, selective automatic ejectors; solid rib, bead front sight. Imported from Italy by Marlin. Introduced 2005.
Price: **$1,884.00**

LEBEAU-COURALLY SIDELOCK SIDE-BY-SIDE SHOTGUN

Gauge: 12, 16, 20, 28, .410-bore. **Barrel:** 25" to 32". **Weight:** To customer specifications. **Stock:** Fancy French walnut. **Features:** Holland & Holland-type action with automatic ejectors; single or double triggers. Custom gun built to customer specifications. Imported from Belgium by Wm. Larkin Moore.
Price: From **$56,000.00**

MERKEL MODEL 47E, 147E SIDE-BY-SIDE SHOTGUNS

Gauge: 12, 3" chambers, 16, 2-3/4" chambers, 20, 3" chambers. **Barrel:** 12, 16 ga.-28"; 20 ga.-26-3/4" (Imp. Cyl. & Mod., Mod. & Full). **Weight:** About 6-3/4 lbs. (12 ga.). **Stock:** Oil-finished walnut; straight English or pistol grip. **Features:** Anson & Deely-type boxlock action with single selective or double triggers, automatic safety, cocking indicators. Color case-hardened receiver with standard arabesque engraving. Imported from Germany by GSI.
Price: Model 47E (H&H ejectors) **$3,295.00**
Price: Model 147E (as above with ejectors) **$3,995.00**

Merkel Model 47SL, 147SL Side-by-Side Shotguns

Similar to Model 47E except H&H style sidelock action with cocking indicators, ejectors. Silver-grayed receiver and sideplates have arabesque engraving, engraved border and screws (Model 47S), or fine hunting scene engraving (Model 147S). Imported from Germany by GSI.
Price: Model 47SL **$5,995.00**
Price: Model 147SL **$7,995.00**
Price: Model 247SL (English-style engraving, large scrolls) **$7,995.00**
Price: Model 447SL (English-style engraving, small scrolls) **$9,995.00**

Merkel Model 280EL, 360EL Shotguns

Similar to Model 47E except smaller frame. Greener cross bolt with double under-barrel locking lugs, fine engraved hunting scenes on silver-grayed receiver, luxury-grade wood, Anson and Deely box-lock action. H&H ejectors, single-selective or double triggers. Introduced 2000. From Merkel.
Price: Model 280EL (28 gauge, 28" barrel, Imp. Cyl. and
Mod. chokes) **$5,795.00**
Price: Model 360EL (.410, 28" barrel, Mod. and
Full chokes) **$5,795.00**
Price: Model 280/360EL two-barrel set (28 and .410 gauge
as above) **$8,295.00**

Piotti Lunik

Rizzini Sidelock

Ruger Gold Label

Stoeger Uplander

Merkel Model 280SL and 360SL Shotguns

Similar to Model 280EL and 360EL except has sidelock action, double triggers, English-style arabesque engraving. Introduced 2000. From Merkel.

Price: Model 280SL (28 gauge, 28" barrel, Imp. Cyl. and
Mod. chokes) **$8,495.00**
Price: Model 360SL (.410, 28" barrel, Mod. and
Full chokes) **$8,495.00**
Price: Model 280/360SL two-barrel set **$11,995.00**

PIOTTI KING NO. 1 SIDE-BY-SIDE SHOTGUN

Gauge: 12, 16, 20, 28, .410. **Barrel:** 25" to 30" (12 ga.), 25" to 28" (16, 20, 28, .410). To customer specs. Chokes as specified. **Weight:** 6-1/2 lbs. to 8 lbs. (12 ga. to customer specs.). **Stock:** Dimensions to customer specs. Finely figured walnut; straight grip with checkered butt with classic splinter forend and hand-rubbed oil finish standard. Pistol grip, beavertail forend. **Features:** Holland & Holland pattern sidelock action, automatic ejectors. Double trigger; non-selective single trigger optional. Coin finish standard; color case-hardened optional. Top rib; level, file-cut; concave, ventilated optional. Very fine, full coverage scroll engraving with small floral bouquets. Imported from Italy by Wm. Larkin Moore.
Price: From **$29,600.00**

Piotti King Extra Side-by-Side Shotgun

Similar to the Piotti King No. 1 except with upgraded engraving. Choice of any type of engraving, including bulino game scene engraving and game scene engraving with gold inlays. Engraved and signed by a master engraver. Other mechanical specifications remain the same. Imported from Italy by Wm. Larkin Moore.
Price: From **$35,000.00**

Piotti Lunik Side-by-Side Shotgun

Similar to the Piotti King No. 1 in overall quality. Has Renaissance-style large scroll engraving in relief. Best quality Holland & Holland-pattern sidelock ejector double with chopper lump (demi-bloc) barrels. Other mechanical specifications remain the same. Imported from Italy by Wm. Larkin Moore.
Price: From **$30,900.00**

PIOTTI PIUMA SIDE-BY-SIDE SHOTGUN

Gauge: 12, 16, 20, 28, .410. **Barrel:** 25" to 30" (12 ga.), 25" to 28" (16, 20, 28, .410). **Weight:** 5-1/2 to 6-1/4 lbs. (20 ga.). **Stock:** Dimensions to customer specs. Straight grip stock with walnut checkered butt, classic splinter forend, hand-rubbed oil finish are standard; pistol grip, beavertail forend, satin luster finish optional. **Features:** Anson & Deeley boxlock ejector double with chopper lump barrels. Level, file-cut rib, light scroll and rosette engraving, scalloped frame. Double triggers; single non-selective optional. Coin finish standard, color case-hardened optional. Imported from Italy by Wm. Larkin Moore.
Price: From **$14,800.00**

RIZZINI SIDELOCK SIDE-BY-SIDE SHOTGUN

Gauge: 12, 16, 20, 28, .410. **Barrel:** 25" to 30" (12, 16, 20 ga.), 25" to 28" (28, .410). To customer specs. Chokes as specified. **Weight:** 6-1/2 lbs. to 8 lbs. (12 ga. to customer specs). **Stock:** Dimensions to customer specs. Finely figured walnut; straight grip with checkered butt with classic splinter forend and hand-rubbed oil finish standard. Pistol grip, beavertail forend. **Features:** Sidelock action, auto ejectors. Double triggers or non-selective single trigger standard. Coin finish standard. Imported from Italy by Wm. Larkin Moore.
Price: 12, 20 ga. From **$66,900.00**
Price: 28, .410 bore. From **$75,500.00**

RUGER GOLD LABEL SIDE-BY-SIDE SHOTGUN

Gauge: 12, 3" chambers. **Barrel:** 28" with skeet tubes. **Weight:** 6-1/2 lbs. **Length:** 45". **Stock:** American walnut straight or pistol grip. **Sights:** Gold bead front, full length rib, serrated top. **Features:** Spring-assisted break-open, SS trigger, auto eject. Five interchangeable screw-in choke tubes, combination safety/barrel selector with auto safety reset.
Price: **$2,000.00**

STOEGER UPLANDER SIDE-BY-SIDE SHOTGUNS

Gauge: 16, 28, 2-3/4 chambers. 12, 20, .410, 3" chambers. **Barrel:** 26", 28". **Weight:** 7.3 lbs. **Sights:** Brass bead. **Features:** Double trigger, IC & M fixed choke tubes with gun.
Price: With fixed chokes **$335.00**
Price: With screw-in chokes) **$350.00**
Price: With English stock . . . . **$335.00 to $350.00**
Price: Upland Special **$375.00**
Price: Upland Supreme with SST, red bar sights **$445.00**
Price: Upland Short Stock (Youth) **$335.00**

Stoeger Silverado Coach

Traditions Uplander V

Tristar Rota Model 411

Price: Uplander III Silver 12, 20 ga. $2,699.00
Price: Uplander V Silver 12, 20 ga. $3,199.00

STOEGER COACH GUN SIDE-BY-SIDE SHOTGUNS
Gauge: 12, 20, .410, 2-3/4", 3" chambers. **Barrel:** 20". **Weight:** 6-1/2 lbs. **Stock:** Brown hardwood, classic beavertail forend. **Sights:** Brass bead. **Features:** IC & M fixed chokes, tang auto safety, auto extractors, black plastic buttplate. 12 ga. and 20 ga. also with English style stock.
Price: $320.00
Price: Nickel $375.00
Price: Silverado $375.00
Price: With English stock $375.00

TRADITIONS ELITE SERIES SIDE-BY-SIDE SHOTGUNS
Gauge: 12, 3"; 20, 3"; 28, 2-3/4"; .410, 3". **Barrel:** 26". **Weight:** 5 lbs., 12 oz. to 6-1/2 lbs. **Length:** 43" overall. **Stock:** Walnut. **Features:** Chrome-lined barrels; fixed chokes (Elite Field III ST, Field I DT and Field I ST) or choke tubes (Elite Hunter ST); extractors (Hunter ST and Field I models) or automatic ejectors (Field III ST); top tang safety. Imported from Fausti of Italy by Traditions.
Price: Elite Field I DT — 12, 20, 28 ga. or .410; IC and Mod. fixed chokes (F and F on .410); double triggers . . . . $789.00 to $969.00
Price: Elite Field I ST — 12, 20, 28 ga. or .410; same as DT but with single trigger . . . . $969.00 to $1,169.00
Price: Elite Field III ST — 28 ga. or .410; gold-engraved receiver; high-grade walnut stock $2,099.00
Price: Elite Hunter ST — 12 or 20 ga.; blued receiver; IC and Mod. choke tubes $999.00

TRADITIONS UPLANDER SERIES SIDE-BY-SIDE SHOTGUNS
Gauge: 12, 3"; 20, 3". **Barrel:** 26", 28". **Weight:** 6-1/4 lbs. to 6-1/2 lbs. **Length:** 43" to 45" overall. **Stock:** Walnut. **Features:** Barrels threaded for choke tubes (Improved Cylinder, Modified and Full); top tang safety, extended trigger guard. Engraved silver receiver with side plates and lavish gold inlays. Imported from Fausti of Italy by Traditions.

TRISTAR ROTA MODEL 411 SIDE-BY-SIDE SHOTGUN
Gauge: 12, 16, 20, .410, 3" chambers; 28, 2-3/4". **Barrel:** 12 ga., 26", 28"; 16, 20, 28 ga., .410-bore, 26"; 12 and 20 ga. have three choke tubes, 16, 28 (Imp. Cyl. & Mod.), .410 (Mod. & Full) fixed chokes. **Weight:** 6-1/2 to 7-1/4 lbs. **Stock:** 14-3/8" l.o.p. Standard walnut with pistol grip, splinter-style forend; hand checkered. **Features:** Engraved, color case-hardened boxlock action; double triggers, extractors; solid barrel rib. Introduced 1998. Imported from Italy by Tristar Sporting Arms, Ltd.
Price: $849.00

Tristar Rota Model 411D Side-by-Side Shotgun
Similar to Model 411 except automatic ejectors, straight English-style stock, single trigger. Solid barrel rib with matted surface; chrome bores; color case-hardened frame; splinter forend. Introduced 1999. Imported from Italy by Tristar Sporting Arms, Ltd.
Price: $1,110.00

Tristar Rota Model 411R Coach Gun Side-by-Side Shotgun
Similar to Model 411 except in 12 or 20 gauge only with 20" barrels and fixed chokes (Cyl. & Cyl.). Double triggers, extractors, choke tubes. Introduced 1999. Imported from Italy by Tristar Sporting Arms, Ltd.
Price: $745.00

Tristar Rota Model 411F Side-by-Side Shotgun
Similar to Model 411 except silver, engraved receiver, ejectors, IC, M and F choke tubes, English-style stock, single gold trigger, cut checkering. Imported from Italy by Tristar Sporting Arms Ltd.
Price: $1,608.00

TRISTAR DERBY CLASSIC SIDE-BY-SIDE SHOTGUN
Gauge: 12. **Barrel:** 28" Mod. & Full fixed chokes. **Features:** Sidelock action, engraved, double trigger, auto ejectors, English straight stock. Made in Europe for Tristar Sporting Arms Ltd.
Price: $1,059.00

Variety of designs for utility and sporting purposes, as well as for competitive shooting.

Browning BT-99 Trap

EAA Baikal IZH18

EAA Baikal IZH18Max

**H&R Model 928
Ultra Slug Hunter Deluxe**

BERETTA DT10 TRIDENT TRAP TOP SINGLE SHOTGUN
Gauge: 12, 3" chamber. **Barrel:** 34"; five Optima Choke tubes (Full, Full, Imp. Modified, Mod. and Imp. Cyl.). **Weight:** 8.8 lbs. **Stock:** High-grade walnut; adjustable. **Features:** Detachable, adjustable trigger group; Optima Bore for improved shot pattern and reduced recoil; slim Optima Choke tubes; raised and thickened receiver for long life. Introduced 2000. Imported from Italy by Beretta USA.
Price: **$6,995.00**

BRNO ZBK 100 SINGLE BARREL SHOTGUN
Gauge: 12 or 20. **Barrel:** 27.5". **Weight:** 5.5 lbs. **Length:** 44" overall. **Stock:** Beech. **Features:** Polished blue finish; sling swivels. Announced 1998. Imported from the Czech Republic by Euro-Imports.
Price: **$185.00**

BROWNING BT-99 TRAP SHOTGUNS
Gauge: 12, 2-3/4" chamber. **Barrel:** 32" or 34"; Invector choke system (full choke tube only included); High Post Rib; back-bored. **Weight:** 8 lbs., 10 oz. (34" bbl.). **Length:** 50-1/2" overall (34" bbl.). **Stock:** Conventional or adjustable comb. **Features:** Reintroduction of the BT-99 Trap Shotgun. Full beavertail forearm; checkered walnut stock; ejector; rubber butt pad. Reintroduced 2001. Imported by Browning.
Price: Conventional stock, 32" or 34" barrel **$1,290.00**
Price: Adj.-comb stock, 32" or 34" barrel **$1,558.00**
Price: Micro (for small-framed shooters) **$1,290.00**

BROWNING GOLDEN CLAYS SHOTGUN
Gauge: 12, 3" chamber. **Barrel:** 32", 34" with Full, Improved Modified, Modified tubes. **Weight:** 8 lbs. 14 oz. to 9 lbs. **Length:** 49" to 51" overall. **Stock:** Adjustable comb; walnut with high gloss finish; cut checkering. GraCoil recoil reduction system. Imported from Japan by Browning.
Price: 34" bbl. **$3,407.00**
Price: 32" bbl. **$3,407.00**

CHIPMUNK 410 YOUTH SHOTGUN
Gauge: .410. **Barrel:** 18-1/4" tapered, blue. **Weight:** 3.25 lbs. **Length:** 33". **Stock:** Walnut. **Features:** Manually cocking single shot bolt, blued receiver.
Price: **$225.95**

EAA BAIKAL IZH18 SINGLE BARREL SHOTGUN
Gauge: 12 (2-3/4" and 3" chambers), 20 (2-3/4" and 3"), 16 (2-3/4"), .410 (3"). **Barrel:** 26-1/2", 28-1/2"; Modified or Full choke (12 and 20 gauge); Full only (16 gauge), Improved cylinder (20 gauge) and Full or Improved Modified (.410). **Stock:** Walnut-stained hardwood; rubber recoil pad. **Features:** Hammer-forged steel barrel; machined receiver; cross-block safety; cocking lever with external cocking indicator; optional automatic ejector, screw-in chokes and rifle barrel. Imported by European American Armory.
Price: IZH18 (12, 16, 20 or .410) **$109.00**
Price: IZH18 (20 gauge w/Imp. Cyl. or .410 w/Imp. Mod.) **$109.00**

EAA BAIKAL IZH18MAX SINGLE BARREL SHOTGUNS
Gauge: 12, 3"; 20, 3"; 410, 3". **Barrel:** 24" (.410), 26" (.410 or 20 ga.) or 28" (12 ga.). **Weight:** 6.4 to 6.6 lbs. **Stock:** Walnut. **Features:** Polished nickel receiver; vent rib; I.C., Mod. and Full choke tubes; titanium-coated trigger; internal hammer; selectable ejector/extractor; rubber butt pad; de-cocking system. Imported by European American Armory.
Price: (12 or 20 ga., choke tubes). **$229.00**
Price: (.410, Full choke only) **$239.00**
Price: Sporting, 12 ga., ported, Monte Carlo stock **$219.00**

HARRINGTON & RICHARDSON SB2-980 ULTRA SLUG SHOTGUN
Gauge: 12, 20, 3" chamber. **Barrel:** 22" (20 ga. Youth) 24", fully rifled. **Weight:** 9 lbs. **Length:** NA. **Stock:** Walnut-stained hardwood. **Sights:** None furnished; comes with scope mount. **Features:** Uses the H&R 10 gauge action with heavy-wall barrel. Monte Carlo stock has sling swivels; comes with black nylon sling. Introduced 1995. Made in U.S. by H&R 1871, LLC.
Price: **$259.00**

H&R Tamer

H&R Topper

H&R Topper Deluxe

H&R Topper Junior

Ljutic Mono Gun

Harrington & Richardson Model 928 Ultra Slug Hunter Deluxe Shotgun
Similar to the SB2-980 Ultra Slug except uses 12 gauge action and 12 gauge barrel blank bored to 20 gauge, and then fully rifled with 1:28" twist. Has hand-checkered camo laminate Monte Carlo stock and forend. Comes with Weaver-style scope base, offset hammer extension, ventilated recoil pad, sling swivels and nylon sling. Introduced 1997. Made in U.S. by H&R 1871 LLC.
Price: **$315.00**

HARRINGTON & RICHARDSON TAMER SHOTGUN
Gauge: .410, 3" chamber. **Barrel:** 20" (Full). **Weight:** 5-6 lbs. **Length:** 33" overall. **Stock:** Thumbhole grip of high density black polymer. **Features:** Uses H&R Topper action with matte electroless nickel finish. Stock holds four spare shotshells. Introduced 1994. From H&R 1871, LLC.
Price: **$164.00**

HARRINGTON & RICHARDSON TOPPER MODEL 098
Gauge: 12, 16, 20, 28 (2-3/4"), .410, 3" chamber. **Barrel:** 12 ga.-28" (Mod.); 16 ga.-28" (Full.); 20 ga.-26" (Mod.); 28 ga.-26" (Mod.); .410 bore-26" (Full). **Weight:** 5-6 lbs. **Stock:** Black-finish hardwood with full pistol grip; semi-beavertail forend. **Sights:** Gold bead front. **Features:** Break-open action with side-lever release, automatic ejector. Satin nickel frame, blued barrel. Reintroduced 1992. From H&R 1871, LLC.
Price: **$145.00**
Price: Topper Junior 098 (as above except 22" barrel, 20 ga. (Mod.), .410-bore (Full), 12-1/2" length of pull) **$152.00**

Harrington & Richardson Topper Deluxe Model 098
Similar to the standard Topper 098 except 12 gauge only with 3-1/2" chamber, 28" barrel with choke tube (comes with Mod. tube, others optional). Satin nickel frame, blued barrel, black-finished wood. Introduced 1992. From H&R 1871, LLC.
Price: **$169.00**

Harrington & Richardson Topper Junior Classic Shotgun
Similar to the Topper Junior 098 except available in 20 gauge (3", Mod.), .410-bore (Full) with 3" chamber; all have 22" barrel. Stock is American black walnut with cut-checkered pistol grip and forend. Ventilated rubber recoil pad. Blued barrel, blued frame. Introduced 1992. From H&R 1871, LLC.
Price: **$184.00**

ITHACA CLASSIC DOUBLES KNICKERBOCKER TRAP GUN
A reissue of the famous Ithaca Knickerbocker trap gun. Custom only. Introduced 2003. Made in U.S.A. by Ithaca Classic Doubles.
Price: From **$9,000.00**

KRIEGHOFF K-80 SINGLE BARREL TRAP GUN
Gauge: 12, 2-3/4" chamber. **Barrel:** 32" or 34" Unsingle. Fixed Full or choke tubes. **Weight:** About 8-3/4 lbs. **Stock:** Four stock dimensions or adjustable stock available. All hand-checkered European walnut. **Features:** Satin nickel finish. Selective mechanical trigger adjustable for finger position. Tapered step vent rib. Adjustable point of impact.
Price: Standard grade Full Unsingle, from **$9,675.00**

KRIEGHOFF KX-5 TRAP GUN
Gauge: 12, 2-3/4" chamber. **Barrel:** 32", 34"; choke tubes. **Weight:** About 8-1/2 lbs. **Stock:** Factory adjustable stock. European walnut. **Features:** Ventilated tapered step rib. Adjustable position trigger, optional release trigger. Fully adjustable rib. Satin gray electroless nickel receiver. Fitted aluminum case. Imported from Germany by Krieghoff International, Inc.
Price: **$5,195.00**

LJUTIC MONO GUN SINGLE BARREL SHOTGUN
Gauge: 12 only. **Barrel:** 34", choked to customer specs; hollow-milled rib, 35-1/2" sight plane. **Weight:** Approx. 9 lbs. **Stock:** To customer specs. Oil finish, hand checkered. **Features:** Custom gun. Pull or release trigger; removable trigger guard contains trigger and hammer mechanism; Ljutic pushbutton opener on front of trigger guard. From Ljutic Industries.
Price: Std., med. or Olympic rib, custom bbls., fixed choke. **$6,995.00**
Price: As above with screw-in choke barrel **$7,395.00**
Price: Stainless steel mono gun **$7,995.00**

Mossberg SSi One

New England Firearms Camo Turkey

New England Firearms Tracker II

New England Firearms Special Purpose

New England Firearms Survivor

Ljutic LTX Pro 3 Deluxe Mono Gun
Deluxe, lightweight version of the Mono gun with high quality wood, upgrade checkering, special rib height, screw-in chokes, ported and cased.
Price: **$8,995.00**
Price: Stainless steel model **$9,995.00**

MOSSBERG SSi-ONE 12 GAUGE SLUG SHOTGUN
Gauge: 12, 3" chamber. **Barrel:** 24", fully rifled. **Weight:** 8 lbs. **Length:** 40" overall. **Stock:** Walnut, fluted and cut checkered; sling-swivel studs; drilled and tapped for scope base. **Sights:** None (scope base supplied). **Features:** Frame accepts interchangeable rifle barrels (see Mossberg SSi-One rifle listing); lever-opening, break-action design; ambidextrous, top-tang safety; internal eject/extract selector. Introduced 2000. From Mossberg.
Price: **$480.00**

Mossberg SSi-One Turkey Shotgun
Similar to SSi-One 12 gauge slug shotgun, but chambered for 12 ga., 3-1/2" loads. Includes Accu-Mag Turkey Tube. Introduced 2001. From Mossberg.
Price: **$459.00**

NEW ENGLAND FIREARMS CAMO TURKEY SHOTGUNS
Gauge: 10, 3-1/2"; 12, 20, 3" chamber. **Barrel:** 24"; extra-full, screw-in choke tube (10 ga.); fixed full choke (12, 20). **Weight:** NA. **Stock:** American hardwood, green and black camouflage finish with sling swivels and ventilated recoil pad. **Sights:** Bead front. **Features:** Matte metal finish; stock counterweight to reduce recoil; patented transfer bar system for hammer-down safety; includes camo sling and trigger lock. Accepts

other factory-fitted barrels. Introduced 2000. From New England Firearms.
Price: . . . . 10 ga. **$278.00**; 12 ga. **$189.00**
Price: 20 ga. Youth model (22" bbl.) **$189.00**

NEW ENGLAND FIREARMS TRACKER II SLUG GUN
Gauge: 12, 20, 3" chamber. **Barrel:** 24" (Cyl.), rifle bore. **Weight:** 5-1/4 lbs. **Length:** 40" overall. **Stock:** Walnut-finished hardwood with full pistol grip, recoil pad. **Sights:** Blade front, fully adjustable rifle-type rear. **Features:** Break-open action with side-lever release; blued barrel, color case-hardened frame. Introduced 1992. From New England Firearms.
Price: Tracker II **$187.00**

NEW ENGLAND FIREARMS SPECIAL PURPOSE SHOTGUNS
Gauge: 10, 3-1/2" chamber. **Barrel:** 28" (Full), 32" (Mod.). **Weight:** 9.5 lbs. **Length:** 44" overall (28" barrel). **Stock:** American hardwood with walnut or matte camo finish; ventilated rubber recoil pad. **Sights:** Bead front. **Features:** Break-open action with side-lever release; ejector. Matte finish on metal. Introduced 1992. From New England Firearms.
Price: Walnut-finish wood sling and swivels **$215.00**
Price: Camo finish, sling and swivels **$278.00**
Price: Camo finish, 32", sling and swivels **$272.00**
Price: Black matte finish, 24", turkey full choke tube,
sling and swivels **$251.00**

NEW ENGLAND FIREARMS SURVIVOR SHOTGUN
Gauge: .410/45 Colt, 3" chamber. **Barrel:** 22" (Mod.); 20" (.410/45 Colt, rifled barrel, choke tube). **Weight:** 6 lbs. **Length:** 36" overall. **Stock:** Black polymer with thumbhole/pistol grip, sling swivels; beavertail forend. **Sights:** Bead front. **Features:** Buttplate removes to expose storage for extra ammunition; forend also holds extra ammunition. Black or nickel finish. Introduced 1993. From New England Firearms.
Price: .410/45 Colt, black **$203.00**
Price: .410/45 Colt, nickel **$221.00**

New England Firearms Standard Pardner

Rossi Single-Shot

Rossi Matched Pair

Savage 210F Slug Warrior

Stoeger Single-Shot

NEW ENGLAND FIREARMS STANDARD PARDNER SHOTGUN
Gauge: 12, 20, .410, 3" chamber; 16, 28, 2-3/4" chamber. **Barrel:** 12 ga. 28" (Full, Mod.), 32" (Full); 16 ga. 28" (Full), 32" (Full); 20 ga. 26" (Full, Mod.); 28 ga. 26" (Mod.); .410-bore 26" (Full). **Weight:** 5-6 lbs. **Length:** 43" overall (28" barrel). **Stock:** Walnut-finished hardwood with full pistol grip. **Sights:** Bead front. **Features:** Transfer bar ignition; break-open action with side-lever release. Introduced 1987. From New England Firearms.
Price: **$132.00**
Price: Youth model (12, 20, 28 ga., .410, 22" barrel, recoil pad) . . . **$141.00**

ROSSI SINGLE-SHOT SHOTGUN
Gauge: 12, 20, 2-3/4" chamber; .410, 3" chamber. **Barrel:** 28" full, 22" Youth. **Weight:** 5 lbs. **Stock:** Stained hardwood. **Sights:** Bead. **Features:** Break-open, positive ejection, internal transfer bar, trigger block.
Price: **$101.00**

ROSSI MATCHED PAIR SINGLE-SHOT SHOTGUN/RIFLE
Gauge: .410, 20 or 12. **Barrel:** 22" (18.5" Youth), 28" (23" full). **Weight:** 4-6 lbs. **Stock:** Hardwood (brown or black finish). **Sights:** Bead front.

Features: Break-open internal transfer bar manual external safety; blued or stainless steel finish; sling-swivel studs; includes matched 22 LR or 22 mag. barrel with fully adjustable front and rear sight. Trigger block system. Introduced 2001. Imported by BrazTech/Taurus.
Price: Blue **$139.95**
Price: Stainless steel **$169.95**

SAVAGE MODEL 210F SLUG WARRIOR SHOTGUN
Gauge: 12, 3" chamber; 2-shot magazine. **Barrel:** 24" 1:35" rifling twist. **Weight:** 7-1/2 lbs. **Length:** 43.5" overall. **Stock:** Glass-filled polymer with positive checkering. **Features:** Based on the Savage Model 110 action; 60-degree bolt lift; controlled round feed; comes with scope mount. Introduced 1996. Made in U.S. by Savage Arms.
Price: **$475.00**
Price: (Camo) **$513.00**

STOEGER SINGLE-SHOT SHOTGUN
Gauge: 12, 20, .410, 2-3/4", 3" chambers. **Barrel:** 26", 28". **Weight:** 5.4 lbs. **Length:** 40-1/2" to 42-1/2" overall. **Sights:** Brass bead. **Features:** .410, Full fixed choke tubes, screw-in. .410 12 ga. hardwood pistol-grip stock and forend. 20 ga. 26" bbl., hardwood forend.
Price: Blue; Youth **$109.00**
Price: Youth with English stock **$119.00**

Tar-Hunt RSG-20 Mountaineer

Thompson/Center Encore Rifled Slug

Thompson/Center Encore Turkey

TAR-HUNT RSG-12 PROFESSIONAL RIFLED SLUG GUN
Gauge: 12, 2-3/4" or 3" chamber, 1-shot magazine. **Barrel:** 23", fully rifled with muzzle brake. **Weight:** 7-3/4 lbs. **Length:** 41-1/2" overall. **Stock:** Matte black McMillan fiberglass with Pachmayr Decelerator pad. **Sights:** None furnished; comes with Leupold windage or Weaver bases. **Features:** Uses rifle-style action with two locking lugs; two-position safety; Shaw barrel; single-stage, trigger; muzzle brake. Many options available. Right- and left-hand models at same prices. Introduced 1991. Made in U.S. by Tar-Hunt Custom Rifles, Inc.
Price: 12 ga. Professional model, right- or left-hand; **$2,750.00**

Tar-Hunt RSG-16 Elite Shotgun
Similar to RSG-12 Professional except 16 gauge; right- or left-hand versions.
Price: **$2,750.00**

Tar-Hunt RSG-20 Mountaineer Slug Gun
Similar to the RSG-12 Professional except chambered for 20 gauge (2-3/4" and 3" shells); 23" Shaw rifled barrel, with muzzle brake; two-lug bolt; one-shot blind magazine; matte black finish; McMillan fiberglass stock with Pachmayr Decelerator pad; receiver drilled and tapped for Rem. 700 bases. Right- or left-hand versions. Weighs 6-1/2 lbs. Introduced 1997. Made in U.S. by Tar-Hunt Custom Rifles, Inc.
Price: **$2,750.00**

THOMPSON/CENTER ENCORE RIFLED SLUG GUN
Gauge: 20, 3" chamber. **Barrel:** 26", fully rifled. **Weight:** About 7 lbs. **Length:** 40-1/2" overall. **Stock:** Walnut with walnut forearm. **Sights:** Steel; click-adjustable rear and ramp-style front, both with fiber optics. **Features:** Encore system features a variety of rifle, shotgun and muzzle-loading rifle barrels interchangeable with the same frame. Break-open design operates by pulling up and back on trigger guard spur. Composite stock and forearm available. Introduced 2000.
Price: **$684.00**

THOMPSON/CENTER ENCORE TURKEY GUN
Gauge: 12 ga. **Barrel:** 24". **Features:** All-camo finish, high definition Realtree Hardwoods HD camo.
Price: **$763.00**

Designs for utility, suitable for and adaptable to competitions and other sporting purposes.

Benelli M3 Convertible

Fabarm Tactical

Fabarm FP6

Mossberg Model 500 Persuader

BENELLI M3 CONVERTIBLE SHOTGUN
Gauge: 12, 2-3/4", 3" chambers, 5-shot magazine. **Barrel:** 19-3/4" (Cyl.). **Weight:** 7 lbs., 4oz. **Length:** 41" overall. **Stock:** High-impact polymer with sling loop in side of butt; rubberized pistol grip on stock. **Sights:** Open rifle, fully adjustable. Ghost ring and rifle type. **Features:** Combination pump/auto action. Alloy receiver with inertia recoil rotating locking lug bolt; matte finish; automatic shell release lever. Introduced 1989. Imported by Benelli USA. Price with pistol grip, open rifle sights.
Price: With standard stock, open rifle sights $1,235.00
Price: With ghost ring sight system, standard stock $1,185.00
Price: With ghost ring sights, pistol grip stock $1,165.00

BENELLI M2 TACTICAL SHOTGUN
Gauge: 12, 2-3/4", 3" chambers, 5-shot magazine. **Barrel:** 18.5" IC, M, F choke tubes. **Weight:** 6.7 lbs. **Length:** 39.75" overall. **Stock:** Black polymer. **Sights:** Rifle type with ghost ring system, tritium night sights optional. **Features:** Semi-auto intertia recoil action. Cross-bolt safety; bolt release button; matte-finish metal. Introduced 1993. Imported from Italy by Benelli USA.
Price: With rifle sights, standard stock. $1,000.00
Price: With ghost ring rifle sights, standard stock $1,065.00
Price: With ghost ring sights, pistol grip stock $1,065.00
Price: With rifle sights, pistol grip stock $1,000.00
Price: ComforTech stock, rifle sights $1,135.00
Price: Comfortech Stock, Ghost-Ring $1,185.00

Benelli M2 Practical Shotgun
Similar to M2 Tactical shotgun, Picatinny receiver rail for scope mounting, nine-round magazine, 26" compensated barrel and ghost ring sights. Designed for IPSC competition.
Price: $1,335.00

CROSSFIRE SHOTGUN/RIFLE
Gauge/Caliber: 12, 2-3/4" Chamber: 4-shot/223 Rem. (5-shot). **Barrel:** 20" (shotgun), 18" (rifle). **Weight:** About 8.6 lbs. **Length:** 40" overall. **Stock:** Composite. **Sights:** Meprolight night sights. Integral Weaver-style scope rail. **Features:** Combination pump-action shotgun, rifle; single selector, single trigger; dual action bars for both upper and lower actions; ambidextrous selector and safety. Introduced 1997. Made in U.S. From Hesco.
Price: About. $1,895.00
Price: With camo finish $1,995.00

FABARM TACTICAL SEMI-AUTOMATIC SHOTGUN
Gauge: 12, 3" chamber. **Barrel:** 20". **Weight:** 6.6 lbs. **Length:** 41.2" overall. **Stock:** Polymer or folding. **Sights:** Ghost ring (tritium night sights optional). **Features:** Gas operated; matte receiver; twin forged action bars; over-sized bolt handle and safety button; Picatinny rail; includes cylinder bore choke tube. New features include polymer pistol grip stock. Introduced 2001. Imported from Italy by Heckler & Koch Inc.
Price: $999.00

FABARM FP6 PUMP SHOTGUN
Gauge: 12, 3" chamber. **Barrel:** 20" (Cyl.); accepts choke tubes. **Weight:** 6.6 lbs. **Length:** 41.25" overall. **Stock:** Black polymer with textured grip, grooved slide handle. **Sights:** Blade front. **Features:** Twin action bars; anodized finish; free carrier for smooth reloading. Introduced 1998. New features include ghost-ring sighting system, low profile Picatinny rail, and pistol grip stock. Imported from Italy by Heckler & Koch, Inc.
Price: (Carbon fiber finish) $499.00
Price: With flip-up front sight, Picatinny rail with rear sight, oversize safety button $499.00

MOSSBERG MODEL 500 PERSUADER SECURITY SHOTGUNS
Gauge: 12, 20, .410, 3" chamber. **Barrel:** 18-1/2", 20" (Cyl.). **Weight:** 7 lbs. **Stock:** Walnut-finished hardwood or black synthetic. **Sights:** Metal bead front. **Features:** Available in 6- or 8-shot models. Top-mounted safety, double action slide bars, swivel studs, rubber recoil pad. Blue, Parkerized, Marinecote finishes. Mossberg Cablelock included. From Mossberg.
Price: 12 ga., 18-1/2", blue, wood or synthetic stock, 6-shot. $353.00
Price: Cruiser, 12 ga., 18-1/2", blue, pistol grip, heat shield $357.00
Price: As above, 20 ga. or .410 bore $345.00

Mossberg Ghost Ring

Mossberg Model HS410

Tactical Response TR-870

Winchester Model 1300 Defender

Mossberg Model 500, 590 Mariner Pump Shotgun
Similar to the Model 500 or 590 Persuader except all metal parts finished with Marinecote metal finish to resist rust and corrosion. Synthetic field stock; pistol grip kit included. Mossberg Cablelock included.
Price: 6-shot, 18-1/2" barrel. **$497.00**
Price: 9-shot, 20" barrel **$513.00**

Mossberg Model 500, 590 Ghost-Ring Shotgun
Similar to the Model 500 Persuader except has adjustable blade front, adjustable Ghost-Ring rear sight with protective "ears." Model 500 has 18.5" (Cyl.) barrel, 6-shot capacity; Model 590 has 20" (Cyl.) barrel, 9-shot capacity. Both have synthetic field stock. Mossberg Cablelock included. Introduced 1990. From Mossberg.
Price: 500 Parkerized **$468.00**
Price: 590 Parkerized **$543.00**
Price: 590 Parkerized Speedfeed stock **$586.00**

Mossberg Model HS410 Shotgun
Similar to the Model 500 Persuader pump except chambered for 20 gauge or .410 with 3" chamber; has pistol grip forend, thick recoil pad, muzzle brake and has special spreader choke on the 18.5" barrel. Overall length is 37.5", weight is 6.25 lbs. Blue finish; synthetic field stock. Mossberg Cablelock and video included. Introduced 1990.
Price: HS 410. . . . . **$355.00**

MOSSBERG MODEL 590 SHOTGUN
Gauge: 12, 3" chamber. **Barrel:** 20" (Cyl.). **Weight:** 7-1/4 lbs. **Stock:** Synthetic field or Speedfeed. **Sights:** Metal bead front. **Features:** Top-mounted safety, double slide action bars. Comes with heat shield, bayonet lug, swivel studs, rubber recoil pad. Blue, Parkerized or Marinecote finish. Mossberg Cablelock included. From Mossberg.
Price: Blue, synthetic stock **$417.00**
Price: Parkerized, synthetic stock **$476.00**
Price: Parkerized, Speedfeed stock **$519.00**

TACTICAL RESPONSE TR-870 STANDARD MODEL SHOTGUNS
Gauge: 12, 3" chamber, 7-shot magazine. **Barrel:** 18" (Cyl.). **Weight:** 9 lbs. **Length:** 38" overall. **Stock:** Fiberglass-filled polypropolene with non-snag recoil absorbing butt pad. Nylon tactical forend houses flashlight. **Sights:**

Trak-Lock ghost ring sight system. Front sight has Tritium insert. **Features:** Highly modified Remington 870P with Parkerized finish. Comes with nylon three-way adjustable sling, high visibility non-binding follower, high performance magazine spring, Jumbo Head safety, and Side Saddle extended 6-shot shell carrier on left side of receiver. Introduced 1991. From Scattergun Technologies, Inc.
Price: Standard model **$815.00**
Price: FBI model **$770.00**
Price: Patrol model **$595.00**
Price: Border Patrol model **$605.00**
Price: K-9 model (Rem. 11-87 action) **$995.00**
Price: Urban Sniper, Rem. 11-87 action **$1,290.00**
Price: Louis Awerbuck model **$705.00**
Price: Practical Turkey model **$725.00**
Price: Expert model **$1,350.00**
Price: Professional model **$815.00**
Price: Entry model **$840.00**
Price: Compact model **$635.00**
Price: SWAT model **$1,195.00**

WINCHESTER MODEL 1300 DEFENDER PUMP GUN SHOTGUNS
Gauge: 12, 20, 3" chamber, 5- or 8-shot capacity. **Barrel:** 18" (Cyl.). **Weight:** 6-3/4 lbs. **Length:** 38-5/8" overall. **Stock:** Walnut-finished hardwood stock and ribbed forend, synthetic or pistol grip. **Sights:** Metal bead front or TruGlo® fiber-optic. **Features:** Cross-bolt safety, front-locking rotary bolt, twin action slide bars. Black rubber butt pad. From U.S. Repeating Arms Co.
Price: Practical Defender **$392.00**
Price: 8-Shot Pistol Grip (pistol grip synthetic stock) **$354.00**

Winchester Model 1300 Coastal Pump Gun Shotgun
Same as the Defender 8-Shot except has bright chrome finish, nickel-plated barrel, bead front sight. Phosphate coated receiver for corrosion resistance.
Price: **$575.00**

Winchester Model 1300 Camp Defender® Shotgun
Same as the Defender 8-Shot except has hardwood stock and forearm, fully adjustable open sights and 22" barrel with WinChoke® choke tube system (cylinder choke tube included). Weighs 6-7/8 lbs. Introduced 2001. From U.S. Repeating Arms Co.
Price: Camp Defender® **$392.00**

Dixie Pennsylvania   Harper's Ferry   Kentucky   Le Page   Lyman Plains Pistol

DIXIE PENNSYLVANIA PISTOL
Caliber: 44 (.430" round ball). **Barrel:** 10", (7/8" octagon). **Weight:** 2-1/2 lbs. **Stocks:** Walnut-stained hardwood. **Sights:** Blade front, open rear drift-adjustable for windage; brass. **Features:** Flintlock only. Brass trigger guard, thimbles, instep, wedge plates; high-luster blue barrel. Imported from Italy by Dixie Gun Works.
Price: Finished. **$215.00**
Price: Kit **$195.00**

FRENCH-STYLE DUELING PISTOL
Caliber: 44. **Barrel:** 10". **Weight:** 35 oz. **Length:** 15-3/4" overall. **Stocks:** Carved walnut. **Sights:** Fixed. **Features:** Comes with velvet-lined case and accessories. Imported by Mandall Shooting Supplies.
Price: **$295.00**

HARPER'S FERRY 1806 PISTOL
Caliber: 58 (.570" round ball). **Barrel:** 10". **Weight:** 40 oz. **Length:** 16" overall. **Stocks:** Walnut. **Sights:** Fixed. **Features:** Case-hardened lock, brass-mounted browned barrel. Replica of the first U.S. gov't.-made flintlock pistol. Imported by Navy Arms, Dixie Gun Works.
Price: . . . . **$275.00 to $405.00**
Price: Kit (Dixie) **$250.00**

KENTUCKY FLINTLOCK PISTOL
Caliber: 44, 45. **Barrel:** 10-1/8". **Weight:** 32 oz. **Length:** 15-1/2" overall. **Stocks:** Walnut. **Sights:** Fixed. **Features:** Specifications, including caliber, weight and length may vary with importer. Case-hardened lock, blued barrel; available also as brass barrel flintlock Model 1821. Imported by Navy Arms, The Armoury, Dixie Gun Works.
Price: **$300.00**
Price: In kit form. From . . . . **$90.00 to $112.00**
Price: Single cased set (Navy Arms) **$360.00**
Price: Double cased set (Navy Arms) **$590.00**

Kentucky Percussion Pistol
Similar to Flint version but percussion lock. Imported by The Armoury, Navy Arms, CVA (50-cal.).
Price: . . . . **$129.95 to $225.00**
Price: Steel barrel (Armoury) **$179.00**

Pedersoli Mang

Price: Single cased set (Navy Arms) **$355.00**
Price: Double cased set (Navy Arms) **$600.00**

LE PAGE PERCUSSION DUELING PISTOL
Caliber: 44. **Barrel:** 10", rifled. **Weight:** 40 oz. **Length:** 16" overall. **Stocks:** Walnut, fluted butt. **Sights:** Blade front, notch rear. **Features:** Double-set triggers. Blued barrel; trigger guard and buttcap are polished silver. Imported by Dixie Gun Works.
Price: **$545.00**

LYMAN PLAINS PISTOL
Caliber: 50 or 54. **Barrel:** 8"; 1:30" twist, both calibers. **Weight:** 50 oz. **Length:** 15" overall. **Stocks:** Walnut half-stock. **Sights:** Blade front, square notch rear adjustable for windage. **Features:** Polished brass trigger guard and ramrod tip, color case-hardened coil spring lock, spring-loaded trigger, stainless steel nipple, blackened iron furniture. Hooked patent breech, detachable belt hook. Introduced 1981. From Lyman Products.
Price: Finished **$244.95**
Price: Kit **$189.95**

PEDERSOLI MANG TARGET PISTOL
Caliber: 38. **Barrel:** 10.5", octagonal; 1:15" twist, **Weight:** 2.5 lbs. **Length:** 17.25" overall. **Stocks:** Walnut with fluted grip. **Sights:** Blade front, open rear adjustable for windage. **Features:** Browned barrel, polished breech plug, remainder color case-hardened. Imported from Italy by Dixie Gun Works.
Price: **$925.00**

Queen Anne

Traditions Pioneer

Traditions William Parker

Traditions Buckhunter Pro

QUEEN ANNE FLINTLOCK PISTOL
Caliber: 50 (.490" round ball). **Barrel:** 7-1/2", smoothbore. **Stocks:** Walnut. **Sights:** None. **Features:** Browned steel barrel, fluted brass trigger guard, brass mask on butt. Lockplate left in the white. Made by Pedersoli in Italy. Introduced 1983. Imported by Dixie Gun Works.
Price: $275.00
Price: Kit $195.00

TRADITIONS BUCKHUNTER PRO IN-LINE PISTOL
Caliber: 50. **Barrel:** 9-1/2", round. **Weight:** 48 oz. **Length:** 14" overall. **Stocks:** Smooth walnut or black epoxy-coated hardwood grip and forend. **Sights:** Beaded blade front, folding adjustable rear. **Features:** Thumb safety; removable stainless steel breech plug; adjustable trigger, barrel drilled and tapped for scope mounting. From Traditions.
Price: With walnut grip. $229.00
Price: Nickel with black grip $239.00
Price: With walnut grip and 12-1/2" barrel $239.00
Price: Nickel with black grip, muzzle brake and 14-3/4" fluted barrel $289.00
Price: 45 cal. nickel w/bl. grip, muzzle brake and 14-3/4" fluted bbl. $289.00

TRADITIONS KENTUCKY PISTOL
Caliber: 50. **Barrel:** 10"; octagon with 7/8" flats; 1:20" twist. **Weight:** 40 oz. **Length:** 15" overall. **Stocks:** Stained beech. **Sights:** Blade front, fixed rear. **Features:** Bird's-head grip; brass thimbles; color case-hardened lock. Percussion only. Introduced 1995. From Traditions.
Price: Finished. $139.00
Price: Kit $109.00

TRADITIONS PIONEER PISTOL
Caliber: 45. **Barrel:** 9-5/8"; 13/16" flats, 1:16" twist. **Weight:** 31 oz. **Length:** 15" overall. **Stocks:** Beech. **Sights:** Blade front, fixed rear. **Features:** V-type mainspring. Single trigger. German silver furniture, blackened hardware. From Traditions.
Price: $139.00
Price: Kit $119.00

TRADITIONS TRAPPER PISTOL
Caliber: 50. **Barrel:** 9-3/4"; 7/8" flats; 1:20" twist. **Weight:** 2-3/4 lbs. **Length:** 16" overall. **Stocks:** Beech. **Sights:** Blade front, adjustable rear.

Features: Double-set triggers; brass buttcap, trigger guard, wedge plate, forend tip, thimble. From Traditions.
Price: Percussion $189.00
Price: Flintlock $209.00
Price: Kit $149.00

TRADITIONS VEST-POCKET DERRINGER
Caliber: 31. **Barrel:** 2-1/4"; brass. **Weight:** 8 oz. **Length:** 4-3/4" overall. **Stocks:** Simulated ivory. **Sights:** Bead front. **Features:** Replica of riverboat gamblers' derringer; authentic spur trigger. From Traditions.
Price: $109.00

TRADITIONS WILLIAM PARKER PISTOL
Caliber: 50. **Barrel:** 10-3/8"; 15/16" flats; polished steel. **Weight:** 37 oz. **Length:** 17-1/2" overall. **Stocks:** Walnut with checkered grip. **Sights:** Brass blade front, fixed rear. **Features:** Replica dueling pistol with 1:20" twist, hooked breech. Brass wedge plate, trigger guard, cap guard; separate ramrod. Double-set triggers. Polished steel barrel, lock. Imported by Traditions.
Price: $269.00

CONSULT

SHOOTER'S MARKETPLACE

Page 74, This Issue

BLACKPOWDER REVOLVERS

Army 1860

Baby Dragoon 1848

Dixie Wyatt Earp

Le Mat Revolver

Navy Arms 1836 Paterson

ARMY 1860 PERCUSSION REVOLVER
Caliber: 44, 6-shot. **Barrel:** 8". **Weight:** 40 oz. **Length:** 13-5/8" overall. **Stocks:** Walnut. **Sights:** Fixed. **Features:** Engraved Navy scene on cylinder; brass trigger guard; case-hardened frame, loading lever and hammer. Some importers supply pistol cut for detachable shoulder stock, have accessory stock available. Imported by Cabela's (1860 Lawman), E.M.F., Navy Arms, The Armoury, Cimarron, Dixie Gun Works (half-fluted cylinder, not roll engraved), Euroarms of America (brass or steel model), Armsport, Traditions (brass or steel), Uberti U.S.A. Inc., United States Patent Fire-Arms.
Price: About $195.00
Price: Hartford model, steel frame, German silver trim,
cartouches (E.M.F.) $215.00
Price: Single cased set (Navy Arms) $300.00
Price: Double cased set (Navy Arms) $490.00
Price: 1861 Navy: Same as Army except 36-cal., 7-1/2" bbl.,
weighs 41 oz., cut for shoulder stock; round cylinder
(fluted available), from Cabela's, CVA (brass frame, 44 cal.),
United States Patent Fire-Arms . . . . $99.95 to $385.00
Price: Steel frame kit (E.M.F., Euroarms) . . . . $125.00 to $216.25
Price: Colt Army Police, fluted cyl., 5-1/2", 36-cal. (Cabela's) $124.95
Price: With nickeled frame, barrel and backstrap, gold-tone fluted cylinder,
trigger and hammer, simulated ivory grips (Traditions) $199.00

BABY DRAGOON 1848, 1849 POCKET, WELLS FARGO
Caliber: 31. **Barrel:** 3", 4", 5", 6"; seven-groove; RH twist. **Weight:** About 21 oz. **Stocks:** Varnished walnut. **Sights:** Brass pin front, hammer notch rear. **Features:** No loading lever on Baby Dragoon or Wells Fargo models. Unfluted cylinder with stagecoach holdup scene; cupped cylinder pin; no grease grooves; one safety pin on cylinder and slot in hammer face; straight (flat) mainspring. From Armsport, Cimarron F.A. Co., Dixie Gun Works, Uberti U.S.A. Inc.
Price: 6" barrel, with loading lever (Dixie Gun Works) $275.00
Price: 4" (Uberti USA Inc.) $335.00

CABELA'S 1860 ARMY SNUBNOSE REVOLVER
Caliber: 44. **Barrel:** 3". **Weight:** 2 lbs., 3 oz. **Length:** 9" overall. **Grips:** Hardwood. **Sights:** Blade front, hammer notch near. **Features:** Shortened barrels without loading lever. Brass loading tool included.
Price: Revolver only $169.99
Price: With starter kit $219.99

CABELA'S 1862 POLICE SNUBNOSE REVOLVER
Caliber: 36. **Barrel:** 3". **Weight:** 2 lbs., 3 oz. **Length:** 8.5" overall. **Grips:** Hardwood. **Sights:** Blade front, hammer notch rear. **Features:** Shortened barrel, removed loading lever. Separate brass loading tool included.
Price: . . . . $159.99 (revolver only); $209.99 (with starter kit).

DIXIE WYATT EARP REVOLVER
Caliber: 44. **Barrel:** 12", octagon. **Weight:** 46 oz. **Length:** 18" overall. **Stocks:** Two-piece walnut. **Sights:** Fixed. **Features:** Highly polished brass frame, backstrap and trigger guard; blued barrel and cylinder; case-hardened hammer, trigger and loading lever. Navy-size shoulder stock ($45) requires minor fitting. From Dixie Gun Works.
Price: $160.00

LE MAT REVOLVER
Caliber: 44/65. **Barrel:** 6-3/4" (revolver); 4-7/8" (single shot). **Weight:** 3 lbs., 7 oz. **Stocks:** Hand-checkered walnut. **Sights:** Post front, hammer notch rear. **Features:** Exact reproduction with all-steel construction; 44-cal. 9-shot cylinder, 65-cal. single barrel; color case-hardened hammer with selector; spur trigger guard; ring at butt; lever-type barrel release. From Navy Arms.
Price: Cavalry model (lanyard ring, spur trigger guard) $595.00
Price: Army model (round trigger guard, pin-type barrel release) . . $595.00
Price: Naval-style (thumb selector on hammer) $595.00

NAVY ARMS NEW MODEL POCKET REVOLVER
Caliber: 31, 5-shot. **Barrel:** 3-1/2", octagon. **Weight:** 15 oz. **Length:** 7-3/4". **Stocks:** Two-piece walnut. **Sights:** Fixed. **Features:** Replica of the Remington New Model Pocket. Available with polished brass frame or nickel-plated finish. Introduced 2000. Imported by Navy Arms.
Price: $300.00

NAVY ARMS 1836 PATERSON REVOLVER
Caliber: 36. **Barrel:** 9". **Weight:** 2 lbs, 11 oz. **Length:** NA. **Stocks:** Walnut. **Sights:** NA. **Features:** Hidden trigger, blued barrel, replica of 5-shooter, roll-engraved with stagecoach holdup scene.
Price: . . . . $340.00 to $499.00

BLACKPOWDER REVOLVERS

North American Companion

New Model
1858 Army Percussion

Pocket Police 1862

Rogers & Spencer

Ruger Old Army

NAVY MODEL 1851 PERCUSSION REVOLVER
Caliber: 36, 44, 6-shot. **Barrel:** 7-1/2". **Weight:** 44 oz. **Length:** 13" overall. **Stocks:** Walnut finish. **Sights:** Post front, hammer notch rear. **Features:** Brass backstrap and trigger guard; some have 1st Model squareback trigger guard, engraved cylinder with navy battle scene; case-hardened frame, hammer, loading lever. Imported by The Armoury, Cabela's, Cimarron F.A. Co., Navy Arms, E.M.F., Dixie Gun Works, Euroarms of America, Armsport, CVA (44-cal. only), Traditions (44 only), Uberti U.S.A. Inc., United States Patent Fire-Arms.

Price: Brass frame . . . . $99.95 to $385.00
Price: Steel frame . . . . $130.00 to $285.00
Price: Kit form . . . . $110.00 to $123.95
Price: Engraved model (Dixie Gun Works) $182.50
Price: Single cased set, steel frame (Navy Arms) $280.00
Price: Double cased set, steel frame (Navy Arms) $455.00
Price: Confederate Navy (Cabela's) $89.99
Price: Hartford model, steel frame, German silver trim, cartouche (E.M.F.) $190.00

NEW MODEL 1858 ARMY PERCUSSION REVOLVER
Caliber: 36 or 44, 6-shot. **Barrel:** 6-1/2" or 8". **Weight:** 38 oz. **Length:** 13-1/2" overall. **Stocks:** Walnut. **Sights:** Blade front, groove-in-frame rear. **Features:** Replica of Remington Model 1858. Also available from some importers as Army Model Belt Revolver in 36-cal., a shortened and lightened version of the 44. Target Model (Uberti U.S.A. Inc., Navy Arms) has fully adjustable target rear sight, target front, 36 or 44. Imported by Cabela's, Cimarron F.A. Co., CVA (as 1858 Army, brass frame, 44 only), Dixie Gun Works, Navy Arms, The Armoury, E.M.F., Euroarms of America (engraved, stainless and plain), Armsport, Traditions (44 only), Uberti U.S.A. Inc.

Price: Steel frame, about . . . . $99.95 to $280.00
Price: Steel frame kit (Euroarms, Navy Arms) . . . . $115.95 to $150.00
Price: Single cased set (Navy Arms) $290.00
Price: Double cased set (Navy Arms) $480.00
Price: Stainless steel Model 1858 (Euroarms, Uberti U.S.A. Inc., Cabela's, Navy Arms, Armsport, Traditions) . . . . $169.95 to $380.00
Price: Target Model, adjustable rear sight (Cabela's, Euroarms, Uberti U.S.A. Inc., Stone Mountain Arms) . . . . $95.95 to $399.00
Price: Brass frame (CVA, Cabela's, Traditions, Navy Arms) . . . . $79.95 to $159.95
Price: As above, kit (Dixie Gun Works, Navy Arms) . . . $145.00 to $188.95
Price: Buffalo model, 44-cal. (Cabela's) $119.99
Price: Hartford model, steel frame, German silver trim, cartouche (E.M.F.) $215.00

NORTH AMERICAN COMPANION PERCUSSION REVOLVER
Caliber: 22. **Barrel:** 1-1/8". **Weight:** 5.1 oz. **Length:** 4-1/2" overall. **Stocks:** Laminated wood. **Sights:** Blade front, notch fixed rear. **Features:** All

stainless steel construction. Uses standard #11 percussion caps. Comes with bullets, powder measure, bullet seater, leather clip holster, gun rag. Long Rifle or Magnum frame size. Introduced 1996. Made in U.S. by North American Arms.

Price: Long Rifle frame $156.00

North American Magnum Companion Percussion Revolver
Similar to the Companion except has larger frame. Weighs 7.2 oz., has 1-5/8" barrel, measures 5-7/16" overall. Comes with bullets, powder measure, bullet seater, leather clip holster, gun rag. Introduced 1996. Made in U.S. by North American Arms.

Price: $215.00

POCKET POLICE 1862 PERCUSSION REVOLVER
Caliber: 36, 5-shot. **Barrel:** 4-1/2", 5-1/2", 6-1/2", 7-1/2". **Weight:** 26 oz. **Length:** 12" overall (6-1/2" bbl.). **Stocks:** Walnut. **Sights:** Fixed. **Features:** Round tapered barrel; half-fluted and rebated cylinder; case-hardened frame, loading lever and hammer; silver or brass trigger guard and backstrap. Imported by Dixie Gun Works, Navy Arms (5-1/2" only), Uberti U.S.A. Inc. (5-1/2", 6-1/2" only), United States Patent Fire-Arms and Cimarron F.A. Co.

Price: About . . . . $139.95 to $335.00
Price: Single cased set with accessories (Navy Arms) $365.00
Price: Hartford model, steel frame, German silver trim, cartouche (E.M.F.) $215.00

ROGERS & SPENCER PERCUSSION REVOLVER
Caliber: 44. **Barrel:** 7-1/2". **Weight:** 47 oz. **Length:** 13-3/4" overall. **Stocks:** Walnut. **Sights:** Cone front, integral groove in frame for rear. **Features:** Accurate reproduction of a Civil War design. Solid frame; extra large nipple cut-out on rear of cylinder; loading lever and cylinder easily removed for cleaning. From Dixie Gun Works, Euroarms of America (standard blue, engraved, burnished, target models), Navy Arms.

Price: . . . . $160.00 to $299.95
Price: Nickel-plated $215.00
Price: Engraved (Euroarms) $287.00
Price: Kit version . . . . $245.00 to $252.00
Price: Target version (Euroarms) . . . . $239.00 to $270.00
Price: Burnished London Gray (Euroarms) . . . . $245.00 to $270.00

BLACKPOWDER REVOLVERS

Spiller & Burr

Texas Paterson

3rd U.S. Model Dragoon

Walker

RUGER OLD ARMY PERCUSSION REVOLVER

Caliber: 45, 6-shot. Uses .457" dia. lead bullets or 454 conical. **Barrel:** 5-1/2", 7-1/2" (6-groove; 1:16" twist). **Weight:** 2-7/8 lbs. **Length:** 11-1/2" and 13-1/2" overall. **Stocks:** Rosewood, simulated ivory. **Sights:** Ramp front, rear adjustable for windage and elevation; or fixed (groove). **Features:** Stainless steel; standard size nipples, chrome-moly steel cylinder and frame, same lockwork as original Super Blackhawk. Also stainless steel. Includes hard case and lock. Made in USA. From Sturm, Ruger & Co.
Price: Blued steel, fixed sight (Model BP-5F) $541.00
Price: Stainless steel, fixed sight (Model KBP-5F-I) $623.00
Price: Stainless steel (Model KBP-7) $577.00
Price: Stainless steel, fixed sight (KBP-7F) $577.00

SHERIFF MODEL 1851 PERCUSSION REVOLVER

Caliber: 36, 44, 6-shot. **Barrel:** 5". **Weight:** 40 oz. **Length:** 10-1/2" overall. **Stocks:** Walnut. **Sights:** Fixed. **Features:** Brass backstrap and trigger guard; engraved navy scene; case-hardened frame, hammer, loading lever. Imported by E.M.F.
Price: Steel frame $169.95
Price: Brass frame $140.00

SPILLER & BURR REVOLVER

Caliber: 36 (.375" round ball). **Barrel:** 7", octagon. **Weight:** 2-1/2 lbs. **Length:** 12-1/2" overall. **Stocks:** Two-piece walnut. **Sights:** Fixed. **Features:** Reproduction of the C.S.A. revolver. Brass frame and trigger guard. Also available as a kit. From Dixie Gun Works, Navy Arms.
Price: $150.00
Price: Kit form (Dixie) $125.00
Price: Single cased set (Navy Arms) $270.00
Price: Double cased set (Navy Arms) $430.00

TEXAS PATERSON 1836 REVOLVER

Caliber: 36 (.375" round ball). **Barrel:** 7-1/2". **Weight:** 42 oz. **Stocks:** One-piece walnut. **Sights:** Fixed. **Features:** Copy of Sam Colt's first commercially-made revolving pistol. Comes with loading tool. From Cimarron F.A. Co., Dixie Gun Works, Navy Arms, Uberti U.S.A. Inc.
Price: About $495.00
Price: With loading lever (Uberti U.S.A. Inc.) $450.00
Price: Engraved (Navy Arms) $485.00

UBERTI 1861 NAVY PERCUSSION REVOLVER

Caliber: 36. **Barrel:** 7-1/2", round. **Weight:** 40-1/2 oz. **Stocks:** One-piece oiled American walnut. **Sights:** Brass pin front, hammer notch rear. **Features:** Rounded trigger guard, German silver blade front sight, "creeping" loading lever. Available with fluted or round cylinder. Imported by Uberti U.S.A. Inc.
Price: Steel backstrap, trigger guard, cut for stock $265.00

1ST U.S. MODEL DRAGOON

Caliber: 44. **Barrel:** 7-1/2", part round, part octagon. **Weight:** 64 oz. **Stocks:** One-piece walnut. **Sights:** German silver blade front, hammer notch rear. **Features:** First model has oval bolt cuts in cylinder, square-back flared trigger guard, V-type mainspring, short trigger. Ranger and Indian scene roll-engraved on cylinder. Color case-hardened frame, loading lever, plunger and hammer; blue barrel, cylinder, trigger and wedge. Available with old-time charcoal blue or standard blue-black finish. Polished brass backstrap and trigger guard. From Cimarron F.A. Co., Dixie Gun Works, Uberti U.S.A. Inc., Navy Arms.
Price: . . . . $295.00 to $435.00

2nd U.S. Model Dragoon Revolver

Similar to the 1st Model except distinguished by rectangular bolt cuts in the cylinder. From Cimarron F.A. Co., Uberti U.S.A. Inc., United States Patent Fire-Arms, Navy Arms, Dixie Gunworks.
Price: . . . . $295.00 to $435.00

3rd U.S. Model Dragoon Revolver

Similar to the 2nd Model except for oval trigger guard, long trigger, modifications to the loading lever and latch. Imported by Cimarron F.A. Co., Uberti U.S.A. Inc., United States Patent Fire-Arms, Dixie Gunworks.
Price: Military model (frame cut for shoulder stock, steel backstrap . . . . $295.00 to $435.00
Price: Civilian (brass backstrap, trigger guard) . . . . $295.00 to $325.00

1861 NAVY PERCUSSION REVOLVER

Caliber: 36, 6-shot. **Barrel:** 7-1/2", 7-groove, round. **Weight:** 2 lbs., 6 oz. **Length:** 13". **Stocks:** One-piece walnut. **Sights:** German silver blade front sight. **Features:** Rounded trigger guard, "creeping" loading lever, fluted or round cylinder, steel backstrap, trigger guard, cut for stock. Imported by Cimarron F.A. Co., Uberti U.S.A. Inc., Dixie Gunworks.
Price: . . . . $255.00 to $300.00

1862 POCKET NAVY PERCUSSION REVOLVER

Caliber: 36, 5-shot. **Barrel:** 5-1/2", 6-1/2", octagonal, 7-groove, LH twist. **Weight:** 27 oz. (5-1/2" barrel). **Length:** 10-1/2" overall (5-1/2" bbl.). **Stocks:** One-piece varnished walnut. **Sights:** Brass pin front, hammer notch rear. **Features:** Rebated cylinder, hinged loading lever, brass or silver-plated backstrap and trigger guard, color-cased frame, hammer, loading lever, plunger and latch, rest blued. Has original-type markings. From Cimarron F.A. Co., Uberti U.S.A. Inc., Dixie Gunworks.
Price: With brass backstrap, trigger guard . . . . $260.00 to $310.00

WALKER 1847 PERCUSSION REVOLVER

Caliber: 44, 6-shot. **Barrel:** 9". **Weight:** 84 oz. **Length:** 15-1/2" overall. **Stocks:** Walnut. **Sights:** Fixed. **Features:** Case-hardened frame, loading lever and hammer; iron backstrap; brass trigger guard; engraved cylinder. Imported by Cabela's, Cimarron F.A. Co., Navy Arms, Dixie Gun Works, Uberti U.S.A. Inc., E.M.F., Cimarron, Traditions, United States Patent Fire-Arms.
Price: About . . . . $225.00 to $445.00
Price: Single cased set (Navy Arms) $405.00
Price: Deluxe Walker with French fitted case (Navy Arms) $540.00
Price: Hartford model, steel frame, German silver trim, cartouche (E.M.F.) $295.00

Austin & Halleck 420 LR In-Line

Austin & Halleck 320 LR In-Line

Austin & Halleck Mountain

Cabela's Blue Ridge

Cabela's
Traditional Hawken

ARMOURY R140 HAWKEN RIFLE
Caliber: 45, 50 or 54. **Barrel:** 29". **Weight:** 8-3/4 to 9 lbs. **Length:** 45-3/4" overall. **Stock:** Walnut, with cheekpiece. **Sights:** Dovetailed front, fully adjustable rear. **Features:** Octagon barrel, removable breech plug; double set triggers; blued barrel, brass stock fittings, color case-hardened percussion lock. From Armsport, The Armoury.
Price: . . . . **$225.00 to $245.00**

AUSTIN & HALLECK MODEL 420 LR IN-LINE RIFLE
Caliber: 45 and 50. **Barrel:** 26", 1" octagon to 3/4" round; 1:28" twist. **Weight:** 7-7/8 lbs. **Length:** 47-1/2" overall. **Stock:** Lightly figured maple in Classic or Monte Carlo style. **Sights:** Ramp front, fully adjustable rear. **Features:** Blue or electroless nickel finish; in-line percussion action with removable weather shroud; Timney adjustable target trigger with sear block safety. Introduced 1998.
Price: Blue **$549.00**
Price: Stainless steel **$549.00**
Price: Blue, hand-select highly figured stock **$709.00**
Price: Stainless steel, select stock **$739.00**

Austin & Halleck Model 320 LR In-Line Rifle
Similar to the Model 420 LR (45 and 50 calibers) except has black resin synthetic stock with checkered grip and forend. Introduced 1998.
Price: Blue **$419.00**
Price: Stainless steel **$449.00**

AUSTIN & HALLECK MOUNTAIN RIFLE
Caliber: 50. **Barrel:** 32"; 1:28" or 1:66" twist; 1" flats. **Weight:** 7-1/2 lbs. **Length:** 49" overall. **Stock:** Curly maple. **Sights:** Silver blade front, buck-horn rear. **Features:** Available in percussion or flintlock; double throw adjustable set triggers; rust brown finish.
Price: Flintlock, fancy wood **$589.00**
Price: Flintlock, select wood **$769.00**
Price: Percussion, fancy wood **$539.00**
Price: Percussion, select wood **$719.00**

BOSTONIAN PERCUSSION RIFLE
Caliber: 45. **Barrel:** 30", octagonal. **Weight:** 7-1/4 lbs. **Length:** 46" overall. **Stock:** Walnut. **Sights:** Blade front, fixed notch rear. **Features:** Color case-hardened lock, brass trigger guard, buttplate, patchbox. Imported from Italy by E.M.F.
Price: **$285.00**

CABELA'S BLUE RIDGE RIFLE
Caliber: 32, 36, 45, 50, .54. **Barrel:** 39", octagonal. **Weight:** About 7-3/4 lbs. **Length:** 55" overall. **Stock:** American black walnut. **Sights:** Blade front, rear drift adjustable for windage. **Features:** Color case-hardened lockplate and cock/hammer, brass trigger guard and buttplate, double set, double-phased triggers. From Cabela's.
Price: Percussion **$429.99**
Price: Flintlock **$549.99**

CABELA'S TRADITIONAL HAWKEN
Caliber: 50, 54. **Barrel:** 29". **Weight:** About 9 lbs. **Stock:** Walnut. **Sights:** Blade front, open adjustable rear. **Features:** Flintlock or percussion. Adjustable double-set triggers. Polished brass furniture, color case-hardened lock. Imported by Cabela's.
Price: Percussion, right-hand **$269.99**
Price: Percussion, left-hand **$269.99**
Price: Flintlock, right-hand **$299.99**

BLACKPOWDER MUSKETS & RIFLES

Cook & Brother

Cabela's Sporterized Hawken Hunter Rifle
Similar to the Traditional Hawken except has more modern stock style with rubber recoil pad, blued furniture, sling swivels. Percussion only, in 50- or 54-caliber.
Price: Carbine or rifle, right-hand **$329.99**

CABELA'S KODIAK EXPRESS DOUBLE RIFLE
Caliber: 50, 54, 58, 72. **Barrel:** Length NA; 1:48" twist. **Weight:** 9.3 lbs. **Length:** 45-1/4" overall. **Stock:** European walnut, oil finish. **Sights:** Fully adjustable double folding-leaf rear, ramp front. **Features:** Percussion. Barrels regulated to point of aim at 75 yards; polished and engraved lock, top tang and trigger guard. From Cabela's.
Price: 50, 54, 58 calibers **$769.99**
Price: 72 caliber **$799.99**

COOK & BROTHER CONFEDERATE CARBINE
Caliber: 58. **Barrel:** 24". **Weight:** 7-1/2 lbs. **Length:** 40-1/2" overall. **Stock:** Select walnut. **Features:** Re-creation of the 1861 New Orleans-made artillery carbine. Color case-hardened lock, browned barrel. Buttplate, trigger guard, barrel bands, sling swivels and nosecap of polished brass. From Euroarms of America.
Price: **$513.00**
Price: Cook & Brother rifle (33" barrel) **$552.00**

CVA BOBCAT RIFLE
Caliber: 50 percussion. **Barrel:** 26"; 1:48" twist, octagonal. **Weight:** 6 lbs. **Length:** 42" overall. **Stock:** Dura-Grip synthetic or wood. **Sights:** Blade front, open rear. **Features:** Oversize trigger guard; wood ramrod; matte black finish. From CVA.
Price: (Wood stock) **$99.95**
Price: (Black synthetic stock) **$69.95**

CVA MOUNTAIN RIFLE
Caliber: 50. **Barrel:** 32"; 1:48" rifling. **Weight:** 8-1/2 lbs. **Length:** NA. **Sights:** Blade front, buckhorn rear. **Features:** Browned steel furniture, patchbox. Made in U.S. From CVA.
Price: **$259.95**

CVA ST. LOUIS HAWKEN RIFLE
Caliber: 50, 54. **Barrel:** 28", octagon; 15/16" across flats; 1:48" twist. **Weight:** 8 lbs. **Length:** 44" overall. **Stock:** Select hardwood. **Sights:** Beaded blade front, fully adjustable open rear. **Features:** Fully adjustable double-set triggers; synthetic ramrod (kits have wood); brass patchbox, wedge plates, nosecap, thimbles, trigger guard and buttplate; blued barrel; color case-hardened, engraved lockplate. V-type mainspring. Button breech. Introduced 1981. From CVA.
Price: St. Louis Hawken, finished (50-, 54-cal.) **$229.95**

CVA FIREBOLT MUSKETMAG BOLT-ACTION IN-LINE RIFLES
Caliber: 45 or 50. **Barrel:** 26". **Weight:** 7 lbs. **Length:** 44". **Stock:** Rubber-coated black or Mossy Oak® Break-Up™ camo synthetic. **Sights:** CVA Illuminator Fiber-Optic Sight System. **Features:** Bolt-action, inline ignition system handles up to 150 grains blackpowder or Pyrodex; nickel or matte blue barrel; removable breech plug; trigger-block safety. Three-way ignition system. From CVA.
Price: FiberGrip/nickel, 50 cal. **$294.95**
Price: Break-Up™/nickel, 50 cal. **$259.95**
Price: FiberGrip/nickel, 45 cal. **$294.95**
Price: Break-Up™/nickel, 45 cal. **$259.95**
Price: FiberGrip/blue, 50 cal. **$199.95**
Price: Break-Up™/blue, 50 cal. **$239.95**

Price: FiberGrip/blue, 45 cal. **$199.95**
Price: Break-Up™/blue, 45 cal. **$239.95**

CVA Hunterbolt 209 Magnum Rifle
Similar to the Firebolt except has 26" barrel and black or Mossy Oak® Break-Up™ synthetic stock. Three-way ignition system. Weighs 6 lbs. From CVA.
Price: 45 or 50 cal. . . . . **$179.95 to $234.95**

CVA OPTIMA PRO 209 BREAK-ACTION RIFLE
Caliber: 45, 50. **Barrel:** 29" fluted, blue or nickel. **Weight:** 8.8 lbs. **Stock:** Ambidextrous Mossy Oak® Camo or black FiberGrip. **Sights:** Adj. fiber-optic. **Features:** Break-action, stainless No. 209 breech plug, aluminum loading rod, cocking spur, lifetime warranty.
Price: Mossy Oak® Camo **$399.95**
Price: Camo, nickel bbl. **$379.95**
Price: Mossy Oak® Camo/blued **$349.95**
Price: Black/nickel **$329.95**
Price: Black/blued **$299.95**
Price: Blued fluted bbl. **$99.95**
Price: Nickel fluted bbl. **$115.95**

CVA Optima 209 Magnum Break-Action Rifle
Similar to Optima Pro but with 26" bbl., nickel or blue finish.
Price: Mossy Oak® Camo/nickel **$299.95**
Price: Mossy Oak® Camo/blue **$279.95**
Price: Black/nickel **$254.95**
Price: Black/blued **$224.95**

CVA Optima Elite
Similar to Optima Pro but chambered for 45, 50 black powder plus 243, 270, 30-06 centerfire cartridges.
Price: Hardwoods Green HD/blue **$415.00**
Price: Black Fleck/blue **$355.00**

CVA BUCKHORN 209 MAGNUM
Caliber: 50. **Barrel:** 24". **Weight:** 6.3 lbs. **Sights:** Illuminator fiber-optic. **Features:** Grip-dot stock, thumb-actuated safety; drilled and tapped for scope mounts.
Price: Black stock, blue barrel **$145.00**

CVA KODIAK MAGNUM RIFLE
Caliber: 45, 50. No. 209 primer ignition. **Barrel:** 28"; 1:28" twist. **Stock:** Ambidextrous black or Mossy Oak® camo. **Sights:** Fiber-optic. **Features:** Blue or nickel finish, recoil pad, lifetime warranty. From CVA.
Price: Mossy Oak® camo; nickel barrel **$355.00**
Price: Mossy Oak® camo; blued barrel **$333.00**
Price: Black stock; nickel barrel **$307.00**
Price: Black stock; blued barrel **$275.00**

DIXIE EARLY AMERICAN JAEGER RIFLE
Caliber: 54. **Barrel:** 27-1/2" octagonal; 1:24" twist. **Weight:** 8-1/4 lbs. **Length:** 43-1/2" overall. **Stock:** American walnut; sliding wooden patchbox on butt. **Sights:** Notch rear, blade front. **Features:** Flintlock or percussion. Browned steel furniture. Imported from Italy by Dixie Gun Works.
Price: Flintlock or percussion **$795.00**

DIXIE DELUXE CUB RIFLE
Caliber: 40. **Barrel:** 28". **Weight:** 6-1/2 lbs. **Stock:** Walnut. **Sights:** Fixed. **Features:** Short rifle for small game and beginning shooters. Brass patchbox and furniture. Flint or percussion. From Dixie Gun Works.
Price: Finished **$450.00**
Price: Kit **$390.00**
Price: Super Cub (50-caliber) **$485.00**

BLACKPOWDER MUSKETS & RIFLES

Dixie Sharps New Model 1859 Military

Dixie U.S. Model 1861 Springfield

Euroarms Volunteer

Euroarms 1861 Springfield

DIXIE 1863 SPRINGFIELD MUSKET
Caliber: 58 (.570" patched ball or .575" Minie). **Barrel:** 50", rifled. **Stock:** Walnut stained. **Sights:** Blade front, adjustable ladder-type rear. **Features:** Bright-finish lock, barrel, furniture. Reproduction of the last of the government regulation muzzleloaders. Imported from Japan by Dixie Gun Works.
Price: Finished $625.00
Price: Kit $550.00

DIXIE INLINE CARBINE
Caliber: 50, 54. **Barrel:** 24"; 1:32" twist. **Weight:** 6.5 lbs. **Length:** 41" overall. **Stock:** Walnut-finished hardwood with Monte Carlo comb. **Sights:** Ramp front with red insert, open fully adjustable rear. **Features:** Sliding bolt fully encloses cap and nipple. Fully adjustable trigger, automatic safety. Aluminum ramrod. Imported from Italy by Dixie Gun Works.
Price: $375.00

DIXIE PEDERSOLI 1857 MAUSER RIFLE
Caliber: 54. **Barrel:** 39-3/8". **Weight:** NA. **Length:** 52" overall. **Stock:** European walnut with oil finish, sling swivels. **Sights:** Fully adjustable rear, lug front. **Features:** Percussion (musket caps). Armory bright finish with color case-hardened lock and barrel tang, engraved lockplate, steel ramrod. Introduced 2000. Imported from Italy by Dixie Gun Works.
Price: $950.00

DIXIE PEDERSOLI 1766 CHARLEVILLE MUSKET
Caliber: 69. **Barrel:** 44-3/4". **Weight:** 10-1/2 lbs. **Length:** 57-1/2" overall. **Stock:** European walnut with oil finish. **Sights:** Fixed rear, lug front. **Features:** Smoothbore flintlock. Armory bright finish with steel furniture and ramrod. Introduced 2000. Imported from Italy by Dixie Gun Works.
Price: $895.00

DIXIE SHARPS NEW MODEL 1859 MILITARY RIFLE
Caliber: 54. **Barrel:** 30", 6-groove; 1:48" twist. **Weight:** 9 lbs. **Length:** 45-1/2" overall. **Stock:** Oiled walnut. **Sights:** Blade front, ladder-style rear. **Features:** Blued barrel, color case-hardened barrel bands, receiver,

hammer, nosecap, lever, patchbox cover and buttplate. Introduced 1995. Imported from Italy by Dixie Gun Works.
Price: $995.00

DIXIE U.S. MODEL 1861 FLINTLOCK MUSKET
Caliber: 69. **Barrel:** 42", smoothbore. **Weight:** 9.75 lbs. **Length:** 56.5" overall. **Stock:** Walnut with oil finish. **Sights:** Blade front. **Features:** All metal finished "National Armory Bright;" three barrel bands with springs; steel ramrod with button-shaped head. Imported by Dixie Gun Works.
Price: $875.00

DIXIE U.S. MODEL 1861 SPRINGFIELD
Caliber: 58. **Barrel:** 40". **Weight:** About 8 lbs. **Length:** 55-13/16" overall. **Stock:** Oil-finished walnut. **Sights:** Blade front, step adjustable rear. **Features:** Exact recreation of original rifle. Sling swivels attached to trigger guard bow and middle barrel band. Lockplate marked "1861" with eagle motif and "U.S. Springfield" in front of hammer; "U.S." stamped on top of buttplate. From Dixie Gun Works.
Price: Kit $550.00

E.M.F. 1863 SHARPS MILITARY CARBINE
Caliber: 54. **Barrel:** 22", round. **Weight:** 8 lbs. **Length:** 39" overall. **Stock:** Oiled walnut. **Sights:** Blade front, military ladder-type rear. **Features:** Color case-hardened lock, rest blued. Imported by E.M.F.
Price: $600.00

EUROARMS VOLUNTEER TARGET RIFLE
Caliber: 451. **Barrel:** 33" (two-band), 36" (three-band). **Weight:** 11 lbs. (two-band). **Length:** 48.75" overall (two-band). **Stock:** European walnut with checkered wrist and forend. **Sights:** Hooded bead front, adjustable rear with interchangeable leaves. **Features:** Alexander Henry-type rifling with 1:20" twist. Color case-hardened hammer and lockplate, brass trigger guard and nosecap, remainder blued. Imported by Euroarms of America, Dixie Gun Works.
Price: Two-band $828.00

EUROARMS 1861 SPRINGFIELD RIFLE
Caliber: 58. **Barrel:** 40". **Weight:** About 10 lbs. **Length:** 55.5" overall. **Stock:** European walnut. **Sights:** Blade front, three-leaf military rear. **Features:** Reproduction of the original three-band rifle. Lockplate marked "1861" with eagle and "U.S. Springfield." White metal. Imported by Euroarms of America.
Price: $579.00

BLACKPOWDER MUSKETS & RIFLES

Gonic Model 93 Thumbhole

Harper's Ferry 1803

J.P. Murray

EUROARMS ZOUAVE RIFLE
Caliber: 58 percussion. **Barrel:** 33". **Overall length:** 49".
Price: $469.00

EUROARMS HARPERS FERRY RIFLE
Caliber: 54 flintlock. **Barrel:** 35". **Overall length:** 50-1/2".
Price: $735.00

EUROARMS RICHMOND RIFLE
Caliber: 58 percussion. **Barrel:** 40". **Overall length:** 49".
Price: $579.00

GONIC MODEL 93 M/L RIFLE
Caliber: 45, 50. **Barrel:** 26"; 1:24" twist. **Weight:** 6-1/2 to 7 lbs. **Length:** 43" overall. **Stock:** American hardwood with black finish. **Sights:** Adjustable or aperture rear, hooded post front. **Features:** Adjustable trigger with side safety; unbreakable ramrod; comes with A. Z. scope bases installed. Introduced 1993. Made in U.S. by Gonic Arms, Inc.
Price: Model 93 Standard (blued barrel) $720.00
Price: Model 93 Standard (stainless brl., 50 cal. only) $782.00

Gonic Model 93 Deluxe M/L Rifle
Similar to the Model 93 except has classic-style walnut or gray laminated wood stock. Introduced 1998. Made in U.S. by Gonic Arms, Inc.
Price: Blue barrel, sights, scope base, choice of stock........... $902.00
Price: Stainless barrel, sights, scope base, choice of stock
(50 cal. only) $964.00

Gonic Model 93 Mountain Thumbhole M/L Rifles
Similar to the Model 93 except has high-grade walnut or gray laminate stock with extensive hand-checkered panels, Monte Carlo cheekpiece and beavertail forend; integral muzzle brake. Introduced 1998. Made in U.S. by Gonic Arms, Inc.
Price: Blued or stainless $2,700.00

H&R SIDEKICK
Caliber: 50, 209 primer ignition. **Barrel:** 24 or 26 (magnum). **Weight:** 6-1/2 lbs. **Length:** 39-1/4 to 41-1/4. **Stock:** Black matte polymer or hardwood. **Sights:** Adjustable fiber-optic open, tapped for scope mounts. **Features:** Break-action single-shot. Uses No. 209 shotgun primer held in place by special primer carrier. Telescoping brass ramrod. Introduced 2004.
Price: (Wood stock, blued finish, case-hardened frame) .... NA
Price: (Stainless, polymer stock) .... NA

H&R HUNTSMAN
Caliber: 50, 209 primer ignition. **Barrel:** 24". **Weight:** 6-1/2 lbs. **Length:** 40". **Stock:** Black matte polymer or hardwood. **Sights:** Fiber-optic open

sights, tapped for scope mounts. **Features:** Break-open action, transfer-bar safety system, breech plug removable for cleaning. Introduced 2004.
Price: Stainless model .... NA
Price: Blued finish .... NA
Price: Combo model (12 ga., .50 cal. muzzleloader, .243 Win) .... NA

HARPER'S FERRY 1803 FLINTLOCK RIFLE
Caliber: 54 or 58. **Barrel:** 35". **Weight:** 9 lbs. **Length:** 59-1/2" overall. **Stock:** Walnut with cheekpiece. **Sights:** Brass blade front, fixed steel rear. **Features:** Brass trigger guard, sideplate, buttplate; steel patchbox. Imported by Euroarms of America, Navy Arms (54-cal. only), Cabela's, and Dixie Gun Works.
Price: .... $495.95 to $729.00
Price: 54-cal. (Navy Arms) $625.00
Price: 54-cal. (Cabela's) $599.99
Price: 54-cal. (Dixie Gun Works) $795.00
Price: 54-cal. (Euroarms) $575.00

HAWKEN RIFLE
Caliber: 45, 50, 54 or 58. **Barrel:** 28", blued, 6-groove rifling. **Weight:** 8-3/4 lbs. **Length:** 44" overall. **Stock:** Walnut with cheekpiece. **Sights:** Blade front, fully adjustable rear. **Features:** Coil mainspring, double-set triggers, polished brass furniture. From Armsport and E.M.F.
Price: .... $220.00 to $345.00

J.P. HENRY TRADE RIFLE
Caliber: 54. **Barrel:** 34"; 1" flats. **Weight:** 8-1/2 lbs. **Length:** 45" overall. **Stock:** Premium curly maple. **Sights:** Silver blade front, fixed buckhorn rear. **Features:** Brass buttplate, side plate, trigger guard and nosecap; browned barrel and lock; L&R Large English percussion lock; single trigger. Made in U.S. by J.P. Gunstocks, Inc.
Price: $965.50

J.P. MURRAY 1862-1864 CAVALRY CARBINE
Caliber: 58 (.577" Minie). **Barrel:** 23". **Weight:** 7 lbs., 9 oz. **Length:** 39" overall. **Stock:** Walnut. **Sights:** Blade front, rear drift adjustable for windage. **Features:** Browned barrel, color case-hardened lock, blued swivel and band springs, polished brass buttplate, trigger guard, barrel bands. From Euroarms of America.
Price: $521.00

KENTUCKIAN RIFLE
Caliber: 44. **Barrel:** 35". **Weight:** 7 lbs. (rifle), 5-1/2 lbs. (carbine). **Length:** 51" overall (rifle), 43" (carbine). **Stock:** Walnut stain. **Sights:** Brass blade front, steel V-ramp rear. **Features:** Octagon barrel, case-hardened and engraved lockplates. Brass furniture. Imported by Dixie Gun Works.
Price: Flintlock or Percussion $395.00

Kentucky Flintlock

Knight 50 Caliber DISC In-Line

Knight Master Hunter DISC Extreme

London Armory 1861

Price: 45 blue walnut	$703.95
Price: 50 blue composite	$549.95
Price: 45 blue composite	$632.45
Price: 50 SS composite	$632.45
Price: 45 SS composite	$703.95

Knight Master Hunter DISC Extreme
Similar to DISC Extreme except fluted barrel, two-tone laminated thumbhole Monte Carlo-style stock, black composite thumbhole field stock included. Jeweled bolt, adjustable premium trigger.
Price: 50 . . . . **$1,044.95**

KNIGHT AMERICAN KNIGHT M/L RIFLE
Caliber: 50. **Barrel:** 22"; 1:28" twist. **Weight:** 6 lbs. **Length:** 41" overall. **Stock:** Black composite. **Sights:** Bead on ramp front, open fully adjustable rear. **Features:** Double safety system; one-piece removable hammer assembly; drilled and tapped for scope mounting. Introduced 1998. Made in U.S. by Knight Rifles.
Price: blued, black comp. **$197.95**
Price: blued, black comp VP **$225.45**

KNIGHT WOLVERINE 209
Caliber: 50. **Barrel:** 22". **Stock:** HD stock with SS barrel, break-up stock blued, black composite thumbhole with stainless steel, standard black composite with blued or SS. **Sights:** Metallic with fiber-optic. **Features:** Double safety system, adjustable match grade trigger, left-hand model available. Full plastic jacket ignition system.
Price: Starting at **$302.45**

KNIGHT REVOLUTION
Caliber: 50, 209 primer ignition. **Barrel:** Stainless, 27". **Weight:** 7 lbs., 14 oz. **Stock:** Walnut, laminated, black composite, Mossy Oak® Break-Up™ or Hardwoods Green finish. **Features:** Blued or stainless finish, adjustable trigger and sights.
Price: . . . . **NA**

LONDON ARMORY 1861 ENFIELD MUSKETOON
Caliber: 58, Minie ball. **Barrel:** 24", round. **Weight:** 7 to 7-1/2 lbs. **Length:** 40-1/2" overall. **Stock:** Walnut, with sling swivels. **Sights:** Blade front, graduated military-leaf rear. **Features:** Brass trigger guard, nosecap, buttplate; blued barrel, bands, lockplate, swivels. Imported by Euroarms of America, Navy Arms.
Price: . . . . **$300.00 to $515.00**
Price: Kit . . . . **$365.00 to $373.00**

KENTUCKY FLINTLOCK RIFLE
Caliber: 44, 45, or 50. **Barrel:** 35". **Weight:** 7 lbs. **Length:** 50" overall. **Stock:** Walnut stained, brass fittings. **Sights:** Fixed. **Features:** Available in carbine model also, 28" bbl. Some variations in detail, finish. Kits also available from some importers. Imported by The Armoury.
Price: About . . . . **$217.95 to $345.00**

Kentucky Percussion Rifle
Similar to Flintlock except percussion lock. Finish and features vary with importer. Imported by The Armoury and CVA.
Price: About **$259.95**
Price: 45 or 50 cal. (Navy Arms) **$425.00**
Price: Kit, 50 cal. (CVA) **$189.95**

KNIGHT 50 CALIBER DISC IN-LINE RIFLE
Caliber: 50. **Barrel:** 24", 26". **Weight:** 7 lbs., 14 oz. **Length:** 43" overall (24" barrel). **Stock:** Checkered synthetic with palm swell grip, rubber recoil pad, swivel studs; black, Advantage or Mossy Oak® Break-Up camouflage. **Sights:** Bead on ramp front, fully adjustable open rear. **Features:** Bolt-action in-line system uses #209 shotshell primer for ignition; primer is held in plastic drop-in Primer Disc. Available in blued or stainless steel. Made in U.S. by Knight Rifles (Modern Muzzleloading).
Price: . . . . **$439.95 to $632.45**

Knight Master Hunter II DISC In-Line Rifle
Similar to Knight 50 caliber DISC rifle except features premium, wood laminated two-tone stock, gold-plated trigger and engraved trigger guard, jeweled bolt and fluted, air-gauged Green Mountain 26" barrel. Length 45" overall, weighs 7 lbs., 7 oz. Includes black composite thumbhole stock. Introduced 2000. Made in U.S. by Knight Rifles (Modern Muzzleloading).
Price: **$1,099.95**

KNIGHT MUZZLELOADER DISC EXTREME
Caliber: 45 fluted, 50. **Barrel:** 26". **Stock:** Stainless steel laminate, blued walnut, black composite thumbhole with blued or SS. **Sights:** Fully adjustable metallic. **Features:** New full plastic jacket ignition system.
Price: 50 SS laminate **$703.95**
Price: 45 SS laminate **$769.95**
Price: 50 blue walnut **$626.95**

Lyman Trade

Lyman Deerstalker

Lyman Great Plains

LONDON ARMORY 2-BAND 1858 ENFIELD
Caliber: .577" Minie, .575" round ball. **Barrel:** 33". **Weight:** 10 lbs. **Length:** 49" overall. **Stock:** Walnut. **Sights:** Folding leaf rear adjustable for elevation. **Features:** Blued barrel, color case-hardened lock and hammer, polished brass buttplate, trigger guard, nosecap. From Navy Arms, Euroarms of America, Dixie Gun Works.
Price: . . . . **$385.00 to $600.00**

LONDON ARMORY 3-BAND 1853 ENFIELD
Caliber: 58 (.577" Minie, .575" round ball, .580" maxi ball). **Barrel:** 39". **Weight:** 9-1/2 lbs. **Length:** 54" overall. **Stock:** European walnut. **Sights:** Inverted "V" front, traditional Enfield folding ladder rear. **Features:** Re-creation of the famed London Armory Company Pattern 1853 Enfield Musket. One-piece walnut stock, brass buttplate, trigger guard and nosecap. Lockplate marked "London Armoury Co." and with a British crown. Blued Baddeley barrel bands. From Dixie Gun Works, Euroarms of America, Navy Arms.
Price: About. . . . . **$350.00 to $645.00**
Price: Assembled kit (Dixie, Euroarms of America) **$495.00**

LYMAN TRADE RIFLE
Caliber: 50, 54. **Barrel:** 28" octagon;1:48" twist. **Weight:** 8-3/4 lbs. **Length:** 45" overall. **Stock:** European walnut. **Sights:** Blade front, open rear adjustable for windage or optional fixed sights. **Features:** Fast twist rifling for conical bullets. Polished brass furniture with blue steel parts, stainless steel nipple. Hook breech, single trigger, coil spring percussion lock. Steel barrel rib and ramrod ferrules. Introduced 1980. From Lyman.
Price: 50 cal. percussion **$581.80**
Price: 50 cal. flintlock **$652.80**
Price: 54 cal. percussion **$581.80**
Price: 54 cal. flintlock **$652.80**

LYMAN DEERSTALKER RIFLE
Caliber: 50, 54. **Barrel:** 24", octagonal; 1:48" rifling. **Weight:** 7-1/2 lbs. **Stock:** Walnut with black rubber buttpad. **Sights:** Lyman #37MA beaded front, fully adjustable fold-down Lyman #16A rear. **Features:** Stock has less drop for quick sighting. All metal parts are blackened, with color case-hardened lock; single trigger. Comes with sling and swivels. Available in flint or percussion. Introduced 1990. From Lyman.
Price: 50 cal. flintlock. **$652.80**

Price: 50 or 54 cal., percussion, left-hand, carbine **$695.40**
Price: 50 or 54 cal., flintlock, left-hand **$645.00**
Price: 54 cal. flintlock **$780.50**
Price: 54 cal. percussion **$821.80**
Price: Stainless steel **$959.80**

LYMAN GREAT PLAINS RIFLE
Caliber: 50, 54. **Barrel:** 32"; 1:60" twist. **Weight:** 9 lbs. **Stock:** Walnut. **Sights:** Steel blade front, buckhorn rear adjustable for windage and elevation and fixed notch primitive sight included. **Features:** Blued steel furniture. Stainless steel nipple. Coil spring lock, Hawken-style trigger guard and double-set triggers. Round thimbles recessed and sweated into rib. Steel wedge plates and toe plate. Introduced 1979. From Lyman.
Price: Percussion **$469.95**
Price: Flintlock **$494.95**
Price: Percussion kit **$359.95**
Price: Flintlock kit **$384.95**
Price: Left-hand percussion **$474.95**
Price: Left-hand flintlock **$499.95**

Lyman Great Plains Hunter Model
Similar to Great Plains model except 1:32" twist shallow-groove barrel and comes drilled and tapped for Lyman 57GPR peep sight.
Price: **$959.80**

MARKESBERY KM BLACK BEAR M/L RIFLE
Caliber: 36, 45, 50, 54. **Barrel:** 24"; 1:26" twist. **Weight:** 6-1/2 lbs. **Length:** 38-1/2" overall. **Stock:** Two-piece American hardwood, walnut, black laminate, green laminate, black composition, X-Tra or Mossy Oak® Break-Up™ camouflage. **Sights:** Bead front, open fully adjustable rear. **Features:** Interchangeable barrels; exposed hammer; Outer-Line Magnum ignition system uses small rifle primer or standard No. 11 cap and nipple. Blue, black matte, or stainless. Made in U.S. by Markesbery Muzzle Loaders.
Price: American hardwood walnut, blue finish **$536.63**
Price: American hardwood walnut, stainless **$553.09**
Price: Black laminate, blue finish **$539.67**
Price: Black laminate, stainless **$556.27**
Price: Camouflage stock, blue finish **$556.46**
Price: Camouflage stock, stainless **$573.73**
Price: Black composite, blue finish **$532.65**
Price: Black composite, stainless **$549.93**
Price: Green laminate, blue finish **$539.00**
Price: Green laminate, stainless **$556.27**

BLACKPOWDER MUSKETS & RIFLES

Markesbery KM Colorado

Mississippi 1841

Markesbery KM Brown Bear Rifle
Similar to KM Black Bear except one-piece thumbhole stock with Monte Carlo comb. Stock in Crotch Walnut composite, green or black laminate, black composite or X-Tra or Mossy Oak® Break-Up™ camouflage. Made in U.S. by Markesbery Muzzle Loaders, Inc.

Price: Black composite, blue finish **$658.83**
Price: Crotch Walnut, blue finish **$658.83**
Price: Camo composite, blue finish **$682.64**
Price: Walnut wood **$662.81**
Price: Black wood **$662.81**
Price: Black laminated wood **$662.81**
Price: Green laminated wood **$662.81**
Price: Camo wood **$684.69**
Price: Black composite, stainless **$676.11**
Price: Crotch Walnut composite, stainless **$676.11**
Price: Camo composite, stainless **$697.69**
Price: Walnut wood, stainless **$680.07**
Price: Black wood, stainless **$680.07**
Price: Black laminated wood, stainless **$680.07**
Price: Green laminate, stainless **$680.07**
Price: Camo wood, stainless **$702.76**

Markesbery KM Grizzly Bear Rifle
Similar to KM Black Bear except thumbhole buttstock with Monte Carlo comb. Stock in Crotch Walnut composite, green or black laminate, black composite or X-Tra or Mossy Oak® Break-Up camouflage. Made in U.S. by Markesbery Muzzle Loaders, Inc.

Price: Black composite, blue finish **$642.96**
Price: Crotch Walnut, blue finish **$642.96**
Price: Camo composite, blue finish **$666.67**
Price: Walnut wood **$646.93**
Price: Black wood **$646.93**
Price: Black laminate wood **$646.93**
Price: Green laminate wood **$646.93**
Price: Camo wood **$670.74**
Price: Black composite, stainless **$660.98**
Price: Crotch Walnut composite, stainless **$660.98**
Price: Black laminate wood, stainless **$664.20**
Price: Green laminate, stainless **$664.20**
Price: Camo wood, stainless **$685.74**
Price: Camo composite, stainless **$684.04**
Price: Walnut wood, stainless **$664.20**
Price: Black wood, stainless **$664.20**

Markesbery KM Polar Bear Rifle
Similar to KM Black Bear except one-piece stock with Monte Carlo comb. Stock in American Hardwood walnut, green or black laminate, black composite, or X-Tra or Mossy Oak® Break-Up™ camouflage. Interchangeable barrel system, Outer-Line ignition system, cross-bolt double safety. Available in 36, 45, 50, 54 caliber. Made in U.S. by Markesbery Muzzle Loaders, Inc.

Price: American Hardwood walnut, blue finish **$539.01**
Price: Black composite, blue finish **$536.63**
Price: Black laminate, blue finish **$541.17**
Price: Green laminate, blue finish **$541.17**
Price: Camo, blue finish **$560.43**
Price: American Hardwood walnut, stainless **$556.27**
Price: Black composite, stainless **$556.04**
Price: Black laminate, stainless **$570.56**
Price: Green laminate, stainless **$570.56**
Price: Camo, stainless **$573.94**

MARKESBERY KM COLORADO ROCKY MOUNTAIN RIFLE
Caliber: 36, 45, 50, 54. **Barrel:** 24"; 1:26" twist. **Weight:** 6-1/2 lbs. **Length:** 38-1/2" overall. **Stock:** American hardwood walnut, green or black laminate. **Sights:** Firesight bead on ramp front, fully adjustable open rear. **Features:** Replicates Reed/Watson rifle of 1851. Straight grip stock with or without two barrel bands, rubber recoil pad, large-spur hammer. Made in U.S. by Markesbery Muzzle Loaders, Inc.

Price: American hardwood walnut, blue finish **$545.92**
Price: Black or green laminate, blue finish **$548.30**
Price: American hardwood walnut, stainless **$563.17**
Price: Black or green laminate, stainless **$566.34**

MDM BUCKWACKA IN-LINE RIFLES
Caliber: 45, 50. **Barrel:** 23", 25". **Weight:** 7 to 7-3/4 lbs. **Stock:** Black, walnut, laminated and camouflage finishes. **Sights:** Williams Fire Sight blade front, Williams fully adjustable rear with ghost-ring peep aperture. **Features:** Break-open action; Incinerating Ignition System incorporates 209 shotshell primer directly into breech plug; 50-caliber models handle up to 150 grains of Pyrodex; synthetic ramrod; transfer bar safety; stainless or blued finish. Made in U.S. by Millennium Designed Muzzleloaders Ltd.

Price: 50 cal., blued finish **$309.95**
Price: 50 cal., stainless **$339.95**
Price: Camouflage stock . . . . **$359.95 to $389.95**

MDM M2K In-Line Rifle
Similar to Buckwacka except adjustable trigger and double-safety mechanism designed to prevent misfires. Made in U.S. by Millennium Designed Muzzleloaders Ltd.

Price: . . . . **$529.00 to $549.00**

MISSISSIPPI 1841 PERCUSSION RIFLE
Caliber: 54, 58. **Barrel:** 33". **Weight:** 9-1/2 lbs. **Length:** 48-5/8" overall. **Stock:** One-piece European walnut full stock with satin finish. **Sights:** Brass blade front, fixed steel rear. **Features:** Case-hardened lockplate marked "U.S." surmounted by American eagle. Two barrel bands, sling swivels. Steel ramrod with brass end, browned barrel. From Navy Arms, Dixie Gun Works, E.M.F., Cabela's, Euroarms of America.

Price: About **$595.00**

BLACKPOWDER MUSKETS & RIFLES

Navy Arms 1763 Charleville

Navy Arms Berdan

Navy Arms 1859 Sharps

Navy Arms 1863 C.S. Richmond

Navy Arms Whitworth

NAVY ARMS 1763 CHARLEVILLE
Caliber: 69. **Barrel:** 44-5/8". **Weight:** 8 lbs., 12 oz. **Length:** 59-3/8" overall. **Stock:** Walnut. **Sights:** Brass blade front. **Features:** Replica of French musket used by American troops during the American Revolution. Imported by Navy Arms.
Price: $1,020.00

NAVY ARMS BERDAN 1859 SHARPS RIFLE
Caliber: 54. **Barrel:** 30". **Weight:** 8 lbs., 8 oz. **Length:** 46-3/4" overall. **Stock:** Walnut. **Sights:** Blade front, folding military ladder-type rear. **Features:** Replica of the Union sniper rifle used by Berdan's 1st and 2nd Sharpshooter regiments. Color case-hardened receiver, patchbox, furniture. Double-set triggers. Imported by Navy Arms.
Price: $1,165.00
Price: 1859 Sharps Infantry Rifle (three-band) $1,100.00

NAVY ARMS 1859 SHARPS CAVALRY CARBINE
Caliber: 54. **Barrel:** 22". **Weight:** 7-3/4 lbs. **Length:** 39" overall. **Stock:** Walnut. **Sights:** Blade front, military ladder-type rear. **Features:** Color case-hardened action, blued barrel. Has saddle ring. Introduced 1991. Imported from Navy Arms.
Price: $1,000.00

NAVY ARMS 1861 SPRINGFIELD RIFLE
Caliber: 58. **Barrel:** 40". **Weight:** 10 lbs., 4 oz. **Length:** 56" overall. **Stock:** Walnut. **Sights:** Blade front, military leaf rear. **Features:** Steel barrel, lock and all furniture have polished bright finish. Has 1855-style hammer. Imported by Navy Arms.
Price: $590.00

NAVY ARMS 1863 C.S. RICHMOND RIFLE
Caliber: 58. **Barrel:** 40". **Weight:** 10 lbs. **Length:** NA. **Stocks:** Walnut. **Sights:** Blade front, adjustable rear. **Features:** Copy of three-band rifle musket made at Richmond Armory for the Confederacy. All steel polished bright. Imported by Navy Arms.
Price: $590.00

NAVY ARMS 1863 SPRINGFIELD
Caliber: 58, uses .575 Minie. **Barrel:** 40", rifled. **Weight:** 9-1/2 lbs. **Length:** 56" overall. **Stock:** Walnut. **Sights:** Open rear adjustable for elevation. **Features:** Full-size, three-band musket. Polished bright metal, including lock. From Navy Arms.
Price: Finished rifle $590.00

NAVY ARMS PARKER-HALE VOLUNTEER RIFLE
Caliber: .451. **Barrel:** 32". **Weight:** 9-1/2 lbs. **Length:** 49" overall. **Stock:** Walnut, checkered wrist and forend. **Sights:** Globe front, adjustable ladder-type rear. **Features:** Recreation of the type of gun issued to volunteer regiments during the 1860s. Rigby-pattern rifling, patent breech, detented lock. Stock is glass bedded for accuracy. Imported by Navy Arms.
Price: $905.00

NAVY ARMS PARKER-HALE WHITWORTH MILITARY TARGET RIFLE
Caliber: 45. **Barrel:** 36". **Weight:** 9-1/4 lbs. **Length:** 52-1/2" overall. **Stock:** Walnut. Checkered at wrist and forend. **Sights:** Hooded post front, open step-adjustable rear. **Features:** Faithful reproduction of Whitworth rifle. Trigger has detented lock, capable of fine adjustments without risk of the sear nose catching on the half-cock notch and damaging both parts. Introduced 1978. Imported by Navy Arms.
Price: $930.00

BLACKPOWDER MUSKETS & RIFLES

Navy Arms Smith Carbine

New England Firearms Huntsman

Peifer TS-93

Remington Model 700 ML

NAVY ARMS SMITH CARBINE
Caliber: 50. **Barrel:** 21-1/2". **Weight:** 7-3/4 lbs. **Length:** 39" overall. **Stock:** American walnut. **Sights:** Brass blade front, folding ladder-type rear. **Features:** Replica of breech-loading Civil War carbine. Color case-hardened receiver, rest blued. Cavalry model has saddle ring and bar, Artillery model has sling swivels. Imported by Navy Arms.
Price: Cavalry model $645.00
Price: Artillery model $645.00

NEW ENGLAND FIREARMS HUNTSMAN
Caliber: 50. **Barrel:** 24". **Weight:** 6-1/2 lbs. **Length:** 40". **Stock:** Walnut-finished American hardwood with pistol grip. **Sights:** Adjustable fiber-optic open sights, tapped for scope base. **Features:** Break-open action, color case-hardened frame, black oxide barrel. Made in U.S.A. by New England Firearms.
Price: $188.00

New England Firearms Stainless Huntsman
Similar to Huntsman, but with matte nickel finish receiver and stainless bbl. Introduced 2003. From New England Firearms.
Price: $81.00

PACIFIC RIFLE MODEL 1837 ZEPHYR
Caliber: 62. **Barrel:** 30", tapered octagon. **Weight:** 7-3/4 lbs. **Length:** NA. **Stock:** Oil-finished fancy walnut. **Sights:** German silver blade front, semi-buckhorn rear. Options available. **Features:** Improved underhammer action. First production rifle to offer Forsyth rifle, with narrow lands and shallow rifling with 1:14" pitch for high-velocity round balls. Metal finish is slow rust brown with nitre blue accents. Optional sights, finishes and integral muzzle brake available. Introduced 1995. Made in U.S. by Pacific Rifle Co.
Price: From $995.00

Pacific Rifle Big Bore African Rifles
Similar to the 1837 Zephyr except in 72-caliber and 8-bore. The 72-caliber is available in standard form with 28" barrel, or as the African with flat buttplate, checkered upgraded wood; weight is 9 lbs. The 8-bore African has dual-cap ignition, 24" barrel, weighs 12 lbs., checkered English walnut, engraving, gold inlays. Introduced 1998. Made in U.S. by Pacific Rifle Co.
Price: 72-caliber, from $1,150.00
Price: 8-bore, from $2,500.00

PEIFER MODEL TS-93 RIFLE
Caliber: 45, 50. **Barrel:** 24" Douglas premium; 1:20" twist in 45; 1:28" in 50. **Weight:** 7 lbs. **Length:** 43-1/4" overall. **Stock:** Bell & Carlson solid composite, with recoil pad, swivel studs. **Sights:** Williams bead front on ramp, fully adjustable open rear. Drilled and tapped for Weaver scope mounts with dovetail for rear peep. **Features:** In-line ignition uses #209 shotshell primer; fast lock time; fully enclosed breech; adjustable trigger; automatic safety; removable primer holder. Blue or stainless. Made in U.S. by Peifer Rifle Co. Introduced 1996.
Price: Blue, black stock $730.00
Price: Blue, wood or camouflage composite stock, or stainless with black composite stock $803.00
Price: Stainless, wood or camouflage composite stock $876.00

PRAIRIE RIVER ARMS PRA BULLPUP RIFLE
Caliber: 50. **Barrel:** 28"; 1:28" twist. **Weight:** 7-1/2 lbs. **Length:** 31-1/2" overall. **Stock:** Hardwood or black all-weather. **Sights:** Blade front, open adjustable rear. **Features:** Bullpup design thumbhole stock. Patented internal percussion ignition system. Left-hand model available. Dovetailed for scope mount. Introduced 1995. Made in U.S. by Prairie River Arms, Ltd.
Price: 4140 alloy barrel, hardwood stock $199.00
Price: All Weather stock, alloy barrel $205.00

REMINGTON MODEL 700 ML, MLS RIFLES
Caliber: 50, new 45 (MLS Magnum). **Barrel:** 24"; 1:28" twist, 26" (Magnum). **Weight:** 7-3/4 lbs. **Length:** 42" to 44-1/2" overall. **Stock:** Black fiberglass-reinforced synthetic with checkered grip and forend; magnum-style butt-pad. **Sights:** Ramped bead front, open fully adjustable rear. Drilled and tapped for scope mounts. **Features:** Uses the Remington 700 bolt action, stock design, safety and trigger mechanisms; removable stainless steel breech plug, No. 11 nipple; solid aluminum ramrod. Comes with cleaning tools and accessories; 3-way ignition.
Price: ML, blued, 50-caliber only $415.00
Price: MLS, stainless, 45 Magnum, 50-caliber $533.00
Price: MLS, stainless, Mossy Oak® Break-Up camo stock $569.00

BLACKPOWDER MUSKETS & RIFLES

C.S. Richmond 1863

Savage 10MLSS-IIXP

Second Model Brown Bess

Thompson/Center Hawken

RICHMOND, C.S., 1863 MUSKET
Caliber: 58. **Barrel:** 40". **Weight:** 11 lbs. **Length:** 56-1/4" overall. **Stock:** European walnut with oil finish. **Sights:** Blade front, adjustable folding leaf rear. **Features:** Reproduction of the three-band Civil War musket. Sling swivels attached to trigger guard and middle barrel band. Lockplate marked "1863" and "C.S. Richmond." All white metal. Brass buttplate and forend cap. Imported by Euroarms of America, Navy Arms, and Dixie Gun Works.
Price: Euroarms **$530.00**
Price: Dixie Gun Works **$675.00**

SAVAGE MODEL 10ML MUZZLELOADER RIFLE SERIES
Caliber: 50. **Barrel:** 24", 1:24 twist, blue or stainless. **Weight:** 7.75 lbs. **Stock:** Black synthetic, Realtree Hardwood JD Camo, brown laminate. **Sights:** Green adjustable rear, Red FiberOptic front. **Features:** XP Models scoped, no sights, designed for smokeless powder, #209 primer ignition. Removeable breech plug and vent liner.
Price: Model 10ML-II **$531.00**
Price: Model 10ML-II Camo **$569.00**
Price: Model 10MLSS-II Camo **$628.00**
Price: Model 10MLBSS-II **$667.00**
Price: Model 10ML-IIXP **$569.00**
Price: Model 10MLSS-IIXP **$628.00**

SECOND MODEL BROWN BESS MUSKET
Caliber: 75, uses .735" round ball. **Barrel:** 42", smoothbore. **Weight:** 9-1/2 lbs. **Length:** 59" overall. **Stock:** Walnut (Navy); walnut-stained hardwood (Dixie). **Sights:** Fixed. **Features:** Polished barrel and lock with brass trigger guard and buttplate. Bayonet and scabbard available. From Navy Arms, Dixie Gun Works, Cabela's.
Price: Finished . . . . **$475.00 to $850.00**
Price: Kit (Dixie Gun Works, Navy Arms) . . . . **$575.00 to $625.00**
Price: Carbine (Navy Arms) **$835.00**
Price: Dixie Gun Works **$765.00**

THOMPSON/CENTER FIRE STORM RIFLE
Caliber: 50. **Barrel:** 26"; 1:28" twist. **Weight:** 7 lbs. **Length:** 41-3/4" overall. **Stock:** Black synthetic with rubber recoil pad, swivel studs. **Sights:** Click-adjustable steel rear and ramp-style front, both with fiber-optic inserts. **Features:** Side hammer lock is the first designed for up to three 50-grain Pyrodex pellets; patented Pyrodex Pyramid breech directs ignition fire 360 degrees around base of pellet. Quick Load Accurizor Muzzle System; aluminum ramrod. Flintlock only. Introduced 2000. Made in U.S. by Thompson/Center Arms.
Price: Blue finish, flintlock model with 1:48" twist for round balls, conicals **$436.00**
Price: SST, flintlock **$488.00**

THOMPSON/CENTER ENCORE 209x50 MAGNUM
Caliber: 50. **Barrel:** 26"; interchangeable with centerfire calibers. **Weight:** 7 lbs. **Length:** 40-1/2" overall. **Stock:** American walnut butt and forend, or black composite. **Sights:** TruGlo fiber-optic front and rear. **Features:** Blue or stainless steel. Uses the stock, frame and forend of the Encore centerfire pistol; break-open design using trigger guard spur; stainless steel universal breech plug; uses #209 shotshell primers. Introduced 1998. Made in U.S. by Thompson/Center Arms.
Price: Stainless wtih camo stock **$772.00**
Price: Blue, walnut stock and forend **$678.00**
Price: Blue, composite stock and forend **$637.00**
Price: Stainless, composite stock and forend **$713.00**
Price: All camo Realtree Hardwoods **$729.00**

THOMPSON/CENTER BLACK DIAMOND RIFLE XR
Caliber: 50. **Barrel:** 26" with QLA; 1:28" twist. **Weight:** 6 lbs., 9 oz. **Length:** 41-1/2" overall. **Stock:** Black Rynite with molded-in checkering and gripcap, or walnut. **Sights:** TruGlo fiber-optic ramp-style front, TruGlo fiber-optic open rear. **Features:** In-line ignition system for musket cap, No. 11 cap, or 209 shotshell primer; removable universal breech plug; stainless steel construction. Selected models available in .45 cal. Made in U.S. by Thompson/Center Arms.
Price: With composite stock, blued **$337.00**
Price: With walnut stock **$412.00**

THOMPSON/CENTER HAWKEN RIFLE
Caliber: 50. **Barrel:** 28" octagon, hooked breech. **Stock:** American walnut. **Sights:** Blade front, rear adjustable for windage and elevation. **Features:** Solid brass furniture, double-set triggers, button rifled barrel, coil-type mainspring. From Thompson/Center Arms.
Price: Percussion model **$590.00**
Price: Flintlock model **$615.00**

Traditions Deerhunter

Traditions Pursuit

Traditions PA Pellet

TRADITIONS BUCKSKINNER CARBINE
Caliber: 50. **Barrel:** 21"; 15/16" flats, half octagon, half round; 1:20" or 1:66" twist. **Weight:** 6 lbs. **Length:** 37" overall. **Stock:** Beech or black laminated. **Sights:** Beaded blade front, fiber-optic open rear click adjustable for windage and elevation or fiber-optics. **Features:** Uses V-type mainspring, single trigger. Non-glare hardware; sling swivels. From Traditions.
Price: Flintlock **$249.00**
Price: Flintlock, laminated stock **$303.00**

TRADITIONS DEERHUNTER RIFLE SERIES
Caliber: 32, 50 or 54. **Barrel:** 24", octagonal; 15/16" flats; 1:48" or 1:66" twist. **Weight:** 6 lbs. **Length:** 40" overall. **Stock:** Stained hardwood or All-Weather composite with rubber buttpad, sling swivels. **Sights:** Lite Optic blade front, adjustable rear fiber-optics. **Features:** Flint or percussion with color case-hardened lock. Hooked breech, oversized trigger guard, blackened furniture, PVC ramrod. All-Weather has composite stock and C-nickel barrel. Drilled and tapped for scope mounting. Imported by Traditions, Inc.
Price: Percussion, 50; blued barrel; 1:48" twist **$189.00**
Price: Percussion, 54 . . . . **$169.00**
Price: Flintlock, 50 caliber only; 1:48" twist **$179.00**
Price: Flintlock, All-Weather, 50-cal. **$239.00**
Price: Redi-Pak, 50 cal. flintlock **$219.00**
Price: Flintlock, left-handed hardwood, 50 cal. **$209.00**
Price: Percussion, All-Weather, 50 or 54 cal. **$179.00**
Price: Percussion, 32 cal. **$199.00**

Traditions Panther Sidelock Rifle
Similar to Deerhunter rifle, but has blade front and windage-adjustable-only rear sights, black composite stock.
Price: **$129.00**

TRADITIONS PURSUIT BREAK-OPEN MUZZLELOADER
Caliber: 45, 54 and 12 gauge. **Barrel:** 28", tapered, fluted; blued, stainless or Hardwoods Green camo. **Weight:** 8-1/4 lbs. **Length:** 44" overall. **Stock:** Synthetic black or Hardwoods Green. **Sights:** Steel fiber-optic rear, bead front. Introduced 2004 by Traditions, Inc.
Price: Steel, blued, 45 or 50 cal., synthetic stock **$279.00**
Price: Steel, nickel, 45 or 50 cal., synthetic stock **$309.00**
Price: Steel, nickel w/Hardwoods Green stock **$359.00**
Price: Matte blued; 12 ga., synthetic stock **$369.00**
Price: Matte blued; 12 ga. w/Hardwoods Green stock **$439.00**

Price: Lightweight model, blued, synthetic stock **$199.00**
Price: Lightweight model, blued, Mossy Oak®
Break-Up™ Camo stock **$239.00**
Price: Lightweight model, nickel, Mossy Oak®
Break-Up™ Camo stock **$279.00**

TRADITIONS EVOLUTION BOLT-ACTION BLACKPOWDER RIFLE
Caliber: 50 percussion. **Barrel:** 26", fluted with porting. **Sights:** Steel fiber-optic. **Weight:** 7 to 7-1/4 lbs. **Length:** 45" overall. **Features:** Bolt-action, cocking indicator, thumb safety, aluminum ramrod, sling studs. Wide variety of stocks and metal finishes. Introduced 2004 by Traditions, Inc.
Price: Synthetic stock **$279.00**
Price: Walnut X-wood **$349.00**
Price: Brown laminated **$469.00**
Price: Advantage Timber **$369.00**
Price: Synthetic, TruGlo sights **$249.00**
Price: Mossy Oak® Break-up™ **$279.00**
Price: Nickel finish **$309.00**
Price: Beech/nickel, Advantage/nickel, Advantage 54 cal. **$289.00**

TRADITIONS PA PELLET FLINTLOCK
Caliber: 50. **Barrel:** 26", blued, nickel. **Weight:** 7 lbs. **Stock:** Hardwood, synthetic and synthetic break-up. **Sights:** Fiber-optic. **Features:** Removeable breech plug, left-hand model with hardwood stock. 1:48" twist.
Price: Hardwood, blued. **$259.00**
Price: Hardwood left, blued **$269.00**

TRADITIONS HAWKEN WOODSMAN RIFLE
Caliber: 50 and 54. **Barrel:** 28"; 15/16" flats. **Weight:** 7 lbs., 11 oz. **Length:** 44-1/2" overall. **Stock:** Walnut-stained hardwood. **Sights:** Beaded blade front, hunting-style open rear adjustable for windage and elevation. **Features:** Percussion only. Brass patchbox and furniture. Double triggers. From Traditions.
Price: 50 or 54. . . . . **$299.00**
Price: 50-cal., left-hand **$279.00**
Price: 50-cal., flintlock **$299.00**

TRADITIONS KENTUCKY RIFLE
Caliber: 50. **Barrel:** 33-1/2"; 7/8" flats; 1:66" twist. **Weight:** 7 lbs. **Length:** 49" overall. **Stock:** Beech; inletted toe plate. **Sights:** Blade front, fixed rear. **Features:** Full-length, two-piece stock; brass furniture; color case-hardened lock. From Traditions.
Price: **$279.00**

BLACKPOWDER MUSKETS & RIFLES

Zouave Percussion

TRADITIONS PENNSYLVANIA RIFLE
Caliber: 50. **Barrel:** 40-1/4"; 7/8" flats; 1:66" twist, octagon. **Weight:** 9 lbs. **Length:** 57-1/2" overall. **Stock:** Walnut. **Sights:** Blade front, adjustable rear. **Features:** Brass patchbox and ornamentation. Double-set triggers. From Traditions.
Price: Flintlock $529.00
Price: Percussion $519.00

TRADITIONS SHENANDOAH RIFLE
Caliber: 36, 50. **Barrel:** 33-1/2" octagon; 1:66" twist. **Weight:** 7 lbs., 3 oz. **Length:** 49-1/2" overall. **Stock:** Walnut. **Sights:** Blade front, buckhorn rear. **Features:** V-type mainspring; double-set trigger; solid brass buttplate, patchbox, nosecap, thimbles, trigger guard. Introduced 1996. From Traditions.
Price: Flintloc $419.00
Price: Percussion $399.00
Price: 36 cal. flintlock, 1:48" twist $419.00
Price: 36 cal. percussion, 1:48" twist $449.00

TRADITIONS TENNESSEE RIFLE
Caliber: 50. **Barrel:** 24", octagon; 15/16" flats; 1:66" twist. **Weight:** 6 lbs. **Length:** 40-1/2" overall. **Stock:** Stained beech. **Sights:** Blade front, fixed rear. **Features:** One-piece stock has inletted brass furniture, cheekpiece; double-set trigger; V-type mainspring. Flint or percussion. From Traditions.
Price: Flintlock $339.00
Price: Percussion $329.00

TRADITIONS TRACKER 209 IN-LINE RIFLES
Caliber: 45, 50. **Barrel:** 22" blued or C-nickel finish; 1:28" twist, 50 cal. 1:20" 45 cal. **Weight:** 6 lbs., 4 oz. **Length:** 41" overall. **Stock:** Black, Advantage Timber® composite, synthetic. **Sights:** Lite Optic blade front, adjustable rear. **Features:** Thumb safety; adjustable trigger; rubber butt pad and sling swivel studs; takes 150 grains of Pyrodex pellets; one-piece breech system takes 209 shotshell primers. Drilled and tapped for scope. From Traditions.
Price: (Black composite or synthetic stock, 22" blued barrel) $129.00
Price: (Black composite or synthetic stock, 22" C-nickel barrel) . . . $139.00
Price: (Advantage Timber® stock, 22" C-nickel barrel) $189.00
Price: (Redi-Pak, black stock and blued barrel, powder flask,
capper, ball starter, other accessories) $179.00
Price: (Redi-Pak, synthetic stock and blued barrel, with scope) . . . $229.00

ULTRA LIGHT ARMS MODEL 209 MUZZLELOADER
Caliber: 45 or 50. **Barrel:** 24" button rifled; 1:32 twist. **Weight:** Under 5 lbs. **Stock:** Kevlar/Graphite. **Features:** Recoil pad, sling swivels included. Some color options available. Adj. Timney trigger, positive primer extraction.
Price: $1,100.00

WHITE MODEL 97 WHITETAIL HUNTER RIFLE
Caliber: 45, 50. **Barrel:** 22", 1:20 twist (45 cal.); 1:24 twist (50 cal.). **Weight:** 7.7 lbs. **Length:** 40" overall. **Stock:** Black laminated or black composite. **Sights:** Marble TruGlo fully adjustable, steel rear with white diamond, red bead front with high-visibility inserts. **Features:** In-line ignition with FlashFire one-piece nipple and breech plug that uses standard or magnum No. 11 caps, fully adjustable trigger, double safety system, aluminum ramrod; drilled and tapped for scope. Hard case. Made in U.S.A. by Split Fire Sporting Goods.
Price: Whitetail w/laminated or composite stock $499.95
Price: Adventurer w/26" stainless barrel & thumbhole stock) $699.95
Price: Odyssey w/24" carbon fiber wrapped
barrel & thumbhole stock $1,299.95

WHITE MODEL 98 ELITE HUNTER RIFLE
Caliber: 45, 50. **Barrel:** 24", 1:24" twist (50 cal). **Weight:** 8.6 lbs. **Length:** 43-1/2" overall. **Stock:** Black laminate wtih swivel studs. **Sights:** TruGlo fully adjustable, steel rear with white diamond, red bead front with high-visibility inserts. **Features:** In-line ignition with FlashFire one-piece nipple and breech plug that uses standard or magnum No. 11 caps, fully adjustable trigger, double safety system, aluminum ramrod, drilled and tapped for scope, hard gun case. Made in U.S.A. by Split Fire Sporting Goods.
Price: Composite or laminate wood stock $499.95

White Thunderbolt Rifle
Similar to the Elite Hunter but is designed to handle 209 shotgun primers only. Has 26" stainless steel barrel, weighs 9.3 lbs. and is 45-1/2" long. Composite or laminate stock. Made in U.S.A. by Split Fire Sporting Goods.
Price: $599.95

WHITE MODEL 2000 BLACKTAIL HUNTER RIFLE
Caliber: 50. **Barrel:** 22", 1:24" twist (50 cal.). **Weight:** 7.6 lbs. **Length:** 39-7/8" overall. **Stock:** Black laminated with swivel studs with laser engraved deer or elk scene. **Sights:** TruGlo fully adjustable, steel rear with white diamond, red bead front with high-visibility inserts. **Features:** Teflon finished barrel, in-line ignition with FlashFire one-piece nipple and breech plug that uses standard or magnum No. 11 caps, fully adjustable trigger, double safety system, aluminum ramrod, drilled and tapped for scope. Hard gun case. Made in U.S.A. by Split Fire Sporting Goods.
Price: Laminate wood stock, w/laser engraved game scene $599.95

WHITE LIGHTNING II RIFLE
Caliber: 45 and 50 percussion. **Barrel:** 24", 1:32 twist. **Sights:** Adj. rear. **Stock:** Black polymer. **Weight:** 6 lbs. **Features:** In-line, 209 primer ignition system, blued or nickel-plated bbl., adj. trigger, Delrin ramrod, sling studs, recoil pad. Made in U.S.A. by Split Fire Sporting Goods.
Price: $299.95

WHITE ALPHA RIFLE
Caliber: 45, 50 percussion. **Barrel:** 27" tapered, stainless. **Sights:** Marble TruGlo rear, fiber-optic front. **Stock:** Laminated. **Features:** Lever action rotating block, hammerless; adj. trigger, positive safety. All stainless metal, including trigger. Made in U.S.A. by Split Fire Sporting Goods.
Price: $449.95

WINCHESTER APEX SWING-ACTION MAGNUM RIFLE
Caliber: 45, 50. **Barrel:** 28". **Stock:** Mossy Oak® Camo, Black Fleck. **Sights:** Adj. fiber-optic. **Weight:** 7 lbs., 12 oz. **Overall length:** 42". **Features:** Monte Carlo cheekpiece, swing-action design, external hammer.
Price: Mossy Oak®/stainless $489.95
Price: Black Fleck/stainless $449.95
Price: Full Mossy Oak® $469.95
Price: Black Fleck/blued $364.95

WINCHESTER X-150 BOLT-ACTION MAGNUM RIFLE
Caliber: 45, 50. **Barrel:** 26". **Stock:** Hardwoods or Timber HD, Black Fleck, Break-Up™. **Weight:** 8 lbs., 3 oz. **Sights:** Adj. fiber-optic. **Features:** No. 209 shotgun primer ignition, stainless steel bolt, stainless fluted bbl.
Price: Mossy Oak®, Timber, Hardwoods/stainless $349.95
Price: Black Fleck/stainless $299.95
Price: Mossy Oak®, Timber, Hardwoods/blued $279.95
Price: Black Fleck/blued $229.95

ZOUAVE PERCUSSION RIFLE
Caliber: 58, 59. **Barrel:** 32-1/2". **Weight:** 9-1/2 lbs. **Length:** 48-1/2" overall. **Stock:** Walnut finish, brass patchbox and buttplate. **Sights:** Fixed front, rear adjustable for elevation. **Features:** Color case-hardened lockplate, blued barrel. From Navy Arms, Dixie Gun Works, E.M.F., Cabela's, Euroarms of America.
Price: . . . . $415.00 to $515.00

Knight TK2000

CABELA'S BLACKPOWDER SHOTGUNS
Gauge: 10, 12, 20. **Barrel:** 10-ga., 30"; 12-ga., 28-1/2" (Extra-Full, Mod., Imp. Cyl. choke tubes); 20-ga., 27-1/2" (Imp. Cyl. & Mod. fixed chokes). **Weight:** 6-1/2 to 7 lbs. **Length:** 45" overall (28-1/2" barrel). **Stock:** American walnut with checkered grip; 12- and 20-gauge have straight stock, 10-gauge has pistol grip. **Features:** Blued barrels, engraved, color case-hardened locks and hammers, brass ramrod tip. From Cabela's.
Price: 10-gauge **$679.99**
Price: 12-gauge **$579.99**
Price: 20-gauge **$549.99**

DIXIE MAGNUM PERCUSSION SHOTGUN
Gauge: 10, 12, 20. **Barrel:** 30" (Imp. Cyl. & Mod.) in 10-gauge; 28" in 12-gauge. **Weight:** 6-1/4 lbs. **Length:** 45" overall. **Stock:** Hand-checkered walnut, 14" pull. **Features:** Double triggers; light hand engraving; case-hardened locks in 12-gauge, polished steel in 10-gauge; sling swivels. From Dixie Gun Works.
Price: Upland **$650.00**
Price: 12-ga. kit **$445.00**
Price: 20-ga. **$525.00**
Price: 10-ga. **$575.00**
Price: 10-ga. kit **$445.00**

KNIGHT TK2000 MUZZLELOADING SHOTGUN (209)
Gauge: 12. **Barrel:** 26", extra-full choke tube. **Weight:** 7 lbs., 9 oz. **Length:** 45" overall. **Stock:** Synthetic black or Advantage Timber HD; recoil pad; swivel studs. **Sights:** Fully adjustable rear, blade front with fiber-optics. **Features:** Receiver drilled and tapped for scope mount; in-line ignition; adjustable trigger; removable breech plug; double safety system; Imp. Cyl. choke tube available. Made in U.S. by Knight Rifles.
Price: . . . . **$349.95 to $399.95**

KNIGHT VERSATILE TK2002
Gauge: 12. **Stock:** Black composite, blued, Advantage Timber HD finish. Both with sling swivel studs installed. **Sights:** Adjustable metallic TruGlo fiber-optic. **Features:** Full plastic jacket ignition system, screw-on choke tubes, load without removing choke tubes, jug-choked barrel design. Improved cylinder and modified choke tubes available.
Price: . . . . **$349.95 to $399.95**

NAVY ARMS STEEL SHOT MAGNUM SHOTGUN
Gauge: 10. **Barrel:** 28" (Cyl. & Cyl.). **Weight:** 7 lbs., 9 oz. **Length:** 45-1/2" overall. **Stock:** Walnut, with cheekpiece. **Features:** Designed specifically for steel shot. Engraved, polished locks; sling swivels; blued barrels. Imported by Navy Arms.
Price: **$605.00**

NAVY ARMS T&T SHOTGUN
Gauge: 12. **Barrel:** 28" (Full & Full). **Weight:** 7-1/2 lbs. **Stock:** Walnut. **Sights:** Bead front. **Features:** Color case-hardened locks, double triggers, blued steel furniture. From Navy Arms.
Price: **$580.00**

WHITE TOMINATOR SHOTGUN
Caliber: 12. **Barrel:** 25" blue, straight, tapered stainless steel. **Weight:** NA. **Length:** NA. **Stock:** Black laminated or black wood. **Sights:** Drilled and tapped for easy scope mounting. **Features:** Internchangeable choke tubes. Custom vent rib with high visibility front bead. Double safeties. Fully adjustable custom trigger. Recoil pad and sling swivel studs. Made in U.S.A. by Split Fire Sporting Goods.
Price: **$349.95**

CONSULT

SHOOTER'S MARKETPLACE

Page 74, This Issue

AIRFORCE TALON SS AIR PISTOL
Caliber: 177, 22. **Barrel:** 12". **Weight:** 5.25 lbs. **Length:** 32.75" overall. **Power:** NA. **Grips:** NA. **Sights:** None, integral mount supplied. **Features:** 400-1000 fps. Fill pressure: 3000 psi. Air tank volume: 490cc.
Price: 22 w/refill clamp, open sights $559.95
Price: 177 w/refill clamp, open sights $559.95
Price: Gun only (22 or 177) $459.95

AirForce Talon Air Pistol
Same as Talon SS but 32.6" long, weights 5.5 lbs.
Price: 22 w/refill clamp, open sights $539.95
Price: 177 w/refill clamp, open sights $539.95
Price: Gun only $439.95

ARS HUNTING MASTER AR6 AIR PISTOL
Caliber: 22 (177 +20 special order). **Barrel:** 12" rifled. **Weight:** 3 lbs. **Length:** 18.25 overall. **Power:** NA. **Grips:** Indonesian walnut with checkered grip. **Sights:** Adjustable rear, blade front. **Features:** 6 shot repeater with rotary magazine, single or double action, receiver grooved for scope, hammer block and trigger block safeties.
Price: . . . . **NA**

BEEMAN P1 MAGNUM AIR PISTOL
Caliber: 177, 5mm, single shot. **Barrel:** 8.4". **Weight:** 2.5 lbs. **Length:** 11" overall. **Power:** Top lever cocking; spring-piston. **Grips:** Checkered walnut. **Sights:** Blade front, square notch rear with click micrometer adjustments for windage and elevation. Grooved for scope mounting. **Features:** Dual power for 177 and 20 cal.: low setting gives 350-400 fps; high setting 500-600 fps. All Colt 45 auto grips fit gun. Dry-firing feature for practice. Optional wood shoulder stock. Imported by Beeman.
Price: 177, 5mm $440.00

BEEMAN P3 AIR PISTOL
Caliber: 177 pellet, single shot. **Barrel:** NA. **Weight:** 1.7 lbs. **Length:** 9.6" overall. **Power:** Single-stroke pneumatic; overlever barrel cocking. **Grips:** Reinforced polymer. **Sights:** Adjustable rear, blade front. **Features:** Velocity 410 fps. Polymer frame; automatic safety; two-stage trigger; built-in muzzle brake.
Price: $180.00
Price: Combo $285.00

BEEMAN/FEINWERKBAU 103 AIR PISTOL
Caliber: 177, single shot. **Barrel:** 10.1", 12-groove rifling. **Weight:** 2.5 lbs. **Length:** 16.5" overall. **Power:** Single-stroke pneumatic, underlever cocking. **Grips:** Stippled walnut with adjustable palm shelf. **Sights:** Blade front, open rear adjustable for windage and elevation. Notch size adjustable for width. Interchangeable front blades. **Features:** Velocity 510 fps. Fully adjustable trigger. Cocking effort 2 lbs. Imported by Beeman.
Price: Right-hand $1,236.00
Price: Left-hand $1,275.00

BEEMAN/FWB P34 MATCH AIR PISTOL
Caliber: 177, single shot. **Barrel:** 10-5/16", with muzzle brake. **Weight:** 2.4 lbs. **Length:** 16.5" overall. **Power:** Precharged pneumatic. **Grips:** Stippled walnut; adjustable match type. **Sights:** Undercut blade front, fully adjustable match rear. **Features:** Velocity to 525 fps; up to 200 shots per CO2 cartridge. Fully adjustable trigger; built-in muzzle brake. Imported from Germany by Beeman.
Price: Right-hand $1,395.00
Price: Left-hand $1,440.00

BEEMAN HW70A AIR PISTOL
Caliber: 177, single shot. **Barrel:** 6-1/4", rifled. **Weight:** 38 oz. **Length:** 12-3/4" overall. **Power:** Spring, barrel cocking. **Grips:** Plastic, with thumbrest. **Sights:** Hooded post front, square notch rear adjustable for windage and elevation. Comes with scope base. **Features:** Adjustable trigger, 31-lb. cocking effort, 440 fps MV; automatic barrel safety. Imported by Beeman.
Price: $190.00

BEEMAN/WEBLEY TEMPEST AIR PISTOL
Caliber: 177, 22, single shot. **Barrel:** 6-7/8". **Weight:** 32 oz. **Length:** 8.9" overall. **Power:** Spring-piston, break barrel. **Grips:** Checkered black plastic with thumbrest. **Sights:** Blade front, adjustable rear. **Features:**

Daisy 662X

Velocity to 500 fps (177), 400 fps (22). Aluminum frame; black epoxy finish; manual safety. Imported from England by Beeman.
Price: $205.00

Beeman/Webley Hurricane Air Pistol
Similar to the Tempest except has extended frame in the rear for a click-adjustable rear sight; hooded front sight; comes with scope mount. Imported from England by Beeman.
Price: $255.00

BENJAMIN SHERIDAN CO2 PELLET PISTOLS
Caliber: 177, 20, 22, single shot. **Barrel:** 6-3/8", rifled brass. **Weight:** 29 oz. **Length:** 9.8" overall. **Power:** 12-gram CO2 cylinder. **Grips:** Walnut. **Sights:** High ramp front, fully adjustable notched rear. **Features:** Velocity to 500 fps. Turnbolt action with cross-bolt safety. Gives about 40 shots per CO2 cylinder. Black or nickel finish. Made in U.S. by Benjamin Sheridan Co.
Price: Black finish, EB17 (177), EB20 (20) $190.00

BENJAMIN SHERIDAN PNEUMATIC PELLET PISTOLS
Caliber: 177, 20, 22, single shot. **Barrel:** 9-3/8", rifled brass. **Weight:** 38 oz. **Length:** 13-1/8" overall. **Power:** Underlever pneumatic, hand pumped. **Grips:** Walnut stocks and pump handle. **Sights:** High ramp front, fully adjustable notch rear. **Features:** Velocity to 525 fps (variable). Bolt action with cross-bolt safety. Choice of black or nickel finish. Made in U.S. by Benjamin Sheridan Co.
Price: Black finish, HB17 (177), HB20 (20) $190.00
Price: HB22 (22) $199.00

BRNO TAU-7 CO2 MATCH AIR PISTOL
Caliber: 177. **Barrel:** 10.24". **Weight:** 37 oz. **Length:** 15.75" overall. **Power:** 12.5-gram CO2 cartridge. **Grips:** Stippled hardwood with adjustable palm rest. **Sights:** Blade front, open fully adjustable rear. **Features:** Comes with extra seals and counterweight. Blue finish. Imported by Great Lakes Airguns.
Price: $299.50

CROSMAN BLACK VENOM AIR PISTOL
Caliber: 177 pellets, BB, 17-shot magazine; darts, single shot. **Barrel:** 4.75" smooth-bore. **Weight:** 16 oz. **Length:** 10.8" overall. **Power:** Spring. **Grips:** NA. **Sights:** Blade front, adjustable rear. **Features:** Velocity to 270 fps (BBs), 250 fps (pellets). Spring-fed magazine; cross-bolt safety. Made in U.S.A. by Crosman Corp.
Price: $60.00

CROSMAN MODEL 1377 AIR PISTOL
Caliber: 177, single shot. **Barrel:** 8", rifled steel. **Weight:** 39 oz. **Length:** 13-5/8". **Power:** Hand pumped. **Grips:** NA. **Sights:** Blade front, rear adjustable for windage and elevation. **Features:** Bolt action, molded plastic grip, hand size pump forearm. Cross-bolt safety. From Crosman.
Price: $60.00

CROSMAN AUTO AIR II PISTOLS
Caliber: BB, 17-shot magazine; 177 pellet, single shot. **Barrel:** 8-5/8" steel, smooth-bore. **Weight:** 13 oz. **Length:** 10-3/4" overall. **Power:** CO2 Powerlet. **Grips:** NA. **Sights:** Blade front, adjustable rear; highlighted system. **Features:** Velocity to 480 fps (BBs), 430 fps (pellets). Semi-automatic action with BBs, single shot with pellets. Black. From Crosman.
Price: AAIIB $38.00
Price: AAIIBRD . . . . **NA**

EAA MP651K

Gamo PT-80

CROSMAN MODEL 1008 REPEAT AIR PISTOL
Caliber: 177, 8-shot pellet clip. **Barrel:** 4.25", rifled steel. **Weight:** 17 oz. **Length:** 8.625" overall. **Power:** CO2 Powerlet. **Grips:** Checkered black plastic. **Sights:** Post front, adjustable rear. **Features:** Velocity about 430 fps. Break-open barrel for easy loading; single or double semi-automatic action; two 8-shot clips included. Optional carrying case available. From Crosman.
Price: **$60.00**
Price: Model 1008SB (silver and black finish), about **$60.00**

CROSMAN SEMI AUTO AIR PISTOL
Caliber: 177, pellets. **Barrel:** Rifled steel. **Weight:** 40 oz. **Length:** 8.63". **Power:** CO2. **Grips:** NA. **Sights:** Blade front, rear adjustable. **Features:** Velocity up to 430 fps. Synthetic grips, zinc alloy frame. From Crosman.
Price: C40 . . . . **NA**

CROSMAN MAGNUM AIR PISTOLS
Caliber: 177, pellets. **Barrel:** Rifled steel. **Weight:** 27 oz. **Length:** 9.38". **Power:** CO2. **Grips:** NA. **Sights:** Blade front, rear adjustable. **Features:** Single/double action accepts sights and scopes with standard 3/8" dovetail mount. Model 3576W features 6" barrel for increased accuracy. From Crosman.
Price: 3574W . . . . **NA**
Price: 3576W . . . . **NA**

DAISY/POWERLINE MODEL 15XT AIR PISTOL
Caliber: 177 BB, 15-shot built-in magazine. **Barrel:** NA. **Weight:** NA. **Length:** 7.21". **Power:** CO2. **Grips:** NA. **Sights:** NA. **Features:** Velocity 425 fps. Made in the U.S.A. by Daisy Mfg. Co.
Price: **$36.95**
New! Price: 15XK Shooting Kit **$59.95**

DAISY/POWERLINE 717 PELLET AIR PISTOL
Caliber: 177, single shot. **Barrel:** 9.61". **Weight:** 2.25 lbs. **Length:** 13-1/2" overall. **Grips:** Molded wood-grain plastic with thumbrest. **Sights:** Blade and ramp front, micro-adjustable notched rear. **Features:** Single pump pneumatic pistol. Rifled steel barrel. Cross-bolt trigger block. Muzzle velocity 385 fps. From Daisy Mfg. Co.
Price: **$71.95**

DAISY/POWERLINE 1270 CO2 AIR PISTOL
Caliber: BB, 60-shot magazine. **Barrel:** Smoothbore steel. **Weight:** 17 oz. **Length:** 11.1" overall. **Power:** CO2 pump action. **Grips:** Molded black polymer. **Sights:** Blade on ramp front, adjustable rear. **Features:** Velocity to 420 fps. Cross-bolt trigger block safety; plated finish. Made in U.S. by Daisy Mfg. Co.
Price: **$39.95**

DAISY/POWERLINE MODEL 93 AIR PISTOL
Caliber: BB, 15-shot magazine. **Barrel:** Smoothbore; steel. **Weight:** 1.1 lbs. **Length:** 7.9" overall. **Power:** CO2 powered semi-auto. **Grips:** Molded brown checkered. **Sights:** Blade on ramp front, fixed open rear. **Features:** Velocity to 400 fps. Manual trigger block. Made in U.S.A. by Daisy Mfg. Co.
Price: **$48.95**

Daisy/Powerline 693 Air Pistol
Similar to Model 93 except has velocity to 235 fps.
Price: **$52.95**

DAISY/POWERLINE 622X PELLET PISTOL
Caliber: 22 (5.5mm), 6-shot. **Barrel:** Rifled steel. **Weight:** 1.3 lbs. **Length:** 8.5". **Power:** CO2. **Grips:** Molded black checkered. **Sights:** Fiber-optic front, fixed open rear. **Features:** Velocity 225 fps. Rotary hammer block. Made by Daisy Mfg. Co.
Price: **$69.95**

DAISY/POWERLINE 45 AIR PISTOL
Caliber: BB, 13-shot magazine. **Barrel:** Rifled steel. **Weight:** 1.25 lbs. **Length:** 8.5" overall. **Power:** CO2 powered semi-auto. **Grips:** Molded black checkered. **Sights:** TruGlo fiber-optic front, fixed open rear. **Features:** Velocity to 224 fps. Manual trigger block. Made in U.S.A. by Daisy Mfg. Co.
Price: **$54.95**

Daisy/Powerline 645 Air Pistol
Similar to Model 93 except has distinctive black and nickel finish.
Price: **$59.95**

EAA/BAIKAL IZH-M46 TARGET AIR PISTOL
Caliber: 177, single shot. **Barrel:** 10". **Weight:** 2.4 lbs. **Length:** 16.8" overall. **Power:** Underlever single-stroke pneumatic. **Grips:** Adjustable wooden target. **Sights:** Micrometer fully adjustable rear, blade front. **Features:** Velocity about 420 fps. Hammer-forged, rifled barrel. Imported from Russia by European American Armory.
Price: **$349.00**

GAMO AUTO 45 AIR PISTOL
Caliber: 177, 12-shot. **Barrel:** 4.25". **Weight:** 1.10 lbs. **Length:** 7.50". **Power:** CO2 cartridge, semi-automatic, 410 fps. **Grips:** Plastic. **Sights:** Rear sights adjusts for windage. **Features:** Glock copy; double-action, manual safety. Imported from Spain by Gamo.
Price: **$99.95**

GAMO COMPACT TARGET PISTOL
Caliber: 177, single shot. **Barrel:** 8.26". **Weight:** 1.95 lbs. **Length:** 12.60". **Power:** Spring-piston, 400 fps. **Grips:** Walnut. **Sights:** Micro-adjustable. **Features:** Rifled steel barrel, adjustable match trigger, recoil and vibration-free. Imported from Spain by Gamo.
Price: **$229.95**

GAMO P-23, P-23 LASER PISTOL
Caliber: 177, 12-shot. **Barrel:** 4.25". **Weight:** 1 lb. **Length:** 7.5". **Power:** CO2 cartridge, semi-automatic, 410 fps. **Grips:** Plastic. **Sights:** NA. **Features:** Walther PPK cartridge pistol copy, optional laser sight. Imported from Spain by Gamo.
Price: . . . . **$89.95**, (with laser) **$129.95**

GAMO PT-80, PT-80 LASER PISTOL
Caliber: 177, 8-shot. **Barrel:** 4.25". **Weight:** 1.2 lbs. **Length:** 7.2". **Power:** CO2 cartridge, semi-automatic, 410 fps. **Grips:** Plastic. **Sights:** 3-dot. **Features:** Optional laser sight and walnut grips available. Imported from Spain by Gamo.
Price: . . . . **$108.95,** (with laser) **$129.95,** (with walnut grip) **$119.95**

"GAT" AIR PISTOL
Caliber: 177, single shot. **Barrel:** 7-1/2" cocked, 9-1/2" extended. **Weight:** 22 oz. **Length:** NA. **Power:** Spring-piston. **Grips:** Cast checkered metal. **Sights:** Fixed. **Features:** Shoots pellets, corks or darts. Matte black finish. Imported from England by Stone Enterprises, Inc.
Price: **$24.95**

AIRGUNS — Handguns

HAMMERLI AP40 AIR PISTOL
Caliber: 177. **Barrel:** 10". **Length:** NA. **Power:** NA. **Grips:** Adjustable orthopedic. **Sights:** Fully adjustable micrometer. **Features:** Sleek, light, well balanced and accurate. Imported from Switzerland by Nygord Precision Products.
Price: **$1,195.00**

MARKSMAN 2000 REPEATER AIR PISTOL
Caliber: 177, 18-shot BB repeater. **Barrel:** 2-1/2", smoothbore. **Weight:** 24 oz. **Length:** 8-1/4" overall. **Power:** Spring. **Grips:** NA. **Sights:** NA. **Features:** Velocity to 200 fps. Thumb safety. Uses BBs, darts, bolts or pellets. Repeats with BBs only. From Marksman Products.
Price: **$27.00**

MARKSMAN 2005 LASERHAWK™ SPECIAL EDITION AIR PISTOL
Caliber: 177, 24-shot magazine. **Barrel:** 3.8", smoothbore. **Weight:** 22 oz. **Length:** 10.3" overall. **Power:** Spring-air. **Grips:** Checkered. **Sights:** Fixed fiber-optic front sight. **Features:** Velocity to 300 fps with Hyper-Velocity pellets. Square trigger guard with skeletonized trigger; extended barrel. Shoots BBs, pellets, darts or bolts. Made in the U.S. From Marksman Products.
Price: **$32.00**

MORINI 162E MATCH AIR PISTOLS
Caliber: 177, single shot. **Barrel:** 9.4". **Weight:** 32 oz. **Length:** 16.1" overall. **Power:** Scuba air. **Grips:** Adjustable match type. **Sights:** Interchangeable blade front, fully adjustable match-type rear. **Features:** Power mechanism shuts down when pressure drops to a preset level. Adjustable electronic trigger. Imported from Switzerland by Nygord Precision Products.
Price: **$825.00**
Price: 162 EI **$1,075.00**

MORINI SAM K-11 AIR PISTOL
Caliber: 177. **Barrel:** 10". **Weight:** 38 oz. **Length:** NA. **Grips:** Fully adjustable. **Sights:** Fully adjustable. **Features:** Improved trigger, more angle adjustment on grip. Sophisticated counter balance system. Deluxe aluminum case, two cylinders and manometer. Imported from Switzerland by Nygord Precision Products.
Price: **$975.00**

PARDINI K58 MATCH AIR PISTOLS
Caliber: 177, single shot. **Barrel:** 9". **Weight:** 37.7 oz. **Length:** 15.5" overall. **Power:** Precharged compressed air; single-stroke cocking. **Grips:** Adjustable match type; stippled walnut. **Sights:** Interchangeable post front, fully adjustable match rear. **Features:** Fully adjustable trigger. Short version K-2 available. Imported from Italy by Nygord Precision Products.
Price: **$795.00**
Price: K2S model, precharged air pistol, introduced in 1998 . . . . . . **$945.00**

RWS 9B/9N AIR PISTOLS
Caliber: 177, single shot. **Barrel:** NA. **Weight:** NA. **Length:** NA. **Power:** NA. **Grips:** Plastic with thumbrest. **Sights:** Adjustable. **Features:** Spring-piston powered; 550 fps. Black or nickel finish. Imported from Spain by Dynamit Nobel-RWS.
Price: 9B **$169.00**
Price: 9N **$185.00**

STEYR LP 5CP MATCH AIR PISTOL
Caliber: 177, 5-shot magazine. **Weight:** 40.7 oz. **Length:** 15.2" overall. **Power:** Precharged air cylinder. **Grips:** Adjustable match type. **Sights:** Interchangeable blade front, adjustable matched rear. **Features:** Adjustable sight radius; adjustable trigger. Barrel compensator. One-shot magazine available. Imported from Austria by Nygord Precision Products.
Price: **$1,100.00**

STEYR LP10P MATCH AIR PISTOL
Caliber: 177, single shot. **Barrel:** 9". **Weight:** 38.7 oz. **Length:** 15.3" overall. **Power:** Scuba air. **Grips:** Adjustable Morini match, palm shelf, stippled walnut. **Sights:** Interchangeable blade in 4mm, 4.5mm or 5mm widths, adjustable open rear, interchangeable 3.5mm or 4mm leaves. **Features:** Velocity about 500 fps. Adjustable trigger, adjustable sight radius from 12.4" to 13.2". With compensator. Recoil elimination. Imported from Austria by Nygord Precision Products.
Price: **$1,175.00**

TECH FORCE SS2 OLYMPIC COMPETITION AIR PISTOL
Caliber: 177 pellet, single shot. **Barrel:** 7.4". **Weight:** 2.8 lbs. **Length:** 16.5" overall. **Power:** Spring piston, sidelever. **Grips:** Hardwood. **Sights:** Extended adjustable rear, blade front accepts inserts. **Features:** Velocity 520 fps. Recoilless design; adjustments allow duplication of a firearm's feel. Match-grade, adjustable trigger; includes carrying case. Imported from China by Compasseco, Inc.
Price: **$295.00**

TECH FORCE 35 AIR PISTOL
Caliber: 177 pellet, single shot. **Weight:** 2.86 lbs. **Length:** 14.9" overall. **Power:** Spring-piston, underlever. **Grips:** Hardwood. **Sights:** Micrometer adjustable rear, blade front. **Features:** Velocity 400 fps. Grooved for scope mount; trigger safety. Imported from China by Compasseco, Inc.
Price: **$39.95**

Tech Force 8 Air Pistol
Similar to Tech Force 35 but with break-barrel action, ambidextrous polymer grips.
Price: **$59.95**

Tech Force S2-1 Air Pistol
Similar to Tech Force 8 except basic grips and sights for plinking.
Price: **$29.95**

WALTHER LP300 MATCH PISTOL
Caliber: 177. **Barrel:** 236mm. **Weight:** 1.018g. **Length:** NA. **Power:** NA. **Grips:** NA. **Sights:** Integrated front with three different widths, adjustable rear. **Features:** Adjustable grip and trigger. Imported from Germany by Nygord Precision Products.
Price: **$1,095.00**

CONSULT
SHOOTER'S
MARKETPLACE
Page 74, This Issue

Crosman 2289G

AIRFORCE CONDOR RIFLE
Caliber: 177, 22. **Barrel:** 24" rifled. **Weight:** 6.5 lbs. **Length:** 38.75" overall. **Power:** NA. **Grips:** NA. **Sights:** None, integral mount supplied. **Features:** 600-1,300 fps. 3,000 psi fill pressure. Automatic safety. Air tank volume: 490cc.
Price: 22 w/refill clamp and open sights **$649.95**
Price: 177 w/refill clamp and open sights **$599.95**
Price: Gun only (22 or 177) **$549.95**

AIRFORCE TALON AIR RIFLE
Caliber: 177, 22, single-shot. **Barrel:** 18". **Weight:** 5.5 lbs. **Length:** 32.6". **Power:** Precharged pneumatic. **Stock:** NA. **Sights:** Intended for scope use, fiber-optic open sights optional. **Features:** Lothar Walther match barrel, adjustable power levels from 400-1000 FPS, operates on high pressure air from scuba tank or hand pump. Accessories attach to multiple dovetailed mounting rails. Manufactured in the U.S.A. by AirForce Airguns.
Price: **$439.95**

AIRFORCE TALON SS AIR RIFLE
Caliber: 177, 22, single-shot. **Barrel:** 12". **Weight:** 5.25 lbs. **Length:** 32.75". **Power:** Precharged pneumatic. **Stock:** NA. **Sights:** Intended for scope use, fiber-optic open sights optional. **Features:** Lothar Walther match barrel, adjustable power levels from 400-1000 FPS. Chamber in front of barrel strips away air turbulence, protects muzzle and reduces firing report. Operates on high pressure air from scuba tank or hand pump. Accessories attach to multiple dovetailed mounting rails. Manufactured in the U.S.A. by AirForce Airguns.
Price: **$439.95**

AIRROW MODEL A-8SRB STEALTH AIR RIFLE
Caliber: 177, 22, 25, 9-shot. **Barrel:** 20"; rifled. **Weight:** 6 lbs. **Length:** 34" overall. **Power:** CO2 or compressed air; variable power. **Stock:** Telescoping CAR-15-type. **Sights:** Variable 3.5-10x scope. **Features:** Velocity 1100 fps in all calibers. Pneumatic air trigger. All aircraft aluminum and stainless steel construction. Mil-spec materials and finishes. From Swivel Machine Works, Inc.
Price: About **$2,299.00**

AIRROW MODEL A-8S1P STEALTH AIR RIFLE
Caliber: #2512 16" arrow. **Barrel:** 16". **Weight:** 4.4 lbs. **Length:** 30.1" overall. **Power:** CO2 or compressed air; variable power. **Stock:** Telescoping CAR-15-type. **Sights:** Scope rings only. 7 oz. rechargeable cylinder and valve. **Features:** Velocity to 650 fps with 260-grain arrow. Pneumatic air trigger. Broadhead guard. All aircraft aluminum and stainless steel construction. Mil-spec materials and finishes. A-8S Models perform to 2,000 PSIG above or below water levels. Waterproof case. From Swivel Machine Works, Inc.
Price: **$1,699.00**

ANSCHUTZ 2002 MATCH AIR RIFLES
Caliber: 177, single shot. **Barrel:** 25.2". **Weight:** 10.4 lbs. **Length:** 44.5" overall. **Stock:** European walnut, blonde hardwood or colored laminated hardwood; stippled grip and forend. Also available with flat-forend walnut stock for benchrest shooting and aluminum. **Sights:** Optional sight set #6834. **Features:** Muzzle velocity 575 fps. Balance, weight match the 1907 ISU smallbore rifle. Uses #5021 match trigger. Recoil and vibration free. Fully adjustable cheekpiece and buttplate; accessory rail under forend. Available in pneumatic and compressed air versions. Imported from Germany by Gunsmithing, Inc., Accuracy International, Champion's Choice.
Price: Right-hand, blonde hardwood stock, with sights **$1,275.00**
Price: Right-hand, walnut stock **$1,275.00**
Price: Right-hand, color laminate stock **$1,300.00**
Price: Right-hand, aluminum stock, butt plate **$1,495.00**
Price: Left-hand, color laminate stock **$1,595.00**
Price: Model 2002D-RT Running Target, right-hand, no sights . . **$1,248.90**
Price: #6834 Sight Set **$227.10**

ARS HUNTING MASTER AR6 AIR RIFLE
Caliber: 22, 6-shot repeater. **Barrel:** 25-1/2". **Weight:** 7 lbs. **Length:** 41-1/4" overall. **Power:** Precompressed air from 3000 psi diving tank. **Stock:** Indonesian walnut with checkered grip; rubber buttpad. **Sights:** Blade front, adjustable peep rear. **Features:** Velocity over 1000 fps with 32-grain pellet. Receiver grooved for scope mounting. Has 6-shot rotary magazine. Imported by Air Rifle Specialists.
Price: **$580.00**

ARS/CAREER 707 AIR RIFLE
Caliber: 22, 6-shot repeater. **Barrel:** 23". **Weight:** 7.75 lbs. **Length:** 40.5" overall. **Power:** Precompressed air; variable power. **Stock:** Indonesian walnut with checkered grip, gloss finish. **Sights:** Hooded post front with interchangeable inserts, fully adjustable diopter rear. **Features:** Velocity to 1000 fps. Lever-action with straight-feed magazine; pressure gauge in lower front air reservoir; scope mounting rail included. Imported from the Philippines by Air Rifle Specialists.
Price: **$580.00**

BEEMAN CROW MAGNUM AIR RIFLE
Caliber: 20, 22, 25, single shot. **Barrel:** 16"; 10-groove rifling. **Weight:** 8.5 lbs. **Length:** 46" overall. **Power:** Gas-spring; adjustable power to 32 foot pounds muzzle energy. Barrel-cocking. **Stock:** Classic-style hardwood; hand checkered. **Sights:** For scope use only; built-in base and 1" rings included. **Features:** Adjustable two-stage trigger. Automatic safety. Available in 22 caliber on special order. Imported by Beeman.
Price: **$1,290.00**

BEEMAN KODIAK AIR RIFLE
Caliber: 25, single shot. **Barrel:** 17.6". **Weight:** 9 lbs. **Length:** 45.6" overall. **Power:** Spring-piston, barrel cocking. **Stock:** Stained hardwood. **Sights:** Blade front, open fully adjustable rear. **Features:** Velocity to 820 fps. Up to 30 foot pounds muzzle energy. Imported by Beeman.
Price: **$670.00**

BEEMAN MAKO MKII AIR RIFLE
Caliber: 177, 22 single shot. **Barrel:** 20", with compensator. **Weight:** 5.5 to 7.8 lbs. **Length:** 39" overall. **Power:** Precharged pneumatic. **Stock:** Stained beech; Monte Carlo cheekpiece; checkered grip. **Sights:** None furnished. **Features:** Velocity to 930 fps. Gives over 50 shots per charge. Manual safety; brass trigger blade; vented rubber buttpad. Requires scuba tank for air. Imported from England by Beeman.
Price: **$999.00**

BEEMAN R1 AIR RIFLE
Caliber: 177, 20 or 22, single shot. **Barrel:** 19.6", 12-groove rifling. **Weight:** 8.5 lbs. **Length:** 45.2" overall. **Power:** Spring-piston, barrel cocking. **Stock:** Walnut-stained beech; cut-checkered pistol grip; Monte Carlo comb and cheekpiece; rubber buttpad. **Sights:** Tunnel front with interchangeable inserts, open rear click-adjustable for windage and elevation. Grooved for scope mounting. **Features:** Velocity 940-1000 fps (177), 860 fps (20), 800 fps (22). Non-drying nylon piston and breech seals. Adjustable metal trigger. Milled steel safety. Right- or left-hand stock. Adjustable cheekpiece and buttplate at extra cost. Custom and Super Laser versions available. Imported by Beeman.
Price: Right-hand **$605.00**
Price: Left-hand **$680.00**

BEEMAN R7 AIR RIFLE
Caliber: 177, 20, single shot. **Barrel:** 17". **Weight:** 6.1 lbs. **Length:** 40.2" overall. **Power:** Spring-piston. **Stock:** Stained beech. **Sights:** Hooded front, fully adjustable micrometer click open rear. **Features:** Velocity to 700 fps (177), 620 fps (20). Receiver grooved for scope mounting; double-jointed cocking lever; fully adjustable trigger; checkered grip. Imported by Beeman.
Price: **$330.00**

BEEMAN R9 AIR RIFLE
Caliber: 177, 20, single shot. **Barrel:** NA. **Weight:** 7.3 lbs. **Length:** 43" overall. **Power:** Spring-piston, barrel cocking. **Stock:** Stained hardwood. **Sights:** Tunnel post front, fully adjustable open rear. **Features:** Velocity to 1000 fps (177), 800 fps (20). Adjustable Rekord trigger; automatic safety; receiver dovetailed for scope mounting. Imported from Germany by Beeman Precision Airguns.
Price: **$360.00**

AIRGUNS — Long Guns

Beeman R9 Deluxe Air Rifle
Same as R9 except has extended forend stock, checkered pistol grip, grip cap, carved Monte Carlo cheekpiece. Globe front sight with inserts. Imported by Beeman.
Price: $440.00

BEEMAN R11 MKII AIR RIFLE
Caliber: 177, single shot. **Barrel:** 19.6". **Weight:** 8.6 lbs. **Length:** 43.5" overall. **Power:** Spring-piston, barrel cocking. **Stock:** Walnut-stained beech; adjustable buttplate and cheekpiece. **Sights:** None furnished. Has dovetail for scope mounting. **Features:** Velocity 910-940 fps. All-steel barrel sleeve. Imported by Beeman.
Price: $620.00

BEEMAN SUPER 12 AIR RIFLE
Caliber: 22, 25, 12-shot magazine. **Barrel:** 19", 12-groove rifling. **Weight:** 7.8 lbs. **Length:** 41.7" overall. **Power:** Precharged pneumatic; external air reservoir. **Stock:** European walnut. **Sights:** None furnished; drilled and tapped for scope mounting; scope mount included. **Features:** Velocity to 850 fps (25-caliber). Adjustable power setting gives 30-70 shots per 400 cc air bottle. Requires scuba tank for air. Imported by Beeman.
Price: $1,940.00

BEEMAN RX-2 GAS-SPRING MAGNUM AIR RIFLE
Caliber: 177, 20, 22, 25, single shot. **Barrel:** 19.6", 12-groove rifling. **Weight:** 8.8 lbs. **Power:** Gas-spring piston air; single stroke barrel cocking. **Stock:** Walnut-finished hardwood, hand checkered, with cheekpiece. Adjustable cheekpiece and buttplate. **Sights:** Tunnel front, click-adjustable rear. **Features:** Velocity adjustable to about 1200 fps. Imported by Beeman.
Price: 177, 20, 22 or 25 regular, right-hand. $670.00

BEEMAN R1 CARBINE
Caliber: 177, 20, 22, 25, single shot. **Barrel:** 16.1". **Weight:** 8.6 lbs. **Length:** 41.7" overall. **Power:** Spring-piston, barrel cocking. **Stock:** Stained beech; Monte Carlo comb and checkpiece; cut checkered pistol grip; rubber buttpad. **Sights:** Tunnel front with interchangeable inserts, open adjustable rear; receiver grooved for scope mounting. **Features:** Velocity up to 1000 fps (177). Non-drying nylon piston and breech seals. Adjustable metal trigger. Machined steel receiver end cap and safety. Right- or left-hand stock. Imported by Beeman.
Price: 177, 20, 22, 25, right-hand . . . . **$605.00**; left-hand **$680.00**

BEEMAN/FEINWERKBAU 603 AIR RIFLE
Caliber: 177, single shot. **Barrel:** 16.6". **Weight:** 10.8 lbs. **Length:** 43" overall. **Power:** Single stroke pneumatic. **Stock:** Special laminated hardwoods and hard rubber for stability. Multi-colored stock also available. **Sights:** Tunnel front with interchangeable inserts, click micrometer match aperture rear. **Features:** Velocity to 570 fps. Recoilless action; double supported barrel; special, short rifled area frees pellet from barrel faster. Fully adjustable match trigger with separately adjustable trigger and trigger slack weight. Trigger and sights blocked when loading latch is open. Imported by Beeman.
Price: Right-hand. $1,625.00
Price: Left-hand $1,775.00
Price: Junior $1,500.00

BEEMAN/FEINWERKBAU 300-S AND 300 JUNIOR MINI-MATCH RIFLE
Caliber: 177, single shot. **Barrel:** 17-1/8". **Weight:** 8.8 lbs. **Length:** 40" overall. **Power:** Spring-piston, single stroke sidelever cocking. **Stock:** Walnut. Stippled grip, adjustable buttplate. Scaled down model for youthful or slightly built shooters. **Sights:** Globe front with interchangeable inserts, micro. adjustable rear. Sights move as a single unit. **Features:** Recoilless, vibration free. Grooved for scope mounts. Steel piston ring. Cocking effort about 9-1/2 lbs. Barrel sleeve optional. Imported by Beeman.
Price: Right-hand . . . . **$1,680.00**; left-hand **$1,825.00**

BEEMAN/FEINWERKBAU P70 AND P70 JUNIOR AIR RIFLE
Caliber: 177, single shot. **Barrel:** 16.6". **Weight:** 10.6 lbs. **Length:** 42.6" overall. **Power:** Precharged pneumatic. **Stock:** Laminated hardwoods and hard rubber for stability. Multi-colored stock also available. **Sights:** Tunnel front with interchangeable inserts, click micrometer match aperture rear. **Features:** Velocity to 570 fps. Recoilless action; double supported barrel; special short rifled area frees pellet from barrel faster. Fully adjustable match trigger with separately adjustable trigger and

trigger slack weight. Trigger and sights blocked when loading latch is open. Imported by Beeman.
Price: P70, precharged, right-hand $1,600.00
Price: P70, precharged, left-hand $1,690.00
Price: P70, precharged, Junior $1,600.00
Price: P70, precharged, right-hand, multi $1,465.00

BEEMAN/HW 97 AIR RIFLE
Caliber: 177, 20, single shot. **Barrel:** 17.75". **Weight:** 9.2 lbs. **Length:** 44.1" overall. **Power:** Spring-piston, underlever cocking. **Stock:** Walnut-stained beech; rubber buttpad. **Sights:** None. Receiver grooved for scope mounting. **Features:** Velocity 830 fps (177). Fixed barrel with fully opening, direct loading breech. Adjustable trigger. Imported by Beeman Precision Airguns.
Price: Right-hand only $605.00

BENJAMIN SHERIDAN PNEUMATIC (PUMP-UP) AIR RIFLE
Caliber: 177 or 22, single shot. **Barrel:** 19-3/8", rifled brass. **Weight:** 5-1/2 lbs. **Length:** 36-1/4" overall. **Power:** Underlever pneumatic, hand pumped. **Stock:** American walnut stock and forend. **Sights:** High ramp front, fully adjustable notched rear. **Features:** Variable velocity to 800 fps. Bolt action with ambidextrous push-pull safety. Black or nickel finish. Made in the U.S. by Benjamin Sheridan Co.
Price: Black finish, Model 397 (177), Model 392 (22) $224.00
Price: Nickel finish, Model S397 (177), Model S392 (22) $245.00

BRNO TAU-200 AIR RIFLES
Caliber: 177, single shot. **Barrel:** 19", rifled. **Weight:** 7-1/2 lbs. **Length:** 42" overall. **Power:** 6-oz. CO2 cartridge. **Stock:** Wood match style with adjustable comb and buttplate. **Sights:** Globe front with interchangeable inserts, fully adjustable open rear. **Features:** Adjustable trigger. Comes with extra seals, large CO2 bottle, counterweight. Imported by Great Lakes Airguns. Available in Standard Universal, Deluxe Universal, International and Target Sporter versions.
Price: Standard Universal (ambidex. stock with buttstock extender, adj. cheekpiece) $349.50
Price: Deluxe Universal (as above but with micro-adj. aperture sight) $449.50
Price: International (like Deluxe Universal but with right- or left-hand stock) $454.50
Price: Target Sporter (like Std. Universal but with 4x scope, no sights) $412.50

BSA MAGNUM GOLDSTAR MAGNUM AIR RIFLE
Caliber: 177, 22, 10-shot repeater. **Barrel:** 17-1/2". **Weight:** 8 lbs., 8 oz. **Length:** 42.5" overall. **Power:** Spring-air, underlever cocking. **Stock:** Oil-finished hardwood; Monte Carlo with cheekpiece, checkered grip; recoil pad. **Sights:** Ramp front, micrometer adjustable rear; comes with Maxi-Grip scope rail. **Features:** Velocity 950 fps (177), 750 fps (22). Patented 10-shot indexing magazine; Maxi-Grip scope rail protects optics from recoil; automatic anti-beartrap plus manual safety; muzzle brake standard. Imported from U.K. by Precision Sales International, Inc.
Price: $499.95

BSA MAGNUM SUPERTEN AIR RIFLE
Caliber: 177, 22 10-shot repeater. **Barrel:** 17-1/2". **Weight:** 7 lbs., 8 oz. **Length:** 37" overall. **Power:** Precharged pneumatic via buddy bottle. **Stock:** Oil-finished hardwood; Monte Carlo with cheekpiece, cut checkered grip; adjustable recoil pad. **Sights:** No sights; intended for scope use. **Features:** Velocity 1000+ fps (177), 1000+ fps (22). Patented 10-shot indexing magazine, bolt-action loading. Left-hand version also available. Imported from U.K. by Precision Sales International, Inc.
Price: $599.95

BSA MAGNUM SUPERSTAR™ MK2 MAGNUM AIR RIFLE, CARBINE
Caliber: 177, 22, 25, single shot. **Barrel:** 18-1/2". **Weight:** 8 lbs., 8 oz. **Length:** 43" overall. **Power:** Spring-air, underlever cocking. **Stock:** Oil-finished hardwood; Monte Carlo with cheekpiece, checkered at grip; recoil pad. **Sights:** Ramp front, micrometer adjustable rear. Maxi-Grip scope rail. **Features:** Velocity 950 fps (177), 750 fps (22), 600 fps (25). Patented rotating breech design. Maxi-Grip scope rail protects optics from recoil; automatic anti-beartrap plus manual safety. Imported from U.K. by Precision Sales International, Inc.
Price: Rifle, MKII Carbine (14" barrel, 39-1/2" overall) $349.95

AIRGUNS — Long Guns

Daisy 7840 Buckmaster

BSA MAGNUM SUPERSPORT™ AIR RIFLE, CARBINE
Caliber: 177, 22, 25, single shot. **Barrel:** 18-1/2". **Weight:** 6 lbs., 8 oz. **Length:** 41" overall. **Power:** Spring-air, barrel cocking. **Stock:** Oil-finished hardwood; Monte Carlo with cheekpiece, recoil pad. **Sights:** Ramp front, micrometer adjustable rear. Maxi-Grip scope rail. **Features:** Velocity 950 fps (177), 750 fps (22), 600 fps (25). Patented Maxi-Grip scope rail protects optics from recoil; automatic anti-beartrap plus manual tang safety. Muzzle brake standard. Imported for U.K. by Precision Sales International, Inc.
Price: **$194.95**
Price: Carbine, 14" barrel, muzzle brake **$214.95**

BSA METEOR MK6 AIR RIFLE
Caliber: 177, 22, single shot. **Barrel:** 18-1/2". **Weight:** 6 lbs. **Length:** 41" overall. **Power:** Spring-air, barrel cocking. **Stock:** Oil-finished hardwood. **Sights:** Ramp front, micrometer adjustable rear. **Features:** Velocity 650 fps (177), 500 fps (22). Automatic anti-beartrap; manual tang safety. Receiver grooved for scope mounting. Imported from U.K. by Precision Sales International, Inc.
Price: Rifle **$144.95**
Price: Carbine **$164.95**

CROSMAN MODEL 66 POWERMASTER AIR RIFLES
Caliber: 177 (single shot pellet) or BB, 200-shot reservoir. **Barrel:** 20", rifled steel. **Weight:** 3 lbs. **Length:** 38-1/2" overall. **Power:** Pneumatic; hand-pumped. **Stock:** Wood-grained ABS plastic; checkered pistol grip and forend. **Sights:** Fiber-optic front, fully adjustable open rear. **Features:** Velocity about 645 fps. Bolt action, cross-bolt safety. From Crosman.
Price: Model 66BX **$60.00**
Price: Model 664X (as above, with 4x scope) **$70.00**
Price: Model 664SB (as above with silver and black finish), about .. **$75.00**

CROSMAN REMINGTON GENESIS AIR RIFLE
Caliber: 177 **Barrel:** Break-action. **Sights:** Fiber-optic front, adj. rear. Dovetailed for scope. **Weight:** 6.5 lbs. **Length:** 43" overall. **Stock:** Synthetic, thumbhole pistol grip. From Crosman.
Price: **$249.99**
Price: W 3-9x40 scope **$279.99**

CROSMAN MODEL 760 PUMPMASTER AIR RIFLES
Caliber: 177 pellets (single shot) or BB (200-shot reservoir). **Barrel:** 19-1/2", rifled steel. **Weight:** 2 lbs., 12 oz. **Length:** 33.5" overall. **Power:** Pneumatic, hand-pump. **Stock:** Walnut-finished ABS plastic stock and forend. **Features:** Velocity to 590 fps (BBs, 10 pumps). Short stroke, power determined by number of strokes. Fiber-optic front sight and adjustable rear sight. Cross-bolt safety. From Crosman.
Price: Model 760B **$40.00**
Price: Model 764SB (silver and black finish), about **$55.00**
Price: Model 760SK .... **NA**
Price: Model 760BRO .... **NA**

CROSMAN MODEL 1077 REPEAT AIR RIFLES
Caliber: 177 pellets, 12-shot clip. **Barrel:** 20.3", rifled steel. **Weight:** 3 lbs., 11 oz. **Length:** 38.8" overall. **Power:** CO2 Powerlet. **Stock:** Textured synthetic or hardwood. **Sights:** Blade front, fully adjustable rear. **Features:** Velocity 590 fps. Removable 12-shot clip. True semi-automatic action. From Crosman.
Price: **$75.00**
Price: 1077W (walnut stock) **$110.00**

CROSMAN 2260 AIR RIFLE
Caliber: 22, single shot. **Barrel:** 24". **Weight:** 4 lbs., 12 oz. **Length:** 39.75" overall. **Power:** CO2 Powerlet. **Stock:** Hardwood. **Sights:** Blade front, adjustable rear open or peep. **Features:** About 600 fps. Made in U.S. by Crosman Corp.
Price: .... **NA**

CROSMAN MODEL 2100 CLASSIC AIR RIFLE
Caliber: 177 pellets (single shot), or BB (200-shot BB reservoir). **Barrel:** 21", rifled. **Weight:** 4 lbs., 13 oz. **Length:** 39-3/4" overall. **Power:** Pump-up, pneumatic. **Stock:** Wood-grained checkered ABS plastic. **Features:** Three pumps give about 450 fps, 10 pumps about 755 fps (BBs). Cross-bolt safety; concealed reservoir holds over 200 BBs. From Crosman.
Price: Model 2100B **$75.00**

CROSMAN MODEL 2200 MAGNUM AIR RIFLE
Caliber: 22, single shot. **Barrel:** 19", rifled steel. **Weight:** 4 lbs., 12 oz. **Length:** 39" overall. **Stock:** Full-size, wood-grained ABS plastic with checkered grip and forend or American walnut. **Sights:** Ramp front, open step-adjustable rear. **Features:** Variable pump power; three pumps give 395 fps, six pumps 530 fps, 10 pumps 595 fps (average). Full-size adult air rifle. Has white line spacers at pistol grip and buttplate. From Crosman.
Price: **$75.00**

DAISY 1938 RED RYDER 60th ANNIVERSARY CLASSIC AIR RIFLE
Caliber: BB, 650-shot repeating action. **Barrel:** Smoothbore steel with shroud. **Weight:** 2.2 lbs. **Length:** 35.4" overall. **Stock:** Walnut stock burned with Red Ryder lariat signature. **Sights:** Post front, adjustable V-slot rear. **Features:** Walnut forend. Saddle ring with leather thong. Lever cocking. Gravity feed. Controlled velocity. From Daisy Mfg. Co.
Price: **$39.95**

DAISY MODEL 840 GRIZZLY AIR RIFLE
Caliber: 177 pellet single shot; or BB 350-shot. **Barrel:** 19", smoothbore, steel. **Weight:** 2.25 lbs. **Length:** 36.8" overall. **Power:** Single pump pneumatic. **Stock:** Molded wood-grain stock and forend. **Sights:** Ramp front, open, adjustable rear. **Features:** Muzzle velocity 320 fps (BB), 300 fps (pellet). Steel buttplate; straight pull bolt action; cross-bolt safety. Forend forms pump lever. From Daisy Mfg. Co.
Price: **$32.95**
Price: 840C Mossy Oak® Break Up™ camo **$49.95**

DAISY MODEL 7840 BUCKMASTER AIR RIFLE
Caliber: 177 pellets, or BB. **Barrel:** Smoothbore steel. **Weight:** 2.25 lbs. **Length:** 36.8" overall. **Power:** Single-pump pneumatic. **Stock:** Molded with checkering and wood-grain. **Sights:** Ramp and blade front, adjustable open rear plus Electronic Point Sight. **Features:** Velocity to 320 fps (BB), 300 fps (pellet). Cross-bolt trigger block safety. From Daisy Mfg. Co.
Price: **$54.95**

DAISY MODEL 105 BUCK AIR RIFLE
Caliber: 177 or BB. **Barrel:** Smoothbore steel. **Weight:** 1.6 lbs. **Length:** 29.8" overall. **Power:** Lever cocking, spring air. **Stock:** Stained solid wood. **Sights:** TruGlo fiber-optic, open fixed rear. **Features:** Velocity to 275. Cross-bolt trigger block safety. From Daisy Mfg. Co.
Price: .... **NA**

Daisy Model 95 Timberwolf Air Rifle
Similar to the 105 Buck except velocity to 325 fps. Weighs 2.4 lbs., overall length 35.2".
Price: **$38.95**

DAISY/POWERLINE 1000 AIR RIFLE
Caliber: 177, single shot. **Barrel:** NA. **Weight:** 6.15 lbs. **Length:** 43" overall. **Power:** Spring-air, barrel cocking. **Stock:** Stained hardwood. **Sights:** Hooded blade front on ramp, adjustable micrometer rear. **Features:** Velocity to 1000 fps. Blued finish; trigger block safety. From Daisy Mfg. Co.
Price: **$208.95**

DAISY/POWERLINE 1170 PELLET RIFLES
Caliber: 177, single shot. **Barrel:** Rifled steel. **Weight:** 5.5 lbs. **Length:** 42.5" overall. **Power:** Spring-air, barrel cocking. **Stock:** Hardwood. **Sights:** Hooded post front, micrometer adjustable open rear. **Features:** Velocity to 800 fps. Monte Carlo comb. From Daisy Mfg. Co.
Price: **$129.95**
Price: Model 131 (velocity to 600 fps) **$117.95**
Price: Model 1150 (black copolymer stock, velocity to 600 fps) **$77.95**

Gamo Sporter

DAISY/POWERLINE 856 PUMP-UP AIR RIFLES
Caliber: 177 pellets (single shot) or BB (100-shot reservoir). **Barrel:** Rifled steel with shroud. **Weight:** 2.7 lbs. **Length:** 37.4" overall. **Power:** Pneumatic pump-up. **Stock:** Molded wood-grain with Monte Carlo cheekpiece. **Sights:** Ramp and blade front, open rear adjustable for elevation. **Features:** Velocity from 315 fps (two pumps) to 650 fps (10 pumps). Shoots BBs or pellets. Heavy die-cast metal receiver. Cross-bolt triggerblock safety. From Daisy Mfg. Co.
Price: $39.95
Price: 856C $59.95

DAISY/POWERLINE 853 AIR RIFLE
Caliber: 177 pellets, single shot. **Barrel:** 20.9"; 12-groove rifling, high-grade solid steel by Lothar Waltherô, precision crowned; bore sized for precision matched pellets. **Weight:** 5.08 lbs. **Length:** 38.9" overall. **Power:** Single-pump pneumatic. **Stock:** Full-length select American hardwood, stained and finished; black buttplate with white spacers. **Sights:** Globe front with four aperture inserts; precision micrometer adjustable rear peep sight mounted on a standard 3/8" dovetailed receiver mount.
Price: $225.00

DAISY/POWERLINE EAGLE 7856 PUMP-UP AIR RIFLE
Caliber: 177 (pellets), BB, 100-shot BB magazine. **Barrel:** Rifled steel with shroud. **Weight:** 3.3 lbs. **Length:** 37.4" overall. **Power:** Pneumatic pump-up. **Stock:** Molded wood-grain plastic. **Sights:** Ramp and blade front, adjustable open rear. **Features:** Velocity from 315 fps (two pumps) to 650 fps (10 pumps). Finger grooved forend. Cross-bolt triggerblock safety. From Daisy Mfg. Co.
Price: With 4x scope, about $49.95

DAISY/POWERLINE 880 AIR RIFLE
Caliber: 177 pellet or BB, 50-shot BB magazine, single shot for pellets. **Barrel:** Rifled steel. **Weight:** 3.7 lbs. **Length:** 37.6" overall. **Power:** Multi-pump pneumatic. **Stock:** Molded wood grain; Monte Carlo comb. **Sights:** Hooded front, adjustable rear. **Features:** Velocity to 685 fps. (BB). Variable power (velocity, range) increase with pump strokes; resin receiver with dovetailed scope mount. Made in U.S.A. by Daisy Mfg. Co.
Price: $50.95

DAISY/YOUTHLINE MODEL 105 AIR RIFLE
Caliber: BB, 400-shot magazine. **Barrel:** 13-1/2". **Weight:** 1.6 lbs. **Length:** 29.8" overall. **Power:** Spring. **Stock:** Molded wood-grain. **Sights:** Blade on ramp front, fixed rear. **Features:** Velocity to 275 fps. Blue finish. Cross-bolt trigger block safety. Made in U.S. by Daisy Mfg. Co.
Price: $28.95

DAISY/YOUTHLINE MODEL 95 AIR RIFLE
Caliber: BB, 700-shot magazine. **Barrel:** 18". **Weight:** 2.4 lbs. **Length:** 35.2" overall. **Power:** Spring. **Stock:** Stained hardwood. **Sights:** Blade on ramp front, open adjustable rear. **Features:** Velocity to 325 fps. Cross-bolt trigger block safety. Made in U.S. by Daisy Mfg. Co.
Price: $38.95

EAA/BAIKAL MP-512 AIR RIFLES
Caliber: 177, single shot. **Barrel:** 17.7". **Weight:** 6.2 lbs. **Length:** 41.3" overall. **Power:** Spring-piston, single stroke. **Stock:** Black synthetic. **Sights:** Adjustable rear, hooded front. **Features:** Velocity 490 fps. Hammer-forged, rifled barrel; automatic safety; scope mount rail. Imported from Russia by European American Armory.
Price: 177 caliber. $49.00
Price: 512M (590 fps) $65.00

EAA/BAIKAL IZH-61 AIR RIFLE
Caliber: 177 pellet, 5-shot magazine. **Barrel:** 17.8". **Weight:** 6.4 lbs. **Length:** 31" overall. **Power:** Spring-piston, side-cocking lever. **Stock:** Black plastic. **Sights:** Adjustable rear, fully hooded front. **Features:** Velocity 490 fps. Futuristic design with adjustable stock. Imported from Russia by European American Armory.
Price: $99.00

EAA/BAIKAL IZHMP-532 AIR RIFLE
Caliber: 177 pellet, single shot. **Barrel:** 15.8". **Weight:** 9.3 lbs. **Length:** 46.1" overall. **Power:** Single-stroke pneumatic. **Stock:** One- or two-piece competition-style stock with adjustable buttpad, pistol grip. **Sights:** Fully adjustable rear, hooded front. **Features:** Velocity 460 fps. Five-way adjustable trigger. Imported from Russia by European American Armory.
Price: $599.00

GAMO DELTA AIR RIFLE
Caliber: 177. **Barrel:** 15.7". **Weight:** 4.2 lbs. **Length:** 37.8". **Power:** Single-stroke pneumatic, 525 fps. **Stock:** Synthetic. **Sights:** TruGlo fiber-optic.
Price: $89.95

GAMO YOUNG HUNTER AIR RIFLE
Caliber: 177. **Barrel:** 17.7". **Weight:** 5.5 lbs. **Length:** 41". **Power:** Single-stroke pneumatic, 640 fps. **Stock:** Wood. **Sights:** TruGlo fiber-optic adjustable. **Features:** Rifled steel barrel, hooded front sight, grooved receiver for scope. Imported from Spain by Gamo.
Price: $129.95
Price: Combo packed with BSA 4x32 scope and rings $169.95

GAMO SPORTER AIR RIFLE
Caliber: 177. **Barrel:** NA. **Weight:** 5.5 lbs. **Length:** 42.5". **Power:** Single-stroke pneumatic, 760 fps. **Stock:** Wood. **Sights:** Adjustable TruGlo fiber-optic. **Features:** Intended to bridge the gap between Gamo's Young Hunter model and the adult-sized Hunter 440. Imported from Spain by Gamo.
Price: $159.95

GAMO HUNTER 440 AIR RIFLES
Caliber: 177, 22. **Barrel:** NA. **Weight:** 6.6 lbs. **Length:** 43.3". **Power:** Single-stroke pneumatifc, 1,000 fps (177), 750 fps (22). **Stock:** Wood. **Sights:** Adjustable TruGlo fiber-optic. **Features:** Adjustable two-stage trigger, rifled barrel, raised scope ramp on receiver. Realtree camo model available.
Price: $229.95
Price: Hunter 440 Combo with BSA 4x32mm scope $259.95

HAMMERLI AR 50 AIR RIFLE
Caliber: 177. **Barrel:** 19.8". **Weight:** 10 lbs. **Length:** 43.2" overall. **Power:** Compressed-air. **Stock:** Anatomically-shaped universal and right-hand; match style; multi-colored laminated wood. **Sights:** Interchangeable element tunnel front, adjustable Hammerli peep rear. **Features:** Vibration-free firing release; adjustable match trigger and trigger stop; stainless air tank, built-in pressure gauge. Gives 270 shots per filling. Imported from Switzerland by SIGARMS, Inc.
Price: $1,653.00

HAMMERLI MODEL 450 MATCH AIR RIFLE
Caliber: 177, single shot. **Barrel:** 19.5". **Weight:** 9.8 lbs. **Length:** 43.3" overall. **Power:** Pneumatic. **Stock:** Match style with stippled grip, rubber buttpad. Beech or walnut. **Sights:** Match tunnel front, Hammerli diopter rear. **Features:** Velocity about 560 fps. Removable sights; forend sling rail; adjustable trigger; adjustable comb. Imported from Switzerland by SIGARMS, Inc.
Price: Beech stock $1,355.00
Price: Walnut stock $1,395.00

MARKSMAN BB BUDDY AIR RIFLE
Caliber: 177, 20-shot magazine. **Barrel:** 10.5" smoothbore. **Weight:** 1.6 lbs. **Length:** 33" overall. **Power:** Spring-air. **Stock:** Molded composition. **Sights:** Blade on ramp front, adjustable V-slot rear. **Features:** Velocity 275 fps. Positive feed; automatic safety. Youth-sized lightweight design. Made in U.S. From Marksman Products.
Price: $27.95

AIRGUNS — Long Guns

MARKSMAN 2015 LASERHAWK™ BB REPEATER AIR RIFLE
Caliber: 177 BB, 20-shot magazine. **Barrel:** 10.5" smoothbore. **Weight:** 1.6 lbs. **Length:** Adjustable to 33", 34" or 35" overall. **Power:** Spring-air. **Stock:** Molded composition. **Sights:** Fixed fiber-optic front sight, adjustable elevation V-slot rear. **Features:** Velocity about 275 fps. Positive feed; automatic safety. Adjustable stock. Made in the U.S. From Marksman Products.
Price: **$33.00**

RWS/DIANA MODEL 24 AIR RIFLES
Caliber: 177, 22, single shot. **Barrel:** 17", rifled. **Weight:** 6 lbs. **Length:** 42" overall. **Power:** Spring-air, barrel cocking. **Stock:** Beech. **Sights:** Hooded front, adjustable rear. **Features:** Velocity of 700 fps (177). Easy cocking effort; blue finish. Imported from Germany by Dynamit Nobel-RWS, Inc.
Price: 24, 24C **$215.00**

RWS/Diana Model 34 Air Rifles
Similar to the Model 24 except has 19" barrel, weighs 7.5 lbs. Gives velocity of 1000 fps (177), 800 fps (22). Adjustable trigger, synthetic seals. Comes with scope rail.
Price: 177 or 22 .... **$290.00**
Price: Model 34N (nickel-plated metal, black epoxy-coated wood stock) **$350.00**
Price: Model 34BC (matte black metal, black stock, 4x32 scope, mounts) **$510.00**

RWS/DIANA MODEL 36 AIR RIFLES
Caliber: 177, 22, single shot. **Barrel:** 19", rifled. **Weight:** 8 lbs. **Length:** 45" overall. **Power:** Spring-air, barrel cocking. **Stock:** Beech. **Sights:** Hooded front (interchangeable inserts available), adjustable rear. **Features:** Velocity of 1000 fps (177-cal.). Comes with scope mount; two-stage adjustable trigger. Imported from Germany by Dynamit Nobel-RWS, Inc.
Price: 36, 36C **$435.00**

RWS/DIANA MODEL 52 AIR RIFLES
Caliber: 177, 22, 25, single shot. **Barrel:** 17", rifled. **Weight:** 8-1/2 lbs. **Length:** 43" overall. **Power:** Spring-air, sidelever cocking. **Stock:** Beech, with Monte Carlo, cheekpiece, checkered grip and forend. **Sights:** Ramp front, adjustable rear. **Features:** Velocity of 1100 fps (177). Blue finish. Solid rubber buttpad. Imported from Germany by Dynamit Nobel-RWS, Inc.
Price: 177, 22 .... **$565.00**
Price: 25 .... **$605.00**
Price: Model 52 Deluxe (177) **$810.00**
Price: Model 48B (as above except matte black metal, black stock) **$535.00**
Price: Model 48 (same as Model 52 except no Monte Carlo cheekpiece or checkering) **$520.00**

RWS/DIANA MODEL 45 AIR RIFLE
Caliber: 177, single shot. **Weight:** 8 lbs. **Length:** 45" overall. **Power:** Spring-air, barrel cocking. **Stock:** Walnut-finished hardwood with rubber recoil pad. **Sights:** Globe front with interchangeable inserts, micro. click open rear with four-way blade. **Features:** Velocity of 820 fps. Dovetailed base for either micrometer peep sight or scope mounting. Automatic safety. Imported from Germany by Dynamit Nobel-RWS, Inc.
Price: **$350.00**

RWS/DIANA MODEL 46 AIR RIFLES
Caliber: 177, 22, single shot. **Barrel:** 18". **Weight:** 8.2 lbs. **Length:** 45" overall. **Stock:** Hardwood; Monte Carlo. **Sights:** Blade front, adjustable rear. **Features:** Underlever cocking spring-air (950 fps in 177, 780 fps in 22); extended scope rail, automatic safety, rubber buttpad, adjustable trigger. Imported from Germany by Dynamit Nobel-RWS, Inc.
Price: **$470.00**
Price: Model 46E (as above except matte black metal, black stock) **$430.00**

RWS/DIANA MODEL 54 AIR RIFLE
Caliber: 177, 22, single shot. **Barrel:** 17". **Weight:** 9 lbs. **Length:** 43" overall. **Power:** Spring-air, sidelever cocking. **Stock:** Walnut with Monte Carlo cheekpiece, checkered grip and forend. **Sights:** Ramp front, fully adjustable rear. **Features:** Velocity to 1000 fps (177), 900 fps (22). Totally recoilless system; floating action absorbs recoil. Imported from Germany by Dynamit Nobel-RWS, Inc.
Price: **$785.00**

RWS/DIANA MODEL 92/93/94 AIR RIFLES
Caliber: 177, 22, single shot. **Barrel:** NA. **Weight:** NA. **Length:** NA. **Stock:** Beechwood; Monte Carlo. **Sights:** Hooded front, fully adjustable rear. **Features:** Break-barrel, spring-air; receiver grooved for scope; adjustable trigger; lifetime warranty. Imported from Spain by Dynamit Nobel-RWS, Inc.
Price: Model 92 (auto safety, 700 fps in 177) .... **NA**
Price: Model 93 (manual safety, 850 fps in 177) .... **NA**
Price: Model 94 (auto safety, 1,000 fps in 177) .... **NA**

RWS/DIANA MODEL 350 MAGNUM AIR RIFLE
Caliber: 177, 22, single shot. **Barrel:** 19-1/2". **Weight:** 8 lbs. **Length:** 48". **Stock:** Beechwood; Monte Carlo. **Sights:** Hooded front, fully adjustable rear. **Features:** Break-barrel, spring-air; 1,250 fps. Imported from Germany by Dynamit Nobel-RWS, Inc.
Price: .... **NA**

TECH FORCE BS4 OLYMPIC COMPETITION AIR RIFLE
Caliber: 177 pellet, single shot. **Barrel:** NA. **Weight:** 10.8 lbs. **Length:** 43.3" overall. **Power:** Spring piston, sidelever action. **Stock:** Wood with semi-pistol grip, adjustable buttplate. **Sights:** Micro-adjustable competition rear, hooded front. **Features:** Velocity 640 fps. Recoilless action; adjustable trigger. Includes carrying case. Imported from China by Compasseco, Inc.
Price: **$595.00**
Price: Optional diopter rear sight **$79.95**

TECH FORCE 6 AIR RIFLE
Caliber: 177 pellet, single shot. **Barrel:** 14". **Weight:** 6 lbs. **Length:** 35.5" overall. **Power:** Spring-piston, sidelever action. **Stock:** Paratrooper-style folding, full pistol grip. **Sights:** Adjustable rear, hooded front. **Features:** Velocity 800 fps. All-metal construction; grooved for scope mounting. Imported from China by Compasseco, Inc.
Price: **$69.95**

Tech Force 51 Air Rifle
Similar to Tech Force 6, but with break-barrel cocking mechanism and folding stock fitted with recoil pad. Overall length, 36". Weighs 6 lbs. From Compasseco, Inc.
Price: **$69.95**

TECH FORCE 25 AIR RIFLE
Caliber: 177, 22 pellet; single shot. **Barrel:** NA. **Weight:** 7.5 lbs. **Length:** 46.2" overall. **Power:** Spring piston, break-action barrel. **Stock:** Oil-finished wood; Monte Carlo stock with recoil pad. **Sights:** Adjustable rear, hooded front with insert. **Features:** Velocity 1,000 fps (177); grooved receiver and scope stop for scope mounting; adjustable trigger; trigger safety. Imported from China by Compasseco, Inc.
Price: 177 or 22 caliber **$125.00**
Price: Includes rifle and Tech Force 96 red dot point sight **$164.95**

TECH FORCE 36 AIR RIFLE
Caliber: 177 pellet, single shot. **Barrel:** NA. **Weight:** 7.4 lbs. **Length:** 43" overall. **Power:** Spring piston, underlever cocking. **Stock:** Monte Carlo hardwood stock; recoil pad. **Sights:** Adjustable rear, hooded front. **Features:** Velocity 900 fps; grooved receiver and scope stop for scope mounting; auto-reset safety. Imported from China by Compasseco, Inc.
Price: **$89.95**

WHISCOMBE JW SERIES AIR RIFLES
Caliber: 177, 20, 22, 25, single shot. **Barrel:** 15", Lothar Walther. Polygonal rifling. **Weight:** 9 lbs., 8 oz. **Length:** 39" overall. **Power:** Dual spring-piston, multi-stroke; underlever cocking. **Stock:** Walnut with adjustable buttplate and cheekpiece. **Sights:** None furnished; grooved scope rail. **Features:** Velocity 660-1000 (JW80) fps (22-caliber, fixed barrel) depending upon model. Interchangeable barrels; automatic safety; muzzle weight; semi-floating action; twin opposed pistons with counter-wound springs; adjustable trigger. All models include Harmonic Optimization Tunable System. Imported from England by Pelaire Products.
Price: JW50, MKII fixed barrel only **$2,085.00**
Price: JW65, MKII **$2,085.00**
Price: JW80, MKII **$2,195.00**

COMPENDIUM OF STATE LAWS GOVERNING FIREARMS

The following chart lists the main provisions of state firearms laws as of the date of publication. In addition to the state provisions, the purchase, sale, and, in certain circumstances, the possession and interstate transportation of firearms are regulated by the Federal Gun Control Act of 1968 as amended by the Firearms Owners' Protection Act of 1986. Also, cities and localities may have their own gun ordinances in addition to federal and state restrictions. Details may be obtained by contacting local law enforcement authorities or by consulting your state's firearms law digest compiled by the NRA Institute for Legislative Action.

STATE	GUN BAN	EXEMPTIONS TO NICS[2]	STATE WAITING PERIOD - NUMBER OF DAYS		LICENSE OR PERMIT TO PURCHASE or other prerequesite		REGISTRATION		RECORD OF SALE REPORTED TO STATE OR LOCAL GOVT.
			HANDGUNS	LONG GUNS	HANDGUNS	LONG GUNS	HANDGUNS	LONG GUNS	
Alabama	—	—	—	—	—	—	—	—	—
Alaska	—	RTC	—	—	—	—	—	—	—
Arizona	—	RTC	—	—	—	—	—	—	—
Arkansas	—	RTC[3]	—	—	—	—	—	—	—
California	X[20]	—	10[14]	10[14,15]	8, 23	—	X	24	X
Colorado	—	—	—	—	—	—	—	—	—
Connecticut	X[20]	—	14[14,15]	14[14,15]	X[16,23]	—	—	24	X
Delaware	—	—	—	—	—	—	—	—	—
Florida	—	GRTC	3[14,15]	—	—	—	—	—	—
Georgia	—	RTC	—	—	—	—	—	—	—
Hawaii	X[20]	L, RTC	—	—	X[16,23]	X[16]	X[12]	X[12]	X
Idaho	—	RTC	—	—	—	—	—	—	—
Illinois	20	—	3	2	X[16]	X[16]	4	4	X
Indiana	—	RTC, O[3]	—	—	—	—	—	—	X
Iowa	—	L, RTC	—	—	X[16]	—	—	—	—
Kansas	—	—	1	—	1	—	1	—	1
Kentucky	—	RTC[3]	—	—	—	—	—	—	—
Louisiana	—	GRTC	—	—	—	—	—	—	—
Maine	—	—	—	—	—	—	—	—	—
Maryland	X[20]	O[3]	7[14]	7[9,14]	8, 23	—	—	—	X
Massachusetts	X[20]	GRTC	—	—	X[16]	X[16]	—	—	X
Michigan	—	O[3]	—	—	X[16,23]	—	X	—	X
Minnesota	—	—	7[16]	16	X[16]	X[16]	—	—	—
Mississippi	—	RTC[3]	—	—	—	—	—	—	—
Missouri	—	—	—	—	X[16]	—	—	—	X
Montana	—	RTC	—	—	—	—	—	—	—
Nebraska	—	L	—	—	X	—	—	—	—
Nevada	—	RTC	1	—	—	—	1	—	—
New Hampshire	—	—	—	—	—	—	—	—	—
New Jersey	X[20]	—	—	—	X[16]	X[16]	—	24	X
New Mexico	—	—	—	—	—	—	—	—	—
New York	X[20]	L, RTC	—	—	X[16,23]	16	X	7	X
North Carolina	—	L, RTC	—	—	X[16]	—	—	—	X
North Dakota	—	RTC	—	—	—	—	—	—	—
Ohio	20	—	1	—	16	—	1	—	1
Oklahoma	—	—	—	—	—	—	—	—	—
Oregon	—	GRTC	—	—	—	—	—	—	X
Pennsylvania	—	—	—	—	—	—	—	—	X
Rhode Island	—	—	7	7	23	—	—	—	X
South Carolina	—	RTC	8	—	8	—	—	—	X
South Dakota	—	GRTC	2	—	—	—	—	—	X
Tennessee	—	—	—	—	—	—	—	—	—
Texas	—	RTC[3]	—	—	—	—	—	—	—
Utah	—	RTC	—	—	—	—	—	—	—
Vermont	—	—	—	—	—	—	—	—	—
Virginia	X[20]	—	1,8	—	1,8	—	—	—	1
Washington	—	O[3]	5[10]	—	—	—	—	—	X
West Virginia	—	—	—	—	—	—	—	—	—
Wisconsin	—	—	2	—	—	—	—	—	—
Wyoming	—	RTC	—	—	—	—	—	—	—
District of Columbia	X[20]	L	—	—	X[16]	X[16]	X[16]	X	X

COMPENDIUM OF STATE LAWS GOVERNING FIREARMS

Since state laws are subject to frequent change, this chart is
not to be considered legal advice or a restatement of the law.

All fifty states have sportsmen's protections laws to halt harrassment.

STATE	STATE PROVISION FOR RIGHT-TO-CARRY CONCEALED	CARRYING OPENLY PROHIBITED	OWNER ID CARDS OR LICENSING	FIREARM RIGHTS CONSTITU- TIONAL PROVISION	STATE FIREARMS PREEMPTION LAWS	RANGE PROTECTION LAW
Alabama	R	X_{11}	—	X	X	X
Alaska	R_{19}	—	—	X	—	X
Arizona	R	—	—	X	X	X
Arkansas	R	X_5	—	X	X	X
California	L	X_6	—	—	X	X
Colorado	R	25	—	X	X_{25}	X
Connecticut	R	X	—	X	X_{17}	X
Delaware	L	—	—	X	X	—
Florida	R	X	—	X	X	X
Georgia	R	X	—	X	X	X
Hawaii	L	X	X	X	—	—
Idaho	R	—	—	X	X	X
Illinois	D	X	X	X	—	X
Indiana	R	X	—	X	X_{18}	X
Iowa	L	X	—	—	X	X
Kansas	D	1	—	X	—	X
Kentucky	R	—	—	X	X	X
Louisiana	R	—	—	X	X	X
Maine	R	—	—	X	X	X
Maryland	L	X	—	—	X	X
Massachusetts	L	X	X	X	X_{17}	X
Michigan	R	X_{11}	—	X	X	X
Minnesota	R	X	—	—	X	—
Mississippi	R	—	—	X	X	X
Missouri	R	—	—	X	X	X
Montana	R	—	—	X	X	X
Nebraska	D	—	—	X	—	—
Nevada	R	—	—	X	X	X
New Hampshire	R	—	—	X	X	X
New Jersey	L	X	X	—	X_{17}	X
New Mexico	R	—	—	X	X	X
New York	L	X	X	—	X_{22}	X
North Carolina	R	—	—	X	X	X
North Dakota	R	X_6	—	X	X	X
Ohio	D	1	16	X	—	X
Oklahoma	R	X_6	—	X	X	X
Oregon	R	—	—	X	X	X
Pennsylvania	R	X_{11}	—	X	X	X
Rhode Island	L	X	—	X	X	X
South Carolina	R	X	—	X	X	X
South Dakota	R	—	—	X	X	X
Tennessee	R	X_5	—	X	X	X
Texas	R	X	—	X	X	X
Utah	R	X_6	—	X	X	X
Vermont	R_{19}	X_5	—	X	X	X
Virginia	R	—	—	X	X	X
Washington	R	X_{21}	—	X	X	—
West Virginia	R	—	—	X	X	X
Wisconsin	D	—	—	X	X	X
Wyoming	R	—	—	X	X	X
District of Columbia	D	X	X	NA	—	—

COMPENDIUM OF STATE LAWS GOVERNING FIREARMS

> With over 20,000 "gun control" laws on the books in America, there are two challenges facing every gun owner. First, you owe it to yourself to become familiar with the federal laws on gun ownership. Only by knowing the laws can you avoid innocently breaking one.
>
> Second, while federal legislation receives much more media attention, state legislatures and city councils make many more decisions regarding your right to own and carry firearms. NRA members and all gun owners must take extra care to be aware of anti-gun laws and ordinances at the state and local levels.

Notes:

1. In certain cities or counties.

2. **National Instant Check System (NICS) exemption codes:**
   RTC-Carry Permit Holders Exempt From NICS
   GRTC-Holders of RTC Permits issued before November 30, 1998 exempt from NICS. Holders of more recent permits are not exempt.
   L-Holders of state licenses to possess or purchase or firearms ID cards exempt from NICS.
   O-Other, See Note 3.

3. **NICS exemption notes: Arkansas**: RTC permits issued prior to 11/30/98 and those issued on and after 4/1/99 qualify. Those issued between 11/1/98 and 3/31/99 do not qualify. **Indiana**: Personal protection, hunting and target permits all qualify for exemptions. **Kentucky**: RTC permits issued after July 15, 1998 and prior to November 30, 1998 are exempt. **Maryland**: There are no exemptions for handgun purchases. For long gun purchases, those holding RTC permits issued before November 30, 1998 are exempt. **Michigan**: No exemptions for handguns, license for long guns. **Mississippi**: Permits issued to security guards do not qualify. **Texas**: Texas Peace Officer License, TCLEOSE Card, is valid only if issued prior to November 30, 1998. **Washington**: RTC permits issued after July 1, 1996 and prior to November 30, 1998 are exempt.

4. Chicago only. No handgun not already registered may be possessed.

5. **Arkansas** prohibits carrying a firearm "with a purpose to employ it as a weapon against a person." **Tennessee** prohibits carrying "with the intent to go armed." **Vermont** prohibits carrying a firearm "with the intent or purpose of injuring another."

6. Loaded.

7. New York City only.

8. A permit is required to acquire another handgun before 30 days have elapsed following the acquisition of a handgun.

9. **Maryland** subjects purchases of "assault weapons" to a 7-day waiting period.

10. May be extended by police to 30 days in some circumstances. An individual not holding a driver's license must wait 90 days.

11. Carrying a handgun openly in a motor vehicle requires a license.

12. Every person arriving in **Hawaii** is required to register any firearm(s) brought into the State within 3 days of arrival of the person or firearm(s), whichever occurs later. Handguns purchased from licensed dealers must be registered within 5 days.

13. Concealed carry laws vary significantly between the states. Ratings reflect the real effect a state's particular laws have on the ability of citizens to carry firearms for self-defense.

14. Purchases from dealers only. **Maryland**: 7 business days. Purchasers of regulated firearms must undergo background checks performed by the State Police, either through a dealer or directly through the State Police.

15. The waiting period does not apply to a person holding a valid permit or license to carry a firearm. In **Connecticut**, a hunting license also exempts the holder for long gun purchasers. **California**: transfers of a long gun to a person's parent, child or grandparent are exempt from the waiting period.

16. **Connecticut:** A certificate of eligibility or a carry permit is required to obtain a handgun and a carry permit is required to transport a handgun outside your home. **District of Columbia:** No handgun may be possessed unless it was registered prior to Sept. 23, 1976 and re-registered by Feb. 5, 1977. A permit to purchase is required for a rifle or shotgun. **Hawaii:** Purchase permits, required for all firearms, may not be issued until 14 days after application. A handgun purchase permit is valid for 10 days, for one handgun; a long gun permit is valid for one year, for multiple long guns. **Illinois:** A Firearm Owner's Identification Card (FOI) is required to possess or purchase a firearm, must be issued to qualified applicants within 30 days, and is valid for 5 years. **Iowa:** A purchase permit is required for handguns, and is valid for one year, beginning three days after issuance. **Massachusetts:** Firearms and feeding devices for firearms are divided into classes. Depending on the class, a firearm identification card (FID) or class A license or class B license is required to possess, purchase, or carry a firearm, ammunition thereof, or firearm feeding device, or "large capacity feeding device." **Michigan:** A handgun purchaser must obtain a license to purchase from local law enforcement, and within 10 days present the license and handgun to obtain a certificate of inspection. **Minnesota:** A handgun transfer or carrying permit, or a 7-day waiting period and handgun transfer report, is required to purchase handguns or "assault weapons" from a dealer. A permit or transfer report must be issued to qualified applicants within 7 days. A permit is valid for one year, a transfer report for

30 days. **Missouri:** A purchase permit is required for a handgun, must be issued to qualified applicants within 7 days, and is valid for 30 days. **New Jersey:** Firearm owners must possess a FID, which must be issued to qualified applicants within 30 days. To purchase a handgun, a purchase permit, which must be issued within 30 days to qualified applicants and is valid for 90 days, is required. An FID is required to purchase long guns. **New York:** Purchase, possession and/or carrying of a handgun require a single license, which includes any restrictions made upon the bearer. New York City also requires a license for long guns. **North Carolina:** To purchase a handgun, a license or permit is required, which must be issued to qualified applicants within 30 days. **Ohio:** Some cities require a permit-to-purchase or firearm owner ID card.

17. Preemption through judicial ruling. Local regulation may be instituted in **Massachusetts** if ratified by the legislature.

18. Except Gary and East Chicago and local laws enacted before January, 1994.

19. **Vermont and Alaska** law respect your right to carry without a permit. Alaska also has a permit to carry system to establish reciprocity with other states.

20. "Assault weapons" are prohibited in **California, Connecticut, New Jersey** and **New York**. Some local jurisdictions in **Ohio** also ban "assault weapons." **Hawaii** prohibits "assault pistols." **California** bans "unsafe handguns." **Illinois:** Chicago, Evanston, Oak Park, Morton Grove, Winnetka, Wilmette, and Highland Park prohibit handguns; some cities prohibit other kinds of firearms. **Maryland** prohibits "assault pistols" and the sale or manufacture of any handgun manufactured after Jan. 1, 1985, that appears on the Handgun Roster. **Massachusetts:** It is unlawful to sell, transfer or possess "any assault weapon or large capacity feeding device" [more than 10 rounds] that was not legally possessed on September 13, 1994. **Ohio:** some cities prohibit handguns of certain magazine capacities." **Virginia** prohibits "Street Sweeper" shotguns. The **District of Columbia** prohibits new acquisition of handguns and any semi-automatic firearm capable of using a detachable ammunition magazine of more than 12 rounds capacity. (With respect to some of these laws and ordinances, individuals may retain prohibited firearms owned previously, with certain restrictions.)

21. Local jurisdictions may opt out of prohibition.

22. Preemption only applies to handguns.

23. Requires proof of safety training for purchase. **California**: Must have Handgun Safety Certificate receipt which is valid for five years. **Connecticut:** To receive certificate of eligibility, must complete a handgun safety course approved by the Commissioner of Public Safety. **Hawaii:** Must have completed an approved handgun safety course. **Maryland:** Must complete an approved handgun safety course. **Michigan:** A person must correctly answer 70% of the questions on a basic safety review questionnaire in order to obtain a license to purchase. **New York:** Some counties require a handgun safety training course to receive a license. **Rhode Island:** Must receive a state-issued handgun safety card.

24. "Assault weapon" registration. **California** had two dates by which assault weapons had to be registered or possession after such date would be considered a felony: March 31, 1992 for the named make and model firearms banned in the 1989 legislation and December 31, 2000 for the firearms meeting the definition of the "assault weapons in the 1999 legislation. In **Connecticut**, those firearms banned by specific make and model in the 1993 law had to be registered by October 1, 1994 or possession would be considered a felony. A recent law requires registration of additional guns by October 1, 2003. In **New Jersey**, any "assault weapon" not registered, licensed, or rendered inoperable pursuant to a state police certificate by May 1, 1991, is considered contraband.

25. Local governments cannot enact ordinances that prohibit the sale, purchase, or possession of a firearm. Municipalities cannot restrict a person's ability to travel into, through, or within their jurisdiction for hunting or personal protection. Local governments, including law enforcement agencies, cannot maintain a database of guns or gun owners. Municipalities may prohibit open carry in government buildings if such prohibition is clearly posted.

Concealed carry codes:

R: Right-to-Carry "Shall issue" or less restrictive discretionary permit system (Ala., Conn.) (See also note #21.)

L: Right-to-Carry Limited by local authority's discretion over permit issuance.

D: Right-to-Carry Denied, no permit system exists; concealed carry is prohibited.

MANUFACTURER'S DIRECTORY

A

A Zone Bullets, 2039 Walter Rd., Billings, MT 59105 / 800-252-3111; FAX: 406-248-1961

A&W Repair, 2930 Schneider Dr., Arnold, MO 63010 / 617-287-3725

A.A. Arms, Inc., 4811 Persimmont Ct., Monroe, NC 28110 / 704-289-5356; or 800-935-1119; FAX: 704-289-5859

A.B.S. III, 9238 St. Morritz Dr., Fern Creek, KY 40291

A.G. Russell Knives, Inc., 1920 North 26th Street, Lowell, AR 72745-8489 / 800-255-9034; FAX: 479-636-8493 ag@agrussell.com agrussell.com

A.R.M.S., Inc., 230 W. Center St., West Bridgewater, MA 02379-1620 / 508-584-7816; FAX: 508-588-8045

A.W. Peterson Gun Shop, Inc., 4255 W. Old U.S. 441, Mt. Dora, FL 32757-3299 / 352-383-4258; FAX: 352-735-1001

A.W. Peterson Gun Shop, Inc., The, 4255 West Old U.S. 441, Mount Dora, FL 32757-3299 / 352-383-4258

AC Dyna-tite Corp., 155 Kelly St., P.O. Box 0984, Elk Grove Village, IL 60007 / 847-593-5566; FAX: 847-593-1304

Acadian Ballistic Specialties, P.O. Box 787, Folsom, LA 70437 / 504-796-0078 gunsmith@neasoft.com

Accuracy Den, The, 25 Bitterbrush Rd., Reno, NV 89523 / 702-345-0225

Accuracy International, Foster, P.O. Box 111, Wilsall, MT 59086 / 406-587-7922; FAX: 406-585-9434

Accuracy Internationl Precision Rifles (See U.S.)

Accuracy Int'l. North America, Inc., P.O. Box 5267, Oak Ridge, TN 37831 / 423-482-0330; FAX: 423-482-0336

Accuracy Unlimited, 7479 S. DePew St., Littleton, CO 80123

Accuracy Unlimited, 16036 N. 49 Ave., Glendale, AZ 85306 / 602-978-9089; FAX: 602-978-9089 fglenn@cox.net www.glenncustom.com

Accura-Site (See All's, The Jim Tembelis Co., Inc.)

Accurate Arms Co., Inc., 5891 Hwy. 230 West, McEwen, TN 37101 / 931-729-4207; FAX: 931-729-4211 burrensburg@aac-ca.com www.accuratepowder.com

Accu-Tek, 4510 Carter Ct., Chino, CA 91710

Ackerman & Co., Box 133 U.S. Highway Rt. 7, Pownal, VT 05261 / 802-823-9874 muskets@togsther.net

Ackerman, Bill (See Optical Services Co.)

Acra-Bond Laminates, 134 Zimmerman Rd., Kalispell, MT 59901 / 406-257-9003; FAX: 406-257-9003 merlins@digisys.net www.acrabondlaminates.com

Action Bullets & Alloy Inc., RR 1, P.O. Box 189, Quinter, KS 67752 / 785-754-3609; FAX: 785-754-3629 bullets@ruraltel.net

Action Direct, Inc., P.O. Box 770400, Miami, FL 33177 / 305-969-0056; FAX: 305-256-3541 www.action-direct.com

Action Products, Inc., 22 N. Mulberry St., Hagerstown, MD 21740 / 301-797-1414; FAX: 301-733-2073

Action Target, Inc., P.O. Box 636, Provo, UT 84603 / 801-377-8033; FAX: 801-377-8096 www.actiontarget.com

Actions by "T" Teddy Jacobson, 16315 Redwood Forest Ct., Sugar Land, TX 77478 / 281-277-4008; FAX: 281-277-9112 tjacobson@houston.rr.com www.actionsbyt.us

AcuSport Corporation, 1 Hunter Place, Bellefontaine, OH 43311-3001 / 513-593-7010; FAX: 513-592-5625

Ad Hominem, 3130 Gun Club Lane, RR #3, Orillia, ON L3V 6H3 CANADA / 705-689-5303; FAX: 705-689-5303

Adair Custom Shop, Bill, 2886 Westridge, Carrollton, TX 75006

ADCO Sales, Inc., 4 Draper St. #A, Woburn, MA 01801 / 781-935-1799; FAX: 781-935-1011

Adkins, Luther, 1292 E. McKay Rd., Shelbyville, IN 46176-8706 / 317-392-3795

Advance Car Mover Co., Rowell Div., P.O. Box 1, 240 N. Depot St., Juneau, WI 53039 / 414-386-4464; FAX: 414-386-4416

Advantage Arms, Inc., 25163 W. Ave. Stanford, Valencia, CA 91355 / 661-257-2290

Adventure 16, Inc., 4620 Alvarado Canyon Rd., San Diego, CA 92120 / 619-283-6314

Aero Peltor, 90 Mechanic St., Southbridge, MA 01550 / 508-764-5500; FAX: 508-764-0188

African Import Co., 22 Goodwin Rd., Plymouth, MA 02360 / 508-746-8552; FAX: 508-746-0404 africanimport@aol.com

AFSCO Ammunition, 731 W. Third St., P.O. Box L, Owen, WI 54460 / 715-229-2516 sailers@webtv.net

Ahlman Guns, 9525 W. 230th St., Morristown, MN 55052 / 507-685-4243; FAX: 507-685-4280 www.ahlmans.com

Ahrends Grips, Box 203, Clarion, IA 50525 / 515-532-3449; FAX: 515-532-3926 ahrends@goldfieldaccess.net

Ahrends, Kim, Box 203, Clarion, IA 50525 / 515-532-3449; FAX: 515-532-3926

Aimtech Mount Systems, P.O. Box 223, Thomasville, GA 31799 / 229-226-4313; FAX: 229-227-0222 mail@aimtech-mounts.com www.aimtech-mounts.com

Air Arms, Hailsham Industrial Park, Diplocks Way, Hailsham, E. Sussex, BN27 3JF ENGLAND / 011-0323-845853; FAX: 1323 440573 general.air-arms.co.uk. www.air-arms.co.uk.

Air Rifle Specialists, P.O. Box 138, 130 Holden Rd., Pine City, NY 14871-0138 / 607-734-7340; FAX: 607-733-3261 ars@stny.rr.com www.air-rifles.com

Air Venture Airguns, 9752 E. Flower St., Bellflower, CA 90706 / 562-867-6355

AirForce Airguns, P.O. Box 2478, Fort Worth, TX 76113 / 817-451-8966; FAX: 817-451-1613 www.airforceairguns.com

Airrow, 11 Monitor Hill Rd., Newtown, CT 06470 / 203-270-6343

Aitor-Cuchilleria Del Norte S.A., Izelaieta, 17, 48260, Ermua, SPAIN / 43-17-08-50 info@aitor.com www.ailor.com

Ajax Custom Grips, Inc., 9130 Viscount Row, Dallas, TX 75247 / 214-630-8893; FAX: 214-630-4942

Aker International, Inc., 2248 Main St., Suite 6, Chula Vista, CA 91911 / 619-423-5182; FAX: 619-423-1363 aker@akerleather.com www.akerleather.com

AKJ Concealco, P.O. Box 871596, Vancouver, WA 98687-1596 / 360-891-8222; FAX: 360-891-8221 Concealco@aol.com www.greatholsters.com

Alana Cupp Custom Engraver, P.O. Box 207, Annabella, UT 84711 / 801-896-4834

Alaska Bullet Works, Inc., 9978 Crazy Horse Drive, Juneau, AK 99801 / 907-789-3834; FAX: 907-789-3433

Alaskan Silversmith, The, 2145 Wagner Hollow Rd., Fort Plain, NY 13339 / 518-993-3983 sidbell@capital.net www.sidbell.cizland.com

Aldis Gunsmithing & Shooting Supply, 502 S. Montezuma St., Prescott, AZ 86303 / 602-445-6723; FAX: 602-445-6763

Alessi Holsters, Inc., 2465 Niagara Falls Blvd., Amherst, NY 14228-3527 / 716-691-5615

Alex, Inc., 3420 Cameron Bridge Rd., Manhattan, MT 59741-8523 / 406-282-7396; FAX: 406-282-7396

Alfano, Sam, 36180 Henry Gaines Rd., Pearl River, LA 70452 / 504-863-3364; FAX: 504-863-7715

All American Lead Shot Corp., P.O. Box 224566, Dallas, TX 75062

All Rite Products, Inc., 9554 Wells Circle, Suite D, West Jordan, UT 84088-6226 / 800-771-8471; FAX: 801-280-8302 info@allriteproducts.com www.allriteproducts.com

Allard, Gary/Creek Side Metal & Woodcrafters, Fishers Hill, VA 22626 / 540-465-3903

Allen Co., Inc., 525 Burbank St., Broomfield, CO 80020 / 303-469-1857; or 800-876-8600; FAX: 303-466-7437

Allen Firearm Engraving, P.O. Box 155, Camp Verde, AZ 86322 / 928-567-6711 rosebudmulgco@netzero.com rosebudmulgco@netzero.com

Allen Mfg., 6449 Hodgson Rd., Circle Pines, MN 55014 / 612-429-8231

Alley Supply Co., P.O. Box 848, Gardnerville, NV 89410 / 775-782-3800; FAX: 775-782-3827 jetalley@aol.com www.alleysupplyco.com

Alliant Techsystems, Smokeless Powder Group, P.O. Box 6, Rt. 114, Bldg. 229, Radford, VA 24141-0096 www.alliantpowder.com

Allred Bullet Co., 932 Evergreen Drive, Logan, UT 84321 / 435-752-6983; FAX: 435-752-6983

All's, The Jim J. Tembelis Co., Inc., 216 Loper Ct., Neenah, WI 54956 / 920-725-5251; FAX: 920-725-5251

Alpec Team, Inc., 201 Ricken Backer Cir., Livermore, CA 94550 / 510-606-8245; FAX: 510-606-4279

Alpha 1 Drop Zone, 2121 N. Tyler, Wichita, KS 67212 / 316-729-0800; FAX: 316-729-4262

Alpha LaFranck Enterprises, P.O. Box 81072, Lincoln, NE 68501 / 402-466-3193

Alpha Precision, Inc., 3238 Della Slaton Rd., Comer, GA 30629-2212 / 706-783-2131 jim@alphaprecisioninc.com www.alphaprecisioninc.com

Alpine Indoor Shooting Range, 2401 Government Way, Coeur d'Alene, ID 83814 / 208-676-8824; FAX: 208-676-8824

Altamont Co., 901 N. Church St., P.O. Box 309, Thomasboro, IL 61878 / 217-643-3125; or 800-626-5774; FAX: 217-643-7973

Alumna Sport by Dee Zee, 1572 NE 58th Ave., P.O. Box 3090, Des Moines, IA 50316 / 800-798-9899

Amadeo Rossi S.A., Rua: Amadeo Rossi, 143, Sao Leopoldo, RS 93030-220 BRAZIL / 051-592-5566 rossi.firearms@pnet.com.br

Amato, Jeff. See: J&M PRECISION MACHINING

AmBr Software Group Ltd., P.O. Box 301, Reisterstown, MD 21136-0301 / 800-888-1917; FAX: 410-526-7212

American Ammunition, 3545 NW 71st St., Miami, FL 33147 / 305-835-7400; FAX: 305-694-0037

American Derringer Corp., 127 N. Lacy Dr., Waco, TX 76705 / 800-642-7817; or 254-799-9111; FAX: 254-799-7935

American Display Co., 55 Cromwell St., Providence, RI 02907 / 401-331-2464; FAX: 401-421-1264

American Gas & Chemical Co., Ltd., 220 Pegasus Ave., Northvale, NJ 07647 / 201-767-7300

American Gunsmithing Institute, 1325 Imola Ave. #504, Napa, CA 94559 / 707-253-0462; FAX: 707-253-7149 www.americangunsmith.com

American Handgunner Magazine, 12345 World Trade Dr., San Diego, CA 92128 / 800-537-3006; FAX: 858-605-0204 www.americanhandgunner.com

American Pioneer Video, P.O. Box 50049, Bowling Green, KY 42102-2649 / 800-743-4675

American Products, Inc., 14729 Spring Valley Road, Morrison, IL 61270 / 815-772-3336; FAX: 815-772-8046

American Safe Arms, Inc., 1240 Riverview Dr., Garland, UT 84312 / 801-257-7472; FAX: 801-785-8156

American Security Products Co., 11925 Pacific Ave., Fontana, CA 92337 / 909-685-9680; or 800-421-6142; FAX: 909-685-9685

American Small Arms Academy, P.O. Box 12111, Prescott, AZ 86304 / 602-778-5623

American Target, 1328 S. Jason St., Denver, CO 80223 / 303-733-0433; FAX: 303-777-0311

American Target Knives, 1030 Brownwood NW, Grand Rapids, MI 49504 / 616-453-1998

Americase, P.O. Box 271, 1610 E. Main, Waxahachie, TX 75165 / 800-880-3629; FAX: 214-937-8373

Ames Metal Products, 4323 S. Western Blvd., Chicago, IL 60609 / 773-523-3230; or 800-255-6937; FAX: 773-523-3854

Amherst Arms, P.O. Box 1457, Englewood, FL 34295 / 941-475-2020; FAX: 941-473-1212

Ammo Load Worldwide, Inc., 815 D St., Lewiston, ID 83501 / 208-743-7418; FAX: 208-746-1703 ammoload@microwavedsl.com

Ammo Load, Inc., 1560 E. Edinger, Suite G, Santa Ana, CA 92705 / 714-558-8858; FAX: 714-569-0319

Amrine's Gun Shop, 937 La Luna, Ojai, CA 93023 / 805-646-2376

Amsec, 11925 Pacific Ave., Fontana, CA 92337

Analog Devices, Box 9106, Norwood, MA 02062

Andela Tool & Machine, Inc., RD3, Box 246, Richfield Springs, NY 13439

Anderson Manufacturing Co., Inc., 22602 53rd Ave. SE, Bothell, WA 98021 / 206-481-1858; FAX: 206-481-7839

Andres & Dworsky KG, Bergstrasse 18, A-3822 Karlstein, Thaya, AUSTRIA / 0 28 44-285; FAX: 0 28 44-28619 andres.dnorsky@wvnet.as

Angelo & Little Custom Gun Stock Blanks, P.O. Box 240046, Dell, MT 59724-0046

Answer Products Co., 1519 Westbury Drive, Davison, MI 48423 / 810-653-2911

Antique American Firearms, P.O. Box 71035, Dept. GD, Des Moines, IA 50325 / 515-224-6552

Antique Arms Co., 1110 Cleveland Ave., Monett, MO 65708 / 417-235-6501

AO Sight Systems, 2401 Ludelle St., Fort Worth, TX 76105 / 888-744-4880; or 817-536-0136; FAX: 817-536-3517

Apel GmbH, Ernst, Am Kirschberg 3, D-97218, Gerbrunn, GERMANY / 0 (931) 707192 info@eaw.de www.eaw.de

Aplan Antiques & Art, James O., HC 80, Box 793-25, Piedmont, SD 57769 / 605-347-5016

AR-7 Industries, LLC, 998 N. Colony Rd., Meriden, CT 06450 / 203-630-3536; FAX: 203-630-3637

Arizona Ammunition, Inc., 21421 No. 14th Ave., Suite E, Phoenix, AZ 85027 / 623-516-9004; FAX: 623-516-9012 www.azammo.com

ArmaLite, Inc., P.O. Box 299, Geneseo, IL 61254 / 800-336-0184; or 309-944-6939; FAX: 309-944-6949

Armament Gunsmithing Co., Inc., 525 Rt. 22, Hillside, NJ 07205 / 908-686-0960; FAX: 718-738-5019 armamentgunsmithing@worldnet.att.net

MANUFACTURER'S DIRECTORY

Armas Garbi, S.A., 12-14 20.600 Urki, 12, Eibar (Guipuzcoa), SPAIN / 943 20 3873; FAX: 943 20 3873 armosgarbi@euskalnet.n

Armas Kemen S. A. (See U.S. Importers)

Armfield Custom Bullets, 10584 County Road 100, Carthage, MO 64836 / 417-359-8480; FAX: 417-359-8497

Armi Perazzi S.P.A., Via Fontanelle 1/3, 1-25080, Botticino Mattina, ITALY / 030-2692591; FAX: 030-2692594

Armi San Marco (See Taylor's & Co.)

Armi San Paolo, 172-A, I-25062, via Europa, ITALY / 030-2751725

Armi Sport (See Cape Outfitters)

Armite Laboratories, 1560 Superior Ave., Costa Mesa, CA 92627 / 213-587-7768; FAX: 213-587-5075

Armoloy Co. of Ft. Worth, 204 E. Daggett St., Fort Worth, TX 76104 / 817-332-5604; FAX: 817-335-6517

Armor (See Buck Stop Lure Co., Inc.)

Armor Metal Products, P.O. Box 4609, Helena, MT 59604 / 406-442-5560; FAX: 406-442-5650

Armory Publications, 2120 S. Reserve St., PMB 253, Missoula, MT 59801 / 406-549-7670; FAX: 406-728-0597 armorypub@aol.com www.armorypub.com

Armoury, Inc., The, Rt. 202, Box 2340, New Preston, CT 06777 / 860-868-0001; FAX: 860-868-2919

Arms & Armour Press, Wellington House, 125 Strand, London, WC2R 0BB ENGLAND / 0171-420-5555; FAX: 0171-240-7265

Arms Corporation of the Philippines, Bo. Parang Marikina, Metro Manila, PHILIPPINES / 632-941-6243; or 632-941-6244; FAX: 632-942-0682

Arms Craft Gunsmithing, 1106 Linda Dr., Arroyo Grande, CA 93420 / 805-481-2830

Arms Software, 4851 SW Madrona St., Lake Oswego, OR 97035 / 800-366-5559; or 503-697-0533; FAX: 503-697-3337

Arms, Programming Solutions (See Arms Software)

Armscor Precision, 5740 S. Arville St. #219, Las Vegas, NV 89118 / 702-362-7750

Armscorp USA, Inc., 4424 John Ave., Baltimore, MD 21227 / 410-247-6200; FAX: 410-247-6205 info@armscorpusa.com www.armscorpusa.com

Arratoonian, Andy (See Horseshoe Leather Products)

Arrieta S.L., Morkaiko 5, 20870, Elgoibar, SPAIN / 34-43-743150; FAX: 34-43-743154

Art Jewel Enterprises Ltd., Eagle Business Ctr., 460 Randy Rd., Carol Stream, IL 60188 / 708-260-0400

Artistry in Wood, 134 Zimmerman Rd., Kalispell, MT 59901 / 406-257-9003; FAX: 406-257-9167 merlins@digisys.net www.acrabondlaminates.com

Art's Gun & Sport Shop, Inc., 6008 Hwy. Y, Hillsboro, MO 63050

Arundel Arms & Ammunition, Inc., A., 24A Defense St., Annapolis, MD 21401 / 410-224-8683

Aspen Outfitting Co., Jon Hollinger, 9 Dean St., Aspen, CO 81611 / 970-925-3406

A-Square Co., 205 Fairfield Ave., Jeffersonville, IN 47130 / 812-283-0577; FAX: 812-283-0375

Astra Sport, S.A., Apartado 3, 48300 Guernica, Espagne, SPAIN / 34-4-6250100; FAX: 34-4-6255186

Atamec-Bretton, 19 rue Victor Grignard, F-42026, St.-Etienne (Cedex 1, FRANCE / 33-77-93-54-69; FAX: 33-77-93-57-98

Atlanta Cutlery Corp., 2143 Gees Mill Rd., Box 839 CIS, Conyers, GA 30207 / 800-883-0300; FAX: 404-388-0246

Atlantic Mills, Inc., 1295 Towbin Ave., Lakewood, NJ 08701-5934 / 800-242-7374

Atsko/Sno-Seal, Inc., 2664 Russell St., Orangeburg, SC 29115 / 803-531-1820; FAX: 803-531-2139 info@atsko.com www.atsko.com

Auguste Francotte & Cie S.A., rue du Trois Juin 109, 4400 Herstal-Liege, BELGIUM / 32-4-248-13-18; FAX: 32-4-948-11-79

Austin & Halleck, Inc., 2150 South 950 East, Provo, UT 84606-6285 / 877-543-3256; or 801-374-9990; FAX: 801-374-9998 www.austinhallek.com

Austin Sheridan USA, Inc., P.O. Box 577, 36 Haddam Quarter Rd., Durham, CT 06422 / 860-349-1772; FAX: 860-349-1771 swalzer@palm.net

Autauga Arms, Inc., Pratt Plaza Mall No. 13, Prattville, AL 36067 / 800-262-9563; FAX: 334-361-2961

Auto Arms, 738 Clearview, San Antonio, TX 78228 / 512-434-5450

Auto-Ordnance Corp., P.O. Box 220, Blauvelt, NY 10913 / 914-353-7770

Autumn Sales, Inc. (Blaser), 1320 Lake St., Fort Worth, TX 76102 / 817-335-1634; FAX: 817-338-0119

Avnda Otaola Norica, 16 Apartado 68, 20600, Eibar, SPAIN

AWC Systems Technology, P.O. Box 41938, Phoenix, AZ 85080-1938 / 623-780-1050; FAX: 623-780-2967 awc@awcsystech.com www.awcsystech.com

Axtell Rifle Co., 353 Mill Creek Road, Sheridan, MT 59749 / 406-842-5814

AYA (See U.S. Importer-New England Custom Gun Serv

B

B&D Trading Co., Inc., 3935 Fair Hill Rd., Fair Oaks, CA 95628 / 800-334-3790; or 916-967-9366; FAX: 916-967-4873

B&P America, 12321 Brittany Cir., Dallas, TX 75230 / 972-726-9069

B.A.C., 17101 Los Modelos St., Fountain Valley, CA 92708 / 435-586-3286

B.B. Walker Co., P.O. Box 1167, 414 E Dixie Dr., Asheboro, NC 27204 / 910-625-1380; FAX: 910-625-8125

B.C. Outdoors, Larry McGhee, PO Box 61497, Boulder City, NV 89006 / 702-294-3056; FAX: 702-294-0413 jdalton@pmcammo.com www.pmcammo.com

B.M.F. Activator, Inc., 12145 Mill Creek Run, Plantersville, TX 77363 / 936-894-2397; FAX: 936-894-2397 bmf25years@aol.com

Baelder, Harry, Alte Goennebeker Strasse 5, 24635, Rickling, GERMANY / 04328-722732; FAX: 04328-722733

Baer's Hollows, P.O. Box 603, Taft, CA 93268 / 719-438-5718

Bagmaster Mfg., Inc., 2731 Sutton Ave., St. Louis, MO 63143 / 314-781-8002; FAX: 314-781-3363 sales@bagmaster.com www.bagmaster.com

Bain & Davis, Inc., 307 E. Valley Blvd., San Gabriel, CA 91776-3522 / 626-573-4241; FAX: 323-283-7449 baindavis@aol.com

Baker, Stan. See: STAN BAKER SPORTS

Baker's Leather Goods, Roy, P.O. Box 893, Magnolia, AR 71754 / 870-234-0344 pholsters@ipa.net

Bald Eagle Precision Machine Co., 101-A Allison St., Lock Haven, PA 17745 / 570-748-6772; FAX: 570-748-4443 bepmachine@aol.com baldeaglemachine.com

Balickie, Joe, 408 Trelawney Lane, Apex, NC 27502 / 919-362-5185

Ballard, Donald. See: BALLARD INDUSTRIES

Ballard Industries, Donald Ballard Sr., P.O. Box 2035, Arnold, CA 95223 / 408-996-0957; FAX: 408-257-6828

Ballard Rifle & Cartridge Co., LLC, 113 W. Yellowstone Ave., Cody, WY 82414 / 307-587-4914; FAX: 307-527-6097 ballard@wyoming.com www.ballardrifles.com

Ballistic Products, Inc., 20015 75th Ave. North, Corcoran, MN 55340-9456 / 763-494-9237; FAX: 763-494-9236 info@ballisticproducts.com www.ballisticproducts.com

Ballistic Program Co., Inc., The, 2417 N. Patterson St., Thomasville, GA 31792 / 912-228-5739 or 800-368-0835

Ballistic Research, 1108 W. May Ave., McHenry, IL 60050 / 815-385-0037

Ballisti-Cast, Inc., P.O. Box 1057, Minot, ND 58702-1057 / 701-497-3333; FAX: 701-497-3335

Bandcor Industries, Div. of Man-Sew Corp., 6108 Sherwin Dr., Port Richey, FL 34668 / 813-848-0432

Bang-Bang Boutique (See Holster Shop, The)

Bansner's Ultimate Rifles, LLC, P.O. Box 839, 261 E. Main St., Adamstown, PA 19501 / 717-484-2370; FAX: 717-484-0523 bansner@aol.com www.bansnersrifle.com

Barbour, Inc., 55 Meadowbrook Dr., Milford, NH 03055 / 603-673-1313; FAX: 603-673-6510

Barnes, 4347 Tweed Dr., Eau Claire, WI 54703-6302

Barnes Bullets, Inc., P.O. Box 215, American Fork, UT 84003 / 801-756-4222; or 800-574-9200; FAX: 801-756-2465 email@barnesbullets.com www.barnesbullets.com

Baron Technology, 62 Spring Hill Rd., Trumbull, CT 06611 / 203-452-0515; FAX: 203-452-0663 dbaron@baronengraving.com www.baronengraving.com

Barraclough, John K., 55 Merit Park Dr., Gardena, CA 90247 / 310-324-2574 johnbar120@aol.com

Barramundi Corp., P.O. Drawer 4259, Homosassa Springs, FL 32687 / 904-628-0200

Barrel & Gunworks, 2601 Lake Valley Rd., Prescott Valley, AZ 86314 / 928-772-4060 www.cutrifle.com

Barrett Firearms Manufacturer, Inc., P.O. Box 1077, Murfreesboro, TN 37133 / 615-896-2938; FAX: 615-896-7313

Bar-Sto Precision Machine, 73377 Sullivan Rd., P.O. Box 1838, Twentynine Palms, CA 92277 / 760-367-2747; FAX: 760-367-2407 barsto@eee.org www.barsto.com

Barta's Gunsmithing, 10231 U.S. Hwy. 10, Cato, WI 54230 / 920-732-4472

Barteaux Machete, 1916 SE 50th Ave., Portland, OR 97215-3238 / 503-233-5880

Bartlett Engineering, 40 South 200 East, Smithfield, UT 84335-1645 / 801-563-5910

Bates Engraving, Billy, 2302 Winthrop Dr. SW, Decatur, AL 35603 / 256-355-3690 bbrn@aol.com www.angelfire.com/al/billybates

Battenfeld Technologies, Inc., 5885 W. Van Horn Tavern Rd., Columbia, MO 65203 / 573-445-9200; FAX: 573-447-4158 battenfeldtechnologies.com

Bauer, Eddie, 15010 NE 36th St., Redmond, WA 98052

Baumgartner Bullets, 3011 S. Alane St., W. Valley City, UT 84120

Bauska Barrels, 105 9th Ave. W., Kalispell, MT 59901 / 406-752-7706

Bear Archery, RR 4, 4600 Southwest 41st Blvd., Gainesville, FL 32601 / 904-376-2327

Bear Arms, 374-A Carson Rd., St. Mathews, SC 29135

Bear Mountain Gun & Tool, 120 N. Plymouth, New Plymouth, ID 83655 / 208-278-5221; FAX: 208-278-5221

Beartooth Bullets, P.O. Box 491, Dept. HLD, Dover, ID 83825-0491 / 208-448-1865 bullets@beartoothbullets.com beartoothbullets.com

Beaver Park Product, Inc., 840 J St., Penrose, CO 81240 / 719-372-6744

BEC, Inc., 1227 W. Valley Blvd., Suite 204, Alhambra, CA 91803 / 626-281-5751; FAX: 626-293-7073

Beeks, Mike. See: GRAYBACK WILDCATS

Beeman Precision Airguns, 5454 Argosy Dr., Huntington Beach, CA 92649 / 714-890-4808; FAX: 714-890-4808

Behlert Precision, Inc., P.O. Box 288, 7067 Easton Rd., Pipersville, PA 18947 / 215-766-8681; or 215-766-7301; FAX: 215-766-8681

Beitzinger, George, 116-20 Atlantic Ave., Richmond Hill, NY 11419 / 718-847-7661

Belding's Custom Gun Shop, 10691 Sayers Rd., Munith, MI 49259 / 517-596-2388

Bell & Carlson, Inc., Dodge City Industrial Park, 101 Allen Rd., Dodge City, KS 67801 / 800-634-8586; or 620-225-6688; FAX: 620-225-6688 email@bellandcarlson.com www.bellandcarlson.com

Bell Reloading, Inc., 1725 Harlin Lane Rd., Villa Rica, GA 30180

Bell's Gun & Sport Shop, 3309-19 Mannheim Rd., Franklin Park, IL 60131

Bell's Legendary Country Wear, 22 Circle Dr., Bellmore, NY 11710 / 516-679-1158

Benchmark Knives (See Gerber Legendary Blades)

Benelli Armi S.P.A., Via della Stazione, 61029, Urbino, ITALY / 39-722-307-1; FAX: 39-722-327427

Benelli USA Corp., 17603 Indian Head Hwy., Accokeek, MD 20607 / 301-283-6981; FAX: 301-283-6988 benelliusa.com

Bengtson Arms Co., L., 6345-B E. Akron St., Mesa, AZ 85205 / 602-981-6375

Benjamin/Sheridan Co., Crosman, Rts. 5 and 20, E. Bloomfield, NY 14443 / 716-657-6161; FAX: 716-657-5405 www.crosman.com

Bentley, John, 128-D Watson Dr., Turtle Creek, PA 15145

Beretta S.P.A., Pietro, Via Beretta, 18, 25063, Gardone Vae Trompia, ITALY / 39-30-8341-1 info@benetta.com www.benetta.com

Beretta U.S.A. Corp., 17601 Beretta Dr., Accokeek, MD 20607 / 301-283-2191; FAX: 301-283-0435

Berger Bullets Ltd., 5443 W. Westwind Dr., Glendale, AZ 85310 / 602-842-4001; FAX: 602-934-9083

Bernardelli, Vincenzo, P.O. Box 460243, Houston, TX 77056-8243 www.bernardelli.com

Bernardelli, Vincenzo, Via Grande, 10, Sede Legale Torbole Casaglia, Brescia, ITALY / 39-30-8912851-2-3; FAX: 39-030-2150963 bernardelli@bernardelli.com www.bernardelli.com

Berry's Mfg., Inc., 401 North 3050 East St., St. George, UT 84770 / 435-634-1682; FAX: 435-634-1683 sales@berrysmfg.com www.berrysmfg.com

Bersa S.A., Benso Bonadimani, Magallanes 775 B1704 FLC, Ramos Mejia, ARGENTINA / 011-4656-2377; FAX: 011-4656-2093+ info@bersa-sa.com.dr www.bersa-sa.com.ar

Bert Johanssons Vapentillbehor, S-430 20 Veddige, SWEDEN

Bertuzzi (See U.S. Importer-New England Arms Co.)

Better Concepts Co., 663 New Castle Rd., Butler, PA 16001 / 412-285-9000

Beverly, Mary, 3201 Horseshoe Trail, Tallahassee, FL 32312

MANUFACTURER'S DIRECTORY

Bianchi International, Inc., 100 Calle Cortez, Temecula, CA 92590 / 909-676-5621; FAX: 909-676-6777

Big Bear Arms & Sporting Goods, Inc., 1112 Milam Way, Carrollton, TX 75006 / 972-416-8051; or 800-400-BEAR; FAX: 972-416-0771

Big Bore Bullets of Alaska, P.O. Box 521455, Big Lake, AK 99652 / 907-373-2673; FAX: 907-373-2673 doug@mtaonline.net ww.awloo.com/bbb/index.

Big Bore Express, 2316 E. Railroad St., Nampa, ID 83651 / 800-376-4010 FAX: 208-466-6927 info@powerbeltbullets.com bigbore.com

Big Spring Enterprises "Bore Stores", P.O. Box 1115, Big Spring Rd., Yellville, AR 72687 / 870-449-5297; FAX: 870-449-4446

Bilal, Mustafa. See: TURK'S HEAD PRODUCTIONS

Bilinski, Bryan. See: FIELDSPORT LTD.

Bill Adair Custom Shop, 2886 Westridge, Carrollton, TX 75006 / 972-418-0950

Bill Austin's Calls, Box 284, Kaycee, WY 82639 / 307-738-2552

Bill Hanus Birdguns, LLC, P.O. Box 533, Newport, OR 97365 / 541-265-7433; FAX: 541-265-7400 www.billhanusbirdguns.com

Bill Russ Trading Post, William A. Russ, 25 William St., Addison, NY 14801-1326 / 607-359-3896

Bill Wiseman and Co., P.O. Box 3427, Bryan, TX 77805 / 409-690-3456; FAX: 409-690-0156

Billeb, Stephen. See: QUALITY CUSTOM FIREARMS

Billings Gunsmiths, 1841 Grand Ave., Billings, MT 59102 / 406-256-8390; FAX: 406-256-6530 blgsgunsmiths@msn.com www.billingsgunsmiths.net

Billingsley & Brownell, P.O. Box 25, Dayton, WY 82836 / 307-655-9344

Bill's Gun Repair, 1007 Burlington St., Mendota, IL 61342 / 815-539-5786

Billy Bates Engraving, 2302 Winthrop Dr. SW, Decatur, AL 35603 / 256-355-3690 bbrn@aol.com www.angelfire.com/al/billybates

Birchwood Casey, 7900 Fuller Rd., Eden Prairie, MN 55344 / 800-328-6156; or 612-937-7933; FAX: 612-937-7979

Birdsong & Assoc., W. E., 1435 Monterey Rd., Florence, MS 39073-9748 / 601-366-8270

Bismuth Cartridge Co., 3500 Maple Ave., Suite 1650, Dallas, TX 75219 / 214-521-5880; FAX: 214-521-9035

Bison Studios, 1409 South Commerce St., Las Vegas, NV 89102 / 702-388-2891; FAX: 702-383-9967

Bitterroot Bullet Co., 2001 Cedar Ave., Lewiston, ID 83501-0412 / 208-743-5635 brootbil@lewiston.com

BKL Technologies, P.O. Box 5237, Brownsville, TX 78523

Black Belt Bullets (See Big Bore Express)

Black Hills Ammunition, Inc., P.O. Box 3090, Rapid City, SD 57709-3090 / 605-348-5150; FAX: 605-348-9827

Black Hills Shooters Supply, P.O. Box 4220, Rapid City, SD 57709 / 800-289-2506

Black Powder Products, 67 Township Rd. 1411, Chesapeake, OH 45619 / 614-867-8047

Black Sheep Brand, 3220 W. Gentry Pkwy., Tyler, TX 75702 / 903-592-3853; FAX: 903-592-0527

Blacksmith Corp., P.O. Box 280, North Hampton, OH 45349 / 937-969-8389; FAX: 937-969-8399 sales@blacksmithcorp.com www.blacksmithcorp.com

BlackStar AccuMax Barrels, 11501 Brittmoore Park Drive, Houston, TX 77041 / 281-721-6040; FAX: 281-721-6041

BlackStar Barrel Accurizing (See BlackStar AccuMax)

Blacktail Mountain Books, 42 First Ave. W., Kalispell, MT 59901 / 406-257-5573

Blammo Ammo, P.O. Box 1677, Seneca, SC 29679 / 803-882-1768

Blaser Jagdwaffen GmbH, D-88316, Isny Im Allgau, GERMANY

Blount, Inc., Sporting Equipment Div., 2299 Snake River Ave., P.O. Box 856, Lewiston, ID 83501 / 800-627-3640; or 208-746-2351; FAX: 208-799-3904

Blount/Outers ATK, P.O. Box 39, Onalaska, WI 54650 / 608-781-5800; FAX: 608-781-0368

Blue and Gray Products Inc. (See Ox-Yoke Originals)

Blue Book Publications, Inc., 8009 34th Ave. S., Ste. 175, Minneapolis, MN 55425 / 952-854-5229; FAX: 952-853-1486 bluebook@bluebookinc.com www.bluebookinc.com

Blue Mountain Bullets, 64146 Quail Ln., Box 231, John Day, OR 97845 / 541-820-4594; FAX: 541-820-4594

Blue Ridge Machinery & Tools, Inc., P.O. Box 536-GD, Hurricane, WV 25526 / 800-872-6500; FAX: 304-562-5311 blueridgemachine@worldnet.att.net www.blueridgemachinery.com

BMC Supply, Inc., 26051 - 179th Ave. SE, Kent, WA 98042

Bob Allen Co., P.O. Box 477, 214 SW Jackson, Des Moines, IA 50315 / 800-685-7020; FAX: 515-283-0779

Bob Allen Sportswear, 220 S. Main St., Osceola, IA 50213 / 210-344-8531; FAX: 210-342-2703 sales@bob-allen.com www.bob-allen.com

Bob Rogers Gunsmithing, P.O. Box 305, 344 S. Walnut St., Franklin Grove, IL 61031 / 815-456-2685; FAX: 815-456-2685

Bob's Gun Shop, P.O. Box 200, Royal, AR 71968 / 501-767-1970; FAX: 501-767-1970 gunparts@hsnp.com www.gun-parts.com

Bob's Tactical Indoor Shooting Range & Gun Shop, 90 Lafayette Rd., Salisbury, MA 01952 / 508-465-5561

Boessler, Erich, Am Vogeltal 3, 97702, Munnerstadt, GERMANY

Boker USA, Inc., 1550 Balsam Street, Lakewood, CO 80214 / 303-462-0662; FAX: 303-462-0668 sales@bokerusa.com bokerusa.com

Boltin, John M., P.O. Box 644, Estill, SC 29918 / 803-625-2185

Bo-Mar Tool & Mfg. Co., 6136 State Hwy. 300, Longview, TX 75604 / 903-759-4784; FAX: 903-759-9141 marykor@earthlink.net bo-mar.com

Bonadimani, Benso. See: BERSA S.A.

Bonanza (See Forster Products), 310 E. Lanark Ave., Lanark, IL 61046 / 815-493-6360; FAX: 815-493-2371

Bond Arms, Inc., P.O. Box 1296, Granbury, TX 76048 / 817-573-4445; FAX: 817-573-5636

Bond Custom Firearms, 8954 N. Lewis Ln., Bloomington, IN 47408 / 812-332-4519

Bonham's & Butterfields, 220 San Bruno Ave., San Francisco, CA 94103 / 415-861-7500; FAX: 415-861-0183 arms@butterfields.com www.butterfields.com

Boone Trading Co., Inc., P.O. Box 669, Brinnon, WA 98320 / 800-423-1945; or 360-796-4330; FAX: 360-796-4511 sales@boonetrading.com boonetrading.com

Boone's Custom Ivory Grips, Inc., 562 Coyote Rd., Brinnon, WA 98320 / 206-796-4330

Boonie Packer Products, P.O. Box 12517, Salem, OR 97309-0517 / 800-477-3244; or 503-581-3244; FAX: 503-581-3191 customerservice@booniepacker.com www.booniepacker.com

Borden Ridges Rimrock Stocks, RR 1 Box 250 BC, Springville, PA 18844 / 570-965-2505; FAX: 570-965-2328

Borden Rifles Inc., RD 1, Box 250 #BC, Springville, PA 18844 / 717-965-2505; FAX: 717-965-2328

Border Barrels Ltd., Riccarton Farm, Newcastleton, SCOTLAND UK

Borovnik K.G., Ludwig, 9170 Ferlach, Bahnhofstrasse 7, AUSTRIA / 042 27 24 42; FAX: 042 26 43 49

Bosis (See U.S. Importer-New England Arms Co.)

Boss Manufacturing Co., 221 W. First St., Kewanee, IL 61443 / 309-852-2131; or 800-447-4581; FAX: 309-852-0848

Bostick Wildlife Calls, Inc., P.O. Box 728, Estill, SC 29918 / 803-625-2210; or 803-625-4512

Bowen Classic Arms Corp., P.O. Box 67, Louisville, TN 37777 / 865-984-3583 www.bowenclassicarms.com

Bowen Knife Co., Inc., P.O. Box 590, Blackshear, GA 31516 / 912-449-4794

Bowerly, Kent, 710 Golden Pheasant Dr., Redmond, OR 97756 / 541-923-3501 jkbowerly@aol.com

Boyds' Gunstock Industries, Inc., 25376 403 Rd. Ave., Mitchell, SD 57301 / 605-996-5011; FAX: 605-996-9878 www.boydsgunstocks.com

Brace, Larry D., 771 Blackfoot Ave., Eugene, OR 97404 / 541-688-1278; FAX: 541-607-5833

Brauer Bros., 1520 Washington Ave., St. Louis, MO 63103 / 314-231-2864; FAX: 314-249-4952 www.brauerbros.com

Break-Free, Inc., 13386 International Pkwy., Jacksonville, FL 32218 / 800-428-0588; FAX: 904-741-5407 contactus@armorholdings.com www.break-free.com

Brennke GmbH, P.O. Box 1646, 30837, Langenhagen, GERMANY / +49-511-97262-0; FAX: +49-511-97262-62 info@brenneke.de brenneke.com

Bridgeman Products, Harry Jaffin, 153 B Cross Slope Ct., Englishtown, NJ 07726 / 732-536-3604; FAX: 732-972-1004

Bridgers Best, P.O. Box 1410, Berthoud, CO 80513

Briese Bullet Co., Inc., 3442 42nd Ave. SE, Tappen, ND 58487 / 701-327-4578; FAX: 701-327-4579

Brigade Quartermasters, 1025 Cobb International Blvd., Dept. VH, Kennesaw, GA 30144-4300 / 404-428-1248; or 800-241-3125; FAX: 404-426-7726

Briganti, A.J. See: BRIGANTI CUSTOM GUNSMITH

Briganti Custom Gunsmith, A.J. Briganti, 512 Rt. 32, Highland Mills, NY 10930 / 845-928-9573

Briley Mfg. Inc., 1230 Lumpkin, Houston, TX 77043 / 800-331-5718; or 713-932-6995; FAX: 713-932-1043

Brill, R. See: ROYAL ARMS INTERNATIONAL

British Sporting Arms, RR 1, Box 130, Millbrook, NY 12545 / 914-677-8303

Broad Creek Rifle Works, Ltd., 120 Horsey Ave., Laurel, DE 19956 / 302-875-5446; FAX: 302-875-1448 bcrw4guns@aol.com

Brockman's Custom Gunsmithing, P.O. Box 357, Gooding, ID 83330 / 208-934-5050

Broken Gun Ranch, 10739 126 Rd., Spearville, KS 67876 / 316-385-2587; FAX: 316-385-2597 nbowlin@ucom.net www.brokengunranch.com

Brooker, Dennis, Rt. 1, Box 12A, Derby, IA 50068 / 515-533-2103

Brooks Tactical Systems-Agrip, 279-C Shorewood Ct., Fox Island, WA 98333 / 253-549-2866 FAX: 253-549-2703 brooks@brookstactical.com www.brookstactical.com

Brown Dog Ent., 2200 Calle Camelia, 1000 Oaks, CA 91360 / 805-497-2318; FAX: 805-497-1618

Brown Precision, Inc., 7786 Molinos Ave., Los Molinos, CA 96055 / 530-384-2506; FAX: 916-384-1638 www.brownprecision.com

Brown Products, Inc., Ed, 43825 Muldrow Trl., Perry, MO 63462 / 573-565-3261; FAX: 573-565-2791 edbrown@edbrown.com www.edbrown.com

Brownells, Inc., 200 S. Front St., Montezuma, IA 50171 / 800-741-0015; FAX: 800-264-3068 orderdesk@brownells.com www.brownells.com

Browning Arms Co., One Browning Place, Morgan, UT 84050 / 801-876-2711; FAX: 801-876-3331 www.browning.com

Browning Arms Co. (Parts & Service), 3005 Arnold Tenbrook Rd., Arnold, MO 63010 / 617-287-6800; FAX: 617-287-9751

BRP, Inc. High Performance Cast Bullets, 1210 Alexander Rd., Colorado Springs, CO 80909 / 719-633-0658

Brunton U.S.A., 620 E. Monroe Ave., Riverton, WY 82501 / 307-856-6559; FAX: 307-857-4702 info@brunton.com www.brunton.com

Bryan & Assoc., R. D. Sauls, P.O. Box 5772, Anderson, SC 29623-5772 / 864-261-6810 bryanandac@aol.com www.huntersweb.com/bryanandac

Brynin, Milton, P.O. Box 383, Yonkers, NY 10710 / 914-779-4333

BSA Guns Ltd., Armoury Rd. Small Heath, Birmingham B11 2PP, ENGLAND / 011-021-772-8543; FAX: 011-021-773-0845 sales@bsagun.com www.bsagun.com

BSA Optics, 3911 SW 47th Ave., Ste. 914, Ft. Lauderdale, FL 33314 / 954-581-2144; FAX: 954-581-3165 4info@basaoptics.com www.bsaoptics.com

B-Square Company, Inc., P.O. Box 11281, 2708 St. Louis Ave., Ft. Worth, TX 76110 / 817-923-0964 or 800-433-2909; FAX: 817-926-7012

Buchsenmachermeister, Peter Hofer Jagdwaffen, A-9170 Ferlach, Kirchgasse 24, Kirchgasse, AUSTRIA / 43 4227 3683; or 43 664 3200216; FAX: 43 4227 368330 peterhofer@hoferwaffen.com www.hoferwaffen.com

Buck Knives, Inc., 1900 Weld Blvd., P.O. Box 1267, El Cajon, CA 92020 / 619-449-1100; or 800-326-2825; FAX: 619-562-5774

Buck Stix-SOS Products Co., Box 3, Neenah, WI 54956

Buck Stop Lure Co., Inc., 3600 Grow Rd. NW, P.O. Box 636, Stanton, MI 48888 / 989-762-5091; FAX: 989-762-5124 buckstop@nethawk.com www.buckstopscents.com

Buckeye Custom Bullets, 6490 Stewart Rd., Elida, OH 45807 / 419-641-4463

Buckhorn Gun Works, 8109 Woodland Dr., Black Hawk, SD 57718 / 605-787-6472

Buckskin Bullet Co., P.O. Box 1893, Cedar City, UT 84721 / 435-586-3286

Budin, Dave, 817 Main St., P.O. Box 685, Margaretville, NY 12455 / 914-568-4103; FAX: 914-586-4105

Budin, Dave. See: DEL-SPORTS, INC.

Buenger Enterprises/Goldenrod Dehumidifier, 3600 S. Harbor Blvd., Oxnard, CA 93035 / 800-451-6797; or 805-985-5828; FAX: 805-985-1534

Buffalo Arms Co., 660 Vermeer Ct., Ponderay, ID 83852 / 208-263-6953; FAX: 208-265-2096 www.buffaloarms.com

Buffalo Bullet Co., Inc., 12637 Los Nietos Rd., Unit A, Santa Fe Springs, CA 90670 / 800-423-8069; FAX: 562-944-5054

MANUFACTURER'S DIRECTORY

Buffalo Gun Center, 3385 Harlem Rd., Buffalo, NY 14225 / 716-833-2581; FAX: 716-833-2265 www.buffaloguncenter.com

Buffalo Rock Shooters Supply, R.R. 1, Ottawa, IL 61350 / 815-433-2471

Buffer Technologies, P.O. Box 104930, Jefferson City, MO 65110 / 573-634-8529; FAX: 573-634-8522

Bull Mountain Rifle Co., 6327 Golden West Terrace, Billings, MT 59106 / 406-656-0778

Bullberry Barrel Works, Ltd., 2430 W. Bullberry Ln., Hurricane, UT 84737 / 435-635-9866; FAX: 435-635-0348 fred@bullberry.com www.bullberry.com

Bullet Metals, Bill Ferguson, P.O. Box 1238, Sierra Vista, AZ 85636 / 520-458-5321; FAX: 520-458-1421 info@theantimonyman.com www.bullet-metals.com

Bullet N Press, 1210 Jones St., Gastonia, NC 28052 / 704-853-0265 bnpress@quik.com www.oldwestgunsmith.com

Bullet Swaging Supply, Inc., P.O. Box 1056, 303 McMillan Rd., West Monroe, LA 71291 / 318-387-3266; FAX: 318-387-7779 leblackmon@colla.com

Bull-X, Inc., 411 E. Water St., Farmer City, IL 61842-1556 / 309-928-2574 or 800-248-3845; FAX: 309-928-2130

Burkhart Gunsmithing, Don, P.O. Box 852, Rawlins, WY 82301 / 307-324-6007

Burnham Bros., P.O. Box 1148, Menard, TX 78659 / 915-396-4572; FAX: 915-396-4574

Burris Co., Inc., P.O. Box 1747, 331 E. 8th St., Greeley, CO 80631 / 970-356-1670; FAX: 970-356-8702

Bushmaster Firearms, Inc., 999 Roosevelt Trail, Windham, ME 04062 / 800-998-7928; FAX: 207-892-8068 info@bushmaster.com www.bushmaster.com

Bushmaster Hunting & Fishing, 451 Alliance Ave., Toronto, ON M6N 2J1 CANADA / 416-763-4040; FAX: 416-763-0623

Bushnell Sports Optics Worldwide, 9200 Cody, Overland Park, KS 66214 / 913-752-3400 or 800-423-3537; FAX: 913-752-3550

Buster's Custom Knives, P.O. Box 214, Richfield, UT 84701 / 435-896-5319; FAX: 435-896-8333 www.warenskiknives.com

Butler Creek Corp., 2100 S. Silverstone Way, Meridian, ID 83642-8151 / 800-423-8327 or 406-388-1356; FAX: 406-388-7204

Butler Enterprises, 834 Oberting Rd., Lawrenceburg, IN 47025 / 812-537-3584

Buzz Fletcher Custom Stockmaker, 117 Silver Road, P.O. Box 189, Taos, NM 87571 / 505-758-3486

C

C&D Special Products (See Claybuster Wads & Harvester Bullets)

C&H Research, 115 Sunnyside Dr., Box 351, Lewis, KS 67552 / 316-324-5445; or 888-324-5445; FAX: 620-324-5984 info@mercuryrecoil.com www.mercuryrecoil.com

C. Palmer Manufacturing Co., Inc., P.O. Box 220, West Newton, PA 15089 / 412-872-8200; FAX: 412-872-8302

C. Sharps Arms Co. Inc./Montana Armory, 100 Centennial Dr., P.O. Box 885, Big Timber, MT 59011 / 406-932-4353; FAX: 406-932-4443

C.S. Van Gorden & Son, Inc., 1815 Main St., Bloomer, WI 54724 / 715-568-2612 vangorden@bloomer.net

C.W. Erickson's L.L.C., 530 Garrison Ave. NE, P.O. Box 522, Buffalo, MN 55313 / 763-682-3665; FAX: 763-682-4328 www.archerhunter.com

Cabanas (See U.S. Importer-Mandall Shooting Supply

Cabela's, One Cabela Drive, Sidney, NE 69160 / 308-254-5505; FAX: 308-254-8420

Cabinet Mtn. Outfitters Scents & Lures, P.O. Box 766, Plains, MT 59859 / 406-826-3970

Cache La Poudre Rifleworks, 140 N. College, Ft. Collins, CO 80524 / 920-482-6913

Cain's Outdoors, Inc., 1832 Williams Hwy., Williamstown, WV 26187 / 304-375-7842; FAX: 304-375-7842 muzzleloading@cainsoutdoor.com www.cainsoutdoor.com

Calhoon Mfg., 4343 U.S. Highway 87, Havre, MT 59501 / 406-395-4079 www.jamescalhoon.com

Cali'co Hardwoods, Inc., 3580 Westwind Blvd., Santa Rosa, CA 95403 / 707-546-4045; FAX: 707-546-4027 calicohardwoods@msn.com

Calico Light Weapon Systems, 1489 Greg St., Sparks, NV 89431

California Sights (See Fautheree, Andy)

Cambos Outdoorsman, 532 E. Idaho Ave., Ontario, OR 97914 / 541-889-3135; FAX: 541-889-2633

Cambos Outdoorsman, Fritz Hallberg, 532 E. Idaho Ave., Ontario, OR 97914 / 541-889-3135; FAX: 541-889-2633

Camdex, Inc., 2330 Alger, Troy, MI 48083 / 810-528-2300; FAX: 810-528-0989

Cameron's, 16690 W. 11th Ave., Golden, CO 80401 / 303-279-7365; FAX: 303-568-1009 ncnoremac@aol.com

Camillus Cutlery Co., 54 Main St., Camillus, NY 13031 / 315-672-8111; FAX: 315-672-8832

Campbell, Dick, 196 Garden Homes Dr., Colville, WA 99114 / 509-684-6080; FAX: 509-684-6080 dicksknives@aol.com

Camp-Cap Products, P.O. Box 3805, Chesterfield, MO 63006 / 866-212-4639; FAX: 636-536-6320 www.langenberghats.com

Cannon Safe, Inc., 216 S. 2nd Ave. #BLD-932, San Bernardino, CA 92400 / 310-692-0636; or 800-242-1055; FAX: 310-692-7252

Canyon Cartridge Corp., P.O. Box 152, Albertson, NY 11507 FAX: 516-294-8946

Cape Outfitters, 599 County Rd. 206, Cape Girardeau, MO 63701 / 573-335-4103; FAX: 573-335-1555

Caraville Manufacturing, P.O. Box 4545, Thousand Oaks, CA 91359 / 805-499-1234

Carbide Checkering Tools (See J&R Engineering)

Carhartt, Inc., P.O. Box 600, 3 Parklane Blvd., Dearborn, MI 48121 / 800-358-3825; or 313-271-8460; FAX: 313-271-3455

Carl Walther GmbH, B.P. 4325, D-89033, Ulm, GERMANY

Carl Zeiss Inc., 13005 N. Kingston Ave., Chester, VA 23836 / 800-441-3005; FAX: 804-530-8481

Carolina Precision Rifles, 1200 Old Jackson Hwy., Jackson, SC 29831 / 803-827-2069

Carrell, William. See: CARRELL'S PRECISION FIREARMS

Carrell's Precision Firearms, William Carrell, 1952 W.Silver Falls Ct., Meridian, ID 83642-3837

Carry-Lite, Inc., P.O. Box 1587, Fort Smith, AR 72902 / 479-782-8971; FAX: 479-783-0234

Carter's Gun Shop, 225 G St., Penrose, CO 81240 / 719-372-6240 rlewiscarter@msn.com

Cascade Bullet Co., Inc., 2355 South 6th St., Klamath Falls, OR 97601 / 503-884-9316

Cascade Shooters, 2155 N.W. 12th St., Redwood, OR 97756

Case & Sons Cutlery Co., W R, Owens Way, Bradford, PA 16701 / 814-368-4123; or 800-523-6350; FAX: 814-768-5369

Case Sorting System, 12695 Cobblestone Creek Rd., Poway, CA 92064 / 619-486-9340

Cash Mfg. Co., Inc., P.O. Box 130, 201 S. Klein Dr., Waunakee, WI 53597-0130 / 608-849-5664; FAX: 608-849-5664

Caspian Arms, Ltd., 14 North Main St., Hardwick, VT 05843 / 802-472-6454; FAX: 802-472-6709

Cast Bullet Association, The, 12857 S. Road, Hoyt, KS 66440-9116 cbamemdir@castbulletassoc.org www.castbulletassoc.org

Cast Performance Bullet Company, P.O. Box 153, Riverton, WY 82501 / 307-857-2940; FAX: 307-857-3132 castperform@wyoming.com castperformance.com

Casull Arms Corp., P.O. Box 1629, Afton, WY 83110 / 307-886-0200

Caswell International, 720 Industrial Dr. No. 112, Cary, IL 60013 / 847-639-7666; FAX: 847-639-7694 www.caswellintl.com

Cathey Enterprises, Inc., P.O. Box 2202, Brownwood, TX 76804 / 915-643-2553; FAX: 915-643-3653

Cation, 2341 Alger St., Troy, MI 48083 / 810-689-0658; FAX: 810-689-7558

Caywood, Shane J., P.O. Box 321, Minocqua, WI 54548 / 715-277-3866

Caywood Gunmakers, 18 Kings Hill Estates, Berryville, AR 72616 / 870-423-4741 www.caywoodguns.com

CBC, Avenida Humberto de Campos 3220, 09400-000, Ribeirao Pires, SP, BRAZIL / 55 11 4822 8378; FAX: 55 11 4822 8323 export@cbc.com.br www.cbc.com.bc

CBC-BRAZIL, 3 Cuckoo Lane, Honley, Yorkshire HD7 2BR, ENGLAND / 44-1484-661062; FAX: 44-1484-663709

CCG Enterprises, 5217 E. Belknap St., Halton City, TX 76117 / 800-819-7464

CCI/Speer Div of ATK, P.O. Box 856, 2299 Snake River Ave., Lewiston, ID 83501 / 800-627-3640 or 208-746-2351

CCL Security Products, 199 Whiting St., New Britain, CT 06051 / 800-733-8588

Cedar Hill Game Calls, LLC, 238 Vic Allen Rd., Downsville, LA 71234 / 318-982-5632; FAX: 318-982-2031

Centaur Systems, Inc., 1602 Foothill Rd., Kalispell, MT 59901 / 406-755-8609; FAX: 406-755-8609

Center Lock Scope Rings, 9901 France Ct., Lakeville, MN 55044 / 952-461-2114; FAX: 952-461-2194 marklee55044@usfamily.net

Central Specialties Ltd. (See Trigger Lock Division)

Century Gun Dist. Inc., 1467 Jason Rd., Greenfield, IN 46140 / 317-462-4524

Century International Arms, Inc., 430 S. Congress Ave. Ste. 1, Delray Beach, FL 33445-4701 / 800-527-1252; FAX: 561-998-1993 support@centuryarms.com www.centuryarms.com

CFVentures, 509 Harvey Dr., Bloomington, IN 47403-1715 paladinwilltravel@yahoo.com www.caversam16.freeserve.co.uk

CH Tool & Die Co. (See 4-D Custom Die Co.), 711 N Sandusky St., P.O. Box 889, Mt. Vernon, OH 43050-0889 / 740-397-7214; FAX: 740-397-6600

Chace Leather Products, 507 Alden St., Fall River, MA 02722 / 508-678-7556; FAX: 508-675-9666 chacelea@aol.com www.chaceleather.com

Chadick's Ltd., P.O. Box 100, Terrell, TX 75160 / 214-563-7577

Chambers Flintlocks Ltd., Jim, 116 Sams Branch Rd., Candler, NC 28715 / 828-667-8361; FAX: 828-665-0852 www.flintlocks.com

Champion Shooters' Supply, P.O. Box 303, New Albany, OH 43054 / 614-855-1603; FAX: 614-855-1209

Champion Target Co., 232 Industrial Parkway, Richmond, IN 47374 / 800-441-4971

Champion's Choice, Inc., 201 International Blvd., LaVergne, TN 37086 / 615-793-4066; FAX: 615-793-4070 champ.choice@earthlink.net www.champchoice.com

Champlin Firearms, Inc., P.O. Box 3191, Woodring Airport, Enid, OK 73701 / 580-237-7388; FAX: 580-242-6922 info@champlinarms.com www.champlinarms.com

Chapman Academy of Practical Shooting, 4350 Academy Rd., Hallsville, MO 65255 / 573-696-5544; FAX: 573-696-2266 hq@chapmanacademy.com chapmanacademy.com

Chapman, J. Ken. See: OLD WEST BULLET MOULDS

Chapman Manufacturing Co., 471 New Haven Rd., P.O. Box 250, Durham, CT 06422 / 860-349-9228; FAX: 860-349-0084 sales@chapmanmfg.com www.chapmanmfg.com

Chapuis Armes, Z1 La Gravoux, BP15, 42380 P.O. Box 15, St. Bonnet-le-Chatea, FRANCE / (33)477.50.06.96; FAX: (33)477 50 10 70 info@chapuis.armes.com www.chapuis-armes.com

Charter 2000, 273 Canal St., Shelton, CT 06484 / 203-922-1652

Checkmate Refinishing, 370 Champion Dr., Brooksville, FL 34601 / 352-799-5774; FAX: 352-799-2986 checkmatecustom.com

Cheddite, France S.A., 99 Route de Lyon, F-26501, Bourg-les-Valence, FRANCE / 33-75-56-4545; FAX: 33-75-56-3587 export@cheddite.com

Chelsea Gun Club of New York City Inc., 237 Ovington Ave., Apt. D53, Brooklyn, NY 11209 / 718-836-9422; or 718-833-2704

Cherry Creek State Park Shooting Center, 12500 E. Belleview Ave., Englewood, CO 80111 / 303-693-1765

CheVron Bullets, RR1, Ottawa, IL 61350 / 815-433-2471

Cheyenne Pioneer Products, P.O. Box 28425, Kansas City, MO 64188 / 816-413-9196; FAX: 816-455-2859 cheyennepp@aol.com www.cartridgeboxes.com

Chicago Cutlery Co., 1536 Beech St., Terre Haute, IN 47804 / 800-457-2665

Chicasaw Gun Works, 4 Mi. Mkr., Pluto Rd., Box 868, Shady Spring, WV 25918-0868 / 304-763-2848; FAX: 304-763-3725

Chip McCormick Corp., P.O. Box 1560, Manchaca, TX 78652 / 800-328-2447; FAX: 512-280-4282 www.chipmccormick.com

Chipmunk (See Oregon Arms, Inc.)

Choate Machine & Tool Co., Inc., P.O. Box 218, 116 Lovers Ln., Bald Knob, AR 72010 / 501-724-6193; or 800-972-6390; FAX: 501-724-5873

Christensen Arms, 192 East 100 North, Fayette, UT 84630 / 435-528-7999; FAX: 435-528-7494 www.christensenarms.com

Christie's East, 20 Rockefeller Plz., New York, NY 10020-1902 / 212-606-0406 christics.com

Chu Tani Ind., Inc., P.O. Box 2064, Cody, WY 82414-2064

Chuck's Gun Shop, P.O. Box 597, Waldo, FL 32694 / 904-468-2264

Churchill (See U.S. Importer-Ellett Bros.)

MANUFACTURER'S DIRECTORY

Churchill, Winston G., 2838 20 Mile Stream Rd., Proctorville, VT 05153 / 802-226-7772

Churchill Glove Co., James, P.O. Box 298, Centralia, WA 98531 / 360-736-2816; FAX: 360-330-0151

CIDCO, 21480 Pacific Blvd., Sterling, VA 22170 / 703-444-5353

Cimarron F.A. Co., P.O. Box 906, Fredericksburg, TX 78624-0906 / 830-997-9090; FAX: 830-997-0802 cimgraph@koc.com www.cimarron-firearms.com

Cincinnati Swaging, 2605 Marlington Ave., Cincinnati, OH 45208

Clark Custom Guns, Inc., 336 Shootout Lane, Princeton, LA 71067 / 318-949-9884; FAX: 318-949-9829

Clark Firearms Engraving, 6347 Avon Ave., San Gabriel, CA 91775-1801 / 818-287-1652

Clarkfield Enterprises, Inc., 1032 10th Ave., Clarkfield, MN 56223 / 612-669-7140

Claro Walnut Gunstock Co., 1235 Stanley Ave., Chico, CA 95928 / 530-342-5188; FAX: 530-342-5199 wally@clarowalnutgunstocks.com www.clarowalnutgunstocks.com

Classic Arms Company, Rt 1 Box 120F, Burnet, TX 78611 / 512-756-4001

Classic Arms Corp., P.O. Box 106, Dunsmuir, CA 96025-0106 / 530-235-2000

Classic Old West Styles, 1060 Doniphan Park Circle C, El Paso, TX 79936 / 915-587-0684

Claybuster Wads & Harvester Bullets, 309 Sequoya Dr., Hopkinsville, KY 42240 / 800-922-6287; or 800-284-1746; FAX: 502-885-8088

Clean Shot Technologies, 21218 St. Andrews Blvd. Ste 504, Boca Raton, FL 33433 / 888-866-2532

Clearview Mfg. Co., Inc., 413 S. Oakley St., Fordyce, AR 71742 / 501-352-8557; FAX: 501-352-7120

Clearview Products, 3021 N. Portland, Oklahoma City, OK 73107

Cleland's Outdoor World, Inc., 10306 Airport Hwy., Swanton, OH 43558 / 419-865-4713; FAX: 419-865-5865 mail@clelands.com www.clelands.com

Clements' Custom Leathercraft, Chas, 1741 Dallas St., Aurora, CO 80010-2018 / 303-364-0403; FAX: 303-739-9824 gryphons@home.com kuntaoslcat.com

Clenzoil Worldwide Corp., Jack Fitzgerald, 25670 1st St., Westlake, OH 44145-1430 / 440-899-0482; FAX: 440-899-0483

Clift Mfg., L. R., 3821 Hammonton Rd., Marysville, CA 95901 / 916-755-3390; FAX: 916-755-3393

Clymer Mfg. Co., 1645 W. Hamlin Rd., Rochester Hills, MI 48309-3312 / 248-853-5555; FAX: 248-853-1530

C-More Systems, P.O. Box 1750, 7553 Gary Rd., Manassas, VA 20108 / 703-361-2663; FAX: 703-361-5881

Cobra Enterprises, Inc., 1960 S. Milestone Drive, Suite F, Salt Lake City, UT 84104 FAX: 801-908-8301 www.cobrapistols@networld.com

Cobra Sport S.R.I., Via Caduti Nei Lager No. 1, 56020 San Romano, Montopoli v/Arno Pi, ITALY / 0039-571-450490; FAX: 0039-571-450492

Coffin, Charles H., 3719 Scarlet Ave., Odessa, TX 79762 / 915-366-4729; FAX: 915-366-4729

Cogar's Gunsmithing, 206 Redwine Dr., Houghton Lake, MI 48629 / 517-422-4591

Coghlan's Ltd., 121 Irene St., Winnipeg, MB R3T 4C7 CANADA / 204-284-9550; FAX: 204-475-4127

Cold Steel Inc., 3036 Seaborg Ave. Ste. A, Ventura, CA 93003 / 800-255-4716; or 800-624-2363; FAX: 805-642-9727

Cole-Grip, 16135 Cohasset St., Van Nuys, CA 91406 / 818-782-4424

Coleman Co., Inc., 3600 N. Hydraulic, Wichita, KS 67219 / 800-835-3278; www.coleman.com

Cole's Gun Works, Old Bank Building, Rt. 4 Box 250, Moyock, NC 27958 / 919-435-2345

Collector's Armoury, Ltd., Tom Nelson, 9404 Gunston Cove Rd., Lorton, VA 22079 / 703-493-9120; FAX: 703-493-9424 www.collectorsarmoury.com

Collings, Ronald, 1006 Cielta Linda, Vista, CA 92083

Colonial Arms, Inc., P.O. Box 636, Selma, AL 36702-0636 / 334-872-9455; FAX: 334-872-9540 colonialarms@mindspring.com www.colonialarms.com

Colonial Repair, 47 Navarre St., Roslindale, MA 02131-4725 / 617-469-4951

Colorado Gunsmithing Academy, RR 3 Box 79B, El Campo, TX 77437 / 719-336-4099; or 800-754-2046; FAX: 719-336-9642

Colorado School of Trades, 1575 Hoyt St., Lakewood, CO 80215 / 800-234-4594; FAX: 303-233-4723

Colt Blackpowder Arms Co., 110 8th Street, Brooklyn, NY 11215 / 718-499-4678; FAX: 718-768-8056

Colt's Mfg. Co., Inc., P.O. Box 1868, Hartford, CT 06144-1868 / 800-962-COLT; or 860-236-6311; FAX: 860-244-1449

Compass Industries, Inc., 104 East 25th St., New York, NY 10010 / 212-473-2614 or 800-221-9904; FAX: 212-353-0826

Compasseco, Ltd., 151 Atkinson Hill Ave., Bardtown, KY 40004 / 502-349-0910

Competition Electronics, Inc., 3469 Precision Dr., Rockford, IL 61109 / 815-874-8001; FAX: 815-874-8181

Competitive Pistol Shop, The, 5233 Palmer Dr., Fort Worth, TX 76117-2433 / 817-834-8479

Competitor Corp., Inc., 26 Knight St. Unit 3, P.O. Box 352, Jaffrey, NH 03452 / 603-532-9483; FAX: 603-532-8209 competitorcorp@aol.com competitor-pistol.com

Component Concepts, Inc., 530 S. Springbrook Road, Newberg, OR 97132 / 503-554-8095; FAX: 503-554-9370 cci@cybcon.com www.phantomonline.com

Concealment Shop, Inc., The, 3550 E. Hwy. 80, Mesquite, TX 75149 / 972-289-8997; or 800-444-7090; FAX: 972-289-4410 info@theconcealmentshop.com www.theconcealmentshop.com

Concept Development Corp., 16610 E. Laser Drive, Suite 5, Fountain Hills, AZ 85268-6644

Conetrol Scope Mounts, 10225 Hwy. 123 S., Seguin, TX 78155 / 830-379-3030; or 800-CONETROL; FAX: 830-379-3030 email@conetrol.com www.conetrol.com

Connecticut Shotgun Mfg. Co., P.O. Box 1692, 35 Woodland St., New Britain, CT 06051 / 860-225-6581; FAX: 860-832-8707

Connecticut Valley Classics (See CVC, BPI)

Conrad, C. A., 3964 Ebert St., Winston-Salem, NC 27127 / 919-788-5469

Cook Engineering Service, 891 Highbury Rd., Vict 3133, 3133 AUSTRALIA

Cooper Arms, P.O. Box 114, Stevensville, MT 59870 / 406-777-0373; FAX: 406-777-5228

Cooper-Woodward Perfect Lube, 4120 Oesterle Rd., Helena, MT 59602 / 406-459-2287 cwperfectlube@mt.net cwperfectlube.com

Corbin Mfg. & Supply, Inc., 600 Industrial Circle, P.O. Box 2659, White City, OR 97503 / 541-826-5211; FAX: 541-826-8669 sales@corbins.com www.corbins.com

Cor-Bon Inc./Glaser LLC, P.O. Box 173, 1311 Industry Rd., Sturgis, SD 57785 / 605-347-4544; or 800-221-3489; FAX: 605-347-5055 email@corbon.com www.corbon.com

Corkys Gun Clinic, 4401 Hot Springs Dr., Greeley, CO 80634-9226 / 970-330-0516

Corry, John, 861 Princeton Ct., Neshanic Station, NJ 08853 / 908-369-8019

Cosmi Americo & Figlio S.N.C., Via Flaminia 307, Ancona, ITALY / 071-888208; FAX: 39-071-887008

Coulston Products, Inc., P.O. Box 30, 201 Ferry St. Suite 212, Easton, PA 18044-0030 / 215-253-0167; or 800-445-9927; FAX: 215-252-1511

Counter Assault, 120 Industrial Court, Kalispell, MT 59901 / 406-257-4740; FAX: 406-257-6674

Country Armourer, The, P.O. Box 308, Ashby, MA 01431-0308 / 508-827-6797; FAX: 508-827-4845

Cousin Bob's Mountain Products, 7119 Ohio River Blvd., Ben Avon, PA 15202 / 412-766-5114; FAX: 412-766-9354

CP Bullets, 1310 Industrial Hwy #5-6, South Hampton, PA 18966 / 215-953-7264; FAX: 215-953-7275

CQB Training, P.O. Box 1739, Manchester, MO 63011

Craftguard, 3624 Logan Ave., Waterloo, IA 50703 / 319-232-2959; FAX: 319-234-0804

Crandall Tool & Machine Co., 19163 21 Mile Rd., Tustin, MI 49688 / 616-829-4430

Creative Craftsman, Inc., The, 95 Highway 29 N., P.O. Box 331, Lawrenceville, GA 30246 / 404-963-2112; FAX: 404-513-9488

Creedmoor Sports, Inc., 3052 Industry St. #103, Oceanside, CA 92054 / 767-757-5529; FAX: 760-757-5558 shoot@creedmoorsports.com www.creedmoorsports.com

Creek Side Metal & Woodcrafters, Fishers Hill, VA 22626 / 703-465-3903

Creighton Audette, 19 Highland Circle, Springfield, VT 05156 / 802-885-2331

Crimson Trace Lasers, 8090 S.W. Cirrus Dr., Beverton, OR 97008 / 800-442-2406; FAX: 503-627-0166 www.crimsontrace.com

Crit'R Call (See Rocky Mountain Wildlife Products)

Crosman Airguns, Rts. 5 and 20, E. Bloomfield, NY 14443 / 716-657-6161; FAX: 716-657-5405

Crosman Blades (See Coleman Co., Inc.)

Crouse's Country Cover, P.O. Box 160, Storrs, CT 06268 / 860-423-8736

CRR, Inc./Marble's Inc., 420 Industrial Park, P.O. Box 111, Gladstone, MI 49837 / 906-428-3710; FAX: 906-428-3711

Crucelegui, Hermanos (See U.S. Importer-Mandall)

Cubic Shot Shell Co., Inc., 98 Fatima Dr., Campbell, OH 44405 / 330-755-0349

Cullity Restoration, 209 Old Country Rd., East Sandwich, MA 02537 / 508-888-1147

Cumberland Arms, 514 Shafer Road, Manchester, TN 37355 / 800-797-8414

Cumberland Mountain Arms, P.O. Box 710, Winchester, TN 37398 / 615-967-8414; FAX: 615-967-9199

Cummings Bullets, 1417 Esperanza Way, Escondido, CA 92027

Cupp, Alana, Custom Engraver, P.O. Box 207, Annabella, UT 84711 / 801-896-4834

Curly Maple Stock Blanks (See Tiger-Hunt)

Curtis Cast Bullets, 527 W. Babcock St., Bozeman, MT 59715 / 406-587-8117; FAX: 406-587-8117

Curtis Gun Shop (See Curtis Cast Bullets)

Custom Bullets by Hoffman, 2604 Peconic Ave., Seaford, NY 11783

Custom Calls, 607 N. 5th St., Burlington, IA 52601 / 319-752-4465

Custom Checkering Service, Kathy Forster, 2124 S.E. Yamhill St., Portland, OR 97214 / 503-236-5874

Custom Firearms (See Ahrends, Kim)

Custom Products (See Jones Custom Products)

Custom Shop, The, 890 Cochrane Crescent, Peterborough, ON K9H 5N3 CANADA / 705-742-6693

Custom Single Shot Rifles, 9651 Meadows Lane, Guthrie, OK 73044 / 405-282-3634

Custom Tackle and Ammo, P.O. Box 1886, Farmington, NM 87499 / 505-632-3539

Cutco Cutlery, P.O. Box 810, Olean, NY 14760 / 716-372-3111

CVA, 5988 Peachtree Corners East, Norcross, GA 30071 / 770-449-4687; FAX: 770-242-8546 info@cva.com www.cva.com

Cylinder & Slide, Inc., William R. Laughridge, 245 E. 4th St., Fremont, NE 68025 / 402-721-4277; FAX: 402-721-0263 bill@cylinder-slide.com www.clinder-slide.com

CZ USA, P.O. Box 171073, Kansas City, KS 66117 / 913-321-1811; FAX: 913-321-4901

D

D&D Gunsmiths, Ltd., 363 E. Elmwood, Troy, MI 48083 / 248-583-1512; FAX: 248-583-1524

D&G Precision Duplicators (See Greenwood Precision)

D&H Precision Tooling, 7522 Barnard Mill Rd., Ringwood, IL 60072 / 815-653-4011

D&L Industries (See D.J. Marketing)

D&L Sports, P.O. Box 651, Gillette, WY 82717 / 307-686-4008

D.C.C. Enterprises, 259 Wynburn Ave., Athens, GA 30601

D.J. Marketing, 10602 Horton Ave., Downey, CA 90241 / 310-806-0891; FAX: 310-806-6231

D.L. Unmussig Bullets, 7862 Brentford Dr., Richmond, VA 23225 / 804-320-1165; FAX: 804-320-4587

Dade Screw Machine Products, 2319 N.W. 7th Ave., Miami, FL 33127 / 305-573-5050

Daisy Outdoor Products, P.O. Box 220, Rogers, AR 72757 / 479-636-1200; FAX: 479-636-0573 www.daisy.com

Dakota (See U.S. Importer-EMF Co., Inc.)

Dakota Arms, Inc., 130 Industry Road, Sturgis, SD 57785 / 605-347-4686; FAX: 605-347-4459 info@dakotaarms.com www.dakotaarms.com

Dakota Corp., 77 Wales St., P.O. Box 543, Rutland, VT 05701 / 802-775-6062; or 800-451-4167; FAX: 802-773-3919

Daly, Charles/KBI, P.O. Box 6625, Harrisburg, PA 17112 / 866-DALY GUN

Da-Mar Gunsmith's, Inc., 102 1st St., Solvay, NY 13209

damascususa@inteliport.com, 149 Deans Farm Rd., Tyner, NC 27980 / 252-221-2010; FAX: 252-221-2010 damascususa@inteliport.com www.damascususa.com

Dan Wesson Firearms, 5169 Rt. 12 South, Norwich, NY 13815 / 607-336-1174; FAX: 607-336-2730 danwessonfirearms@citlink.net danwessonfirearms.com

Dangler, Homer L., 2870 Lee Marie Dr., Adrian, MI 49221 / 517-266-1997

MANUFACTURER'S DIRECTORY

Danner Shoe Mfg. Co., 12722 N.E. Airport Way, Portland, OR 97230 / 503-251-1100; or 800-345-0430; FAX: 503-251-1119

Dan's Whetstone Co., Inc., 418 Hilltop Rd., Pearcy, AR 71964 / 501-767-1616; FAX: 501-767-9598 questions@danswhetstone.com www.danswhetstone.com

Danuser Machine Co., 550 E. Third St., P.O. Box 368, Fulton, MO 65251 / 573-642-2246; FAX: 573-642-2240 sales@danuser.com www.danuser.com

Dara-Nes, Inc. (See Nesci Enterprises, Inc.)

D'Arcy Echols & Co., P.O. Box 421, Millville, UT 84326 / 435-755-6842

Darlington Gun Works, Inc., P.O. Box 698, 516 S. 52 Bypass, Darlington, SC 29532 / 803-393-3931

Dart Bell/Brass (See MAST Technology Inc.)

Darwin Hensley Gunmaker, P.O. Box 329, Brightwood, OR 97011 / 503-622-5411

Data Tech Software Systems, 19312 East Eldorado Drive, Aurora, CO 80013

Dave Norin Schrank's Smoke & Gun, 2010 Washington St., Waukegan, IL 60085 / 708-662-4034

Dave's Gun Shop, P.O. Box 2824, Casper, WY 82602-2824 / 307-754-9724

David Clark Co., Inc., P.O. Box 15054, Worcester, MA 01615 / 508-756-6216; FAX: 508-753-5827 sales@davidclark.com www.davidclark.com

David Condon, Inc., 109 E. Washington St., Middleburg, VA 22117 / 703-687-5642

David Miller Co., 3131 E. Greenlee Rd., Tucson, AZ 85716 / 520-326-3117

David R. Chicoine, 1210 Jones Street, Gastonia, NC 28052 / 704-853-0265 bnpress@quik.com www.oldwestgunsmith.com

David W. Schwartz Custom Guns, 2505 Waller St., Eau Claire, WI 54703 / 715-832-1735

Davide Pedersoli and Co., Via Artigiani 57, Gardone VT, Brescia 25063, ITALY / 030-8915000; FAX: 030-8911019 info@davidepedersoli.com www.davide_pedersoli.com

Davis, Don, 1619 Heights, Katy, TX 77493 / 713-391-3090

Davis Industries (See Cobra Enterprises, Inc.)

Davis Products, Mike, 643 Loop Dr., Moses Lake, WA 98837 / 509-765-6178; or 509-766-7281

Daystate Ltd., Birch House Lanee, Cotes Heath Staffs, ST15.022, ENGLAND / 01782-791755; FAX: 01782-791617

Dayton Traister, 4778 N. Monkey Hill Rd., P.O. Box 593, Oak Harbor, WA 98277 / 360-679-4657; FAX: 360-675-1114

D-Boone Ent., Inc., 5900 Colwyn Dr., Harrisburg, PA 17109

Dead Eye's Sport Center, 76 Baer Rd., Shickshinny, PA 18655 / 570-256-7432 deadeyeprizz@aol.com

Deepeeka Exports Pvt. Ltd., D-78, Saket, Meerut-250-006, INDIA / 011-91-121-640363 or ; FAX: 011-91-121-640988 deepeeka@poboxes.com www.deepeeka.com

Defense Training International, Inc., 749 S. Lemay, Ste. A3-337, Ft. Collins, CO 80524 / 303-482-2520; FAX: 303-482-0548

deHaas Barrels, 20049 W. State Hwy. Z, Ridgeway, MO 64481 / 660-872-6308

Del Rey Products, P.O. Box 5134, Playa Del Rey, CA 90296-5134 / 213-823-0494

Delhi Gun House, 1374 Kashmere Gate, New Delhi 110 006, INDIA / 2940974; or 394-0974; FAX: 2917344 dgh@vsnl.com

Delorge, Ed, 6734 W. Main, Houma, LA 70360 / 985-223-0206 delorge@triparish.net www.eddelorge.com

Del-Sports, Inc., Dave Budin, P.O. Box 685, 817 Main St., Margaretville, NY 12455 / 845-586-4103; FAX: 845-586-4105

Delta Arms Ltd., P.O. Box 1000, Delta, VT 84624-1000

Delta Enterprises, 284 Hagemann Drive, Livermore, CA 94550

Delta Frangible Ammunition LLC, P.O. Box 2350, Stafford, VA 22555-2350 / 540-720-5778; or 800-339-1933; FAX: 540-720-5667 dfa@dfanet.com www.dfanet.com

Dem-Bart Checkering Tools, Inc., 1825 Bickford Ave., Snohomish, WA 98290 / 360-568-7356 walt@dembartco.com www.dembartco.com

Denver Instrument Co., 6542 Fig St., Arvada, CO 80004 / 800-321-1135; or 303-431-7255; FAX: 303-423-4831

DeSantis Holster & Leather Goods, Inc., 431 Bayview Ave., Amityville, NY 11701 / 631-841-6300; FAX: 631-841-6320 www.desantisholster.com

Desert Mountain Mfg., P.O. Box 130184, Coram, MT 59913 / 800-477-0762; or 406-387-5361; FAX: 406-387-5361

Detonics USA, 53 Perimeter Center East #200, Atlanta, GA 30346 / 866-759-1169

DGR Custom Rifles, 4191 37th Ave. SE, Tappen, ND 58487 / 701-327-8135

DGS, Inc., Dale A. Storey, 1117 E. 12th, Casper, WY 82601 / 307-237-2414; FAX: 307-237-2414 dalest@trib.com www.dgsrifle.com

DHB Products, 336 River View Dr., Verona, VA 24482-2547 / 703-836-2648

Diamond Machining Technology Inc. (See DMT)

Diamond Mfg. Co., P.O. Box 174, Wyoming, PA 18644 / 800-233-9601

Dibble, Derek A., 555 John Downey Dr., New Britain, CT 06051 / 203-224-2630

Dietz Gun Shop & Range, Inc., 421 Range Rd., New Braunfels, TX 78132 / 210-885-4662

Dilliott Gunsmithing, Inc., 657 Scarlett Rd., Dandridge, TN 37725 / 865-397-9204 gunsmithd@aol.com dilliottgunsmithing.com

Dillon Precision Products, Inc., 8009 East Dillon's Way, Scottsdale, AZ 85260 / 480-948-8009; or 800-762-3845; FAX: 480-998-2786 sales@dillonprecision.com www.dillonprecision.com

Dina Arms Corporation, P.O. Box 46, Royersford, PA 19468 / 610-287-0266; FAX: 610-287-0266

Dixie Gun Works, P.O. Box 130, Union City, TN 38281 / 731-885-0700; FAX: 731-885-0440 info@dixiegunworks.com www.dixiegunworks.com

Dixon Muzzleloading Shop, Inc., 9952 Kunkels Mill Rd., Kempton, PA 19529 / 610-756-6271 dixonmuzzleloading.com

DKT, Inc., 14623 Vera Dr., Union, MI 49130-9744 / 800-741-7083 orders; FAX: 616-641-2015

DLO Mfg., 10807 SE Foster Ave., Arcadia, FL 33821-7304

DMT-Diamond Machining Technology, Inc., 85 Hayes Memorial Dr., Marlborough, MA 01752 FAX: 508-485-3924

Dohring Bullets, 100 W. 8 Mile Rd., Ferndale, MI 48220

Dolbare, Elizabeth, P.O. Box 502, Dubois, WY 82513-0502 / 307-450-7500 edolbare@hotmail.com www.scrimshaw-engraving.com

Domino, P.O. Box 108, 20019 Settimo Milanese, Milano, ITALY / 1-39-2-33512040; FAX: 1-39-2-33511587

Don Klein Custom Guns, 433 Murray Park Dr., Ripon, WI 54971 / 920-748-2931 daklein@charter.net www.donkleincustomguns.com

Donnelly, C. P., 405 Kubli Rd., Grants Pass, OR 97527 / 541-846-6604

Doskocil Mfg. Co., Inc., P.O. Box 1246, 4209 Barnett, Arlington, TX 76017 / 817-467-5116; FAX: 817-472-9810

Douglas Barrels, Inc., 5504 Big Tyler Rd., Charleston, WV 25313-1398 / 304-776-1341; FAX: 304-776-8560 www.benchrest.com/douglas

Downsizer Corp., P.O. Box 710316, Santee, CA 92072-0316 / 619-448-5510 www.downsizer.com

DPMS (Defense Procurement Manufacturing Services, Inc.), 13983 Industry Ave., Becker, MN 55308 / 800-578-DPMS; or 763-261-5600; FAX: 763-261-5599

Dr. O's Products Ltd., P.O. Box 111, Niverville, NY 12130 / 518-784-3333; FAX: 518-784-2800

Drain, Mark, SE 3211 Kamilche Point Rd., Shelton, WA 98584 / 206-426-5452

Dremel Mfg. Co., 4915-21st St., Racine, WI 53406

Dri-Slide, Inc., 411 N. Darling, Fremont, MI 49412 / 616-924-3950

Dropkick, 1460 Washington Blvd., Williamsport, PA 17701 / 717-326-6561; FAX: 717-326-4950

DS Arms, Inc., P.O. Box 370, 27 West 990 Industrial Ave., Barrington, IL 60010 / 847-277-7258; FAX: 847-277-7259 www.dsarms.com

DTM International, Inc., 40 Joslyn Rd., P.O. Box 5, Lake Orion, MI 48362 / 313-693-6670

Duane A. Hobbie Gunsmithing, 2412 Pattie Ave., Wichita, KS 67216 / 316-264-8266

Duane's Gun Repair (See DGR Custom Rifles)

Dubber, Michael W., P.O. Box 312, Evansville, IN 47702 / 812-424-9000; FAX: 812-424-6551

Duffy, Charles E. (See Guns Antique & Modern DBA), Williams Ln., P.O. Box 2, West Hurley, NY 12491 / 914-679-2997

Du-Lite Corp., 171 River Rd., Middletown, CT 06457 / 203-347-2505; FAX: 203-347-9404

Dumoulin, Ernest, Rue Florent Boclinville 8-10, 13-4041, Votten, BELGIUM / 41 27 78 92

Duncan's Gun Works, Inc., 1619 Grand Ave., San Marcos, CA 92069 / 760-727-0515

DunLyon R&D, Inc., 52151 E. U.S. Hwy. 60, Miami, AZ 85539 / 928-473-9027

Duofold, Inc., RD 3 Rt. 309, Valley Square Mall, Tamaqua, PA 18252 / 717-386-2666; FAX: 717-386-3652

Dybala Gun Shop, P.O. Box 1024, FM 3156, Bay City, TX 77414 / 409-245-0866

Dykstra, Doug, 411 N. Darling, Fremont, MI 49412 / 616-924-3950

Dynalite Products, Inc., 215 S. Washington St., Greenfield, OH 45123 / 513-981-2124

Dynamit Nobel-RWS, Inc., 81 Ruckman Rd., Closter, NJ 07624 / 201-767-7971; FAX: 201-767-1589

E

E&L Mfg., Inc., 4177 Riddle Bypass Rd., Riddle, OR 97469 / 541-874-2137; FAX: 541-874-3107

E. Arthur Brown Co. Inc., 4353 Hwy. 27 E., Alexandria, MN 56308 / 320-762-8847; FAX: 320-763-4310 www.eabco.com

E.A.A. Corp., P.O. Box 1299, Sharpes, FL 32959 / 407-639-4842; or 800-536-4442; FAX: 407-639-7006

Eagan, Donald V., P.O. Box 196, Benton, PA 17814 / 717-925-6134

Eagle Arms, Inc. (See ArmaLite, Inc.)

Eagle Grips, Eagle Business Center, 460 Randy Rd., Carol Stream, IL 60188 / 800-323-6144; or 708-260-0400; FAX: 708-260-0486

Eagle Imports, Inc., 1750 Brielle Ave., Unit B1, Wanamassa, NJ 07712 / 732-493-0333; FAX: 732-493-0301 gsodini@aol.com www.bersa-llama.com

E-A-R, Inc., Div. of Cabot Safety Corp., 5457 W. 79th St., Indianapolis, IN 46268 / 800-327-3431; FAX: 800-488-8007

EAW (See U.S. Importer-New England Custom Gun Serv

Eckelman Gunsmithing, 3125 133rd St. SW, Fort Ripley, MN 56449 / 218-829-3176

Ed Brown Products, Inc., P.O. Box 492, Perry, MO 63462 / 573-565-3261; FAX: 573-565-2791 edbrown@edbrown.com www.edbrown.com

Edenpine, Inc. c/o Six Enterprises, Inc., 320 D Turtle Creek Ct., San Jose, CA 95125 / 408-999-0201; FAX: 408-999-0216

EdgeCraft Corp., S. Weiner, 825 Southwood Rd., Avondale, PA 19311 / 610-268-0500; or 800-342-3255; FAX: 610-268-3545 www.edgecraft.com

Edmisten Co., P.O. Box 1293, Boone, NC 28607

Edmund Scientific Co., 101 E. Gloucester Pike, Barrington, NJ 08033 / 609-543-6250

Ed's Gun House, Ed Kukowski, P.O. Box 62, Minnesota City, MN 55959 / 507-689-2925

Effebi SNC-Dr. Franco Beretta, via Rossa, 4, 25062, ITALY / 030-2751955; FAX: 030-2180414

Eggleston, Jere D., 400 Saluda Ave., Columbia, SC 29205 / 803-799-3402

Eichelberger Bullets, Wm., 158 Crossfield Rd., King Of Prussia, PA 19406

Ekol Leather Care, P.O. Box 2652, West Lafayette, IN 47906 / 317-463-2250; FAX: 317-463-7004

El Paso Saddlery Co., P.O. Box 27194, El Paso, TX 79926 / 915-544-2233; FAX: 915-544-2535 info@epsaddlery.com www.epsaddlery.com

Electro Prismatic Collimators, Inc., 1441 Manatt St., Lincoln, NE 68521

Electronic Shooters Protection, Inc., 15290 Gadsden Ct., Brighton, CO 80603 / 800-797-7791; FAX: 303-659-8668 esp@usa.net espamerican.com

Eley Ltd., Selco Way Minworth Industrial Estate, Minworth Sutton Coldfield, West Midlands, B76 1BA ENGLAND / 44 0 121-313-4567; FAX: 44 0 121-313-4568 www.eley.co.uk

Elite Ammunition, P.O. Box 3251, Oakbrook, IL 60522 / 708-366-9006

Ellett Bros., 267 Columbia Ave., P.O. Box 128, Chapin, SC 29036 / 803-345-3751; or 800-845-3711; FAX: 803-345-1820 www.ellettbrothers.com

Ellicott Arms, Inc. / Woods Pistolsmithing, 8390 Sunset Dr., Ellicott City, MD 21043 / 410-465-7979

EMAP USA, 6420 Wilshire Blvd., Los Angeles, CA 90048 / 213-782-2000; FAX: 213-782-2867

Emerging Technologies, Inc. (See Laseraim Technologies, Inc.)

EMF Co. Inc., 1900 E. Warner Ave., Suite 1-D, Santa Ana, CA 92705 / 949-261-6611; FAX: 949-756-0133

MANUFACTURER'S DIRECTORY

Empire Cutlery Corp., 12 Kruger Ct., Clifton, NJ 07013 / 201-472-5155; FAX: 201-779-0759
Empire Rifles, P.O. Box 406, Meriden, NH 03770 info@empirerifles.com www.empirerifles.com
English, Inc., A.G., 708 S. 12th St., Broken Arrow, OK 74012 / 918-251-3399 www.agenglish.com
Engraving Artistry, 36 Alto Rd., Burlington, CT 06013 / 860-673-6837 bobburt44@hotmail.com
Enguix Import-Export, Alpujarras 58, Alzira, Valencia, SPAIN / (96) 241 43 95; FAX: (96) 241 43 95
Enhanced Presentations, Inc., 5929 Market St., Wilmington, NC 28405 / 910-799-1622; FAX: 910-799-5004
Enlow, Charles, Box 895, Beaver, OK 73932 / 405-625-4487
Ensign-Bickford Co., The, 660 Hopmeadow St., Simsbury, CT 06070
Entreprise Arms, Inc., 5321 Irwindale Ave., Irwindale, CA 91706 / 626-962-8712; FAX: 626-962-4692 www.entreprise.com
EPC, 1441 Manatt St., Lincoln, NE 68521 / 402-476-3946
Erhardt, Dennis, 4508 N. Montana Ave., Helena, MT 59602 / 406-442-4533
Essex Arms, P.O. Box 363, Island Pond, VT 05846 / 802-723-6203; FAX: 802-723-6203
Estate Cartridge, Inc., 900 Bob Ehlen Dr., Anoka, MN 55303-7502 / 409-856-7277; FAX: 409-856-5486
Euber Bullets, No. Orwell Rd., Orwell, VT 05760 / 802-948-2621
Euroarms of America, Inc., P.O. Box 3277, Winchester, VA 22604 / 540-662-1863; FAX: 540-662-4464 www.euroarms.net
Euro-Imports, 2221 Upland Ave. S., Pahrump, NV 89048 / 775-751-6671; FAX: 775-751-6671
European American Armory Corp. (See E.A.A. Corp.)
Eversull Co., Inc., 1 Tracemont, Boyce, LA 71409 / 318-793-8728; FAX: 318-793-5483 bestguns@aol.com
Evolution Gun Works, Inc., 48 Belmont Ave., Quakertown, PA 18951-1347 www.egw-guns.com
Excalibur Electro Optics, Inc., P.O. Box 400, Fogelsville, PA 18051-0400 / 610-391-9105; FAX: 610-391-9220
Excalibur Publications, P.O. Box 89667, Tucson, AZ 85752 / 520-575-9057 excalibureditor@earthlink.net
Excel Industries, Inc., 4510 Carter Ct., Chino, CA 91710 / 909-627-2404; FAX: 909-627-7817
Executive Protection Institute, P.O. Box 802, Berryville, VA 22611 / 540-554-2540; FAX: 540-554-2558 ruk@crosslink.net www.personalprotecion.com
Eze-Lap Diamond Prods., P.O. Box 2229, 15164 W. State St., Westminster, CA 92683 / 714-847-1555; FAX: 714-897-0280
E-Z-Way Systems, P.O. Box 4310, Newark, OH 43058-4310 / 614-345-6645; or 800-848-2072; FAX: 614-345-6600

F

F&W Publications, Inc., 700 E. State St., Iola, WI 54990 / 715-445-2214; FAX: 715-445-4087
F.A.I.R., Via Gitti, 41, 25060 Marcheno Bresc, ITALY / 030 861162-8610344; FAX: 030 8610179 info@fair.it www.fair.it
Fabarm S.p.A., Via Averolda 31, 25039 Travagliato, Brescia, ITALY / 030-6863629; FAX: 030-6863684 info@fabarm.com www.fabarm.com
Fagan Arms, 22952 15 Mile Rd., Clinton Township, MI 48035 / 810-465-4637; FAX: 810-792-6996
Faith Associates, P.O. Box 549, Flat Rock, NC 28731-0549 FAX: 828-697-6827
Falcon Industries, Inc., P.O. Box 1690, Edgewood, NM 87015 / 505-281-3783; FAX: 505-281-3991 shines@ergogrips.net www.ergogrips.net
Far North Outfitters, Box 1252, Bethel, AK 99559
Farm Form Decoys, Inc., 1602 Biovu, P.O. Box 748, Galveston, TX 77553 / 409-744-0762; or 409-765-6361; FAX: 409-765-8513
Farr Studio, Inc., 17149 Bournbrook Ln., Jeffersonton, VA 22724-1796 / 615-638-8825
Farrar Tool Co., Inc., 11855 Cog Hill Dr., Whittier, CA 90601-1902 / 310-863-4367; FAX: 310-863-5123
Faulhaber Wildlocker, Dipl.-Ing. Norbert Wittasek, Seilergasse 2, A-1010 Wien, AUSTRIA / 43-1-5137001; FAX: 43-1-5137001 faulhaber1@utanet.at
Faulk's Game Call Co., Inc., 616 18th St., Lake Charles, LA 70601 / 337-436-9726; FAX: 337-494-7205
Faust Inc., T. G., 544 Minor St., Reading, PA 19602 / 610-375-8549; FAX: 610-375-4488
Fautheree, Andy, P.O. Box 4607, Pagosa Springs, CO 81157 / 970-731-5003; FAX: 970-731-5009

Feather, Flex Decoys, 4500 Doniphan Dr., Neosho, MO 64850 / 318-746-8596; FAX: 318-742-4815
Federal Cartridge Co., 900 Ehlen Dr., Anoka, MN 55303 / 612-323-2300; FAX: 612-323-2506
Federal Champion Target Co., 232 Industrial Pkwy., Richmond, IN 47374 / 800-441-4971; FAX: 317-966-7747
Federated-Fry (See Fry Metals)
FEG, Budapest, Soroksariut 158, H-1095, HUNGARY
Feinwerkbau Westinger & Altenburger, Neckarstrasse 43, 78727, Oberndorf a. N., GERMANY / 07423-814-0; FAX: 07423-814-200 info@feinwerkbau.de www.feinwerkbau.de
Felk Pistols, Inc., P.O. Box 33, Bracey, VA 23919 / 434-636-2537; FAX: 208-988-4834
Ferguson, Bill, P.O. Box 1238, Sierra Vista, AZ 85636 / 520-458-5321; FAX: 520-458-9125
Ferguson, Bill. See: BULLET METALS
FERLIB, Via Parte 33 Marcheno/BS, Marcheno/BS, ITALY / 00390308610191; FAX: 00390308966882 info@ferlib.com www.ferlib.com
Ferris Firearms, 7110 F.M. 1863, Bulverde, TX 78163 / 210-980-4424
Fibron Products, Inc., P.O. Box 430, Buffalo, NY 14209-0430 / 716-886-2378; FAX: 716-886-2394
Fieldsport Ltd., Bryan Bilinski, 3313 W. South Airport Rd., Traverse City, MI 49684 / 616-933-0767
Fiocchi Munizioni S.A. (See U.S. Importer-Fiocch
Fiocchi of America, Inc., 5030 Fremont Rd., Ozark, MO 65721 / 417-725-4118; or 800-721-2666; FAX: 417-725-1039
Firearm Brokers, 4143 Taylor Blvd., Louisville, KY 40215 / 502-366-0555 firearmbrokers@aol.com www.firearmbrokers.com
Firearm Training Center, The, 9555 Blandville Rd., West Paducah, KY 42086 / 502-554-5886
Firearms Co. Ltd. / Alpine (See U.S. Importer-Mandall
Firearms Engraver's Guild of America, 3011 E. Pine Dr., Flagstaff, AZ 86004 / 928-527-8427 fegainfo@fega.com
Fisher, Jerry A., 631 Crane Mt. Rd., Big Fork, MT 59911 / 406-837-2722
Fisher Custom Firearms, 2199 S. Kittredge Way, Aurora, CO 80013 / 303-755-3710
Fitzgerald, Jack. See: CLENZOIL WORLDWIDE CORP.
Flambeau, Inc., 15981 Valplast Rd., Middlefield, OH 44062 / 216-632-1631; FAX: 216-632-1581 www.flambeau.com
Flayderman & Co., Inc., P.O. Box 2446, Fort Lauderdale, FL 33303 / 954-761-8855 www.flayderman.com
Fleming Firearms, 7720 E. 126th St. N., Collinsville, OK 74021-7016 / 918-665-3624
Fletcher-Bidwell, LLC, 305 E. Terhune St., Viroqua, WI 54665-1631 / 866-637-1860 fbguns@netscape.net
Flintlocks, Etc., 160 Rossiter Rd., P.O. Box 181, Richmond, MA 01254 / 413-698-3822; FAX: 413-698-3866 flintetc@berkshire.rr.com
Flitz International Ltd., 821 Mohr Ave., Waterford, WI 53185 / 414-534-5898; FAX: 414-534-2991
Fluoramics, Inc., 18 Industrial Ave., Mahwah, NJ 07430 / 800-922-0075; FAX: 201-825-7035
Flynn's Custom Guns, P.O. Box 7461, Alexandria, LA 71306 / 318-455-7130
FN Manufacturing, P.O. Box 24257, Columbia, SC 29224 / 803-736-0522
Folks, Donald E., 205 W. Lincoln St., Pontiac, IL 61764 / 815-844-7901
Foothills Video Productions, Inc., P.O. Box 651, Spartanburg, SC 29304 / 803-573-7023; or 800-782-5358
Foredom Electric Co., Rt. 6, 16 Stony Hill Rd., Bethel, CT 06801 / 203-792-8622
Forgett, Valmore. See: NAVY ARMS COMPANY
Forgreens Tool & Mfg., Inc., P.O. Box 955, Robert Lee, TX 76945 / 915-453-2800; FAX: 915-453-2460
Forkin Custom Classics, 205 10th Ave. S.W., White Sulphur Spring, MT 59645 / 406-547-2344
Forrest Tool Co., P.O. Box 768, 44380 Gordon Ln., Mendocino, CA 95460 / 707-937-2141; FAX: 717-937-1817
Forster, Kathy (See Custom Checkering)
Forster, Larry L., Box 212, 216 Hwy. 13 E., Gwinner, ND 58040-0212 / 701-678-2475
Forster Products, Inc., 310 E. Lanark Ave., Lanark, IL 61046 / 815-493-6360; FAX: 815-493-2371 info@forsterproducts.com www.forsterproductscom
Fort Hill Gunstocks, 12807 Fort Hill Rd., Hillsboro, OH 45133 / 513-466-2763
Fort Knox Security Products, 1051 N. Industrial Park Rd., Orem, UT 84057 / 801-224-7233; or 800-821-5216; FAX: 801-226-5493

Forthofer's Gunsmithing & Knifemaking, 5535 U.S. Hwy. 93S, Whitefish, MT 59937-8411 / 406-862-2674
Fortune Products, Inc., 205 Hickory Creek Rd., Marble Falls, TX 78654 / 210-693-6111; FAX: 210-693-6394 randy@accusharp.com
Forty-Five Ranch Enterprises, Box 1080, Miami, OK 74355-1080 / 918-542-5875
Foster, . See: ACCURACY INTERNATIONAL
Fountain Products, 492 Prospect Ave., West Springfield, MA 01089 / 413-781-4651; FAX: 413-733-8217
Fowler Bullets, 806 Dogwood Dr., Gastonia, NC 28054 / 704-867-3259
Fowler, Bob (See Black Powder Products)
Fox River Mills, Inc., P.O. Box 298, 227 Poplar St., Osage, IA 50461 / 515-732-3798; FAX: 515-732-5128
Frank Knives, 13868 NW Keleka Pl., Seal Rock, OR 97376 / 541-563-3041; FAX: 541-563-3041
Frank Mittermeier, Inc., P.O. Box 1, Bronx, NY 10465
Franzen International, Inc. (See U.S. Importer-Importer Co.)
Fred F. Wells/Wells Sport Store, 110 N. Summit St., Prescott, AZ 86301 / 928-445-3655 www.wellssportstore@cableone.net
Freedom Arms, Inc., P.O. Box 150, Freedom, WY 83120 / 307-883-2468; FAX: 307-883-2005
Fremont Tool Works, 1214 Prairie, Ford, KS 67842 / 316-369-2327
Front Sight Firearms Training Institute, P.O. Box 2619, Aptos, CA 95001 / 800-987-7719; FAX: 408-684-2137
Frontier, 2910 San Bernardo, Laredo, TX 78040 / 956-723-5409; FAX: 956-723-1774
Frontier Arms Co., Inc., 401 W. Rio Santa Cruz, Green Valley, AZ 85614-3932
Frontier Products Co., 2401 Walker Rd., Roswell, NM 88201-8950 / 614-262-9357
Frontier Safe Co., 3201 S. Clinton St., Fort Wayne, IN 46806 / 219-744-7233; FAX: 219-744-6678
Frost Cutlery Co., P.O. Box 22636, Chattanooga, TN 37422 / 615-894-6079; FAX: 615-894-9576
Fry Metals, 4100 6th Ave., Altoona, PA 16602 / 814-946-1611
Fujinon, Inc., 10 High Point Dr., Wayne, NJ 07470 / 201-633-5600; FAX: 201-633-5216
Fullmer, Geo. M., 2499 Mavis St., Oakland, CA 94601 / 510-533-4193
Fulton Armory, 8725 Bollman Place No. 1, Savage, MD 20763 / 301-490-9485; FAX: 301-490-9547 www.fulton.armory.com
Furr Arms, 91 N. 970 West, Orem, UT 84057 / 801-226-3877; FAX: 801-226-3877

G

G&H Decoys, Inc., P.O. Box 1208, Hwy. 75 North, Henryetta, OK 74437 / 918-652-3314; FAX: 918-652-3400
G.C. Bullet Co., Inc., 40 Mokelumne River Dr., Lodi, CA 95240
G.G. & G., 3602 E. 42nd Stravenue, Tucson, AZ 85713 / 520-748-7167; FAX: 520-748-7583 ggg&3@aol.com www.ggg&3.com
G.H. Enterprises Ltd., Bag 10, Okotoks, AB T0L 1T0 CANADA / 403-938-6070
G.U., Inc. (See U.S. Importer-New SKB Arms Co.)
G96 Products Co., Inc., 85 5th Ave., Bldg. #6, Paterson, NJ 07544 / 973-684-4050; FAX: 973-684-3848 g96prod@aol
Gage Manufacturing, 663 W. 7th St., A, San Pedro, CA 90731 / 310-832-3546
Gaillard Barrels, Box 68, St. Brieux, SK S0K 3V0 CANADA / 306-752-3769; FAX: 306-752-5969
Galati International, P.O. Box 10, 616 Burley Ridge Rd., Wesco, MO 65586 / 636-584-0785; FAX: 573-775-4308 support@galatiinternational.com www.galatiinternational.com
Galaxy Imports Ltd., Inc., P.O. Box 3361, Victoria, TX 77903 / 361-573-4867; FAX: 361-576-9622 galaxy@cox-internet.com
GALCO International Ltd., 2019 W. Quail Ave., Phoenix, AZ 85027 / 623-474-7070; FAX: 623-582-6854 customerservice@usgalco.com www.usgalco.com
Galena Industries AMT, 5463 Diaz St., Irwindale, CA 91706 / 626-856-8883; FAX: 626-856-8878
Gamba S.p.A. Societa Armi Bresciane Srl, Renato, Via Artigiani 93, ITALY / 30-8911640; FAX: 30-8911648
Gamba, USA, P.O. Box 60452, Colorado Springs, CO 80960 / 719-578-1145; FAX: 719-444-0731
Game Haven Gunstocks, 13750 Shire Rd., Wolverine, MI 49799 / 616-525-8257

MANUFACTURER'S DIRECTORY

Gamebore Division, Polywad, Inc., P.O. Box 7916, Macon, GA 31209 / 478-477-0669; or 800-998-0669

Gamo (See U.S. Importers-Arms United Corp., Daisy M

Gamo USA, Inc., 3911 SW 47th Ave., Suite 914, Fort Lauderdale, FL 33314 / 954-581-5822; FAX: 954-581-3165 gamousa@gate.net www.gamo.com

Gander Mountain, Inc., 12400 Fox River Rd., Wilmont, WI 53192 / 414-862-6848

GAR, 590 McBride Ave., West Paterson, NJ 07424 / 973-754-1114; FAX: 973-754-1114 garreloading@aol.com www.garreloading.com

Garcia National Gun Traders, Inc., 225 SW 22nd Ave., Miami, FL 33135 / 305-642-2355

Garrett Cartridges, Inc., P.O. Box 178, Chehalis, WA 98532 / 360-736-0702 www.garrettcartridges.com

Garthwaite Pistolsmith, Inc., Jim, 12130 State Route 405, Watsontown, PA 17777 / 570-538-1566; FAX: 570-538-2965 www.garthwaite.com

Gary Goudy Classic Stocks, 1512 S. 5th St., Dayton, WA 99328 / 509-382-2726 goudy@innw.net

Gary Reeder Custom Guns, 2601 7th Ave. E., Flagstaff, AZ 86004 / 928-526-3313; FAX: 928-527-0840 gary@reedercustomguns.com www.reedercustomguns.com

Gator Guns & Repair, 7952 Kenai Spur Hwy., Kenai, AK 99611-8311

Gaucher Armes, S.A., 46 rue Desjoyaux, 42000, Saint-Etienne, FRANCE / 04-77-33-38-92; FAX: 04-77-61-95-72

GDL Enterprises, 409 Le Gardeur, Slidell, LA 70460 / 504-649-0693

Gehmann, Walter (See Huntington Die Specialties)

Genco, P.O. Box 5704, Asheville, NC 28803

Genecco Gun Works, 10512 Lower Sacramento Rd., Stockton, CA 95210 / 209-951-0706; FAX: 209-931-3872

Gene's Custom Guns, P.O. Box 10534, White Bear Lake, MN 55110 / 651-429-5105; FAX: 651-429-7365

Gentex Corp., 5 Tinkham Ave., Derry, NH 03038 / 603-434-0311; FAX: 603-434-3002 sales@derry.gentexcorp.com www.derry.gentexcorp.com

Gentner Bullets, 109 Woodlawn Ave., Upper Darby, PA 19082 / 610-352-9396 dongentner@rcn.com www.gentnerbullets.com

Gentry Custom LLC, 314 N. Hoffman, Belgrade, MT 59714 / 406-388-GUNS gentryshop@earthlink.net www.gentrycustom.com

George & Roy's, P.O. Box 2125, Sisters, OR 97759-2125 / 503-228-5424; or 800-553-3022; FAX: 503-225-9409

George Hoenig, 6521 Morton Dr., Boise, ID 83704 / 208-375-1116; FAX: 208-375-1116

George Ibberson (Sheffield) Ltd., 25-31 Allen St., Sheffield, S3 7AW ENGLAND / 0114-2766123; FAX: 0114-2738465 sales@eggintongroupco.uk www.eggintongroup.co.uk

Gerber Legendary Blades, 14200 SW 72nd Ave., Portland, OR 97223 / 503-639-6161; or 800-950-6161; FAX: 503-684-7008

Gervais, Mike, 3804 S. Cruise Dr., Salt Lake City, UT 84109 / 801-277-7729

Getz Barrel Company, P.O. Box 88, 426 E. Market St., Beavertown, PA 17813 / 570-658-7263; FAX: 570-658-4110 www.getzbrl.com

Giacomo Sporting USA, 6234 Stokes Lee Center Rd., Lee Center, NY 13363

Gibbs Rifle Co., Inc., 219 Lawn St., Martinsburg, WV 25401 / 304-262-1651; FAX: 304-262-1658 support@gibbsrifle.com www.gibbsrifle.com

Gil Hebard Guns, Inc., 125 Public Square, Knoxville, IL 61448 / 309-289-2700; FAX: 309-289-2233

Gilbert Equipment Co., Inc., 960 Downtowner Rd., Mobile, AL 36609 / 205-344-3322

Gillmann, Edwin, 33 Valley View Dr., Hanover, PA 17331 / 717-632-1662 gillmaned@superpa.net

Gilmore Sports Concepts, Inc., 5949 S. Garnett Rd., Tulsa, OK 74146 / 918-250-3810; FAX: 918-250-3845 info@gilmoresports.com www.gilmoresports.com

Glacier Glove, 4890 Aircenter Circle, Suite 210, Reno, NV 89502 / 702-825-8225; FAX: 702-825-6544

Glaser LLC, P.O. Box 173, Sturgis, SD 57785 / 605-347-4544; or 800-221-3489; FAX: 605-347-5055 email@corbon.com www.safetyslug.com

Glaser Safety Slug, Inc., P.O. Box 8223, Foster City, CA 94404 / 800-221-3489; FAX: 510-785-6685 safetyslug.com

Glass, Herb, P.O. Box 25, Bullville, NY 10915 / 914-361-3021

Glimm, Jerome. See: GLIMM'S CUSTOM GUN ENGRAVING

Glimm's Custom Gun Engraving, Jerome C. Glimm, 19 S. Maryland, Conrad, MT 59425 / 406-278-3574 jandlglimm@mcn.net www.gunengraver.biz

Glock GmbH, P.O. Box 50, A-2232, Deutsch, Wagram, AUSTRIA

Glock, Inc., P.O. Box 369, Smyrna, GA 30081 / 770-432-1202; FAX: 770-433-8719

Glynn Scobey Duck & Goose Calls, Rt. 3, Box 37, Newbern, TN 38059 / 731-643-6128

GML Products, Inc., 394 Laredo Dr., Birmingham, AL 35226 / 205-979-4867

Goens, Dale W., P.O. Box 224, Cedar Crest, NM 87008 / 505-281-5419

Goergen's Gun Shop, Inc., 17985 538th Ave., Austin, MN 55912 / 507-433-9280

GOEX, Inc., P.O. Box 659, Doyline, LA 71023-0659 / 318-382-9300; FAX: 318-382-9303 mfahringer@goexpowder.com www.goexpowder.com

Golden Age Arms Co., 115 E. High St., Ashley, OH 43003 / 614-747-2488

Golden Bear Bullets, 3065 Fairfax Ave., San Jose, CA 95148 / 408-238-9515

Gonic Arms North American Arms, Inc., 134 Flagg Rd., Gonic, NH 03839 / 603-332-8456; or 603-332-8457

Goodling's Gunsmithing, 1950 Stoverstown Rd., Spring Grove, PA 17362 / 717-225-3350

Goodwin, Fred. See: GOODWIN'S GUNS

Goodwin's Guns, Fred Goodwin, Silver Ridge, ME 04776 / 207-365-4451

Gotz Bullets, 11426 Edgemere Ter., Roscoe, IL 61073-8232

Gould & Goodrich Leather, Inc., 709 E. McNeil St., Lillington, NC 27546 / 910-893-2071; FAX: 910-893-4742 info@gouldusa.com www.gouldusa.com

Gournet Artistic Engraving, Geoffroy Gournet, 820 Paxinosa Ave., Easton, PA 18042 / 610-559-0710 www.geoffroygournet.com

Gournet, Geoffroy. See: GOURNET ARTISTIC ENGRAVING

Grace, Charles E., 718 E. 2nd, Trinidad, CO 81082 / 719-846-9435 chuckgrace@sensonics.org

Grace Metal Products, P.O. Box 67, Elk Rapids, MI 49629 / 616-264-8133

Graf & Sons, 4050 S. Clark St., Mexico, MO 65265 / 573-581-2266; FAX: 573-581-2875 customerservice@grafs.com www.grafs.com

Grand Slam Hunting Products, Box 121, 25454 Military Rd., Cascade, MD 21719 / 301-241-4900; FAX: 301-241-4900 rlj6call@aol.com

Granite Mountain Arms, Inc., 3145 W. Hidden Acres Trail, Prescott, AZ 86305 / 520-541-9758; FAX: 520-445-6826

Grant, Howard V., Hiawatha 15, Woodruff, WI 54568 / 715-356-7146

Graphics Direct, P.O. Box 372421, Reseda, CA 91337-2421 / 818-344-9002

Graves Co., 1800 Andrews Ave., Pompano Beach, FL 33069 / 800-327-9103; FAX: 305-960-0301

Grayback Wildcats, Mike Beeks, 5306 Bryant Ave., Klamath Falls, OR 97603 / 541-884-1072; FAX: 541-884-1072 graybackwildcats@aol.com

Graybill's Gun Shop, 1035 Ironville Pike, Columbia, PA 17512 / 717-684-2739

Great American Gunstock Co., 3420 Industrial Drive, Yuba City, CA 95993 / 800-784-4867; FAX: 530-671-3906 gunstox@hotmail.com www.gunstocks.com

Great Lakes Airguns, 6175 S. Park Ave., Hamburg, NY 14075 / 716-648-6666; FAX: 716-648-6666 www.greatlakesairguns.com

Green, Arthur S., 485 S. Robertson Blvd., Beverly Hills, CA 90211 / 310-274-1283

Green, Roger M., P.O. Box 984, 435 E. Birch, Glenrock, WY 82637 / 307-436-9804

Green Head Game Call Co., RR 1, Box 33, Lacon, IL 61540 / 309-246-2155

Green Mountain Rifle Barrel Co., Inc., P.O. Box 2670, 153 W. Main St., Conway, NH 03818 / 603-447-1095; FAX: 603-447-1099 info@gmriflebarrel.com www.gmriflebarrel.com

Greenwood Precision, P.O. Box 407, Rogersville, MO 65742 / 417-725-2330

Greg Gunsmithing Repair, 3732 26th Ave. N., Robbinsdale, MN 55422 / 612-529-8103

Greg's Superior Products, P.O. Box 46219, Seattle, WA 98146

Greider Precision, 431 Santa Marina Ct., Escondido, CA 92029 / 760-480-8892; FAX: 760-480-9800 greider@msn.com

Gre-Tan Rifles, 29742 W.C.R. 50, Kersey, CO 80644 / 970-353-6176; FAX: 970-356-5940 www.gtrtooling.com

Grier Hard Cast Bullets, P.O. Box 41, Tillamook, OR 97141-0041 / 503-963-8796

Grier's Hard Cast Bullets, 1107 11th St., LaGrande, OR 97850 / 503-963-8796

Griffin & Howe, Inc., 340 W. Putnam Ave., Greenwich, CT 06830 / 203-618-0270 info@griffinhowe.com www.griffinhowe.com

Griffin & Howe, Inc., 33 Claremont Rd., Bernardsville, NJ 07924 / 908-766-2287; FAX: 908-766-1068 info@griffinhowe.com www.griffinhowe.com

Grifon, Inc., 58 Guinam St., Waltham, MS 02154

Groenewold, John. See: JG AIRGUNS, LLC

GRS/Glendo Corp., P.O. Box 1153, 900 Overlander St., Emporia, KS 66801 / 620-343-1084; or 800-836-3519; FAX: 620-343-9640 glendo@glendo.com www.glendo.com

Grulla Arms, Apartado 453, Avda Otaloa 12, Eiber, SPAIN

Gruning Precision, Inc., 7101 Jurupa Ave., No. 12, Riverside, CA 92504 / 909-289-4371; FAX: 909-689-7791 gruningprecision@earthlink.net www.gruningprecision.com

GSI, Inc., 7661 Commerce Ln., Trussville, AL 35173 / 205-655-8299

GTB-Custom Bullets, 482 Comerwood Court, S. San Francisco, CA 94080 / 650-583-1550

Guarasi, Robert. See: WILCOX INDUSTRIES CORP.

Guardsman Products, 411 N. Darling, Fremont, MI 49412 / 616-924-3950

Gun City, 212 W. Main Ave., Bismarck, ND 58501 / 701-223-2304

Gun Doc, Inc., 5405 NW 82nd Ave., Miami, FL 33166 / 305-477-2777; FAX: 305-477-2778 www.gundoc.com

Gun Doctor, The, 435 E. Maple, Roselle, IL 60172 / 708-894-0668

Gun Hunter Books (See Gun Hunter Trading Co.), 5075 Heisig St., Beaumont, TX 77705 / 409-835-3006; FAX: 409-838-2266 gunhuntertrading@hotmail.com

Gun Hunter Trading Co., 5075 Heisig St., Beaumont, TX 77705 / 409-835-3006; FAX: 409-838-2266 gunhuntertrading@hotmail.com

Gun Leather Limited, 116 Lipscomb, Fort Worth, TX 76104 / 817-334-0225; FAX: 800-247-0609

Gun List (See F&W Publications), 700 E. State St., Iola, WI 54990 / 715-445-2214; FAX: 715-445-4087

Gun Room Press, The, 127 Raritan Ave., Highland Park, NJ 08904 / 732-545-4344; FAX: 732-545-6686 gunbooks@rutgersgunbooks.com www.rutgersgunbooks.com

Gun Room, The, 1121 Burlington, Muncie, IN 47302 / 765-282-9073; FAX: 765-282-5270 bshstleguns@aol.com

Gun Shop, The, 62778 Spring Creek Rd., Montrose, CO 81401

Gun Shop, The, 5550 S. 900 East, Salt Lake City, UT 84117 / 801-263-3633

Gun South, Inc. (See GSI, Inc.)

Gun Vault, 7339 E. Acoma Dr., Ste. 7, Scottsdale, AZ 85260 / 602-951-6855

Gun Works, The, 247 S. 2nd St., Springfield, OR 97477 / 541-741-4118; FAX: 541-988-1097 gunworks@worldnet.att.net www.thegunworks.com

Gun-Alert, 1010 N. Maclay Ave., San Fernando, CA 91340 / 818-365-0864; FAX: 818-365-1308

Guncraft Books (See Guncraft Sports, Inc.), 10737 Dutchtown Rd., Knoxville, TN 37932 / 865-966-4545; FAX: 865-966-4500 findit@guncraft.com www.guncraft.com

Guncraft Sports, Inc., 10737 Dutchtown Rd., Knoxville, TN 37932 / 865-966-4545; FAX: 865-966-4500 findit@guncraft.com www.usit.net/guncraft

Guncraft Sports, Inc., Marie C. Wiest, 10737 Dutchtown Rd., Knoxville, TN 37932 / 865-966-4545; FAX: 865-966-4500 findit@guncraft.com www.guncraft.com

Guncrafter Industries, 171 Madison 1510, Huntsville, AR 72740 / 479-665-2466 www.guncrafterindustries.com

Gun-Ho Sports Cases, 110 E. 10th St., St. Paul, MN 55101 / 612-224-9491

Gunline Tools, 2950 Saturn St., "O", Brea, CA 92821 / 714-993-5100; FAX: 714-572-4128

Gunnerman Books, P.O. Box 81697, Rochester Hills, MI 48308 / 248-608-2856 gunnermanbks@att.net

Guns Antique & Modern DBA / Charles E. Duffy, Williams Lane, West Hurley, NY 12491 / 914-679-2997

Guns Div. of D.C. Engineering, Inc., 8633 Southfield Fwy., Detroit, MI 48228 / 313-271-7111; or 800-886-7623;

MANUFACTURER'S DIRECTORY

FAX: 313-271-7112 guns@rifletech.com www.rifletech.com

GUNS Magazine, 12345 World Trade Dr., San Diego, CA 92128-3743 / 619-297-5350; FAX: 619-297-5353

Gunsight, The, 1712 N. Placentia Ave., Fullerton, CA 92631

Gunsite Training Center, P.O. Box 700, Paulden, AZ 86334 / 520-636-4565; FAX: 520-636-1236

Gunsmithing Ltd., 57 Unquowa Rd., Fairfield, CT 06824 / 203-254-0436; FAX: 203-254-1535

Gunsmithing, Inc., 30 W. Buchanan St., Colorado Springs, CO 80907 / 719-632-3795; FAX: 719-632-3493 www.nealsguns.com

Gurney, F. R., Box 13, Sooke, BC V0S 1N0 CANADA / 604-642-5282; FAX: 604-642-7859

H

H&B Forge Co., Rt. 2, Geisinger Rd., Shiloh, OH 44878 / 419-895-1856

H&P Publishing, 7174 Hoffman Rd., San Angelo, TX 76905 / 915-655-5953

H&R 1871.LLC, 60 Industrial Rowe, Gardner, MA 01440 / 508-632-9393; FAX: 508-632-2300 hr1871@hr1871.com www.hr1871.com

H. Krieghoff Gun Co., Boschstrasse 22, D-89079, Ulm, GERMANY / 731-401820; FAX: 731-4018270

H.K.S. Products, 7841 Founion Dr., Florence, KY 41042 / 606-342-7841; or 800-354-9814; FAX: 606-342-5865

H.P. White Laboratory, Inc., 3114 Scarboro Rd., Street, MD 21154 / 410-838-6550; FAX: 410-838-2802 info@hpwhite.com www.hpwhite.com

Hafner World Wide, Inc., P.O. Box 1987, Lake City, FL 32055 / 904-755-6481; FAX: 904-755-6595 hafner@isgroupe.net

Hakko Co. Ltd., 1-13-12, Narimasu, Itabashiku Tokyo, JAPAN / 03-5997-7870/2; FAX: 81-3-5997-7840

Half Moon Rifle Shop, 490 Halfmoon Rd., Columbia Falls, MT 59912 / 406-892-4409 halfmoonrs@centurytel.net

Hall Manufacturing, 142 CR 406, Clanton, AL 35045 / 205-755-4094

Hall Plastics, Inc., John, P.O. Box 1526, Alvin, TX 77512 / 713-489-8709

Hallberg, Fritz. See: CAMBOS OUTDOORSMAN

Hallowell & Co., P.O. Box 1445, Livingston, MT 59047 / 406-222-4770; FAX: 406-222-4792 morris@hallowellco.com www.hallowellco.com

Hally Caller, 443 Wells Rd., Doylestown, PA 18901 / 215-345-6354; FAX: 215-345-6354 info@hallycaller.com www.hallycaller.com

Hamilton, Alex B. (See Ten-Ring Precision, Inc.)

Hammans, Charles E., P.O. Box 788, 2022 McCracken, Stuttgart, AR 72160-0788 / 870-673-1388

Hammerli AG, Industrieplaz, a/Rheinpall, CH-8212 Neuhausen, SWITZERLAND info@hammerli.com www.haemmerliich.com

Hammerli Service-Precision Mac, Rudolf Marent, 9711 Tiltree St., Houston, TX 77075 / 713-946-7028 rmarent@webtv.net

Hammerli USA, 19296 Oak Grove Circle, Groveland, CA 95321 FAX: 209-962-5311

Hammond Custom Guns Ltd., 619 S. Pandora, Gilbert, AZ 85234 / 602-892-3437

HandCrafts Unltd. (See Clements' Custom Leathercraft), 1741 Dallas St., Aurora, CO 80010-2018 / 303-364-0403; FAX: 303-739-9824 gryphons@home.com kuntaoslcat.com

Handgun Press, P.O. Box 406, Glenview, IL 60025 / 847-657-6500; FAX: 847-724-8831 handgunpress@comcast.net

Hank's Gun Shop, Box 370, 50 W. 100 South, Monroe, UT 84754 / 435-527-4456 hanksgs@compuvision.com

Hanned Line, The, 4463 Madoc Way, San Jose, CA 95130 smith@hanned.com www.hanned.com

Hanned Precision (See The Hanned Line)

Hansen & Co., 244-246 Old Post Rd., Southport, CT 06490 / 203-259-6222; FAX: 203-254-3832

Hanson's Gun Center, Dick, 233 Everett Dr., Colorado Springs, CO 80911

Harford (See U.S. Importer-EMF Co., Inc.)

Harper's Custom Stocks, 928 Lombrano St., San Antonio, TX 78207 / 210-732-7174

Harrell's Precision, 5756 Hickory Dr., Salem, VA 24153 / 540-380-2683

Harrington & Richardson (See H&R 1871, Inc.)

Harris Engineering Inc., Dept. GD54, 999 Broadway, Barlow, KY 42024 / 270-334-3633; FAX: 270-334-3000

Harris Enterprises, P.O. Box 105, Bly, OR 97622 / 503-353-2625

Harris Hand Engraving, Paul A., 113 Rusty Ln., Boerne, TX 78006-5746 / 512-391-5121

Harris Publications, 1115 Broadway, New York, NY 10010 / 212-807-7100; FAX: 212-627-4678

Harrison Bullets, 6437 E. Hobart St., Mesa, AZ 85205

Harry Lawson Co., 3328 N. Richey Blvd., Tucson, AZ 85716 / 520-326-1117; FAX: 520-326-1117

Hart & Son, Inc., Robert W., 401 Montgomery St., Nescopeck, PA 18635 / 717-752-3655; FAX: 717-752-1088

Hart Rifle Barrels, Inc., P.O. Box 182, 1690 Apulia Rd., Lafayette, NY 13084 / 315-677-9841; FAX: 315-677-9610 hartrb@aol.com hartbarrels.com

Hartford (See U.S. Importer-EMF Co. Inc.)

Hartmann & Weiss GmbH, Rahlstedter Bahnhofstr. 47, 22143, Hamburg, GERMANY / (40) 677 55 85; FAX: (40) 677 55 92 hartmannundweiss@t-online.de

Harvey, Frank, 218 Nightfall, Terrace, NV 89015 / 702-558-6998

Hastings, P.O. Box 135, Clay Center, KS 67432 / 785-632-3169; FAX: 785-632-6554

Hatfield Gun, 224 N. 4th St., St. Joseph, MO 64501

Hawk Laboratories, Inc. (See Hawk, Inc.), 849 Hawks Bridge Rd., Salem, NJ 08079 / 609-299-2700; FAX: 609-299-2800

Hawk, Inc., 849 Hawks Bridge Rd., Salem, NJ 08079 / 609-299-2700; FAX: 609-299-2800 info@hawkbullets.com www.hawkbullets.com

Hawken Shop, The, P.O. Box 593, Oak Harbor, WA 98277 / 206-679-4657; FAX: 206-675-1114

Hawken Shop, The (See Dayton Traister)

Haydel's Game Calls, Inc., 5018 Hazel Jones Rd., Bossier City, LA 71111 / 318-746-3586; FAX: 318-746-3711 www.haydels.com

Hecht, Hubert J., Waffen-Hecht, P.O. Box 2635, Fair Oaks, CA 95628 / 916-966-1020

Heckler & Koch GmbH, P.O. Box 1329, 78722 Oberndorf, Neckar, GERMANY / 49-7423179-0; FAX: 49-7423179-2406

Heckler & Koch, Inc., 21480 Pacific Blvd., Sterling, VA 20166-8900 / 703-450-1900; FAX: 703-450-8160 www.hecklerkoch-usa.com

Hege Jagd-u. Sporthandels GmbH, P.O. Box 101461, W-7770, Ueberlingen a. Boden, GERMANY

Heidenstrom Bullets, Dalghte 86-3660 Rjukan, 35091818, NORWAY, olau.joh@online.tuo

Heilmann, Stephen, P.O. Box 657, Grass Valley, CA 95945 / 530-272-8758; FAX: 530-274-0285 sheilmann@jps.net www.metalwood.com

Heinie Specialty Products, 301 Oak St., Quincy, IL 62301-2500 / 217-228-9500; FAX: 217-228-9502 rheinie@heinie.com www.heinie.com

Helwan (See U.S. Importer-Interarms)

Henigson & Associates, Steve, P.O. Box 2726, Culver City, CA 90231 / 310-305-8288; FAX: 310-305-1905

Henriksen Tool Co., Inc., 8515 Wagner Creek Rd., Talent, OR 97540 / 541-535-2309; FAX: 541-535-2309

Henry Repeating Arms Co., 110 8th St., Brooklyn, NY 11215 / 718-499-5600; FAX: 718-768-8056 info@henryrepeating.com www.henryrepeating.com

Hensley, Gunmaker, Darwin, P.O. Box 329, Brightwood, OR 97011 / 503-622-5411

Heppler, Keith. See: KEITH'S CUSTOM GUNSTOCKS

Hercules, Inc. (See Alliant Techsystems Smokeless Powder Group)

Heritage Firearms (See Heritage Mfg., Inc.)

Heritage Manufacturing, Inc., 4600 NW 135th St., Opa Locka, FL 33054 / 305-685-5966; FAX: 305-687-6721 infohmi@heritagemfg.com www.heritagemfg.com

Heritage/VSP Gun Books, P.O. Box 887, McCall, ID 83638 / 208-634-4104; FAX: 208-634-3101 heritage@gunbooks.com www.gunbooks.com

Herrett's Stocks, Inc., P.O. Box 741, Twin Falls, ID 83303 / 208-733-1498

Herter's Manufacturing Inc., 111 E. Burnett St., P.O. Box 518, Beaver Dam, WI 53916-1811 / 414-887-1765; FAX: 414-887-8444

Hesco-Meprolight, 2139 Greenville Rd., LaGrange, GA 30241 / 706-884-7967; FAX: 706-882-4683

Hesse Arms, Robert Hesse, 1126 70th St. E., Inver Grove Heights, MN 55077-2416 / 651-455-5760; FAX: 612-455-5760

Hesse, Robert. See: HESSE ARMS

Heydenberk, Warren R., 1059 W. Sawmill Rd., Quakertown, PA 18951 / 215-538-2682

Hickman, Jaclyn, Box 1900, Glenrock, WY 82637

Hidalgo, Tony, 12701 SW 9th Pl., Davie, FL 33325 / 954-476-7645

High Bridge Arms, Inc., 3185 Mission St., San Francisco, CA 94110 / 415-282-8358

High North Products, Inc., P.O. Box 2, Antigo, WI 54409 / 715-627-2331; FAX: 715-623-5451

High Performance International, 5734 W. Florist Ave., Milwaukee, WI 53218 / 414-466-9040; FAX: 414-466-7050 mike@hpirifles.com hpirifles.com

High Precision, Bud Welsh, 80 New Road, E. Amherst, NY 14051 / 716-688-6344; FAX: 716-688-0425 welsh5168@aol.com www.high-precision.com

High Standard Mfg. Co./F.I., Inc., 5200 Mitchelldale St., Ste. E17, Houston, TX 77092-7222 / 713-462-4200; or 800-272-7816; FAX: 713-681-5665 info@highstandard.com www.highstandard.com

High Tech Specialties, Inc., P.O. Box 839, 293 E Main St., Rear, Adamstown, PA 19501 / 717-484-0405; FAX: 717-484-0523 bansner@aol.com www.bansmersrifle.com/hightech

Highline Machine Co., Randall Thompson, Randall Thompson, 654 Lela Place, Grand Junction, CO 81504 / 970-434-4971

Highwood Special Products, 1531 E. Highwood, Pontiac, MI 48340

Hill, Loring F., 304 Cedar Rd., Elkins Park, PA 19027

Hill Speed Leather, Ernie, 4507 N 195th Ave., Litchfield Park, AZ 85340 / 602-853-9222; FAX: 602-853-9235

Hinman Outfitters, Bob, 107 N Sanderson Ave., Bartonville, IL 61607-1839 / 309-691-8132

Hi-Performance Ammunition Company, 484 State Route 366, Apollo, PA 15613 / 304-674-9000; FAX: 304-675-6700

HIP-GRIP Barami Corp., P.O. Box 252224, West Bloomfield, MI 48325-2224 / 248-738-0462; FAX: 248-738-2542 hipgripja@aol.com www.hipgrip.com

Hi-Point Firearms/MKS Supply, 8611-A North Dixie Dr., Dayton, OH 45414 / 877-425-4867; FAX: 937-454-0503 www.hi-pointfirearms.com

Hiptmayer, Armurier, RR 112 750, P.O. Box 136, Eastman, PQ J0E 1P0 CANADA / 514-297-2492

Hiptmayer, Heidemarie, RR 112 750, P.O. Box 136, Eastman, PQ J0E 1P0 CANADA / 514-297-2492

Hiptmayer, Klaus, RR 112 750, P.O. Box 136, Eastman, PQ J0E 1P0 CANADA / 514-297-2492

Hirtenberger AG, Leobersdorferstrasse 31, A-2552, Hirtenberg, AUSTRIA / 43(0)2256 81184; FAX: 43(0)2256 81808 www.hirtenberger.ot

HJS Arms, Inc., P.O. Box 3711, Brownsville, TX 78523-3711 / 956-542-2767; FAX: 956-542-2767

Hoag, James W., 8523 Canoga Ave., Suite C, Canoga Park, CA 91304 / 818-998-1510

Hobson Precision Mfg. Co., 210 Big Oak Ln., Brent, AL 35034 / 205-926-4662; FAX: 205-926-3193 cahobbob@dbtech.net

Hodgdon Powder Co., 6231 Robinson, Shawnee Mission, KS 66202 / 913-362-9455; FAX: 913-362-1307

Hodgman, Inc., 1750 Orchard Rd., Montgomery, IL 60538 / 708-897-7555; FAX: 708-897-7558

Hodgson, Richard, 9081 Tahoe Lane, Boulder, CO 80301

Hoehn Sales, Inc., 2045 Kohn Road, Wright City, MO 63390 / 636-745-8144; FAX: 636-745-7868 hoehnsal@usmo.com

Hofer Jagdwaffen, P., A9170 Ferlach, Kirchgasse 24, Kirchgasse, AUSTRIA / 43 4227 3683; or 43 664 3200216; FAX: 43 4227 368330 peterhofer@hoferwaffen.com www.hoferwaffen.com

Hoffman New Ideas, 821 Northmoor Rd., Lake Forest, IL 60045 / 312-234-4075

Hogue Grips, P.O. Box 1138, Paso Robles, CA 93447 / 800-438-4747 or 805-239-1440; FAX: 805-239-2553

Holland & Holland Ltd., 33 Bruton St., London, ENGLAND / 44-171-499-4411; FAX: 44-171-408-7962

Holland's Gunsmithing, P.O. Box 69, Powers, OR 97466 / 541-439-5155; FAX: 541-439-5155

Hollinger, Jon. See: ASPEN OUTFITTING CO.

Hollywood Engineering, 10642 Arminta St., Sun Valley, CA 91352 / 818-842-8376; FAX: 818-504-4168 cadqueenel1@aol.com

Homak, 350 N. La Salle Dr. Ste. 1100, Chicago, IL 60610-4731 / 312-523-3100; FAX: 312-523-9455

Hoppe's Div. Penguin Industries, Inc., P.O. Box 1690, Oregon City, OR 97045-0690 / 610-384-6000

Horizons Unlimited, P.O. Box 426, Warm Springs, GA 31830 / 706-655-3603; FAX: 706-655-3603

Hornady Mfg. Co., P.O. Box 1848, Grand Island, NE 68802 / 800-338-3220 or 308-382-1390; FAX: 308-382-5761

MANUFACTURER'S DIRECTORY

Horseshoe Leather Products, Andy Arratoonian, The Cottage Sharow, Ripon, ENGLAND U.K. / 44-1765-605858 andy@horseshoe.co.uk www.holsters.org

House of Muskets, Inc., The, PO Box 4640, Pagosa Springs, CO 81157 / 970-731-2295

Houtz & Barwick, P.O. Box 435, W. Church St., Elizabeth City, NC 27909 / 800-775-0337; or 919-335-4191; FAX: 919-335-1152

Howa Machinery, Ltd., Sukaguchi, Shinkawa-cho Nishikasugai-gun, Aichi 452-8601, JAPAN / 81-52-408-1231; FAX: 81-52-401-4999 howa@howa.co.jp http://www.howa.cojpl

Howell Machine, Inc., 815 D St., Lewiston, ID 83501 / 208-743-7418; FAX: 208-746-1703

H-S Precision, Inc., 1301 Turbine Dr., Rapid City, SD 57701 / 605-341-3006; FAX: 605-342-8964

HT Bullets, 244 Belleville Rd., New Bedford, MA 02745 / 508-999-3338

Hubert J. Hecht Waffen-Hecht, P.O. Box 2635, Fair Oaks, CA 95628 / 916-966-1020

Huebner, Corey O., P.O. Box 564, Frenchtown, MT 59834 / 406-721-7168 bugsboys@hotmail.com

Huey Gun Cases, 820 Indiana St., Lawrence, KS 66044-2645 / 785-842-0062; FAX: 785-842-0062 hueycases@aol.com www.hueycases.com

Hume, Don, P.O. Box 351, Miami, OK 74355 / 800-331-2686; FAX: 918-542-4340 info@donhume.com www.donhume.com

Hunkeler, A. (See Buckskin Machine Works), 3235 S 358th St., Auburn, WA 98001 / 206-927-5412

Hunter Co., Inc., 3300 W. 71st Ave., Westminster, CO 80030 / 303-427-4626; FAX: 303-428-3980 debbiet@huntercompany.com www.huntercompany.com

Hunterjohn, P.O. Box 771457, St. Louis, MO 63177 / 314-531-7250 www.hunterjohn.com

Hunter's Specialties Inc., 6000 Huntington Ct. NE, Cedar Rapids, IA 52402-1268 / 319-395-0321; FAX: 319-395-0326

Hunters Supply, Inc., P.O. Box 313, Tioga, TX 76271 / 940-437-2458; FAX: 940-437-2228 hunterssupply@hotmail.com www.hunterssupply.net

Huntington Die Specialties, 601 Oro Dam Blvd., Oroville, CA 95965 / 530-534-1210; FAX: 530-534-1212 buy@huntingtons.com www.huntingtons.com

Hutton Rifle Ranch, P.O. Box 170317, Boise, ID 83717 / 208-345-8781 www.martinbrevik@aol.com

Hydrosorbent Products, P.O. Box 437, Ashley Falls, MA 01222 / 800-448-7903; FAX: 413-229-8743 orders@dehumidify.com www.dehumidify.com

I

I.A.B. (See U.S. Importer-Taylor's & Co., Inc.)

I.D.S.A. Books, 1324 Stratford Drive, Piqua, OH 45356 / 937-773-4203; FAX: 937-778-1922

I.N.C. Inc. (See Kickeez I.N.C., Inc.)

I.S.W., 106 E. Cairo Dr., Tempe, AZ 85282

IAR Inc., 33171 Camino Capistrano, San Juan Capistrano, CA 92675 / 949-443-3642; FAX: 949-443-3647 sales@iar-arms.com iar-arms.com

Ide, Ken. See: STURGEON VALLEY SPORTERS

IGA (See U.S. Importer-Stoeger Industries)

Image Ind. Inc., 11220 E. Main St., Huntley, IL 60142-7369 / 630-766-2402; FAX: 630-766-7373

Impact Case & Container, Inc., P.O. Box 1129, Rathdrum, ID 83858 / 877-687-2452; FAX: 208-687-0632 bradk@icc-case.com www.icc-case.com

Imperial (See E-Z-Way Systems), P.O. Box 4310, Newark, OH 43058-4310 / 614-345-6645; FAX: 614-345-6600 ezway@infinet.com www.jcunald.com

Imperial Magnum Corp., P.O. Box 249, Oroville, WA 98844 / 604-495-3131; FAX: 604-495-2816

Imperial Miniature Armory, 1115 FM 359, Houston, TX 77035-3305 / 800-646-4288; FAX: 832-595-8787 miniguns@houston.rr.com www.1800miniature.com

Imperial Schrade Corp., 7 Schrade Ct., Box 7000, Ellenville, NY 12428 / 914-647-7601; FAX: 914-647-8701 csc@schradeknives.com www.schradeknives.com

Import Sports Inc., 1750 Brielle Ave., Unit B1, Wanamassa, NJ 07712 / 732-493-0302; FAX: 732-493-0301 gsodini@aol.com www.bersa-llama.com

IMR Powder Co., 1080 Military Turnpike, Suite 2, Plattsburgh, NY 12901 / 518-563-2253; FAX: 518-563-6916

Info-Arm, P.O. Box 1262, Champlain, NY 12919 / 514-955-0355; FAX: 514-955-0357 infoarm@qc.aira.com

Innovative Weaponry Inc., 2513 E. Loop 820 N., Fort Worth, TX 76118 / 817-284-0099 or 800-334-3573

INTEC International, Inc., P.O. Box 5708, Scottsdale, AZ 85261 / 602-483-1708

Inter Ordnance of America LP, 3305 Westwood Industrial Dr., Monroe, NC 28110-5204 / 704-821-8337; FAX: 704-821-8523

Intercontinental Distributors, Ltd., P.O. Box 815, Beulah, ND 58523

International Shooters Service, P.O. Box 185234, Ft. Worth, TX 76181 / 817-595-2090; FAX: 817-595-2090 is_s_@sbcglobal.net

Intrac Arms International, 5005 Chapman Hwy., Knoxville, TN 37920

Ion Industries, Inc., 3508 E Allerton Ave., Cudahy, WI 53110 / 414-486-2007; FAX: 414-486-2017

Iosso Products, 1485 Lively Blvd., Elk Grove Village, IL 60007 / 847-437-8400; FAX: 847-437-8478

Iron Bench, 12619 Bailey Rd., Redding, CA 96003 / 916-241-4623

Ironside International Publishers, Inc., P.O. Box 1050, Lorton, VA 22199

Ironsighter Co., P.O. Box 85070, Westland, MI 48185 / 734-326-8731; FAX: 734-326-3378 www.ironsighter.com

Irwin, Campbell H., 140 Hartland Blvd., East Hartland, CT 06027 / 203-653-3901

Israel Arms Inc., 5625 Star Ln. #B, Houston, TX 77057 / 713-789-0745; FAX: 713-914-9515 www.israelarms.com

Ithaca Classic Doubles, Stephen Lamboy, No. 5 Railroad St., Victor, NY 14564 / 716-924-2710; FAX: 716-924-2737 ithacadoubles.com

Ithaca Gun Company LLC, 901 Rt. 34 B, King Ferry, NY 13081 / 315-364-7171; FAX: 315-364-5134 info@ithacagun.com

Ivanoff, Thomas G. (See Tom's Gun Repair)

J

J J Roberts Firearm Engraver, 7808 Lake Dr., Manassas, VA 20111 / 703-330-0448; FAX: 703-264-8600 james.roberts@angelfire.com www.angelfire.com/va2/engraver

J&D Components, 75 East 350 North, Orem, UT 84057-4719 / 801-225-7007 www.jdcomponents.com

J&J Products, Inc., 9240 Whitmore, El Monte, CA 91731 / 818-571-5228; FAX: 800-927-8361

J&J Sales, 1501 21st Ave. S., Great Falls, MT 59405 / 406-727-9789 mtshootingbench@yahoo.com www.j&jsales.us

J&L Superior Bullets (See Huntington Die Specialties)

J&M Precision Machining, Jeff Amato, RR 1 Box 91, Bloomfield, IN 47424

J&R Engineering, P.O. Box 77, 200 Lyons Hill Rd., Athol, MA 01331 / 508-249-9241

J&R Enterprises, 4550 Scotts Valley Rd., Lakeport, CA 95453

J&S Heat Treat, 803 S. 16th St., Blue Springs, MO 64015 / 816-229-2149; FAX: 816-228-1135

J. Dewey Mfg. Co., Inc., P.O. Box 2014, Southbury, CT 06488 / 203-264-3064; FAX: 203-262-6907 deweyrods@worldnet.att.net www.deweyrods.com

J. Korzinek Riflesmith, RD 2, Box 73D, Canton, PA 17724 / 717-673-8512

J.A. Blades, Inc. (See Christopher Firearms Co.)

J.A. Henckels Zwillingswerk Inc., 9 Skyline Dr., Hawthorne, NY 10532 / 914-592-7370

J.G. Anschutz GmbH & Co. KG, Daimlerstr. 12, D-89079 Ulm, Ulm, GERMANY / 49 731 40120; FAX: 49 731 4012700 JGA-info@anschuetz-sport.com www.anschuetz-sport.com

J.G. Dapkus Co., Inc., Commerce Circle, P.O. Box 293, Durham, CT 06422 www.explodingtargets.com

J.I.T. Ltd., P.O. Box 230, Freedom, WY 83120 / 708-494-0937

J.J. Roberts / Engraver, 7808 Lake Dr., Manassas, VA 20111 / 703-330-0448 jjrengraver@aol.com www.angelfire.com/va2/engraver

J.R. Williams Bullet Co., 2008 Tucker Rd., Perry, GA 31069 / 912-987-0274

J.W. Morrison Custom Rifles, 4015 W. Sharon, Phoenix, AZ 85029 / 602-978-3754

Jack A. Rosenberg & Sons, 12229 Cox Ln., Dallas, TX 75234 / 214-241-6302

Jack Dever Co., 8520 NW 90th St., Oklahoma City, OK 73132 / 405-721-6393 jbdever1@home.com

Jack First, Inc., 1201 Turbine Dr., Rapid City, SD 57703 / 605-343-8481; FAX: 605-343-9420

Jack Jonas Appraisals & Taki, 13952 E. Marina Dr., #604, Aurora, CO 80014

Jackalope Gun Shop, 1048 S. 5th St., Douglas, WY 82633 / 307-358-3441

Jaffin, Harry. See: BRIDGEMAN PRODUCTS

Jagdwaffen, Peter. See: BUCHSENMACHERMEISTER

James Churchill Glove Co., PO Box 298, Centralia, WA 98531 / 360-736-2816; FAX: 360-330-0151 churchillglove@localaccess.com

James Wayne Firearms for Collectors and Investors, 2608 N. Laurent, Victoria, TX 77901 / 361-578-1258; FAX: 361-578-3559

Jamison International, Marc Jamison, 3551 Mayer Ave., Sturgis, SD 57785 / 605-347-5090; FAX: 605-347-4704 jbell2@masttechnology.com

Jamison, Marc. See: JAMISON INTERNATIONAL

Jamison's Forge Works, 4527 Rd. 6.5 NE, Moses Lake, WA 98837 / 509-762-2659

Jantz Supply, 309 West Main Dept HD, Davis, OK 73030-0584 / 580-369-2316; FAX: 580-369-3082 jantz@brightok.net www.knifemaking.com

Jarrett Rifles, Inc., 383 Brown Rd., Jackson, SC 29831 / 803-471-3616 www.jarrettrifles.com

Jarvis, Inc., 1123 Cherry Orchard Lane, Hamilton, MT 59840 / 406-961-4392

Javelina Lube Products, P.O. Box 337, San Bernardino, CA 92402 / 909-350-9556; FAX: 909-429-1211

Jay McCament Custom Gunmaker, Jay McCament, 1730-134th St. Ct. S., Tacoma, WA 98444 / 253-531-8832

JB Custom, P.O. Box 6912, Leawood, KS 66206 / 913-381-2329

Jeff Flannery Engraving, 11034 Riddles Run Rd., Union, KY 41091 / 859-384-3127; FAX: 859-384-2222 engraving@fuse.net http://home.fuse.net/engraving/

Jeffredo Gunsight, P.O. Box 669, San Marcos, CA 92079 / 760-728-2695

Jena Eur, P.O. Box 319, Dunmore, PA 18512

Jenco Sales, Inc., P.O. Box 1000, Manchaca, TX 78652 / 800-531-5301; FAX: 800-266-2373 jencosales@sbcglobal.net

Jenkins Recoil Pads, 5438 E. Frontage Ln., Olney, IL 62450 / 618-395-3416

Jensen Bullets, RR 1 Box 187, Arco, ID 83213 / 208-785-5590

Jensen's Custom Ammunition, 5146 E. Pima, Tucson, AZ 85712 / 602-325-3346; FAX: 602-322-5704

Jensen's Firearms Academy, 1280 W. Prince, Tucson, AZ 85705 / 602-293-8516

Jericho Tool & Die Co., Inc., 121 W. Keech Rd., Bainbridge, NY 13733-3248 / 607-563-8222; FAX: 607-563-8560 jerichotool.com www.jerichotool.com

Jerry Phillips Optics, P.O. Box L632, Langhorne, PA 19047 / 215-757-5037; FAX: 215-757-7097

Jesse W. Smith Saddlery, 0499 County Road J, Pritchett, CO 81064 / 509-325-0622

Jester Bullets, Rt. 1 Box 27, Orienta, OK 73737

Jewell Triggers, Inc., 3620 Hwy. 123, San Marcos, TX 78666 / 512-353-2999; FAX: 512-392-0543

JG Airguns, LLC, John Groenewold, P.O. Box 830, Mundelein, IL 60060 / 847-566-2365; FAX: 847-566-4065 jgairguns@jgairguns www.jgairguns.com

JGS Precision Tool Mfg., LLC, 60819 Selander Rd., Coos Bay, OR 97420 / 541-267-4331; FAX: 541-267-5996 jgstools@harborside.com www.jgstools.com

Jim Blair Engraving, P.O. Box 64, Glenrock, WY 82637 / 307-436-8115 jblairengrav@msn.com

Jim Noble Co., 204 W. 5th St., Vancouver, WA 98660 / 360-695-1309; FAX: 360-695-6835 jnobleco@aol.com

Jim Norman Custom Gunstocks, 14281 Cane Rd., Valley Center, CA 92082 / 619-749-6252

Jim's Precision, Jim Ketchum, 1725 Moclips Dr., Petaluma, CA 94952 / 707-762-3014

JLK Bullets, 414 Turner Rd., Dover, AR 72837 / 501-331-4194

Johanssons Vapentillbehor, Bert, S-430 20, Veddige, SWEDEN

John Hall Plastics, Inc., P.O. Box 1526, Alvin, TX 77512 / 713-489-8709

John J. Adams & Son Engravers, 7040 VT Rt 113, Vershire, VT 05079 / 802-685-0019

John Masen Co. Inc., 1305 Jelmak, Grand Prairie, TX 75050 / 817-430-8732; FAX: 817-430-1715

MANUFACTURER'S DIRECTORY

John Partridge Sales Ltd., Trent Meadows Rugeley, Staffordshire, WS15 2HS ENGLAND

John Rigby & Co., 500 Linne Rd. Ste. D, Paso Robles, CA 93446 / 805-227-4236; FAX: 805-227-4723 jrigby@calinet www.johnrigbyandco.com

John's Custom Leather, 523 S. Liberty St., Blairsville, PA 15717 / 724-459-6802; FAX: 724-459-5996

Johnson Wood Products, 34897 Crystal Road, Strawberry Point, IA 52076 / 563-933-6504 johnsonwoodproducts@yahoo.com

Jonad Corp., 2091 Lakeland Ave., Lakewood, OH 44107 / 216-226-3161

Jonathan Arthur Ciener, Inc., 8700 Commerce St., Cape Canaveral, FL 32920 / 321-868-2200; FAX: 321-868-2201 www.22lrconversions.com

Jones Co., Dale, 680 Hoffman Draw, Kila, MT 59920 / 406-755-4684

Jones Custom Products, Neil A., 17217 Brookhouser Rd., Saegertown, PA 16433 / 814-763-2769; FAX: 814-763-4228 njones@mdul.net neiljones.com

Jones, J. See: SSK INDUSTRIES

Jones Moulds, Paul, 4901 Telegraph Rd., Los Angeles, CA 90022 / 213-262-1510

JP Enterprises, Inc., P.O. Box 378, Hugo, MN 55038 / 651-426-9196; FAX: 651-426-2472 www.jprifles.com

JP Sales, Box 307, Anderson, TX 77830

JRP Custom Bullets, RR2 2233 Carlton Rd., Whitehall, NY 12887 / 518-282-0084 or 802-438-5548

JSL Ltd. (See U.S. Importer-Specialty Shooters Supply)

Juenke, Vern, 25 Bitterbush Rd., Reno, NV 89523 / 702-345-0225

Jungkind, Reeves C., 509 E. Granite St., Llano, TX 78643-3055 / 325-247-1151

Jurras, L. See: L. E. JURRAS & ASSOC.

Justin Phillippi Custom Bullets, P.O. Box 773, Ligonier, PA 15658 / 412-238-9671

K

K&M Industries, Inc., Box 66, 510 S. Main, Troy, ID 83871 / 208-835-2281; FAX: 208-835-5211

K&M Services, 5430 Salmon Run Rd., Dover, PA 17315 / 717-292-3175; FAX: 717-292-3175

K. Eversull Co., Inc., 1 Tracemont, Boyce, LA 71409 / 318-793-8728; FAX: 318-793-5483 bestguns@aol.com

K.B.I. Inc., P.O. Box 6625, Harrisburg, PA 17112 / 717-540-8518; FAX: 717-540-8567

Ka Pu Kapili, P.O. Box 745, Honokaa, HI 96727 / 808-776-1644; FAX: 808-776-1731

KA-BAR Knives, 200 Homer St., Olean, NY 14760 / 800-282-0130; FAX: 716-790-7188 info@ka-bar.com www.ka-bar.com

Kahles A. Swarovski Company, 2 Slater Rd., Cranston, RI 02920 / 401-946-2220; FAX: 401-946-2587

Kahr Arms, P.O. Box 220, 630 Route 303, Blauvelt, NY 10913 / 845-353-7770; FAX: 845-353-7833 www.kahr.com

Kailua Custom Guns Inc., 51 N. Dean Street, Coquille, OR 97423 / 541-396-5413 kailuacustom@aol.com www.kailuacustom.com

Kalispel Case Line, P.O. Box 267, Cusick, WA 99119 / 509-445-1121

Kamik Outdoor Footwear, 554 Montee de Liesse, Montreal, PQ H4T 1P1 CANADA / 514-341-3950; FAX: 514-341-1861

Kane, Edward, P.O. Box 385, Ukiah, CA 95482 / 707-462-2937

Kapro Mfg. Co. Inc. (See R.E.I.)

Kasenit Co., Inc., 39 Park Ave., Highland Mills, NY 10930 / 845-928-9595; FAX: 845-986-8038

Kaswer Custom, Inc., 13 Surrey Drive, Brookfield, CT 06804 / 203-775-0564; FAX: 203-775-6872

KDF, Inc., 2485 Hwy. 46 N., Seguin, TX 78155 / 830-379-8141; FAX: 830-379-5420

KeeCo Impressions, Inc., 346 Wood Ave., North Brunswick, NJ 08902 / 800-468-0546

Kehr, Roger, 2131 Agate Ct. SE, Lacy, WA 98503 / 360-491-0691

Keith's Bullets, 942 Twisted Oak, Algonquin, IL 60102 / 708-658-3520

Keith's Custom Gunstocks, Keith M. Heppler, 540 Banyan Circle, Walnut Creek, CA 94598 / 925-934-3509; FAX: 925-934-3143 kmheppler@hotmail.com

Kelbly, Inc., 7222 Dalton Fox Lake Rd., North Lawrence, OH 44666 / 216-683-4674; FAX: 216-683-7349

Keller Co., The, P.O. Box 4057, Port Angeles, WA 98363-0997 / 214-770-8585

Kelley's, P.O. Box 125, Woburn, MA 01801-0125 / 800-879-7273; FAX: 781-272-7077 kels@star.net www.kelsmilitary.com

Kellogg's Professional Products, 325 Pearl St., Sandusky, OH 44870 / 419-625-6551; FAX: 419-625-6167 skwigton@aol.com

Kelly, Lance, 1723 Willow Oak Dr., Edgewater, FL 32132 / 904-423-4933

Kel-Tec CNC Industries, Inc., P.O. Box 236009, Cocoa, FL 32923 / 407-631-0068; FAX: 407-631-1169

Kemen America, 2550 Hwy. 23, Wrenshall, MN 55797 / 218-384-3670 patrickl@midwestshootingschool.com midwestshootingschool.com

Ken Eyster Heritage Gunsmiths, Inc., 6441 Bisop Rd., Centerburg, OH 43011 / 740-625-6131; FAX: 740-625-7811

Ken Starnes Gunmaker, 15940 SW Holly Hill Rd., Hillsboro, OR 97123-9033 / 503-628-0705; FAX: 503-443-2096 kstarnes@kdsa.com

Keng's Firearms Specialty, Inc./US Tactical Systems, 875 Wharton Dr., P.O. Box 44405, Atlanta, GA 30336-1405 / 404-691-7611; FAX: 404-505-8445

Kennebec Journal, 274 Western Ave., Augusta, ME 04330 / 207-622-6288

Kennedy Firearms, 10 N. Market St., Muncy, PA 17756 / 717-546-6695

Kenneth W. Warren Engraver, P.O. Box 2842, Wenatchee, WA 98807 / 509-663-6123; FAX: 509-665-6123

Ken's Kustom Kartridges, 331 Jacobs Rd., Hubbard, OH 44425 / 216-534-4595

Kent Cartridge America, Inc., P.O. Box 849, 1000 Zigor Rd., Kearneysville, WV 25430

Keowee Game Calls, 608 Hwy. 25 North, Travelers Rest, SC 29690 / 864-834-7204; FAX: 864-834-7831

Kershaw Knives, 18600 SW Teton Ave., Tualatin, OR 97062 / 503-682-1966; or 800-325-2891; FAX: 503-682-7168

Kesselring Gun Shop, 4024 Old Hwy. 99N, Burlington, WA 98233 / 360-724-3113; FAX: 360-724-7003 info@kesselrings.com www.kesselrings.com

Ketchum, Jim (See Jim's Precision)

Keystone Sporting Arms, Inc. (Crickett Rifles), 8920 State Route 405, Milton, PA 17847 / 800-742-2777; FAX: 570-742-1455

Kickeez I.N.C., Inc., 301 Industrial Dr., Carl Junction, MO 64834-8806 / 419-649-2100; FAX: 417-649-2200 kickeez@gbronline.com www.kickeez.net

Kilham & Co., Main St., P.O. Box 37, Lyme, NH 03768 / 603-795-4112

Kimar (See U.S. Importer-IAR, Inc.)

Kimber of America, Inc., 1 Lawton St., Yonkers, NY 10705 / 800-880-2418; FAX: 914-964-9340

King & Co., P.O. Box 1242, Bloomington, IL 61702 / 309-473-3964; or 800-914-5464; FAX: 309-473-2161

King's Gun Works, 1837 W. Glenoaks Blvd., Glendale, CA 91201 / 818-956-6010; FAX: 818-548-8606

Kirkpatrick Leather Co., P.O. Box 677, Laredo, TX 78040 / 956-723-6631; FAX: 956-725-0672 mike@kirkpatrickleather.com www.kirkpatrickleather.com

KK Air International (See Impact Case & Container Co., Inc.)

Kleen-Bore, Inc., 16 Industrial Pkwy., Easthampton, MA 01027 / 413-527-0300; FAX: 413-527-2522 info@kleen-bore.com www.kleen-bore.com

Kleinendorst, K. W., RR 1, Box 1500, Hop Bottom, PA 18824 / 717-289-4687

Klingler Woodcarving, P.O. Box 141, Thistle Hill, Cabot, VT 05647 / 802-426-3811 www.vermartcrafts.com

Knifeware, Inc., P.O. Box 3, Greenville, WV 24945 / 304-832-6878

Knight Rifles, 21852 Hwy. J46, P.O. Box 130, Centerville, IA 52544 / 515-856-2626; FAX: 515-856-2628 www.knightrifles.com

Knight Rifles (See Modern Muzzleloading, Inc.)

Knight's Manufacturing Co., 701 Columbia Blvd., Titusville, FL 32780 / 321-607-9900; FAX: 321-268-1498 civiliansales@knightarmco.com www.knightarmco.com

Knock on Wood Antiques, 355 Post Rd., Darien, CT 06820 / 203-655-9031

Knoell, Doug, 9737 McCardle Way, Santee, CA 92071 / 619-449-5189

Knopp, Gary. See: SUPER 6 LLC

Koevenig's Engraving Service, Box 55 Rabbit Gulch, Hill City, SD 57745 / 605-574-2239 ekoevenig@msn.com

KOGOT, 410 College, Trinidad, CO 81082 / 719-846-9406; FAX: 719-846-9406

Kolar, 1925 Roosevelt Ave., Racine, WI 53406 / 414-554-0800; FAX: 414-554-9093

Kolpin Outdoors, Inc., P.O. Box 107, 205 Depot St., Fox Lake, WI 53933 / 414-928-3118; FAX: 414-928-3687 cdutton@kolpin.com www.kolpin.com

Korth Germany GmbH, Robert Bosch Strasse, 11, D-23909, 23909 Ratzeburg, GERMANY / 4541-840363; FAX: 4541-84 05 35 info@korthwaffen.de www.korthwaffen.com

Korth USA, 437R Chandler St., Tewksbury, MA 01876 / 978-851-8656; FAX: 978-851-9462 info@kortusa.com www.korthusa.com

Korzinek Riflesmith, J., RD 2 Box 73D, Canton, PA 17724 / 717-673-8512

Koval Knives, 5819 Zarley St., Suite A, New Albany, OH 43054 / 614-855-0777; FAX: 614-855-0945 koval@kovalknives.com www.kovalknives.com

Kowa Optimed, Inc., 20001 S. Vermont Ave., Torrance, CA 90502 / 310-327-1913; FAX: 310-327-4177 scopekowa@kowa.com www.kowascope.com

KP Books Division of F&W Publications, 700 E. State St., Iola, WI 54990-0001 / 715-445-2214

Kramer Designs, P.O. Box 129, Clancy, MT 59634 / 406-933-8658; FAX: 406-933-8658

Kramer Handgun Leather, P.O. Box 112154, Tacoma, WA 98411 / 800-510-2666; FAX: 253-564-1214 www.kramerleather.com

Krico Deutschland GmbH, Nurnbergerstrasse 6, D-90602, Pyrbaum, GERMANY / 09180-2780; FAX: 09180-2661

Krieger Barrels, Inc., 2024 Mayfield Rd, Richfield, WI 53076 / 262-628-8558; FAX: 262-628-8748

Krieghoff Gun Co., H., Boschstrasse 22, D-89079 Elm, GERMANY / 731-4018270

Krieghoff International,Inc., 7528 Easton Rd., Ottsville, PA 18942 / 610-847-5173; FAX: 610-847-8691

Kukowski, Ed. See: ED'S GUN HOUSE

Kulis Freeze Dry Taxidermy, 725 Broadway Ave., Bedford, OH 44146 / 216-232-8352; FAX: 216-232-7305 jkulis@kastaway.com kastaway.com

KVH Industries, Inc., 110 Enterprise Center, Middletown, RI 02842 / 401-847-3327; FAX: 401-849-0045

Kwik-Site Co., 5555 Treadwell St., Wayne, MI 48184 / 734-326-1500; FAX: 734-326-4120 kwiksiteco@aol.com

L

L&R Lock Co., 2328 Cains Mill Rd., Sumter, SC 29154 / 803-481-5790; FAX: 803-481-5795

L&S Technologies Inc. (See Aimtech Mount Systems)

L. Bengtson Arms Co., 6345-B E. Akron St., Mesa, AZ 85205 / 602-981-6375

L. E. Jurras & Assoc., L. E. Jurras, P.O. Box 680, Washington, IN 47501 / 812-254-6170; FAX: 812-254-6170 jurras@sbcglobal.net www.leejurras.com

L.A.R. Mfg., Inc., 4133 W. Farm Rd., West Jordan, UT 84088 / 801-280-3505; FAX: 801-280-1972

L.B.T., Judy Smith, HCR 62, Box 145, Moyie Springs, ID 83845 / 208-267-3588

L.E. Wilson, Inc., Box 324, 404 Pioneer Ave., Cashmere, WA 98815 / 509-782-1328; FAX: 509-782-7200

L.L. Bean, Inc., Freeport, ME 04032 / 207-865-4761; FAX: 207-552-2802

L.P.A. Inc., Via Alfieri 26, Gardone V.T., Brescia, ITALY / 30-891-14-81; FAX: 30-891-09-51

L.R. Clift Mfg., 3821 Hammonton Rd., Marysville, CA 95901 / 916-755-3390; FAX: 916-755-3393

La Clinique du .45, 1432 Rougemont, Chambly, PQ J3L 2L8 CANADA / 514-658-1144

Labanu Inc., 2201-F Fifth Ave., Ronkonkoma, NY 11779 / 516-467-6197; FAX: 516-981-4112

LaBoone, Pat. See: MIDWEST SHOOTING SCHOOL, THE

LaBounty Precision Reboring, Inc, 7968 Silver Lake Rd., PO Box 186, Maple Falls, WA 98266 / 360-599-2047; FAX: 360-599-3018

LaCrosse Footwear, Inc., 18550 NE Riverside Parkway, Portland, OR 97230 / 503-766-1010; or 800-323-2668; FAX: 503-766-1015

LaFrance Specialties, P.O. Box 87933, San Diego, CA 92138 / 619-293-3373; FAX: 619-293-0819 timlafrance@att.net lafrancespecialties.com

Lake Center Marina, P.O. Box 670, St. Charles, MO 63302 / 314-946-7500

Lakefield Arms Ltd. (See Savage Arms, Inc.)

Lakewood Products LLC, 275 June St., Berlin, WI 54923 / 800-872-8458; FAX: 920-361-7719 lakewood@centurytel.net www.lakewoodproducts.com

Lamboy, Stephen. See: ITHACA CLASSIC DOUBLES

Lampert, Ron, Rt. 1, 44857 Schoolcraft Trl., Guthrie, MN 56461 / 218-854-7345

MANUFACTURER'S DIRECTORY

Lamson & Goodnow Mfg. Co., 45 Conway St., Shelburne Falls, MA 03170 / 413-625-6564; or 800-872-6564; FAX: 413-625-9816 www.lamsonsharp.com
Lansky Levine, Arthur. See: LANSKY SHARPENERS
Lansky Sharpeners, Arthur Lansky Levine, P.O. Box 50830, Las Vegas, NV 89016 / 702-361-7511; FAX: 702-896-9511
LaPrade, P.O. Box 250, Ewing, VA 24248 / 423-733-2615
LaRocca Gun Works, 51 Union Place, Worcester, MA 01608 / 508-754-2887; FAX: 508-754-2887 www.laroccagunworks.com
Larry Lyons Gunworks, 110 Hamilton St., Dowagiac, MI 49047 / 616-782-9478
Laser Devices, Inc., 2 Harris Ct. A-4, Monterey, CA 93940 / 831-373-0701; FAX: 831-373-0903 sales@laserdevices.com www.laserdevices.com
Laseraim Technologies, Inc., P.O. Box 3548, Little Rock, AR 72203 / 501-375-2227
Laserlyte, 2201 Amapola Ct., Torrance, CA 90501
LaserMax, Inc., 3495 Winton Place, Bldg. B, Rochester, NY 14623-2807 / 800-527-3703; FAX: 716-272-5427 customerservice@lasermax-inc.com www.lasermax.com
Lassen Community College, Gunsmithing Dept., P.O. Box 3000, Hwy. 139, Susanville, CA 96130 / 916-251-8800; FAX: 916-251-8838 staylor@lassencollege.edu www.lassencommunitycollege.edu
Lathrop's, Inc., 5146 E. Pima, Tucson, AZ 85712 / 520-881-0266; or 800-875-4867; FAX: 520-322-5704
Laughridge, William R. (See Cylinder & Slide, Inc.)
Laurel Mountain Forge, P.O. Box 52, Crown Point, IN 46308 / 219-548-2950; FAX: 219-548-2950
Laurona Armas Eibar, S.A.L., Avenida de Otaola 25, P.O. Box 260, Eibar 20600, SPAIN / 34-43-700600; FAX: 34-43-700616
Lawrence Brand Shot (See Precision Reloading, Inc.)
Lawrence Leather Co., P.O. Box 1479, Lillington, NC 27546 / 910-893-2071; FAX: 910-893-4742
Lawson Co., Harry, 3328 N Richey Blvd., Tucson, AZ 85716 / 520-326-1117; FAX: 520-326-1117
Lawson, John. See: SIGHT SHOP, THE
Lawson, John G. (See Sight Shop, The)
Lazzeroni Arms Co., P.O. Box 26696, Tucson, AZ 85726 / 888-492-7247; FAX: 520-624-4250
Le Clear Industries (See E-Z-Way Systems)
Leapers, Inc., 7675 Five Mile Rd., Northville, MI 48167 / 248-486-1231; FAX: 248-486-1430
Leatherman Tool Group, Inc., 12106 NE Ainsworth Cir., P.O. Box 20595, Portland, OR 97294 / 503-253-7826; FAX: 503-253-7830
Lebeau-Courally, Rue St. Gilles, 386 4000, Liege, BELGIUM / 042-52-48-43; FAX: 32-4-252-2008 info@lebeau-courally.com www.lebeau-courally.com
Leckie Professional Gunsmithing, 546 Quarry Rd., Ottsville, PA 18942 / 215-847-8594
Ledbetter Airguns, Riley, 1804 E Sprague St., Winston Salem, NC 27107-3521 / 919-784-0676
Lee Precision, Inc., 4275 Hwy. U, Hartford, WI 53027 / 262-673-3075; FAX: 262-673-9273 info@leeprecision.com www.leeprecision.com
Lee Supplies, Mark, 9901 France Ct., Lakeville, MN 55044 / 612-461-2114
LeFever Arms Co., Inc., 6234 Stokes, Lee Center Rd., Lee Center, NY 13363 / 315-337-6722; FAX: 315-337-1543
Legacy Sports International, 206 S. Union St., Alexandria, VA 22314 / 703-548-4837 www.legacysports.com
Leica USA, Inc., 156 Ludlow Ave., Northvale, NJ 07647 / 201-767-7500; FAX: 201-767-8666
Leonard Day, 3 Kings Hwy., West Hatfield, MA 01027-9506 / 413-337-8369
Les Baer Custom, Inc., 29601 34th Ave., Hillsdale, IL 61257 / 309-658-2716; FAX: 309-658-2610 www.lesbaer.com
LesMerises, Felix. See: ROCKY MOUNTAIN ARMOURY
Lethal Force Institute (See Police Bookshelf), P.O. Box 122, Concord, NH 03301 / 603-224-6814; FAX: 603-226-3554
Lett Custom Grips, 672 Currier Rd., Hopkinton, NH 03229-2652 / 800-421-5388; FAX: 603-226-4580 info@lettgrips.com www.lettgrips.com
Leupold & Stevens, Inc., 14400 NW Greenbrier Pky., Beaverton, OR 97006 / 503-646-9171; FAX: 503-526-1455
Lever Arms Service Ltd., 2131 Burrard St., Vancouver, BC V6J 3H7 CANADA / 604-736-2711; FAX: 604-738-3503 leverarms@leverarms.com www.leverarms.com
Lew Horton Dist. Co., Inc., 15 Walkup Dr., Westboro, MA 01581 / 508-366-7400; FAX: 508-366-5332

Lewis Lead Remover, The (See Brownells, Inc.)
Liberty Metals, 2233 East 16th St., Los Angeles, CA 90021 / 213-581-9171; FAX: 213-581-9351 libertymfgsolder@hotmail.com
Liberty Safe, 999 W. Utah Ave., Payson, UT 84651-1744 / 800-247-5625; FAX: 801-489-6409
Liberty Shooting Supplies, P.O. Box 357, Hillsboro, OR 97123 / 503-640-5518; FAX: 503-640-5518 info@libertyshootingsupplies.com www.libertyshootingsupplies.com
Lightning Performance Innovations, Inc., RD1 Box 555, Mohawk, NY 13407 / 315-866-8819; FAX: 315-867-5701
Lilja Precision Rifle Barrels, P.O. Box 372, Plains, MT 59859 / 406-826-3084; FAX: 406-826-3083 lilja@riflebarrels.com www.riflebarrels.com
Lincoln, Dean, Box 1886, Farmington, NM 87401
Linder Solingen Knives, 4401 Sentry Dr. #B, Tucker, GA 30084 / 770-939-6915; FAX: 770-939-6738
Lindsay Engraving & Tools, Steve Lindsay, 3714 W. Cedar Hills, Kearney, NE 68845 / 308-236-7885 steve@lindsayengraving.com www.handgravers.com
Lindsay, Steve. See: LINDSAY ENGRAVING & TOOLS
Lindsley Arms Cartridge Co., P.O. Box 757, 20 College Hill Rd., Henniker, NH 03242 / 603-428-3127
Linebaugh Custom Sixguns, P.O. Box 455, Cody, WY 82414 / 307-645-3332 www.sixgunner.com
Lion Country Supply, P.O. Box 480, Port Matilda, PA 16870
List Precision Engineering, Unit 1 Ingley Works, 13 River Road, Barking, ENGLAND / 011-081-594-1686
Lithi Bee Bullet Lube, 1728 Carr Rd., Muskegon, MI 49442 / 616-788-4479 lithibee@att.net
"Little John's" Antique Arms, 1740 W. Laveta, Orange, CA 92668
Littler Sales Co., 20815 W. Chicago, Detroit, MI 48228 / 313-273-6889; FAX: 313-273-1099 littlersales@aol.com
Littleton, J. F., 275 Pinedale Ave., Oroville, CA 95966 / 916-533-6084
Ljutic Industries, Inc., 732 N. 16th Ave., Suite 22, Yakima, WA 98902 / 509-248-0476; FAX: 509-576-8233 ljuticgun@earthlink.net www.ljuticgun.com
Llama Gabilondo Y Cia, Apartado 290, E-01080, Victoria, SPAIN
Lock's Philadelphia Gun Exchange, 6700 Rowland Ave., Philadelphia, PA 19149 / 215-332-6225; FAX: 215-332-4800 locks.gunshop@verizon.net
Lodewick, Walter H., 2816 NE Halsey St., Portland, OR 97232 / 503-284-2554 wlodewick@aol.com
Lodgewood Mfg., P.O. Box 611, Whitewater, WI 53190 / 262-473-5444; FAX: 262-473-6448 lodgewd@idcnet.com lodgewood.com
Log Cabin Sport Shop, 8010 Lafayette Rd., Lodi, OH 44254 / 330-948-1082; FAX: 330-948-4307 logcabin@logcabinshop.com www.logcabinshop.com
Logan, Harry M., Box 745, Honokaa, HI 96727 / 808-776-1644
Logdewood Mfg., P.O. Box 611, Whitewater, WI 53190 / 262-473-5444; FAX: 262-473-6448 lodgewd@idcnet.com www.lodgewood.com
Lohman Mfg. Co., Inc., 4500 Doniphan Dr., P.O. Box 220, Neosho, MO 64850 / 417-451-4438; FAX: 417-451-2576
Lomont Precision Bullets, 278 Sandy Creek Rd., Salmon, ID 83467 / 208-756-6819; FAX: 208-756-6824 www.klomont.com
London Guns Ltd., Box 3750, Santa Barbara, CA 93130 / 805-683-4141; FAX: 805-683-1712
Lone Star Gunleather, 1301 Brushy Bend Dr., Round Rock, TX 78681 / 512-255-1805
Lone Star Rifle Company, 11231 Rose Road, Conroe, TX 77303 / 936-856-3363; FAX: 936-856-3363 dave@lonestar.com
Long, George F., 1402 Kokanee Ln., Grants Pass, OR 97527 / 541-476-0836
Lortone Inc., 2856 NW Market St., Seattle, WA 98107
Lothar Walther Precision Tool Inc., 3425 Hutchinson Rd., Cumming, GA 30040 / 770-889-9998; FAX: 770-889-4919 lotharwalther@mindspring.com www.lothar-walther.com
LPS Laboratories, Inc., 4647 Hugh Howell Rd., P.O. Box 3050, Tucker, GA 30084 / 404-934-7800
Lucas, Edward E, 32 Garfield Ave., East Brunswick, NJ 08816 / 201-251-5526
Lupton, Keith. See: PAWLING MOUNTAIN CLUB
Lyman Instant Targets, Inc. (See Lyman Products Corp.)
Lyman Products Corp., 475 Smith St., Middletown, CT 06457-1541 / 800-423-9704; FAX: 860-632-1699 lymansales@cshore.com www.lymanproducts.com

M

M.H. Canjar Co., 6510 Raleigh St., Arvada, CO 80003 / 303-295-2638; FAX: 303-295-2638
MA Systems, Inc., P.O. Box 894, Pryor, OK 74362-0894 / 918-824-3705; FAX: 918-824-3710
Mac-1 Airgun Distributors, 13974 Van Ness Ave., Gardena, CA 90249-2900 / 310-327-3581; FAX: 310-327-0238 mac1@maclairgun.com www.mac1airgun.com
Machinist's Workshop-Village Press, P.O. Box 1810, Traverse City, MI 49685 / 800-447-7367; FAX: 616-946-3289
Madis Books, 2453 West Five Mile Pkwy., Dallas, TX 75233 / 214-330-7168
Madis, George. See: WINCHESTER CONSULTANTS
MAG Instrument, Inc., 1635 S. Sacramento Ave., Ontario, CA 91761 / 909-947-1006; FAX: 909-947-3116
Magma Engineering Co., P.O. Box 161, 20955 E. Ocotillo Rd., Queen Creek, AZ 85242 / 602-987-9008; FAX: 602-987-0148
Mag-Na-Port International, Inc., 41302 Executive Dr., Harrison Twp., MI 48045-1306 / 586-469-6727; FAX: 586-469-0425 email@magnaport.com www.magnaport.com
Magnum Power Products, Inc., P.O. Box 17768, Fountain Hills, AZ 85268
Magnum Research, Inc., 7110 University Ave. NE, Minneapolis, MN 55432 / 800-772-6168 or 763-574-1868; FAX: 763-574-0109 info@magnumresearch.com
Magnus Bullets, P.O. Box 239, Toney, AL 35773 / 256-420-8359; FAX: 256-420-8360 bulletman@mchsi.com www.magnusbullets.com
Mag-Pack Corp., P.O. Box 846, Chesterland, OH 44026 / 440-285-9480 magpack@hotmail.com
MagSafe Ammo Co., 4700 S US Highway 17/92, Casselberry, FL 32707-3814 / 407-834-9966; FAX: 407-834-8185 www.magsafeonline.com
Magtech Ammunition Co. Inc., 6845 20th Ave. S., Ste. 120, Centerville, MN 55038 / 651-762-8500; FAX: 651-429-9485 www.magtechammunition.com
Mahony, Philip Bruce, 67 White Hollow Rd., Lime Rock, CT 06039-2418 / 860-435-9341 filbalony-redbeard@snet.net
Mahovsky's Metalife, R.D. 1, Box 149a Eureka Road, Grand Valley, PA 16420 / 814-436-7747
Makinson, Nicholas, RR 3, Komoka, ON N0L 1R0 CANADA / 519-471-5462
Mallardtone Game Calls, 10406 96th St., Court West, Taylor Ridge, IL 61284 / 309-798-2481; FAX: 309-798-2501
Mandall Shooting Supply Inc., 5442 E. Cambridge Ave., Phoenix, AZ 85008-1721 / 602-952-0097; FAX: 480-949-0734
Marble Arms (See CRR, Inc./Marble's Inc.)
Marchmon Bullets, 6502 Riverdale Rd., Whitmore Lake, MI 48189
Marent, Rudolf. See: HAMMERLI SERVICE-PRECISION MAC
Mark Lee Supplies, 9901 France Ct., Lakeville, MN 55044 / 952-461-2114; FAX: 952-461-2194 marklee55044@usfamily.net
Markell, Inc., 422 Larkfield Center 235, Santa Rosa, CA 95403 / 707-573-0792; FAX: 707-573-9867
Markesbery Muzzle Loaders, Inc., 7785 Foundation Dr., Ste. 6, Florence, KY 41042 / 606-342-5553 or 606-342-2380
Marksman Products, 5482 Argosy Dr., Huntington Beach, CA 92649 / 714-898-7535; or 800-822-8005; FAX: 714-891-0782
Marlin Firearms Co., 100 Kenna Dr., North Haven, CT 06473 / 203-239-5621; FAX: 203-234-7991 www.marlinfirearms.com
Marocchi F.lli S.p.A, Via Galileo Galilei 8, I-25068 Zanano, ITALY
Marsh, Mike, Croft Cottage, Main St., Derbyshire, DE4 2BY ENGLAND / 01629 650 669
Marshall Enterprises, 792 Canyon Rd., Redwood City, CA 94062
Marshall Fish Mfg. Gunsmith Sptg. Co., 87 Champlain Ave., Westport, NY 12993 / 518-962-4897; FAX: 518-962-4897
Martin B. Retting Inc., 11029 Washington, Culver City, CA 90232 / 213-837-2412 retting@retting.com
Martini & Hagn, 1264 Jimsmith Lake Rd., Cranbrook, BC V1C 6V6 CANADA / 250-417-2926; FAX: 250-417-2928
Martin's Gun Shop, 937 S. Sheridan Blvd., Lakewood, CO 80226 / 303-922-2184
Martz, John V., 8060 Lakeview Lane, Lincoln, CA 95648 FAX: 916-645-3815

MANUFACTURER'S DIRECTORY

Marvel, Alan, 3922 Madonna Rd., Jarretsville, MD 21084 / 301-557-6545

Marx, Harry (See U.S. Importer for FERLIB)

Maryland Paintball Supply, 8507 Harford Rd., Parkville, MD 21234 / 410-882-5607

MAST Technology, Inc., 14555 US Hwy. 95 S., P.O. Box 60969, Boulder City, NV 89006 / 702-293-6969; FAX: 702-293-7255 info@masttechnology.com www.bellammo.com

Master Lock Co., 2600 N. 32nd St., Milwaukee, WI 53245 / 414-444-2800

Match Prep-Doyle Gracey, P.O. Box 155, Tehachapi, CA 93581 / 661-822-5383; FAX: 661-823-8680 gracenotes@csurpers.net www.matchprep.com

Mathews Gun Shop & Gunsmithing, Inc., 10224 S. Paramount Blvd., Downey, CA 90241 / 562-928-2129; FAX: 562-928-8629

Matthews Cutlery, 4401 Sentry Dr. #B, Tucker, GA 30084 / 770-939-6915

Mauser Werke Oberndorf Waffensysteme GmbH, Postfach 1349, 78722, Oberndorf/N., GERMANY

Maverick Arms, Inc., 7 Grasso Ave., P.O. Box 497, North Haven, CT 06473 / 203-230-5300; FAX: 203-230-5420

Maxi-Mount Inc., P.O. Box 291, Willoughby Hills, OH 44096-0291 / 440-944-9456; FAX: 440-944-9456 maximount454@yahoo.com

Mayville Engineering Co. (See MEC, Inc.)

Mazur Restoration, Pete, 13083 Drummer Way, Grass Valley, CA 95949 / 530-268-2412

McCament, Jay. See: JAY MCCAMENT CUSTOM GUNMAKER

McCann, Tom, 14 Walton Dr., New Hope, PA 18938 / 215-862-2728

McCann Industries, P.O. Box 641, Spanaway, WA 98387 / 253-537-6919; FAX: 253-537-6919 mccann.machine@worldnet.att.net www.mccannindustries.com

McCluskey Precision Rifles, 10502 14th Ave. NW, Seattle, WA 98177 / 206-781-2776

McCombs, Leo, 1862 White Cemetery Rd., Patriot, OH 45658 / 740-256-1714

McDonald, Dennis, 8359 Brady St., Peosta, IA 52068 / 319-556-7940

McFarland, Stan, 2221 Idella Ct., Grand Junction, CO 81505 / 970-243-4704

McGhee, Larry. See: B.C. OUTDOORS

McGowen Rifle Barrels, 5961 Spruce Lane, St. Anne, IL 60964 / 815-937-9816; FAX: 815-937-4024

Mchalik, Gary. See: ROSSI FIREARMS

McKenzie, Lynton, 6940 N. Alvernon Way, Tucson, AZ 85718 / 520-299-5090

McMillan Fiberglass Stocks, Inc., 1638 W. Knudsen Dr. #102, Phoenix, AZ 85027 / 623-582-9635; FAX: 623-581-3825 mfsinc@mcmfamily.com www.mcmfamily.com

McMillan Optical Gunsight Co., 28638 N. 42nd St., Cave Creek, AZ 85331 / 602-585-7868; FAX: 602-585-7872

McMillan Rifle Barrels, P.O. Box 3427, Bryan, TX 77805 / 409-690-3456; FAX: 409-690-0156

McMurdo, Lynn, P.O. Box 404, Afton, WY 83110 / 307-886-5535

MCS, Inc., 166 Pocono Rd., Brookfield, CT 06804-2023 / 203-775-1013; FAX: 203-775-9462

McWelco Products, 6730 Santa Fe Ave., Hesperia, CA 92345 / 619-244-8876; FAX: 619-244-9398 products@mcwelco.com www.mcwelco.com

MDS, P.O. Box 1441, Brandon, FL 33509-1441 / 813-653-1180; FAX: 813-684-5953

Meacham Tool & Hardware Co., Inc., 37052 Eberhardt Rd., Peck, ID 83545 / 208-486-7171 smeacham@clearwater.net www.meachamrifles.com

Measurement Group Inc., Box 27777, Raleigh, NC 27611

Measures, Leon. See: SHOOT WHERE YOU LOOK

MEC, Inc., 715 South St., Mayville, WI 53050 reloaders@mayvl.com www.mecreloaders.com

MEC-Gar S.R.L., Via Madonnina 64, Gardone V.T. Brescia, ITALY / 39-030-3733668; FAX: 39-030-3733687 info@mec-gar.it www.mec-gar.it

MEC-Gar U.S.A., Inc., Hurley Farms Industr. Park, 115, Hurley Road 6G, Oxford, CT 06478 / 203-262-1525; FAX: 203-262-1719 mecgar@aol.com www.mec-gar.com

Mech-Tech Systems, Inc., 1602 Foothill Rd., Kalispell, MT 59901 / 406-755-8055

Meister Bullets (See Gander Mountain)

Mele, Frank, 201 S. Wellow Ave., Cookeville, TN 38501 / 615-526-4860

Menck, Gunsmith Inc., T.W., 5703 S 77th St., Ralston, NE 68127

Mendez, John A., 1309 Continental Dr., Daytona Beach, FL 32117-3807 / 407-344-2791

Men-Metallwerk Elisenhuette GmbH, P.O. Box 1263, Nassau/Lahn, D-56372 GERMANY / 2604-7819

Meprolight (See Hesco-Meprolight)

Mercer Custom Guns, 216 S. Whitewater Ave., Jefferson, WI 53549 / 920-674-3839

Merit Corp., P.O. Box 9044, Schenectady, NY 12309 / 518-346-1420 sales@meritcorporation.com www.meritcorporation.com

Merkel, Schutzenstrasse 26, D-98527 Suhl, Suhl, GERMANY FAX: 011-49-3681-854-203 www.merkel-waffen.de

Metal Merchants, P.O. Box 186, Walled Lake, MI 48390-0186

Metalife Industries (See Mahovsky's Metalife)

Michael's Antiques, Box 591, Waldoboro, ME 04572

Michaels of Oregon Co., P.O. Box 1690, Oregon City, OR 97045 www.michaels-oregon.com

Micro Sight Co., 242 Harbor Blvd., Belmont, CA 94002 / 415-591-0769; FAX: 415-591-7531

Microfusion Alfa S.A., Paseo San Andres N8, P.O. Box 271, Eibar 20600, 20600 SPAIN / 34-43-11-89-16; FAX: 34-43-11-40-38

Mid-America Recreation, Inc., 1328 5th Ave., Moline, IL 61265 / 309-764-5089; FAX: 309-764-5089 fmilcusguns@aol.com www.midamericarecreation.com

Middlebrooks Custom Shop, 7366 Colonial Trail East, Surry, VA 23883 / 757-357-0881; FAX: 757-365-0442

Midway Arms, Inc., 5875 W. Van Horn Tavern Rd., Columbia, MO 65203 / 800-243-3220; FAX: 800-992-8312 www.midwayusa.com

Midwest Gun Sport, 1108 Herbert Dr., Zebulon, NC 27597 / 919-269-5570

Midwest Shooting School, The, Pat LaBoone, 2550 Hwy. 23, Wrenshall, MN 55797 / 218-384-3670 shootingschool@starband.net

Midwest Sport Distributors, Box 129, Fayette, MO 65248

Mike Davis Products, 643 Loop Dr., Moses Lake, WA 98837 / 509-765-6178; or 509-766-7281

Mike Yee Custom Stocking, 29927 56 Pl. S., Auburn, WA 98001 / 253-839-3991

Military Armament Corp., P.O. Box 120, Mt. Zion Rd., Lingleville, TX 76461 / 817-965-3253

Millennium Designed Muzzleloaders, P.O. Box 536, Routes 11 & 25, Limington, ME 04049 / 207-637-2316

Miller Arms, Inc., P.O. Box 260 Purl St., St. Onge, SD 57779 / 605-642-5160; FAX: 605-642-5160

Miller Custom, 210 E. Julia, Clinton, IL 61727 / 217-935-9362

Miller Single Trigger Mfg. Co., 6680 Rt. 5-20, P.O. Box 471, Bloomfield, NY 14469 / 585-657-6338

Millett Sights, 7275 Murdy Circle, Adm. Office, Huntington Beach, CA 92647 / 714-842-5575 or 800-645-5388; FAX: 714-843-5707

Mills Jr., Hugh B., 3615 Canterbury Rd., New Bern, NC 28560 / 919-637-4631

Milstor Corp., 80-975 Indio Blvd. C-7, Indio, CA 92201 / 760-775-9998; FAX: 760-775-5229 milstor@webtv.net

Minute Man High Tech Industries, 10611 Canyon Rd. E., Suite 151, Puyallup, WA 98373 / 800-233-2734

Mirador Optical Corp., P.O. Box 11614, Marina Del Rey, CA 90295-7614 / 310-821-5587; FAX: 310-305-0386

Mitchell, Jack, c/o Geoff Gaebe, Addieville East Farm, 200 Pheasant Dr., Mapleville, RI 02839 / 401-568-3185

Mitchell Bullets, R.F., 430 Walnut St., Westernport, MD 21562

Mitchell Mfg. Corp., P.O. Box 9295, Fountain Valley, CA 92728 / 714-444-2220

Mitchell Optics, Inc., 2072 CR 1100 N, Sidney, IL 61877 / 217-688-2219; or 217-621-3018; FAX: 217-688-2505 mitchell@attglobal.net

Mitchell's Accuracy Shop, 68 Greenridge Dr., Stafford, VA 22554 / 703-659-0165

Mitchell's Mauser, P.O. Box 9295, Fountain Valley, CA 92728 / 714-979-7663; FAX: 714-899-3660

MI-TE Bullets, 1396 Ave. K, Ellsworth, KS 67439 / 785-472-4575; FAX: 785-472-5579

Mittleman, William, P.O. Box 65, Etna, CA 96027

Mixson Corp., 7635 W. 28th Ave., Hialeah, FL 33016 / 305-821-5190; or 800-327-0078; FAX: 305-558-9318

MJK Gunsmithing, Inc., 417 N. Huber Ct., E. Wenatchee, WA 98802 / 509-884-7683

MKS Supply, Inc. (See Hi-Point Firearms)

MMC, 2700 W. Sahara Ave. Ste. 440, Las Vegas, NV 89102-1703 / 817-831-9557; FAX: 817-834-5508

MOA Corporation, 2451 Old Camden Pike, Eaton, OH 45320 / 937-456-3669 www.moaguns.com

Mobile Area Networks, Inc., 2772 Depot St., Sanford, FL 32773 / 407-333-2350; FAX: 407-333-9903 georgew@mobilan.com

Modern Gun Repair School, P.O. Box 846, Saint Albans, VT 05478 / 802-524-2223; FAX: 802-524-2053 jfwp@dlilearn.com www.mgsinfoadlifearn.com

Modern Muzzleloading, Inc., P.O. Box 130, Centerville, IA 52544 / 515-856-2626

Moeller, Steve, 1213 4th St., Fulton, IL 61252 / 815-589-2300

Mogul Co./Life Jacket, 500 N. Kimball Rd., Ste. 109, South Lake, TX 76092

Monell Custom Guns, 228 Red Mills Rd., Pine Bush, NY 12566 / 914-744-3021

Moneymaker Guncraft Corp., 1420 Military Ave., Omaha, NE 68131 / 402-556-0226

Montana Armory, Inc., 100 Centennial Dr., P.O. Box 885, Big Timber, MT 59011 / 406-932-4353; FAX: 406-932-4443

Montana Outfitters, Lewis E. Yearout, 308 Riverview Dr. E., Great Falls, MT 59404 / 406-761-0859; or 406-727-4560

Montana Precision Swaging, P.O. Box 4746, Butte, MT 59702 / 406-494-0600; FAX: 406-494-0600

Montana Rifleman, Inc., 2593A Hwy. 2 East, Kalispell, MT 59901 / 406-755-4867

Montana Vintage Arms, 2354 Bear Canyon Rd., Bozeman, MT 59715

Morini (See U.S. Importers-Mandall Shooting Supplies, Inc.)

Morrison Custom Rifles, J. W., 4015 W Sharon, Phoenix, AZ 85029 / 602-978-3754

Morrison Precision, 6719 Calle Mango, Hereford, AZ 85615 / 520-378-6207 morprec@c2i2.com

Morrow, Bud, 11 Hillside Lane, Sheridan, WY 82801-9729 / 307-674-8360

Morton Booth Co., P.O. Box 123, Joplin, MO 64802 / 417-673-1962; FAX: 417-673-3642

Mo's Competitor Supplies (See MCS, Inc.)

Moss Double Tone, Inc., P.O. Box 1112, 2101 S. Kentucky, Sedalia, MO 65301 / 816-827-0827

Mountain Plains Industries, 3720 Otter Place, Lynchburg, VA 24503 / 800-687-3000; FAX: 434-845-6594 MPItargets@verizon.com

Mowrey Gun Works, P.O. Box 246, Waldron, IN 46182 / 317-525-6181; FAX: 317-525-9595

Mowrey's Guns & Gunsmithing, 119 Fredericks St., Canajoharie, NY 13317 / 518-673-3483

MPC, P.O. Box 450, McMinnville, TN 37110-0450 / 615-473-5513; FAX: 615-473-5516 thebox@blomand.net www.mpc-thebox.com

MPI Stocks, P.O. Box 83266, Portland, OR 97283 / 503-226-1215; FAX: 503-226-2661

MSR Targets, P.O. Box 1042, West Covina, CA 91793 / 818-331-7840

MTM Molded Products Co., Inc., 3370 Obco Ct., Dayton, OH 45414 / 937-890-7461; FAX: 937-890-1747

Mulberry House Publishing, P.O. Box 2180, Apache Junction, AZ 85217 / 888-738-1567; FAX: 480-671-1015

Mulhern, Rick, Rt. 5, Box 152, Rayville, LA 71269 / 318-728-2688

Mullins Ammunition, Rt. 2 Box 304N, Clintwood, VA 24228 / 276-926-6772; FAX: 276-926-6092 mammo@extremeshockusa.com www.extremeshockusa.com

Mullis Guncraft, 3523 Lawyers Road E., Monroe, NC 28110 / 704-283-6683

Multiplex International, 26 S. Main St., Concord, NH 03301 FAX: 603-796-2223

Multipropulseurs, La Bertrandiere, 42580, FRANCE / 77 74 01 30; FAX: 77 93 19 34

Mundy, Thomas A., 69 Robbins Road, Somerville, NJ 08876 / 201-722-2199

Murmur Corp., 2823 N. Westmoreland Ave., Dallas, TX 75222 / 214-630-5400

Murphy, R.R. Murphy Co., Inc. See: MURPHY, R.R. CO., INC.

Murphy, R.R. Co., Inc., R.R. Murphy, Co., Inc. Murphy, P.O. Box 102, Ripley, TN 38063 / 901-635-4003; FAX: 901-635-2320

Murray State College, 1 Murray Campus St., Tishomingo, OK 73460 / 508-371-2371 darnold@mscol.edu

Muscle Products Corp., 112 Fennell Dr., Butler, PA 16002 / 800-227-7049; or 724-283-0567; FAX: 724-283-8310 mpc@mpc_home.com www.mpc_home.com

Muzzleloaders Etcetera, Inc., 9901 Lyndale Ave. S., Bloomington, MN 55420 / 952-884-1161 www.muzzleloaders-etcetera.com

MWG, P.O. Box 971202, Miami, FL 33197 / 800-428-9394; or 305-253-8393; FAX: 305-232-1247

MANUFACTURER'S DIRECTORY

N

N.B.B., Inc., 24 Elliot Rd., Sterling, MA 01564 / 508-422-7538; or 800-942-9444

N.C. Ordnance Co., P.O. Box 3254, Wilson, NC 27895 / 919-237-2440; FAX: 919-243-9845

Nagel's Custom Bullets, 100 Scott St., Baytown, TX 77520-2849

Nalpak, 1937-C Friendship Drive, El Cajon, CA 92020 / 619-258-1200

Nammo Lapua Oy, P.O. Box 5, Lapua, FINLAND / 358-6-4310111; FAX: 358-6-4310317 info@nammo.ti www.lapua.com

Nastoff, Steve. See: NASTOFFS 45 SHOP, INC.

Nastoffs 45 Shop, Inc., Steve Nastoff, 1057 Laverne Dr., Youngstown, OH 44511

National Bullet Co., 1585 E. 361 St., Eastlake, OH 44095 / 216-951-1854; FAX: 216-951-7761

National Target Co., 3958-D Dartmouth Ct., Frederick, MD 21703 / 800-827-7060; FAX: 301-874-4764

Nationwide Airgun Repair, 2310 Windsor Forest Dr., Louisville, KY 40272 / 502-937-2614; FAX: 812-637-1463 shortshoestring@insightbb.com

Naval Ordnance Works, 467 Knott Rd., Sheperdstown, WV 25443 / 304-876-0998; FAX: 304-876-0998 nvordfdy@earthlink.net

Navy Arms Co., 219 Lawn St., Martinsburg, WV 25401 / 304-262-9870; FAX: 304-262-1658

Navy Arms Company, Valmore J. Forgett Jr., 815 22nd Street, Union City, NJ 07087 / 201-863-7100; FAX: 201-863-8770 info@navyarms.com www.navyarms.com

NCP Products, Inc., 3500 12th St. N.W., Canton, OH 44708 / 330-456-5130; FAX: 330-456-5234

Necessary Concepts, Inc., P.O. Box 571, Deer Park, NY 11729 / 516-667-8509; FAX: 516-667-8588

NEI Handtools, Inc., 10960 Gary Player Dr., El Paso, TX 79935

Neil A. Jones Custom Products, 17217 Brookhouser Road, Saegertown, PA 16433 / 814-763-2769; FAX: 814-763-4228

Nelson, Gary K., 975 Terrace Dr., Oakdale, CA 95361 / 209-847-4590

Nelson, Stephen. See: NELSON'S CUSTOM GUNS, INC.

Nelson's Custom Guns, Inc., Stephen Nelson, 7430 Valley View Dr. N.W., Corvallis, OR 97330 / 541-745-5232 nelsons-custom@attbi.com

Nesci Enterprises Inc., P.O. Box 119, Summit St., East Hampton, CT 06424 / 203-267-2588

Nesika Bay Precision, 22239 Big Valley Rd., Poulsbo, WA 98370 / 206-697-3830

Nettestad Gun Works, 38962 160th Avenue, Pelican Rapids, MN 56572 / 218-863-1338

Neumann GmbH, Am Galgenberg 6, 90575, GERMANY / 09101/8258; FAX: 09101/6356

New England Ammunition Co., 1771 Post Rd. East, Suite 223, Westport, CT 06880 / 203-254-8048

New England Arms Co., Box 278, Lawrence Lane, Kittery Point, ME 03905 / 207-439-0593; FAX: 207-439-0525 info@newenglandarms.com www.newenglandarms.com

New England Custom Gun Service, 438 Willow Brook Rd., Plainfield, NH 03781 / 603-469-3450; FAX: 603-469-3471 bestguns@adelphia.net www.newenglandcustom.com

New Orleans Jewelers Supply Co., 206 Charters St., New Orleans, LA 70130 / 504-523-3839; FAX: 504-523-3836

New SKB Arms Co., C.P.O. Box 1401, Tokyo, JAPAN / 81-3-3943-9550; FAX: 81-3-3943-0695

New Ultra Light Arms, LLC, P.O. Box 340, Granville, WV 26534

Newark Electronics, 4801 N. Ravenswood Ave., Chicago, IL 60640

Newell, Robert H., 55 Coyote, Los Alamos, NM 87544 / 505-662-7135

Newman Gunshop, 2035 Chester Ave. #411, Ottumwa, IA 52501-3715 / 515-937-5775

NgraveR Co., The, 67 Wawecus Hill Rd., Bozrah, CT 06334 / 860-823-1533; FAX: 860-887-6252 ngraver98@aol.com www.ngraver.com

Nicholson Custom, 17285 Thornlay Road, Hughesville, MO 65334 / 816-826-8746

Nickels, Paul R., 4328 Seville St., Las Vegas, NV 89121 / 702-435-5318

Niemi Engineering, W. B., Box 126 Center Rd., Greensboro, VT 05841 / 802-533-7180; FAX: 802-533-7141

Nikon, Inc., 1300 Walt Whitman Rd., Melville, NY 11747 / 516-547-8623; FAX: 516-547-0309

Noreen, Peter H., 5075 Buena Vista Dr., Belgrade, MT 59714 / 406-586-7383

Norica, Avnda Otaola, 16 Apartado 68, Eibar, SPAIN

Norinco, 7A Yun Tan N, Beijing, CHINA

Norincoptics (See BEC, Inc.)

Norma Precision AB (See U.S. Importers-Dynamit)

Normark Corp., 10395 Yellow Circle Dr., Minnetonka, MN 55343-9101 / 612-933-7060; FAX: 612-933-0046

North American Arms, Inc., 2150 South 950 East, Provo, UT 84606-6285 / 800-821-5783; or 801-374-9990; FAX: 801-374-9998

North American Correspondence Schools, The Gun Pro, Oak & Pawney St., Scranton, PA 18515 / 717-342-7701

North American Shooting Systems, P.O. Box 306, Osoyoos, BC V0H 1V0 CANADA / 250-495-3131; FAX: 250-495-3131 rifle@cablerocket.com

North Devon Firearms Services, 3 North St., Braunton, EX33 1AJ ENGLAND / 01271 813624; FAX: 01271 813624

North Mountain Pine Training Center (See Executive Protection Institute)

North Star West, P.O. Box 488, Glencoe, CA 95232 / 209-293-7010 northstarwest.com

Northern Precision, 329 S. James St., Carthage, NY 13619 / 315-493-1711

Northside Gun Shop, 2725 NW 109th, Oklahoma City, OK 73120 / 405-840-2353

Northwest Arms, 26884 Pearl Rd., Parma, ID 83660 / 208-722-6771; FAX: 208-722-1062

Northwest Custom Projectile, P.O. Box 127, Butte, MT 59703-0127 www.customprojectile.com

No-Sho Mfg. Co., 10727 Glenfield Ct., Houston, TX 77096 / 713-723-5332

Nosler, Inc., P.O. Box 671, Bend, OR 97709 / 800-285-3701; or 541-382-3921; FAX: 541-388-4667 www.nosler.com

Novak's, Inc., 1206 I/2 30th St., P.O. Box 4045, Parkersburg, WV 26101 / 304-485-9295; FAX: 304-428-6722 www.novaksights.com

Nowlin Mfg. Co., 20622 S 4092 Rd., Claremore, OK 74017 / 918-342-0689; FAX: 918-342-0624 nowlinguns@msn.com nowlinguns.com

NRI Gunsmith School, P.O. Box 182968, Columbus, OH 43218-2968

Nu Line Guns, 8150 CR 4055, Rhineland, MO 65069 / 573-676-5500; FAX: 314-447-5018 nlg@ktis.net

Null Holsters Ltd. K.L., 161 School St. N.W., Resaca, GA 30735 / 706-625-5643; FAX: 706-625-9392 ken@klnullholsters.com www.klnullholsters.com

Numrich Gun Parts Corporation, 226 Williams Lane, P.O. Box 299, West Hurley, NY 12491 / 866-686-7424; FAX: 877-GUNPART info@gunpartscorp.com www.e-gunparts.com

Nygord Precision Products, Inc., P.O. Box 12578, Prescott, AZ 86304 / 928-717-2315; FAX: 928-717-2198 nygords@northlink.com www.nygordprecision.com

O

O.F. Mossberg & Sons, Inc., 7 Grasso Ave., North Haven, CT 06473 / 203-230-5300; FAX: 203-230-5420

Oakman Turkey Calls, RD 1, Box 825, Harrisonville, PA 17228 / 717-485-4620

Obermeyer Rifled Barrels, 23122 60th St., Bristol, WI 53104 / 262-843-3537; FAX: 262-843-2129 www.obermeyerbarrels.com

October Country Muzzleloading, P.O. Box 969, Dept. GD, Hayden, ID 83835 / 208-772-2068; FAX: 208-772-9230 ocinfo@octobercountry.com www.octobercountry.com

Oehler Research, Inc., P.O. Box 9135, Austin, TX 78766 / 512-327-6900; or 800-531-5125; FAX: 512-327-6903 www.oehler-research.com

Oil Rod and Gun Shop, 69 Oak St., East Douglas, MA 01516 / 508-476-3687

OK Weber, Inc., P.O. Box 7485, Eugene, OR 97401 / 541-747-0458; FAX: 541-747-5927 okweber@pacinfo www.okweber.com

Oker's Engraving, P.O. Box 126, Shawnee, CO 80475 / 303-838-6042

Oklahoma Ammunition Co., 3701A S. Harvard Ave., No. 367, Tulsa, OK 74135-2265 / 918-396-3187; FAX: 918-396-4270

Oklahoma Leather Products, Inc., 500 26th NW, Miami, OK 74354 / 918-542-6651; FAX: 918-542-6653

Olathe Gun Shop, 716-A South Rogers Road, Olathe, KS 66062 / 913-782-6900; FAX: 913-782-6902 info@olathegunshop.com www.olathegunshop.com

Old Wagon Bullets, 32 Old Wagon Rd., Wilton, CT 06897

Old West Bullet Moulds, J. Ken Chapman, P.O. Box 519, Flora Vista, NM 87415 / 505-334-6970

Old West Reproductions, Inc. R.M. Bachman, 446 Florence S. Loop, Florence, MT 59833 / 406-273-2615; FAX: 406-273-2615 rick@oldwestreproductions.com www.oldwestreproductions.com

Old Western Scrounger Ammunition Inc., 50 Industrial Parkway, Carson City, NV 89706 / 775-246-2091; FAX: 775-246-2095 www.ows-ammunition.com

Old World Gunsmithing, 2901 SE 122nd St., Portland, OR 97236 / 503-760-7681

Ole Frontier Gunsmith Shop, 2617 Hwy. 29 S., Cantonment, FL 32533 / 904-477-8074

Olson, Myron, 989 W. Kemp, Watertown, SD 57201 / 605-886-9787

Olson, Vic, 5002 Countryside Dr., Imperial, MO 63052 / 314-296-8086

Olympic Arms Inc., 620-626 Old Pacific Hwy. SE, Olympia, WA 98513 / 360-456-3471; FAX: 360-491-3447 info@olyarms.com www.olyarms.com

Olympic Optical Co., P.O. Box 752377, Memphis, TN 38175-2377 / 901-794-3890; or 800-238-7120; FAX: 901-794-0676

Omega Sales, P.O. Box 1066, Mt. Clemens, MI 48043 / 810-469-7323; FAX: 810-469-0425

One Of A Kind, 15610 Purple Sage, San Antonio, TX 78255 / 512-695-3364

One Ragged Hole, P.O. Box 13624, Tallahassee, FL 32317-3624

Op-Tec, P.O. Box L632, Langhorn, PA 19047 / 215-757-5037; FAX: 215-757-7097

Optical Services Co., P.O. Box 1174, Santa Teresa, NM 88008-1174 / 505-589-3833

Orchard Park Enterprise, P.O. Box 563, Orchard Park, NY 14127 / 616-656-0356

Ordnance Works, The, 2969 Pigeon Point Rd., Eureka, CA 95501 / 707-443-3252

Oregon Arms, Inc. (See Rogue Rifle Co., Inc.)

Oregon Trail Bullet Company, P.O. Box 529, Dept. P, Baker City, OR 97814 / 800-811-0548; FAX: 514-523-1803

Original Box, Inc., 700 Linden Ave., York, PA 17404 / 717-854-2897; FAX: 717-845-4276

Original Deer Formula Co., The, P.O. Box 1705, Dickson, TN 37056 / 800-874-6965; FAX: 615-446-0646 deerformula1@aol.com www.deerformula.com

Orion Rifle Barrel Co., RR2, 137 Cobler Village, Kalispell, MT 59901 / 406-257-5649

Orvis Co., The, Rt. 7, Manchester, VT 05254 / 802-362-3622; FAX: 802-362-3525

Otis Technology, Inc., RR 1 Box 84, Boonville, NY 13309 / 315-942-3320

Ottmar, Maurice, Box 657, 113 E. Fir, Coulee City, WA 99115 / 509-632-5717

Outa-Site Gun Carriers, 219 Market St., Laredo, TX 78040 / 210-722-4678; or 800-880-9715; FAX: 210-726-4858

Outdoor Connection, Inc., The, 7901 Panther Way, Waco, TX 76712-6556 / 800-533-6076; FAX: 254-776-3553 info@outdoorconnection.com www.outdoorconnection.com

Outdoor Edge Cutlery Corp., 4699 Nautilus Ct. S. Ste. 503, Boulder, CO 80301-5310 / 303-530-7667; FAX: 303-530-7020 www.outdooredge.com

Outdoor Enthusiast, 3784 W. Woodland, Springfield, MO 65807 / 417-883-9841

Outdoor Sports Headquarters, Inc., 967 Watertower Ln., West Carrollton, OH 45449 / 513-865-5855; FAX: 513-865-5962

Outers Laboratories Div. of ATK, Route 2, P.O. Box 39, Onalaska, WI 54650 / 608-781-5800; FAX: 608-781-0368

Ox-Yoke Originals, Inc., 34 Main St., Milo, ME 04463 / 800-231-8313; or 207-943-7351; FAX: 207-943-2416

Ozark Gun Works, 11830 Cemetery Rd., Rogers, AR 72756 / 479-631-1024; FAX: 479-631-1024 ozarkgunworks@cox.net www.geocities.com

P

P&M Sales & Services, LLC, 4697 Tote Rd. Bldg. H-B, Comins, MI 48619 / 989-848-8364; FAX: 989-848-8364 info@pmsales-online.com

P.S.M.G. Gun Co., 10 Park Ave., Arlington, MA 02174 / 781-646-1699; FAX: 781-643-7212 psmg2@aol.com

Pachmayr Div. Lyman Products, 475 Smith St., Middletown, CT 06457 / 860-632-2020; or 800-225-9626; FAX: 860-632-1699 lymansales@cshore.com www.pachmayr.com

MANUFACTURER'S DIRECTORY

Pacific Armament Corp, 4813 Enterprise Way, Unit K, Modesto, CA 95356 / 209-545-2800 gunsparts@att.net

Pacific Rifle Co., P.O. Box 841, Carlton, OR 97111 / 503-852-6276 pacificrifle@aol.com

PAC-NOR Barreling, 99299 Overlook Rd., P.O. Box 6188, Brookings, OR 97415 / 503-469-7330; FAX: 503-469-7331 info@pac-nor.com www.pac-nor.com

PACT, Inc., P.O. Box 535025, Grand Prairie, TX 75053 / 972-641-0049; FAX: 972-641-2641

Page Custom Bullets, P.O. Box 25, Port Moresby, NEW GUINEA

Pagel Gun Works, Inc., 2 SE 1st St., Grand Rapids, MN 55744

Pager Pal, 200 W Pleasantview, Hurst, TX 76054 / 800-561-1603; FAX: 817-285-8769 www.pagerpal.com

Paintball Games International Magazine Aceville, Castle House 97 High St., Essex, ENGLAND / 011-44-206-564840

Palsa Outdoor Products, P.O. Box 81336, Lincoln, NE 68501 / 402-488-5288; FAX: 402-488-2321

Pansch, Robert F, 1004 Main St. #10, Neenah, WI 54956 / 920-725-8175

Paragon Sales & Services, Inc., 2501 Theodore St., Crest Hill, IL 60435-1613 / 815-725-9212; FAX: 815-725-8974

Para-Ordnance Mfg., Inc., 980 Tapscott Rd., Scarborough, ON M1X 1E7 CANADA / 416-297-7855; FAX: 416-297-1289

Para-Ordnance, Inc., 1919 NE 45th St., Ste 215, Ft. Lauderdale, FL 33308 info@paraord.com www.paraord.com

Pardini Armi Srl, Via Italica 154, 55043, Lido Di Camaiore Lu, ITALY / 584-90121; FAX: 584-90122

Paris, Frank J., 17417 Pershing St., Livonia, MI 48152-3822

Park Rifle Co., Ltd., The, Unit 6a Dartford Trade Park, Power Mill Lane, Dartford DA7 7NX, ENGLAND / 011-0322-222512

Parker & Sons Shooting Supply, 9337 Smoky Row Road, Strawberry Plains, TN 37871 / 865-933-3286; FAX: 865-932-8586

Parker Gun Finishes, 9337 Smokey Row Rd., Strawberry Plains, TN 37871 / 865-933-3286; FAX: 865-932-8586 parcraft7838@netzero.com

Parsons Optical Mfg. Co., PO Box 192, Ross, OH 45061 / 513-867-0820; FAX: 513-867-8380 psscopes@concentric.net

Partridge Sales Ltd., John, Trent Meadows, Rugeley, ENGLAND

Pasadena Gun Center, 206 E. Shaw, Pasadena, TX 77506 / 713-472-0417; FAX: 713-472-1322

Passive Bullet Traps, Inc. (See Savage Range Systems, Inc.)

Paterson Gunsmithing, 438 Main St., Paterson, NJ 07502 / 201-345-4100

Pathfinder Sports Leather, 2920 E. Chambers St., Phoenix, AZ 85040 / 602-276-0016

Patrick W. Price Bullets, 16520 Worthley Drive, San Lorenzo, CA 94580 / 510-278-1547

Pattern Control, 114 N. Third St., P.O. Box 462105, Garland, TX 75046 / 214-494-3551; FAX: 214-272-8447

Paul A. Harris Hand Engraving, 113 Rusty Lane, Boerne, TX 78006-5746 / 512-391-5121

Paul and Sharon Dressel, 209 N. 92nd Ave., Yakima, WA 98908 / 509-966-9233; FAX: 509-966-3365 dressels@nwinfo.net www.dressels.com

Paul Co., The, 27385 Pressonville Rd., Wellsville, KS 66092 / 785-883-4444; FAX: 785-883-2525

Paul D. Hillmer Custom Gunstocks, 7251 Hudson Heights, Hudson, IA 50643 / 319-988-3941

Paul Jones Moulds, 4901 Telegraph Rd., Los Angeles, CA 90022 / 213-262-1510

Paulsen Gunstocks, Rt. 71, Box 11, Chinook, MT 59523 / 406-357-3403

Pawling Mountain Club, Keith Lupton, P.O. Box 573, Pawling, NY 12564 / 914-855-3825

Paxton Quigley's Personal Protection Strategies, 9903 Santa Monica Blvd., 300, Beverly Hills, CA 90212 / 310-281-1762 www.defend-net.com/paxton

Payne Photography, Robert, Robert, P.O. Box 141471, Austin, TX 78714 / 512-272-4554

Peacemaker Specialists, P.O. Box 157, Whitmore, CA 96096 / 530-472-3438 www.peacemakerspecialists.com

Pearce Grip, Inc., P.O. Box 40367, Fort Worth, TX 76140 / 817-568-9704; FAX: 817-568-9707 info@pearcegrip.com www.pearcegrip.com

PECAR Herbert Schwarz GmbH, Kreuzbergstrasse 6, 10965, Berlin, GERMANY / 004930-785-7383; FAX: 004930-785-1934 michael.schwart@pecar-berlin.de www.pecar-berlin.de

Pecatonica River Longrifle, 5205 Nottingham Dr., Rockford, IL 61111 / 815-968-1995; FAX: 815-968-1996

Pedersen, C. R., 2717 S. Pere Marquette Hwy., Ludington, MI 49431 / 231-843-2061; FAX: 231-845-7695 fega@fega.com

Pedersen, Rex C., 2717 S. Pere Marquette Hwy., Ludington, MI 49431 / 231-843-2061; FAX: 231-845-7695 fega@fega.com

Peifer Rifle Co., P.O. Box 220, Nokomis, IL 62075

Pejsa Ballistics, 1314 Marquette Ave., Apt 906, Minneapolis, MN 55403 / 612-332-5073; FAX: 612-332-5204 pejsa@sprintmail.com pejsa.com

Peltor, Inc. (See Aero Peltor)

PEM's Mfg. Co., 5063 Waterloo Rd., Atwater, OH 44201 / 216-947-3721

Pence Precision Barrels, 7567 E. 900 S., S. Whitley, IN 46787 / 219-839-4745

Pendleton Royal, c/o Swingler Buckland Ltd., 4/7 Highgate St., Birmingham, ENGLAND / 44 121 440 3060; or 44 121 446 5898; FAX: 44 121 446 4165

Pendleton Woolen Mills, P.O. Box 3030, 220 N.W. Broadway, Portland, OR 97208 / 503-226-4801

Penn Bullets, P.O. Box 756, Indianola, PA 15051

Pennsylvania Gun Parts Inc., RR 7 Box 150, Mount Pleasant, PA 15666

Pennsylvania Gunsmith School, 812 Ohio River Blvd., Avalon, Pittsburgh, PA 15202 / 412-766-1812; FAX: 412-766-0855 pgs@pagunsmith.com www.pagunsmith.com

Penrod, Mark. See: PENROD PRECISION

Penrod Precision, Mark Penrod, 312 College Ave., P.O. Box 307, N. Manchester, IN 46962 / 260-982-8385; FAX: 260-982-1819 markpenrod@kconline.com

Pentax U.S.A., Inc., 600 12th St. Ste. 300, Golden, CO 80401 / 303-799-8000; FAX: 303-460-1628 www.pentaxlightseeker.com

Pentheny de Pentheny, c/o H.P. Okelly, 321 S. Main St., Sebastopol, CA 95472 / 707-824-1637; FAX: 707-824-1637

Perazone-Gunsmith, Brian, Cold Spring Rd., Roxbury, NY 12474 / 607-326-4088; FAX: 607-326-3140 bpgunsmith@catskill.net www.bpgunsmith@catskill.net

Perazzi U.S.A. Inc., 1010 West Tenth, Azusa, CA 91702 / 626-334-1234; FAX: 626-334-0344 perazziusa@aol.com

Performance Specialists, 308 Eanes School Rd., Austin, TX 78746 / 512-327-0119

Perugini Visini & Co. S.r.l., Via Camprelle, 126, 25080 Nuvolera, ITALY / 30-6897535; FAX: 30-6897821 peruvisi@virgilia.it

Pete de Coux Auction House, 14940 Brenda Dr., Prescott, AZ 86305-7447 / 928-776-8285; FAX: 928-776-8276 pdbullets@commspeed.net

Pete Mazur Restoration, 13083 Drummer Way, Grass Valley, CA 95949 / 530-268-2412; FAX: 530-268-2412

Pete Rickard, Inc., 115 Roy Walsh Rd, Cobleskill, NY 12043 / 518-234-2731: FAX: 518-234-2454 rickard@telenet.net www.peterickard.com

Peter Dyson & Son Ltd., 3 Cuckoo Lane, Honley, Holmfirth, West Yorkshire, HD9 6AS ENGLAND / 44-1484-661062; FAX: 44-1484-663709 peter@peterdyson.co.uk fega@peterdyson.co.uk

Peter Hale/Engraver, 997 Maple Dr., Spanish Fork, UT 84660-2524 / 801-798-8215

Peters Stahl GmbH, Stettiner Strasse 42, D-33106, Paderborn, GERMANY / 05251-750025; FAX: 05251-75611

Peterson Gun Shop, Inc., A.W., 4255 W. Old U.S. 441, Mt. Dora, FL 32757-3299 / 352-383-4258; FAX: 352-735-1001

Petro-Explo Inc., 7650 U.S. Hwy. 287, Suite 100, Arlington, TX 76017 / 817-478-8888

Pettinger Books, Gerald, 47827 300th Ave., Russell, IA 50238 / 641-535-2239 gpettinger@lisco.com

Pflumm Mfg. Co., 10662 Widmer Rd., Lenexa, KS 66215 / 800-888-4867; FAX: 913-451-7857

PFRB Co., P.O. Box 1242, Bloomington, IL 61702 / 309-473-3964; or 800-914-5464; FAX: 309-473-2161

Philip S. Olt Co., P.O. Box 550, 12662 Fifth St., Pekin, IL 61554 / 309-348-3633; FAX: 309-348-3300

Phillippi Custom Bullets, Justin, P.O. Box 773, Ligonier, PA 15658 / 724-238-2962; FAX: 724-238-9671 jrp@wpa.net http://www.wpa.net~jrphil

Phillips & Rogers, Inc., 852 FM 980 Rd., Conroe, TX 77320 / 409-435-0011

Phoenix Arms, 4231 Brickell St., Ontario, CA 91761 / 909-937-6900; FAX: 909-937-0060

Piedmont Community College, P.O. Box 1197, Roxboro, NC 27573 / 336-599-1181; FAX: 336-597-3817 www.piedmont.cc.nc.us

Pietta (See U.S. Importers-Navy Arms Co, Taylor's

Pine Technical College, 1100 4th St., Pine City, MN 55063 / 800-521-7463; FAX: 612-629-6766

Pinetree Bullets, 133 Skeena St., Kitimat, BC V8C 1Z1 CANADA / 604-632-3768; FAX: 604-632-3768

Pioneer Arms Co., 355 Lawrence Rd., Broomall, PA 19008 / 215-356-5203

Piotti (See U.S. Importer-Moore & Co., Wm. Larkin)

Piquette, Paul. See: PIQUETTE'S CUSTOM ENGRAVING

Piquette's Custom Engraving, Paul R. Piquette, 511 Southwick St., Feeding Hills, MA 01030 / 413-789-4582 ppiquette@comcast.net www.pistoldynamics.com

Plaza Cutlery, Inc., 3333 Bristol, 161 South Coast Plaza, Costa Mesa, CA 92626 / 714-549-3932

Plum City Ballistic Range, N2162 80th St., Plum City, WI 54761 / 715-647-2539

PlumFire Press, Inc., 30-A Grove Ave., Patchogue, NY 11772-4112 / 800-695-7246; FAX: 516-758-4071

PMC/Eldorado Cartridge Corp., P.O. Box 62508, 12801 U.S. Hwy. 95 S., Boulder City, NV 89005 / 702-294-0025; FAX: 702-294-0121 kbauer@pmcammo.com www.pmcammo.com

Poburka, Philip (See Bison Studios)

Pointing Dog Journal, Village Press Publications, P.O. Box 968, Dept. PGD, Traverse City, MI 49685 / 800-272-3246; FAX: 616-946-3289

Police Bookshelf, P.O. Box 122, Concord, NH 03301 / 603-224-6814; FAX: 603-226-3554

Polywad, Inc., P.O. Box 7916, Macon, GA 31209 / 478-477-0669; or 800-998-0669 FAX: 478-477-0666 polywadmpb@aol.com www.polywad.com

Ponsness, Warren, 7634 W. Ohio St., Rathdrum, ID 83858 / 800-732-0706; FAX: 208-687-2233 www.reloaders.com

Pony Express Reloaders, 608 E. Co. Rd. D, Suite 3, St. Paul, MN 55117 / 612-483-9406; FAX: 612-483-9884

Pony Express Sport Shop, 23404 Lyons Ave., PMB 448, Newhall, CA 91321-2511 / 818-895-1231

Potts, Wayne E., 1580 Meade St. Apt. A, Denver, CO 80204-5930 / 303-355-5462

Powder Horn Ltd., P.O. Box 565, Glenview, IL 60025 / 305-565-6060

Powell & Son (Gunmakers) Ltd., William, 35-37 Carrs Lane, Birmingham, B4 7SX ENGLAND / 121-643-0689; FAX: 121-631-3504 sales@william-powell.co.uk www.william-powell.co.uk

Powell Agency, William, 22 Circle Dr., Bellmore, NY 11710 / 516-679-1158

Power Custom, Inc., 29739 Hwy. J, Gravois Mills, MO 65037 / 573-372-5684; FAX: 573-372-5799 rwpowers@laurie.net www.powercustom.com

Power Plus Enterprises, Inc., P.O. Box 38, Warm Springs, GA 31830 / 706-655-2132

Powley Computer (See Hutton Rifle Ranch)

Practical Tools, Inc., 7067 Easton Rd., P.O. Box 133, Pipersville, PA 18947 / 215-766-7301; FAX: 215-766-8681

Prairie Gun Works, 1-761 Marion St., Winnipeg, MB R2J 0K6 CANADA / 204-231-2976; FAX: 204-231-8566

Prairie River Arms, 1220 N. Sixth St., Princeton, IL 61356 / 815-875-1616; or 800-445-1541; FAX: 815-875-1402

Pranger, Ed G., 1414 7th St., Anacortes, WA 98221 / 206-293-3488

Precision Airgun Sales, Inc., 5247 Warrensville Ctr Rd., Maple Hts., OH 44137 / 216-587-5005; FAX: 216-587-5005

Precision Cast Bullets, 101 Mud Creek Lane, Ronan, MT 59864 / 406-676-5135

Precision Delta Corp., P.O. Box 128, Ruleville, MS 38771 / 662-756-2810; FAX: 662-756-2590

Precision Firearm Finishing, 25 N.W. 44th Avenue, Des Moines, IA 50313 / 515-288-8680; FAX: 515-244-3925

Precision Gun Works, 104 Sierra Rd., Dept. GD, Kerrville, TX 78028 / 830-367-4587

Precision Reloading, Inc., P.O. Box 122, Stafford Springs, CT 06076 / 860-684-7979; FAX: 860-684-6788 info@precisionreloading.com www.precisionreloading.com

Precision Shooting, Inc., 222 McKee St., Manchester, CT 06040 / 860-645-8776; FAX: 860-643-8215 www.theaccuraterifle.com or precisionshooting.com

Precision Small Arms Inc., 9272 Jeronimo Rd., Ste. 121, Irvine, CA 92618 / 800-554-5515; or 949-768-3530; FAX: 949-768-4808 www.tcbebe.com

MANUFACTURER'S DIRECTORY

Precision Specialties, 131 Hendom Dr., Feeding Hills, MA 01030 / 413-786-3365; FAX: 413-786-3365

Precision Sport Optics, 15571 Producer Lane, Unit G, Huntington Beach, CA 92649 / 714-891-1309; FAX: 714-892-6920

Premier Reticles, 920 Breckinridge Lane, Winchester, VA 22601-6707 / 540-722-0601; FAX: 540-722-3522

Prescott Projectile Co., 1808 Meadowbrook Road, Prescott, AZ 86303

Preslik's Gunstocks, 4245 Keith Ln., Chico, CA 95926 / 916-891-8236

Price Bullets, Patrick W., 16520 Worthley Dr., San Lorenzo, CA 94580 / 510-278-1547

Prime Reloading, 30 Chiswick End, Meldreth, ROYSTON UK / 0763-260636

Primedia Publishing Co., 6420 Wilshire Blvd., Los Angeles, CA 90048 / 213-782-2000; FAX: 213-782-2867

Primos Hunting Calls, 604 First St., Flora, MS 39071 / 601-879-9323; FAX: 601-879-9324 www.primos.com

PRL Bullets, c/o Blackburn Enterprises, 114 Stuart Rd., Ste. 110, Cleveland, TN 37312 / 423-559-0340

Pro Load Ammunition, Inc., 5180 E. Seltice Way, Post Falls, ID 83854 / 208-773-9444; FAX: 208-773-9441

Professional Gunsmiths of America, Rt 1 Box 224, Lexington, MO 64067 / 660-259-2636

Professional Hunter Supplies, P.O. Box 608, 468 Main St., Ferndale, CA 95536 / 707-786-9140; FAX: 707-786-9117 wmebride@humboldt.com

PrOlixr Lubricants, P.O. Box 1348, Victorville, CA 92393 / 760-243-3129; FAX: 760-241-0148 prolix@accex.net www.prolixlubricant.com

Pro-Mark Div. of Wells Lamont, 6640 W. Touhy, Chicago, IL 60648 / 312-647-8200

Proofmark Corp., P.O. Box 357, Burgess, VA 22432 / 804-453-4337; FAX: 804-453-4337 proofmark@direzway.com www.proofmarkbullets.com

Pro-Port Ltd., 41302 Executive Dr., Harrison Twp., MI 48045-1306 / 586-469-6727; FAX: 586-469-0425 e-mail@magnaport.com www.magnaport.com

Pro-Shot Products, Inc., P.O. Box 763, Taylorville, IL 62568 / 217-824-9133; FAX: 217-824-8861 www.proshotproducts.com

Protector Mfg. Co., Inc., The, 443 Ashwood Pl., Boca Raton, FL 33431 / 407-394-6011

Protektor Model, 1-11 Bridge St., Galeton, PA 16922 / 814-435-2442 mail@protektormodel.com www.protektormodel.com

Prototech Industries, Inc., 10532 E Road, Delia, KS 66418 / 785-771-3571 prototec@grapevine.net

ProWare, Inc., 15847 NE Hancock St., Portland, OR 97230 / 503-239-0159

PWL Gunleather, P.O. Box 450432, Atlanta, GA 31145 / 800-960-4072; FAX: 770-822-1704 covert@pwlusa.com www.pwlusa.com

PWM Sales Ltd., N.D.F.S., Gowdall Lane, Pollington DN14 0AU, ENGLAND / 01405862688; FAX: 01405862622 Paulwelburn9@aol.com

Pyramyd Stone Inter. Corp., 2447 Suffolk Lane, Pepper Pike, OH 44124-4540

Q

Quack Decoy & Sporting Clays, 4 Ann & Hope Way, P.O. Box 98, Cumberland, RI 02864 / 401-723-8202; FAX: 401-722-5910

Quaker Boy, Inc., 5455 Webster Rd., Orchard Parks, NY 14127 / 716-662-3979; FAX: 716-662-9426

Quality Arms, Inc., Box 19477, Dept. GD, Houston, TX 77224 / 281-870-8377 arrieta2@excite.com www.arrieta.com

Quality Cartridge, P.O. Box 445, Hollywood, MD 20636 / 301-373-3719 www.qual-cart.com

Quality Custom Firearms, Stephen Billeb, 22 Vista View Dr., Cody, WY 82414 / 307-587-4278; FAX: 307-587-4297 stevebilleb@wyoming.com

Quarton Beamshot, 4538 Centerview Dr., Ste. 149, San Antonio, TX 78228 / 800-520-8435; FAX: 210-735-1326 www.beamshot.com

Que Industries, Inc., P.O. Box 2471, Everett, WA 98203 / 425-303-9088; FAX: 206-514-3266 queinfo@queindustries.com

Queen Cutlery Co., P.O. Box 500, Franklinville, NY 14737 / 800-222-5233; FAX: 800-299-2618

R

R&C Knives & Such, 2136 CANDY CANE WALK, Manteca, CA 95336-9501 / 209-239-3722; FAX: 209-825-6947

R&D Gun Repair, Kenny Howell, RR1 Box 283, Beloit, WI 53511

R&J Gun Shop, 337 S. Humbolt St., Canyon City, OR 97820 / 541-575-2130 rjgunshop@highdesertnet.com

R&S Industries Corp., 8255 Brentwood Industrial Dr., St. Louis, MO 63144 / 314-781-5169 ron@miraclepolishingcloth.com www.miraclepolishingcloth.com

R. Murphy Co., Inc., 13 Groton-Harvard Rd., P.O. Box 376, Ayer, MA 01432 / 617-772-3481 www.r.murphyknives.com

R.A. Wells Custom Gunsmith, 3452 1st Ave., Racine, WI 53402 / 414-639-5223

R.E. Seebeck Assoc., P.O. Box 59752, Dallas, TX 75229

R.E.I., P.O. Box 88, Tallevast, FL 34270 / 813-755-0085

R.E.T. Enterprises, 2608 S. Chestnut, Broken Arrow, OK 74012 / 918-251-GUNS; FAX: 918-251-0587

R.F. Mitchell Bullets, 430 Walnut St., Westernport, MD 21562

R.T. Eastman Products, P.O. Box 1531, Jackson, WY 83001 / 307-733-3217; or 800-624-4311

Rabeno, Martin, 530 The Eagle Pass, Durango, CO 81301 / 970-382-0353 fancygun@aol.com

Radack Photography, Lauren, 21140 Jib Court L-12, Aventura, FL 33180 / 305-931-3110

Radiator Specialty Co., 1900 Wilkinson Blvd., P.O. Box 34689, Charlotte, NC 28234 / 800-438-6947; FAX: 800-421-9525 tkrossell@gunk.com www.gunk.com

Radical Concepts, P.O. Box 1473, Lake Grove, OR 97035 / 503-538-7437

Rainier Ballistics, 4500 15th St. East, Tacoma, WA 98424 / 800-638-8722; FAX: 253-922-7854 sales@rainierballistics.com www.rainierballistics.com

Ralph Bone Engraving, 718 N. Atlanta St., Owasso, OK 74055 / 918-272-9745

Ram-Line ATK, P.O. Box 39, Onalaska, WI 54650

Ramon B. Gonzalez Guns, P.O. Box 370, Monticello, NY 12701 / 914-794-4515; FAX: 914-794-4515

Rampart International, 2781 W. MacArthur Blvd., B-283, Santa Ana, CA 92704 / 800-976-7240 or 714-557-6405

Ranch Products, P.O. Box 145, Malinta, OH 43535 / 313-277-3118; FAX: 313-565-8536

Randall-Made Knives, P.O. Box 1988, Orlando, FL 32802 / 407-855-8075

Randco UK, 286 Gipsy Rd., Welling, DA16 1JJ ENGLAND / 44 81 303 4118

Randolph Engineering, Inc., Ranger Shooting Glasses, 26 Thomas Patten Dr., Randolph, MA 02368 / 800-541-1405; FAX: 781-986-0337 sales@randolphusa.com www.randolphusa.com

Randy Duane Custom Stocks, 7822 Church St., Middletown, VA 22645-9521

Range Brass Products Company, P.O. Box 218, Rockport, TX 78381

Ransom International Corp., 1027 Spire Dr., Prescott, AZ 86305 / 928-778-7899; FAX: 928-778-7993 ransom@cableone.net www.ransomrest.com

Rapine Bullet Mould Mfg. Co., 9503 Landis Lane, East Greenville, PA 18041 / 215-679-5413; FAX: 215-679-9795

Ravell Ltd., 289 Diputacion St., 08009, Barcelona, SPAIN / 34(3) 4874486; FAX: 34(3) 4881394

Ray Riling Arms Books Co., 6844 Gorsten St., Philadelphia, PA 19119 / 215-438-2456; FAX: 215-438-5395 sales@rayrilingarmsbooks.com www.rayrilingarmsbooks.com

Ray's Gunsmith Shop, 3199 Elm Ave., Grand Junction, CO 81504 / 970-434-6162; FAX: 970-434-6162

Raytech Div. of Lyman Products Corp., 475 Smith Street, Middletown, CT 06457-1541 / 860-632-2020 or 800-225-9626; FAX: 860-632-1699 raysales@cshore.com www.raytech-ind.com

RCBS Operations/ATK, 605 Oro Dam Blvd., Oroville, CA 95965 / 530-533-5191 or 800-533-5000; FAX: 530-533-1647 www.rcbs.com

RCBS/ATK, 605 Oro Dam Blvd., Oroville, CA 95965 / 800-533-5000; FAX: 916-533-1647

Reardon Products, P.O. Box 126, Morrison, IL 61270 / 815-772-3155

Red Diamond Dist. Co., 1304 Snowdon Dr., Knoxville, TN 37912

Redding Reloading Equipment, 1089 Starr Rd., Cortland, NY 13045 / 607-753-3331; FAX: 607-756-8445 techline@redding-reloading.com www.redding-reloading.com

Redfield Media Resource Center, 4607 N.E. Cedar Creek Rd., Woodland, WA 98674 / 360-225-5000; FAX: 360-225-7616

Redman's Rifling & Reboring, 189 Nichols Rd., Omak, WA 98841 / 509-826-5512

Redwood Bullet Works, 3559 Bay Rd., Redwood City, CA 94063 / 415-367-6741

Reed, Dave, Rt. 1, Box 374, Minnesota City, MN 55959 / 507-689-2944

Reimer Johannsen, Inc., 438 Willow Brook Rd., Plainfield, NH 03781 / 603-469-3450; FAX: 603-469-3471

Reloaders Equipment Co., 4680 High St., Ecorse, MI 48229

Reloading Specialties, Inc., Box 1130, Pine Island, MN 55463 / 507-356-8500; FAX: 507-356-8800

Remington Arms Co., Inc., 870 Remington Drive, P.O. Box 700, Madison, NC 27025-0700 / 800-243-9700; FAX: 910-548-8700

Remington Double Shotguns, 7885 Cyd Dr., Denver, CO 80221 / 303-429-6947

Renato Gamba S.p.A.-Societa Armi Bresciane Srl., Via Artigiani 93, 25063 Gardone, Val Trompia (BS), ITALY / 30-8911640; FAX: 30-8911648

Renegade, P.O. Box 31546, Phoenix, AZ 85046 / 602-482-6777; FAX: 602-482-1952

Renfrew Guns & Supplies, R.R. 4, Renfrew, ON K7V 3Z7 CANADA / 613-432-7080

Reno, Wayne, 2808 Stagestop Road, Jefferson, CO 80456

Republic Arms, Inc. (See Cobra Enterprises, Inc.)

Retting, Inc., Martin B., 11029 Washington, Culver City, CA 90232 / 213-837-2412

RG-G, Inc., P.O. Box 935, Trinidad, CO 81082 / 719-845-1436

RH Machine & Consulting Inc., P.O. Box 394, Pacific, MO 63069 / 314-271-8465

Rhino, P.O. Box 787, Locust, NC 28097 / 704-753-2198

Rhodeside, Inc., 1704 Commerce Dr., Piqua, OH 45356 / 513-773-5781

Rice, Keith (See White Rock Tool & Die)

Richards MicroFit Stocks, Inc., P.O. Box 1066, Sun Valley, CA 91352 / 800-895-7420; FAX: 818-771-1242 sales@rifle-stocks.com www.rifle-stocks.com

Ridgeline, Inc., Bruce Sheldon, P.O. Box 930, Dewey, AZ 86327-0930 / 800-632-5900; FAX: 520-632-5900

Ridgetop Sporting Goods, P.O. Box 306, 42907 Hilligoss Ln. East, Eatonville, WA 98328 / 360-832-6422; FAX: 360-832-6422

Ries, Chuck, 415 Ridgecrest Dr., Grants Pass, OR 97527 / 503-476-5623

Rifles, Inc., 3580 Leal Rd., Pleasanton, TX 78064 / 830-569-2055; FAX: 830-569-2297

Riggs, Jim, 206 Azalea, Boerne, TX 78006 / 210-249-8567

Riley Ledbetter Airguns, 1804 E. Sprague St., Winston Salem, NC 27107-3521 / 919-784-0676

Rim Pac Sports, Inc., 1034 N. Soldano Ave., Azusa, CA 91702-2135

Ringler Custom Leather Co., 31 Shining Mtn. Rd., Powell, WY 82435 / 307-645-3255

Ripley Rifles, 42 Fletcher Street, Ripley, Derbyshire, DE5 3LP ENGLAND / 011-0773-748353

Rizzini F.lli (See U.S. Importers-Wm. Larkin Moore & Co., N.E. Arms Corp.)

Rizzini SNC, Via 2 Giugno, 7/7Bis-25060, Marcheno (Brescia), ITALY

RLCM Enterprises, 110 Hill Crest Drive, Burleson, TX 76028

RMS Custom Gunsmithing, 4120 N. Bitterwell, Prescott Valley, AZ 86314 / 520-772-7626 www.customstockmaker.com

Robar Co., Inc., The, 21438 N. 7th Ave., Suite B, Phoenix, AZ 85027 / 623-581-2648; FAX: 623-582-0059 info@robarguns.com www.robarguns.com

Robert Evans Engraving, 332 Vine St., Oregon City, OR 97045 / 503-656-5693

Robert Valade Engraving, 931 3rd Ave., Seaside, OR 97138 / 503-738-7672

Robinett, R. G., P.O. Box 72, Madrid, IA 50156 / 515-795-2906

Robinson, Don, Pennsylvania Hse, 36 Fairfax Crescent, W Yorkshire, ENGLAND / 0422-364458 donrobinsonuk@yahoo.co.uk www.guns4u2.co.uk

Robinson Armament Co., P.O. Box 16776, Salt Lake City, UT 84116 / 801-355-0401; FAX: 801-355-0402 zdf@robarm.com www.robarm.com

Robinson Firearms Mfg. Ltd., 1699 Blondeaux Crescent, Kelowna, BC V1Y 4J8 CANADA / 604-868-9596

Robinson H.V. Bullets, 3145 Church St., Zachary, LA 70791 / 504-654-4029

Rochester Lead Works, 76 Anderson Ave., Rochester, NY 14607 / 716-442-8500; FAX: 716-442-4712

Rock River Arms, 101 Noble St., Cleveland, IL 61241

MANUFACTURER'S DIRECTORY

Rockwood Corp., Speedwell Division, 136 Lincoln Blvd., Middlesex, NJ 08846 / 800-243-8274; FAX: 980-560-7475

Rocky Mountain Armoury, Mr. Felix LesMerises, 610 Main Street, P.O. Box 691, Frisco, CO 80443-0691 / 970-668-0136; FAX: 970-668-4484 felix@rockymountainarmoury.com

Rocky Mountain Arms, Inc., 1813 Sunset Pl., Unit D, Longmont, CO 80501 / 800-375-0846; FAX: 303-678-8766

Rocky Mountain Target Co., 3 Aloe Way, Leesburg, FL 34788 / 352-365-9598

Rocky Mountain Wildlife Products, P.O. Box 999, La Porte, CO 80535 / 970-484-2768; FAX: 970-484-0807 critrcall@larinet.net www.critrcall.com

Rocky Shoes & Boots, 294 Harper St., Nelsonville, OH 45764 / 800-848-9452; or 614-753-1951; FAX: 614-753-4024

Rogue Rifle Co., Inc., 1140 36th St. N., Ste. B, Lewiston, ID 83501 / 208-743-4355; FAX: 208-743-4163

Rogue River Rifleworks, 500 Linne Road #D, Paso Robles, CA 93446 / 805-227-4706; FAX: 805-227-4723 rrrifles@calinet.com

Rohner, Hans, 1148 Twin Sisters Ranch Rd., Nederland, CO 80466-9600

Rohner, John, 186 Virginia Ave., Asheville, NC 28806 / 828-281-3704

Rohrbaugh, P.O. Box 785, Bayport, NY 11705 / 631-363-2843; FAX: 631-363-2681 API380@aol.com

Romain's Custom Guns, Inc., RD 1, Whetstone Rd., Brockport, PA 15823 / 814-265-1948 romwhetstone@penn.com

Ron Frank Custom Classic Arms, 7131 Richland Rd., Ft. Worth, TX 76118 / 817-284-9300; FAX: 817-284-9300 rfrank3974@aol.com

Rooster Laboratories, P.O. Box 414605, Kansas City, MO 64141 / 816-474-1622; FAX: 816-474-7622

Rorschach Precision Products, 417 Keats Cir., Irving, TX 75061 / 214-790-3487

Rosenberg & Son, Jack A., 12229 Cox Ln., Dallas, TX 75234 / 214-241-6302

Ross, Don, 12813 West 83 Terrace, Lenexa, KS 66215 / 913-492-6982

Rosser, Bob, 2809 Crescent Ave., Suite 20, Homewood, AL 35209 / 205-870-4422; FAX: 205-870-4421 www.hand-engravers.com

Rossi Firearms, Gary Mchalik, 16175 NW 49th Ave., Miami, FL 33014-6314 / 305-474-0401; FAX: 305-623-7506

Rottweil Compe, 1330 Glassell, Orange, CA 92667

Roy Baker's Leather Goods, P.O. Box 893, Magnolia, AR 71754 / 870-234-0344

Royal Arms Gunstocks, 919 8th Ave. NW, Great Falls, MT 59404 / 406-453-1149 royalarms@lmt.net www.lmt.net/~royalarms

Royal Arms International, R J Brill, P.O. Box 6083, Woodland Hills, CA 91365 / 818-704-5110; FAX: 818-887-2059 royalarms.com

Roy's Custom Grips, 793 Mt. Olivet Church Rd., Lynchburg, VA 24504 / 434-993-3470

RPM, 15481 N. Twin Lakes Dr., Tucson, AZ 85739 / 520-825-1233; FAX: 520-825-3333

Rubright Bullets, 1008 S. Quince Rd., Walnutport, PA 18088 / 215-767-1339

Rucker Dist. Inc., P.O. Box 479, Terrell, TX 75160 / 214-563-2094

Ruger (See Sturm Ruger & Co., Inc.)

Ruger, Chris. See: RUGER'S CUSTOM GUNS

Ruger's Custom Guns, Chris Ruger, 1050 Morton Blvd., Kingston, NY 12401 / 845-336-7106; FAX: 845-336-7106 rugerscustom@outdrs.net rugergunsmith.com

Rundell's Gun Shop, 6198 Frances Rd., Clio, MI 48420 / 313-687-0059

Rupert's Gun Shop, 2202 Dick Rd., Suite B, Fenwick, MI 48834 / 517-248-3252 17rupert@pathwaynet.com

Russ Haydon's Shooters' Supply, 15018 Goodrich Dr. NW, Gig Harbor, WA 98329 / 877-663-6249; FAX: 253-857-7884 info@shooters-supply.com www.shooters-supply.com

Russ, William. See: BILL RUSS TRADING POST

Rusteprufe Laboratories, 1319 Jefferson Ave., Sparta, WI 54656 / 608-269-4144; FAX: 608-366-1972 rusteprufe@centurytel.net www.rusteprufe.com

Rusty Duck Premium Gun Care Products, 7785 Foundation Dr., Suite 6, Florence, KY 41042 / 606-342-5553; FAX: 606-342-5556

Rutgers Book Center, 127 Raritan Ave., Highland Park, NJ 08904 / 732-545-4344; FAX: 732-545-6686 gunbooks@rutgersgunbooks.com www.rutgersgunbooks.com

Rutten (See U.S. Importer-Labanu Inc.)

RWS (See U.S. Importer-Dynamit Nobel-RWS, Inc.), 81 Ruckman Rd., Closter, NJ 07624 / 201-767-7971; FAX: 201-767-1589

S

S&K Scope Mounts, RD 2 Box 21C, Sugar Grove, PA 16350 / 814-489-3091; or 800-578-9862; FAX: 814-489-5466 comments@scopemounts.com www.scopemounts.com

S&S Firearms, 74-11 Myrtle Ave., Glendale, NY 11385 / 718-497-1100; FAX: 718-497-1105 info@ssfirearms.com ssfirearms.com

S.A.R.L. G. Granger, 66 cours Fauriel, 42100, Saint Etienne, FRANCE / 04 77 25 14 73; FAX: 04 77 38 66 99

S.C.R.C., P.O. Box 660, Katy, TX 77492-0660 FAX: 281-492-6332

S.D. Meacham, 1070 Angel Ridge, Peck, ID 83545

S.I.A.C.E. (See U.S. Importer-IAR Inc.)

Sabatti SPA, Via A Volta 90, 25063 Gandome V.T.(BS), Brescia, ITALY / 030-8912207-831312; FAX: 030-8912059 info@sabatti.it www.sabatti.com

SAECO (See Redding Reloading Equipment)

Safari Arms/Schuetzen Pistol Works, 620-626 Old Pacific Hwy. SE, Olympia, WA 98513 / 360-459-3471; FAX: 360-491-3447 info@olyarms.com www.olyarms.com

Safari Press, Inc., 15621 Chemical Lane B, Huntington Beach, CA 92649 / 714-894-9080; FAX: 714-894-4949 info@safaripress.com www.safaripress.com

Safariland Ltd., Inc., 3120 E. Mission Blvd., P.O. Box 51478, Ontario, CA 91761 / 909-923-7300; FAX: 909-923-7400

SAFE, P.O. Box 864, Post Falls, ID 83877 / 208-773-3624; FAX: 208-773-6819 staysafe@safe-llc.com www.safe-llc.com

Sako Ltd. (See U.S. Importer-Stoeger Industries)

Sam Welch Gun Engraving, Sam Welch, HC 64 Box 2110, Moab, UT 84532 / 435-259-8131

Samco Global Arms, Inc., 6995 NW 43rd St., Miami, FL 33166 / 305-593-9782; FAX: 305-593-1014 samco@samcoglobal.com www.samcoglobal.com

Sampson, Roger, 2316 Mahogany St., Mora, MN 55051 / 612-679-4868

San Marco (See U.S. Importers-Cape Outfitters-EMF Co., Inc.

Sandia Die & Cartridge Co., 37 Atancacio Rd. NE, Albuquerque, NM 87123 / 505-298-5729

Sarco, Inc., 323 Union St., Stirling, NJ 07980 / 908-647-3800; FAX: 908-647-9413

Sarsilmaz Shotguns-Turkey (see B.C. Outdoors)

Sauer (See U.S. Importers-Paul Co., The Sigarms Inc.)

Sauls, R. See: BRYAN & ASSOC.

Saunders Gun & Machine Shop, 145 Delhi Rd., Manchester, IA 52057 / 563-927-4026

Savage Arms (Canada), Inc., 248 Water St., P.O. Box 1240, Lakefield, ON K0L 2H0 CANADA / 705-652-8000; FAX: 705-652-8431 www.savagearms.com

Savage Arms, Inc., 100 Springdale Rd., Westfield, MA 01085 / 413-568-7001; FAX: 413-562-7764

Savage Range Systems, Inc., 100 Springdale Rd., Westfield, MA 01085 / 413-568-7001; FAX: 413-562-1152 snailtraps@savagearms.com www.snailtraps.com

Saville Iron Co. (See Greenwood Precision)

Scansport, Inc., P.O. Box 700, Enfield, NH 03748 / 603-632-7654

Sceery Game Calls, P.O. Box 6520, Sante Fe, NM 87502 / 505-471-9110; FAX: 505-471-3476

Schaefer Shooting Sports, P.O. Box 1515, Melville, NY 11747-0515 / 516-643-5466; FAX: 516-643-2426 robert@robertschaefer.com www.schaefershooting.com

Scharch Mfg., Inc.-Top Brass, 10325 Co. Rd. 120, Salida, CO 81201 / 800-836-4683; FAX: 719-539-3021 topbrass@scharch.com www.handgun-brass.com

Scherer, Liz. See: SCHERER SUPPLIES

Scherer Supplies, Liz Scherer, Box 250, Ewing, VA 24248 FAX: 423-733-2073

Schiffman, Mike, 8233 S. Crystal Springs, McCammon, ID 83250 / 208-254-9114

Schmidt & Bender, Inc., P.O. Box 134, Meriden, NH 03770 / 603-469-3565; FAX: 603-469-3471 scopes@adelphia.net www.schmidtbender.com

Schmidtke Group, 17050 W. Salentine Dr., New Berlin, WI 53151-7349

Schneider Bullets, 3655 West 214th St., Fairview Park, OH 44126

Schneider Rifle Barrels, Inc., 1403 W. Red Baron Rd., Payson, AZ 85541 / 602-948-2525

School of Gunsmithing, The, 6065 Roswell Rd., Atlanta, GA 30328 / 800-223-4542

Schroeder Bullets, 1421 Thermal Ave., San Diego, CA 92154 / 619-423-3523; FAX: 619-423-8124

Schulz Industries, 16247 Minnesota Ave., Paramount, CA 90723 / 213-439-5903

Schumakers Gun Shop, 512 Prouty Corner Lp. A, Colville, WA 99114 / 509-684-4848

Scope Control, Inc., 5775 Co. Rd. 23 SE, Alexandria, MN 56308 / 612-762-7295

Score High Gunsmithing, 9812-A, Cochiti SE, Albuquerque, NM 87123 / 800-326-5632; or 505-292-5532; FAX: 505-292-2592 scorehi@scorehi.com www.probed2000.com

Scot Powder, Rt. 1 Box 167, McEwen, TN 37101 / 800-416-3006; FAX: 615-729-4211

Scott Fine Guns Inc., Thad, P.O. Box 412, Indianola, MS 38751 / 601-887-5929

Searcy Enterprises, P.O. Box 584, Boron, CA 93596 / 760-762-6771; FAX: 760-762-0191

Second Chance Body Armor, P.O. Box 578, Central Lake, MI 49622 / 616-544-5721; FAX: 616-544-9824

Seebeck Assoc., R.E., P.O. Box 59752, Dallas, TX 75229

Segway Industries, P.O. Box 783, Suffern, NY 10901-0783 / 914-357-5510

Seligman Shooting Products, Box 133, Seligman, AZ 86337 / 602-422-3607 shootssp@yahoo.com

Sellier & Bellot, USA, Inc., P.O. Box 27006, Shawnee Mission, KS 66225 / 913-685-0916; FAX: 913-685-0917

Selsi Co., Inc., P.O. Box 10, Midland Park, NJ 07432-0010 / 201-935-0388; FAX: 201-935-5851

Semmer, Charles (See Remington Double Shotguns), 7885 Cyd Dr., Denver, CO 80221 / 303-429-6947

Sentinel Arms, P.O. Box 57, Detroit, MI 48231 / 313-331-1951; FAX: 313-331-1456

Servus Footwear Co., 1136 2nd St., Rock Island, IL 61204 / 309-786-7741; FAX: 309-786-9808

Shappy Bullets, 76 Milldale Ave., Plantsville, CT 06479 / 203-621-3704

Sharp Shooter Supply, 4970 Lehman Road, Delphos, OH 45833 / 419-695-3179

Sharps Arms Co., Inc., C., 100 Centennial, Box 885, Big Timber, MT 59011 / 406-932-4353

Shaw, Inc., E. R. (See Small Arms Mfg. Co.)

Shay's Gunsmithing, 931 Marvin Ave., Lebanon, PA 17042

Sheffield Knifemakers Supply, Inc., P.O. Box 741107, Orange City, FL 32774-1107 / 386-775-6453; FAX: 386-774-5754

Sheldon, Bruce. See: RIDGELINE, INC.

Shepherd Enterprises, Inc., Box 189, Waterloo, NE 68069 / 402-779-2424; FAX: 402-779-4010 ssshepherd@shepherdscopes.com www.shepherdscopes.com

Sherwood, George, 46 N. River Dr., Roseburg, OR 97470 / 541-672-3159

Shilen, Inc., 205 Metro Park Blvd., Ennis, TX 75119 / 972-875-5318; FAX: 972-875-5402

Shiloh Rifle Mfg., P.O. Box 279, Big Timber, MT 59011

Shockley, Harold H., 204 E. Farmington Rd., Hanna City, IL 61536 / 309-565-4524

Shoot Where You Look, Leon Measures, Dept GD, 408 Fair, Livingston, TX 77351

Shooters Arms Manufacturing, Inc., Rivergate Mall, Gen. Maxilom Ave., Cebu City 6000, PHILIPPINES / 6332-254-8478 www.shootersarms.com.ph

Shooter's Choice Gun Care, 15050 Berkshire Ind. Pkwy., Middlefield, OH 44062 / 440-834-8888; FAX: 440-834-3388 www.shooterschoice.com

Shooter's Edge Inc., 3313 Creekstone Dr., Fort Collins, CO 80525

Shooters Supply, 1120 Tieton Dr., Yakima, WA 98902 / 509-452-1181

Shooter's World, 3828 N. 28th Ave., Phoenix, AZ 85017 / 602-266-0170

Shooters, Inc., 5139 Stanart St., Norfolk, VA 23502 / 757-461-9152; FAX: 757-461-9155 gflocker@aol.com

Shootin' Shack, 357 Cypress Drive, No. 10, Tequesta, FL 33469 / 561-842-0990; FAX: 561-545-4861

Shooting Gallery, The, 8070 Southern Blvd., Boardman, OH 44512 / 216-726-7788

Shoot-N-C Targets (See Birchwood Casey)

Shotgun Sports, P.O. Box 6810, Auburn, CA 95604 / 530-889-2220; FAX: 530-889-9106 custsrv@shotgunsportsmagazine.com shotgunsportsmagazine.com

MANUFACTURER'S DIRECTORY

Shotgun Sports Magazine, dba Shootin' Accessories Ltd., P.O. Box 6810, Auburn, CA 95604 / 916-889-2220 custsrv@shotgunsportsmagazine.com shotgunsportsmagazine.com

Shotguns Unlimited, 2307 Fon Du Lac Rd., Richmond, VA 23229 / 804-752-7115

Siegrist Gun Shop, 8752 Turtle Road, Whittemore, MI 48770 / 989-873-3929

Sierra Bullets, 1400 W. Henry St., Sedalia, MO 65301 / 816-827-6300; FAX: 816-827-6300

Sierra Specialty Prod. Co., 1344 Oakhurst Ave., Los Altos, CA 94024 FAX: 415-965-1536

SIG, CH-8212 Neuhausen, SWITZERLAND

Sigarms Inc., 18 Industrial Dr., Exeter, NH 03833 / 603-772-2302; FAX: 603-772-9082 www.sigarms.com

Sight Shop, The, John G. Lawson, 1802 E. Columbia Ave., Tacoma, WA 98404 / 253-474-5465 parahellum9@aol.com www.thesightshop.org

Sightron, Inc., 1672B Hwy. 96, Franklinton, NC 27525 / 919-528-8783; FAX: 919-528-0995 info@sightron.com www.sightron.com

SIG-Sauer (See U.S. Importer-Sigarms, Inc.)

Silencio/Safety Direct, 56 Coney Island Dr., Sparks, NV 89431 / 800-648-1812; or 702-354-4451; FAX: 702-359-1074

Silent Hunter, 1100 Newton Ave., W. Collingswood, NJ 08107 / 609-854-3276

Silhouette Leathers, 8598 Hwy. 51 N. #4, Millington, TN 38053 silhouetteleathers@yahoo.com silhouetteleathers.com

Silver Eagle Machining, 18007 N. 69th Ave., Glendale, AZ 85308

Silver Ridge Gun Shop (See Goodwin Guns)

Simmons, Jerry, 715 Middlebury St., Goshen, IN 46528-2717 / 574-533-8546

Simmons Gun Repair, Inc., 700 S. Rogers Rd., Olathe, KS 66062 / 913-782-3131; FAX: 913-782-4189

Simmons Outdoor Corp., 6001 Oak Canyon, Irvine, CA 92618 / 949-451-1450; FAX: 949-451-1460 www.meade.com

Sinclair International, Inc., 2330 Wayne Haven St., Fort Wayne, IN 46803 / 260-493-1858; or 800-717-8211; FAX: 260-493-2530 sales@sinclairintl.com www.sinclairintl.com

Singletary, Kent, 4538 W. Carol Ave., Glendale, AZ 85302 / 602-526-6836 kent@kscustom www.kscustom.com

Siskiyou Gun Works (See Donnelly, C. P.)

Six Enterprises, 320-D Turtle Creek Ct., San Jose, CA 95125 / 408-999-0201; FAX: 408-999-0216

SKB Shotguns, 4325 S. 120th St., Omaha, NE 68137 / 800-752-2767; FAX: 402-330-8040 skb@skbshotguns.com www.skbshotguns.com

Skeoch, Brian R., P.O. Box 279, Glenrock, WY 82637 / 307-436-9655 skeochbrian@netzero.net

Skip's Machine, 364 29 Road, Grand Junction, CO 81501 / 303-245-5417

Sklany's Machine Shop, 566 Birch Grove Dr., Kalispell, MT 59901 / 406-755-4257

Slug Site, Ozark Wilds, 21300 Hwy. 5, Versailles, MO 65084 / 573-378-6430 john@ebeling.com john.ebeling.com

Small Arms Mfg. Co., 5312 Thoms Run Rd., Bridgeville, PA 15017 / 412-221-4343; FAX: 412-221-4303

Small Arms Specialists, 443 Firchburg Rd., Mason, NH 03048 / 603-878-0427; FAX: 603-878-3905 miniguns@empire.net miniguns.com

Smires, C. L., 5222 Windmill Lane, Columbia, MD 21044-1328

Smith & Wesson, 2100 Roosevelt Ave., Springfield, MA 01104 / 413-781-8300; FAX: 413-731-8980

Smith, Art, P.O. Box 645, Park Rapids, MN 56470 / 218-732-5333

Smith, Mark A., P.O. Box 182, Sinclair, WY 82334 / 307-324-7929

Smith, Michael, 2612 Ashmore Ave., Red Bank, TN 37415 / 615-267-8341

Smith, Ron, 5869 Straley, Fort Worth, TX 76114 / 817-732-6768

Smith, Sharmon, 4545 Speas Rd., Fruitland, ID 83619 / 208-452-6329 sharmon@fmtc.com

Smith Abrasives, Inc., 1700 Sleepy Valley Rd., Hot Springs, AR 71902-5095 / 501-321-2244; FAX: 501-321-9232 www.smithabrasives.com

Smith, Judy. See: L.B.T.

Smith Saddlery, Jesse W., 0499 County Road J, Pritchett, CO 81064 / 509-325-0622

Smokey Valley Rifles, E1976 Smokey Valley Rd., Scandinavia, WI 54977 / 715-467-2674

Snapp's Gunshop, 6911 E. Washington Rd., Clare, MI 48617 / 989-386-9226 snapp@glccomputers.com

Sno-Seal, Inc. (See Atsko/Sno-Seal, Inc.)

Societa Armi Bresciane Srl (See U.S. Importer-Cape Outfitters)

SOS Products Co. (See Buck Stix-SOS Products Co.), Box 3, Neenah, WI 54956

Sotheby's, 1334 York Ave. at 72nd St., New York, NY 10021 / 212-606-7260

Sound Tech Silencers, Box 391, Pelham, AL 35124 / 205-664-5860 silenceio@wmconnect.com www.soundtechsilencers.com

South Bend Replicas, Inc., 61650 Oak Rd., South Bend, IN 46614 / 219-289-4500

Southeastern Community College, 1015 S. Gear Ave., West Burlington, IA 52655 / 319-752-2731

Southern Ammunition Co., Inc., 4232 Meadow St., Loris, SC 29569-3124 / 803-756-3262; FAX: 803-756-3583

Southern Armory, The, 25 Millstone Rd., Woodlawn, VA 24381 / 703-238-1343; FAX: 703-238-1453

Southern Bloomer Mfg. Co., P.O. Box 1621, Bristol, TN 37620 / 615-878-6660; FAX: 615-878-8761

Southern Security, 1700 Oak Hills Dr., Kingston, TN 37763 / 423-376-6297; FAX: 800-251-9992

Sparks, Milt, 605 E. 44th St. No. 2, Boise, ID 83714-4800

Spartan-Realtree Products, Inc., 1390 Box Circle, Columbus, GA 31907 / 706-569-9101; FAX: 706-569-0042

Specialty Gunsmithing, Lynn McMurdo, P.O. Box 404, Afton, WY 83110 / 307-886-5535

Specialty Shooters Supply, Inc., 3325 Griffin Rd., Suite 9mm, Fort Lauderdale, FL 33317

Speer Bullets, P.O. Box 856, Lewiston, ID 83501 / 208-746-2351 www.speer-bullets.com

Spegel, Craig, P.O. Box 387, Nehalem, OR 97131 / 503-368-5653

Speiser, Fred D., 2229 Dearborn, Missoula, MT 59801 / 406-549-8133

Spencer Reblue Service, 1820 Tupelo Trail, Holt, MI 48842 / 517-694-7474

Spencer's Rifle Barrels, Inc., 4107 Jacobs Creek Dr., Scottsville, VA 24590 / 804-293-6836; FAX: 804-293-6836 www.spencersriflebarrels.com

SPG LLC, P.O. Box 1625, Cody, WY 82414 / 307-587-7621; FAX: 307-587-7695 spg@cody.wtp.net www.blackpowderspg.com

Sphinx Systems Ltd., Gesteigtstrasse 12, CH-3800, Matten, BRNE, SWITZERLAND

Splitfire Sporting Goods, L.L.C., P.O. Box 1044, Orem, UT 84059-1044 / 801-932-7950; FAX: 801-932-7959 www.splitfireguns.com

Spolar Power Load, Inc., 17376 Filbert, Fontana, CA 92335 / 800-227-9667

Sport Flite Manufacturing Co., 637 Kingsley Trl., Bloomfield Hills, MI 48304-2320 / 248-647-3747

Sporting Clays Of America, 9257 Bluckeye Rd., Sugar Grove, OH 43155-9632 / 740-746-8334; FAX: 740-746-8605

Sports Afield Magazine, 15621 Chemical Lane B, Huntington Beach, CA 92649 / 714-894-9080; FAX: 714-894-4949 info@sportsafield.com www.sportsafield.com

Sports Innovations, Inc., P.O. Box 5181, 8505 Jacksboro Hwy., Wichita Falls, TX 76307 / 817-723-6015

Sportsman Safe Mfg. Co., 6309-6311 Paramount Blvd., Long Beach, CA 90805 / 800-266-7150; or 310-984-5445

Sportsman's Communicators, 588 Radcliffe Ave., Pacific Palisades, CA 90272 / 800-538-3752

Sportsmatch U.K. Ltd., 16 Summer St. Leighton, Buzzard Beds, Bedfordshire, LU7 1HT ENGLAND / 4401525-381638; FAX: 4401525-851236 info@sportsmatch-uk.com www.sportsmatch-uk.com

Sportsmen's Exchange & Western Gun Traders, Inc., 813 Doris Ave., Oxnard, CA 93030 / 805-483-1917

Spradlin's, 457 Shannon Rd., Texas Creek Cotopaxi, CO 81223 / 719-275-7105; FAX: 719-275-3852 spradlins@prodigy.net www.spradlins.net

Springfield Armory, 420 W. Main St., Geneseo, IL 61254 / 309-944-5631; FAX: 309-944-3676 sales@springfield-armory.com www.springfieldarmory.com

Springfield Sporters, Inc., RD 1, Penn Run, PA 15765 / 412-254-2626; FAX: 412-254-9173

Springfield, Inc., 420 W. Main St., Geneseo, IL 61254 / 309-944-5631; FAX: 309-944-3676

Spyderco, Inc., 820 Spyderco Way, Golden, CO 80403 / 800-525-7770; or 800-525-7770; FAX: 303-278-2229 sales@spyderco.com www.spyderco.com

SSK Industries, J. D. Jones, 590 Woodvue Lane, Wintersville, OH 43953 / 740-264-0176; FAX: 740-264-2257 www.sskindustries.com

Stackpole Books, 5067 Ritter Rd., Mechanicsburg, PA 17055-6921 / 717-796-0411; or 800-732-3669; FAX: 717-796-0412 tmanney@stackpolebooks.com www.stackpolebooks.com

Stalker, Inc., P.O. Box 21, Fishermans Wharf Rd., Malakoff, TX 75148 / 903-489-1010

Stalwart Corporation, P.O. Box 46, Evanston, WY 82931 / 307-789-7687; FAX: 307-789-7688

Stan Baker Sports, Stan Baker, 10000 Lake City Way, Seattle, WA 98125 / 206-522-4575

Stan De Treville & Co., 4129 Normal St., San Diego, CA 92103 / 619-298-3393

Stanley Bullets, 2085 Heatheridge Ln., Reno, NV 89509

Star Ammunition, Inc., 5520 Rock Hampton Ct., Indianapolis, IN 46268 / 800-221-5927; FAX: 317-872-5847

Star Custom Bullets, P.O. Box 608, 468 Main St., Ferndale, CA 95536 / 707-786-9140; FAX: 707-786-9117 wmebridge@humboldt.com

Star Machine Works, P.O. Box 1872, Pioneer, CA 95666 / 209-295-5000

Starke Bullet Company, P.O. Box 400, 605 6th St. NW, Cooperstown, ND 58425 / 888-797-3431

Starkey Labs, 6700 Washington Ave. S., Eden Prairie, MN 55344

Starkey's Gun Shop, 9430 McCombs, El Paso, TX 79924 / 915-751-3030

Starlight Training Center, Inc., Rt. 1, P.O. Box 88, Bronaugh, MO 64728 / 417-843-3555

Starline, Inc., 1300 W. Henry St., Sedalia, MO 65301 / 660-827-6640; FAX: 660-827-6650 info@starlinebrass.com http://www.starlinebrass.com

Starr Trading Co., Jedediah, P.O. Box 2007, Farmington Hills, MI 48333 / 810-683-4343; FAX: 810-683-3282

Starrett Co., L. S., 121 Crescent St., Athol, MA 01331 / 978-249-3551; FAX: 978-249-8495

Steelman's Gun Shop, 10465 Beers Rd., Swartz Creek, MI 48473 / 810-735-4884

Steffens, Ron, 18396 Mariposa Creek Rd., Willits, CA 95490 / 707-485-0873

Stegall, James B., 26 Forest Rd., Wallkill, NY 12589

Steve Henigson & Associates, P.O. Box 2726, Culver City, CA 90231 / 310-305-8288; FAX: 310-305-1905

Steve Kamyk Engraver, 9 Grandview Dr., Westfield, MA 01085-1810 / 413-568-0457 stevek201@comcast.net

Steven Dodd Hughes, P.O. Box 545, Livingston, MT 59047 / 406-222-9377; FAX: 406-222-9377

Steves House of Guns, Rt. 1, Minnesota City, MN 55959 / 507-689-2573

Stewart Game Calls, Inc., Johnny, P.O. Box 7954, 5100 Fort Ave., Waco, TX 76714 / 817-772-3261; FAX: 817-772-3670

Stewart's Gunsmithing, P.O. Box 5854, Pietersburg North 0750, Transvaal, SOUTH AFRICA / 01521-89401

Steyr Mannlicher GmbH & Co. KG, Mannlicherstrasse 1, 4400 Steyr, Steyr, AUSTRIA / 0043-7252-896-0; FAX: 0043-7252-78620 office@steyr-mannlicher.com www.steyr-mannlicher.com

STI International, 114 Halmar Cove, Georgetown, TX 78628 / 800-959-8201; FAX: 512-819-0465 www.stiguns.com

Stiles Custom Guns, 76 Cherry Run Rd., Box 1605, Homer City, PA 15748 / 712-479-9945 glstiles@yourinter.net www.yourinter.net/glstiles

Stillwell, Robert, 421 Judith Ann Dr., Schertz, TX 78154

Stoeger Industries, 17603 Indian Head Hwy., Suite 200, Accokeek, MD 20607-2501 / 301-283-6300; FAX: 301-283-6986 www.stoegerindustries.com

Stoeger Publishing Co. (See Stoeger Industries)

Stone Enterprises Ltd., 426 Harveys Neck Rd., P.O. Box 335, Wicomico Church, VA 22579 / 804-580-5114; FAX: 804-580-8421

Stone Mountain Arms, 5988 Peachtree Corners E., Norcross, GA 30071 / 800-251-9412

Stoney Point Products, Inc., P.O. Box 234, 1822 N. Minnesota St., New Ulm, MN 56073-0234 / 507-354-3360; FAX: 507-354-7236 stoney@newulmtel.com www.stoneypoint.com

Storm, Gary, P.O. Box 5211, Richardson, TX 75083 / 214-385-0862

Stott's Creek Armory, Inc., 2526 S. 475W, Morgantown, IN 46160 / 317-878-5489; FAX: 317-878-9489 sccalendar@aol.com www.Sccalendar.aol.com

Stratco, Inc., P.O. Box 2270, Kalispell, MT 59901 / 406-755-1221; FAX: 406-755-1226

Strayer, Sandy. See: STRAYER-VOIGT, INC.

MANUFACTURER'S DIRECTORY

Strayer-Voigt, Inc., Sandy Strayer, 3435 Ray Orr Blvd., Grand Prairie, TX 75050 / 972-513-0575

Strong Holster Co., 39 Grove St., Gloucester, MA 01930 / 508-281-3300; FAX: 508-281-6321

Strutz Rifle Barrels, Inc., W. C., P.O. Box 611, Eagle River, WI 54521 / 715-479-4766

Stuart, V. Pat, Rt. 1, Box 447-S, Greenville, VA 24440 / 804-556-3845

Sturgeon Valley Sporters, Ken Ide, P.O. Box 283, Vanderbilt, MI 49795 / 989-983-4338 k.ide@mail.com

Sturm Ruger & Co. Inc., 200 Ruger Rd., Prescott, AZ 86301 / 928-541-8820; FAX: 520-541-8850 www.ruger.com

Sullivan, David S. (See Westwind Rifles, Inc.)

"Su-Press-On", Inc., P.O. Box 09161, Detroit, MI 48209 / 313-842-4222

Sun Welding Safe Co., 290 Easy St. No. 3, Simi Valley, CA 93065 / 805-584-6678; or 800-729-SAFE; FAX: 805-584-6169 sunwelding.com

Sunny Hill Enterprises, Inc., W1790 Cty. HHH, Malone, WI 53049 / 920-795-4722; FAX: 920-795-4822

Super 6 LLC, Gary Knopp, 3806 W. Lisbon Ave., Milwaukee, WI 53208 / 414-344-3343; FAX: 414-344-0304

Surecase Co., The, 233 Wilshire Blvd., Ste. 900, Santa Monica, CA 90401 / 800-92ARMLOC

Sure-Shot Game Calls, Inc., P.O. Box 816, 6835 Capitol, Groves, TX 77619 / 409-962-1636; FAX: 409-962-5465

Svon Corp., 2107 W. Blue Heron Blvd., Riviera Beach, FL 33404 / 508-881-8852

Swampfire Shop, The (See Peterson Gun Shop, Inc., A.W.)

Swann, D. J., 5 Orsova Close, Eltham North Vic., 3095 AUSTRALIA / 03-431-0323

Swanndri New Zealand, 152 Elm Ave., Burlingame, CA 94010 / 415-347-6158

Swanson, Mark, 975 Heap Avenue, Prescott, AZ 86301 / 928-778-4423

Swarovski Optik North America Ltd., 2 Slater Rd., Cranston, RI 02920 / 401-946-2220; or 800-426-3089; FAX: 401-946-2587

Sweet Home, Inc., P.O. Box 900, Orrville, OH 44667-0900

Swenson's 45 Shop, A. D., 3839 Ladera Vista Rd., Fallbrook, CA 92028-9431

Swift Bullet Co., P.O. Box 27, 201 Main St., Quinter, KS 67752 / 913-754-3959; FAX: 913-754-2359

Swift Instruments, Inc., 952 Dorchester Ave., Boston, MA 02125 / 617-436-2960; FAX: 617-436-3232

Swift River Gunworks, 450 State St., Belchertown, MA 01007 / 413-323-4052

Szweda, Robert (See RMS Custom Gunsmithing)

T

T&S Industries, Inc., 1027 Skyview Dr., W. Carrollton, OH 45449 / 513-859-8414; FAX: 937-859-8404 keith.tomlinson@tandsshellcatcher.com www.tandsshellcatcher.com

T.F.C. S.p.A., Via G. Marconi 118, B, Villa Carcina 25069, ITALY / 030-881271; FAX: 030-881826

T.G. Faust, Inc., 544 Minor St., Reading, PA 19602 / 610-375-8549; FAX: 610-375-4488

T.K. Lee Co., 1282 Branchwater Ln., Birmingham, AL 35216 / 205-913-5222 odonmich@aol.com www.scopedot.com

T.W. Menck Gunsmith, Inc., 5703 S. 77th St., Ralston, NE 68127 guntools@cox.net http://llwww.members.cox.net/guntools

Tabler Marketing, 2554 Lincoln Blvd., Suite 555, Marina Del Rey, CA 90291 / 818-386-0373; FAX: 818-386-0373

Taconic Firearms Ltd., Perry Lane, P.O. Box 553, Cambridge, NY 12816 / 518-677-2704; FAX: 518-677-5974

Tactical Defense Institute, 2174 Bethany Ridges, West Union, OH 45693 / 937-544-7228; FAX: 937-544-2887 tdiohio@dragonbbs.com www.tdiohio.com

Talley, Dave, P.O. Box 369, Santee, SC 29142 / 803-854-5700; or 307-436-9315; FAX: 803-854-9315 talley@diretway www.talleyrings.com

Talon Industries Inc. (See Cobra Enterprises, Inc.)

Tamarack Products, Inc., P.O. Box 625, Wauconda, IL 60084 / 708-526-9333; FAX: 708-526-9353

Tanfoglio Fratelli S.r.l., via Valtrompia 39, 41, Brescia, ITALY / 011-39-030-8910361; FAX: 011-39-030-8910183 info@tanfoglio.it www.tanfoglio.it

Tanglefree Industries, 1261 Heavenly Dr., Martinez, CA 94553 / 800-982-4868; FAX: 510-825-3874

Tank's Rifle Shop, P.O. Box 474, Fremont, NE 68026-0474 / 402-727-1317 jtank@tanksrifleshop.com www.tanksrifleshop.com

Tanner (See U.S. Importer-Mandall Shooting Supplies, Inc.)

Taracorp Industries, Inc., 1200 Sixteenth St., Granite City, IL 62040 / 618-451-4400

Target Shooting, Inc., P.O. Box 773, Watertown, SD 57201 / 605-882-6955; FAX: 605-882-8840

Tar-Hunt Custom Rifles, Inc., 101 Dogtown Rd., Bloomsburg, PA 17815 / 570-784-6368; FAX: 570-389-9150 www.tar-hunt.com

Tarnhelm Supply Co., Inc., 431 High St., Boscawen, NH 03303 / 603-796-2551; FAX: 603-796-2918 info@tarnhelm.com www.tarnhelm.com

Tasco Sales, Inc., 2889 Commerce Pkwy., Miramar, FL 33025

Taurus Firearms, Inc., 16175 NW 49th Ave., Miami, FL 33014 / 305-624-1115; FAX: 305-623-7506

Taurus International Firearms (See U.S. Importer Taurus Firearms, Inc.)

Taurus S.A. Forjas, Avenida Do Forte 511, Porto Alegre, RS BRAZIL 91360 / 55-51-347-4050; FAX: 55-51-347-3065

Taylor & Robbins, P.O. Box 164, Rixford, PA 16745 / 814-966-3233

Taylor's & Co., Inc., 304 Lenoir Dr., Winchester, VA 22603 / 540-722-2017; FAX: 540-722-2018 info@taylorsfirearms.com www.taylorsfirearms.com

TCCI, P.O. Box 302, Phoenix, AZ 85001 / 602-237-3823; FAX: 602-237-3858

TCSR, 3998 Hoffman Rd., White Bear Lake, MN 55110-4626 / 800-328-5323; FAX: 612-429-0526

TDP Industries, Inc., P.O. Box 249, Ottsville, PA 18942-0249 / 215-345-8687; FAX: 215-345-6057

Techno Arms (See U.S. Importer- Auto-Ordnance Corp.)

Tecnolegno S.p.A., Via A. Locatelli, 6 10, 24019 Zogno, ITALY / 0345-55111; FAX: 0345-55155

Ted Blocker Holsters, Inc., 9396 S.W. Tigard St., Tigard, OR 97223 / 800-650-9742; FAX: 503-670-9692 www.tedblocker.com

Tele-Optics, 630 E. Rockland Rd., P.O. Box 6313, Libertyville, IL 60048 / 847-362-7757; FAX: 847-362-7757

Tennessee Valley Mfg., 14 County Road 521, Corinth, MS 38834 / 601-286-5014 tvm@avsia.com www.avsia.com/tvm

Ten-Ring Precision, Inc., Alex B. Hamilton, 1449 Blue Crest Lane, San Antonio, TX 78232 / 210-494-3063; FAX: 210-494-3066

TEN-X Products Group, 1905 N. Main St., Suite 133, Cleburne, TX 76031-1305 / 972-243-4016; or 800-433-2225; FAX: 972-243-4112

Tepeco, P.O. Box 342, Friendswood, TX 77546 / 713-482-2702

Terry K. Kopp Professional Gunsmithing, Rt 1 Box 224, Lexington, MO 64067 / 816-259-2636

Testing Systems, Inc., 220 Pegasus Ave., Northvale, NJ 07647

Tetra Gun Care, 8 Vreeland Rd., Florham Park, NJ 07932 / 973-443-0004; FAX: 973-443-0263

Tex Shoemaker & Sons, Inc., 714 W. Cienega Ave., San Dimas, CA 91773 / 909-592-2071; FAX: 909-592-2378 texshoemaker@texshoemaker.com www.texshoemaker.com

Texas Armory (See Bond Arms, Inc.)

Texas Platers Supply Co., 2453 W. Five Mile Parkway, Dallas, TX 75233 / 214-330-7168

Thad Rybka Custom Leather Equipment, 2050 Canoe Creek Rd., Springvale, AL 35146-6709

Thad Scott Fine Guns, Inc., P.O. Box 412, Indianola, MS 38751 / 601-887-5929

Theis, Terry, 21452 FM 2093, Harper, TX 78631 / 830-864-4438

Thiewes, George W., 14329 W. Parada Dr., Sun City West, AZ 85375

Things Unlimited, 235 N. Kimbau, Casper, WY 82601 / 307-234-5277

Thirion Gun Engraving, Denise, P.O. Box 408, Graton, CA 95444 / 707-829-1876

Thomas, Charles C., 2600 S. First St., Springfield, IL 62704 / 217-789-8980; FAX: 217-789-9130 books@ccthomas.com ccthomas.com

Thompson Bullet Lube Co., P.O. Box 409, Wills Point, TX 75169 / 866-476-1500; FAX: 866-476-1500 thompsonbulletlube.com www.thompsonbulletlube.com

Thompson Precision, 110 Mary St., P.O. Box 251, Warren, IL 61087 / 815-745-3625

Thompson, Randall. See: HIGHLINE MACHINE CO.

Thompson Target Technology, 4804 Sherman Church Ave. S.W., Canton, OH 44710 / 330-484-6480; FAX: 330-491-1087 www.thompsontarget.com

Thompson Tool Mount, 1550 Solomon Rd., Santa Maria, CA 93455 / 805-934-1281 ttm@pronet.net www.thompsontoolmount.com

Thompson/Center Arms, P.O. Box 5002, Rochester, NH 03866 / 603-332-2394; FAX: 603-332-5133 tech@tcarms.com www.tcarms.com

Thunden Ranch, HCR 1, Box 53, Mountain Home, TX 78058 / 830-640-3138

Tiger-Hunt Longrifle Gunstocks, Box 379, Beaverdale, PA 15921 / 814-472-5161 tigerhunt4@aol.com www.gunstockwood.com

Tikka (See U.S. Importer-Stoeger Industries)

Time Precision, 4 Nicholas Sq., New Milford, CT 06776-3506 / 860-350-8343; FAX: 860-350-6343 timeprecision@aol.com

Tinks & Ben Lee Hunting Products (See Wellington Outdoors)

Tink's Safariland Hunting Corp., P.O. Box 244, 1140 Monticello Rd., Madison, GA 30650 / 706-342-4915; FAX: 706-342-7568

Tioga Engineering Co., Inc., P.O. Box 913, 13 Cone St., Wellsboro, PA 16901 / 570-724-3533; FAX: 570-724-3895 tiogaeng@epix.net

Tippman Pneumatics, Inc., 2955 Adams Center Rd., Fort Wayne, IN 46803

Tirelli, Snc Di Tirelli Primo E.C., Via Matteotti No. 359, Gardone V.T. Brescia, ITALY / 0039-030-8912819; FAX: 0039-030-832240 tirelli@tirelli.it www.tirelli.it

TM Stockworks, 6355 Maplecrest Rd., Fort Wayne, IN 46835 / 219-485-5389

Tom Forrest, Inc., P.O. Box 326, Lakeside, CA 92040 / 619-561-5800; FAX: 888-GUN-CLIP info@gunmag.com www.gunmags.com

Tombstone Smoke`n' Deals, PO Box 31298, Phoenix, AZ 85046 / 602-905-7013; FAX: 602-443-1998

Tom's Gun Repair, Thomas G. Ivanoff, 76-6 Rt. Southfork Rd., Cody, WY 82414 / 307-587-6949

Tom's Gunshop, 3601 Central Ave., Hot Springs, AR 71913 / 501-624-3856

Tonoloway Tack Drives, HCR 81, Box 100, Needmore, PA 17238

Torel, Inc./Tandy Brands Outdoors/AA & E, 208 Industrial Loop, Yoakum, TX 77995 / 361-293-6366; FAX: 361-293-9127

TOZ (See U.S. Importer-Nygord Precision Products, Inc.)

Track of the Wolf, Inc., 18308 Joplin St. NW, Elk River, MN 55330-1773 / 763-633-2500; FAX: 763-633-2550

Traditions Performance Firearms, P.O. Box 776, 1375 Boston Post Rd., Old Saybrook, CT 06475 / 860-388-4656; FAX: 860-388-4657 info@traditionsfirearms.com www.traditionsfirearms.com

Trafalgar Square, P.O. Box 257, N. Pomfret, VT 05053 / 802-457-1911

Trail Visions, 5800 N. Ames Terrace, Glendale, WI 53209 / 414-228-1328

Trax America, Inc., P.O. Box 898, 1150 Eldridge, Forrest City, AR 72335 / 870-633-0410; or 800-232-2327; FAX: 870-633-4788 trax@ipa.net www.traxamerica.com

Treadlok Gun Safe, Inc., 1764 Granby St. NE, Roanoke, VA 24012 / 800-729-8732; or 703-982-6881; FAX: 703-982-1059

Treebone Carving, P.O. Box 551, Cimarron, NJ 87714 / 505-376-2145 treebonecarving.com

Treemaster, P.O. Box 247, Guntersville, AL 35976 / 205-878-3597

Trevallion Gunstocks, 9 Old Mountain Rd., Cape Neddick, ME 03902 / 207-361-1130

Trico Plastics, 28061 Diaz Rd., Temecula, CA 92590 / 909-676-7714; FAX: 909-676-0267 ustinfo@ustplastics.com www.tricoplastics.com

Trigger Lock Division / Central Specialties Ltd., 220-D Exchange Dr., Crystal Lake, IL 60014 / 847-639-3900; FAX: 847-639-3972

Trijicon, Inc., 49385 Shafer Ave., P.O. Box 930059, Wixom, MI 48393-0059 / 248-960-7700; or 800-338-0563

Trilby Sport Shop, 1623 Hagley Rd., Toledo, OH 43612-2024 / 419-472-6222

Trilux, Inc., P.O. Box 24608, Winston-Salem, NC 27114 / 910-659-9438; FAX: 910-768-7720

Trinidad St. Jr. Col. Gunsmith Dept., 600 Prospect St., Trinidad, CO 81082 / 719-846-5631; FAX: 719-846-5667

Triple-K Mfg. Co., Inc., 2222 Commercial St., San Diego, CA 92113 / 619-232-2066; FAX: 619-232-7675 sales@triplek.com www.triplek.com

MANUFACTURER'S DIRECTORY

Tristar Sporting Arms, Ltd., 1814 Linn St. #16, N. Kansas City, MO 64116-3627 / 816-421-1400; FAX: 816-421-4182 tristar@blitz-it.net www.tristarsportingarms

Trius Traps, Inc., P.O. Box 25, 221 S. Miami Ave., Cleves, OH 45002 / 513-941-5682; FAX: 513-941-7970 triustraps@fuse.net www.triustraps.com

Trooper Walsh, 2393 N. Edgewood St., Arlington, VA 22207

Trotman, Ken, 135 Ditton Walk, Unit 11, Cambridge, CB5 8PY ENGLAND / 01223-211030; FAX: 01223-212317 www.kentrolman.com

Tru-Balance Knife Co., P.O. Box 140555, Grand Rapids, MI 49514 / 616-647-1215

True Flight Bullet Co., 5581 Roosevelt St., Whitehall, PA 18052 / 610-262-7630; FAX: 610-262-7806

Truglo, Inc., P.O. Box 1612, McKinna, TX 75070 / 972-774-0300; FAX: 972-774-0323 www.truglosights.com

Trulock Tool, P.O. Box 530, Whigham, GA 31797 / 229-762-4678; FAX: 229-762-4050 trulockchokes@hotmail.com trulockchokes.com

Tru-Nord Compass, 1504 Erick Lane, Brainerd, MN 56401 / 218-829-2870; FAX: 218-829-2870 www.trunord.com

Tru-Square Metal Products, Inc., 640 First St. SW, P.O. Box 585, Auburn, WA 98071 / 253-833-2310; or 800-225-1017; FAX: 253-833-2349 t-tumbler@qwest.net

Tucker, James C., P.O. Box 366, Medford, OR 97501 / 541-664-9160 jctstocker@yahoo.com

Tucson Mold, Inc., 930 S. Plumer Ave., Tucson, AZ 85719 / 520-792-1075; FAX: 520-792-1075

Turk's Head Productions, Mustafa Bilal, 908 NW 50th St., Seattle, WA 98107-3634 / 206-782-4164; FAX: 206-783-5677 info@turkshead.com www.turkshead.com

Turnbull Restoration, Doug, 6680 Rts. 5 & 20, P.O. Box 471, Bloomfield, NY 14469 / 585-657-6338; FAX: 585-657-6338 turnbullrest@mindspring.com www.turnbullrestoration.com

Tuttle, Dale, 4046 Russell Rd., Muskegon, MI 49445 / 616-766-2250

U

U.S. Importer-Wm. Larkin Moore, 8430 E. Raintree Ste. B-7, Scottsdale, AZ 85260

U.S. Optics, A Division of Zeitz Optics U.S.A., 5900 Dale St., Buena Park, CA 90621 / 714-994-4901; FAX: 714-994-4904 www.usoptics.com

U.S. Repeating Arms Co., Inc., 275 Winchester Ave., Morgan, UT 84050-9333 / 801-876-3440; FAX: 801-876-3737 www.winchester-guns.com

U.S. Tactical Systems (See Keng's Firearms Specialty, Inc.)

Ugartechea S. A., Ignacio, Chonta 26, Eibar, SPAIN / 43-121257; FAX: 43-121669

Ultra Dot Distribution, P.O. Box 362, 6304 Riverside Dr., Yankeetown, FL 34498 / 352-447-2255; FAX: 352-447-2266

Ultralux (See U.S. Importer-Keng's Firearms Specialty, Inc.)

UltraSport Arms, Inc., 1955 Norwood Ct., Racine, WI 53403 / 414-554-3237; FAX: 414-554-9731

Uncle Bud's, HCR 81, Box 100, Needmore, PA 17238 / 717-294-6000; FAX: 717-294-6005

Uncle Mike's (See Michaels of Oregon, Co.)

Unertl Optical Co., Inc., 103 Grand Avenue, P.O. Box 895, Mars, PA 16046-0895 / 724-625-3810; FAX: 724-625-3819 unertl@nauticom.net www.unertloptics.net

UniTec, 1250 Bedford SW, Canton, OH 44710 / 216-452-4017

United Binocular Co., 9043 S. Western Ave., Chicago, IL 60620

United Cutlery Corp., 1425 United Blvd., Sevierville, TN 37876 / 865-428-2532; or 800-548-0835; FAX: 865-428-2267 www.unitedcutlery.com

United States Products Co., 518 Melwood Ave., Pittsburgh, PA 15213-1136 / 412-621-2130; FAX: 412-621-8740 sales@us-products.com www.usporepaste.com

Universal Sports, P.O. Box 532, Vincennes, IN 47591 / 812-882-8680; FAX: 812-882-8680

Upper Missouri Trading Co., P.O. Box 100, 304 Harold St., Crofton, NE 68730-0100 / 402-388-4844 www.uppermotradingco.com

USAC, 4500-15th St. East, Tacoma, WA 98424 / 206-922-7589

Uselton/Arms, Inc., 842 Conference Dr., Goodlettsville, TN 37072 / 615-851-4919

Utica Cutlery Co., 820 Noyes St., Utica, NY 13503 / 315-733-4663; FAX: 315-733-6602

V

V. H. Blackinton & Co., Inc., 221 John L. Dietsch, Attleboro Falls, MA 02763-0300 / 508-699-4436; FAX: 508-695-5349

Valdada Enterprises, P.O. Box 773122, 31733 County Road 35, Steamboat Springs, CO 80477 / 970-879-2983; FAX: 970-879-0851 www.valdada.com

Valtro USA, Inc., 1281 Andersen Dr., San Rafael, CA 94901 / 415-256-2575; FAX: 415-256-2576

VAM Distribution Co. LLC, 1141-B Mechanicsburg Rd., Wooster, OH 44691 www.rex10.com

Van Gorden & Son Inc., C. S., 1815 Main St., Bloomer, WI 54724 / 715-568-2612

Van Horn, Gil, P.O. Box 207, Llano, CA 93544

Van Patten, J. W., P.O. Box 145, Foster Hill, Milford, PA 18337 / 717-296-7069

Vann Custom Bullets, 2766 N. Willowside Way, Meridian, ID 83642

Van's Gunsmith Service, 224 Route 69-A, Parish, NY 13131 / 315-625-7251

Varmint Masters, LLC, Rick Vecqueray, P.O. Box 6724, Bend, OR 97708 / 541-318-7306; FAX: 541-318-7306 varmintmasters@bendcable.com www.varmintmasters.net

Vecqueray, Rick. See: VARMINT MASTERS, LLC

Vector Arms, Inc., 270 W. 500 N., North Salt Lake, UT 84054 / 801-295-1917; FAX: 801-295-9316 vectorarms@bbscmail.com www.vectorarms.com

Vega Tool Co., c/o T. R. Ross, 4865 Tanglewood Ct., Boulder, CO 80301 / 303-530-0174 clanlaird@aol.com www.vegatool.com

Venco Industries, Inc. (See Shooter's Choice Gun Care)

Venus Industries, P.O. Box 246, Sialkot-1, PAKISTAN FAX: 92 432 85579

Verney-Carron, 54 Boulevard Thiers-B.P. 72, 42002 St. Etienne Cedex 1, St. Etienne Cedex 1, FRANCE / 33-477791500; FAX: 33-477790702 email@verney-carron.com www.verney-carron.com

Vest, John, 1923 NE 7th St., Redmond, OR 97756 / 541-923-8898

VibraShine, Inc., P.O. Box 577, Taylorsville, MS 39168 / 601-785-9854; FAX: 601-785-9874 rdbeke@vibrashine.com www.vibrashine.com

Vibra-Tek Co., 1844 Arroya Rd., Colorado Springs, CO 80906 / 719-634-8611; FAX: 719-634-6886

Vic's Gun Refinishing, 6 Pineview Dr., Dover, NH 03820-6422 / 603-742-0013

Victory Ammunition, P.O. Box 1022, Milford, PA 18337 / 717-296-5768; FAX: 717-296-9298

Victory USA, P.O. Box 1021, Pine Bush, NY 12566 / 914-744-2060; FAX: 914-744-5181

Vihtavuori Oy, FIN-41330 Vihtavuori, FINLAND, / 358-41-3779211; FAX: 358-41-3771643

Vihtavuori Oy/Kaltron-Pettibone, 1241 Ellis St., Bensenville, IL 60106 / 708-350-1116; FAX: 708-350-1606

Viking Video Productions, P.O. Box 251, Roseburg, OR 97470

Village Restorations & Consulting, Inc., P.O. Box 569, Claysburg, PA 16625 / 814-239-8200; FAX: 814-239-2165 www.villagerestoration@yahoo.com

Vincent's Shop, 210 Antoinette, Fairbanks, AK 99701

Viper Bullet and Brass Works, 11 Brock St., Box 582, Norwich, ON N0J 1P0 CANADA

Viramontez Engraving, Ray Viramontez, 601 Springfield Dr., Albany, GA 31721 / 229-432-9683 sgtvira@aol.com

Viramontez, Ray. See: VIRAMONTEZ ENGRAVING

Virgin Valley Custom Guns, 450 E 800 N. #20, Hurricane, UT 84737 / 435-635-8941; FAX: 435-635-8943 vvcguns@infowest.com www.virginvalleyguns.com

Visible Impact Targets, Rts. 5 & 20, E. Bloomfield, NY 14443 / 716-657-6161; FAX: 716-657-5405

Vitt/Boos, 1195 Buck Hill Rd., Townshend, VT 05353 / 802-365-9232

Voere-KGH GmbH, Untere Sparchen 56, A-6330 Kufstein, Tirol, AUSTRIA / 0043-5372-62547; FAX: 0043-5372-65752 voere@aon.com www.voere.com

Volquartsen Custom Ltd., 24276 240th Street, P.O. Box 397, Carroll, IA 51401 / 712-792-4238; FAX: 712-792-2542 vcl@netins.net www.volquartsen.com

Vorhes, David, 3042 Beecham St., Napa, CA 94558 / 707-226-9116; FAX: 707-253-7334

VSP Publishers (See Heritage/VSP Gun Books), P.O. Box 887, McCall, ID 83638 / 208-634-4104; FAX: 208-634-3101 heritage@gunbooks.com www.gunbooks.com

VTI Gun Parts, P.O. Box 509, Lakeville, CT 06039 / 860-435-8068; FAX: 860-435-8146 mail@vtigunparts.com www.vtigunparts.com

Vulpes Ventures, Inc., Fox Cartridge Division, P.O. Box 1363, Bolingbrook, IL 60440-7363 / 630-759-1229

W

W. Square Enterprises, 9826 Sagedale Dr., Houston, TX 77089 / 281-484-0935; FAX: 281-464-9940 lfdw@pdq.net www.loadammo.com

W. Waller & Son, Inc., 2221 Stoney Brook Rd., Grantham, NH 03753-7706 / 603-863-4177 www.wallerandson.com

W.B. Niemi Engineering, Box 126 Center Road, Greensboro, VT 05841 / 802-533-7180; or 802-533-7141

W.C. Wolff Co., P.O. Box 458, Newtown Square, PA 19073 / 610-359-9600; or 800-545-0077 mail@gunsprings.com www.gunsprings.com

W.E. Birdsong & Assoc., 1435 Monterey Rd., Florence, MS 39073-9748 / 601-366-8270

W.E. Brownell Checkering Tools, 9390 Twin Mountain Cir., San Diego, CA 92126 / 858-695-2479; FAX: 858-695-2479

W.J. Riebe Co., 3434 Tucker Rd., Boise, ID 83703

W.R. Case & Sons Cutlery Co., Owens Way, Bradford, PA 16701 / 814-368-4123; or 800-523-6350; FAX: 814-368-1736 jsullivan@wrcase.com www.wrcase.com

Wagoner, Vernon G., 2325 E. Encanto St., Mesa, AZ 85213-5917 / 480-835-1307

Waldron, Herman, Box 475, 80 N. 17th St., Pomeroy, WA 99347 / 509-843-1404

Walker Arms Co., Inc., 499 County Rd. 820, Selma, AL 36701 / 334-872-6231; FAX: 334-872-6262

Wallace, Terry, 385 San Marino, Vallejo, CA 94589 / 707-642-7041

Walls Industries, Inc., P.O. Box 98, 1905 N. Main, Cleburne, TX 76033 / 817-645-4366; FAX: 817-645-7946 www.wallsoutdoors.com

Walters Industries, 6226 Park Lane, Dallas, TX 75225 / 214-691-6973

Walters, John. See: WALTERS WADS

Walters Wads, John Walters, 500 N. Avery Dr., Moore, OK 73160 / 405-799-0376; FAX: 405-799-7727 www.tinwadman@cs.com

Walther America, P.O. Box 22, Springfield, MA 01102 / 413-747-3443 www.walther-usa.com

Walther GmbH, Carl, B.P. 4325, D-89033 Ulm, GERMANY

Walt's Custom Leather, Walt Whinnery, 1947 Meadow Creek Dr., Louisville, KY 40218 / 502-458-4361

WAMCO-New Mexico, P.O. Box 205, Peralta, NM 87042-0205 / 505-869-0826

Ward & Van Valkenburg, 114 32nd Ave. N., Fargo, ND 58102 / 701-232-2351

Ward Machine, 5620 Lexington Rd., Corpus Christi, TX 78412 / 512-992-1221

Wardell Precision Handguns Ltd., P.O. Box 391, Clyde, AZ 79510-0391 / 602-465-7995

Warenski Engraving, Julie Warenski, 590 E. 500 N., Richfield, UT 84701 / 435-896-5319; FAX: 435-896-8333 julie@warenskiknives.com

Warenski, Julie. See: WARENSKI ENGRAVING

Warne Manufacturing Co., 9057 SE Jannsen Rd., Clackamas, OR 97015 / 503-657-5590; or 800-683-5590; FAX: 503-657-5695 info@warnescopemounts.com www.warnescopemounts.com

Warren Muzzleloading Co., Inc., Hwy. 21 North, P.O. Box 100, Ozone, AR 72854 / 501-292-3268

Washita Mountain Whetstone Co., P.O. Box 20378, Hot Springs, AR 71903 / 501-525-3914 www.hsnp.com

Wasmundt, Jim, P.O. Box 130, Powers, OR 97466-0130

Watson Bros., 39 Redcross Way, London Bridge SE1 1H6, London, ENGLAND FAX: 44-171-403-336

Watson Bullets, 231 Allies Pass, Frostproof, FL 33843 / 863-635-7948 cbestbullet@aol.com

Wayne Specialty Services, 260 Waterford Drive, Florissant, MO 63033 / 413-831-7083

WD-40 Co., 1061 Cudahy Pl., San Diego, CA 92110 / 619-275-1400; FAX: 619-275-5823

Weatherby, Inc., 3100 El Camino Real, Atascadero, CA 93422 / 805-466-1767; FAX: 805-466-2527 www.weatherby.com

Weaver Products ATK, P.O. Box 39, Onalaska, WI 54650 / 800-648-9624; or 608-781-5800; FAX: 608-781-0368

MANUFACTURER'S DIRECTORY

Weaver Scope Repair Service, 1121 Larry Mahan Dr., Suite B, El Paso, TX 79925 / 915-593-1005

Webb, Bill, 6504 North Bellefontaine, Kansas City, MO 64119 / 816-453-7431

Weber & Markin Custom Gunsmiths, 4-1691 Powick Rd., Kelowna, BC V1X 4L1 CANADA / 250-762-7575; FAX: 250-861-3655 www.weberandmarkinguns.com

Webley and Scott Ltd., Frankley Industrial Park, Tay Rd., Birmingham, B45 0PA ENGLAND / 011-021-453-1864; FAX: 0121-457-7846 guns@webley.co.uk www.webley.co.uk

Webster Scale Mfg. Co., P.O. Box 188, Sebring, FL 33870 / 813-385-6362

Weems, Cecil, 510 W. Hubbard St., Mineral Wells, TX 76067-4847 / 817-325-1462

Weigand Combat Handguns, Inc., 1057 South Main Rd., Mountain Top, PA 18707 / 570-868-8358; FAX: 570-868-5218 sales@jackweigand.com www.jackweigand.com

Weihrauch KG, Hermann, Industriestrasse 11, 8744 Mellrichstadt, Mellrichstadt, GERMANY

Welch, Sam. See: SAM WELCH GUN ENGRAVING

Wellington Outdoors, P.O. Box 244, 1140 Monticello Rd., Madison, GA 30650 / 706-342-4915; FAX: 706-342-7568

Wells, Rachel, 110 N. Summit St., Prescott, AZ 86301 / 928-445-3655 wellssportstore@cableone.net

Wells Creek Knife & Gun Works, 32956 State Hwy. 38, Scottsburg, OR 97473 / 541-587-4202; FAX: 541-587-4223

Welsh, Bud. See: HIGH PRECISION

Wenger North America/Precise Int'l., 15 Corporate Dr., Orangeburg, NY 10962 / 800-431-2996; FAX: 914-425-4700

Wenig Custom Gunstocks, 103 N. Market St., P.O. Box 249, Lincoln, MO 65338 / 660-547-3334; FAX: 660-547-2881 gustock@wenig.com www.wenig.com

Werth, T. W., 1203 Woodlawn Rd., Lincoln, IL 62656 / 217-732-1300

Wescombe, Bill (See North Star West)

Wessinger Custom Guns & Engraving, 268 Limestone Rd., Chapin, SC 29036 / 803-345-5677

West, Jack L., 1220 W. Fifth, P.O. Box 427, Arlington, OR 97812

Western Cutlery (See Camillus Cutlery Co.)

Western Mfg. Co., 550 Valencia School Rd., Aptos, CA 95003 / 831-688-5884 lotsabears@eathlink.net

Western Missouri Shooters Alliance, P.O. Box 11144, Kansas City, MO 64119 / 816-597-3950; FAX: 816-229-7350

Western Nevada West Coast Bullets, P.O. BOX 2270, DAYTON, NV 89403-2270 / 702-246-3941; FAX: 702-246-0836

Westley Richards & Co. Ltd., 40 Grange Rd., Birmingham, ENGLAND / 010-214722953; FAX: 010-214141138 sales@westleyrichards.com www.westleyrichards.com

Westley Richards Agency USA (See U.S. Importer

Westwind Rifles, Inc., David S. Sullivan, P.O. Box 261, 640 Briggs St., Erie, CO 80516 / 303-828-3823

Weyer International, 2740 Nebraska Ave., Toledo, OH 43607 / 419-534-2020; FAX: 419-534-2697

Whildin & Sons Ltd., E.H., RR 2 Box 119, Tamaqua, PA 18252 / 717-668-6743; FAX: 717-668-6745

Whinnery, Walt (See Walt's Custom Leather)

White Barn Wor, 431 County Road, Broadlands, IL 61816

White Pine Photographic Services, Hwy. 60, General Delivery, Wilno, ON K0J 2N0 CANADA / 613-756-3452

White Rifles, Inc., 234 S. 1250 W., Linden, UT 84042 / 801-932-7950 www.whiterifles.com

White Rock Tool & Die, 6400 N. Brighton Ave., Kansas City, MO 64119 / 816-454-0478

Whitestone Lumber Corp., 148-02 14th Ave., Whitestone, NY 11357 / 718-746-4400; FAX: 718-767-1748 whstco@aol.com

Wichita Arms, Inc., 923 E. Gilbert, Wichita, KS 67211 / 316-265-0661; FAX: 316-265-0760 sales@wichitaarms.com www.wichitaarms.com

Wick, David E., 1504 Michigan Ave., Columbus, IN 47201 / 812-376-6960

Widener's Reloading & Shooting Supply, Inc., P.O. Box 3009 CRS, Johnson City, TN 37602 / 615-282-6786; FAX: 615-282-6651

Wideview Scope Mount Corp., 13535 S. Hwy. 16, Rapid City, SD 57702 / 605-341-3220; FAX: 605-341-9142 wvdon@rapidnet.com www.wideviewscopemount.com

Wiebe, Duane, 5300 Merchant Cir. #2, Placerville, CA 95667 / 530-344-1357; FAX: 530-344-1357 wiebe@d-wdb.com

Wiest, Marie. See: GUNCRAFT SPORTS, INC.

Wilcox All-Pro Tools & Supply, 4880 147th St., Montezuma, IA 50171 / 515-623-3138; FAX: 515-623-3104

Wilcox Industries Corp., Robert F. Guarasi, 53 Durham St., Portsmouth, NH 03801 / 603-431-1331; FAX: 603-431-1221

Wild Bill's Originals, P.O. Box 13037, Burton, WA 98013 / 206-463-5738; FAX: 206-465-5925 wildbill@halcyon.com billcleaver@centurytel.net

Wild West Guns, 7521 Old Seward Hwy., Unit A, Anchorage, AK 99518 / 800-992-4570; or 907-344-4500; FAX: 907-344-4005 wwguns@ak.net www.wildwestguns.com

Wilderness Sound Products Ltd., 4015 Main St. A, Springfield, OR 97478

Wildey F. A., Inc., 45 Angevin Rd., Warren, CT 06754-1818 / 860-355-9000; FAX: 860-354-7759 wildeyfa@optonline.net www.wildeyguns.com

Wildlife Research Center, Inc., 1050 McKinley St., Anoka, MN 55303 / 763-427-3350; or 800-USE-LURE; FAX: 763-427-8354 www.wildlife.com

Will-Burt Co., 169 S. Main, Orrville, OH 44667

William E. Phillips Firearms, 38 Avondale Rd., Wigston, Leicester, ENGLAND / 0116 2886334; FAX: 0116 2810644 william.phillips2@tesco.net

William Powell Agency, 22 Circle Dr., Bellmore, NY 11710 / 516-679-1158

Williams Gun Sight Co., 7389 Lapeer Rd., Box 329, Davison, MI 48423 / 810-653-2131; or 800-530-9028; FAX: 810-658-2140 williamsgunsight.com

Williams Mfg. of Oregon, 110 East B St., Drain, OR 97435 / 503-836-7461; FAX: 503-836-7245

Williams Shootin' Iron Service, The Lynx-Line, Rt. 2 Box 223A, Mountain Grove, MO 65711 / 417-948-0902; FAX: 417-948-0902

Williamson Precision Gunsmithing, 117 W. Pipeline, Hurst, TX 76053 / 817-285-0064; FAX: 817-280-0044

Willow Bend, P.O. Box 203, Chelmsford, MA 01824 / 978-256-8508; FAX: 978-256-8508

Wilsom Combat, 2234 CR 719, Berryville, AR 72616-4573 / 800-955-4856; FAX: 870-545-3310

Wilson Arms Co., The, 63 Leetes Island Rd., Branford, CT 06405 / 203-488-7297; FAX: 203-488-0135

Wilson Case, Inc., P.O. Box 1106, Hastings, NE 68902-1106 / 800-322-5493; FAX: 402-463-5276 sales@wilsoncase.com www.wilsoncase.com

Wilson Combat, 2234 CR 719, Berryville, AR 72616-4573 / 800-955-4856

Winchester Consultants, George Madis, P.O. Box 545, Brownsboro, TX 75756 / 903-852-6480; FAX: 903-852-5486 gmadis@earthlink.com www.georgemadis.com

Winchester Div. Olin Corp., 427 N. Shamrock, E. Alton, IL 62024 / 618-258-3566; FAX: 618-258-3599

Winchester Sutler, Inc., The, 270 Shadow Brook Lane, Winchester, VA 22603 / 540-888-3595; FAX: 540-888-4632

Windish, Jim, 2510 Dawn Dr., Alexandria, VA 22306 / 703-765-1994

Winfield Galleries LLC, 748 Hanley Industrial Ct., St. Louis, MO 63144 / 314-645-7636; FAX: 314-781-0224 info@winfieldgalleries.com www.winfieldgalleries.com

Wingshooting Adventures, 0-1845 W. Leonard, Grand Rapids, MI 49544 / 616-677-1980; FAX: 616-677-1986

Winter, Robert M., P.O. Box 484, 42975-287th St., Menno, SD 57045 / 605-387-5322

Wise Custom Guns, 1402 Blanco Rd., San Antonio, TX 78212-2716 / 210-828-3388

Wise Guns, Dale, 1402 Blanco Rd., San Antonio, TX 78212 / 210-734-9999

Wiseman and Co., Bill, P.O. Box 3427, Bryan, TX 77805 / 409-690-3456; FAX: 409-690-0156

Wisners, Inc., P.O. Box 58, Adna, WA 98522 / 360-748-4590; FAX: 360-748-6028 parts@wisnersinc.com www.wisnersinc.com

Wolf Performance Ammunition, 2201 E. Winston Rd., Ste. K, Anaheim, CA 92806-5537 / 702-837-8506; FAX: 702-837-9250

Wolfe Publishing Co., 2625 Stearman Rd., Ste. A, Prescott, AZ 86301 / 928-445-7810; or 800-899-7810; FAX: 928-778-5124

Wolverine Footwear Group, 9341 Courtland Dr. NE, Rockford, MI 49351 / 616-866-5500; FAX: 616-866-5658

Woodleigh (See Huntington Die Specialties)

Woods Wise Products, P.O. Box 681552, Franklin, TN 37068 / 800-735-8182; FAX: 615-726-2637

Woodstream, P.O. Box 327, Lititz, PA 17543 / 717-626-2125; FAX: 717-626-1912

Woodworker's Supply, 1108 North Glenn Rd., Casper, WY 82601 / 307-237-5354

Woolrich, Inc., Mill St., Woolrich, PA 17701 / 800-995-1299; FAX: 717-769-6234/6259

World of Targets (See Birchwood Casey)

World Trek, Inc., 7170 Turkey Creek Rd., Pueblo, CO 81007-1046 / 719-546-2121; FAX: 719-543-6886

Worthy Products, Inc., RR 1, P.O. Box 213, Martville, NY 13111 / 315-324-5298

Wright's Gunstock Blanks, 8540 SE Kane Rd., Gresham, OR 97080 / 503-666-1705 doyal@wrightsguns.com www.wrightsguns.com

WTA Manufacturing, P.O. Box 164, Kit Carson, CO 80825 / 719-962-3570; or 719-962-3570 wta@rebeltec.net http://www.members.aol.com/ductman249/wta.html

Wyant Bullets, Gen. Del., Swan Lake, MT 59911

Wyoming Custom Bullets, 1626 21st St., Cody, WY 82414

Wyoming Knife Corp., 101 Commerce Dr., Fort Collins, CO 80524 / 303-224-3454

X

XS Sight Systems, 2401 Ludelle St., Fort Worth, TX 76105 / 888-744-4880; FAX: 800-734-7939

X-Spand Target Systems, 26-10th St. SE, Medicine Hat, AB T1A 1P7 CANADA / 403-526-7997; FAX: 403-528-2362

Y

Yankee Gunsmith "Just Glocks", 2901 Deer Flat Dr., Copperas Cove, TX 76522 / 817-547-8433; FAX: 254-547-8887 ed@justglocks.com www.justglocks.com

Yavapai College, 1100 E. Sheldon St., Prescott, AZ 86301 / 520-776-2353; FAX: 520-776-2355

Yavapai Firearms Academy Ltd., P.O. Box 27290, Prescott Valley, AZ 86312 / 928-772-8262; FAX: 928-772-0062 info@yfainc.com www.yfainc.com

Yearout, Lewis E. (See Montana Outfitters)

Yellowstone Wilderness Supply, P.O. Box 129, West Yellowstone, MT 59758 / 406-646-7613

Yesteryear Armory & Supply, P.O. Box 408, Carthage, TN 37030

York M-1 Conversion, 12145 Mill Creek Run, Plantersville, TX 77363 / 936-894-2397; FAX: 936-894-2397 bmf25years@aol.com

Young Country Arms, William, 1409 Kuehner Dr. #13, Simi Valley, CA 93063-4478

Z

Zabala Hermanos S.A., P.O. Box 97, Elbar Lasao, 6, Elgueta, Guipuzcoa, 20600 SPAIN / 34-943-768076; FAX: 34-943-768201 imanol@zabalahermanos.com www.zabalahermanos.com

Zander's Sporting Goods, 7525 Hwy. 154 West, Baldwin, IL 62217-9706 / 800-851-4373; FAX: 618-785-2320

Zanotti Armor, Inc., 123 W. Lone Tree Rd., Cedar Falls, IA 50613 / 319-232-9650 www.zanottiarmor.com

Zeeryp, Russ, 1601 Foard Dr., Lynn Ross Manor, Morristown, TN 37814 / 615-586-2357

Zero Ammunition Co., Inc., 1601 22nd St. SE, P.O. Box 1188, Cullman, AL 35056-1188 / 800-545-9376; FAX: 205-739-4683 zerobulletco@aoz.com www.zerobullets.com

Ziegel Engineering, 1390 E. Bunnett St. "F", Signal Hill, CA 90755 / 562-596-9481; FAX: 562-598-4734 ziegel@aol.com www.ziegeleng.com

Zim's, Inc., 4370 S. 3rd West, Salt Lake City, UT 84107 / 801-268-2505

Z-M Weapons, 203 South St., Bernardston, MA 01337 / 413-648-9501; FAX: 413-648-0219

Numbers

100 Straight Products, Inc., P.O. Box 6148, Omaha, NE 68106 / 402-556-1055; FAX: 402-556-1055

3-Ten Corp., P.O. Box 269, Feeding Hills, MA 01030 / 413-789-2086; FAX: 413-789-1549 www.3-ten.com

4-D Custom Die Co., 711 N. Sandusky St., P.O. Box 889, Mt. Vernon, OH 43050-0889 / 740-397-7214; FAX: 740-397-6600 info@ch4d.com ch4d.com